Licensing Law in Scotland

To Josephine

Licensing Law in Scotland

J C Cummins, MA, LLB
Solicitor

Butterworths/Law Society of Scotland
Edinburgh
1993

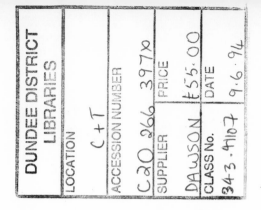
United Kingdom	Butterworth & Co (Publishers) Ltd, 4 Hill Street, EDINBURGH EH2 3JZ and 88 Kingsway, LONDON WC2B 6AB
Australia	Butterworths, SYDNEY, MELBOURNE, BRISBANE, ADELAIDE, PERTH, CANBERRA and HOBART
Canada	Butterworth Canada Ltd, TORONTO and VANCOUVER
Ireland	Butterworth (Ireland) Ltd, DUBLIN
Malaysia	Malayan Law Journal Sdn Bhd, KUALA LUMPUR
New Zealand	Butterworths of New Zealand Ltd, WELLINGTON and AUCKLAND
Puerto Rico	Butterworth of Puerto Rico, Inc, SAN JUAN
Singapore	Butterworths, Asia, SINGAPORE
USA	Butterworth Legal Publishers, CARLSBAD, California; and SALEM, New Hampshire

Law Society of Scotland
26 Drumsheugh Gardens, EDINBURGH EH3 7YR

A CIP Catalogue record for this book is available from the British Library.

ISBN 0 406 11547 8

Typeset by Phoenix Photosetting, Chatham, Kent
Printed and bound by Butler and Tanner Ltd, Frome, Somerset

Foreword

Few of the members of the Clayson Committee whose report on Scottish licensing law formed the basis of the Licensing (Scotland) Act 1976 expected that their recommendations would be enacted quite so quickly, but equally none of those who welcomed the passing into law of that Act can have anticipated the extent to which the courts would be called upon to interpret its provisions or those of subsequent amending legislation. Prior to 1976, judicial scrutiny of liquor licensing law was virtually unknown since legislation gave an apparently unfettered discretion to the licensing court which few were able to challenge. The scheme of licensing introduced by the 1976 Act and in particular the right of appeal under section 39 to the sheriff court and thereafter to the Court of Session swiftly and inevitably gave rise to a substantial body of case law, much of which was required to provide interpretation of novel statutory provisions introduced for the first time by the Act.

Liquor licensing has always attracted a corps of specialist practitioners but so great has been the impact of the 1976 Act that increasingly lawyers with no previous experience have found themselves engaged in licensing work.

This book has been written by a specialist but its logical and clear approach should commend it to expert and novice alike. The author has in a practical way analysed the mass of judicial decisions which have flowed since 1976 and provided easily understood explanations of these and the statutory provisions which they seek to explain. Jack Cummins has made a significant contribution to Scottish licensing law by his diligence and clarity of expression.

Menzies Campbell
Advocates' Library
Parliament House
Edinburgh
November 1993

v

'It does seem to me to be at least difficult to find a clear pattern or consistent philosophy in the legislation embodied in the Licensing Act'.

Lord Clyde: *Argyll Arms (McManus) Ltd v Lorn etc Divisional Licensing Board* 1988 SCLR 241 at 243.

Preface

See: 'Dog'.

This solitary reference under 'Licence' in the computer index of a Scottish university library epitomises licensing law's 'wilderness years' during which the subject appears to have attracted little interest.

Now, a renaissance is under way, fuelled by an increasing resort to litigation, a concomitant increase in the reporting of cases, the government's apparent intention of using Scottish licensing law as a model for the remainder of Great Britain and (paradoxically) unremitting difficulties with the legislation in practice.

In his preface to the eighth edition of *Purves's Scottish Licensing Laws*, Sheriff A G Walker was able to suggest that the Licensing (Scotland) Act 1959, as a consolidating measure, produced a 'coherent whole' by knitting together the tattered remnants of various statutes. The modern practitioner's experience of the Licensing (Scotland) Act 1976 and the Law Reform (Miscellaneous Provisions) (Scotland) Act 1990 precludes such unalloyed approval. In the volatile period of two years preceding the publication of this book, the mechanism has creaked loudly; and, regrettably, there is no apparent prospect of the necessary legislative lubrication. Although a Law Lord has said that in this kind of legislation 'precision and simplicity' are all* these highly desirable features are conspicuously absent.

Several penumbral areas are explored and solutions suggested. In the process, I have drawn upon a bank of unreported cases which may usefully see the light of day. Reference is made to a number of decisions with *Greens' Weekly Digest* citations where it has been possible to provide extracts from the unpublished opinions.

The subject of seamen's canteens is now of highly marginal interest and has been virtually ignored.

The forbearance of my partners during the development of the manuscript requires recognition. I also owe a debt of gratitude to a number of colleagues: Janet Hood, Depute Clerk, Kincardine and Deeside District Licensing Board, who read the manuscript and supplied a valuable user's viewpoint; Brian M Hughes, solicitor, Glasgow, who brought his special skills to bear by revising Chapter 12; Peter Coulson, editor of *Licensing Review*, who supplied advice and encouragement; and Josephine Cummins, who undertook research. Of course, I accept responsibility for the finished work.

I have attempted to take account of all developments up to 30 July 1993.

J C Cummins
Glasgow
August 1993

---

* *Carter v Bradbeer* [1975] 1 WLR 1204 at 1221 per Lord Edmund-Davies.

Contents

Table of statutes

Table of cases

C

G

Abbreviations

REFERENCES

Unless otherwise stated, all statutory references are to the Licensing (Scotland) Act 1976 (c 66), as amended ('the Act').

The Law Reform (Miscellaneous Provisions) (Scotland) Act 1990 (c 40) is referred to as 'the 1990 Act'.

'Maximum penalty' references are to levels on the standard scale set out in s 289G of the Criminal Procedure (Scotland) Act (c 21) (added by the Criminal Justice Act 1982 (c 48), s 54).

BIBLIOGRAPHY

Clayson:	*Report of the Departmental Committee on Scottish Licensing Law* (Cmnd 5354) (1973) (chaired by Dr Christopher Clayson)
Gordon:	G H Gordon *The Criminal Law of Scotland* (2nd edn, 1978; Supplement 1992, W Green)
Macphail:	I D Macphail *Sheriff Court Practice* (1988, W Green)
Purves:	J Purves *Scottish Licensing Laws* (edition as specified: sixth edition by Shearer (1949) or eighth edition by Walker (1961))
Stair Memorial Encyclopaedia	*The Laws of Scotland: Stair Memorial Encyclopaedia* (Butterworths/Law Society of Scotland)

LAW REPORTS

AC	Law Reports, Appeal Cases (House of Lords and Privy Council) 1890–
Adam	Adam's Justiciary Reports 1894–1919
All ER	All England Law Reports 1936–
All ER Rep	All England Law Reports Reprint
B&S	Best and Smith's Reports (Queen's Bench) 1861–70
BSMD	Brewers' Society Monthly Digest
BTRLR	Brewing Trade Review Law Reports 1836–1972
Brewing Tr Rev	Brewing Trade Review 1836–1972
C & P	Carrington and Payne's Reports 1823–41
Ch	Law Reports, Chancery Division 1890–
Ch App	Law Reports, Chancery Appeals 1865–75
Coup	Couper's Justiciary Reports 1868–85
CPD	Law Reports, Common Pleas Division
Crim LR	Criminal Law Review
D	Dunlop's Session Cases 1838–62
F	Fraser's Session Cases 1898–1906
F(J)	Justiciary Cases in Fraser's Session Cases 1898–1906
GWD	Green's Weekly Digest 1986–
IRLR	Industrial Relations Law Reports 1972–
JC	Justiciary Cases 1917–
JP	Justice of the Peace Reports 1837–
JPN	Justice of the Peace Journal
KB	Law Reports, King's Bench Division 1900–52
LGR	Knight's Local Government Reports 1902–
LR	Licensing Review
LS Gaz R	Law Society's Gazette 1903–
M	Macpherson's Session Cases 1862–73
QB	Law Reports, Queen's Bench Division 1891–1901, 1952–
QBD	Law Reports, Queen's Bench Division 1875–90
R	Rettie's Session Cases 1873–98
R(J)	Justiciary Cases in Rettie's Session Cases 1873–98
SC	Session Cases 1907–
SC (HL)	House of Lords Cases in Session Cases 1907–
SC (J)	Justiciary Cases in Session Cases 1907–16
SCCR	Scottish Criminal Case Reports 1981–
SCCR (Supp)	Scottish Criminal Case Reports Supplement 1950–80
SCLR	Scottish Civil Law Reports 1987–
Sh Ct Rep	Sheriff Court Reports in Scottish Law Review
SJ	Solicitors' Journal
SLR	Scottish Law Reporter 1865–1925
SLT	Scots Law Times 1893–1908, and 1909–

SLT (Notes)	Notes of Recent Decisions in Scots Law Times 1946–81
SLT (Sh Ct)	Sheriff Court Reports in Scots Law Times 1893–
TLR	Times Law Reports 1884–1952
WLR	Weekly Law Reports 1953–

CHAPTER 1

Administration of liquor licensing

LICENSING BOARDS

Constitution
The administration of liquor licensing in Scotland is entrusted to licensing boards constituted for each district and islands area or for separate divisions therein (s 1(2))[1]. A decision to create or discontinue divisions must be notified 'forthwith' to the Secretary of State by the district or islands council; provision is also made for newspaper advertisement (s 1(3)).

A board must consist of not less than one-quarter of the district or islands council members, subject to an absolute minimum of five such members (s 1(4)); and, where divisions have been created, not less than one-third of the divisional licensing board members shall be councillors for a ward or electoral division within the area of the division 'unless the Secretary of State otherwise directs' (s 1(5)).

Election of licensing board members

Board members are elected at the first district or islands council meeting held after the ordinary (four-yearly) council elections (s 1(6), (7)) and hold office until the next board election (s 1(8)) (even if not re-elected at the council election) (s 1(9)). A board election is not vitiated by any 'technical defect' which has not prejudiced a candidate's interests (s 1(12)). Where a timeous election does not take place or insufficient members are elected, the Secretary of State may 'by order provide for the holding of an election or elections' to rectify the omission or deficiency (s 1(11)).

Retiring board members are eligible for re-election (provided, of course, that they remain council members) (s 1(8)).

A board vacancy arising from 'death, resignation, disqualification[2] or other cause' may be filled at the next following council meeting. The newly-appointed member holds office for the remainder of the life of the board (s 1(10)).

The board elects its chairman annually from one of its number (s 6(1)). If the election results in an equality of voting for two or more persons, the result is determined by lot (the form of which is at the discretion of the board (s 6(2)). In

---

1 The rationale of the system is explained in the *Report of the Departmental Committee on Scottish Licensing Law* (Cmnd 5354) (*Clayson*), paras 5.21ff. Boards also perform functions under the Betting, Gaming and Lotteries Act 1963 and the Gaming Act 1968: see s 133.
2 For Disqualification: see below.

the chairman's absence at any meeting or pending his election, a chairman is elected for a particular meeting (s 6(1)). The chairman has a second or casting vote 'at any meeting of a licensing board' (s 6(3)).

Categories of statutory disqualification[1]

Certain persons are absolutely prohibited from being a licensing board member[2]:
(1) 'A person who is, or who is in partnership with any person, as a brewer, maltster, distiller or dealer in or retailer of alcoholic liquor' (s 2(1))[3] and
(2) 'a person who is an employee of a holder of a licence' under the Act[4] and 'any other person engaged in a business which deals in alcoholic liquor, including directors, officers and employees of companies so engaged' (s 2(3)).

In addition, a licensing board member who is otherwise qualified may not act in certain circumstances, namely:
(a) where he holds a 'disqualifying interest' in a company he may not take part in any proceedings in which that company is an applicant or objector (s 2(2)). The interest is 'disqualifying' where the member holds a beneficial interest[5] in shares or stocks of a close company[6] which have a total nominal value exceeding £50 or which amount to more than one-hundredth of the nominal value of the issued share capital or stock or any class of such capital or stock; or
(b) where he is 'the proprietor, tenant or sub-tenant' of premises he may not act 'in the granting of a licence' in respect of those premises' (s 2(4))[7].

Anything done by a disqualified person 'shall be void' (s 2(6))[8] but the grant of a new licence 'shall not be liable to objection on the ground that the members of the licensing board, or any of them, were not qualified to grant a licence' (s 2(6), proviso). This proviso does not protect a new licence from challenge on common law grounds (see Chapter 15).

Any person who 'knowingly and wilfully contravenes' s 2 is guilty of an offence (s 2(5))[9] It is not sufficient that he 'knowingly' acts as a board member while disqualified: there must be a deliberate intent to perform the prohibited deed[10].

---

1 See also Chapter 15 for circumstances in which a breach of the rules of natural justice may occur because of common law disqualification.
2 There is nothing to prevent councillors falling within these categories from taking part in the election of the board under s 1(6), (7).
3 'Dealer' no doubt includes a wholesaler.
4 The expression 'holder of a licence' includes the employee or agent of a non-natural person: s 11(3).
5 A trustee would not appear to be disqualified.
6 Section 2(2) defines 'close company' by reference to the Income and Corporation Taxes Act 1970, s 282. The definition is now to be found in the Income and Corporation Taxes Act 1988, s 414.
7 'Grant' includes grant by way of renewal; s 139(1). In *Blaik v Anderson* (1899) 7 SLT 299 the Lord Ordinary 'greatly doubted' whether a shareholder of a joint stock company could be said to be 'even a part proprietor of its heritable subjects'.
8 In *Blaik* above, the Lord Ordinary observed that a statutory objection would 'probably go no further than to discount the vote'. Cf. *Goodall v Bilsland* 1909 SC 1152, (1909) 1 SLT 376.
9 Maximum penalty: level 5 on the standard scale; Sch 5. The prosecution must take place in the sheriff court: s 128(1)(c).
10 See discussion of 'wilful' in Sheriff G H Gordon's *The Criminal Law of Scotland*, 2nd edn, at para 7.31, and cases cited. Cf. *Attorney-General v Cozens* (1934) 50 TLR 320, in which a disqualified justice was convicted of 'knowingly' acting as such, although there was no deliberate intent to contravene the relevant statutory provision.

Proceedings against board members and others

Proceedings against 'any sheriff, justice of the peace, sheriff clerk, member of a licensing board, clerk of a licensing board, procurator fiscal, constable[1] or other person' arising from anything done in the execution of the Act must be commenced 'within two months[2] after the cause of such proceedings has arisen' (s 130).

The personal actions contemplated by this provision are virtually unknown. In the solitary, modern example, *Ballantyne v City of Glasgow District Licensing Board*[3], where a licenceholder sought to recover damages as a result of the board's failure to treat applications as timeously lodged, Lord Jauncey said:

'I deduce two propositions [from the authorities cited] . . . namely: (1) that a public officer or body will not be liable for a mere error of judgment while acting in the ordinary course of duty; and (2) that such an officer or body will not be liable for exceeding his or its powers if he or it genuinely and with reason believed that the relevant actions were within those powers'.

Ballantyne was argued solely on the question of the *vires* of the board's actions and, 'as a very general proposition' loss arising from the public exercise of judicial or administrative duties was actionable 'where the exercise can be shown to have been actuated by malice or to have exceeded the powers conferred upon the exerciser'[4].

Canvassing, bribery and corruption

An attempt by an applicant, either by himself or by another person at his instigation, to influence a member of a licensing board to support certain types of applications before they are considered is an offence (s 19(1), amended by the Licensing (Amendment) (Scotland) Act 1992, s 2)[5] only triable in the sheriff court (s 128(1)(c)). The relevant applications are those for: grant, renewal, permanent transfer, temporary transfer (under s 25(1)(A)), confirmation of a transfer (under s 25(4)), and the regular (but not the occasional) extension of permitted hours (s 128(1)(c)).

Where proceedings for this offence are pending, the application to which they relate may be adjourned until the proceedings are concluded (s 19(2)); and, in the event of a conviction, the board may refuse to consider the application (s 19(3)).

Canvassing (as distinct from bribery or corruption; see above) by objectors or potential objectors (s 16) is not prohibited. Indeed, licensing board members *qua* district councillors frequently receive representations from their constituents[6];

1 For the meaning of 'constable': see definition in s 139(1).
2 'Month' means 'calendar month': Interpretation Act 1978, Sch 1.
3 1987 SLT 745.
4 At 746L.
5 The maximum penalty is level 3 on the standard scale (Sch 5). Where the offence is committed by a licenceholder both he and the premises concerned are liable to disqualification, despite a confusing indication to the contrary in column 4 of Sch 5: see the express provision for disqualification in s 67(3).
6 A practice approved in *Walsh v Magistrates of Pollokshaws* 1907 SC (HL) 1, although cases decided under earlier legislation are now of little assistance as respects the exercise of discretion by licensing boards: see *Freeland v City of Glasgow District Licensing Board* 1979 SC 226, 1980 SLT 101 at 104.

but any information thereby gathered which may have a bearing on an application must be disclosed to the applicant at the hearing[1]. The canvassing of licensing board members by another member may vitiate a decision[2].

Bribery of a licensing board member is an offence at common law[3]; but a local councillor who accepted payment from an applicant against a promise to use his influence in the procurement of a licence but who was not a member of the licensing authority, committed no offence[4]. In relation to public officials statutory provision is made for the offence of corruption in the Public Bodies Corrupt Practices Act 1889, the Prevention of Corruption Act 1906[5], and the Prevention of Corruption Act 1916[6].

While an offence under s 19 simply attracts a level 3 (maximum) penalty (Sch 5) and no doubt a refusal by the board to consider the application in quo (s 19(3)), where a licenceholder (not simply an applicant) commits an offence under the Prevention of Corruption Acts 1889 to 1916 'in connection with an application to a licensing board' the court of conviction may (in addition to any other penalty) make either or both of the following orders:

'(a) that the licenceholder shall be disqualified from holding a licence for a period not exceeding five years in respect of the premises to which the application relates or related[7];
(b) that the premises to which the application relates or related shall be disqualified from being used as licensed premises for a period not exceeding five years' (s 67(4)).

THE CLERK

The clerk of the board is appointed by the district or islands council. He may occupy the position on a full- or part-time basis and must be an advocate or solicitor (s 7(1)). In addition, the council must appoint 'such other persons as may be necessary' to assist him 'or to act on his behalf as clerk or assistant clerk' (s 7(1)); there is no requirement that these persons be legally qualified. The clerk may be appointed from the private sector (although all but one of the clerks currently holding office are local authority employees); and both he and his assistant may be regional council officers placed at the district council's disposal (s 7(2)).

1 See *Robertson v Inverclyde Licensing Board* 1979 SLT (Sh Ct) 16; *Freeland v City of Glasgow District Licensing Board* 1979 SC 226, 1980 SLT 101; and Chapter 15.
2 *Macdougall v Miller* (1900) 8 SLT 284. See also *Ahmed v Stirling District Licensing Board* 1980 SLT (Sh Ct) 51; *R v Ferguson* (1890) 54 JP 101. Cf. *R v London Justices ex parte Kerfoot* (1896) 60 JP 726, (1896) 13 TLR 2.
3 See *Gordon* 2nd edn at paras 44.03 and 50.04; and *Logue v HM Advocate* 1932 JC 1.
4 *HM Advocate v Dick* (1901) 3 Adam 344. See *Gordon*, p 1010, fn 11.
5 This Act is principally concerned with the corruption of agents. A member of a licensing court was not an 'agent' of the court: see *Copeland v Johnston* 1967 SLT (Sh Ct) 28.
6 For a full analysis, see *Gordon*; paras 21.22ff, 44.03ff, and Second Supplement to the principal work. See also *Campbell v HM Advocate* 1941 JC 86, 1942 SLT 19 where it was held that a burgh licensing court was a 'public body' within the meaning of s 4(2) of the 1916 Act.
7 A person may not be disqualified from being a licenceholder as such: see *Canavan v Carmichael* 1989 SCCR 480; *Devaux v MacPhail* 1991 GWD 7-396; *Matchett v Douglas* 1992 SCCR 617.

Where the incumbent is in private practice, neither he nor his partner nor his employee may 'act as solicitor to, or agent for, any person in any proceedings before that board or in any appellate proceedings which may result therefrom'. Contravention of this provision is an offence (s 7(3))[1].

Powers and duties

All applications made under the Act are lodged with the clerk. Lodgement by facsimile transmission may be competent[2] but the clerk is entitled to insist that the application be accompanied by the appropriate fee.

He is bound to keep 'a register of applications for licences', including occasional licences under s 33[3]: which is to be available for inspection by 'any member of the public' at times and places determined by him (s 20). Decisions taken on all applications are to be entered in the register 'at the end of each day's meeting of the board' (s 20). In addition, a variety of applications lodged for consideration at a particular quarterly meeting are, 'together with the documents lodged therewith', subject to public inspection 'during normal office hours' (s 10(7)).

He must also 'cause to be published in one or more newspapers circulating in the area of the board' prescribed details of 'all competent applications' made to the board for (a) the grant, including the provisional grant, of a new licence and (b) the regular extension of permitted hours (s 12)[4].

If a request is made in terms of s 139(5)[5] he must arrange for publication of an agent's address, rather than that of the applicant and/or his employee or agent.

The advertisement will usually (but need not) summarise the procedure for objections. Publication must take place 'not later than three weeks' before the first day of the board meeting at which the applications are to be considered, which means, in effect, that the advertisement must appear at least 21 *clear* days before the meeting[6].

The extent of the clerk's power to reject applications as incompetent, particularly having regard to the requirement that only 'competent' applications be advertised, has been considered by the court on a number of occasions. In *Main v City of Glasgow District Licensing Board*[7] the clerk refused to accept an application for the regular extension of permitted hours on the ground that it had been presented out-of-time[8]. The Lord Ordinary (Morison) said:

'In my view the provisions of s 12 necessarily involve the clerk in taking a view as to the competency of any application. He is enjoined to publish only "all competent applica-

1 Maximum penalty: level 5 (Sch 5). A prosecution must be taken in the sheriff court: s 128(1)(c).
2 See *Hastie & Jenkerson v McMahon* (1990) The Times, 3 April, Independent, 20 April.
3 See *Hollywood Bowl (Scotland) Ltd v Horsburgh* 1993 SLT 241.
4 See s 12(2) and 12(3) for the prescribed details. It is doubtful whether 'freesheets' may legitimately be used for this purpose: some may not qualify as 'newspapers'. Provided that the newspaper 'circulates' in the area it need not be a local newspaper: *R v Westminster Betting Licensing Committee ex parte Peabody Donation Fund* [1963] 2 QB 750.
5 Added by the 1990 Act, Sch 8, para 18.
6 See *Main v City of Glasgow District Licensing Board* 1987 SLT 305.
7 1987 SLT 305, discussed in articles at 1987 SLT (News) 157 and 353.
8 Time-limits are discussed at p 10.

tions", and no machinery is afforded whereby he can refer to the board to determine what is or is not competent'.

On the other hand, rejection of a renewal application lodged out-of-time was reversed in *Tait v Horsborough*[1], having regard to the provisions of s 13(2), which allow for discretionary consideration of defective (including late) applications at an adjourned meeting in cases of 'inadvertence or misadventure'[2]. An application for renewal does not require to be advertised, but the ratio of *Tait* applies equally to late applications for the grant, including the provisional grant of a new licence, which are also capable of benefitting from s 13(2); in those cases, however, the advertisement requirement may cause time-scale problems[3].

In *M Milne Ltd v City of Glasgow District Licensing Board*[4] the sheriff held that the clerk's refusal to accept a late renewal application amounted to 'a refusal to renew the licence by the board' and could competently be the subject of an appeal, rejecting the board's argument that the appellants could only proceed by way of judicial review. It is submitted that this decision is wrong and that the proper course was followed in *Tait v Horsborough* above. While the 'constructive refusal' theory is superficially attractive, it sits uncomfortably with the provisions of s 39(6), in terms of which the sheriff may, on upholding an appeal, either (a) remit the case to the board for reconsideration of *its* decision or (b) reverse or modify its decision. Clearly, in the circumstances of *M Milne Ltd*, the sheriff was in no position to reach any view on the merits of the renewal application; indeed, a substantive disposal would have resulted in the total demolition of the scheme of the Act as respects renewal applications[5]. In addition, the appeals procedure is usually initiated by a statement of reasons for the board's decision, requested under s 18, which refers to 'the hearing' at which the decision was taken (see s 18(2), (3)).

Further clarification of the clerk's powers is provided by *Kelvinside Community Council v Glasgow District Licensing Board*[6]. Where an application for a new licence is refused, a subsequent application 'in respect of the same premises' is not to be entertained within two years of the refusal, unless a contrary direction (commonly known as a 'section 14 direction') is made at the time of the refusal (s 14). In this case, the Second Division, distinguishing *Main*, held that whether two applications were in respect of 'the same premises' fell to be determined by the board, rather than the clerk, and accorded a restricted meaning to 'competent' for the purposes of s 12. The Lord Justice-Clerk (Ross) rejected the argument that the advertisement provisions of s 12 'showed that the clerk was the judge of competency' and defined 'competent' simply by reference to the preliminary procedural requirements contained in ss 10 and 11.

An analysis of these various authorities enables the following propositions to be made:

1 1987 SCLR 310, sub nom *Tait v City of Glasgow District Licensing Board* 1987 SLT 340, discussed at 1987 SLT (News) 157.
2 See discussion of late renewal applications in chapter 9.
3 See J C Cummins 'Late Licensing Applications' 1987 SLT (News) 157.
4 1987 SLT (Sh Ct) 145.
5 See 1987 SLT (Sh Ct) 145 at 148J, K.
6 1990 SCLR 110, 1990 SLT 725.

(1) The clerk has no power to reject late or otherwise defective applications for the renewal, grant or provisional grant of a new licence[1].

(2) The advertisement provisions of s 12 preclude the acceptance of a late application for the regular extension of permitted hours, which, in any event, may not benefit from the discretionary power provided by s 13(2).

(3) Whether an application is in respect of 'the same premises' for the purposes of s 14 is a matter for the board, not the clerk[2].

(4) Although applications for the permanent transfer of a licence and a children's certificate do not require to be advertised, no mechanism is provided whereby any procedural failure (normally late-lodging) may be cured. Thus, the clerk has power to reject late applications.

Objected applications are in practice always placed before the board even where doubt may arise as to the competency of the objection[3].

The clerk 'shall accompany the board' when it retires from a public meeting to consider a decision, 'unless the board otherwise directs' (s 5(7)). In the unusual circumstances of *Low v Kincardineshire Licensing Court*[4] it was held that the rules of natural justice had been breached where the depute-clerk, who had lodged an objection to a betting office licence on behalf of the local authority, retired with the court when the application was considered. By parity of reasoning it would be unwise for a clerk or depute clerk to become involved in any objection submitted on behalf of the district council by virtue of s 16(1)(f).

The clerk or any person appointed to assist him may discharge the board's functions (as may a committee of the board or a member or members of the board) under what is commonly known as a 'delegated powers' arrangement, except in relation to the matters listed in s 5(2) (qv) (see s 5(1))[5].

The reasons which a licensing board may be required to give in terms of s 18 for any decision mentioned in s 5(2) are issued by the clerk and should be composed in consultation with board members[6].

The clerk is under an obligation to issue 'a licence' to 'every person to whom a licence is granted by the board', within 28 days of the grant (s 21(1), amended by 1990 Act, Sch 8, para 8)[7]. Application may be made by any person (not necessarily the holder) for a duplicate licence, which the clerk shall certify as 'a true copy of the original licence'[8]. The duplicate shall be 'sufficient evidence of the facts therein contained and of the terms of the original licence' (s 21(2)).

---

1 Although new licence applications require to be advertised; see J C Cummins 'Late Licensing Applications' 1987 SLT (News) 157.

2 The same reasoning would apply to a further application for a children's certificate where waiver has not been granted under the 1990 Act, Sch 5, para 5.

3 See *Cooper v City of Edinburgh District Licensing Board* 1991 SLT 47. The provisions of s 5(2) may conceivably suggest that a competency decision in relation to an objected *renewal* application is the preserve of the clerk. Section 5(2)(b) (read with s 5(6)) has the effect of requiring the application to be considered at a quarterly meeting 'where a competent objection has been received'; otherwise it may be granted (but not refused) under a 'delegated powers' arrangement made under s 5(1) (see below).

4 1974 SLT (Sh Ct) 54.

5 The clerk could thus grant, for example, an unopposed renewal application.

6 See *Ladbroke Racing (Strathclyde) Ltd v Cunninghame District Licensing Board* 1978 SLT (Sh Ct) 77.

7 A number of *dies non* are excluded from the 28 day period: see s 21(3). See definitions of 'grant' and 'licence' in s 139(1).

8 A fee is payable: currently £12.

While the factual background to *Tait v Horsborough*[1] appears to be confused and complicated, it appears that the petitioner incorrectly believed that he was the holder of a licence on the basis of a duplicate containing erroneous information. It was argued on his behalf that the copy licence was ex facie valid until reduced, while counsel for the board submitted that it provided prima facie but not conclusive evidence of fact. The question did not require to be resolved but the latter view is perhaps to be preferred.

Where a licenceholder is convicted of any offence under the Act in relation to his premises, a certified extract of the conviction is to be transmitted to the clerk of the board by the clerk of court within six days (s 129).

Although some clerks issue reminders to licenceholders relative to the expiry of licences or other permissions, they are under no obligation to do so.

Proceedings against inter alia the clerk 'on account of anything done in the execution of [the] Act' require to be commenced within two months 'after the cause of such proceedings has arisen' (s 130).

FEES FOR APPLICATIONS

The fees payable in respect of liquor licensing applications are prescribed by statutory instrument, currently the Liquor Licensing (Fees) (Scotland) Order 1990, SI 1990/2458, as amended by the Liquor Licensing (Fees) (Scotland) (Variation) Order 1992, SI 1992/1011 (s 8). An application may not be accepted unless accompanied by the correct fee.

Where application is made for the regular extension of permitted hours in terms of s 64, only a single fee (presently £60) may be required, even where the additional hours sought are referable to more than one part of a day or days. Where a clerk required separate fees for each component of an application (mornings and evenings) the opinion was expressed that his practice was 'wholly misconceived' and 'without statutory warrant'[2]. It is extremely doubtful whether, in the absence of any provision, fees may be charged for applications submitted in terms of byelaws made under s 38(1)(f). There is no basis for the imposition of the additional fee imposed in at least one district to defray administrative costs in connection with the processing of transfer applications.

As more fully explained in chapter 4, applications for new licences (other than off-sale licences) require to be accompanied, in terms of s 23, by certificates of suitability in relation to planning, building control and food hygiene matters. A number of local authorities levy a charge for the supply of these certificates: in one case, the fee (£100) is higher than the actual licensing dues. This practice has yet to be challenged but the decision of the House of Lords in *McCarthy & Stone Ltd v Richmond upon Thames London Borough Council*[3], where it was held that a local authority had no power to impose a charge for pre-application planning consultations, casts considerable doubt upon its lawfulness.

1 1987 SCLR 310, sub nom *Tait v City of Glasgow District Licensing Board* 1987 SLT 340.
2 *Moriarty v City of Edinburgh District Licensing Board* 1993 GWD 19-1185, OH.
3 [1991] 4 All ER 897, revsg [1990] 2 All ER 852.

LICENSING BOARD MEETINGS

Licensing boards are required to hold so-called 'quarterly meetings' in January, March, June and October of each year. The date of the first day of the meeting requires to be fixed at least eight weeks in advance (s 4(1)(a)). Re-scheduling of that date within the eight-week period (a rare but not unknown occurrence) should be achieved by means of an adjournment (s 4(2): see below), for which purpose there need not be a quorum (s 5(4)), rather than by cancellation[1]. There is no provision for formal public intimation. As explained below, certain applications and other items of business may be considered only at these meetings[2]. In addition, the board 'may hold such other meetings as appear to the board to be appropriate', (s 4(1)(b)) at which it may deal with matters which cannot be delegated under s 5(1) (see below).

The board may proceed to business at these meetings only if it is quorate. A quorum consists of one half of the members of the board, subject to a minimum of three (s 5(3)). Any vacancy is ignored (s 5(5)). Where there is no quorum the chairman or, if he is absent, the clerk may call a further meeting (s 5(4)). This sensible provision is clearly designed to preserve the *status quo ad interim* but since the inquorate meeting cannot dispose of any business doubt may arise as to the continuing validity of regular extensions of the permitted hours. In terms of s 64(3) these are valid 'during such period in the year succeeding the date of the grant' as may be specified and, on a strict construction of this provision, do not automatically continue in force until the date of an adjourned meeting.

Meetings for the discharge of the functions listed in s 5(2) are held in public (s 5(7)). Some boards hold private 'pre-meetings', ostensibly so that the clerk may outline the business about to be conducted[3]. Decisions relative to possible hearings under s 31 (suspension of licence), s 32 (closure order) and s 65 (restriction of permitted hours) are usually taken in camera.

In terms of s 4(2), any meeting (not simply a quarterly meeting) may be adjourned 'from time to time during the period of one month[4] next following the first day of such meeting, but no longer'. An adjourned sitting of a quarterly meeting is merely a continuation of the initial meeting:

'In our opinion, the language used in section 4 makes it plain that the meeting of the licensing board of 7 October 1988, although extended to the adjourned meeting on 4 November 1988, was still the quarterly meeting of the board for October. The reference to the meeting "beginning on a date in each such month" clearly shows that the meeting may end on a later date'[5].

Where an adjourned March meeting takes place after the election of a new board following district or island council elections the outgoing board is 'deemed to constitute the licensing board' for the disposal of outstanding business (s 1(13)).

---

1 See *Ballantyne v City of Glasgow District Licensing Board* 1987 SLT 745 at 748.
2 See s 5(2)(a)–(i) and 5(l), read with s 5(6).
3 The difficulties which this practice may create were focused in *Ahmed v Stirling District Licensing Board* 1980 SLT (Sh Ct) 51.
4 'Month' means calendar month: Interpretation Act 1978, Sch 1.
5 *Tarditi v Drummond* 1989 SCLR 201, 1989 SLT 554.

Applications for the renewal of a licence or for the grant or provisional grant of a new licence which have not been lodged timeously (s 10(1)), or which are defective as respects other preliminary requirements, due to 'inadvertence or misadventure', may be continued to an adjourned meeting if the board 'thinks fit' and 'upon such terms as the board thinks proper'[1]. Any of these applications submitted after the first day of a quarterly meeting but before an adjourned meeting must be accepted by the clerk for consideration by the board in terms of s 13(2)[2].

Doubt arises as to whether such an adjournment is subject to the one-month limitation contained in s 4(2). In practice, boards usually regard themselves as empowered to continue beyond one month the consideration of business which is competently before them at any time up until the conclusion of the final day of the meeting.

Consideration of applications and other business

(1) Time-limits

The time-limits set down in the Act for the lodgement of applications and for the performance of other procedural requirements (such as the service of notices), noted at the appropriate section of the text, are normally expressed by the use of the phrases 'not later than' or 'not less than' a number of days or weeks.

In *Main v City of Glasgow District Licensing Board*[3] the expression 'not later than five weeks' was interpreted as meaning:

'not later than five weeks before the inception of the day on which the meeting takes place, ie, in the present case at midnight between 3 and 4 October. The application should therefore have been lodged before midnight between 29 and 30 August'.

A period expressed as being 'not later' or 'not less' than a number of days is computed by the exclusion of the first and last day, so that, for example, 'not less than seven days' means 'not less than seven *clear* days'[4].

Lodgement of an application or an objection with the clerk probably requires to take place during the hours when his public office is open[5].

A difficulty may arise where the time-limit expires on a Sunday or other *dies non*[6]. The prescribed period should normally be extended until the first day on

---

1 Section 13(2)) makes similar provision for the death of an applicant or objector. The board will usually require the cost of any advertisement required in terms of s 12 to be borne by the applicant; semble no additional fees may be charged as such.
2 See *Indpine Ltd v City of Dundee District Licensing Board* 1992 SCLR 113 (OH), 1992 SCLR 353, 1992 SLT 473 (IH), discussed in Chapter 9.
3 1987 SLT 305. See also D C Coull '"Not Later Than" Defined' 1987 SLT (News) 353.
4 *Re Hector Whaling Ltd* [1936] Ch 208, followed in *Main*, above; *McMillan v HM Advocate* 1982 SCCR 309, 1983 SLT 24.
5 Despite the Lord Ordinary's reference to 'before midnight' in *Main* (above). See 22 *Stair Memorial Encyclopaedia* para 823.
6 See 22 *Stair Memorial Encyclopaedia* para 825.

which the requisite act may be performed[1]. Incorrectly, it is suggested, a number of clerks fix the *preceding* working day as the last day. For example, where the first day of a quarterly meeting is due to take place on Monday 17 June, an objection would require to be lodged (s 16(2)(a)) no later than Friday 7 June, rather than Monday 10 June.

(2) Method of disposal

Section 5 divides applications and other items of business into various categories as respects the method of disposal.

(a) A number of decisions may be taken under a 'delegated powers' arrangement 'by a committee of the board, a member or members of the board, the clerk of the board or any other person appointed to assist the clerk' (s 5(1))[2].

(b) Certain decisions are to be taken at a meeting of the board, which need not be a quarterly meeting, (s 5(2)(j), (k), (m), read with s 5(6)), namely decisions on: (i) the suspension of a licence (ss 31, 36(4)); (ii) a closure order (s 32), and (iii) confirmation under s 25(4) of an interim transfer made under s 25(2) or (3). An application to affirm the provisional grant of a new licence made under s 26(2) may be considered 'at any meeting of the board held not earlier than 14 days after the making of the application' (s 26(3)), although the delegated powers procedure is in practice sometimes employed.

(c) The following applications may be considered only at a quarterly meeting: (i) for the grant, including the provisional grant, of a new licence (s 5(2)(a)); (ii) for the renewal of a licence where a competent objection has been lodged (s 5(2)(b)); (iii) for the permanent transfer of a licence (s 5(2)(d)); (iv) for the regular extension of permitted hours (s 5(2)(e)); and (v) for a children's certificate (s 5(2)(l)).

(d) A number of sanction-related decisions must be taken at a quarterly meeting, as respects: (i) the restriction of 'the terminal permitted hour' (s 5(2)(f)); (ii) the restoration of 'restricted hours' (s 5(2)(g)), and (iii) the imposition of a Sunday restriction order (s 5(2)(i)). A decision to refuse an application for the renewal of a licence falls into the same category (s 5(2)(c)).

(3) Attendance at meetings

The provisions of section 15, which provide for the attendance or representation of applicants at board meetings may be divided into two parts[3]:

(i) All applications except renewal and permanent transfer. The board 'may decline to consider' the application if the applicant or his representative does not

---

1 *McNiven v Glasgow Corporation* 1920 SC 584, 1920 2 SLT 57. See also *Craig-Na-Brro Sales v Munro Furniture Ltd* 1974 SLT (Sh Ct) 107. Cf *Swainston v Hetton Victory Club* [1983] IRLR 164: 'presentation' of an application to an industrial tribunal did not require any action on the part of the recipient and should have been effected when the tribunal's office was closed (on a Sunday).

2 The relevant decisions are identified at the appropriate section of the text.

3 Where a competent objector elects not to attend the meeting his objection must nevertheless be considered (s 16(5)) but he will have no right of appeal against the board's decision; see s 17(5).

attend the meeting (s 15(1)). Despite this automatic requirement a number of boards nevertheless issue citations (see below) or at least remind applicants of the possible consequence of non-appearance.

In *Bury v Kilmarnock and Loudoun District Licensing Board*[1] the applicant's solicitor, who had been instructed to appear in support of the application for the regular extension of permitted hours (s 64: see chapter 10) failed to do so. The board declined to consider the application simply on the basis of non-representation and non-attendance, without any other substantive reason, essentially, it may be suspected, *pour encourager les autres*. Ordering the board to hold a new meeting to consider the application, the Lord Ordinary (Prosser) held that the words 'may decline' in s 15 afforded a board a discretion which required to be exercised rationally. While the requirement for attendance or representation had a clear purpose, since it allowed board members to raise issues and ask questions, in this case the absence of the applicant or his agent should not have prevented the board from disposing of the application on its merits:

'[I]t appears to me that in the exercise of its discretion under section 15 a board such as the respondents could not reasonably refuse to consider an application without asking itself whether the non-representation and non-attendance was of any significance to [its] decision on the merits of the application'.

Nevertheless, one board which is almost invariably disposed to grant uncontentious applications on a motion to do so made either by the applicant or his agent will nevertheless continue the matter to an adjourned meeting in the event that no one appears in support of the application. Another board will decline to hear an application if the applicant is not present before them, even though represented, unless the agent is able to produce satisfactory evidence of his client's incapacity.

Both practices are clearly wrong, although it may be remarked that, in practical terms, an agent dealing with even a mildly contentious application puts himself in the position of being unable to obtain proper instructions in the cut-and-thrust of the proceedings if he does not arrange for the applicant or the applicant's manager to be at his side.

A declinature to consider an application is not a refusal for the purposes of s 14[2] or s 64(9)[3].

(ii) Renewal and permanent transfer applications. An applicant for the renewal or permanent transfer of a licence need not attend the meeting unless cited by the board (s 15(1), proviso)[4]. Where an applicant fails to obtemper a citation the application may be *refused*[5] in his absence (s 15(2)). Otherwise, there may be no refusal without a hearing[6].

1 1988 SCLR 436, 1989 SLT 110.
2 Where an application for a new licence is refused a further application may not be entertained in the ensuing two years unless the board directs otherwise.
3 One year prohibition on further application for extended hours without direction to the contrary.
4 Intimation of an objection (s 16) or of police observations (s 16A) does not operate as a citation.
5 Cf 'may decline to consider' in s 15(1).
6 Note, however, that in *CRS Leisure Ltd v Dumbarton District Licensing Board* 1989 SCLR 566, 1990 SLT 200 the Lord Ordinary rejected an argument that this specific provision did not indicate a legislative intention to deprive applicants of a hearing in relation to other types of application (in this case for the regular extension of permitted hours).

No form of citation is prescribed, although postal service is expressly authorised by s 134, and recorded delivery letters are usually employed. In *Dolan v City of Glasgow District Council*[1] an applicant was deemed to have been 'notified' of a hearing[2] where recorded delivery letters had been sent by the licensing authority to his former address (returned by the Post Office marked 'gone away') and his new address (returned as 'not called for'). The sheriff held that the authority had acted 'more than reasonably'. Although it offended against natural justice that a person, for whatever reason, had been unable to put forward his case, the applicant had no room for complaint since the address change had come to light only as a result of information supplied by the chief constable[3].

The citation need not specify the reason for its issue, but an applicant who is met with unintimated material at the hearing will usually be entitled to an adjournment. In the absence of any prescribed time-limit, it will generally be reasonable to give the applicant at least seven days' notice. This period will, however, inevitably be shorter where the citation is issued following lodgement of an objection with the clerk at the last possible moment[4].

Separate provision is made for the licenceholder's attendance in connection with hearings under ss 31, 32 and 65, where 'due notice' is required[5].

(4) Order of consideration

Section 13(1) provides that 'the cases of applicants for new licences' are not to be heard until all other applications 'have been disposed of'. The expression 'new licence' means 'a licence granted in respect of premises for which, at the time of the application for such grant, either no licence was in force or a licence in a form different from the form of licence so granted was in force' (s 139(1)) and includes (for application purposes) the provisional grant of a new licence[6], but does not include a replacement licence (of the same type) where premises have been destroyed 'by fire, tempest or other unforeseen cause'[7].

The purpose of the provision is presumably to give a licensing board a clear view of the number of licensed premises in a locality when a new licence application comes before it. As more fully explained in chapter 4, the application is to be refused if the board finds that overprovision would otherwise result, having regard to the number of licensed and provisionally licensed premises in the locality *at the time the application is considered* (s 17(1)(d))[8].

The mandatory scheduling of new licence applications after applications for

---

1 1990 SCLR 553.
2 For the purposes of the Civic Government (Scotland) Act 1982, Sch 1, para 4(2).
3 Cf *Jolly v Hamilton District Council* 1992 SCLR 88, 1992 SLT 28.
4 Ie, seven (clear) days before the meeting: s 16(2)(a).
5 These sections relate, respectively, to suspension orders, closure orders and the restriction of the permitted hours.
6 See *Kelvinside Community Council v Glasgow District Licensing Board* 1990 SCLR 110, 1990 SLT 725.
7 See proviso to 'new licence' definition in s 139(1); and *Stevenson v Hunter* (1903) 5 F 761, (1903) 10 SLT 754.
8 See *Chung v Wigtown District Licensing Board* 1993 SCLR 256.

renewal should thus, in theory, lend a degree of precision to this exercise[1]. The reality is somewhat different. Since the consideration of applications may be adjourned, the requirement that other cases be 'disposed of' cannot possibly mean that a final determination is obligatory; otherwise, lengthy delays would result[2]. A board may thus be required to decide upon a new licence application while the fate of one or more renewal applications remains to be resolved[3].

Where competing applications for a new licence are to be considered at the same meeting:

'[T]he order in which each application is considered is likely to be critical. There can be no fairer way to proceed than to consider and dispose of each application in the order in which the applications were lodged with the board'[4].

By extension, applications should also be stamped as to the time of receipt.

Section 13(1) is subject to the proviso that 'where more than one application for a licence has been made in respect of the premises, the licensing board may hear and consider such applications together'. This is, in turn, subject to the important qualification that the consideration of two new licence applications should not be conjoined for the irrelevant purpose of considering the *actual* facilities which the applicants propose to provide[4]. However, applications (usually for permanent transfer) are sometimes heard together where one or more applicants claim to be entitled to occupy premises (see s 25(1)). Although it has been observed that 'a licensing authority cannot resolve a dispute about title or authority between rival applicants'[5], boards may prefer one applicant to another on the basis of appropriate documentary evidence.

(5) Voting

Although the board may retire to consider its decision, voting must take place in public[6]. A board member who has been absent for part of the hearing should not vote[7] nor should he take part in the board's private discussions[8].

In terms of s 6(3) the chairman has 'in a case of equality in voting' a casting vote. Until removed by the 1990 Act, Sch 8, para 4 the subsection was subject to the proviso that an application for the grant or provisional grant of a new licence could be granted 'only by a majority of the members . . . present and voting'.

---

1 A number of boards interpret s 13(1) in this purposive way by ensuring that applications for new licences are heard after renewal applications, but not necessarily at the very end of the agenda (which the letter of the Act requires).
2 The Licensing (Scotland) Act 1903, s 16 required that the daily deliverance, to be signed by the chairman, should indicate whether applications were 'granted or refused or continued for further inquiry, or how otherwise disposed of'.
3 These renewal applications would, of course, have relevance to the determination of a new licence application only if they related to premises in the same locality: see s 17(1)(d).
4 *Chung v Wigtown District Licensing Board* 1993 SCLR 256, examined at p 80 below.
5 *Edward Barrett Ltd v City of Dundee District Licensing Board* 1992 SLT 963, decided under betting legislation.
6 See Chapter 15 for a detailed consideration of cases on this subject.
7 *Goodall v Bilsland* 1909 SC 1152, (1909) 1 SLT 376. See also *McGhee v Moncur* (1899) 1 F 594.
8 *Black v Perth and Kinross District Council* (5 November 1991, unreported), Perth Sh Ct.

Since an application for inter alia a new licence can be refused only if the board 'finds' that a ground of refusal applies (s 17(1)), it had been held that s 6(3) was essentially an erroneous re-enactment of s 26 of the Licensing (Scotland) Act 1959 and required to be ignored: an equality of voting resulted in grant of the application[1].

Since the repeal of the proviso, licensing boards have so far proceeded on the basis that the casting vote has been reinstated. While this is an understandable conclusion, it is nevertheless open to considerable doubt. It is more probable that the amendment simply gives effect to the decision in *Hart v City of Edinburgh District Council*, above[2]. The Sheriff-Principal (R D Ireland, QC) said:

'The only way in which the board can find that any ground [of refusal] applies is to hold a vote as to whether it does. If the votes are equally divided the motion to find that the ground applies has failed, and the board has no option but to grant the application. The board never gets to the stage envisaged by [the unamended] s 6(3) of holding a vote on whether the licence should be granted or not. The "mischief" which the 1976 Act sought to correct was the unfettered discretion of the old licensing courts, and the remedy provided was the restriction imposed by s 17'.

Similar reasoning would, of course, apply where votes are tied in an application for renewal[3] or permanent transfer of a licence where, again, a refusal may only follow a 'finding' of a ground of refusal.

On any view equality of voting creates a difficulty where a statement of reasons for the board's 'decision' is requested in terms of s 18. In *Clive v Nithsdale District Licensing Board*[4] the sheriff (K Barr) considered that a refusal following a 'tie' 'would defeat not only the provisions of s 17 . . . but would also make the provisions of s 18, which requires the board to give reasons for the decision, completely valueless'. It requires to be borne in mind, however, that the grant of an application may result in a request for a statement of reasons by a competent objector. In such a circumstance it is difficult to envisage the manner in which reasons could be satisfactorily formulated: it may be thought that, if the board has not reached a 'finding', neither has it reached a 'decision'.

(6) Finality of decisions

Section 37(3) of the Licensing (Scotland) Act 1959, which prohibited the alteration at an adjourned half-yearly meeting of anything done on any previous day in 'granting or refusing to grant a certificate', was not re-enacted in the 1976 Act. Nevertheless, it seems clear that once a decision has been intimated the board is functus In *Matchett v Dunfermline District Council*[5] the Lord Ordinary expressed the opinion that the purported reversal of a decision to refuse an amusement-

---

1 *Hart v City of Edinburgh District Licensing Board* 1987 SLT (Sh Ct) 54; see also *Knowles v Stirling District Licensing Board* 1980 SLT (Sh Ct) 87; *Clive v Nithsdale District Licensing Board* 1987 SLT (Sh Ct) 113.
2 See also *Allan and Chapman's* commentary to the Act (3rd edn by Agnew and Baillie), p 55.
3 Including the Sunday permitted hours component: s 17(2A).
4 1987 SLT 113.
5 1993 SLT 537.

with-prizes machine permit was *ultra vires*, where an appeal to the sheriff against the licensing authority's original decision had been sisted[1].

The rehearing of an application may be ordered where an appeal is upheld (s 39(6)(a))[2]; or by the Court of Session as a result of a judicial review petition[3].

(7) Defective decisions

In terms of s 9(5) 'A licence granted otherwise than at a properly constituted meeting of a licensing board[4] or otherwise in accordance with the provisions of this Act[5] shall be void'. Section 9 is concerned with the grant of a licence 'for the sale by retail or supply of alcoholic liquor'. While 'grant' includes grant by way of renewal (s 139(1)), the subsection, derived from s 32(4) of the Licensing (Scotland) Act 1959, has not been modernised and enlarged to reflect the range of functions carried out by licensing boards.

The defective grant of a licence is not *ipso facto* void and requires to be reduced. Where a licensing court granted licences for the playing of bingo without a quorum being present, in an appeal against the subsequent refusal of a similar licence the sheriff rejected an argument that the *ex facie* valid licences ought to have been disregarded:

'I agree with the submissions made by counsel [for the licensing court] that the licences are ex facie valid and remain so until they are reduced, withdrawn, or recalled, and that it is for the licensing court to withdraw them or for the appellants to raise actions of reduction'[6].

A number of irregularities which would once have required Court of Session proceedings may now provide a ground of appeal under s 39: for example, a failure to vote in public in terms of s 5(7)[7].

---

1 See also *Thomson v City of Glasgow District Council* 1992 SLT 805, decided under the Civic Government (Scotland) Act 1982, in which a decision to rehear applications for taxi operators' licences was held to be ultra vires.
2 The board's subsequent decision is 'valid as if reached at a quarterly meeting as mentioned in section 4(1)(a)'; s 39(7).
3 See, for example, *Bantop v City of Glasgow District Licensing Board* 1989 SCLR 731, 1990 SLT 366.
4 Eg, where there is no quorum; s 5(3).
5 Eg, where the premises are in a motorway service area and, in terms of s 28, cannot be licensed.
6 *Mecca Ltd v Kirkcaldy Burgh Licensing Court* 1975 SLT (Sh Ct) 50.
7 See *McKay v Banff and Buchan Western Division Licensing Board* 1991 SCLR 15, 1991 SLT 20.

CHAPTER 2

Requirement for a licence

THE SALE OF ALCOHOLIC LIQUOR

A licence is required for the retail sale of alcoholic liquor. Beyond this super-ficially simple proposition lies a Byzantine maze of regulation, without 'a clear pattern or consistent philosophy'[1], at whose heart lies s 90(a). If any person: 'trafficks in any alcoholic liquor in any premises or place without holding a licence in that behalf . . . he shall be guilty of an offence'[2]. 'Trafficking' means: 'barter-ing, selling, dealing in, trading in, or exposing or offering for sale, by retail' (s 139(1)). The different methods by which the offence of 'trafficking' may be committed are examined later in this chapter; but we begin by confining our attention to three expressions of primary importance.

(1) 'Alcoholic liquor'

Section 139(1)[3] provides the following definition:

'"Alcoholic liquor" includes spirits, wine, porter, ale, beer, cider, perry and made-wine, but does not include –
(a) any liquor which on analysis of a sample thereof at any time is found to be of an original gravity[4] not exceeding 1,016 degrees and to be of a strength not exceeding 1.2% of ethyl alcohol by volume (at a temperature of 20 degrees Celsius);
(b) perfumes;
(c) flavouring essences recognised by the Commissioners[5] as not being intended for consumption as or with dutiable alcoholic liquor;
(d) spirits, wine or made-wine so medicated as to be, in the opinion of the Commissioners[5] intended for use as a medicine and not as a beverage'.

The expressions 'wine' and 'made-wine' are defined by reference to s 1 of the Alcoholic Liquor Duties Act 1979 (s 139(1), as amended by Alcoholic Liquor Duties Act 1979, Sch 3, para 9(a)).
Wine. 'Wine' means 'any liquor obtained from the alcoholic fermentation of

---

1 *Argyll Arms (McManus) Ltd v Lorn, Mid-Argyll, Kintyre and Islay Divisional Licensing Board* 1988 SCLR 241, 1988 SLT 290, per Lord Clyde.
2 Maximum penalty: level 5 (Sch 5). The offence is usually known simply as 'trafficking'.
3 As amended by: Licensing (Scotland) Act Amendment Regulations 1979, SI 1979/1755; Finance Act 1981, Sch 19; Law Reform (Miscellaneous Provisions) Scotland Act 1985, s 53.
4 For 'original gravity': see Alcoholic Liquor Duties Act 1979, s 3(1).
5 'Commissioners' means 'Commissioners of Customs and Excise': s 139(1).

fresh grapes or of the must of fresh grapes, whether or not the liquor is fortified with spirits or flavoured with aromatic extracts' (1979 Act, s 1(4)).

Made-wine. 'Made-wine' means 'any liquor obtained from the alcoholic fermentation of any substance or by mixing a liquor so obtained or derived from a liquor so obtained with any other liquor or substance but does not include wine, beer, black beer, spirits or cider' (1979 Act, s 1(5))[1].

Otherwise, no definition of the named types of liquor is offered, although these varieties acquire added significance in a number of contexts:

(1) While a licence normally authorises the sale by retail of any alcoholic liquor (s 29(1)) the licence may be granted (or renewed) in a restricted form so that the sale of spirits by 'the licenceholder or his employee or agent' constitutes an offence (s 29(1), (2))[2]. Nevertheless, the only statutory definition of 'spirits' is to be found in the Alcoholic Liquor Duties Act 1979, s 1 which defines alcoholic liquors subject to excise duty: '"Spirits" means . . . spirits of any description and includes all liquors mixed with spirits and all mixtures, compounds or preparations made with spirits but does not include methylated spirits'[3].

(2) The 'type of alcoholic liquor' which may be sold under an occasional licence may be the subject of a condition imposed by a licensing board; s 33(3) and see chapter 7.

(3) A licensing board byelaw may require that 'all wines, made-wines and spirits sold by the holder of an off-sale licence' shall be supplied in corked, stoppered or sealed containers (s 38(1)(c), subject to exceptions; see chapter 8).

(4) The holder of an off-sale licence or his employee or agent commits an offence if 'he sells wine (including made-wine) in an open vessel' (s 97(4))[4].

(5) A person who has attained the age of 16 may purchase 'beer, wine, made-wine, porter, cider or perry' for consumption with his meal in an area of licensed premises which is not a 'bar' (s 68(4)). 'Beer' (which includes 'porter' as well as 'ale' and 'stout') and 'cider or perry' are the subject of definitions in, respectively, s 1(3) and 1(6) of the Alcoholic Liquor Duties Act 1979[5] which are offered to the reader *quantum valeat*[6].

Low- and no-alcohol products

A number of drinks which are non-alcoholic when supplied to the consumer fall to be treated as 'alcoholic liquor' at the first stage of production. The definition in

---

1 Subject to s 1(10) which permits certain beverages made with beer or cider to be categorised as such, rather than as made-wine, by means of a statutory instrument.

2 The grant of an occasional or regular extension of permitted hours (s 64) may be similarly restricted. Maximum penalty: level 5. Licenceholder and premises liable to disqualification (s 67, Sch 5). In terms of s 90(b), the bartering or retail sale of spirits without a licence is also an offence, for historical reasons which are now irrelevant; maximum penalty : level 5 (Sch 5).

3 Alcoholic Liquor Duties Act 1979, s 1(2), subject to a number of esoteric exceptions, including angostura bitters, in s 1(7), 1(8) and 1(9). Angostura bitters are also excluded from the meaning of 'spirits' in *licensing* legislation by the Finance Act 1970, s 6(2)(b).

4 Maximum penalty: level 3. Licenceholder and premises liable to disqualification; s 67, Sch 5.

5 As amended by the Finance Act 1984, s 1(5).

6 In *Wood v Mackenzie* 1925 JC 13 at 17 the Lord Justice-Clerk (Alness) homologated the importation of revenue legislation definitions for licensing purposes.

s 139(1) refers to analysis of a sample of liquor '*at any time*'. The use of a similar expression in s 201 of the Licensing Act 1964[1] has resulted in de-alcoholised products requiring to be treated as 'alcoholic liquor', notwithstanding their non-alcoholic strength at the time of sale[2]. This interpretation has not been adopted in Scotland.

Shandy (the combination of beer or ginger beer and lemonade) and other similar *pre-packed* mixtures whose strength falls below the prescribed levels are regarded as falling outwith the statutory definition[3]. However, in *Hall v Hyder*[4] the Queen's Bench Division held that beer and lemonade mixed by a publican *at the time of sale* (and then consumed by an under-age person) constituted 'intoxicating' liquor:

'[W]hat the publican does when he sells shandy is to sell beer and, separately, either lemonade or ginger beer, and then, as agent for the purchaser and as agent only, to pour one into the other . . . . If one starts from that, it seems to me that, if what is being sold is beer, it is perfectly apt to say that beer is consumed, albeit it is mixed with some other ingredient'[5].

This decision rested substantially upon the publican's inability to sell diluted beer[6] and it is doubtful whether a Scottish court would take such an arguably artificial view.

Alcoholic liquor in confectionery

The provisions of the Act relating to 'the sale, supply, purchase, delivery or consumption of alcoholic liquor' have no effect in relation to alcoholic liquor in 'confectionery' which:

'(a) does not contain alcoholic liquor in a proportion greater than 200 millilitres of liquor of a strength of 57 per cent of ethyl alcohol by volume (at a temperature of 20 degrees celsius) per kilogramme of the confectionery, and

(b) either consists of separate pieces weighing not more than 50 grammes or is designed to be broken into such pieces for the purpose of consumption'[7].

---

1 Section 201 defines 'intoxicating liquor' subject to the exclusion of inter alia 'any liquor which, whether made on the premises of a brewer for sale or elsewhere, is found on analysis of a sample thereof at any time to be of an original gravity not exceeding 1016° and of a strength not exceeding 1.2 per cent'.
2 This curious result is corrected in the Licensing (Low Alcohol Drinks) Act 1990, discussed below.
3 See the *Report of the Departmental Committee on Scottish Licensing Law* (Cmnd 5354) (*Clayson*), para 15.27, where it was considered that the consumption of shandy and similar beverages by persons under 18 was 'unlikely to have harmful medical or social consequences'. In terms of current food labelling regulations 'shandy' must have an alcoholic strength by volume ('abv') of at least 0.9 per cent: Food Labelling (Scotland) Regulations 1984, SI 1984/1519, Sch 7.
4 [1966] 1 All ER 661, [1966] 1 WLR 410.
5 Per Lord Parker, CJ.
6 Customs and Excise Act 1952, s 163, replaced by Alcoholic Liquor Duties Act 1979, s 72.
7 Section 127(1), as amended by the Licensing (Scotland) Act Amendment Regulations 1979, SI 1979/1755, made under the European Communities Act 1972, s 2(2).

However, while confectionery conforming to this description may thus be sold without a licence, no alcoholic liquor in *any* confectionery may 'knowingly' be sold to a person under the age of 16 (s 127(2))[1]. While the purpose of s 127 is to create a limited exception for liqueur chocolates[2] 'confectionery' is not defined and doubtless admits of a wider interpretation.

Licensing (Low Alcohol Drinks) Act 1990

This Act amends the definition of 'alcoholic liquor' in s 139(1) by substituting the words: 'is of a strength not exceeding 0.5%' for the words: from 'on analysis of' to the words '1.2%'[3]. The reference to 'original gravity' is thus removed; and a licence will be required for the sale of a number of products, typically beers or lagers with an abv of around 0.9%, currently available from unlicensed outlets[4].

If no commencement order is made before 1 January 1994, the Act will automatically come into force on that day[5]. The delay to date is due to necessary, consequential amendments to food labelling regulations which require to be approved by the European Commission and other EC member states[6].

Alcoholic liquor and offences

Proof that a particular liquid falls within the definition of 'alcoholic liquor' is, of course, central to the prosecution of a large number of offences under the Act.

Any liquid found in a (sealed or open) container is presumed to conform to the description on the container (s 127(2))[7]. A similar presumption applies where the contents of an open container defy analysis because there is insufficient liquid or where an open container is found to be empty: if the container was sealed when sold or supplied it shall be presumed to have contained at that time liquid matching the container description (s 127(3)).

Provided that the accused in any proceedings gives 'not less than seven days' notice (s 127(4))[8] to the prosecutor prior to the trial, he may rebut these presumptions (on the balance of probabilities)[9] by showing that: 'at the time of the sale or supply, the liquid in the container did not conform to the description of the liquid on the container' (s 127(5)).

Corroboration is not required:

'Where . . . an assumption falls to be made unless an accused proves otherwise, it is, we consider, in accordance with principle that the evidence led by the accused for this purpose

---

1 Maximum penalty: level 3 (Sch 5).
2 The corresponding provision of the Licensing Act 1964 (s 167) is headed: 'Saving for liqueur chocolates'.
3 Licensing (Low Alcohol Drinks) Act 1990, s 2.
4 See further '"Liquor" to be re-defined' [1990] 1 LR 1.
5 Licensing (Low Alcohol Drinks) Act 1990, s 3(2).
6 Food Labelling Directive 79/112/EEC.
7 Section 127(2)–(6) substituted by the 1990 Act, s 55(1).
8 Not less than seven *clear* days' notice is required: *McMillan v HM Advocate* 1982 SCCR 309, 1983 SLT 24; *Main v City of Glasgow Licensing Board* 1987 SLT 305.
9 *Neish v Stevenson* 1969 SLT 229. See also *HM Advocate v Mitchell* 1951 JC 53, 1951 SLT 200.

need not be corroborated: all that is required is that the court accepts the evidence led by the accused as being credible and reliable'[1].

It is sufficient for the Crown to prove that the liquid *in quo* is of an original gravity exceeding 1,016 degrees *or* of a strength above 1.2 per cent abv[2]. Thus, subject to the possible displacement of the statutory presumption, a bottle of beer with the label description 'Alc 6% vol.' contains 'alcoholic liquor' despite the absence of so-called 'gravity banding'[3].

However, where a cider bottle label described the contents as having been fermented to 'full strength' but gave no indication of original gravity or proof strength, in the absence of expert analysis, the High Court was drawn to the 'absurd' conclusion that the accused required to be acquitted[4].

Similarly, in *Grieve v Hillary*[5] the High Court held that a justice had not been entitled to conclude that three sealed cans of 'Schlitz', marked 'great American beer since 1849', contained 'intoxicating liquor'[6].

This area of licensing law has been significantly developed by a recent case, *Matchett v Douglas*[7]. A licenceholder was charged with the sale of alcoholic liquor to a number of persons under the age of 18[8]. Police officers investigating the offence were unable to obtain for analysis purposes samples of the liquor actually supplied but, several months later, procured samples of similar liquors from other licensed premises. Dismissing an appeal against conviction, the court endorsed 'brand sampling':

'It seems to us that if a named brand of alcoholic liquor is on sale at a given time, it is a reasonable inference that when the same named brand is found to be on sale elsewhere, either on the same date or at some different date, it will have the same properties so far as its original gravity and strength of ethyl alcohol by volume are concerned'.

On the other hand, no inference may be drawn which reaches the required standard that an *unnamed brand* will have characteristics equal to a *particular* brand of similar liquor. Accordingly, where an accused has sold an unknown brand of, say, lager to an under-age person, an analysis of a can of 'Skol' lager is (not surprisingly) evidentially worthless.

(2) The 'sale' of alcoholic liquor

While the reference to 'barter' in various sections of the Act is for the purpose of 'avoiding cavil and technical objection as to whether the Act was, strictly speak-

---

1 *King v Lees* 1993 SCCR 28 at 32, per the Lord Justice-Clerk, a road traffic case.
2 *Matchett v Douglas* 1992 SCLR 617, [1993] 12 LR 29.
3 The new definition of 'alcoholic liquor' to be introduced by the Licensing (Low Alcohol Drinks) Act 1990 (see above) dispenses with the reference to an original gravity figure.
4 *Tudhope v McDonald* 1986 SCCR 32. Note, however, that the definition of 'alcoholic liquor' is incorrectly stated in the court's opinion: the reference to '2 degree of proof' had been replaced by the 1.2 per cent abv figure.
5 1987 SCCR 317.
6 The prosecution was taken under British Rail byelaws which referred to the definition of 'intoxicating liquor' in the Licensing Act 1964, which is in point for the purpose of this discussion.
7 1992 SCCR 617, [1993] 12 LR 29.
8 Contrary to s 68(1) and (7).

ing, a sale or not; and not at all to create a new offence'[1] the concept of 'sale' is, itself, less than straightforward.

While 'a publican does not, more than any other of the lieges, require a certificate to supply his household with food and drink, or to entertain his friends or relatives'[2] there may be a 'sale' of alcoholic liquor although the transaction is structured as a gift[3]. Such a conclusion may be reached without difficulty where the price of one commodity has been adjusted to allow for the accompanying 'free' provision of alcohol. A number of English decisions indicate that a 'sale' takes place although it is impossible to ascribe any part of a purchase price to the 'free' article. In *Scott & Co v Solomon*[4] a conviction for dealing in plate without a licence was upheld where packets of tea, sold at their normal price, were accompanied by coupons which, if collected in sufficient quantities, could be exchanged for inter alia gold watches. The Lord Chief Justice (Alverstone) said:

'Each of the various purchasers got in return for the payment they made, not only the tea, but also this coupon. Of course the suggestion that full value in tea was given in return for the price paid, meaning that there was nothing charged for these coupons, is simply absurd'[5].

On the broadly similar facts of *Taylor v Smetten*[6] it was 'impossible to suppose that the aggregate prices charged and obtained for the [tea] did not include the aggregate prices of the tea and the prizes'.

'Sale' does not mean 'sale at a pr ᶜt': 'It appears to me immaterial whether the sum [paid for] the liquor is equal to or more or less than the cost price. The transaction does not become the more or less a sale on that account'[7]. Licensing boards have no control over the price at which alcoholic liquor is sold on licensed premises, although 'loss leader' promotions in entertainment licensed premises may conceivably be struck at by a condition imposed in terms of s 101(2)[8]. While the 'long pull' provisions of the Licensing (Scotland) Act 1959 are omitted from the 1976 Act[9], the ethos of the earlier legislation lives on in some areas where the gratuitous supply of alcohol by licenceholders is met with opprobrium.

Alcoholic liquor which has been paid for need not be identifiable as the purchaser's property. In *Doak v Bedford*[10] an organiser of 'social parties' collected sums of money in advance from 'guests' who thereby acquired the right to help themselves to drink. No money changed hands at the parties and there was no

---

1 *Bruce v Linton* (1861) 24 D 184 at 191, per the Lord Justice-Clerk (Inglis).
2 *Smith v Stirling* (1878) 5 R (J) 24. The actual decision in this case is no longer of relevance as respects gratuitous supply outwith the permitted hours: see *Jack v Thom* 1952 JC 41, 1952 SLT 161.
3 A bona fide gift is not a 'sale': *Petherick v Sargent* (1862) 26 JP 135. It may, however, constitute 'supply': see below.
4 [1905] 1 KB 577.
5 See also the House of Lords decision in *Imperial Tobacco Ltd v Attorney-General* [1981] AC 718, [1980] 1 All ER 866, [1980] 2 WLR 466, in which payment for a packet of cigarettes, at their normal price, amounted to payment for the chance of a prize.
6 (1883) 11 QBD 207. Coupons with packets of tea entitled the purchaser to a 'mystery' prize.
7 *Graff v Evans* (1882) 8 QBD 373 at 378, per Field J.
8 See the consideration of entertainment licences in general in chapter 3.
9 Section 149 of the 1959 Act prohibited the sale or supply of a quantity of liquor in excess of the amount requested by the purchaser. *Clayson* (para 15.18) considered that the prohibition no longer served any useful purpose. Cf Licensing Act 1964, s 165.
10 [1964] 2 QB 587.

restriction on the amount of alcohol which could be consumed. The transactions were held to amount to 'sales': 'If I pay a sum of money for the right, inter alia, to pick out such goods as I desire from a shelf and make those mine, in my judgment when I so pick out such goods, those goods have been sold to me'[1].

Where the proprietor of unlicensed premises (usually a restaurant) or one of his staff makes a purchase purely as agent for a customer, no illegal 'sale' takes place[2], provided, of course, that no 'mark-up' is applied[3]. It has been held that a number of sales to different persons on different days constituted one offence for 'the charge is not of effecting sales but of trafficking without a licence'[4].

Restriction on credit sales

Section 87 restricts the sale (or supply) of alcoholic liquor on credit where consumption is to take place in licensed premises or in the premises of a registered club: subject to the exceptions explained below, the liquor must be 'paid for before or at the time when it is supplied or sold' (s 87(1))[5]. An offence is committed by any person who sells or supplies[6] or consumes[7] in contravention of this provision (s 87(2)).

Credit sales are not prohibited in the following circumstances:
(1) Where the liquor is (a) sold or supplied for consumption *at* a meal, (b) supplied *at the same time* as the meal, (c) consumed *with* the meal, and (d) paid for with the meal (s 87(1), proviso (a)). This exemption does not apply where the drink is simply 'ancillary' to the meal[8], with the result that a pre- or post-prandial drink cannot be added to a food bill; but where the conditions of the exemption are met, settlement of a food and drink account may take place a considerable time after the sale or supply.
(2) Where the liquor is sold or supplied for consumption by (a) a person residing in the premises (see s 139(3))[9] or (b) a resident's 'private friend' at the former's expense[10] with the liquor and accommodation being paid for at the same time (whenever payment takes place) (s 87(1), proviso (b)).
(3) Where the liquor is paid for by production of 'a credit token within the meaning of the Consumer Credit Act 1974, s 14' in premises which are the

---

1 At 596, per Paull J.
2 *Langmuir v Persichini* 1935 JC 73, 1935 SLT 399. See, however, s 97(3).
3 *Taylor v Oram* (1862) 27 JP 8. See also the discussion of agency sales at [1991] 4 LR 26, 27.
4 *McCluskey v Boyd* 1916 JC 31, (1916) 1 SLT 322. See also *Manson v MacLeod* 1918 JC 60, (1918) 1 SLT 230. Cf *Lord Advocate v D&J Nicol* 1915 SC (J) 735, (1915) 1 SLT 274.
5 It need not, of course, be paid for by the person actually supplied. *Clayson* (para 15.19) considered that this provision 'serves a useful purpose' by avoiding 'any encouragement towards excessive drinking or financial extravagance as a result of a too liberal grant of credit'. The committee recommended that the reforming legislation should, however, give limited recognition to the use of credit cards, which indicated 'some degree of financial responsibility' on the part of the card-holder: see below.
6 Maximum penalty: level 3. Licenceholder and premises liable to disqualification (s 67, Sch 5).
7 Maximum penalty: level 3 (Sch 5).
8 See discussion of 'ancillary' at p 42 below.
9 Under certain circumstances a person 'resides' in premises although occupying sleeping accommodation in a separate building.
10 Cf s 54(3)(e), discussed in Chapter 10; and see *Jack v Thom* 1952 JC 41, 1952 SLT 161.

subject of a hotel, restricted hotel licence, restaurant or entertainment licence *but not* in a 'public bar' of such premises (s 87(1), proviso (c))[1].

The following are examples of a 'credit token': credit cards issued to business users by hotel groups; Access and Visa cards; and 'checks' or vouchers issued by finance companies. The expression does *not* include 'charge' cards such as those issued by American Express, nor the so-called 'Gold' forms of Access and Visa cards, where payment of the account balance is required in full at the expiry of a certain period[2].

However, the Court of Appeal has now recognised 'the popular perception of the role of credit cards in modern retail trade as "plastic money"'[3], holding that garage customers using charge cards to pay for petrol had absolutely discharged their obligations to the retailer. The (inferential) prohibition on the use of a 'credit token' in public houses and hotel bars is irreconcilable with this decision.

Nothing contained in s 87 prohibits or restricts the sale or supply of alcoholic liquor 'to any canteen in which the sale or supply of alcoholic liquor is carried on under the authority of the Secretary of State or to any authorised mess of the members of Her Majesty's naval, military or air forces' (s 87(4))[4].

Sale and 'supply'

While a licence may be granted 'to any person for the sale by retail or supply of alcoholic liquor' (s 9(1)), the word 'supply' does not appear within the definition of trafficking in s 139(1)[5]; but it is no doubt the case that 'only a licensed person can supply liquor'[6] and a commercial 'supply'[7] will normally amount to trafficking in one of its forms for the purpose of s 90(a).

However, the word 'supply' (not defined in the Act) *is* employed in relation to certain offences, apparently as a 'catch all' to embrace the provision or distribution of alcoholic liquor *otherwise than by way of sale*[8] and import a 'universal prohibition'[9]: for example, except in certain circumstances, gratuitous supply

---

1 Note, however, that premises for which a restricted hotel or restaurant licence is held may not, in any event, contain a 'bar'; and it is at least arguable that a drinking area in entertainment-licensed premises does not constitute a 'bar', since, by definition, the sale or supply of alcoholic liquor is an 'ancillary' activity. See examination of various types of licences in chapter 3.
2 Consumer Credit Act 1974, s 14 provides inter alia that: 'A credit-token is a card, check, voucher, coupon, stamp, form, booklet or other document or thing given to an individual by a person carrying on a consumer credit business', the production of which procures the supply of cash, goods or services on credit.
3 *In re Charge Card Services Ltd* [1988] 3 WLR 764 at 775, per Sir Nicolas Browne-Wilkinson V-C. No distinction was drawn between credit and charge cards.
4 The reference to the Secretary of State includes a reference to the service authorities of a visiting force and the reference to members of Her Majesty's forces includes a reference to members of a visiting force: Visiting Forces and International Headquarters (Application of Law) Order 1965, SI 1965/1536; and Visiting Forces (Designation) (Colonies) (Amendment) Order 1958, SI 1958/1262.
5 See *Macdonald v Skinner* 1979 JC 29, 1978 SLT (Notes) 52.
6 *Bennet v Hanks* [1954] Brewing Tr Rev 410.
7 See *John v Matthews* [1970] 2 QB 443, [1970] 2 WLR 1246.
8 See *Emerson v Hall-Dalwood* (1918) 82 JP 50.
9 *Sinclair v Beattie* 1934 JC 24.

outwith the permitted hours is forbidden[1], while 'supply' is disjunctively associated with 'sale' and 'trafficking' in a number of sections (eg, in s 99)[2].

The 'sale' of alcoholic liquor to a member in a registered club[3] is, in fact, a 'supply'[4], although the liquor is 'sold' at a profit paid into the club's funds[5].

(3) Sale 'by retail'

Apart from the limited constraints on wholesale dealing, discussed below, the Act is concerned only with 'retail' sales of alcoholic liquor, but fails to furnish an appropriate definition[6]. The difference between 'wholesale' and 'retail' selling is, however, determined by reference to the quantity supplied, having regard to the provisions of revenue legislation[7]. Thus, in *Wood v Mackenzie*[8] the High Court rejected the prosecution argument that a 'retail' sale took place where the purchaser was simply a member of the public:

'[T]he criterion of a wholesale transaction, as distinguished from a retail transaction, in the [Finance (1909–1910) Act 1910][9] is simply and solely one of quantity sold, and there is no suggestion that, provided that quantity is sold, it is in the least degree material to inquire to whom it is sold'[10].

For the purpose of the Licensing (Scotland) Act 1959, 'sale by retail' was defined by reference to s 148(4) of the Customs and Excise Act 1952, now repealed[11]. The current revenue definition is to be found in s 4(4) of the Alcoholic Liquor Duties Act 1979[12] which prescribes maxima for the purpose of 'selling by retail'. No doubt confusingly, however, the line between 'wholesale' and 'retail' is drawn by reference to the definition of 'wholesale' in s 4(1) of the 1979 Act:

'"wholesale", in relation to dealing in dutiable alcoholic liquor, means the sale at any one time to any one person of quantities not less than the following, namely –
(a) in the case of spirits, wine or made-wine, 9 litres or 1 case; or
(b) in the case of beer or cider, 20 litres or 2 cases'[13].

---

1 See *Jack v Thom* 1952 JC 41, 1952 SLT 161.
2 In an unusual wartime case, *Mackenna v Brady* 1918 JC 37, the owner of licensed premises was convicted of 'supplying' himself with his own stock outwith permitted hours.
3 For registered clubs: see Chapter 16.
4 *Crossgates British Legion Club v Davidson* 1954 JC 35, 1954 SLT 124. Cf *John v Matthews* [1970] 2 QB 443, [1970] 2 WLR 1246.
5 *Graff v Evans* (1882) 8 QBD 373.
6 Cf Licensing Act 1964, s 201.
7 For a criticism of this approach, see James Scott 'Wholesaling of alcoholic liquor' [1992] 11 LR 3.
8 1925 JC 13, 1925 SLT 28.
9 Which prescribed the minimum quantity of inter alia beer which could be sold to one person at any one time under a wholesale dealer's licence, and the maximum under a retail dealer's licence. These excise liquor licences are, of course, no longer required.
10 Per Lord Justice-Clerk Alness, 1925 JC 13 at 17.
11 Finance Act 1981, Sch 19.
12 As amended by Alcoholic Liquors (Amendment of Enactments Relating to Strength and to Units of Measurement) Order 1979, SI 1979/241, arts 4, 8(b).
13 This definition has been expressly adopted for the purpose of s 90A: see below.

'Case' means:

'1 dozen units each consisting of a container holding not less than 65 nor more than 80 centilitres, or the equivalent of that number of such units made up wholly or partly of containers of a larger or smaller size'[1].

Where a wholesale quantity has been demanded and paid for, the transaction does not assume a 'retail' character where, through inadvertence, the quantity actually delivered falls marginally short of the wholesale minimum:

'In my opinion it does not change the character of the transaction and transform it into a retail transaction that . . . it was subsequently ascertained that there was a shortage of quantity'[2].

The delivery of alcoholic liquor in retail quantities to a customer pursuant to an antecedent wholesale purchase does not constitute a 'sale by retail'[3].

Wholesalers

Section 138(2)(b) removes the sale of alcoholic liquor by a wholesaler from the ambit of the Act, 'save as expressly provided'[4]. Following the abolition of the wholesaler's excise licence by the Finance Act 1981, Sch 19, the bulk sale of alcoholic liquor became wholly deregulated. Evidence of abuse prompted the imposition of limited controls[5]. In terms of s 90A(1)[6] a 'wholesaler'[7] or his employee or agent commits an offence if he 'barters, sells, or exposes or offers for sale' alcoholic liquor unless:

'(a) he does so from premises which are used exclusively for wholesale[8] trading (whether solely of alcoholic liquor or not); or
(b) he does so from licensed premises, a licensed canteen or a registered club during the hours in respect of which it is lawful to sell alcohol by retail from or in these premises, that canteen or that club'[9].

Very few 'cash-and-carry' warehouses are used 'exclusively' for wholesale trading, if one accepts that wholesale dealing consists of sales to a retailer in

---

1 Alcoholic Liquor Duties Act 1979, s 4(1), as amended by Alcoholic Liquors (Amendment of Enactments Relating to Strength and to Units of Measurement) Order 1979, SI 1979/241, arts 4, 8(a))(ii).
2 *Wood v Mackenzie* 1925 JC 13 at 20, per Lord Anderson.
3 *Hales v Buckley* (1911) 75 JP 214.
4 Although the holders of restaurant (s 99(b)), refreshment (s 100(b)), entertainment (s 101(1)) and (with a limited exception) restricted hotel licences (s 98(2)) may not traffick in or supply alcoholic liquor for consumption off the premises, s 138(2)(b) appears to legitimise wholesale dealing.
5 Restrictions on the sale of alcoholic liquor by or to persons under 18 are considered in Chapter 14.
6 Added by 1990 Act, s 52.
7 '"Wholesaler" means a person who deals wholesale in dutiable alcoholic liquor': Alcoholic Liquor Duties Act 1979, s 4(1), applied by s 90A(6), so far as relating to the sale of alcoholic liquor. 'Dutiable alcoholic liquor' is defined in s 1(1) of the 1979 Act.
8 'Wholesale': the definition contained in s 4(1) of the Alcoholic Liquor Duties Act 1979 (above) is applied by s 90A(6), so far as relating to the sale of alcoholic liquor.
9 Maximum penalty: level 5. The wholesaler has vicarious responsibility (s 67, Sch 5). The 'due diligence' defence provided by s 71 is available (s 90A(5)). For permitted and trading hours: see Chapter 10.

quantities larger than those sold to the final consumer. The majority allow customers to purchase at least certain commodities singly. Even if alcoholic liquor sales are restricted to the wholesale minimum, the 'exclusively' test is not satisfied in such cases. However, where exemption may properly be claimed, unlicensed warehouses may be used for the sale of alcoholic liquor without restriction as to trading hours.

The majority of 'cash-and-carry' warehouses (and some brewery distribution depots) are off-sale licensed for the purpose of occasional sales in retail quantities and are thus restricted to the trading hours specified in s 119, which prohibits the serving of customers with liquor on Sundays (s 119(3))[1].

TRAFFICKING

We have observed that the offence of 'trafficking' in alcoholic liquor without a licence, constituted by s 90(a), embraces 'bartering, selling, dealing in, trading in, or exposing or offering for sale, by retail'[2], and that a 'sale' may take place under a variety of guises.

In all its forms the offence may only be committed 'in any premises or place', that is to say, a location which is capable of being licensed, either on the usual, permanent basis or by means of an occasional licence under s 33[3]. Thus, the sale of liquor in a public street is excluded, but will amount to the separate offence of 'hawking'[4], discussed below. In *Hutcheon v Cadenhead*[5] the word 'place' was construed 'in the fullest sense of the term': it certainly included a tent in a grass field and could include the whole field, the Lord Justice-Clerk considering that a licence could be granted for 'a spot under a particular tree'.

While no offence is committed where a licenceholder or his traveller visits customers and obtains orders for future delivery from licensed premises[6], convictions have been upheld where orders have been accepted at unlicensed premises for execution at licensed premises[7].

We now consider the various modes of commission[8].

---

1 Trading hours are restricted to the period between 8 am and 10 pm on Mondays to Saturdays. Prior to the insertion of s 90A, a number of cash-and-carry operators had lawfully sold liquor in wholesale quantities on Sundays.
2 Definition of 'trafficking' in s 139(1).
3 *Hamilton v Inglis* (1879) 6 R (J) 45. Semble a sale outwith the hours authorised by an occasional licence constitutes trafficking: the Act's provisions anent 'permitted hours' do not apply (s 33(6)) so that the offence is not committed under s 54(1), (4) (sale or supply outwith permitted hours).
4 *Hamilton v Inglis*, above.
5 (1892) 19 R (J) 32.
6 *Cameron v Buchan* (1896) 23 R (J) 46, (1896) 3 SLT 269. See discussion of 'Hawking', below.
7 *Guild v Freeman* (1898) 25 R (J) 106; *Elias v Dunlop* [1906] 1 KB 266, both decided under now repealed revenue legislation.
8 Ignoring 'barter', the inclusion of which is purely for the avoidance of 'cavil and technical objection'; *Bruce v Linton* (1861) 24 D 184 at 191 per the Lord Justice-Clerk (Inglis).

Sales other than by licenceholder

While trafficking in its simplest form occurs where alcoholic liquor is sold from unlicensed premises, it requires to be kept in view that the authority conferred by a licence in force is personal to the licenceholder. Section 9(1) permits the grant of a licence 'to any person' for the sale or supply of alcoholic liquor '*by that person*'. Axiomatically, the sale by any other person amounts to trafficking. Purchasers and new tenants of licensed premises wishing to commence business pending the determination of a transfer application[1] require to be reminded that they may not lawfully do so[2]. The licence may not be 'negotiated' by the endorsement of the holder's consent[3].

The transfer of a licence precludes the continuation or resumption of trading by the transferor[4]. Care requires to be taken that a prospective transferee's date of entry is synchronised with the date of transfer.

The 'personal' nature of licenceholding suggests that the profit from liquor sales should accrue to the licenceholder alone. This proposition requires refinement. Section 17(1)(a) directs a licensing board to refuse an application for inter alia the grant of a new licence where it finds that the applicant *or* 'the person on whose behalf or for whose benefit the applicant will manage the premises' is not a 'fit and proper person'. This provision: 'clearly envisages . . . a situation in which the owner of premises appoints a manager to run his licensed business' and act as licenceholder[5]. Such an expedient is adopted where the proprietor of a number of premises is unable to hold more than a certain quota of licences[6].

However, while s 11 provides that a licence may be held by a non-natural person (usually a partnership or limited company) with a named employee or agent, (a) no parallel provision is made for 'agency' licenceholding by one non-natural person on behalf of another[7]; and (b) a natural person should not hold a licence in his own name on behalf of a juristic persona[8]. Indeed, while only a non-natural person which is a trading entity should hold a licence, so-called 'shelf' companies are routinely purchased *purely* for licenceholding purposes: the whole share capital may be procured by the purchaser of the business, omitting the necessity to have the licence transferred and circumventing any potential difficulties with the transferability of ancillary permissions (principally the regular extension of permitted hours) (s 64: see Chapter 10). It is suggested that this practice involves a contravention of s 90(a).

Facilities for the sale of alcoholic liquor are sometimes franchised to an outside organisation by the owner of the principal business conducted at the premises: for example, the operation of a bar or restaurant within an entertainment complex

---

1 Transfers of licences: see Chapter 5.
2 See Note by John A Loudon, (1988) JLSS 34.
3 *Hawick Heritable Investment Bank Ltd v Huggan* (1902) 5 F 75, (1902) 10 SLT 320, (1902) 40 SLR 33.
4 *Miller v Linton* (1888) 15 R (J) 37; *Campbell v Neilson* (1897) 24 R (J) 28, (1897) 4 SLT 269.
5 *Tominey v City of Glasgow District Licensing Board* 1984 SLT (Sh Ct) 2.
6 Local practices vary. Some licensing boards will not allow an individual to be the holder of more than one licence; in other areas the maximum number is two or (rarely) three.
7 See the First Division's interpretation of s 17(1)(a) in *Fereneze Leisure Ltd v Renfrew District Licensing Board* 1991 SCLR 751, 1992 SLT 604.
8 See *Paterson v City of Glasgow District Licensing Board* 1982 SLT (Sh Ct) 37.

may be entrusted to a catering company. Although the nature of the contract between the parties will require to be considered, the franchisee's position will normally be approximate to that of a tenant and he will properly hold the licence, although the franchiser may receive royalty-type payments linked to turnover.

Where an insolvent licenceholder grants a trust deed for behoof of his creditors the licence neither lapses nor becomes part of the trust estate and he may carry on business through a manager[1].

Dealing and trading

A consideration of the authorities suggests that the court is reluctant to hold that 'dealing' or 'trading' have taken place where the conduct *in quo* does not amount to a sale[2].

In *Robertson v Provident Clothing and Supply Co Ltd*[3], clients of a finance company ('Provident') were afforded credit facilities for their purchase of parcels containing alcoholic liquor from nominated suppliers. Payment was made by Provident's 'checks', the face value of which was repaid to them by their clients over a number of weeks, with the addition of a 'poundage fee'; Provident made payment to the suppliers at a discount[4]. Upholding Provident's acquittal on a charge of trafficking in 'exciseable liquor', the High Court held that the company, in the role of financiers, was solely concerned with a contract for the provision of credit and, 'without unduly stretching the meaning of the words', it could not be said that it was 'trading or dealing' in liquor.

On the more persuasive facts of *Macdonald v Skinner*[5], the High Court was not prepared to find that the largesse of a hotel proprietor who dispensed free drinks to customers, following the loss of his licence, amounted to 'dealing in' alcoholic liquor by retail. While there was no evidence of covert payment[6], the *Macdonald* decision has generally been regarded as surprising and there may yet be circumstances in which the court will take a stricter view.

'Exposing or offering' for sale

A well-established distinction falls to be drawn between an 'offer to sell' and 'an invitation to treat':

'It is perfectly clear that according to the ordinary law of contract the display of an article with a price on it in a shop window is merely an invitation . . . [I]t is to be observed that in many statutes and orders which prohibit selling and offering for sale of goods it is very

---

1 *Wylie v Thom* (1889) 16 R (J) 90. A similar opinion was expressed obiter in *Rattray v White* (1891) 19 R (J) 23.
2 'Trade in its largest sense is the business of selling, with a view to profit, goods which the trader has either manufactured or himself purchased': *Grainger & Son v Gough* [1896] AC 325 at 345, 346 per Lord Davey.
3 1961 JC 16, 1961 SLT 170.
4 All the elements of a credit-card purchase are present and this case, if otherwise decided may have had a stultifying effect on the use of third-party credit facilities for the purchase of alcohol.
5 1979 JC 29, 1978 SLT (Notes) 52.
6 Cf *Scott & Co v Solomon* [1905] 1 KB 577.

common when it is so desired to insert the words "offering or exposing for sale", "exposing for sale" being clearly words which would cover the display of goods in a shop window"[1].

Similarly, the display of goods in a 'self-service' setting does not per se constitute an 'offer to sell'[2]; and 'strictly you do not offer goods for sale by inserting an advertisement in a newspaper'[3].

An auctioneer does not 'offer to sell' but invites 'offers to buy' from persons attending the auction[4]. The offer of credit to facilitate the purchase of alcoholic liquor by a finance company's customers is not an 'offer to sell' the liquor[5].

Police entry to unlicensed premises

A police officer occupying the rank of inspector or above has power to inspect and enter at any time 'any temperance hotel, restaurant, shop, vessel or other place where food and drink is sold for consumption on the premises or in which he has reasonable grounds for believing that alcoholic liquor is being trafficked in unlawfully' (s 86(1)).

An officer of a lower rank may also exercise this power but must first have obtained the authority in writing of (a) a justice of the peace or (b) an officer of or above the rank of inspector; such authority is valid only for eight days and may only be exercised 'on such time or times' as specified (s 86(1), proviso).

Any person who fails to admit a police officer demanding entry or obstructs his entry is guilty of an offence (s 86(2))[6].

Proof of trafficking

Section 122 provides that there shall be 'sufficient evidence' that a person has been trafficking without a licence 'in any premises or place'[7] if it is proved:

'(a) that a person other than the owner or occupier of such premises or place was at the time charged found therein[8] drunk[9] or drinking[10], or having had drink supplied to him therein; and

---

1 *Fisher v Bell* [1961] 1 QB 394 at 399 per Lord Parker, CJ. A shopkeeper who displayed a flick-knife in his window was acquitted of 'offering to sell' the article. Cf the observations of Lord Parker, CJ in *John v Mathews* [1970] 2 WLR 1246 at 1250. For an example of 'exposure for sale' in the context of s 39(2) of the Civic Government (Scotland) Act 1982, see *Joseph Dunn (Bottlers) Ltd v MacDougall* 1987 SCCR 290.
2 *Pharmaceutical Society of Great Britain v Boots Cash Chemists (Southern) Ltd* [1953] 1 QB 401, [1953] 2 WLR 427.
3 *British Car Auctions Ltd v Wright* [1972] 1 WLR 1519, per Lord Widgery, CJ, referring to the decision in *Partridge v Crittenden* [1968] 2 All ER 421, [1968] 1 WLR 1204.
4 *British Car Auctions Ltd v Wright*, above.
5 *Robertson v Provident Clothing and Supply Co Ltd* 1961 JC 16, 1961 SLT 170.
6 Maximum penalty: level 3 (Sch 5). The police officer is under an obligation to make his identity known: *Alexander v Rankin* (1899) 1 F (J) 58.
7 Which, as explained above, must be capable of being licensed.
8 For a consideration of 'found in any premises', see *Maclean v Paterson* 1968 JC 67, 1968 SLT 374 in which the phrase was considered to mean 'found physically on the premises at the relevant moment'; cf *Marr v Heywood* 1993 SCCR 441.
9 'Drunk': see Chapter 13.
10 A person found 'drunk or drinking' in unlicensed premises is guilty of an offence (s 82). Maximum penalty: level 1 (Sch 5).

(b) either that such premises are or such place is, by repute, kept for the illegal sale of alcoholic liquor or that at the time charged such premises or place contained drinking utensils and fittings usually found in licensed premises'.

In *Macdonald v Skinner*[1] the Crown conceded (correctly, in the opinion of the court) that the omission of the words 'in the absence of any contrary evidence', which had appeared in the corresponding provisions of earlier Acts[2], did not exclude the potential displacement of the presumption by evidence which established that what took place was not 'trafficking'.

Where evidence was led that the accused's premises were, by repute, kept as a shebeen, it was held that the statutory presumption need not have been libelled, nor was it necessary for the prosecutor to give notice in the complaint that he intended to prove such repute[3].

Section 312(v) of the Criminal Procedure (Scotland) Act 1975 provides that:

'Any exception, exemption, proviso, excuse or qualification . . . may be proved by the accused, but need not be specified or negatived in the complaint, and no proof in relation to such exception, exemption, proviso, excuse or qualification shall be required on behalf of the prosecution'.

In *McCluskey v Boyd*[4] the High Court held that, by virtue of a similar provision[5]: 'it was wholly unnecessary for the prosecutor to allege or prove that the accused had no licence, but it was certainly open to her both to allege and to prove that she had'[6].

No reliance should be placed on this decision, which has been the subject of considerable criticism[7].

Exemptions

Section 138 removes from the scope of the Act 'trafficking' in:
(a) *Service canteens* held 'under the authority of the Secretary of State' (s 138(1)(a))[8]. The sale or supply of alcoholic liquor to these canteens is authorised outwith the permitted hours (s 54(3)(j)); they are also expressly exempted from the general prohibition on credit sales (s 87(3)).
(b) *Theatres erected before 1 January 1904* (s 138(1)(b)). These theatres are 'treated for the purposes of the sale or supply of alcoholic liquor' as if an entertainment licence[9] were in force (s 121). They are not otherwise integrated into the scheme of the Act. The notional licence is 'held' on a permanent basis, there is no

1 1979 JC 29, 1978 SLT (Notes) 52.
2 See *Purves's Scottish Licensing Laws* (8th edn, 1961, ed Walker), p 199.
3 *Mann v Cadenhead* (1886) 13 R (J) 60, (1886) 23 SLR 640.
4 1916 JC 31, (1916) 1 SLT 322.
5 Summary Jurisdiction (Scotland) Act 1908, s 19.
6 Cf *Zaino v Malloch* (1902) 4 F (J) 94.
7 See *Renton and Brown's Criminal Procedure* (5th edn), paras 13–52, 13–53 and cases cited.
8 Service canteens are operated by the Navy, Army and Air Force Institutes ('NAAFI') under rules published by the Ministry of Defence. The reference to the Secretary of State includes a reference to the service authorities of a visiting force: Visiting Forces and International Headquarters (Application of Law) Order 1965, SI 1965/1536; and Visiting Forces (Designation) (Colonies) (Amendment) Order 1958, SI 1958/1262.
9 Entertainment licences in general are discussed in Chapter 3.

notional licenceholder, the conduct of the theatre is beyond the supervision of the licensing board, and there are no 'permitted hours'[1]. In terms of Schedule 1, where an entertainment licence is in force the holder is authorised to 'sell by retail or supply alcoholic liquor to persons frequenting the premises for consumption on the premises as an ancillary to the entertainment provided'. Sale or supply in any other circumstances is not *ipso facto* an offence: while compliance may normally be secured by the attachment of a condition by the licensing board in terms of s 101(2), no such facility exists in relation to the notional entertainment licence, so that alcoholic liquor may apparently be sold without any form of accountability.

The Act's deficiencies in this regard were to some extent focused on in *Standard Taverns v McAneny*[2], a petition for interdict arising from the operation of a café bar within the Theatre Royal in Glasgow, operated independently of the theatre and essentially as a public house, on the basis of the exemption provided by s 138(1)(b). The Lord Ordinary (Cullen) refused interim interdict[3]:

'Standing the terms of section 138(1)(b) I was not satisfied that the petitioners had demonstrated that the sale or supply of alcohol which they sought to prevent was at least prima facie unlawful. That provision is in unqualified terms. It also appeared to me to be of some significance that the Act did not contain any indication that in the case of a "deemed entertainment licence" it was intended that the sale or supply of alcohol in a way which would go beyond the scope of the definition of an actual entertainment licence would constitute an offence'.

(c) *Aircraft*. The sale or supply of alcoholic liquor to aircraft passengers is unregulated while the 'plane is airborne' (s 138(1)(c)).
(d) *Railway passenger vehicles*, provided that 'passengers can be supplied with food' (s 138(1)(c))[4].
(e) *Passenger vessels* while in the course of being navigated (s 138(1)(c))[5].

HAWKING

Any person who 'hawks alcoholic liquor' is guilty of an offence (s 90(c))[6]. In terms of s 139(1)[7] 'hawking' means 'trafficking in or about the roads or other places or

---

1 Leading to the suggestion that 'alcoholic liquor may be provided at any time that the theatre is open for business as an ancillary to the entertainment provided': *2 Stair Memorial Encyclopaedia* para 26; but see below as to the absence of an enforcement mechanism.
2 Outer House, 14 May 1993, unreported.
3 At the date of completion of this text, the petition, brought by the proprietors of neighbouring public houses, had not further progressed. A question as to whether the café bar formed part of the 'theatre' had yet to be resolved.
4 It may be observed that no provision is made for the sale of alcohol on coaches, which are not capable of being licensed.
5 The sale or supply of alcoholic liquor on Sundays is restricted to the periods between 12.30 pm and 2.30 pm and 6.30 pm to 11 pm where the vessel is travelling between two places in Scotland or engaged in a voyage departing from and returning to the same place in Scotland: see s 93.
6 Maximum penalty: level 3. Where the offence is committed by the holder of a licence, both he and the premises in respect of which the licence is held are liable to disqualification, (s 67, Sch 5) although, as explained below, 'hawking' takes place other than in licensed premises. See also s 97(3).
7 As amended by the Roads (Scotland) Act 1984, Sch 9.

in or from any boat or vessel[1] on the water'. In contradistinction to 'trafficking' in any premises or place, this offence may only be committed in a place which *cannot* be licensed. The difference was carefully considered in *Hutcheon v Cadenhead*[2], Lord Rutherfurd Clark observing that 'if there must be some building' to justify the grant of an occasional licence, 'it may be granted for the outside as well as the inside of the building'; indeed, according to circumstances, such a licence could be granted for a field. Thus, it may not be said with complete precision that hawking will always take place outdoors. Indeed, sales which 'are made in private premises of any kind' probably do not fall within the definition[3].

Hutcheon supplies the classic judicial interpretation of 'hawking', based on an earlier (and virtually identical) statutory definition:

'A hawker is an itinerant trader who brings the goods to his customers wherever they may be . . . I doubt if the language of [the definition] can be construed apart altogether from the ordinary meaning of the word which it is intended to define, and I am disposed to think that it means nothing more than that a single act of sale shall be held to be hawking[4] although that word in its ordinary sense signifies a trade or practice. But the sales which fall within the definition are not the less sales irrespective of trade premises'[5].

The hawker carries his goods with him[6]. A licenceholder or his representative may visit customers and solicit orders for future delivery, even on a public road, provided that the goods are appropriated to the purchaser at the licensed premises (which must, of course, be licensed for off-sales)[7]. *Per contra*, where jars of beer were delivered to customers at their homes in implement of previous orders but the containers were not labelled with the names of the purchasers, it was held that sales had not taken place at the licensed premises[8].

The offence was not made out where a club member made a single purchase of whisky inside club premises, purely as mandatory for a member of the public, and delivered the liquor in the street[9]; but a conviction was warranted where three similar transactions took place, at a profit, on the same day[10]. Note, however, that in terms of s 95(1) off-sales from the premises of a registered club are prohibited, except for personal consumption by a member or where the sale is to the holder of a licence.

1 Licences have been granted for permanently-moored craft: cf *Gate v Bath Justices* (1983) 147 JP 289.
2 (1892) 19 R (J) 32.
3 *Hutcheon v Cadenhead*, above, at 35 per Lord Rutherfurd Clark. As to specification of the locus, see *Hamilton v Inglis* (1879) 6 R (J) 46.
4 Similarly, in *Russell v Paton* (1902) 4 F (J) 77, (1902) 10 SLT 94 it was considered sufficient for the prosecutor to libel one act of sale in a street.
5 Per Lord Rutherfurd Clark; see above.
6 *Cameron v Buchan* (1896) 23 R (J) 46, (1896) 3 SLT 269. See also *Robertson v Provident Clothing and Supply Co Ltd*, 1961 JC 16, 1961 SLT 170.
7 *Cameron v Buchan*, above; *Pletts v Beattie* [1896] 1 QB 519. See also *Titmus v Littlewood* [1916] 1 KB 732; *Mizen v Old Florida Ltd* (1934) 50 TLR 349.
8 *Pletts v Campbell* [1895] 2 QB 299. For provisions regulating deliveries from vehicles etc, see s 91 and Chapter 13.
9 *Dewart v Neilson* (1900) 2 F (J) 57, (1900) 8 SLT 147.
10 *Neilson v Dunsmore* (1900) 3 F (J) 6, (1900) 8 SLT 339.

CHAPTER 3

Types of licences

The types of licences which may be granted (s 9(3)) and the authority which they confer for the sale of alcoholic liquor (Sch 1) are now considered[1].

PUBLIC HOUSE LICENCE

A public house licence is 'a licence granted in respect of a public house specified therein which authorises the holder thereof to sell by retail alcoholic liquor for consumption on or off the premises' (Sch 1). The expression 'public house' includes 'an inn, ale-house, victualling house or other premises in which alcoholic liquor is sold by retail for consumption on or off the premises' (s 139(1). Because of the very broad authority which it confers for the sale or supply of alcoholic liquor, this licence lends itself to a variety of applications beyond the traditional 'pub'. For example:
(a) A department store containing restaurant and off-sale sections could not be operated under any other licence: refreshment and restaurant licences do not permit the sale of alcoholic liquor for consumption off the premises (s 100(a) (refreshment); s 99(b) (restaurant)) while alcoholic liquor may not be sold for consumption in off-sale premises (s 97(1)). Since the normal permitted hours for public house premises commence at 11 am on weekdays (s 53(1)) the licence would require to be subject to a condition in terms of s 119, permitting off-sales from 8 am until 10 pm; but where this condition applies the off-sale part 'shall not be open for the serving of customers with [alcoholic liquor] on Sundays' (s 119(3)).
(b) Public house licences have been granted for hospitals. Although hospitals clearly have residents they do not contain 'apartments set apart exclusively for the sleeping accommodation of travellers'[2].
(c) A public house licence will be required in respect of premises providing entertainment where it is intended to sell or supply alcoholic liquor when entertainment is not available[3].
  A public house (or possibly a refreshment) licence will be required in respect of premises predominantly used as a restaurant but which provide facilities, even of

---

1 Note that a board may promulgate a byelaw permitting the grant of a licence other than that applied for (s 38(1)(g)).
2 See definition of 'hotel' in s 139(1).
3 See discussion of entertainment licences below.

an extremely limited nature, for customers simply having a refreshment or a drink with food not amounting to a 'meal'[1].

As part of popular licensing mythology it is often suggested that the holder of a public house licence has no right to refuse or restrict the entry of customers[2]. On that account some licensing boards have promulgated a byelaw under s 38(1)(f) purporting to prohibit an admission charge (which licenceholders sometimes impose where entertainment is provided), unless the board's consent has been obtained. Such a stipulation is probably *ultra vires*[3]. In terms of s 41(2)(f) of the Civic Government (Scotland) Act 1982 a public entertainment licence, normally necessary for premises providing entertainment or recreation facilities subject to payment, is not required for licensed premises when permitted hours are in operation. It may be argued that, *ex hypothesi*, admission charges are lawful and cannot be rendered unlawful by a byelaw[4].

In fact, subject to exceptions created by race relations and sex discrimination legislation[5], a licenceholder can refuse service as he pleases and is under no obligation to explain his decision[6]. In *R v Rymer*[7] it was observed that 'no one has a right to insist on being served, any more than in any other shop'[8].

Nevertheless, the refusal to cater for customers could conceivably reach such a level as to justify the refusal of a renewal application, having regard to 'the nature and extent of the proposed use of the premises, and the persons likely to resort to the premises' (s 17(1)(b)).

OFF-SALE LICENCE

An off-sale licence 'is a licence granted in respect of premises specified therein which authorises the holder thereof to sell by retail alcoholic liquor for consumption off the premises only' (Sch 1).

An offence is committed where wine (including made-wine)[9] is sold in an open vessel[10]. Licensing boards are entitled to impose a broader prohibition by means of a byelaw made under s 38(1)(c) requiring 'all wines, made-wines and spirits sold by the holder of an off-sale licence to be sold in corked, stoppered or sealed

---

1 See discussion of restaurant licences at p 41. See also *Leisure Inns (UK) Ltd v Perth and Kinross District Licensing Board* 1991 SCLR 721 at 726, where the significance of planning restrictions upon the operation of a proposed 'public house' is discussed.
2 He must not, of course, serve a drunken person: s 76.
3 For a more detailed consideration of the *vires* of byelaws purporting to require the board's consent for certain activities, see Chapter 8.
4 See *White v Morley* [1899] 2 QB 34.
5 See the Race Relations Act 1976, s 20; Sex Discrimination Act 1975, s 29.
6 Note, however, that special considerations apply to hotels: see below.
7 (1877) 2 QBD 136.
8 At 140 per Kelly, CB. See also *Sealey v Tandy* [1902] 1 KB 296; and *R v Sussex Confirming Authority, ex parte Tamplin & Sons* [1937] 4 All ER 106 at 111 per Humphreys, J.
9 'Made-wine' has the meaning given by the Alcoholic Liquor Duties Act 1979, s 1 (1976 Act, s 139(1)).
10 Maximum penalty: level 3. Licenceholder, who has vicarious responsibility, and premises liable to disqualification: s 67, Sch 5.

vessels, cans, jars or casks' but not in respect of licensed premises 'where no groceries are kept or sold and where a bona fide wholesale business in alcoholic liquor is carried on' (s 38(1), proviso).

Apart from its familiar application, this type of licence is sometimes obtained in respect of:

(a) premises predominantly used for wholesale selling where there may be an occasional requirement to sell in retail quantities;

(b) catering premises which are not open to the public where the sole purpose of the licence is to allow application to be made for occasional licences (s 33)[1] in respect of events taking place outwith the premises;

(c) distribution depots where staff purchases are to be permitted.

Licensing boards will sometimes call for undertakings in respect of these types of operation: for example, that there will be no sales to the public. While it is perfectly legitimate to seek 'assurances', undertakings of this nature are not legally enforceable; but their breach could be visited with a closure order (s 32) or a refusal to renew the licence.

Until recently, the Act imposed a complete prohibition on the consumption of alcoholic liquor on off-sale premises[2]. This embargo does not now apply where the liquor is supplied gratuitously (s 97(1), as amended by the 1990 Act, Sch 8, para. 15). Otherwise, 'the holder of an off-sale licence or his employee or agent'[3] commits an offence if he 'sells to any person' alcoholic liquor to be consumed on the premises[4]. An offence is also committed by any person who 'induces'[5] a sale and proceeds to consume the liquor 'or any part thereof' on the premises (s 97(2), as amended by the 1990 Act, Sch 8. para 15)[6]. Semble no offence is committed by the licenceholder if a customer drinks his purchase on the premises without any prior indication of his intention so to do.

Section 97(3) imposes further restrictions. The holder of an off-sale licence or his employee or agent is guilty of an offence[7] if he 'takes, or causes or permits[8] any other person to take' alcoholic liquor from the premises for any of the following purposes:

(a) the selling or hawking[9] of the liquor 'on his account or for his benefit or profit' (s 93(3)(a)); or

(b) the consumption of the liquor 'for his benefit or profit in any house or other premises belonging to him, or hired, used or occupied by him, or in which he may be interested' (s 97(3)(b)).

---

1 See Chapter 7.
2 Although an offence under earlier legislation of 'permitting or suffering' drink to be consumed on a licensed grocer's premises was not made out where a grocer had permitted his customer to test a purchase of whisky: *Lennox v Ferguson* (1882) 5 Coup 33.
3 The word 'or' is conjunctive: see *Stainton and Seiler v McNaughtan* 1991 SCCR 339, 1993 SLT 119.
4 Maximum penalty: level 3 (Sch 5). Licenceholder, who has vicarious responsibility, and premises liable to disqualification: s 67, Sch 5.
5 See *Wilson v Danny Quastel (Rotherhithe) Ltd* [1966] 1 QB 125, [1965] 2 All ER 541.
6 Maximum penalty: level 3 (Sch 5).
7 Maximum penalty: level 1. Licenceholder, who has vicarious responsibility, and premises liable to disqualification: s 67, Sch 5.
8 For a consideration of 'causing and permitting', see Sheriff G H Gordon's *The Criminal Law of Scotland* (2nd edn) paras 8.68ff.
9 'Hawking' is defined in s 139(1) as 'trafficking in or about the roads or other places or in or from any boat or other vessel in the water'. See also s 90 and Chapter 2.

The latter offence appears to legislate for circumstances such as those disclosed in *Pasquier v Neale*[1]. The proprietor of an unlicensed restaurant was also a partner in a nearby licensed wine dealer's business. A restaurant customer's wine order was executed by a restaurant employee who purchased claret at the wine shop. The High Court upheld the magistrate's finding that the restaurateur had sold wine without a licence at the restaurant premises (but observed that a conviction could not be supported where it is proved that a restaurant servant acts as agent for the customer)[2]. In terms of s 97(3)(b) an offence is committed in this situation by the off-sale licence holder (or his employee or agent).

It appears, incidentally, that the parallel provision in the Licensing Act 1964 (s 164(3)) is apt to cause difficulties in the case of holiday villages or camps where the resort operator provides an off-sale licensed shop for residents[3].

HOTEL LICENCE

In terms of s 139(1) a 'hotel' is:

'(a) in towns and suburbs thereof, a house containing at least four apartments set apart exclusively for the sleeping accommodation of travellers[4];
 (b) in rural districts and populous places not exceeding 1,000 inhabitants according to the census for the time being last taken, a house containing at least two such apartments'.

A hotel licence (Sch 1):

'is a licence granted in respect of a hotel specified therein which authorises the holder thereof to sell by retail alcoholic liquor for consumption on or off the premises'.

The premises need not consist of a single structure. In *Chief Constable, Northern Constabulary v Lochaber District Licensing Board*[5] motel premises consisted of two buildings about twelve yards apart:

'There is nothing in the Act which in our view requires the provision of [facilities] to be in the same structural building, but the connection between the two should be sufficiently close as to demonstrate that collectively they can be regarded as a single unit . . . How close that physical connection requires to be to satisfy the concept of a combined single operational establishment involving two separate buildings is no doubt a matter of circumstance and degree'.

Indeed, in terms of s 139(3):

'a person shall be treated as residing in premises, notwithstanding that he occupies sleeping accommodation in a separate building, if he is provided with that accommodation in the course of a business of providing board and lodging for reward at those premises and the building is habitually used for the purpose by way of annex or overflow in connection with those premises and is occupied and managed with those premises'.

---

1 [1902] 2 KB 287, (1902) 67 JP 49. Cf *Taylor v Oram* (1862) 27 JP 8.
2 See *Langmuir v Persichini* 1935 JC 73, 1935 SLT 399.
3 See Field & Pink *Liquor Licensing Law and Practice* (2nd edn) para 2.17.
4 For a consideration of 'traveller', see *Orchard v Bush* [1898] 2 QB 284.
5 1985 SLT 410.

This provision acquires particular significance in relation to the protection afforded to residents by various exemptions: for example, the permitted hours do not apply to 'the sale or supply to, or consumption by' any resident of alcoholic liquor (s 54(3)(c)).

At common law hoteliers as 'innkeepers' have long been regarded as public servants. They owe a special duty to travellers[1], who are entitled to food and lodging unless there is 'good personal objection' and provided that they are 'decently behaved'; a failure to honour this obligation may result in damages[2]. The common law position has now been enacted by the Hotel Proprietors Act 1956, in terms of which the expression 'hotel' means:

'an establishment held out by the proprietor as offering food, drink and, if so required, sleeping accommodation without special contract, to any traveller presenting himself who appears able and willing to pay a reasonable sum for the services and facilities provided and who is in a fit state to be received'[3].

Although an innkeeper 'is not to select his guests'[4], provided he does not act 'capriciously or maliciously'[5], he may on reasonable grounds refuse to entertain travellers. The innkeeper's rejection was regarded as lawful in the following circumstances:

(a) Where the guest was a money-lender with a past history of annoying other residents by attempts to solicit their business[6].

(b) Where no bedroom accommodation was available and the traveller's request to be allowed to sleep on a coffee room bench was refused[7].

(c) Where the traveller was accompanied by a fearsome dog which he refused to leave outside[8].

(d) Where the guest had ceased to be a traveller and has become a long-term resident[9].

It has also been suggested that the obligation to supply food and drink does not extend to the provision of alcoholic liquor: 'So far as appears, the public interest to have travellers accommodated in an inn licensed for the sale of liquor does not extend to the supplying of them with liquor'[10].

The closure of hotels for part of the year may be sanctioned by a seasonal licence (s 62).

Where hotels offer leisure facilities a public entertainment licence may be required for their operation outwith the permitted hours[11].

1 See *Williams v Linnitt* [1951] 1 KB 565, [1951] 1 All ER 278 where the term was held to embrace a person who had no desire to be accommodated overnight. The length of the traveller's journey is immaterial: *Orchard v Bush* [1898] 2 QB 284.
2 *Ewing v Campbells* (1877) 5 R 234, 15 SLR 145.
3 Hotel Proprietors Act 1956, s 1(3). The innkeeper's responsibility for guests' property in terms of the Act is summarised in K Pain 'Five stars – but still an inn' [1992] 11 LR 17.
4 *R v Ivens* (1835) 7 C & P 213.
5 *Strathearn Hydropathic Co Ltd v Inland Revenue* (1881) 8 R 798.
6 *Rothfield v North British Railway Co* 1920 SC 805, 1920 2 SLT 269.
7 *Browne v Brandt* [1902] 1 KB 696.
8 *R v Rymer* (1877) 2 QBD 136.
9 *Lamond v Richard* [1897] 1 QB 541.
10 *West Wemyss United Services Club, Applicants* 1948 SLT (Sh Ct) 33.
11 See the Civic Government (Scotland) Act 1982, s 41(1), (2)(f).

RESTRICTED HOTEL LICENCE

For the purposes of a restricted hotel licence, premises must fall within the definition of hotel in s 139(1) and may be classified as a hotel for the purposes of the Hotel Proprietors Act 1956, with the holder subject to an innkeeper's obligations (see above).

Schedule 1 sets out adaptation and use requirements, providing that this type of licence:

'(a) is granted in respect of a hotel specified therein which –
   (i)   is structurally adapted and bona fide used, or intended to be used, for the purpose of habitually providing the customary main meal at midday or in the evening or both for the accommodation of persons frequenting the premises of such hotel;
   (ii) so far as it is used or intended to be used for the purpose of providing meals to persons who are not residing there, is principally used, or intended to be used, for providing the customary main meal at midday or in the evening or both; and
   (iii) does not contain a bar counter'.

Thus, in addition to the sleeping accommodation for travellers desiderated by s 139(1), the premises must contain proper restaurant facilities which those operating under a (full) hotel licence are not obliged to provide. The expressions 'meal' and 'bar counter' are considered below in the context of restaurant licences.

The authority conferred for the sale and supply of alcoholic liquor is expressed in serpentine terms, broadly with the effect of creating a hybrid between a hotel and restaurant licence; indeed the English equivalent is known as the 'residential and restaurant licence'[1]. Alcoholic liquor may only be sold or supplied to the following classes of person:

(1) Those taking table meals (who need not be residents), 'for consumption by such a person as an ancillary to his meal' (Sch 1 definition, (b)(i)). The meanings of 'table meal' and 'ancillary' are considered below in the discussion of restaurant and entertainment licences. Since consumption must be 'by such a person', a customer may only purchase drink for another diner, unless he is a resident purchasing for a private friend (see next paragraph).

(2) A resident for consumption by himself or by his 'private friend', provided that the latter is 'bona fide entertained by and at the expense of' the former. (Consumption may only take place on the premises; Sch 1 definition, (b)(ii)). A meal need not be taken. The onus of establishing 'resident' and 'private friend' status rests on the defence in the event of a prosecution under s 98(1)[2]. In addition, the *supply* of drink to a 'private friend' of a resident in this situation is expressly authorised (Sch 1 definition, (b)(iii)). The meaning of 'private friend' and 'entertainment' were considered in *Jack v Thom*[3], in which a party of police officers held a party at a hotel with the permission but not at the invitation of the certificate-holder. No payment was required for the drink supplied. The Lord-Justice Clerk said:

---

1 Licensing Act 1964, s 94.
2 *Jack v Thom* 1952 JC 41, 1952 SLT 161. See also *Atkins v Agar* [1914] 1 KB 26.
3 See above.

'Entertainment seems to me to be a mutual affair and the thing to be looked at is the whole circumstances and particularly the character of the entertainment. The Court must look at the substance of the matter and ask themselves in terms of the statute whether the recipients of the hospitality were private friends of the [licenceholder] and bona fide entertained by him'[1].

The permitted hours do not apply to the sale or supply to, or consumption by, residents (s 54(3)(c)); nor to the supply to, or consumption by, 'private friends' in the circumstances described above (s 54(3)(e)).

(3) Residents who have been supplied with a meal 'at, but to be consumed off' the premises (a packed lunch, for example), provided that the alcoholic liquor is 'ancillary' to the meal and consumption is by the resident or 'any private friend of such a person who is bona fide entertained by, and at the expense of that person'. The permitted hours do not apply to this class of transaction (s 54(3)(d)). It will have been appreciated that the sale or supply of alcoholic liquor for consumption off the premises is otherwise prohibited.

Where 'application is made in that behalf'[2], the sale or supply of alcoholic liquor may be restricted by the exclusion of the authority normally conferred in relation to persons taking table meals (paragraph (1) above) (Sch 1 definition, para (b)(v)): in other words, service is confined to residents and their private friends, in terms of the Schedule 1 definition, paragraph (b) (ii), (iii) and (iv). No procedure is prescribed, but it is not open to the board to impose the limitation *ex proprio motu*[3]. A request may certainly be made when application is made for the grant of the licence and, presumably, when the licence is renewed; the possibility of a request being made at other times is apparently open.

Restricted hotel licences are suitable for those wishing to operate a hotel with a public restaurant but no public bar facilities. The holder will, however, have difficulty in catering for functions which normally involve the sale or supply of alcoholic liquor to non-residents following the conclusion of a meal, in circumstances where it will be impossible to argue that the drink is still 'ancillary' thereto. Doubt arises as to whether an occasional licence under s 33 may be obtained in order to obviate this difficulty[4].

In terms of s 98 'the holder of a restricted hotel licence or his employee or agent' is guilty of an offence if he sells or supplies alcoholic liquor for consumption on the premises, except in certain circumstances, which essentially mirror the authority conferred by the Schedule 1 definition, paragraphs (b)(i), (ii) and (iii) (and thus are not repeated here)[5]; or if he 'trafficks[6] in or supplies' alcoholic liquor for consumption off the premises except as provided in the Schedule 1 definition, paragraph (b)(iv). The offences attract a level 3 (maximum) penalty

---

1 1952 JC 41 at 46.
2 It would appear that the request may be made orally at the time the application for the licence is heard: see *Quinn v Paisley Magistrates* 1909 SC 1085, (1909) 2 SLT 35.
3 See *Boyd v Hislop* (1909) 9 SLT 466.
4 See Chapter 7; and *Donald v Stirling District Licensing Board* 1992 SLT 75 at 78.
5 Note, however, that s 98 does not take account of the possible 'resident's only' restriction which, as explained above, may be requested by an applicant.
6 'Trafficking' is defined in s 139(1) as 'bartering, selling, dealing in, trading in, or exposing for sale, by retail': see *MacDonald v Skinner* 1978 SLT (Notes) 52.

(Sch 5). The licenceholder, who has vicarious responsibility, and the premises are liable to disqualification (s 67, Sch 5).

RESTAURANT LICENCE

Sometimes erroneously referred to as a 'table licence', a restaurant licence is a licence granted in respect of premises which:

'(i) are structurally adapted and bona fide used, or intended to be used, for the purpose of habitually providing meals for the accommodation of persons frequenting the premises;

(ii) so far as they are used, or intended to be used, for the said purpose, are principally to be used, or intended to be used, for providing the customary main meal at midday or in the evening, or both; and

(iii) do not contain a bar counter'[1].

No guidance is given as to the manner in which structural adaptation is to be assessed, although the adequacy of kitchen facilities will clearly be taken into account. An applicant for a licence must, in any event, produce a food hygiene certificate in terms of s 23(4).

The Act does not provide a definition of 'meal' and, perhaps surprisingly, there is a paucity of case law to provide clarification, particularly in Scotland. Two English decisions suggest that light meals, amounting to little more than bar snacks, could qualify. In *Timmis v Millman*[2], the latest reported case, obiter approval was given to a decision that a substantial sandwich accompanied by salad items could be sufficient. Similarly, in *Solomon v Green*[3] sandwiches and sausages on sticks qualified as a 'meal' by a narrow margin. No issue appears to have been taken with a 'basket-type supper' in *Stainton and Seiler v McNaughtan*[4].

However, it must be kept in view that, as explained below, the sale or supply of alcoholic liquor requires to be 'ancillary' to the taking of table meals. Thus, the consumption of alcohol out of proportion to the food supplied may in some circumstances suggest that no 'meal' has been provided[5].

The meaning of 'bar counter' is apt to cause confusion. Whether the familiar physical structure amounts to a 'bar counter' does not depend upon its appearance, but rather upon the manner in which it is used for the service of alcoholic liquor. In terms of s 139(2), a 'bar counter' does not include:

'a counter which is bona fide used, or intended to be used –

(a) as a place at which meals are served to persons sitting thereat and at which alcoholic liquor is supplied to persons taking such meals for consumption by such a person while seated at such counter and as an ancillary to his meal; or

(b) as a place at which alcoholic liquor is dispensed to the holder of the licence in respect

---

1 Sch 1.
2 [1965] Brewing Tr Rev 23, (1965) 109 SJ 31.
3 [1955] Brewing Tr Rev 313, (1955) 119 JP 289.
4 1991 SCCR 339.
5 See *Robertson v Mackenzie* 1975 JC 72, 1975 SLT 222.

of the premises or any servant or agent of his, but to no other person, and is so dispensed in order that it may be supplied to persons frequenting the premises; or

(c) for both of the purposes mentioned in the two foregoing paragraphs;

and for no other purpose'.

Paragraph (a) recognises that many bona fide restaurants provide dining facilities other than at conventional tables, while (b) legitimises the operation of a dispense bar for the waiter service of customers seated at 'normal' tables. Self-service restaurants (except those operating under a public house licence) may not allow customers to help themselves to drink at the servery counter.

The licence granted on the basis of the above adaptation and use requirements authorises the holder 'to sell by retail or supply alcoholic liquor in the said premises to persons taking table meals[1] there, for consumption by such a person as an ancillary to his meal' (Sch 1).

Since consumption must be 'by such a person', a meal-taking customer is disabled from making a purchase of alcoholic liquor for someone who is not having a table meal but may, of course, extend hospitality to other diners.

The expression 'table meal' means:

'a meal eaten by a person sitting at a table, or at a counter or other structure which serves the purpose of a table and is not used for the service of refreshments for consumption by persons not seated at a table or structure serving the purpose of a table'[2].

In other words, a meal will fall outwith the definition if it is taken at 'a counter or other structure' at which even one other customer is served refreshments (not necessarily alcoholic liquor) while standing.

'Ancillary' means 'subservient or subordinate'[3]. Subject to the drinking-up time *caveat* explained below, the consumption of alcoholic liquor may be 'ancillary' to the table meal although not taken at the same time. In *Healy v McIntyre*[4] a party of restaurant customers were served with a round of drinks half-an-hour after the conclusion of their meal. The High Court held that pre-prandial drinks and digestifs could be regarded as 'ancillary':

'The question when they cease to be ancillary must be a question of fact in the circumstances of each case. There must, I think, come a point in time when drinks served considerably after the end of the meal cease to be ancillary thereto'[5].

It is essential to compare the relative importance of the food and drink[6]; but while alcohol is not to be sold 'under the cloak of meals', it is not a legitimate exercise to examine the total amount of business carried on in the premises as between the two[7]. Where the consumption of food is a 'subterfuge to enable customers to drink' there will be no genuine taking of a meal. In *Robertson v*

---

1 Not necessarily a customary main meal.
2 Section 139(1).
3 *Young v O'Connell*, The Times, 25 May 1985, unreported.
4 1965 JC 1, 1965 SLT 81.
5 Per the Lord Justice-Clerk (Grant). Cf *Stainton and Seiler v McNaughtan* 1991 SCCR 339, 1993 SLT 119. See also *Loosefoot Entertainment Ltd v Glasgow District Licensing Board* 1990 SCLR (Sh Ct) 584 at 590B, C.
6 *Young v O'Connell*, above.
7 *R v Liverpool Licensing Justices ex parte Tynan* [1961] 2 All ER 363, [1961] 1 WLR 837.

Mackenzie[1] the High Court held that an offence had been made out where the ordering of sandwiches was 'a mere pretext on which to obtain exciseable liquor and this is or should have been known to the supplier'.

The concept of 'ancillary drinking' was introduced by the Licensing (Scotland) Act 1962, but remnants of the former references to 'consumption *at* a meal' result in certain paradoxes. While thirty minutes drinking-up time may be added to the conclusion of the permitted hours (where the liquor was supplied during those hours), merely 'ancillary' consumption is insufficient: drink must be 'served at the same time as the meal and for consumption at the meal' (s 54(3)(h)).

Similarly, s 87, derived from s 150 of the Licensing (Scotland) Act 1959, exempts from a general prohibition on credit sales (where liquor is sold for consumption on licensed premises) the sale or supply of liquor 'for consumption at a meal', supplied at the same time and consumed with the meal, with the result that a pre-dinner drink cannot simply be added to the food bill.

Indeed, possibly because of this historical dichotomy, the licensing board in one large district has for many years taken the view (erroneously, it is suggested) that a restaurant with a separate cocktail bar must be operated under a public house licence, even where the bar is purely used as a dispense bar (falling within the exemption created by s 139(2), explained above) and the sale or supply of drink is purely 'ancillary' to the taking of meals.

Since the concept of 'breach of certificate' was swept away by the 1976 Act, and the operation of premises outwith the parameters of the Schedule 1 definition is not *ipso facto* unlawful, the Act has necessarily created substantive offences. Thus, the holder of a restaurant licence 'or his employee or agent' commits an offence if he sells or supplies alcoholic liquor for consumption on the premises 'except to persons taking table meals in the premises for consumption by such a person as an ancillary to his meal' (s 99(a)); or 'trafficks in or supplies any alcoholic liquor for consumption off the premises in respect of which the licence is held' (s 99(b))[2]. In both cases a conviction attracts a level 3 (maximum) penalty. The licenceholder has vicarious responsibility; both he and the premises are liable to disqualification (s 67, Sch 5).

In *Stainton and Seiler v McNaughtan*[3] the appellants were found guilty of two contraventions of s 99(a). Evidence to the effect that customers were supplied with drink without the provision of a meal over a period of two hours and ten minutes justified one conviction[4]. As respects the second charge, however, police officers observing the restaurant left the premises for a period which, although 'relatively short', raised the possibility, which the Crown did not rule out, that drink was supplied to customers who had consumed, or were about to consume, a meal. Quashing this conviction, the Lord Justice-Clerk (Ross) said:

'[T]he possibility that the drink which [the Crown witnesses] saw being supplied [was] by way of an aperitif has not been excluded nor has it been excluded that the drink which they saw supplied may have been drink supplied to persons who had already had a meal, the debris of which had been cleared away from the table'.

1 1975 JC 72, 1975 SLT 222. See also *Miller v MacKnight* 1945 JC 107, 1945 SLT 251.
2 'Trafficking' is defined in s 139(1) as 'bartering, selling, dealing in, trading in, or exposing for sale, by retail': see *MacDonald v Skinner* 1978 SLT (Notes) 52.
3 1991 SCCR 339.
4 Cf *Healy v McIntyre* 1965 JC 1, 1965 SLT 81.

A meal must be taken *in the premises*. Restaurants offering a carry-out meals service must not supply alcoholic liquor to customers who are waiting for their food order.

REFRESHMENT LICENCE

In order to qualify for a refreshment licence, premises require to be 'structurally adapted and bona fide used or intended to be used for the provision of refreshments including food and non-alcoholic beverages for consumption on the premises' (Sch 1 definition).

The food provided need not amount to a 'meal' and the level of catering facilities will generally be lower than those found in restaurants. There must be no bar counter (Sch 1 definition)[1].

The taking of food is not a prerequisite of alcoholic consumption. The licence authorises the sale or supply of alcoholic liquor on the premises 'when food and non-alcoholic beverages are also on sale, provided no alcoholic liquor is sold or supplied for consumption off the premises' (Sch 1 definition).

The holder of a refreshment licence or his employee or agent commits an offence if:

'(a) he trafficks[2] in or sells any alcoholic liquor for consumption off the premises in respect of which the licence is held, or
 (b) he sells or supplies alcoholic liquor at any time when other refreshments, including food and non-alcoholic beverages, are not available for sale'[3].

Introduced by the 1976 Act, refreshment licences have proved to be disappointingly unpopular. While *Clayson*[4] recorded a large measure of public support for 'café-type premises which would sell not only alcoholic drinks but also soft drinks, tea, coffee and snacks' (on the basis that 'such a place would keep the family together and make the occasion more enjoyable')[5], this enthusiasm was not matched by the licensed trade's response. Indeed, the new form of licence was greeted with a wave of apathy. In 1988 a total of 212 refreshment licences were in force throughout Scotland (compared with, for example, 4,788 public house and 1,338 restaurant licences)[6]. Three years later this figure had increased marginally to 236; five licensing board areas had *no* refreshment-licensed premises, with 23 districts having less than three[7]. The latest available figures indicate that refreshment licences represent only 1.5 per cent of the Scottish total[8].

There are possibly two reasons for the low uptake. Section 64, as originally enacted, did not allow the holder of a refreshment licence to make application for

---

1 'Bar counter': see above.
2 See definition of 'trafficking' in s 139(1).
3 Section 100. Maximum penalty in all cases: level 3 (Sch 5). Licenceholder, who has vicarious responsibility, and premises liable to disqualification: s 67, Sch 5.
4 Paras 7.19 ff.
5 Access by children is discussed below.
6 Source: 'Scottish Licensing Statistics', [1990] 3 LR 9.
7 Source: Scottish Office Statistical Bulletin, CRJ/1992/5, August 1992.
8 Source: Scottish Office Statistical Bulletin, CRJ/1993/4, July, 1993.

the regular extension of permitted hours[1]. Until standard weekday opening from 11 am to 11 pm was introduced by the 1990 Act[2] the premises could have no permitted hours between 2.30 pm and 5 pm, unless the licenceholder invoked s 57, permitting the sale or supply of drink with table meals until 4 pm in an area 'usually set apart' for that purpose (s 57(3)(a); but, of course, the whole *raison d'être* of the refreshment licence was thereby substantially defeated.

In addition, the Act's provisions regarding the presence of children on the premises were seen as cumbersome and restrictive. While *Clayson*[3] saw no need for access controls, in terms of s 70(1)[4] the holder of a refreshment licence or his employee or agent commits an offence if he allows a person under 14: '(a) to be in the premises at any time during the permitted hours, unless accompanied by a person of 18 or over[5]; or (b) to remain in the premises after eight in the evening. (It is sometimes erroneously believed that the 8 pm watershed simply places an embargo upon *admission* after that hour)[6]. No offence is committed where the person under 14 is either (1) a child of the licenceholder or (2) resides in the premises but is not employed there. (s 70(2))[7].

In broad terms, refreshment-licensed premises are subject to a régime similar to that which applies where a children's certificate is in force by virtue of s 49 of the 1990 Act[8] but, in the absence of any power to attach conditions, licensing boards have been unable to exact from licenceholders the sometimes bizarre requirements imposed in relation to certificates[8].

The primary purpose of refreshment-licensed premises is clearly the provision of refreshments, as described in the Schedule 1 'definition'. They are not and do not contain a 'bar', which 'includes': 'any place exclusively or mainly used for the sale and consumption of alcoholic liquor' (s 139(1))[9].

Thus, the legislature has chosen to regulate the presence of children in refreshment-licensed premises in the self-contained s 70, rather than by modification of s 69, which, subject to a number of exceptions, provides that a licenceholder may not allow persons under the age of 14 to be in a bar of the premises during the permitted hours[10]. It may also be observed that while the employment of persons under 18 in bars is prohibited by s 72, the separate provisions of s 73 prevent the service of alcohol by them in refreshment-licensed premises.

1 The lacuna has now been filled: para 12 of Sch 8 to the 1990 Act makes the appropriate amendment to s 64(1).
2 New s 53 substituted by the 1990 Act, s 45(1).
3 Para 7.21.
4 As amended by the 1990 Act, Sch 8, para 14.
5 The Act originally provided that the accompanying adult required to be at least 21.
6 Maximum penalty: level 3 (Sch 5). Licenceholder, who has vicarious responsibility, and premises liable to disqualification: s 67, Sch 5. See also defence provided by s 71.
7 Persons under 18 may not be employed to serve alcoholic liquor in refreshment licensed premises: s 73.
8 See Chapter 14.
9 See *Clayson*, para 7. 21: 'We envisage that a refreshment house certificate would be granted for premises in which refreshments are served to persons seated at tables. There should be no bar on the premises, that is to say they should not include any place exclusively or mainly used for the sale and consumption of exciseable liquor'.
10 See also the 1990 Act, s 49(3) which modifies s 69 vis-à-vis premises or parts of premises which are the subject of a children's certificate.

Since this approach to the drafting of the Act is wholly consistent with the proposition that there is no 'bar', there appears to be a surprising hiatus. Restrictions on the purchase and consumption of alcoholic liquor (s 68(2) and (3)) by persons under 18 do not, in certain circumstances[1], prevent consumption by such a person *other than in a bar*.

The holder of a refreshment licence may not apply for an occasional licence in order to cater for an event taking place outwith his premises (s 33(10)).

ENTERTAINMENT LICENCE

Clayson recognised a trend towards the sale of alcohol in 'ancillary outlets' such as dance halls, discothèques, cinemas and other places of public entertainment. This development, in the committee's opinion, was to be encouraged 'as it might help to promote civilised drinking and break down the attitude that regards the consumption of liquor as an end in itself'[2]. A new form of certificate was considered desirable. The entertainment licence introduced by the Act may be granted in respect of places of public entertainment 'such as cinemas, theatres, dance halls and proprietary clubs' and:

'authorises the holder to sell by retail or supply alcoholic liquor to persons frequenting the premises for consumption on the premises as an ancillary to the entertainment provided, subject to such conditions as the licensing board may determine to ensure that such sale or supply is ancillary to the entertainment provided'[3].

Although commercially problematic, often requiring substantial investment and sometimes utterly dependent upon the discretionary grant of a regular extension of the evening hours (s 64), entertainment licences have proved to be comparatively popular[4].

The holder of an entertainment licence or his employee or agent commits an offence 'if he trafficks in[5] or supplies alcoholic liquor for consumption off the premises in respect of which the licence is held'[6]. In terms of s 101(2), a licensing board may, when granting[7] an entertainment licence, attach conditions 'including conditions placing restrictions on the permitted hours, in order to secure that the sale or supply of alcoholic liquor is ancillary to the entertainment'[8]. Contravention of a condition by the licenceholder or his employee or agent is an offence[9].

---

1 As more fully explained in Chapter 14.
2 *Clayson*, para 7.16.
3 Sch 1.
4 A total of 766 entertainment licences were in force at the end of 1991. Source: Scottish Office Statistical Bulletin, CRJ/1992/5, August 1992.
5 'Trafficking': see s 139(1).
6 Maximum penalty: level 3 (Sch 5). Licenceholder, who has vicarious responsibility, and premises liable to disqualification: s 67, Sch 5.
7 'Granting' includes granting by way of renewal: see s 139(1).
8 Note that conditions may also be imposed by virtue of a byelaw: see s 38(1)(f).
9 Maximum penalty: level 3 (Sch 5). Licenceholder, who has vicarious responsibility, and premises liable to disqualification: s 67, Sch 5.

The possibility of a limitation of the permitted hours is clearly designed to prevent evening-orientated premises such as discothèques selling liquor during the afternoon when entertainment is unlikely to be provided. Otherwise, the extent of a licensing board's power to impose conditions appears to be the subject of some perplexity, exacerbated by the absence of any reported cases to date.

The sale or supply of drink otherwise than in an entertainment context is not *ipso facto* an offence. The argument that such activity would constitute 'trafficking' (s 90(a)), while certainly colourable, encounters the difficulty that in the circumstance postulated there is a licence in force. Since the sale of drink in a restaurant to non-diners is prohibited (s 99(a)) one might reasonably have expected an analogous offence in relation to entertainment licences. There is no such provision. It is suggested that s 101(2) is designed, at least in part, to afford boards the power to create the potential for an offence which is, so to speak, tailored to individual circumstances. Conditions should be carefully framed to meet that objective. Nevertheless, in practice, entertainment licences are sometimes granted *de plano*.

The *vires* of conditions attached to an entertainment licence was the subject of close scrutiny in *Granite City Bowling Centre Ltd v City of Aberdeen District Licensing Board*[1]. The company appellants held an entertainment licence expressed to be subject to a number of conditions to ensure that the sale or supply of alcoholic liquor was 'ancillary to entertainment provided'. The conditions provided inter alia that:

(a) The appellants' premises were 'to be run as a proprietary club'.
(b) The permitted entertainment was to be 'bowling, and from 8.00 pm on Fridays and Saturdays, live entertainment for members and guests only'.
(c) Any public notice or advertisement required to indicate clearly the nature of the entertainment and 'must not stipulate or imply that anything other than the said entertainment constitutes the principal activity to be carried on there'.

The board found that conditions had been contravened on five occasions and refused a renewal application on the ground that the appellants were no longer 'fit and proper persons' to hold a licence. It was argued on the appellants' behalf that the conditions set out above were *ultra vires*. The sheriff held that a condition attached to an entertainment licence specifying the nature of the entertainment was 'perfectly reasonable' for the purpose of ensuring that the supply of alcoholic liquor was ancillary thereto. He said:

'One cannot have an ancillary activity without an identifiable principal activity. Without such specification a licensee could run what was simply a drinking establishment and claim that he was providing entertainment because he employed a singing barman or waitresses dressed as rabbits'.

On the other hand, the board had no power to insist that the premises be operated as a proprietary club[2] nor that admission be restricted at certain times to members and guests. (*Ex hypothesi*, those boards which purport to exercise control over the content of a proprietary club's rules may not lawfully do so.)

---

1 Aberdeen Sheriff Court, 31 October 1991, unreported.
2 See *Clayson*, para 7.17 where it was considered that no special provision should be made for proprietary clubs.

The sheriff further found that condition (c) was *intra vires*:

'On a reasonable construction the purpose of the condition is to ensure that persons are not encouraged to resort to the premises with the dominant purpose of doing something other than participate in the permitted entertainment'.

If this view is correct, it holds considerable significance for so-called 'happy hours' (when alcoholic liquor is sold at markedly reduced prices for a limited period) in entertainment-licensed premises, as well as during promotional evenings when sales of a particular brand of drink are financially supported by the manufacturer or distributor. Police authorities and licensing boards often view these activities with displeasure as providing an inducement to drink rather than participate in entertainment. It would appear that the 'mischief' may be prevented by an appropriate condition.

The legitimacy of the imposition of an occupant capacity for premises, even where desirable for safety reasons, is open to doubt. Proposals which would have allowed licensing boards to limit the number of customers in any licensed premises were defeated during the Parliamentary progress of the 1990 Act; and the Secretary of State for Scotland has refused to confirm draft byelaws which contain such a power. Conceivably, however, a condition of this nature could be *intra vires* where only a certain number of customers could plausibly be associated with the entertainment facilities.

The cases considered above in connection with 'ancillary' restaurant drinking will no doubt be of relevance in the present context. Thus, it would appear that the supply of alcohol before or after the provision of entertainment is permissible, provided that there is a sufficient *nexus* between the two[1].

Although entertainment licences are not subject to a preliminary 'adaptation and use' requirement, the suitability of the premises nevertheless falls to be considered for the purpose of s 17(1)(b) which, as further discussed in Chapter 4, provides that an application for a new licence shall be refused if premises are found to be 'not suitable or convenient' for the sale of alcoholic liquor. A question may thus arise as to whether the applicant's description of the facilities proposed to be provided demonstrates that the supply of alcohol would be ancillary to entertainment. In *Loosefoot Entertainment Ltd v Glasgow District Licensing Board*[2] trade competitors objected to the provisional grant of a new entertainment licence in respect of a proposed nightclub, arguing, inter alia, that the premises were to be regarded as a discothèque with a wholly inadequate dancing area (130 square metres for approximately 1,600 people). An Extra Division of the Inner House upheld the following approach adopted by the sheriff:

'The question whether one of a number of activities is ancillary to the rest, or is on a par with them, or indeed is the primary activity, is very much a question of balance and impression, and it is not for me to substitute what might be my own assessment . . . for the assessment made by the board themselves. Given the information provided by [the applicant's agent] as to the general nature of the facilities offered, given the information the board were provided with relating to the [applicant's] general activities as providers of cabaret, and given that the board specifically considered the problem of the size of the

---

1 By analogy with *Healy v McIntyre* 1965 JC 1, 1965 SLT 81.
2 1990 SCLR 584 (Sh Ct), aff'd 1991 SLT 843 (IH).

dancing area, and rejected dancing as something which in itself would justify the grant of an entertainment licence, I do not think that it can be said that they exercised their discretion so unreasonably as to entitle me to interfere . . .'

A question also arises as to whether drinking is 'ancillary' where entertainment facilities are inadequate *on a particular occasion*. In the *Granite City Bowling* case[1] a dinner-dance attended by over 600 people was held at the appellants' premises. The bowling area, with the exception of two rinks, was placed out of commission. The sheriff said:

'Having regard to the numbers involved [the board was] quite entitled to take the view that the supply of liquor was not ancillary to bowling; indeed I should have thought it perverse to hold otherwise. The maximum number of bowlers who can play on one rink at one time is eight. I do not think that any sensible person observing sixteen people playing bowls and 634 people engaged in a dinner-dance could conclude that bowling was the principal activity taking place. If bowling was not the principal acitivity the supply of liquor was not ancillary thereto'.

On the other hand, the position is less than clear where perfectly adequate entertainment facilities are not utilised by a large number of customers: for example, where discothèque patrons choose not to dance, perhaps because their primary motivation for resorting to the premises is the availability of cheap drink (discussed above). In *Richards v Bloxham (Binks)*[2] a special hours certificate[3] had been granted on the basis that the ballroom premises were 'structurally adapted and bona fide used, or intended to be used' for the provision of music and dancing and substantial refreshment to which the sale of drink would be ancillary. Evidence was led that very few customers took 'substantial refreshment'. Police applied for revocation of the certificate on the ground that 'on the whole' persons resorted to the premises for the purpose of obtaining intoxicating liquor 'rather than for the purpose of dancing or of obtaining refreshments other than intoxicating liquor'[3]. The application was unsuccessful on the basis that the certificate-holder was only obligated to *provide* the appropriate facilities. Nevertheless, action could no doubt be taken by a licensing board under s 32[4] if a pattern of non-use, or, perhaps more appropriately, abuse, became established.

In the *Granite City Bowling* case[5] the sheriff rejected an assertion that the appellants were bound to observe the purported conditions because they had been accepted without complaint (when the licence was originally granted or last renewed), holding that 'The appellants had no choice as to what conditions [the board] imposed on their licence'. This statement (which is, of course, perfectly accurate in terms) ignores the potential for an appeal against conditions created by s 17(6)[6]. Nevertheless, the sheriff was no doubt correct in his view that an invalid condition could not be made valid by acquiescence.

---

1 Aberdeen Sheriff Court, 31 October 1991, unreported.
2 (1968) 112 SJ 543, (1968) 66 LGR 739.
3 Licensing Act 1964, s 77.
4 Which empowers a board to make a closure order.
5 See above.
6 'Any person entitled . . . to appeal to the sheriff against the grant or refusal of a licence may appeal to the sheriff against a decision of a licensing board to attach . . . a condition to a licence, being a condition mentioned in . . . [section] 101(2) of this Act'.

As the reader will be reminded at various parts of the text, the operator of entertainment-licensed premises should consider the advisability of obtaining a public entertainment licence under s 41 of and Schedule 1 to the Civic Government (Scotland) Act 1982. Section 41(2)[1] provides that such a licence is required for 'any place where, on payment of money or money's worth, members of the public are admitted or may use any facilities for the purpose of entertainment or recreation', except where the entertainment is provided during permitted hours under the 1976 Act[2]. Where premises are operated under a public entertainment licence outwith the permitted hours, conditions imposed under s 101(2) do not apply[3]. The holder of an entertainment licence is disabled from applying for an occasional licence under s 33 (s 33(10)).

PROVISIONAL LICENCE

The Act allows a licensing board to grant a 'provisional licence' (not to be confused with the provisional grant of a new licence under s 26) to the holder of any type of licence so that he may 'carry on business in temporary premises during the reconstruction of his premises' (s 27). This type of licence is a *rara avis*. No procedure is prescribed, although boards are entitled to make regulations in terms of s 37. All references in the Act to a 'licence' and a 'licence-holder' are relevant[4] but not those to a 'new licence'. In the result, a provisional licence may be granted under a 'delegated powers' arrangement by virtue of s 5(1) and is not subject to the grounds of refusal set out in s 17(1); its refusal cannot be appealed under s 17(4). Objection to an application may be taken in terms of s 16. Police have powers of entry to the premises by virtue of s 85.

SEASONAL LICENCE[5]

Any licence may be made 'seasonal' at the request of an applicant for its grant or transfer. Provided that the board is 'satisfied that the requirements of the area for which the board is constituted make it desirable', a condition may be inserted allowing for removal of the permitted hours (or, in the case of off-sale licensed premises, 'trading hours') for a part or parts of the year to a maximum of 180 days (s 62(1))[6].

Hotels may be allowed to continue the operation of a public bar or restaurant

---

1 Section 41 has effect in a licensing authority's area only if and in so far as the authority have so resolved: see the 1982 Act, s 9.
2 1982 Act, s 42(2)(f).
3 *Granite City Bowling Ltd v City of Aberdeen District Licensing Board*, Aberdeen Sheriff Court, 31 October 1991, unreported.
4 See definition of these terms in s 139(1).
5 Section 62.
6 Permitted and 'trading' hours are examined in Chapter 10.

when letting facilities are not available (s 62(1)(b))[1]; but, curiously, the restriction of permitted hours to the non-residential parts would not prevent the sale or supply of alcohol to 'out-of-season' residents (see s 54(3)(c)).

It appears that an oral request for a seasonal licence may competently be made at the hearing of the application[2]. The board is not empowered to impose a condition *ex proprio motu*. Application forms for the grant or provisional grant of a new licence (and for transfer) usually enquire as to whether a seasonal licence is requested. Although renewal application forms are almost invariably silent on the matter, it requires to be kept in view that the board's ability to attach the condition may be exercised on the 'granting' of a licence, a term which includes grant by way of renewal[3]. Accordingly, the condition (if the applicant desires) must be attached *de novo* at each renewal.

The refusal of a seasonal licence may be appealed to the sheriff[4], although no express right of appeal is conferred[5].

1 The plain reference here to 'hotel premises' no doubt includes premises which are the subject of a restricted hotel licence, bearing in mind that, as explained above, they *must* not have public bar facilities and *may* not have a public restaurant.
2 See *Quinn v Magistrates of Paisley* 1909 SC 1085, (1902) 2 SLT 35.
3 See definition of 'grant' in s 139(1).
4 See *Wallace v Kyle and Carrick Licensing Board* 1979 SLT (Sh Ct) 12.
5 Cf s 17(6).

CHAPTER 4

Applying for a new licence

MEANING OF 'NEW LICENCE'

In terms of s 139(1), 'new licence' means 'a licence granted in respect of premises for which, at the time of the application for such a grant, either no licence was in force or a licence in a form different from the form of licence[1] so granted was in force' (and includes for application purposes the provisional grant of a new licence)[2] subject to the proviso that:

'a licence granted[3] in respect of premises which have been rebuilt after having been destroyed by fire, tempest or other unforeseen cause, and for which, at the time they were so destroyed, a licence in the same form as the first-mentioned licence was in force, shall be deemed not to be a new licence'[4].

The proviso appears to give effect to the decision in *Stevenson v Hunter*[5]. Licensed premises were rebuilt with an altered internal layout, increased floor area and slightly different outside measurements; no new certificate was required as the identity of the premises had not changed and the existing licence (which had not ceased to be valid) could competently be renewed[6].

Apart from the familiar situation in which it is intended to license premises for the first time, the procedure is also employed where:

(a) The type of licence is to be changed; or premises are to be divided into two or more parts with licences of the same or different types.

(b) Existing licensed premises are to be 'materially' altered[7].

---

1 The expression 'form of licence' refers to the various types of licences specified in Sch 1, is derived from 'form of certificate' in s 199(1) of the Licensing (Scotland) Act 1959 and does not relate to the physical characteristics of the premises.

2 *Kelvinside Community Council v Glasgow District Licensing Board* 1990 SCLR 110, 1990 SLT 725. Note, however, that the provisional grant of a new licence is not a licence 'in force': see *Ginera Ltd v City of Glasgow District Licensing Board* 1982 SLT 136; *Baljaffray Residents' Association v Milngavie and Bearsden District Council Licensing Board* 1981 SLT (Sh Ct) 106.

3 'Grant' includes grant by way of renewal: s 139(1).

4 The rationale of the definition, which virtually repeats the definition of 'new certificate' in s 199(1) of the Licensing (Scotland) Act 1959, is explained in *Purves's Scottish Licensing Laws* (8th edn, 1961, ed Walker) p 52.

5 (1903) 5 F 761, (1903) 10 SLT 754.

6 But see Chapter 11 as to the necessity for licensing board consent to alterations. See also *Craig v Peebles* (1875) 2 R (J) 90, in which a certificate-holder was acquitted of trafficking where he continued to trade after the substantial destruction of his premises.

7 Some licensing boards require a new licence application where *any* extension of the premises is contemplated. A material internal rearrangement may also necessitate a new licence: this approach is criticised at Chapter 11.

(c) It is desired to release a licence from a condition attached under, for example, s 29[1].
(d) The type of entertainment provided in entertainment licensed premises is to be changed[2].
(e) The layout of premises approved by the board for the purpose of an earlier application for the provisional grant of a new licence is to be materially altered[3].
(f) A part or parts of licensed premises are to be 'de-licensed'.

DISQUALIFIED PREMISES AND APPLICANTS

Statutory disqualifications

An application for a new licence may not competently be made and any purported grant would be void (s 9(5)) where:
(1) Premises are disqualified from being licensed premises because of their situation:

> 'on land acquired or appropriated by a special road authority, and for the time being used, for the provision of facilities to be used in connection with the use of a special road provided for the use of traffic of class 1 (with or without other classes)'[4].

This provision enacts the recommendation in the *Report of the Departmental Committee on Scottish Licensing Law*[5] that licences should not be available for motorway service stations.

Although s 9(4A) and (4B) of the Licensing Act 1964[6] prohibits the grant of a justices' licence in respect of garage premises used for the retailing of motor fuel or the sale or maintenance of motor vehicles, there is no parallel provision in the 1976 Act and a number of off-sale licences have been granted for grocers' shops within petrol stations, despite the emotive connection between drinking and driving.

(2) The applicant has been disqualified from holding a licence for the premises or the premises have been disqualified from being used as licensed premises by order of the court[7].

---

1 Which may be employed to prevent the sale of spirits. *Quaere*, however, whether a licence subject to this restriction is in a 'different form'.
2 A new licence is indubitably required where the form of entertainment is circumscribed by a condition attached to the existing licence by virtue of s 101(2); in other cases, a new licence is usually obtained to protect the revamped operation of the premises from challenge.
3 As explained at Chapter 4, in terms of s 26(4)(b), deviations from the approved plan are permitted only where they are of 'minor importance' and have not 'materially altered' the character of the premises or the facilities for the supply of liquor.
4 Section 28, as amended by the Roads (Scotland) Act 1984, Sch 9. 'Special road', 'special road authority' and 'class 1' are defined by reference to the 1984 Act: see s 28(2).
5 (Cmnd 5354) (*Clayson*) paras 15.31, 15.32.
6 As amended by the Licensing Act 1988.
7 Where there has been a conviction in respect of certain offences: see s 67(3) and (4) and Sch 5. A licenceholder's disqualification may only relate to 'the premises concerned' and a general disqualification is incompetent: see *Devaux v MacPhail* 1991 GWD 7-396; *Matchett v Douglas* 1992 SCCR 617.

Incompetent applications

(1) Further application following refusal

In addition, where a licensing board has refused an application for a new licence 'in respect of any premises', it shall not 'within two years of its refusal entertain a subsequent application for a new licence'[1] unless a contrary direction is made at the time of the original refusal (s 14). Where a further application is submitted which prima facie relates to the same premises the competency of its consideration is a matter for the board, rather than the clerk. In *Kelvinside Community Council v Glasgow District Licensing Board*[2] the board's decision to entertain a second application, distinguished from an earlier application by the inclusion of an outside drinking area, was upheld by the Second Division.

(2) 'Double licensing'

Premises may not be the subject of two licences at the same time and, where it is desired to replace one licence with another, grant of the new licence application must be conditional upon surrender of the existing licence[3]. A new licence application may, however, be competent where the holder of an ex facie current licence has ceased to possess the premises[4].

(3) Licensing of 'premises'

A licensing board may only grant an application in respect of 'premises' within its own area (s 9(2)). Whether 'premises' are suitable for licensed use falls to be considered in the context of the grounds of refusal provided by s 17(1)(b) and (c)[5] but a licence may not competently be granted other than for some fixed, permanent structure[6]. It has been held that hotel premises may consist of more than one building[7]. Local authority premises are not disqualified (s 124).

---

1 The refusal of an application for the *renewal* of a licence does not (as sometimes suggested) necessitate a 'section 14 direction' to allow the presentation of a new licence application in respect of the same premises.
2 1990 SCLR 110, 1990 SLT 726.
3 As to whether premises may be the subject of a 'permanent' and occasional (s 33) licence at the same time, see Chapter 7.
4 See *West Wemyss United Services Club, Applicants* 1948 SLT (Sh Ct) 33, where a public house certificate 'fell to all effects with the surrender of possession'; and, more recently, in the context of betting legislation, *Edward Barrett Ltd v City of Dundee District Licensing Board* 1992 SLT 963.
5 A question may arise as to whether a licence may be granted for only part of premises. See p 73 below.
6 *Gate v Bath Justices* (1983) 147 JP 289. In this case justices refused to grant a licence for a barge which occasionally left its berth for pleasure cruises. Licences have, however, been granted for permanently-moored vessels.
7 *Chief Constable, Northern Constabulary v Lochaber District Licensing Board* 1985 SLT 410.

THE APPLICATION PROCEDURE

Types of application

There are three application procedures, outlined here and thereafter subjected to detailed consideration.

(1) Grant of a new licence

This procedure is only appropriate where, at the time of application, the premises are complete. It may be employed where, for example, existing retail premises are to be put to off-sale use; where it is desired to extend existing premises by the inclusion of a beer garden; or where application requires to be made following a failure to renew a licence. The application must be supported by detailed plans and certificates of suitability in relation to planning, building control and food hygiene.

(2) Provisional grant of a new licence (section 26(1))

In the majority of cases, the intending licenceholder will clearly be unwilling to carry out a new building project on a speculative basis. Application for the provisional grant of a new licence may be made in terms of s 26(1) for 'premises about to be constructed or in the course of construction', on the basis of detailed plans and subject to the production of certificates of suitability required by s 23 in relation to planning, building control and food hygiene. The board 'may' make a provisional grant if satisfied:

'(a) that the premises will be fit and convenient for their purpose, and
 (b) that, if the premises had been completed in accordance with the plan thereof . . . the board would on application have granted such a licence in respect thereof'[1].

Where the application is granted and the premises are completed in accordance with the approved plans (with minor deviations being permissible), the provisional grant is converted to a licence 'in force' by an application for 'finalisation'. This type of provisional grant will be referred to as a 'full provisional grant'.

(3) Provisional grant of a new licence (section 26(2))

An intending applicant may wish to avoid the substantial (and potentially fruitless) costs which are usually incurred in the preparation of detailed plans; or he may hold planning permission for his project but not a building warrant. In such a case, application may be made under s 26(2) for an 'outline provisional grant', the expression which will be employed to distinguish this permission from the 'full

---

1 Section 26(1)(a), (b). Despite the use of the word 'may', the application requires to be granted unless one of the grounds of refusal set out in s 17(1) is found to exist: see p 66 below.

provisional grant'. The application need only be accompanied by a site plan, a general description of the proposed facilities and a certificate of suitability relative to planning. If the application is granted, the outline provisional grant must be 'affirmed' within the ensuing 12 months on the basis of detailed drawings (such as would have accompanied a full provisional grant application) and the production of certificates of suitability in relation to building control and food hygiene. Affirmation is followed by finalisation when the premises have been completed.

Types of applicant

Application may be made by:

(a) An individual natural person alone, including, it would appear, a manager on behalf of the beneficial owner[1]. It is suggested, however, that in view of the provisions of s 11 (see (b) below) a natural person should not hold a licence where the business is to be conducted for the profit of a limited company, partnership or other juristic *persona*[2].

(b) A non-natural person with a nominated employee or agent. Section 11 provides that where an application is made for a new licence[3] 'by an applicant who is not an individual natural person', the application (s 11(1)) 'shall name both the applicant[4] and the employee or agent of the applicant whom the applicant intends should have the responsibility for the day to day running of the premises to which the application relates'.

It requires to be observed, however, that an application for a full or outline provisional grant is made simply by 'any person interested in premises' (s 26(1)); and that where such a grant is held 'by a person other than an individual natural person' the *finalisation* application must include 'the name of the employee or agent whom it is intended should have the day to day running of the premises' (s 26(4)). Accordingly, the provisional application should proceed in the name of the non-natural person alone. A minority of licensing boards have nevertheless insisted upon a nomination at the outset. Such a requirement is not only hopelessly impractical where a management appointment has yet to be made but also incurs a substantial risk. Since a provisional grant is not a licence 'in force', the transfer provisions of s 25 do not apply[5] and where the employee or agent dies or

---

1 *Tominey v City of Glasgow District Licensing Board* 1984 SLT (Sh Ct) 2.
2 See also *Paterson v City of Glasgow Licensing Board* 1982 SLT (Sh Ct) 37, in which a manager of a limited company was held not to be an 'occupant' for transfer purposes.
3 Or for the renewal or permanent transfer of a licence.
4 In the case of a partnership, some licensing boards accept applications in the firm name alone, without reference to the individual partners; others will require the partners to be named and designed, although no mechanism is provided whereby subsequent changes in the constitution of the partnership are to be brought to the attention of the board. On the whole, the legal status of juristic *personae* seems to be poorly understood: see, for example, *Singh and Kaur v Kirkcaldy District Licensing Board* 1988 SLT 286. Application should not be made simply in name of the partners without reference to the firm.
5 *Baljaffray Residents' Association v Milngavie and Bearsden District Council Licensing Board* 1981 SLT (Sh Ct) 106. See also *Ginera Ltd v City of Glasgow District Licensing Board* 1982 SLT 136.

ceases to be connected with the project prior to finalisation no mechanism exists whereby he may be replaced[1].

While the expression 'any person interested' has yet to be the subject of judicial consideration in Scotland, it has been held that the similar phrase occurring in s 6 of the Licensing Act 1964:

'should be construed in each case by the justices looking broadly at the circumstances of the individual application and what is proposed to be carried out and by whom, so that an occupier of the premises who has no interest in the land as such and no firm contract with the owner may be allowed to make application'[2].

Since a person whose legal interest in the premises has yet to crystallise may conceivably be qualified to make an application, it requires to be kept in view that the refusal of his application without a direction in terms of s 14 would prohibit consideration of a further application in respect of 'the same premises' in the ensuing two years and may substantially prejudice the owner.

In terms of regulations made under s 37, a licensing board may require the provision of character references.

Content of the application

The application is made in 'such form as may be prescribed' (s 10(1))[3] but should take into account certain matters, as follows.

Sunday permitted hours

An applicant for the grant or provisional grant of a new public house or refreshment licence shall 'state whether [he] intends the premises to be open for the sale or supply of alcoholic liquor during the permitted hours on a Sunday' (s 10(3A), inserted by the 1990 Act, s 46)[4]. The importance of compliance with this requirement cannot be over-emphasised. As a result of the amendments introduced by the 1990 Act, Sunday opening permission can no longer be obtained by application to any quarterly board meeting and must be requested in the context of the grant, provisional grant or renewal of a licence (1990 Act, s 46).

Children's certificates

An applicant for the grant or provisional grant of a new public house or hotel licence requires to state whether application is also made for a children's certificate (1990 Act, Sch 5, para 6)[5]. Application for the certificate must be made

---

1 In relation to 'full' licences the substitution procedure is provided by s 25(3): see Chapter 5.
2 *R v Dudley Crown Court ex parte Pask* (1983) 147 JP 417.
3 'Prescribed' means 'prescribed by regulations made under section 37': s 139(1).
4 No separate application is required. The permitted hours on Sundays are the periods between 12.30 pm and 2.30 pm and 6.30 pm and 11 pm. For permitted hours in general, see Chapter 10.
5 Children's certificates are considered in Chapter 14. It is doubtful whether an outline provisional grant application would provide information sufficient to establish the suitability of the premises or the part in respect of which application is made.

separately and requires to be intimated by the applicant to the chief constable (1990 Act, Sch 5, para 4), while the new licence application itself is exempt from such a requirement.

Seasonal licences

The applicant may request that the licence be subject to a 'seasonal' condition in terms of s 62[1].

Restricted hotel licences

An applicant for a restricted hotel licence may request that the sale or supply of alcoholic liquor be limited by the exclusion of the authority normally conferred in relation to the operation of a public restaurant, so that service is confined to residents and their private friends[2]. Application forms are usually silent as to this possibility, but the request may be made orally at the hearing[3].

Off-sale parts

An applicant for the grant or provisional grant of a public house or hotel licence may request that part of the premises be specially designated for off-sale use only (s 119(2))[4]. The board requires to be satisfied that:

(a) the relevant part is 'structurally adapted for the sale and supply of alcoholic liquor for consumption off the premises' (s 119(2)(a)); and

(b) there is no internal communication available to the customers connecting the off-sale part with a drinking area or any such communication is capable of being closed to customers (s 119(2)(b)).

Where these criteria are met the board 'shall' insert conditions prohibiting in the off-sale part the sale or supply of alcoholic liquor for consumption on the premises; requiring any internal communication between the off-sale part and a drinking area to be closed to customers 'during any time when customers are present in any part of the premises'; and preventing customers from using 'any internal communication for the purpose of passing from one part of the premises to another part thereof' (s 119(2)(i), (ii) and (iii))[5].

While the licence is subject to these conditions the off-sale part enjoys off-sale 'trading hours' on Mondays to Saturdays from 8 am to 10 pm (rather than normal permitted hours) and 'shall not be opened for the serving of customers' with alcoholic liquor on Sundays (s 119(3))[6].

---

1 Seasonal licences are considered at Chapter 3.
2 Schedule 1 definition of 'restricted hotel licence', para (b)(v).
3 *Quinn v Paisley Magistrates* 1909 SC 1085, (1909) 2 SLT 35.
4 A similar request may be made when a licence is renewed or transferred.
5 Contravention of a condition by the holder of a licence or his employee or agent is an offence: s 119(4). Maximum penalty: level 3 (Sch 5). Licenceholder has vicarious responsibility: s 67, Sch 5.
6 Sunday trading in liquor is an offence: s 119(4). Maximum penalty: level 3 (Sch 5). Licenceholder has vicarious responsibility: s 67, Sch 5. The off-sale part may be open for the sale of other commodities.

Since public houses (with Sunday permitted hours) and hotels enjoy seven-day trading with an inbuilt off-sale facility and often possess regular extensions of the permitted hours beyond 11 pm[1], the concession made available by s 119 is normally considered unattractive.

Confidentiality of applicant's address

The application may contain a request that the agent's address be published in terms of s 12, rather than the address of the applicant, in which case any intimation requirement (normally in relation to an objection; s 16(2), (3)) may be satisfied by intimation to the agent (s 139(5), (6), added by the 1990 Act, Sch 8, para 18).

Time-limit for submission

An application for the grant or provisional grant of a new licence may only be considered at a quarterly licensing board meeting (s 5(2)(a), (6)), requiring to be 'completed and signed by the applicant or his agent'[2] and lodged with the clerk 'not later than five weeks before the first day of the meeting'[3].

Where an application is lodged out-of-time due to 'inadvertence or misadventure', its consideration may be postponed to an adjourned meeting (held in terms of s 4(2)), at the board's discretion and 'upon such terms as the board thinks proper'[4].

The clerk is bound to accept for consideration in terms of s 13(2) an application lodged after the first day of a quarterly meeting but before the date of any adjourned meeting[5].

Plans

An application for the grant of a new licence (except an off-sale licence) (s 10(2)(a))[6] or for a *full* provisional grant (s 10(3)(a)) must be accompanied by a plan of the premises.

Plans often require to be prepared to a particular specification, prescribed by regulations (s 37), and will require to show the whole premises, including, for

---

1 In terms of s 64. Note, however, that regular extensions are sometimes granted subject to a condition imposed under s 64(6) prohibiting off-sales after a certain time.
2 The 'agent' need not be a law agent.
3 'Not later than five weeks' means 'not later than five weeks before the inception of the day on which the meeting takes place': *Main v City of Glasgow District Licensing Board* 1987 SLT 305. See also discussion of time limits at Chapter 1.
4 Section 13(2), which is also available where there has been a failure to comply with any other 'preliminary requirement': eg the display/service of a notice in terms of s 10(2)(b), (3)(b) and (5) (see below).
5 See *Indpine Ltd v City of Dundee District Licensing Board* 1992 SCLR 113 (OH), 1992 SCLR 353, 1992 SLT 473 (IH).
6 Note, however, that licensing boards will generally require the production of a drawing for off-sales applications, although it may generally be prepared to a lower standard than in other cases.

example, the bedroom block of a hotel[1]. At this stage, consideration should be given as to whether an outside drinking area is to be included. Delay and unnecessary additional expense is likely to be avoided if plans are prepared by a suitably qualified architect.

The clerk will circulate the plans to the police, the building control and environmental health departments, the firemaster[2] and (possibly) the local planning department[3].

Most licensing board clerks are prepared to allow the amendment of plans up to a reasonable time before the board meeting; and an adjournment of an application is sometimes allowed for this purpose.

An application for an *outline* provisional grant need only be accompanied by 'a plan sufficient to identify the site of the premises, together with such description of the premises as will give a general indication of their proposed size and character (with reference in particular to the sale of alcoholic liquor)'. (s 26(2))[4].

Applicants will normally wish to avail themselves of the wide latitude which this provision affords; but it requires to be kept in view that affirmation of the provisional grant may be refused where the detailed plans later submitted 'deviate materially from the site plan and description' (s 26(3)).

Certificates of suitability

Unless certificates of suitability are produced to the board in accordance with the provisions of s 23, an application for the grant or provisional grant of a new licence (other than an off-sale licence) 'shall not be entertained' by the board (s 23(1))[5]. An application for the grant of a new licence or for a full provisional grant (s 26(1)) must be supported by certificates in relation to planning (s 23(2)), building control (s 23(3)) and food hygiene (s 23(4)); in relation to an outline provisional grant (s 26(2)) only a planning certificate need be produced, but building control and food hygiene certificates are required at the affirmation stage (s 23(6)).

(1) Planning

The certificate from 'the appropriate authority'[6] should state that:

---

1 As explained at p 73 below, licensing boards may not be prepared to grant a licence restricted to part of premises and, in some cases, interconnection with unlicensed premises will not be permitted.

2 The board is obliged to consult the firemaster in terms of s 23(5). Where application has been made for an outline provisional grant, consultation is deferred until the affirmation stage: s 23(6). He is empowered to object to a grant or provisional grant application: s 16(1)(e).

3 The plans also require to be made available, with the application, for public inspection: s 10(7).

4 Despite the minimalism of this requirement, it is suggested that reference should be made to any proposed outside drinking area as the board may otherwise take the view that potential objectors have been prejudiced: see *Kelvinside Community Council v Glasgow District Licensing Board* 1990 SCLR 110, 1990 SLT 725.

5 Modified by s 23(5) as respects outline provisional grant applications: see below.

6 The 'appropriate authority' in the case of the Highland, Borders, and Dumfries and Galloway Regions is the regional council and, in any other case, is the district or islands council: s 23(7).

'the applicant has obtained in respect of the premises planning permission under the Town and Country Planning (Scotland) Act 1972 or, in the case of an application for the provisional grant of a licence, outline planning permission under sections 39 and 40 of that Act, or, in either case, a determination under section 51 of that Act that planning permission is not required or a certificate under section 90A of that Act that the proposed use or operations would be lawful as mentioned in the said section 90A'[1].

Despite the somewhat inept reference to 'the applicant', clerks appear content to accept that planning consents relate to the premises, rather than any individual; it is thus considered immaterial that consent has been granted to an individual other than the applicant for the licence.

Determinations under s 51 of the Town and Country Planning (Scotland) Act 1972 ('the 1972 Act') were abolished with effect from 25 September 1992 by the Planning and Compensation Act 1991 ('the 1991 Act'). Provision is now made for certificates of lawfulness of proposed use or development, in terms of s 90A of the 1972 Act[2]. The 1991 Act contained no consequential amendment to the 1976 Act, causing considerable difficulty until the oversight was corrected by the Licensing (Amendment) (Scotland) Act 1993 (s 1)[3]. Section 90A provides that if any person wishes to ascertain whether:

'(a) any proposed use of buildings or other land; or
(b) any operations proposed to be carried out in, on, over or under land',

would be lawful, he may apply to the planning authority with a description of the use or operations in question[4]. Where the authority is satisfied that the use or operations 'would be lawful if instituted or begun at the time of the application', they are required to issue a certificate to that effect[5].

Otherwise, an application for change of use may be required. The Town and Country Planning (Use Classes) (Scotland) Order 1989, SI 1989/147 ('the 1989 Order') lists 16 classes of use, the most significant for licensing purposes being:

Class 1: shops used for inter alia the retail sale of goods (but excluding hot food). This will usually embrace off-sale premises[6].
Class 3: use for the sale of food or drink for consumption on the premises or of hot food for consumption off the premises. Restaurants clearly fall within this category.
Class 12: use as inter alia a hotel where 'no significant element of care is provided, other than premises licensed for the sale of alcoholic liquor to persons other than residents or to persons other than persons consuming meals on the premises'. This classification effectively excludes hotels other than those to be operated under a restricted hotel licence.
Class 16: use as a '(a) cinema; (b) concert hall; (c) bingo hall or casino; (d) dance hall or discothèque; or (e) swimming bath, skating rink, gymnasium or area for

1 Section 23(2), as amended by the Licensing (Amendment) (Scotland) Act 1993, s 1.
2 As inserted by the 1991 Act, s 42.
3 This Act came into force on 1 July 1993. Ad interim, the Secretary of State considered that licensing boards could not consider an application which was supported only by a planning certificate proceeding upon a s 90A certificate.
4 1972 Act, s 90A(1).
5 1972 Act, s 90A(2).
6 No certificates of suitability are required for an off-sale application.

other indoor or outdoor sports or recreation, not involving motorised vehicles or firearms'. Premises which are to be the subject of an entertainment licence will normally come within Class 16.

Nothing in any class includes use as a public house or as a theatre[1]. In practice, problems are frequently encountered in relation to the planning status of a restaurant which is to be operated under a public house licence. As explained elsewhere[2], at least one licensing board considers that a public house licence, with corresponding planning consent, is required for a restaurant with a dispense bar, although alcohol is only served to persons taking table meals. In many areas, however, Class 3 use will be considered appropriate for (a) this type of bona fide restaurant operating under a restaurant licence or (b) a restaurant with a public house licence where the predominant use is the provision of meals[3].

Although refreshment-licensed premises would appear to fall squarely within Class 3, public house consent may be necessary in some districts on the view that the consumption of alcohol need not be associated with the taking of food.

For a case in which the grant of a licence was reversed on appeal because of the inadequacy of the planning certificate, see *Donald v Stirling District Licensing Board*[4].

Where listed building consent is required, some authorities will withhold the certificate of suitability until this has been obtained.

(2) *Building control*

Where application has been made for the grant of a new licence, the certificate 'from the appropriate authority'[5] should state:

'(i) either that a warrant for the construction of the premises has been granted under section 6 of the Building (Scotland) Act 1959 and a certificate of completion has been granted under section 9 of that Act, or that no warrant for construction of the premises is required; and
(ii) either that a warrant for the change of use of the premises has been granted under the said section 6 or that no such warrant is required'[6].

Otherwise, in the case of provisional grant applications, the certificate confirms:

'(i) that a warrant for the construction of the premises has been granted under section 6 of the said Act of 1959; and
(ii) either that a warrant for the change of use of the premises has been granted under the said section 6, or that on completion of the construction of the premises in accordance with the warrant a warrant for the change of use will be granted, or that no such warrant is required'[7].

---

1 1989 Order, para 3(5).
2 See Chapter 3.
3 Enforcement procedure may, however, be taken by the planning authority where there is a significant change of emphasis.
4 1992 SCLR (Notes) 369, 1992 SLT (Sh Ct) 75.
5 The 'appropriate authority' in the case of the Highland, Borders, and Dumfries and Galloway Regions is the regional council and, in any other case, is the district or islands council: s 23(7).
6 Section 23(3)(a).
7 Section 23(3)(b).

(3) Food hygiene

The certificate from 'the appropriate authority'[1] should:

'in the case of an application for a new licence, state that the premises to which the application relates comply, or in the case of an application for the provisional grant of a new licence, would comply, with the requirements of regulations made under section 16 of the Food Safety Act 1990, relating to construction, layout, drainage, ventilation, lighting and water supply or concerned with the provision of sanitary and washing facilities'[2].

In certain licensing board areas application for these certificates is made on forms supplied by the departments concerned; otherwise, application is simply made by letter. A number of district councils require payment of a fee and, while this practice has yet to be challenged, the decision in *McCarthy & Stone Ltd v Richmond upon Thames London Borough Council*[3] casts considerable doubt upon its legitimacy.

The Act prescribes no time-limit for production of the certificates, a *lacuna* frequently filled by a licensing board's regulation (s 37). Difficulties are likely to arise where the applicant is obliged to submit certificates with the application no later than the last lodging date for the quarterly meeting. It is suggested that such a requirement is *ultra vires* as it purports to elide the possibility of a motion in terms of s 13(2)[4], which is always available where the application itself has been lodged late. Indeed, while s 23(1) enjoins a board not to 'entertain' an application which is not suitably supported by certificates, it appears that the application is nevertheless 'competent' for advertisement purposes, having regard to the dictum of the Lord Justice-Clerk (Ross) in *Kelvinside Community Council v Glasgow District Licensing Board*[5].

While many licensing boards are prepared to grant a continuation to an adjourned meeting where certificates are awaited, at least one clerk is of the opinion that a motion for that purpose may not be considered as the application cannot be 'entertained' in terms of s 23(1).

A situation may arise in which a local authority department attempts to exact from an applicant requirements beyond those necessary for the issue of the certificate. Such an eventuality, far from unknown in practice, was foreseen by *Clayson*[6]:

'It may be that a local authority consider that the proposed premises, although meeting statutory requirements, are in some way unsuitable bearing in mind desirable standards for licensed premises in their area. In that case there should be no question of the local authority refusing the certificate'.

---

1 Ie the district or islands council: s 23(7).
2 Section 23(4), as amended by the Food Safety Act 1990, Sch 3, para 19.
3 [1991] 4 All ER 897, revsg [1990] 2 All ER 852. The House of Lords held that a local authority had no power to impose a charge for pre-planning consultations.
4 See 'Time-limit for submission', above. Cf *Clayson*, para 14.23 where it appears to be assumed that the certificates would be obtained before application is made.
5 1990 SCLR 110, 1990 SLT 725.
6 Para. 8.26.

The committee also considered, however, that the local authority's reservations could nevertheless be brought to the licensing board's attention and taken into account. At least one licensing board has drawn up a set of standards for licensed premises, with the result that the environmental health department (for example) may issue a certificate in terms of s 23 and yet comment adversely upon an application.

An unjustifiable refusal to issue a certificate may be the subject of review by petition under s 45 of the Court of Session Act 1988[1], which provides the remedy of specific performance where there has been a failure to perform a statutory duty[2]. In *Annan v Leith Magistrates*[3] such a procedure was, however, considered inappropriate where magistrates had failed to furnish a report as to the suitability of premises: this decision has been criticised as 'unsound'[4].

Notices

A notice intimating the application requires to be (a) displayed at the premises or site (s 10(2)(b), (3)(b)) and (b) given to neighbouring occupiers (s 10(5)). In the case of public house and refreshment licence applications both notices should state whether the applicant intends the premises to be open for the sale or supply of alcoholic liquor during the Sunday permitted hours (s 10(8), added by the 1990 Act, s 46)[5]. Only the agent's address should be given for the intimation of objections where a 'confidentiality' request has been made in terms of s 139(5).

Notice at premises or site

The applicant must arrange for the display of this notice 'in the prescribed form'[6] for a period of at least 21 days before the first day of the quarterly meeting[7] 'in a place and at a height where it can conveniently be read by the public' (s 10(2)(b)). In *Tevan v Motherwell District Licensing Board (No. 1)*[8] display of a notice in a post office was held to conform to this requirement but it was suggested that display within a public house would not be adequate. The applicant's only safe course is to ensure that the general public have unrestricted access to the notice 24 hours a day.

The applicant is not to be treated as having failed to comply with the display requirement where:

---

1 Formerly Court of Session Act 1868, s 91. See 1 *Stair Memorial Encyclopaedia* para 335.
2 For an unusual case in which the procedure was employed (competently but unsuccessfully) see *Noble Developments Ltd v City of Glasgow District Council* 1989 SCLR 622.
3 (1901) 9 SLT 63.
4 1 *Stair Memorial Encyclopaedia* para 335.
5 As explained above, a similar statement requires to be made in the application form itself: s 10(3A).
6 Ie prescribed by a regulation made under s 37. The time-limit for objections is invariably stated, together with a précis of the objections procedure.
7 Ie 21 clear days: *Main v City of Glasgow District Licensing Board* 1987 SLT 305.
8 1985 SLT (Sh Ct) 14.

'the notice is, without any fault or intention of his, removed, obscured or defaced before the first day of the meeting at which the application is to be considered, so long as he has taken reasonable steps for its protection and, if need be, replacement'[1].

Otherwise, in a case of defective or non-compliance through 'inadvertence or misadventure' the applicant may move the board to exercise its discretion in terms of s 13(2) and continue consideration of the application to an adjourned meeting so that the notice may properly be displayed *ad interim*[2].

Notice to occupiers

'Not later than three weeks' before the first day of the board meeting[3], the applicant must give 'notice in writing of the application to every occupier of premises situated in the same building as the premises to which the application relates' (s 10(5)).

This notice (often referred to somewhat erroneously as the 'neighbourhood notification notice') will normally be in identical terms to the notice displayed at the premises or site.

The terms 'occupier' and 'building' are not defined. For the purposes of earlier legislation 'occupier' was considered to mean 'an occupier within the meaning of the Lands Valuation (Scotland) Act 1854, although entries in the Valuation Roll [were] not necessarily conclusive of the matter'[4]; a person residing in property was not automatically to be regarded as possessing the requisite status[5]. In current practice, correctly or otherwise, such arcane considerations are ignored and notice will be given to 'occupiers' in the plain sense of the word.

Premises are generally treated as being 'in the same building' where they share with the application premises the same roof and gables[6], but whether two adjacent structures form one building will require to be determined on the facts of each case[7].

The method of service is not prescribed but notices may, of course, be sent by post (s 134)[8]. Otherwise delivery should be effected in the presence of a witness.

Certificates of compliance

The proper display of the notice at the premises or site will usually be checked by the police. In addition, a number of licensing boards require the applicant to

---

1 Section 10(4).
2 A similar motion may be made where there has been a failure to comply with s 10(5): see below.
3 The period of three weeks ends at midnight on the day before the first day of the meeting: *Main v City of Glasgow District Licensing Board* 1987 SLT 305.
4 *Purves*, 8th edn, p 44.
5 *McDonald v Chambers* 1956 SC 542, (sub nom *McDonald v Finlay*) 1957 SLT 81. The meaning of 'occupier' for objection purposes is considered at Chapter 6.
6 See *City of Edinburgh District Council v Gardner* 1990 SLT 600 at 603I, J.
7 *Assessor for Lothian Region v City of Edinburgh District Council* 1990 SLT 382. See further *Allan and Chapman's* commentary to the Act 3rd edn by Agnew and Baillie, p 60, and cases cited.
8 A number of licensing boards have promulgated regulations under s 37 requiring the first class recorded service to be employed.

submit to the clerk a certificate confirming that he has complied with the Act's requirements, accompanied, where appropriate, by recorded delivery receipts to vouch service upon adjoining occupiers.

Advertisement

The clerk of the board must 'not later than three weeks before the first day of the meeting'[1] cause 'a list of all competent applications' for inter alia the grant and provisional grant of a new licence to be published 'in one or more newspapers circulating in the area of the board' (s 12)[2]. In *Kelvinside Community Council v Glasgow District Licensing Board*[3] it was considered that 'a list of all competent applications' means:

'[A]pplications made under the preceding sections, that is sections 10 and 11. In other words, what the clerk requires to publish is a list of all applications which have been lodged in accordance with the provisions of sections 10 and 11. Thus it is for the clerk to ensure that applications comply with the requirements of sections 10 and 11. They must be signed by the applicant or his agent and lodged within the specified period; an application must be accompanied by a plan[4], and arrangements must be made for display of the necessary notices'[5].

Objections

An objection to an application for the grant or provisional grant of a new licence may competently be made by persons 'owning or occupying property' in the neighbourhood of the premises; an organisation representing such persons; the community council for the area; an organised church representing 'a significant body of opinion among persons residing in the neighbourhood'; the chief constable; the fire authority; the local authority (s 16(1)). Objections require to be lodged with the clerk and intimated to the applicant not later than seven (clear) days before the board meeting (s 16(2), (3))[6].

In addition, the chief constable is empowered to make observations, to which the board 'shall have regard' (s 16A)[7].

Grounds of refusal

Under earlier legislation the licensing court had complete discretion to grant certificates 'to such and so many persons as the court shall think fit'[8]. The 1976

---

1 The period of three weeks ends at midnight on the day before the first day of the meeting: *Main v City of Glasgow District Licensing Board* 1987 SLT 305.
2 For the information to be specified in the advertisement as respects each application, see s 12(2).
3 1990 SCLR 110, 1990 SLT 725.
4 As respects off-sales premises only a provisional grant application need be accompanied by a plan: see s 10(2).
5 Note, however, that a failure to display the notice will not become apparent until after publication of the advertisement. The clerk's powers in this area are examined further at Chapter 1.
6 Late or otherwise defective objections may be considered at an adjourned meeting: s 13(2).
7 The procedure for objections and observations is examined in further detail at Chapter 6.
8 Licensing Act 1959, s 32.

Act provides that the application shall be refused if one or more of the four competent grounds of refusal is found to exist; otherwise the application shall be granted (s 17(1)).

(1) Suitability of the applicant

The board is bound to refuse the application where:

'the applicant, or the person on whose behalf or for whose benefit the applicant will manage the premises or, in the case of an application to which section 11 . . . applies, the applicant or the employee or agent named in the application is not a fit and proper person to be the holder of a licence'[1].

When considering this ground, the board may 'have regard to any misconduct . . . whether or not constituting a breach of [the] Act or any byelaw [s 38] made thereunder, which in the opinion of the board has a bearing on his fitness to hold a licence' (s 17(3)). Normally, fitness to hold a licence becomes an issue only where the chief constable objects to the application or submits observations, based on the applicant's previous criminal convictions (as discussed below). The licensing board will also wish to be satisfied that the applicant has appropriate experience in the licensed trade and may require the production of character references[2], although the scope of the enquiry as to 'fitness' is generally not as comprehensive as *Clayson* envisaged. The committee considered that, in the exercise of a 'wide discretion', the board should have regard to 'health, general competence and ability as regards the conduct of the premises' (as well as 'character')[3].

On that account, the approach taken in *J & J Inns Ltd v Angus District Licensing Board*[4] is, at least in part, atypical. An application to substitute a new employee in terms of s 25(3) was refused primarily on the ground that the proposed manageress was 'unfit' because of her association with certain individuals. The board also considered significant her previous failure to ensure that an application for renewal of (a different) public house licence was submitted timeously; and a disinclination to visit the application premises supposedly indicated 'a lack of interest, hence a lack of ability'. While the Lord Ordinary (Weir) appears to have entertained doubts as to the weight which could be accorded to these ancillary reasons, he was not prepared to hold that the board's decision proceeded upon irrelevant considerations.

It may be remarked in passing that an application made in terms of s 25(4) for confirmation of a transfer approved on an interim basis under s 25(2) or (3)[5] may only be *granted* where the board is 'satisfied' as to 'fitness'[6], while an application

---

1 Section 17(1)(a). Where the provisional grant of a new licence is made in name of a non-natural person alone, the application for finalisation must be refused if the employee or agent put forward at that stage is not 'a fit and proper person': s 26(6). Finalisation: see p 84 below.
2 By virtue of regulations: s 37. Perth and Kinross District Licensing Board (uniquely, it is believed) operate induction seminars for intending licenceholders in the area.
3 Para 8.14. See also *R v Hyde Justices (or Cooke) ex parte Atherton* [1912] 1 KB 645, in which 'fitness' was considered to embrace 'health, temper and disposition'.
4 1992 SCLR 683, 1992 SLT 930.
5 See further: Chapter 5.
6 *Pace* the Lord Ordinary in *J & J Inns Ltd* the same test requires to be applied at the interim stage.

for the grant or provisional grant of a new licence may only be *refused* if the board *'finds'* the applicant to be unfit. In *J & J Inns Ltd* the Lord Ordinary held that:

'it is for the applicant to satisfy the board that the employee or agent which [sic] is put forward is a fit and proper person. On the other hand, in deciding to refuse to grant the application, there is no onus on the board in giving its reasons to demonstrate positively that the applicant is not a fit and proper person'.

It may be considered that the scheme of s 17(1) is rather different and that the board is obliged to make a sustainable finding of 'unfitness' if the new licence application is to be refused.

Although there is no minimum (or maximum) age for licenceholding[1] an application by a person in minority has no prospect of success, standing the Act's provisions regarding the employment of persons under the age of 18 (see ss 72, 73) and the virtual certainty that he will be unable to demonstrate relevant experience.

The suitability of an applicant will also be open to question where his knowledge of the English language is so basic as to give rise to communication difficulties.

Much emphasis has traditionally been placed upon the principle of 'one man, one certificate'[2]: the proper conduct of licensed premises is considered to be promoted by the personal supervision of an accountable licenceholder. For that reason, many licensing boards will not countenance multiple licenceholding; others fix a limit of two or, rarely, three licences. A natural person who owns a number of licensed businesses may obviate this difficulty by arranging for licences to be held by his managers[3]. Where a licence is to be granted to a non-natural person and a nominated employee (or agent) in terms of s 11, the latter has 'responsibility for the day to day running of the premises' (s 11(2)). *In extremis*, a board may be prepared to approve dual licenceholding by a nominee for a limited period only but never on a permanent basis.

Where an applicant's criminal record is to be taken into account, a question may arise as to whether 'spent' convictions may be disclosed. In terms of the Rehabilitation of Offenders Act 1974[4], with certain exceptions[5], a conviction becomes spent after a period of rehabilitation fixed according to the sentence imposed[6]: for example, an absolute discharge is spent after six months[7], a fine after five years[8] and a custodial sentence not exceeding thirty months after ten years[9]. No evidence of a spent conviction is admissible in any proceedings before a

---

1 *Bootland v McFarlane* (1900) 2 F 1014, (1900) 8 SLT 63.
2 See *Clayson*, paras 8.01ff; and *Aldridge v Simpson-Bell* 1971 SC 87, 1971 SLT 188.
3 *Tominey v City of Glasgow District Licensing Board* 1984 SLT (Sh Ct) 2.
4 For a commendably lucid exposition of the Act's somewhat complicated provisions, see the annotations to the Act by John Rear in 'Current Law Statutes'.
5 Rehabilitation of Offenders Act 1974, s 5(1).
6 Ibid, s 5(2)ff.
7 Ibid, s 5(3).
8 Ibid, s 5(2) and Table A.
9 Ibid, s 5(2) and Table A. Rehabilitation periods commence on the date of conviction. In certain circumstances a further conviction during the period may result in its extension or completely exclude rehabilitation.

'judicial authority'[1], an expression which has been held to include a licensing authority[2], except where the authority is satisfied at 'any stage' that 'justice' cannot otherwise be done[3]. In *Morton v City of Dundee District Council*[4] the licensing authority considered details of spent convictions relating to an applicant for a taxi driver's licence before a preliminary decision had been taken as to whether they should be examined. The sheriff (A L Stewart) held that the authority had erred in law and said:

'What should, in my opinion, have happened is that the committee should have been informed by the chief constable that the [applicant] had "spent" convictions (without going into detail at that stage). On consideration of the whole circumstances, including the very serious conviction which was not "spent", the [committee] should then have taken a decision on whether they were satisfied that justice could not be done without admitting in evidence the "spent" convictions. If they so decided, then full details of these convictions would have been made available to them'[5].

Nevertheless, the fact that the applicant had an unspent conviction entitled the committee to base its decision on his whole criminal record and discretion had not been exercised in such a way that the court was entitled to interfere.

In *Cashley v City of Dundee District Council*[6] an application for a taxi licence[7] was refused on the basis of spent convictions, to which the licensing authority had regard as a matter of policy. An Extra Division held that such a policy required to be applied 'fairly and evenly'; discretion had been exercised unreasonably and the policy applied 'in an arbitrary fashion' where other, successful applicants had criminal records which 'appeared to be significantly more serious and more relevant'[8].

It is doubtful whether details of spent convictions may be demanded in an application form: at this point there are no 'proceedings' before a judicial authority[9].

Licensing boards are not empowered to make their own investigation into the existence or otherwise of an applicant's convictions, which will only come to their notice where the chief constable elects to object or make observations[10].

1 Ibid, s 4(1)(a). For the definition of 'judicial authority', see s 4(6).
2 *Francey v Cunninghame District Council* 1987 SCLR 6. A concession to that effect was made in *Morton v City of Dundee District Council* 1992 SLT (Sh Ct) 2.
3 Rehabilitation of Offenders Act 1974, s 7(3). A 'party' to proceedings may consent to the admission of the evidence: ibid, s 7(2)(f).
4 1992 SLT (Sh Ct) 2.
5 It has been suggested, very properly, that evidence of spent convictions should never be read aloud in public but should simply be handed to the bench: Field & Pink *Liquor Licensing Law and Practice* 2nd edn, para 1.64.
6 Inner House (Ex Div), 11 June 1993, unreported.
7 Civic Government (Scotland) Act 1982, s 10.
8 As to the consistency of licensing board decisions in general, see Chapter 16.
9 Cf *Francey v Cunninghame District Licensing Board* 1987 SCLR 6. The correctness of this decision is doubted in the Commentary to the report (at 9) and by the sheriff in *Morton v City of Dundee District Council* 1992 SLT (Sh Ct) 2 at 3J.
10 A licenceholder's conviction for any offence under the Act is, however, to be transmitted to the clerk of the board: s 129. It is interesting to note that where a licensing authority may make 'such reasonable enquiries as they think fit', (Civic Government (Scotland) Act 1982, Sch 1, para 4(1)) the refusal of an application on the basis of previous convictions thus disclosed by the police, considered to be minor or insufficiently serious by the sheriff, has been supported by the Inner House, despite the absence of the chief constable's objection. See, for example, *Ranachan v Renfrew District Council* 1991 SLT 625; *Hughes v Hamilton District Council* 1991 SLT 628.

Apart from breaches of the Act, convictions brought to the attention of licensing boards normally relate to dishonesty and violence, although minor assaults are frequently ignored. Road traffic offences are unlikely to be taken into account, unless of a particularly serious nature: a single drink-driving conviction is unlikely to create a barrier to licenceholding but a second offence may give cause for concern[1]. Although *Muir v Chief Constable of Edinburgh*[2] was decided under betting and gaming legislation[3], there is much to commend in the approach desiderated by the sheriff:

'It is impossible to lay down any hard and fast rule . . . Each application must, therefore, be considered on its own facts and circumstances and upon its own merits. Criminal convictions must be looked at carefully and assessed as to their seriousness and as to the extent to which they reflect upon an applicant's present character. If there is a series of offences carrying on to a comparatively recent date, they probably give a good indication of present character. If the conviction is an isolated one occurring a long time ago followed by a lengthy period of blameless behaviour, then I think it should be ignored unless it be for an offence of unusual gravity'[4].

Before a licensing board can make a finding of unfitness it 'must have some information before it other than the mere fact of a conviction'[5], although responsibility for advancing this information no doubt rests with the applicant:

'If the board were to take [a conviction for theft] otherwise than at face value as indicating . . . an offence of dishonesty, then it was for the [applicant's] representative when he was given the opportunity to have explained the circumstances to the board and to have attempted to persuade them that the [applicant] was a fit and proper person to hold a licence notwithstanding the conviction'[6].

In *Anwar v Clydesdale District Licensing Board*[7] the renewal of an off-sale licence had been refused simply on the ground of the applicant's conviction for selling alcohol to a person under the age of 18. The sheriff (I Dean) allowed his appeal, taking into account the fact that the offence had been committed vicariously by an employee, the relatively modest penalty imposed (a fine of £150) and the justice's failure to make a disqualification order[8]:

'In the circumstances the only conclusion I can come to is that the [board] paid no attention to anything other than the mere fact of the conviction and that their view that the conviction was "so severe" was merely capricious and that their discretion was exercised unreasonably'[9].

1 See further C Manchester 'Liquor licensing and applicants with criminal records' (1990) 154 JP 684.
2 1961 SLT (Sh Ct) 41.
3 An application for the grant or renewal of a bookmaker's permit was liable to refusal where the applicant was not a 'fit and proper person'.
4 See also *Williamson v Edinburgh Licensing Authority* 1976 SLT (Sh Ct) 35 for approval of this dictum.
5 *Hussain v Motherwell District Licensing Board*, Hamilton Sheriff Court, 9 September 1982, unreported.
6 *McTaggart v Inverclyde District Licensing Board*, Greenock Sheriff Court, 10 October 1985, unreported.
7 Lanark Sheriff Court, 17 June 1991, unreported.
8 Section 67(3), Sch 5.
9 A similar approach was taken in a number of other unreported cases referred to by the sheriff: *Hussain v Motherwell District Licensing Board* Hamilton Sheriff Court, 9 September 1982; *Raza v Hamilton District Licensing Board*, Hamilton Sheriff Court, 22 September 1988; *Siddique v Motherwell District Licensing Board*, Hamilton Sheriff Court, 20 June 1990.

It is submitted, however, that a criminal court's failure to disqualify in terms of s 67(3) deserves to be afforded very limited weight: a licensing board is entitled to the exercise of its own discretion[1].

The Court of Session has consistently indicated that it will rarely disturb a licensing authority's assessment of the importance to be attached to an applicant's criminal record or other matters which may have a bearing on fitness, provided that only relevant material is taken into account. For example:

'[T]he question as to what weight fell to be attached to the recorded convictions was plainly a matter upon which the committee was obliged to form an opinion. Once there is relevant material before a licensing authority the question as to the weight to be attached to that material and the significance of any balancing factors must be for the authority to assess'[2].

Where it is alleged that 'the person on whose behalf or for whose benefit the applicant will manage the premises' is not a 'fit and proper person' (s 17(1)(a))[3] it must of course be established that such a management arrangement exists: often this is no easy matter.

A partnership is not necessarily unfit to hold a licence simply by reason of one partner's previous convictions, particularly where another partner is responsible for the day to day running of the premises[4].

The Act's provisions permitting the holding of licences by juristic *personae* gave effect to a recommendation by *Clayson*[5]:

'[I]t is not practicable, even if it were desirable, to prevent companies being the real owners of licensed premises and their businesses. Since this fact sits uneasily on the law it must be the law that changes to fit the fact, and not vice versa'[6].

Although it was not suggested to the committee 'that the question of determining whether a company, as distinct from an individual, was a "fit and proper person" . . . would present any difficulty', such determinations have, in fact, become extremely problematic. Where application is made by a partnership or company, the police will make enquiries into the background of partners and directors (and possibly shareholders, where practical); but the salient weakness of this form of licenceholding stems from the fact that:

'The affairs of the company are conducted by individuals; if the licence is held by the company individuals in charge of the premises may change without the transfer procedure which enables [scrutiny of] a change in management where licences are held by the individuals concerned'[7].

1 See also *Clayson*, para 10.38. The committee considered it appropriate that a board should be empowered to suspend a licence following a conviction where no 'forfeiture' was ordered by the criminal court, a recommendation enacted in s 31.
2 *Hughes v Hamilton District Council* 1991 SLT 628. See also *J & J Inns Ltd v Angus District Licensing Board* 1992 SCLR 683, 1992 SLT 930.
3 This does not entitle the board to examine the fitness of an applicant's company's directors; but see below for a discussion of *Fereneze Leisure Ltd v Renfrew District Licensing Board* 1991 SCLR 751, 1992 SLT 604.
4 *Singh and Kaur v Kirkcaldy District Licensing Board* 1988 SLT 286. The board had failed to appreciate that the partnership was a separate legal *persona*.
5 Paras 8.02ff.
6 *Clayson*, para 8.06.
7 *Paterson's Licensing Acts* 101st edn, p 333. A change of *manager* in Scotland is of course subject to the scrutiny of the licensing board: s 25(3), (4).

The problems posed by corporate licenceholding were focused on in *Fereneze Leisure Ltd v Renfrew District Licensing Board*[1]. At first instance, the sheriff held that the board had erred in law by concentrating:

'solely on the character of two directors instead of applying their collective minds to whether there was sufficient material before them upon which they could hold that the company itself was unfit'[2].

The First Division upheld the sheriff's decision that company directors were not 'persons for whose benefit the business will be conducted' for the purpose of s 17(1)(a) and (3) but found that he had erred in law by considering that only the conduct of the company itself fell to be scrutinised. The Lord President said:

'[I]t would be highly artificial and unsatisfactory if a licensing board could not consider the character and reputation of the person or persons who actually controlled the company . . . [The board] should have asked themselves the correct question, namely, whether the applicant company was a fit and proper person to hold the licence for the premises. In deciding that question, however, they were entitled to take into account inter alia the general character and reputation of the two named directors and consider whether, in the whole circumstances, the application should have been granted'[3].

The 'character' of a corporate applicant *qua company* cannot, of course, be ignored; indeed, the Lord President's use of the words 'inter alia' points to an examination of the company itself. In *David Kelbie Properties Ltd v City of Dundee Licensing Board*[4] the sheriff (A L Stewart) considered that the board's failure to address this issue was fatal:

'It is plain . . . that the refusal was based entirely on the unsuitability of the directors and not on that of the applicant company itself. In my opinion this clearly indicates that the [board] failed to direct their minds to the true question in issue, which was whether the company was "a fit and proper person". The fact that the individual directors would not themselves have been considered fit and proper persons is only of limited relevance and, following *Fereneze*, is certainly not conclusive of the matter . . . [The board] thus erred in law'.

No doubt the tests desiderated by the sheriff in *Fereneze* are perfectly apposite:

'A number of factors may be relevant in considering a company application, such as whether the company has any criminal convictions which might reflect on its management capacity, or whether there is any history of difficulties with other premises (licensed or not) owned by the company. Does the company obey the law with respect to the health and safety of its employees? What about the company's reputation, if any?'[5]

---

1 1991 SCLR 751, 1992 SLT 604.
2 The sheriff court proceedings are reported at 1990 SCLR 436.
3 Approving the opinion of Griffiths, LJ in *R v Knightsbridge Crown Court ex parte International Sporting Club (London) Ltd* [1982] QB 304 at 317A-B; and following *Singh and Kaur v Kirkcaldy District Licensing Board* 1988 SLT 286.
4 Dundee Sheriff Court, 7 August 1991, unreported.
5 See 1990 SCLR 436 at 442. On a broadly similar approach, *Clayson* (para 8.14) considered as important matters inter alia 'the general standing of the company' and 'the likely effectiveness of higher management in maintaining the condition and controlling the conduct of the premises'. For the difficulties likely to be encountered, see 1990 SCLR 436 at 442 and 443.

(2) Suitability of the premises

The application must be refused where the board finds that:

'the premises to which the application relates are not suitable or convenient for the sale of alcoholic liquor, having regard to their location, their character and condition, the nature and extent of the proposed use of the premises, and the persons likely to resort to the premises'[1].

This ground is widely framed to allow consideration of structure, layout, physical condition, suitability for a particular locality, potential effect on amenity and the likely clientele[2].

Location and access. The Act permits the licensing of 'premises' (s 9(2)). In *Commissioners of Customs and Excise v Griffiths*[3] the Court of Appeal rejected an argument that licensing justices were not empowered to grant a licence for part of a building, in this case a restaurant in 'Harrods' which was in direct internal communication with the various store departments:

'[I] do not find anything in the Licensing Act which limits the word "premises" to an entire building. In my opinion any part of a building which is defined by metes and bounds is "premises" in respect of which a licence can be granted, provided it is in the justices' opinion structurally adapted for the sale of liquor. I can quite understand that the justices will be slow to grant a licence to a part of a large building . . . because of the difficulty of police supervision where the building has several exits and entrances . . . But it appears to me that this is a matter which affects the discretion of the justices rather than their jurisdiction'[4].

It is suggested that this opinion accurately reflects the current position in Scotland. The availability of access for the purpose of police supervision, to which his Lordship referred, is usually considered to be highly relevant and has occupied the attention of the court in the following cases[5].

In *University Court of the University of Glasgow v City of Glasgow District Licensing Board*[6] a licence for staff dining rooms was refused because the premises were not self-contained; the board considered that the police would thereby be deprived from exercising their power to enter the premises without a warrant (s 85) as it would be 'impossible to gain access . . . without going through unlicensed premises'. Observing that the right of police entry to private property is limited and that the powers conferred by s 86 did not avail the applicants, the sheriff (J Jardine) said:

'In my opinion, it is not unreasonable to insist that [police access] should depend upon clear right, as opposed to assurances about constant access given at the time of the application, although the responsible nature of those assurances was not in the slightest

---

1 Section 17(1)(b).
2 See *Clayson*, para 8.22.
3 [1924] 1 KB 735.
4 At 746, 747 per Scrutton, L J.
5 See also *Bruce v Chief Constable of Edinburgh* 1962 SLT (Sh Ct) 9, in which it was held that a licensing authority could not, as a matter of policy, refuse to grant a betting office licence for premises on the upper floor of a tenemental block because of supervisory difficulties.
6 Glasgow Sheriff Court, 26 October 1981, unreported.

questioned. Likewise, I have found that I am unable to say that it is unreasonable to require that premises be self-contained'.

On the other hand, in the circumstances of *Chief Constable of Strathclyde v Glasgow District Licensing Board*[1] the First Division found that the board had been entitled to accept an assurance given by the prospective owners of a commercial complex that the police would, at all times, enjoy unrestricted access to licensed shop units, agreeing with the sheriff that:

'Each case requires to be considered on its own merits, but it is entirely a matter within the discretion of the board to decide whether the [access] arrangements made are indeed satisfactory'[2].

Where a board was entitled to conclude that delivery vehicles would require to use a pathway in a public park, a refusal based on the unsatisfactory location of premises for access purposes was reasonable, even where application was simply made for an outline provisional grant (s 26(2))[3].

Location and amenity. The broad interpretation of 'location' favoured by the court[4] permits a consideration of 'amenity'[5]. Such an exercise has proved to be problematic standing the prior existence of planning permission, which must, of course be vouched by production of a certificate under s 23 before the application may be 'entertained', except as respects off-sales applications[6].

Two Inner House decisions indicate that while a licensing board's discretion is not fettered by a planning decision, a refusal which takes no account of planning restrictions and has no factual foundation will not be sustained.

In *J E Sheeran (Amusement Arcades) Ltd v Hamilton District Council*[7], an amusement-machine permit[8] relative to the operation of a leisure centre was refused partly because of an apprehended increase in pedestrian traffic leading to congestion. The earlier refusal of planning permission on the same ground had been reversed on appeal to the Secretary of State. The applicant argued in vain

---

1 1988 SCLR 18, 1988 SLT 128.
2 The sheriff had considered that the situation in *University Court of the University of Glasgow*, above, 'was entirely different' as the application in that case 'related to a private staff dining-room to which neither the public nor students of the university had access'.
3 *Lipoltan Ltd v Glasgow District Licensing Board* 1988 SCLR 443.
4 See, for example, *William Hill (Scotland) Ltd v Kyle and Carrick District Licensing Board* 1991 SCLR 375, 1991 SLT 559. An application for the grant or renewal of a betting office licence may be refused on the ground of (inter alia) an unsuitable 'location' (Betting, Gaming and Lotteries Act 1963, Sch 1, para 19). The litigiosity of bookmakers, particularly in the 1960s, has produced a substantial number of reported decisions on 'location'. For example, in *Burns v Bryce* (1962) 78 Sh Ct Rep 125 the sheriff considered that 'location' should be given 'its full natural meaning': loss of amenity to surrounding properties was a relevant factor. See also the discussion of 'location' in Smith & Monkcom *The Law of Betting, Gaming and Lotteries*, pp 32, 33.
5 *Leisure Inns (UK) Ltd v Perth and Kinross District Licensing Board* 1991 SCLR 721.
6 *Clayson* wished to 'find a means of associating local authorities with the licensing process in such a way as to give them substantially the final say on matters within their statutory responsibility (para 8.21); but believed that local authority certification should not operate to exclude the licensing board's consideration of the same matters in dealing with an application (para 8.27).
7 1986 SLT 289.
8 Gaming Act 1968, s 34.

that the licensing authority had failed to consider the matter 'independently and of new'. In the opinion of the Second Division:

'The planning decision was made by [the Secretary of State's representative] as a result of a view which he took of the evidence before him. Another body, discharging a different statutory function for a different purpose under discretionary powers, was perfectly entitled to reach a different conclusion'.

On the other hand, where applicants intending to operate a restaurant and café bar with a public house licence had obtained detailed planning permission, subject to conditions designed to protect the amenity of adjacent residential property, a refusal based on the location of the premises was overturned[1]. The Lord Justice-Clerk (Ross) re-affirmed the view he had expressed in *William Hill (Scotland) Ltd v Kyle and Carrick District Licensing Board*[2]: the words 'having regard to their location' should be given a wider rather than a restricted interpretation and loss of amenity to surrounding properties was a relevant consideration. However, standing the grant of planning permission and in the absence of any material to support their finding, the board should 'have been slow to hold that any detrimental effect on amenity was to be apprehended'[3].

Character, condition and proposed use. Very little consideration has required to be given to the meaning of 'character'. It has been suggested that 'character' and 'condition' are of equivalent meaning and 'can connote more than a physical state'[4]. In *Leisure Inns (UK) Ltd v Perth and Kinross District Licensing Board* the board's reference to the 'use of premises as a public house' ignored their 'particular character' as a restaurant and café bar[5]. Although licensing boards have granted off-sale licences for retail shops within petrol station sites, this type of principal use would no doubt be a relevant consideration for the purpose of s 17(1)(b).

In *Loosefoot Entertainment Ltd v City of Glasgow District Licensing Board*[6] it was competently argued that 'suitability' could be referable to the sufficiency or otherwise of entertainment facilities in an application for an entertainment licence, even where premises were physically suitable for the sale of alcohol[7].

In the relatively rare cases when application is made for the grant of a new licence, the condition of the premises should be assessed at the time of the application[8]. The issue of certificates in relation to building control and food

1 *Leisure Inns (UK) Ltd v Perth and Kinross District Licensing Board* 1991 SCLR 721.
2 1991 SCLR 375, 1991 SLT 559.
3 See also Smith & Monkcom *The Law of Betting, Gaming and Lotteries*, p 33: 'Where planning permission [for a betting office] has been granted . . . the impact of the proposed use of the premises upon the amenities of the locality will have been considered. This fact, it is submitted, should be given great weight by the committee, and where an inspector has come to a conclusion on a specific issue there would have to be a good reason for rejecting the inspector's view'.
4 *Mount Charlotte Investments plc v City of Glasgow Licensing Board* 1992 SCLR 311.
5 1991 SCLR 721 at 727 per Lord Morison.
6 1990 SCLR 597, affirmed 1991 SLT 843.
7 For a case in which premises were to be used as a leisure complex, see discussion of *Fife Regional Council v Kirkcaldy District Licensing Board (No 2)* 1991 GWD 18-1110, 2nd Div, below.
8 See *Ahmed v City of Glasgow District Licensing Board* 1987 GWD 5-156, Sh Ct; *Bantop v City of Glasgow District Licensing Board* 1989 SCLR 731, 1990 SLT 366.

hygiene in terms of s 23 does not conclusively demonstrate suitability. A building warrant may conceivably be granted for premises which are nevertheless unsuitable: for example, because the internal layout is not conducive to proper supervision.

'Persons likely to resort'. The 'persons likely to resort to the premises' may also have a bearing upon amenity[1]. While a sheriff has colourfully postulated, 'a bothy erected in the middle of waste ground frequented by alcoholic down-and-outs'[2], opposition to new licence applications frequently stems from local experience with existing licensed premises. For example, in *Transition Interiors Ltd v Eastwood District Licensing Board*[3]:

'The reasons submitted by [the board] indicate that the apparent apprehensions of objectors were based on the attendance of youths at nearby "off-sales" licensed premises . . . I could not feel that the board erred in law in listening to objection on this ground'.

Thus, to an extent, s 17(1)(b) overlaps with the 'public nuisance' ground of refusal provided by s 17(1)(c), discussed below.

Since children 'resort' to off-sale licensed premises, licensing boards are properly concerned to ensure that satisfactory arrangements will be made to prevent under-age purchases of alcohol. The 'open plan' style of operation favoured by supermarkets, once contentious in certain areas, is now well accepted, although licensing boards have been known to demand 'constant supervision' undertakings. There is frequently a reluctance to grant a licence (especially an off-sale licence) for premises situated close to a school.

In *Scott Catering & Offshore Services Ltd v City of Aberdeen Licensing Board*[4] application had been made for the grant of a new public house licence in respect of premises adjoining and to be interconnected with a licensed fish restaurant and take-away (all in the same ownership)[5]. The sheriff upheld a refusal based on the board's conclusion that unaccompanied children and young persons frequenting the existing premises were 'likely' to frequent the public house.

The fact that children and young persons attending a leisure complex 'may be unduly exposed to drink' justified the refusal of an entertainment licence in *Fife Regional Council v Kirkcaldy District Licensing Board (No 2)*[6]. The first floor of the premises contained a partitioned-off bar area (overlooking the games hall) to which the sale of drink was to be restricted and a separate cafeteria where alcohol could be consumed. In the opinion of the court:

---

1 'Persons likely to resort' appears to refer to potential clientele; but in *McKay v Banff and Buchan Western Division Licensing Board* 1991 SCLR 15, 1991 SLT 20 the reference in s 31(3)(b) to 'persons frequenting licensed premises' applied to persons who had been refused admission.
2 *Crolla v City of Edinburgh District Licensing Board* 1983 SLT (Sh Ct) 11 at 14.
3 Paisley Sheriff Court, 2 May 1990, unreported.
4 1987 GWD 22-823, Sh Ct.
5 It was noted (at p 72 above) that licensing boards have a discretion to consider as unsuitable premises which are not self-contained. Similarly, some licensing boards are not prepared to approve the interconnection of one set of licensed premises with another because of apprehended supervisory difficulties.
6 1991 GWD 18-1110, 2nd Div. The court had previously accepted that the words 'unduly exposed to drink' were sufficiently clear: see 1991 GWD 10-611.

'[I]t was plain . . . that the [board] were satisfied that the premises were not suitable for the sale of alcoholic liquor having regard to the proposed use of the premises and having regard also to the fact that children and young persons were likely to resort there. Although it is no doubt true that children under 14 will be prohibited from the actual bar, it is plain that both children under 14 and children above the age of 14 will be entitled to be in the refreshment area'.

This is a curious case which may indicate confusion as to the presence of children in entertainment-licensed premises. The passage quoted above refers to the exclusion of children from 'the actual bar'; and the board had considered that the location of the bar would operate to exclude children and young persons from the games hall viewing area[1]. It requires to be kept in view, however, that:

(1) No provision is made for a children's certificate application[2] by the holder of an entertainment licence, suggesting that the *ancillary* nature of alcohol supply (Sch 1) may never amount to the *'exclusive or main'* use for the sale and consumption of alcohol which is the hallmark of a 'bar' (s 139(1)). This hypothesis is fortified by the fact that the holders of restaurant and restricted hotel licences (whose premises cannot contain a bar) are similarly disabled.

(2) In any event, by virtue of s 69(4), the general prohibition on the presence of children under 14 in a 'bar' does not extend to 'a bar which is in any railway refreshment room or other premises constructed, fitted and intended to be used bona fide for any purpose to which the holding of a licence is merely ancillary'. Further, children have access to refreshment-licensed premises (subject to certain restrictions) where they are no doubt 'exposed' to drink without the provision of any other facilities (other than the availability of food and non-alcoholic beverages); and, on one view, the decision here that children's access to the cafeteria area was undesirable sits uneasily with the scheme of the legislation.

(3) Public nuisance

Section 17(1)(c) provides as a ground of refusal that 'the use of the premises for the sale of alcoholic liquor is likely to cause undue public nuisance, or a threat to public order or safety'. The term 'public' includes those who are likely to be affected by the conduct of the premises, as well as customers[3]. As one would imagine, this ground is more frequently invoked in the context of renewal applications[4] where premises have an established 'track record'. In a case of an application for a new licence, it may only be sustained on the basis of factual material beyond mere speculation. For example, in *Augustus Barnett Ltd v Ross and Cromarty District Licensing Board*[5], there was no evidence 'that the existing

1 This conclusion (as a matter of law) was not challenged by the Division but the opinion was expressed that this aspect of the board's concerns was a matter for regulation by management.
2 Broadly speaking, the grant of a children's certificate allows children under 14 to be in a bar area: see Chapter 14.
3 *Sangha v Bute and Cowal Divisional Licensing Board* 1990 SCLR 409.
4 See Chapter 9.
5 Tain Sheriff Court, 9 March 1993, unreported.

problems will be increased if the pursuers' application were granted. There is no more than a belief based upon an assertion'[1].

On the other hand, where application was made for a new entertainment licence in respect of discothèque premises to be operated between 10 pm and 2 am, the board was entitled to take into account a history of late-night noise nuisance associated with the applicant's neighbouring public house premises[2]. Although a licence by itself only authorises the operation of premises until 11 pm, the Inner House appears to place little weight on the fact that nuisance has largely been confined to the extended rather than permitted hours[3].

In *Kenny's Restaurants (Aberdeen) Ltd v City of Aberdeen Licensing Board*[4], where application had been made for a public house licence to replace an existing restaurant licence, the chief constable's objection founded on s 17(1)(c) was sustained. Despite any history of nuisance or disorder associated with the premises, the board was entitled to take into account the police view that licensed premises in the area already placed a strain on their resources and that the change in the type of licence would exacerbate this problem[5].

(4) Over provision

The most troublesome ground of refusal is found in s 17(1)(d)[6]:

'that, having regard to –
  (i) the number of licensed premises in the locality at the time the application is considered; and
  (ii) the number of premises in respect of which the provisional grant of a new licence is in force,
the board is satisfied that the grant of the application would result in the over provision of licensed premises in the locality'.

As 'an essential first step in the reasoning process'[7] the board must define the 'locality' under review; default in this regard will provide a ground of appeal under s 39(4)(b)[8]. It has been held, however, that a board's failure to challenge the applicant's description of the locality was not a breach of natural justice: it was sufficient that his agent had been given an opportunity to address the board on the matter[9].

1 See also *Leisure Inns (UK) Ltd v Perth and Kinross District Licensing Board* 1991 SCLR 721.
2 *Harpspot Ltd v City of Glasgow Licensing Board* 1992 GWD 6-311, 1st Div.
3 See *Sangha v Bute and Cowal Divisional Licensing Board*; and *McKay v Banff and Buchan Western Division Licensing Board* 1991 SCLR 15, 1991 SLT 20.
4 Aberdeen Sheriff Court, 15 January 1992, unreported.
5 This decision is echoed in *Lidster v Owen* [1983] 1 All ER 1012, [1983] 1 WLR 516. The Court of Appeal upheld the refusal of an application to renew a licence for public music, singing and dancing, where the chief constable's objection had drawn attention to manpower difficulties caused by the redeployment of officers into central Bournemouth from other districts.
6 As amended by the 1990 Act, Sch 8, para 6.
7 *Art Wells Ltd (t/a Corals) v Glasgow District Licensing Board* 1988 SCLR (Sh Ct) 48, aff'd 1988 SCLR 531 (IH).
8 Ie that the board based its decision on an incorrect material fact.
9 *Khullar v City of Glasgow Licensing Board*, Glasgow Sheriff Court, 21 August 1991, unreported. A refusal on the ground of over provision was unfair where s 17(1)(d) had not been put in issue by the board at the hearing: *Tomkins v City of Glasgow Licensing Board* 1991 GWD 39-2410, Ex Div. It is suggested, however, that as a matter of good practice, the applicant should address the potential for over provision.

There is no statutory definition of 'locality', either in the Act or where it is found in the Betting, Gaming and Lotteries Act 1963 (Sch 1, para 19(b)(ii))[1]. Where a board decided that a section of a busy main road formed a natural boundary between distinct localities, it was held that they had reached a 'wholly unreasonable' conclusion based on this fact alone[2]. While it has been suggested that 'locality' involves 'some sense of identity of a community which is not necessarily confined within definitive physical boundaries'[3], the court has been prepared to support a more arbitrary approach, at least in a city centre context, recognising that such a location serves a 'floating clientele' and 'is not on the whole going to have any local residents within the immediate neighbourhood as regular customers'[4]. Thus, in *Lazerdale v City of Glasgow District Licensing Board*[5] a radius of 200 metres from the application premises was acceptable:

'[The board] clearly took the view that if the "locality" was related to the source of customers there was no way in which it could be defined short of including the whole of Glasgow and its environs. In those circumstances they related the "locality" to the existing facilities within a given radius of the premises. Bearing in mind that they were dealing with premises in the city centre this was an intelligible and sensible approach. Further we cannot agree that there was no good reason for the adoption of a radius of 200 metres . . . In our view [the board] were entitled to take the area within that radius as a practical way of defining the "locality" in a city centre location'.

Equally, 'Glasgow city centre' was 'an appropriate locality' for the purpose of an entertainment licence application in *Loosefoot Entertainment Ltd v City of Glasgow District Licensing Board*[6]: although 'not defined by reference to map or distance', the area was of 'known character and fairly well-defined boundaries'. The sheriff (G H Gordon, QC) was inclined 'to go so far as to say that it makes much more sense as a description of locality than any arbitrary selection of a radius of so many yards'[7].

Since the actual facilities which an applicant proposes to provide are not to be taken into account (see below), a question arises as to whether 'locality' boundaries may be mapped out by reference to 'the catchment area from which . . . customers are, or may be expected to be drawn'[8]. If not, an off-sale licence for a superstore in a regional shopping centre could conceivably be refused on the basis of premises licensed for off-sale consumption within the immediate neighbourhood.

Prior to amendment by para 6 of Sch 8 to the 1990 Act, s 17(1)(d) directed

1 Cases decided under the 1963 Act are of relevance here.
2 *Art Wells Ltd (t/a Corals) v Glasgow District Licensing Board* 1988 SCLR (Sh Ct) 48, aff'd 1988 SCLR 531 (IH).
3 *Art Wells Ltd (t/a Corals) v Glasgow District Licensing Board* 1988 SCLR 531 at 533.
4 *Beard Hotels Ltd v City of Glasgow Licensing Board*, Glasgow Sheriff Court, 20 June 1990, unreported.
5 1st Div, 14 October 1988, unreported.
6 1990 SCLR 597, aff'd 1991 SLT 843.
7 See also *R v Peterborough City Council ex parte Quietlynn* (1987) 85 LGR 249, in which the Court of Appeal considered that 'relevant locality' in the broadly analogous provisions of the Local Government (Miscellaneous Provisions) Act 1982 (s 2, Sch 3, para 12(3)) carried no connotation of precise boundaries but could not encompass an entire town or the whole of a licensing authority's administrative area.
8 Smith & Monkcom *The Law of Betting, Gaming and Lotteries*, p 34.

licensing boards to have regard to 'facilities of the same or similar kind already available in the locality' or which were to be provided in terms of provisional grants in force. Although *Collins v Hamilton District Licensing Board*[1] appeared to require a very narrow construction of 'facilities', based on the authority for the sale of alcoholic liquor conferred by each type of licence (so that, as in this case, public houses could relevantly be taken into account in an off-sale application), the Inner House was not prepared to endorse a 'numerical tally' approach. In subsequent cases it was considered that an assessment of 'facilities' required a qualitative examination of proposals. Thus, an applicant for a new off-sale licence could pray in aid the superior choice of wine which he would offer[2]; and in *Mohammed v Docherty*[3] it was held that the board required to consider not only the licensed facilities which *could* be provided but also 'what present facilities are actually being provided or could be provided in the future'.

Parliament appears to have considered that *Augustus Barnett Ltd* and *Mohammed* represented a 'mischief' which required to be corrected. Indeed, on occasions, arcane comparisons had required to be made: for example, was a nightclub 'just an upmarket disco' or 'something different'[4]. In the result, the approach required by the amended s 17(1)(d) is carefully set forth by the Lord President (Hope) in *Chung v Wigtown District Licensing Board*[5]. Declining to find that a consideration of over provision had become a simple arithmetical exercise, he said:

'[T]he proper approach to the amended section 17(1)(d) is to count up the number of premises falling within each of the two categories, namely (i) the number of licensed premises in the locality at the time and (ii) the number of premises in respect of which the provisional grant of a new licence is in force. Consideration must then be given to the question whether to grant the licence sought by the applicant would result in over provision. In their consideration of this question the board are entitled to examine the number of licences of each type listed in Sch 1 to the Act and the facilities which, in terms of that Schedule, a holder of that type of licence is authorised to provide in the premises. It is, however, no longer relevant to examine the particular way in which each licence holder is in fact operating the premises for the time being or to consider the particular facilities which the applicant proposes to provide'.

Yet, the abolition of the qualitative approach and the virtual enactment of the decision in *Collins v Hamilton District Licensing Board*[6] is likely to produce fresh difficulties; and possibly bizarre results. Consider the following passage from the sheriff's note in *Loosefoot Entertainment Ltd v City of Glasgow District Licensing Board*[7], decided prior to the amendment to the sub-section, and which required a comparison of entertainment 'facilities':

'[W]hen is one facility for the provision of alcohol similar to another? It cannot just be when both provide drink. [Counsel for the objectors] indicated that he might be prepared

1 1984 SLT 230.
2 *Augustus Barnett v Bute and Cowal Divisional Licensing Board* 1989 SCLR 413, 1989 SLT 572.
3 1992 SLT 488.
4 *Loosefoot Entertainment Ltd v City of Glasgow District Licensing Board* 1990 SCLR 597, affirmed 1991 SLT 843.
5 1993 SCLR 256.
6 1984 SLT 230.
7 1990 SCLR 597, affirmed 1991 SLT 843.

to argue that it was when both premises provided drink as ancillary to entertainment, but that he did not need to go that far in this case. [Senior counsel for the successful applicants] sought to demolish any such argument by pointing out that it was absurd to say that a decision whether or not to give an entertainment licence to a concert hall required account to be taken of discothèques and nightclubs'.

The alteration to the basis of assessment leaves this potential for absurdity firmly in place. In the concert hall application postulated by senior counsel account *would* require to be taken of all other entertainment licences in the area, irrespective of the entertainment facilities actually provided. As a further example, an application for an off-sale licence for a superstore could be jeopardised by the existence of public houses and hotels in the locality.

While an application for a new entertainment licence will only invite a consideration of other entertainment licensed premises[1] and off-sale, public house and hotel licensed premises require to be equiparated to the extent that all authorise the sale of alcohol for consumption off the premises, difficult questions are bound to arise as to the validity of other comparisons. For example:

(1) It appears that public house and restaurant licences are distinguishable on the basis that the former only authorise the sale of drink ancillary to meals, although many restaurants are, in fact, operated under public house licences.

(2) Since refreshment licensed premises need only make food available comparison probably falls to be made with public houses rather than restaurants.

(3) Despite the distinctive definitions of 'hotel' and 'public house' in s 139(1), the authority for the sale of alcoholic liquor is, in terms of Sch 1, the same for each type of licence.

Where a number of applications for new licences in a locality fall to be considered at the same board meeting, it is not unreasonable to hear the applications in the order in which they have been lodged[2]. If a licence is granted without opposition from a compearing objector, the licence comes into effect immediately (s 30(1))[3], and must accordingly be taken into account in the consideration of subsequent applications at the same meeting[4]. Obversely, the potential for appeal by a competent objector places the grant of an application in suspense (s 30(1)) and it must be discounted. It will also be appreciated that the agenda order of applications may be disrupted for a number of mundane reasons. Success or failure may therefore depend on purely chance factors. In *Chung*, the sheriff asked 'What was the significance of the numbers? What considerations had [the board] in mind to give the number concerned significance?' In very many cases, particularly those involving town or city-centre locations, a licensing board will find it practically impossible to give a rational explanation as to why 'x' licences fall just short of critical mass, while 'x plus one' licences would result in over provision; nor will such an explanation normally be required by the court. In *Latif v Motherwell District Licensing Board*[5] the Lord President said:

1 Although provisional grants of new licences must, of course, also be considered.
2 *Chung v Wigtown District Licensing Board* 1993 SCLR 256. The order of consideration also seems to have been critical in *J E Sheeran (Amusement Arcades) Ltd v Hamilton District Council* 1986 SLT 289.
3 Note, however, that a provisional grant does not become a licence 'in force' until it is declared final: s 26(4).
4 *Chung v Wigtown District Licensing Board*, above.
5 1993 GWD 20-1256, 1st Div.

'A board cannot be expected to lay down an exact number of licensed premises which can be permitted in any locality as circumstances can vary and change, and the question of over provision is always a matter of fact and degree for the decision of the board to be decided at the time they are considering the application'.

Until the decision in *Chung*, it appears to have been assumed that a proposed change in the type of licence held for premises would escape scrutiny under s 17(1)(d), simply on the basis that the number of licensed premises in the locality would be undisturbed. This assumption sometimes led to the concern that an application for, say, a restaurant licence was no more than a 'stalking horse' for a public house licence: a subsequent application would not be open to refusal on a pure 'numbers count'. Now, a licensing board may be entitled to apply the 'Sch 1 facilities' test desiderated by the Lord President.

Refusal of Sunday permitted hours

The Sunday permitted hours component of an application for the grant or provisional grant of a new public house or refreshment licence may be refused (without prejudice to the permitted hours on other days) where the board finds that 'the opening and use on a Sunday of the premises to which the application relates would cause undue disturbance or public nuisance in the locality' (s 17(2A), inserted by the 1990 Act, s 46(4)(a))[1].

Disposal of the application

The board may grant the application, subject to a restriction prohibiting the sale of spirits (s 29(1)). Where power is conferred by a byelaw (s 38(1)(g)), a licence may be granted 'of a type other than that applied for'[2]. In the event of refusal, a statement of reasons for the board's decision should be requested (s 18)[3]. It is particularly important that a direction is sought in terms of s 14: without such dispensation 'a subsequent application for a new licence in respect of the same premises' may not be entertained within the ensuing two years[4]. A motion for the direction *must be made at the time of refusal*.

An appeal to the sheriff[5] lies at the instance of (a) the applicant (s 17(4), which also confers a right of appeal against the refusal of Sunday permitted hours) and (b) 'any competent objector who appeared at the hearing' of the application (s 17(5), which is silent as to a right of appeal against the grant of Sunday permitted hours). The refusal of a 'section 14 direction' is final[6]; but the grant of a direction is open to challenge by an objector[7].

---

1 A refusal may be appealed to the sheriff: s 17(4), as amended by the 1990 Act, s 46(4)(b). Sunday permitted hours are examined further at Chapter 9.
2 Such a power should only be exercised having regard to the extant planning permission.
3 An unsuccessful objector should also make a request.
4 The purpose of this provision is to prevent well-funded applicants waging a war of attrition against objectors.
5 Appeals: see Chapter 15.
6 *Fife and Kinross Motor Auctions Ltd v Perth and Kinross District Licensing Board* 1981 SLT 106.
7 *Kelvinside Community Council v City of Glasgow District Licensing Board* 1990 SCLR 110, 1990 SLT 725.

Related applications

In some districts it is possible to obtain a regular extension of the permitted hours (s 64) at the same time as application is made for the grant or provisional grant of a new licence, which in the latter case will effectively be held 'in suspense' until the finalisation stage[1]. Otherwise, on the basis that application may only be made by 'the holder of a licence', consideration may require to be deferred until the quarterly meeting following grant of the licence; or after finalisation of the provisional grant.

Bye-law permissions may be necessary for the provision of entertainment facilities (s 38)[2].

Consideration should be given as to whether a public entertainment or late hours catering licence will be required in terms of the Civic Government (Scotland) Act 1982[3].

Registration of the premises will be necessary under the Food Premises (Registration) Regulations 1991, SI 1991/2825.

Affirmation of outline provisional grant

An outline provisional grant made under s 26(2) becomes 'ineffective' unless 'affirmed' within 12 months (s 26(2)(b)). The application for affirmation must be accompanied by a detailed plan of the premises (s 26(2)(b)), such as would have been lodged with an application for a full provisional grant under s 26(1), and cannot be entertained unless supported by certificates of suitability in relation to building control (s 23(3), (6)) and food hygiene (s 23(4), (6)). At this stage the board must consult the fire authority for the area (s 23(5), (6)).

Consideration of the application is to take place 'at any meeting of the board held not earlier than 14 days' after it has been made (s 26(3)). Some licensing boards will only deal with affirmation at a quarterly meeting, possibly because the reference to a 'meeting' may suggest that the application cannot be disposed of under a 'delegated powers' arrangement under s 5(1)[4]. The board 'shall' affirm the provisional grant if 'satisfied' that:

'the premises, if completed in accordance with the [detailed] plan . . ., will be fit and convenient for their purpose and that the said plan does not deviate materially from the site plan and description of the premises . . .'.[5]

No provision is made for objections. While an applicant may appeal to the sheriff against a refusal (s 26(10)), the board is not obliged to give reasons for its decision (s 18(1), read with s 5(2)).

1 Finalisation: see below.
2 See Chapter 8.
3 Civic Government (Scotland) Act 1982, ss. 41, 42.
4 Note, however, that affirmation is not specifically excluded from such an arrangement by virtue of s 5(2).
5 Section 26(3).

Declaration of finality

A provisional grant is converted to a licence 'in force' by being 'declared final' (s 26(4)). The board requires to be given such notice 'as may be prescribed' (s 26(5))[1]. In almost every district the application will be disposed of under a 'delegated powers' arrangement (s 5(1))[2]; and considerable hardship may be experienced if a licensing board elects to restrict consideration to quarterly meetings (as it is entitled to do). *Clayson*[3] considered that there was 'no good reason' why finalisation should be subject to this sort of delay:

'We think it should be left to the discretion of the licensing authority to decide how applications to have provisional certificates declared final should be entertained and dealt with between their quarterly meetings'.

Where the provisional grant was made in the name of a non-natural person alone, the finalisation application must include 'the name of the employee or agent whom it is intended should have the day to day running of the premises' (s 26(6))[4]. Unless the board finds that the nominee 'is not a fit and proper person to be the holder of a licence' (s 26(6))[5], the board 'shall' declare the provisional grant final if 'satisfied' either:

'(a) that the premises . . . have been completed in accordance with the plan thereof lodged with the board, or

(b) that the premises have been completed and that such deviations from the said plan as exist are of minor importance and have not materially altered the character of the premises or the facilities for the supply of alcoholic liquor thereat'[6].

Until the decision in *Baljaffray Residents' Association v Milngavie and Bearsden District Council Licensing Board*[7], in which it was held that a licence provisionally granted was not 'in force', it was possible to obtain the comfort of the board's consent to proposed deviations by means of an application made under s 35. Now, where it is intended to alter the intended layout, the holder of the provisional grant may rely upon the dispensing power afforded by s 26(4)(b), usually after informal discussion with the police, building control and environmental health; but in the rare cases where it is considered that the alterations are 'material' it will be necessary to make fresh application for a provisional grant.

No further local authority certificates are required by the Act at this stage but, in practice, the board will wish to be satisfied that a certificate of completion has been issued as evidence that the finished works comply with the original building warrant[8].

---

1 'Prescribed' means 'prescribed by regulations made under section 37': s 139(1).
2 Some boards are only prepared to delegate a grant of finalisation if moved to do so by the applicant at the time the provisional grant is made.
3 Para 14.33.
4 Both the non-natural person and the nominee become the holder of the licence after finalisation: s 26(7). See also s 11.
5 While the chief constable has no power to object, the proposed nominee will invariably be the subject of a police report, a practice effectively legitimised by the decision in *J & J Inns Ltd v Angus District Licensing Board* 1992 SCLR 683, 1992 SLT 930.
6 Section 26(4)(a), (b).
7 1981 SLT (Sh Ct) 106.
8 Building (Scotland) Act 1959, s 9, as variously amended.

Although an applicant for finalisation is not entitled to a statement of reasons in the event of refusal (s 18(1), read with s 5(2)), an appeal lies to the sheriff (s 26(10)).

Where the provisional grant of a new licence has been obtained in respect of existing licensed premises because of (a) an extension to the building and/or (b) internal rearrangement considered to be material by the board or the clerk of the board[1], a question sometimes arises as to whether trading may resume in the altered premises pending finalisation. In practice (and no doubt quite correctly) extensions are not opened to the public until finalisation has been granted. In other cases, there would appear to be nothing to prevent the interim resumption of business; the premises continue to be licensed, so that the offence of trafficking (s 90) is not committed[2]; of course, as a logical extension of this argument (which should not be followed in practice) application need *never* be made for finalisation, an absurdity which perhaps strengthens the suggestion that a *new* certificate is never appropriate where there is no increase in the size of the building.

1 See Chapter 11 for the suggestion that the practice of requiring a new licence for purely internal alterations is wrong.
2 See *Craig v Peebles* (1875) 2 R (J) 90, in which a certificate-holder was acquitted of trafficking where he continued to trade in his premises after their substantial destruction by fire.

CHAPTER 5

Transfer of licences

TO 'A NEW TENANT OR TO A NEW OR EXISTING OCCUPANT'

Prior to the amendment of s 25 by s 51 of the 1990 Act a licence could only be transferred to 'a new tenant or occupant' and the transfer could only take place at a quarterly meeting of a licensing board. These restrictions caused two serious difficulties. Application could not be made by an existing occupant, such as the wife of the current licenceholder[1] and, strictly speaking, licensed business could only change hands four times a year, although various devices were (and continue to be) employed to circumvent the statutory mechanism[2]. So-called 'shelf' companies are routinely purchased by intending licensed trade operators simply to act as a licence-holding vehicle so that the whole share capital may be acquired by a purchaser of the business, thus eliding the necessity to have the licence transferred and eliminating any potential problems with the transferability of the regular extension[3]. The amendment permits transfers to be granted to 'a new tenant or to a new or existing occupant'. Where a licensed business is operated by a limited company the licence should properly be held by that company and a nominee in terms of s 11 or s 26. It has been held that the new manager of licensed premises operated by a company, making application for a transfer in his own name alone, is not an 'occupant'[4]; but where the proprietor of the business is a natural person his new manager has been so regarded[5].

More significantly, a new, two-step system of transfers (temporary and permanent) was introduced and the single step permanent transfer abolished. As a result of enormous difficulties[6], some of which remain (as discussed below), the Licensing (Amendment)(Scotland) Act 1992[7] reinstated the one-step permanent transfer as an option.

Both systems (described below) share a number of common features:
(a) Application may be made by (i) a natural person alone or (ii) a non-natural person nominating an employee or agent to have responsibility for the day to day running of the premises (s 11).

---

1 *Chief Constable of Tayside v Angus District Licensing Board* 1980 SLT (Sh Ct) 31.
2 See Note by J A Loudon (1988) 33 JLS 34.
3 See J C Cummins 'Licensing Reform' 1991 SLT (News) 271 and commentaries to *Fereneze Leisure Ltd v Renfrew District Licensing Board* 1990 SCLR 436 (OH) at 442, 1991 SCLR 751 (IH) at 758.
4 *Paterson v City of Glasgow District Licensing Board* 1982 SLT (Sh Ct) 37.
5 *Tominey v City of Glasgow District Licensing Board* 1984 SLT (Sh Ct) 2.
6 See J A Loudon 'Licensing Nightmare' 1990 SLT (News) 374 and J A Scott 'Licensing Transfers – Some Answers?' 1991 SLT (News) 58.
7 See J C Cummins 'Licensing Transfers – Another Try' 1992 SLT (News) 141.

(b) The applicant for transfer may require to produce character references[1].

(c) The board may require to be satisfied as to the applicant's status as a new tenant or a new or existing occupant, for example by the production to the clerk of missives for purchase or lease.

(d) In a number of areas a natural person may only hold one licence. Rarely will he be permitted to hold more than two[2]. This difficulty is, of course, avoided if a limited company or partnership is formed to hold a number of licences with different managers.

(e) Some boards require the applicant to produce the current licenceholder's consent to the proposed transfer[3]. Occasionally it may require to be lodged with the transfer application or be *in gremio* thereof. Of course, in a variety of situations such a consent will not be available: for example, where the licensed premises are to be sold or leased by a heritable creditor who has entered into possession. In that event it should be sufficient for the would-be transferee to produce documentary evidence vouching his entitlement to occupy the premises, such as an extract decree in an action of ejection and the heritable creditor's consent. In difficult cases the clerk may consider it prudent to cite the current licenceholder whose consent has been withheld to a hearing of the issue.

The transfer may not be withheld simply because no consent has been produced[4]. A consent once given may be withdrawn at any time prior to the transfer.

(f) Where a licence is transferred it is subject to the conditions on which it was originally granted (s 25(6)). For example, a restriction in terms of s 29 as to the type of alcoholic liquor which may be sold will continue to apply.

(g) A transfer applicant may request a seasonal licence (s 62) and as respects public house and hotel licences the board may be asked to insert a condition under s 119 relative to an off-sale part.

(h) A transfer has no effect upon the suspension of a licence (s 31) or a closure order (s 32)[5].

(i) The provisional grant of a licence may not be transferred: the premises in respect of which the grant is held are not 'licensed premises'[6]. While applications of that nature are nevertheless accepted by at least one licensing board the person intending to acquire the premises will generally require to make fresh application for a provisional grant.

The available procedures are now as follows.

---

1 In terms of regulations made by the board under s 37.
2 See *Aldridge v Simpson-Bell* 1971 SLT (Notes) 23, in which it was held that a licensing court was entitled to take into account the degree of personal supervision which would be exercised by an applicant.
3 Again in terms of regulations.
4 See *Hawick Heritable Investment Bank Ltd v Huggan* (1902) 5 F 75, (1902) 10 SLT 320, (1902) 40 SLR 33.
5 Suspension and closure orders are considered in Chapter 9.
6 *Baljaffray Residents' Association v Milngavie and Bearsden District Licensing Board* 1981 SLT (Sh Ct) 106.

Temporary and permanent transfer

An application may be made at any time for the temporary transfer of a licence to a person in one of the categories described above (s 25(1A)). The application will usually be disposed of under a 'delegated powers' arrangement made under s 5(1).

No procedure is prescribed by the Act. In particular, no provision is made for police (or any other) objections or observations, no ground of refusal is specified, the board is not obliged to give reasons for its decision and there is no right of appeal[1].

Nevertheless, in *J & J Inns Ltd v Angus District Licensing Board*[2] Lord Weir held that the board had a discretion to refuse an application to substitute a new employee under s 25(3)[3] and was perfectly entitled to take into consideration the terms of a police report. If this decision is correct the ratio would apply equally to a temporary transfer application[4].

Where a transfer takes place the licence (not simply the transfer) has effect until 'the appropriate [quarterly] meeting of the board', defined as:

'(a) the next meeting of the board; or
 (b) where the temporary transfer has been made within the period of six weeks before the first day of the next meeting, the next following meeting of the board'[5].

At the appropriate meeting the board shall make a decision on the permanent transfer of the licence (s 25(1B)). The application in that regard requires to be lodged not later than five weeks before the first day of the meeting (s 10(1)). Any person mentioned in s 16(1) may object. The chief constable is additionally empowered to make observations (s 16(1A)). There is no requirement for newspaper advertisement. As to the applicant's attendance at the meeting, see under 'Permanent transfer' below.

The application must be refused if the board finds:

'that the applicant, or the person on whose behalf or for whose benefit the applicant will manage the premises or, in the case of an application to which section 11 . . . applies, the applicant or the employee or agent named in the application is not a fit and proper person to be the holder of a licence'[6].

The condition of premises is irrelevant as such but may reflect on an applicant's suitability[7]. The transfer may not be granted subject to restrictions. In *R v*

---

1 A refusal may, of course, be challenged by judicial review. There is nothing to prevent the subsequent consideration of an application for one-step permanent transfer, the refusal of which is susceptible to appeal: s 17(4).
2 1992 SCLR 683, 1992 SLT 930.
3 This procedure is explained below.
4 For a full discussion of *J & J Inns Ltd*, see the commentary to the case report at 1992 SCLR 691.
5 Section 25(1A).
6 Section 17(1)(a). See Chapter 4 sub voce 'Suitability of the applicant' and *Fereneze Leisure Ltd v Renfrew District Licensing Board* 1991 SCLR 751, 1992 SLT 604, *J & J Inns Ltd v Angus District Licensing Board* 1992 SCLR 683, 1992 SLT 930.
7 See *London Borough of Haringey v Sandhu*, The Times, 6 May 1987, unreported; *Coppola v Midlothian District Licensing Board* 1983 SLT (Sh Ct) 95; *Farquhar v City of Glasgow District Licensing Board*, Glasgow Sheriff Court, 31 October 1980, unreported.

Licensing Committee for Inner London South Eastern Division ex parte Papaspyrou[1] the court overturned a refusal to transfer a licence where the applicant was unwilling to undertake to keep the premises closed in the evening.

In the event of refusal the licence has effect 'until the time within which an appeal may be made has elapsed or, if an appeal has been lodged, until the appeal has been abandoned or determined' (s 25(1C); see also s 17(4), (5)).

It may well be that if the licence ceases to have effect it is not lost entirely but simply placed in a form of 'suspended animation' from which it may be revived by a further, successful transfer[2]; but it is perhaps significant that the *licence* rather than the *transfer* is jeopardised. A statement of reasons may be requested.

The two-step system is highly unsatisfactory for a number of reasons, which led to the passing of the amending legislation:

(1) The absence of a prescribed procedure for the disposal of temporary transfer applications has been interpreted by some boards as requiring the enquiry as to the applicant's fitness to be reserved until the permanent transfer application is lodged. In addition, police forces in some parts of the country interpret the absence of a right to object as an indication that the chief constable may not submit a report to the clerk (although they will generally be prepared to produce a report if the temporary and permanent transfer applications are lodged more or less contemporaneously).

It is therefore possible for a board to be without any reliable means of assessing an applicant's suitability with the result that the temporary transfer is simply 'rubber-stamped', leaving open the possibility of police objection or observations at the second stage. The decision in *J & J Inns Ltd v Angus District Licensing Board*[3] may persuade licensing boards and chief constables that their reticence is unjustified.

Where the applicant for temporary transfer is subject to scrutiny it is perfectly conceivable that, by reason of some misconduct ad interim, he will have ceased to be a 'fit and proper person' to hold a licence when the permanent transfer application is considered.

Understandably, brewers and lending institutions are reluctant to advance funds to prospective purchasers of licensed premises on the strength of a fragile temporary transfer. Vendors are, of course, properly counselled not to part with possession of the property until the purchase price is paid in full and, in any event, heritable creditors will usually forbid such a course.

(2) Subject to the 'suspended animation' possibility mentioned above, the actual licence may stand at risk if the permanent transfer application is refused. In the Parliamentary debate[4] on the provisions of the Licensing (Amendment) (Scotland) Act 1992, Menzies Campbell, QC drew attention to this danger:

'[A] problem arises if the transfer takes place but it is not confirmed and the appeal to the sheriff is unsuccessful. The licence would cease to exist. The attempt to transfer it would

---

1 QBD, The Times, 4 July 1989, unreported.
2 By analogy with *Argyll Arms (McManus) Ltd v Lorn, Mid-Argyll, Kintyre and Islay Divisional Licensing Board* 1988 SCLR 241, 1988 SLT 290, discussed below, in which a distinction was drawn between the 'expiry' and 'effect' of a licence.
3 1992 SCLR 683, 1992 SLT 930. See below, sub voce 'Substitution of employee or agent'.
4 'Official Report', First Scottish Standing Committee, 19 July 1990, col 982.

have vitiated it. That happened in the 1897 case of *Campbell v Neilson*[1] when Lord Justice-General Robertson said that if the transfer was null and void, it would not revert to the person who had attempted to transfer it. That could have horrific consequences . . . Appeals to the sheriff can only be taken by the person who seeks the transfer not by the person who effects it. If the attempt to transfer the licence was rejected and the subsequent appeal to the sheriff was unsuccessful, the right to sell alcohol on the premises would be vitiated'.

In *Campbell* magistrates refused to renew a transfer which had been granted some two months earlier, subject to a condition which was not fulfilled. The original certificate holder, who then resumed possession of the premises, was convicted of trafficking.

It has also been held that where the certificate holder ceases to possess the premises 'from whatever cause' then 'the sale of exciseable liquor in these premises becomes illegal unless and until authorised of new by the appropriate licensing authority'[2]. In modern practice, however, where the licenceholder simply quits the premises (leaving aside the difficulty which may be occasioned by an abortive transfer), authority for the sale of alcoholic liquor is reinstated by a transfer of the licence[3].

Where the permanent transfer is refused following the grant of a temporary transfer the person to whom the licence has been transferred may either gamble the existence (or at least the effectiveness) of the licence upon the outcome of an appeal or arrange for a fresh transfer to a suitable individual; but, of course, he would be well advised to set an appeal in motion to preserve the validity of the licence *pro tem*.

Similar difficulties are likely to occur where a permanent transfer application has been granted despite formal objection from (usually) the chief constable. In the event that a competent objector exercises his right of appeal (s 17(5)) the board's decision may well be reversed by the sheriff. Even if the grant of the application is upheld there remains the possibility of ultimate reversal by the Inner House. At least one loss of licence insurer is not prepared to continue cover where a permanent transfer applicant has been unsuccessfully opposed.

An objector's appeal against the grant of a permanent transfer does not, of course, 'freeze' the licence in the name of the transferor[4].

(3) The problems described above are exacerbated by the requirement that a permanent transfer be delayed until the next following meeting of the board 'where the temporary transfer has been made within the period of six weeks before the first day of the next meeting' (s 25(1A)). There may therefore be a gap of up to five months between the temporary and permanent transfer stages. This provision has been strictly construed by the court[5] and some (but not all) clerks

---

1 (1897) 24 R (J) 28.
2 *West Wemyss United Services Club, Applicants* 1948 SLT (Sh Ct) 33. See also *Miller v Linton* (1888) 15 R (J) 37.
3 Cf *Edward Barrett Ltd v City of Dundee District Licensing Board* 1992 SLT 963, in which it was held that a betting office licence ceased to have effect and 'could not be transferred' where the holder was no longer the tenant of the premises' (bearing in mind that there is no formal mechanism for the transfer of such licences).
4 Cf s 30(1) which prevents a new licence coming into effect pending an appeal.
5 *Kerr v McAuslin* 1992 SCLR 135, 1992 SLT 367.

who had previously been prepared to take a pragmatic approach now feel constrained to follow this decision. Nevertheless, one clerk has been willing to arrange for the consideration of a temporary transfer application on the morning of the quarterly meeting at which the permanent transfer is due to be heard, on the perfectly arguable basis that a temporary transfer granted at the pre-meeting on that day is not granted within the period of six weeks before *the first day of the meeting*.

(4) If the person to whom the licence has been transferred omits to make timeous application for permanent transfer of the licence at the 'appropriate meeting' the licence is thereby jeopardised. The board has no discretion to accept a late application[1]. In such a circumstance the licenceholder will require to arrange for the lodgement of an 'emergency' application for the temporary transfer of the licence to 'a new tenant or to a new or existing occupant' and do everything in his power to have that application granted before the meeting at which the permanent transfer application ought to have been considered. Otherwise the licence ceases to have effect.

(5) As discussed elsewhere[2], difficulties may well occur where the temporary transfer coincides with the necessity to 'renew' the regular extension of permitted hours. Problems have also been known to arise where the licence itself is due for renewal. An application to renew a licence may competently be made only by the current licenceholder. Where the application is submitted and a temporary transfer application is granted thereafter, the last lodgement date for the quarterly meeting having passed, the licence will no longer stand in name of the renewal applicant when the renewal application comes to be considered. Pragmatic clerks will simply alter the renewal application by substituting the details of the person to whom the licence has been temporarily transferred for those originally given. Others are not so inclined: while the renewal application does not require to be advertised a change of applicant at the hand of the clerk could complicate the position of objectors. In some cases, the clerk has required the temporary transferee to submit his own, late application for renewal for consideration in terms of s 13(2) which affords the board a discretionary power to continue to an adjourned meeting applications for inter alia the renewal of a licence where the applicant 'has, through inadvertence or misadventure, failed to comply with any of the preliminary requirements' of the Act (s 13(2)(a)). It is doubtful whether the circumstances described constitute 'inadvertence or misadventure' and the difficulty requires legislative correction.

(6) Permits for amusement with prizes machines, which are granted under s 34 of and Sch 9 to the Gaming Act 1968[3] are not transferable. The person to whom the licence has been transferred must submit his own application for a permit. In many parts of the country applications of this nature are only considered at quarterly meetings so that the new licenceholder may be unable to operate 'fruit' machines for an extended period.

---

1 Cf s 13(2).
2 See Chapter 10.
3 See Chapter 12.

Permanent transfer

The uncertainties and risks which attach to the two-step procedure may largely be avoided if application is simply made to a quarterly meeting of the board for the permanent transfer of the licence (s 25(1)).

The application must be lodged no later than five weeks before the first day of the meeting (s 10(1)). It does not require to be advertised.

The applicant need not attend or be represented when the application is considered unless cited to the meeting by the board (s 15(1)). The application may only be refused without a hearing if the applicant, having been cited, fails to attend the meeting (s 15(2)).

Any person listed in s 16(1) may object and the chief constable may also make observations (s 16(1A)). The only ground of refusal is as explained above (s 17(1)(a)). An appeal to the sheriff lies at the instance of the applicant (s 17(4)) and a competent objector (s 17(5)). A statement of reasons may be requested (s 18). Where the application has been refused the licence simply remains with the transferor[1]. However, if the transfer is granted but reversed on appeal it is an open question as to whether the licence has been lost in the process[2].

Under either system, a permanent transfer does not affect the currency of the licence and, where already granted, occasional and regular extensions of the permitted hours (s 64(3A)). Sunday permitted hours (which are essentially an integral part of the licence) and a children's certificate (with any conditions attached)[3] continue in force.

Where a licensing board requires its permission to be obtained for entertainment facilities in terms of byelaws[4] these are invariably regarded as transferring with the licence.

A permit for amusement with prizes machines is personal to the holder and the transferee will require to make his own application[5]. As regards public house and hotel licensed premises applications are submitted to the licensing board[6]. They are usually considered at the quarterly meeting which will dispose of the permanent transfer application. Strictly speaking, application may only be made by the holder of a licence[7] with the unhappy result that, in a minority of licensing board areas, applications will not be accepted until a one-step permanent transfer has been granted (although, of course, where a temporary transfer has already been approved, the permit application may competently be lodged immediately thereafter, normally for consideration with the permanent transfer).

So far as other types of licences are concerned jurisdiction lies with the district council[8] (but, confusingly, some licensing boards nevertheless deal with applications themselves). In these cases, application may be made by 'the person who is,

1 *Andrews v Denton* [1897] 2 QB 37; *Lawrence v O'Hara* (1903) 67 JP 369.
2 *Miller v Linton* (1888) 15 R (J) 37; *Campbell v Neilson* (1897) 24 R (J) 28; *West Wemyss United Services Club, Applicants* 1948 SLT (Sh Ct) 33.
3 1990 Act, s 49(10).
4 As explained in Chapter 8.
5 Under s 34 of and Sch 9 to the Gaming Act 1968.
6 Ibid, Sch 9, para 1(c).
7 Ibid, Sch 9, para 5(1)(a).
8 Ibid, Sch 9, para 1(d).

or by any person who proposes if the permit is granted to become, the occupier of the premises'[1].

Conveyancing aspects

Those concerned with the acquisition of licensed premises should require the vendor to warrant that:

(1) There is in force a (specified) regular extension of the permitted hours granted without conditions (with the relevant certificate to be exhibited).
(2) No application for the regular extension of permitted hours has ever been the subject of objection or observations.
(3) The premises enjoy Sunday opening or Sunday permitted hours (public house and refreshment licences only) which have never been the subject of objection.
(4) In the case of an entertainment licence, no conditions have been attached in terms of s 101(2)[2].
(5) No complaint has been intimated to the licensing board in terms of s 31 (suspension of licence) or s 65 (restriction of permitted hours).
(6) No hearing is pending in terms of s 32[3].
(7) No application has been made to the licensing board in terms of s 66[4].
(8) He is not aware of any circumstances which could give rise to a complaint, hearing or application as referred to above.
(9) The present physical layout of the premises and their external appearance conform to plans approved by the licensing board or its predecessors and no alterations, extensions or reconstruction affecting the premises or any part of them have been or are in the course of being carried out without the consent of the licensing board.
(10) No order for structural alterations has been made by the licensing board in terms of s 36.
(11) All necessary consents and permissions for all forms of entertainment and amusement and games facilities currently provided at the premises have been obtained.
(12) No notice has been served by the local authority in terms of s 58(1) of the Control of Pollution Act 1974.
(13) No undertakings have been given to the licensing board, the police, or any local authority department relative to the conduct of the premises.
(14) No prosecutions are pending in connection with the premises, whether under the Act or otherwise.
(15) The premises are registered in terms of the Food Premises (Registration) Regulations 1991, SI 1991/2825. (See also the Environmental Protection (Duty of Care) Regulations 1991, SI 1991/2839).
(16) If applicable, a full fire certificate has been obtained, which will be exhibited, and there are no outstanding requirements, recommendations or

1 Ibid, Sch 9, para 5(1)(b).
2 See the consideration of entertainment licences in Chapter 3.
3 Which provides for the making of a closure order.
4 Temporary restriction of permitted hours.

orders issued by the firemaster for repairs, improvements or alterations to the premises.
(17) If applicable, a public entertainment licence has been obtained under s 41 of the Civic Government (Scotland) Act 1982.

In addition, the vendor should be obligated to lodge licensing applications (for example, for the occasional extension of permitted hours) at the request and at the expense of the purchaser, and steps should be taken to apportion the HM Customs and Excise Ordinary Gaming Machine Licence relative to any amusement with prizes machines.

Of course, this list is hardly exhaustive, nor is likely to meet with a *de plano* acceptance, but it will assist in uncovering possible areas of concern.

It should also be borne in mind, when the date of entry is stipulated, that a plain reference to the transfer of the licence at a quarterly meeting of the board includes an adjournment of that meeting[1]. The transaction will naturally be subject to the successful transfer of the licence. It is perfectly conceivable that the licence will be due for renewal at the board meeting which is to consider a one step permanent transfer. In the event that the renewal is refused, the board must nevertheless consider the transfer application on the basis of the applicant's fitness alone (irrespective of any factors which led to the refusal of the renewal, such as the condition of the premises)[2]. By virtue of s 30(5)(b) the licence continues to have effect 'until the time within which an appeal may be made has elapsed or, if an appeal has been lodged, until the appeal has been abandoned or determined'. In addition, the renewal may be granted despite objections, leaving open the possibility of a successful appeal by an objector (s 17(5)), and the transfer granted thereafter. The transferee would require to accept that the condition of the bargain stipulating the successful transfer of the licence had been purified, but would face the risk of being in possession of unlicensed premises (or, at best, premises with no operable licence). It is therefore extremely important that missives properly address these hazards.

Where the two-step procedure is employed, subject to the remarks above, once the temporary transfer application is granted responsibility for the successful renewal of the licence rests squarely with the new licenceholder.

IN THE CASE OF DEATH, BANKRUPTCY OR INCAPACITY

Provision has long been made for the temporary transfer of a licence following the holder's death, bankruptcy or incapacity. Section 25 (2) provides that a licensing board may transfer a licence to:

'(a) the executors, representatives or disponees of any person who held a licence in respect of premises situated within the area of the board and who has died before the expiry of the licence; or
 (b) the trustee, judicial factor or curator bonis of any person holding such a licence who has become bankrupt, insolvent or incapable before the expiry of the licence'.

---

1 *Tarditi v Drummond* 1989 SCLR 201, 1989 SLT 554, discussed (1993) 39 SPEL 39.
2 See commentary to *C R S Leisure Ltd v Dumbarton District Licensing Board* 1989 SCLR 566 at 572.

The applicant must be in possession of the premises and thus in a position to carry on the business[1].

Applications are normally processed under 'delegated powers' (s 5(1)). No provision is made for advertisement, a hearing, objections or observations, a statement of reasons for the board's decision, or a right of appeal. Under s 47(2) of the Licensing (Scotland) Act 1959 (the predecessor of s 25(2)) application was made to two or more members of the licensing court who required to be satisfied that the applicant was 'a fit person to hold a certificate'. This requirement is no longer stated[2]. Nevertheless, character references and other requirements may be prescribed by regulations made under s 37.

In all cases, any existing occasional or regular extensions of the permitted hours (s 64(3A)), Sunday permitted hours and children's certificate[3] continue to be valid and the licence is transferred 'subject to the conditions on which it was originally granted' (s 25(6)), with the expiry date unaltered.

The transferee will require to make his own application for an amusement with prizes machine permit (as explained above relative to temporary and permanent transfers), except that where a permit holder has died provision is made for the limited prolongation of the permit[4].

Transfers on death

Although a licence may be transferred following the death of the holder, it appears to be ineffective *pro tem*. Although the Act is silent on this matter[5], in *Cook v Gray*[6] the Lord President (Robertson) observed:

'There is no doubt that a person requires, in order to carry on a public-house, to have a certificate from the magistrates and a licence from the Excise authorities. These are personal, and on the death of the persons to whom they are issued they fall . . . [T]he representatives should as soon as possible furnish themselves with a licence. . .'.

Boards are no doubt entitled to require production of the confirmation of executors, so that lengthy delays are possible.

Separate provision is made where the licenceholder lodges a renewal application but dies before the board meeting at which it is to be considered. In such a circumstance the board 'may, if it thinks fit, and upon such terms as the board thinks proper, postpone consideration of the application . . . to an adjourned meeting' (s 13(2)) at which it may proceed to grant the licence to the executors, representatives or disponees, provided that they are 'possessed of the premises' (s 13(3)).

---

1 See *Budge v Goudie* (1895) 2 SLT 406.
2 But see discussion of *J & J Inns Ltd v Angus District Licensing Board* 1992 SCLR 683, 1992 SLT 930, sub voce 'Substitution of employee or agent' below.
3 1990 Act, s 49(10).
4 See Gaming Act 1968, Sch 9, para 20(2).
5 Cf s 11(4), discussed below.
6 (1891) SLR 247 at 249, commented upon in *Argyll Arms (McManus) Ltd v Lorn, Mid-Argyll, Kintyre and Islay Divisional Licensing Board* 1988 SCLR 241, 1988 SLT 290.

Transfers following bankruptcy or incapacity

Application is made for transfer to the trustee where the licenceholder has become bankrupt and, in relatively rare instances, to a curator bonis or judicial factor in the case of incapacity.

Sometimes a transfer is sought by a trustee acting under a trust deed for creditors but such an arrangement:

'. . . is not a matter with which the public authorities are concerned. Such deeds do not generally displace the trader from the management of his business. Indeed, the chief reason of preference for a private trust over a sequestration is that it does not involve the sacrifice of a going business and very often the deed provides for the business being carried on by the truster under supervision. I am unable to see how the granting of such a deed can have the effect of depriving the licensee of the benefit of his certificate'[1].

Equally, in such a situation, the truster may carry on business through a manager[2].

The provisions of s 25(2) relate only to natural persons (but *not*, as sometimes supposed, to employees or agents nominated under ss 11 and 26). They have no applicability to limited companies. Where a company is in liquidation, administration or receivership it retains its persona for licenceholding purposes.

Where a licence is transferred by virtue of s 25(2) the transfer requires to be confirmed at the next meeting of the board[3].

SUBSTITUTION OF EMPLOYEE OR AGENT

Where a licence is held by a non-natural person and an employee or agent[4] by virtue of s 11 or s 26 an application to substitute a new nominee must be effected 'within eight weeks from the time when the employee or agent named in a licence ceases to be responsible for the day to day running of the premises', otherwise 'the licence shall cease to have effect' (s 11 (4)).

Whether a nominee 'ceases to be responsible' for premises is plainly a matter of fact but it is also a question of degree where, as sometimes happens, a nominee is prevented from performing his duties because of long-term illness. In such a circumstance a substitution is desirable. Indeed, it may be that a person incapacitated by reason of sickness is not a 'fit and proper person' to be the holder of a licence. There is English authority for the proposition that 'health, temper and disposition' may be considered[5].

The possible distinction between 'ceasing to be responsible' and 'ceasing to exercise responsibility' appears to have been canvassed but not resolved in *Argyll Arms (McManus) Ltd v Lorn, Mid-Argyll, Kintyre and Islay Divisional Licensing*

1 *Wylie v Thom* (1889) 16 R (J) 90 at 92 per Lord McLaren.
2 *Wylie v Thom*, above.
3 See below.
4 Both generally referred to in this section as a 'nominee'.
5 *R v Hyde Justices (or Cooke) ex parte Atherton* [1912] 1 KB 645. See also the *Report of the Departmental Committee on Scottish Licensing Law* (Cmnd 5354) (*Clayson*) para 8.14.

Board[1]. It is not without significance where premises close for an extended period pending a disposal and the ultimate intention is to effect a transfer of the licence to the purchaser. Clearly, the nominee at the time of closure cannot thereafter be responsible in any meaningful way for the 'day to day running of the premises', but where he remains in the employ of the licenceholding company the effectiveness of the licence is unlikely to be challenged. Otherwise, it is suggested that a token substitution is initiated.

The mechanism for a substitution is supplied by s 25(3)[2], which provides that:

'A licensing board may on an application made to it in that behalf by a person other than an individual natural person, substitute another employee or agent of the applicant for the employee or agent mentioned in section 11 or section 26 of this Act'.

Applications are almost invariably considered under 'delegated powers' (s 5(1)). The process is susceptible to regulations made under s 37 so that, for example, character references may be required. At least one board requires the former nominee to consent to the substitution application. This is palpably wrong.

It is universally accepted that a nominee may not be the joint holder of more than one licence: the Act clearly envisages that he will have responsibility only for one set of premises. Similarly, boards regard as unsuitable for nominee purposes persons such as brewery area managers who, by the nature of their position, cannot exercise close supervision on a daily basis. Exceptionally, however, where premises have been acquired by a company which has yet to appoint a manager, the board may sanction the nomination of someone such as an area manager on a purely temporary basis.

There are only two reported cases concerning the operation of s 25(3). Both deserve careful attention.

In *Argyll Arms (McManus) Ltd v Lorn, Mid-Argyll, Kintyre and Islay Divisional Licensing Board*[3] application was made to the board to substitute a new nominee outwith the eight-week period referred to above. The board took the view that the application could not competently be considered as the licence had ceased to have effect in terms of s 11(4). It may be remarked in the passing that the board's position was not unprecedented: a number of boards had required new licences to be obtained where the eight-week watershed was breached.

In the result, the Lord Ordinary (Clyde) held that the application could be validly entertained, with result that the expiry of the eight-week period simply places the licence in a form of 'suspended animation' from which it is revived by the grant of the substitution application, and in so doing made a number of important observations (with author's emphasis):

(1) '[T]he view put forward by the [board] leaves the whole life and existence of the licence at the mercy of the administrative procedures of the board. It may be that a transfer can readily be managed within a space of eight weeks but the provision in s 11(4) *is expressly related, not to the making of the application, but to the date of the transfer*'.

---

1 1988 SCLR 241, 1988 SLT 290.
2 The procedure is incorrectly described in *J & J Inns Ltd v Angus District Licensing Board* 1992 SCLR 683, as explained in the commentary thereto at 691.
3 1988 SCLR 241, 1988 SLT 290.

It is very frequently and quite erroneously believed that it is sufficient to submit an application within the eight-week period. Some boards' regulations require that the application be lodged within a specified period or 'as soon as possible'. Although the *vires* of such a provision is open to considerable doubt, especially since no time limit is specified in the Act and there may be no positive sanction for non-compliance, failure to comply may provide the board with an argument that the applicant has not afforded sufficient time for processing (see below). Of course, the board could not decline to consider an application submitted outwith the prescribed period.

(2) 'It would seem to me unreasonable to conclude that because of delays which might occur for a number of reasons, innocent or culpable, the whole life of the licence should be at risk depending on the date upon which the board may be able to meet and the transference achieved'.

In practice, as observed above, applications are rarely heard at a board meeting but are generally disposed of under 'delegated powers,' by the clerk alone or by the clerk and one or two board members, usually following a police report (see below); but disconcerting delays commonly occur through no fault of the applicant. In the absence of his culpability police action is virtually unknown but no reliance should be placed on this informal indulgence. While the Lord Ordinary rejected the view that 'the whole life and existence of the licence' should be at the mercy of administrative procedures it remains an uncomfortable fact that the continuing *effectiveness* of the licence *does* depend on these procedures.

(3) '[S]ince no elaborate procedure is usually intended to be adopted the likelihood is that no great investigation is expected to be made and yet it is such an elaborate investigation which may be required if an enquiry has to be made of the date on which a person ceased to be responsible . . . Such an investigation may be more appropriate in the context of enforcement procedures or criminal procedures in a case in which it may be suggested that an unlawful use has been made of the premises at a date after the licence became ineffective'.

In other words, the continued sale of alcoholic liquor outwith the eight-week period will constitute the offence of trafficking without a licence (s 90(a)) and, strictly speaking, it is no defence that the board was dilatory in disposing of the application. The issue is brought into sharp focus by those boards which require the applicant for substitution to state the date on which the previous nominee ceased to be responsible for the premises. Holders of entertainment licences should, in appropriate cases, obtain a public entertainment licence[1] to allow their businesses to continue in operation without the sale of alcoholic liquor until such time as the substitution application is granted since, in the circumstance described, no exemption is available for the entertainment use of the premises[2].

No provision is made for objections or observations, the applicant has no express right to be heard, the board need not state reasons for its decision and there is no right of appeal. There is no express requirement that the board be satisfied (at this stage) as to the applicant's fitness.

1 Civic Government (Scotland) Act 1982, s 41.
2 Civic Government (Scotland) Act 1982, s 41(2)(f).

In *Argyll Arms (McManus) Ltd*[1] Lord Clyde appeared to interpret these procedural *lacunae* as suggesting that the substitution should be accomplished as a 'single and simple administrative step'. However, any conception that the process is simply one of 'rubber-stamping' was firmly dispelled in *J & J Inns Ltd v Angus District Licensing Board*[2]. The petitioners brought judicial review proceedings following the board's decision to refuse a substitution application on the ground that the proposed new nominee was not a fit and proper person, principally because of her association with certain named individuals themselves adjudged unsuitable to hold a licence, but also taking into account her failure to ensure the timeous renewal of the licence in respect of premises where she had been manageress and her failure to visit the application premises.

The Lord Ordinary (Weir) rejected the petitioners' arguments that the question of fitness required to be reserved until consideration of the confirmation application (see below) and that the board ought not to have taken into consideration information laid before them by the police, holding inter alia that:

(a) the use of the word 'may' in s 25(3) indicated that the board had a discretion to refuse the application[3]; and

(b) they could not be expected to exercise their discretion 'in the dark'.

While the case may have significant ramifications for all types of interim transfers, whether under s 25(1A), (2) or (3), it is difficult to accept the Lord Ordinary's suggestion that his decision 'does no violence to the scheme of the Act,' for a number of reasons:

(1) As explained below, a transfer by way of substitution requires to be confirmed at the next board meeting, when the board is directed to 'consider whether it is satisfied that the person to whom the licence *has been transferred* [author's emphasis] is a fit and proper person' (s 24(4)). It is tempting to conclude that if such a requirement is desiderated in s 25(3) but not in s 25(4) then, quite simply, the maxim *expressio unius, exclusio alterius* applies.

(2) Since provision is made for an application to be disposed of under a simple 'delegated powers' arrangement (s 5(1)) it is difficult to conceive that Parliament intended that the fitness of an individual to hold a licence be placed on a par with, say, an application for an occasional extension of permitted hours. Indeed, other matters which may involve the applicant's suitability may not be delegated and are susceptible to appeal (see s 5(2)(a), (b), (c), (d), (j) and (m)).

(3) If the decision is correct, the ratio would apply equally to a temporary transfer application made under s 25(1A); but in such a circumstance the person refused a temporary transfer could obtain a hearing before the full board and secure a right of appeal to the sheriff simply by proceeding to present a one-step permanent transfer application in terms of s 25(1). In *J & J Inns Ltd* the issue was in fact the subject of a proper hearing but the Lord Ordinary reserved his opinion as to whether this need have taken place. It is however

1 1988 SCLR 241, 1988 SLT 290.
2 1992 SCLR 683, 1992 SLT 930.
3 For a consideration of the words 'may refuse' in betting and gaming legislation see *Patmor Ltd v City of Edinburgh District Licensing Board* 1987 SLT 492; and *Mecca Bookmakers (Scotland) Ltd v East Lothian District Licensing Board* 1988 SLT 520.

inconceivable that the applicant could be denied the right to make represen-tations[1]. By parity of reasoning the applicant would be entitled to the disclo-sure of the contents of any objection.

It is perhaps of some significance that s 47(2) of the Licensing (Scotland) Act 1959, upon which s 25(2) of the 1976 Act is based, provided that two or more members of a licensing court 'may' grant an interim transfer subject to being satisfied as to the applicant's fitness to hold a certificate. Notwithstanding the use of the word 'may' it was accepted that the members had no discretion in the matter if the suitability criterion was satisfied. *A fortiori* the omission of the fitness requirement in s 25(2) and the 'new' forms of interim of transfer is an indication of Parliament's deliberate intention that this issue be reserved *pro tem* and the continued use of the word 'may' is no more than one of the many drafting infelici-ties in the Act.

From a practical point of view, however, where a substitution application is refused, having regard to the eight-week watershed, the only sensible remedy is the submission of a fresh application.

The grant of a substitution application does not affect the validity of a regular or occasional extension of the permitted hours. Section 64(3A)[2] provides that, where a licence has been transferred by virtue of s 25 and such an extension has been granted to the previous holder of the licence, references in s 64(2) and (3) to the person whose application has been granted 'shall include a reference to the person to whom the licence has been transferred'. This amendment was designed to cure the 'mischief' of *Archyield v City of Glasgow Licensing Board*[3]. While difficulties continue to be experienced with the coincidence of temporary and permanent transfers and applications to 'renew' (or indeed supplement) regular extensions[4] the possible effect of the grant of a substitution application in name of the non-natural person and the former nominee after the last lodgement date and before the board meeting which will consider the extension application seems to be fortuitously ignored.

Sunday permitted hours and children's certificates[5] remain in force notwith-standing the substitution. Permits for amusement with prizes machines are more problematic, at least so far as public house and hotel licensed premises are con-cerned. Some boards take the view that since the existing permit has been granted to the 'holder of a licence'[6] and both the non-natural person and nominee fall into that category by virtue of s 11 (3) (at least for the purposes of the 1976 Act) any change of nominee precipitates a requirement for a new permit. The problem should not arise with other types of licences, where the permit will have been obtained by the 'occupier' of the premises[7] and it is generally accepted that the identity of the occupier is not altered by a nominee's substitution.

---

1 See *Inland Revenue v Barrs* 1961 SLT 343, HL; *Devana Investments Ltd v City of Aberdeen Licensing Board* 1992 SCLR 616; and Lord Prosser's remarks in *C R S Leisure Ltd v Dumbarton District Licensing Board* 1989 SCLR 566 at 570 and 1990 SLT 200 at 202 and 203.
2 Inserted by s 51(5) of the 1990 Act.
3 1987 SCLR 191, 1987 SLT 547, doubted in *C R S Leisure Ltd v Dumbarton District Licensing Board* 1989 SCLR 566, 1990 SLT 200.
4 See Chapter 10.
5 1990 Act, s 49(10).
6 Gaming Act 1968, Sch 9, para 5(1)(a).
7 Ibid, Sch 9, para 5(1)(b).

As explained above, where a licence is temporarily transferred by virtue of s 25(1A) a permanent transfer must then go before an 'appropriate meeting' of the board. If the temporary transfer is granted to a non-natural person and a nominee it is perfectly possible that a substitution in terms of s 25(3) will require to be effected before the meeting at which the permanent transfer will be considered. A question arises as to the effect (if any) of the substitution upon the permanent transfer. It would appear that the permanent transfer application should proceed in name of the non-natural person and the original nominee; and that the substitution should be independently confirmed in the usual way, in terms of s 25(4) (as explained in the next section).

Pending the grant of the substitution application the employee who has ceased to be responsible for the day to day running of the premises remains *prima facie* responsible for a wide range of offences because of his continuing status as the holder of a licence.

CONFIRMATION OF TRANSFERS GRANTED UNDER S 25(2) OR (3)

A licence transferred by virtue of s 25(2) or (3) has effect until the *next* meeting of the board when the transfer requires to be confirmed (s 25(4)). The next meeting need not be a quarterly meeting (see s 5(2)(m) read with s 5(6)).

No time limit for lodgement of the confirmation application is specified. The omission is one of considerable significance since the continuing validity of the licence depends upon this second stage.

In practice, the next meeting will usually be a quarterly meeting and the confirmation is ordinarily, but purely as a matter of convention, subjected to the five-week lodgement deadline for 'major' applications. The application need not be advertised so that a shorter deadline is perfectly feasible. While one may be tempted to suppose that a time limit could be specified by a regulation made under s 37, a question inevitably arises as to procedure to be followed when an application is lodged 'late' (however that is defined). It is doubtful whether a regulation could have the effect of placing a late confirmation applicant in a worse position than a late renewal applicant. It may be that the board is obliged to consider an application lodged at *any* time prior to the next meeting, including any adjournment of that meeting[1].

The difficulty will be all the more acute where an interim transfer is granted very shortly before a board meeting. Section 25(4) unambiguously provides that 'A licence transferred by virtue of subsection (2) or (3) above shall have effect until the next meeting of the board'. While the 'old' s 25(4) was notoriously unsatisfactory it was generally (but not universally) regarded as requiring the interim transfer to be 'renewed' by way of a permanent transfer or renewal application, both of which may only be considered at a quarterly meeting and must be lodged five weeks in advance. In the circumstance postulated above the

---

1 See *Tarditi v Drummond* 1989 SCLR 201, 1989 SLT 554; *Indpine Ltd v City of Dundee Licensing Board* 1992 SCLR 113 (OH) 1992 SCLR 353, 1992 SLT 473 (IH).

renewal or permanent transfer was held over until the next following quarterly meeting. Strictly construed, the 'new' s 25(4) may give rise to problems.

At the confirmation stage the board is directed to consider 'whether it is satisfied that the person to whom the licence has been transferred is a fit and proper person to be the holder of a licence' and 'may have regard to any misconduct on his part, whether or not constituting a breach of this Act or any byelaw thereunder which in its opinion has a bearing on his fitness to hold a licence' (s 25(4), (4A)[1].

As the reader will have appreciated, s 25(4) is procedurally deficient. No provision is made for objections from the police or any other source, or for police observations. These hiatuses are particularly surprising. As Lord Weir observed in *J & J Inns Ltd v Angus District Licensing Board*[2] it would be 'absurd' if the board required to consider the fitness of an applicant with 'no information whatsoever' and, while that case may not be the last word on the subject, it will meantime fortify the position of any board which decides to obtain a police report, as invariably happens in practice. Paradoxically, however, the decision in *J & J Inns Ltd* suggests that the fitness issue may legitimately be resolved at the interim stage, so that the confirmation application is a 'rubber-stamping' process.

Where the board is satisfied as to fitness the transfer is confirmed and the expiry date of the licence is not affected (s 25(4B)). The grant of a confirmation application is not itself a transfer.

Otherwise, a refusal to confirm the transfer may be appealed to the sheriff, in which case 'the licence shall have effect until the time within which an appeal may be made has elapsed or, if an appeal has been lodged, until the appeal has been abandoned or determined' (s 25(4C)). A statement of reasons may be requested (s 18, read with s 5(2)(m)). It is possible that in the event of an unsuccessful appeal the licence may be irretrievably lost[3]. The alternative view is that the licence enters a form of 'suspended animation' from which it may be resurrected by a further transfer[4]. Much misery would have been avoided had the draftsman chosen to provide that the *transfer* rather than the *licence* has effect on the dependency of an appeal.

1 The expression 'is satisfied' means 'makes up its mind on the evidence': *Blyth v Blyth* [1966] 1 All ER 524, [1966] 2 WLR 634. It has been held that a licensing board cannot be 'satisfied' as to matters in contention unless it hears evidence: *Lennon v Monklands District Licensing Board*, Airdrie Sheriff Court, 24 May 1978, unreported.
2 1992 SCLR 683, 1992 SLT 930.
3 See *Campbell v Neilson* (1897) 24 R (J) 28 and *Miller v Linton* (1888) 15 R (J) 37.
4 *Argyll Arms (McManus) Ltd v Lorn, Mid-Argyll, Kintyre and Islay Divisional Licensing Board* 1988 SCLR 241, 1988 SLT 290.

CHAPTER SIX

Objections and observations

OBJECTIONS

To the grant, renewal or permanent transfer of a licence

Competent objectors

Objection to an application for the grant (including the provisional grant), renewal or permanent transfer of a licence[1] may competently be made by the following persons and bodies (s 16(1)) on one or more of the grounds of refusal provided by s 17 (s 16(5)).

(a) **Neighbouring proprietors and occupiers.** This category embraces 'any person[2] owning or occupying property situated in the neighbourhood of the premises to which the application relates or any organisation which in the opinion of the board represents such persons' (s 16(1)(a)).

In practice, there is a tendency to accept prima facie evidence of an objector's residence in the neighbourhood as providing the necessary qualification; but, strictly speaking, residence per se is insufficient[3]. Whether or not a person 'occupies' property may be difficult to determine. The only reported licensing case[4] suggests that the phrase 'occupier of property' is to be construed in terms of valuation law: a daughter living in her father's house and acting as his house-keeper did not by reason of her exclusive use of a bedroom possess the necessary status[5]. A degree of permanence is essential to rateable occupation but not conclusive[6].

The Act provides no definition of 'neighbourhood' but it is generally accepted that owners or occupiers whose amenity may possibly be prejudiced have locus[7].

---

1 No provision is made for objections to an application for temporary transfer under s 25(1A) or s 25(2) or for substitution of an employee/agent under s 25(3), but see *J & J Inns Ltd v Angus District Licensing Board* 1992 SCLR 683, 1992 SLT 930.
2 '"Person" includes a body of persons corporate or unincorporate': Interpretation Act 1978, Sch 1.
3 See 2 *Stair Memorial Encyclopaedia* para 49.
4 *McDonald v Chambers* 1956 SC 542, (sub nom *McDonald v Finlay*) 1957 SLT 81, decided under the Licensing (Scotland) Act 1903 which employed similar terminology.
5 See also *Wright v Assessor for Glasgow* 1936 SC 345 in which the distinction between persons in rateable occupation and lodgers was considered.
6 See *Forest Hills Trossachs Club v Assessor for Central Region* 1992 SLT 295.
7 It is extremely rare for neighbourhood objections to be based on s 17(1)(a) (applicant not a fit and proper person).

In *Freeland v City of Glasgow District Licensing Board*[1] the sheriff observed: '[E]very nuisance, such as an offensive odour, must have a locality of its own, and those members of the public who will be affected by it will be those round about . . .'.

Whether an organisation represents qualified owners or occupiers is a matter of fact for the board to determine. Only on surprisingly rare occasions do applicants' agents challenge the standing of representative organisations by enquiring as to the manner in which their mandate was obtained.

Where a competent objector presented to the board a petition containing over 1,000 signatures which had not been served upon the applicant the sheriff treated consideration of the petition as an exercise of the board's power to 'obtain information to enable them to discharge their functions in whatever way and by whatever means they choose'[2].

(b) Community councils. The community council requires to have been 'established in accordance with the provisions [of Part IV] of the Local Government (Scotland) Act 1973' (s 16(1)(b)). In terms of s 51 of the 1973 Act the general purpose of a community council shall be:

'to ascertain, co-ordinate and express to the local authorities for its area . . . the views of the community which it represents, in relation to matters for which those authorities are responsible, and to take such action in the interests of that community as appears to it to be expedient and practicable'.

Only the council 'for the area in which the premises are situated' (s 16(1)(b)) may object. An argument that the community council for an adjoining area could claim to be qualified in terms of s 16(1)(a) was raised but not resolved in *Kelvinside Community Council v Glasgow District Licensing Board*[3].

The *Report of the Departmental Commitee on Scottish Licensing Law*[4] attached 'considerable importance to the expression of local opinion on licensing matters' and believed that it was 'entirely appropriate that community councils which will be set up for the purpose of expressing local opinion should be given a statutory right to object' to applications. These councils have, however, made little impact on the licensing process.

(c) Churches. The church must be 'organised' and in the opinion of the licensing board represent 'a significant body of opinion among persons residing[5] in the neighbourhood of the premises' (s 16(1)(c)).

(d) The Chief Constable (s 16(1)(d)).[6] In *Lorimer's Breweries Ltd v City of Glasgow District Licensing Board*[7] it was held that an assistant chief constable who signed a letter of objection could competently do so as the chief constable's agent

---

1 1980 SLT (Sh Ct) 125.
2 *Fitzpatrick v Glasgow District Licensing Board* 1978 SLT (Sh Ct) 63.
3 1990 SCLR 110, 1990 SLT 725.
4 (Cmnd 5354) (*Clayson*) para 8.33.
5 Cf the owner/occupier provisions of s 16(1)(a).
6 The chief constable is also uniquely empowered to make observations: see below.
7 Glasgow Sheriff Court, 20 October 1980, unreported.

in terms of s 16(2)[1]. On a construction of s 5(1) of the Police (Scotland) Act 1967 a deputy chief constable was empowered to sign a complaint (under s 31) 'during any absence' of the chief constable[2]. In certain parts of the country objections are made on behalf of the chief constable by officers of lower rank (usually the local Chief Superintendent) under the authority of the force's standing orders, but they are not entitled to express their personal views[3].

(e) **The fire authority.** The fire authority[4] for the area in which the premises are situated was added to the list of competent objectors (s 16(1)(e)) by para 5 of Sch 8 to the 1990 Act. The licensing board is obliged to consult the fire authority in relation to applications for the grant (s 23(5)) and renewal (s 24(1)) of a licence[5].

(f) **The local authority.** Similarly, the local authority for the area in which the premises are situated is now empowered to object (s 16(1)(f), added by para 5 of Sch 8 to the 1990 Act).

In terms of s 235(1) of the Local Government (Scotland) Act 1973 'local authority' means 'a regional, islands or district council'.

Since the Act came into force the environmental health and building control departments of many district councils have played an increasingly prominent role in the licensing process, reporting to licensing boards the unsatisfactory condition of licensed premises[6].

In a number of unreported appeal cases it was unsuccessfully argued that local authorities were essentially conferring upon themselves the status of objector which had been denied by Parliament. For example, in *Farquhar v City of Glasgow District Licensing Board*[7] the sheriff (I D Macphail) held that the board had not acted *ultra vires* by considering departmental reports and observed that:

'I understand the law to be that a body such as the Board is entitled to obtain information in any way they think best, provided that they always give a fair opportunity to those who are parties in the controversy to correct or contradict any relevant statement prejudicial to their view . . .'.

Local authorities have been noticeably reluctant to exercise the new freedom to object. There is anecdotal evidence that this hesitancy is based on the specious view that a local authority department is not *the* local authority. It has also been suggested that the passing of a resolution to object is a lengthy process inimical to the time limit for objections. Nevertheless, s 56 of the Local Government (Scotland) Act 1973 allows the delegation of functions to an officer of a local authority; there appears to be nothing to prevent the delegation of an objection to, say, a director of environmental health.

In the result, in several parts of the country district council departments simply

---

1 Which requires that a written notice of objection be signed by the objector or his agent.
2 *Stephen v City of Aberdeen District Licensing Board* 1989 SLT 94.
3 See *Mecca Ltd v Kirkcaldy Burgh Licensing Court* 1975 SLT (Sh Ct) 50.
4 '"Fire authority" has the same meaning as in s 38 of the Fire Services Act 1947': s 139(1).
5 Consultation is also to take place as respects applications for consent to alter licensed premises (s 35(3)). There is no formal mechanism for objections.
6 Even where the condition of premises was irrelevant to the consideration of an application: see *Bantop Ltd v Glasgow District Licensing Board* 1989 SCLR 731, 1990 SLT 366.
7 Glasgow Sheriff Court, 31 October 1980, unreported.

continue to make 'observations' to the board. The legitimacy of this approach is highly suspect. In *Centralbite Ltd v Kincardine and Deeside District Licensing Board*[1] the chief constable 'recommended' the curtailment of extended hours. In subsequent judicial review proceedings the Lord Ordinary held that any document which made it clear that the author objected to the grant of an application fell to be treated as an objection irrespective of whether the word 'object' was used or not. *Ex hypothesi*, 'observations' from a qualified objector, such as a local authority, which are tantamount to an objection may be open to challenge.

Indeed, the chief constable is now empowered to make 'observations' (s 16A)[2]. The following syllogism has considerable attraction: the chief constable is empowered to object and to make observations; a local authority is only provided with express power to object; *ergo* a local authority has no power to make observations.

Licensing boards are inclined to argue that they cannot be expected to reach a conclusion as to the suitability of premises for the sale of alcoholic liquor unless provided with appropriate reports. It may equally be suggested that the fitness of a person to hold a licence cannot be decided without the assistance of the chief constable, whose power to bring information before the board is circumscribed by the mechanism for objections and observations.

Difficulties may also arise in cases where a board member has taken part in a district council committee decision to object to an application or to refuse planning permission. It has, however, been decided in England that members of a city council which had withheld planning approval for an application site were not disqualified from membership of the licensing confirming authority[3]. In *Low v Kincardineshire Licensing Court*[4], two bailies present at a town council meeting which resolved to object to an application for a betting office licence were among the eleven members who sat on the licensing court which considered the application. The sheriff observed:

'Although this might seem surprising to one's sense of natural justice . . . it is neither incompetent or illegal, so far as I can see upon a study of the legislation, and is no more than a curious reflection on the somewhat unsatisfactory framework which Parliament has given us . . .'.

Preliminary procedure

The procedure prescribed for the lodgement of objections with the clerk of the board and intimation to the applicant is particularly demanding and frequently misunderstood. The notice of objection must:
(a) be in writing, signed by the objector or his agent (s 16(2)(a))[5];
(b) specify[6] the grounds of objection (s 16(2)(a)); and

---

1 1989 SCLR 652, 1990 SLT 231.
2 See below.
3 *R v Sheffield Confirming Authority ex parte Truswell's Brewery Co Ltd* [1937] 4 All ER 114.
4 1974 SLT (Sh Ct) 54.
5 If a licensing board finds that an objection to the renewal of a licence is unauthorised the putative agent may be found liable in expenses to such extent as the board thinks fit: s 16(5).
6 For the standard of specification, see below.

(c) be lodged with the clerk of the board (s 16(2)(a)) and intimated to the applicant (s 16(2)(b)) 'not later than seven days before the meeting of the licensing board at which the application is to be considered' (s 16(2)).

A licensing board may only entertain an objection which 'is proved or admitted' to have been correctly intimated (s 16(2)).

The phrase 'not later than seven days' means 'not later than seven *clear* days'[1].

In *Indpine Ltd v City of Dundee District Licensing Board*[2] it was held that the word 'meeting' (in s 10(1)) was intended to cover all of the days on which a board meets for the discharge of its functions. In the result, a renewal application lodged after the first day of the meeting but before an adjourned meeting could competently be considered for the possible exercise of the board's discretion in terms of s 13(2).

Clearly, where the board is in a position to consider an application on the first day of its meeting, having received no objection, the ratio of *Indpine Ltd* confers no benefit upon a potential objector. *Semble*, however, that where the application is adjourned in terms of s 4(2) there is nothing to prevent the lodgement and intimation of an objection ad interim.

Indeed, such a proposition may not rest upon the decision in *Indpine Ltd*. Section 10(1) requires that an application for the renewal of a licence be lodged 'not later than five weeks before *the first day* of the meeting of the board at which the application is to be considered' (author's emphasis). As respects objections, s 16(2) simply fixes as the deadline the date not later than seven days 'before the meeting'[3].

In the result *Indpine Ltd* may only be of significance in this context if the expressions 'the meeting' and 'the first day of the meeting' are synonymous.

The time limit for lodgement and intimation of the objection is not to be reckoned using the *naturalis computatio* method by reference to the *time* of the board meeting. Where the meeting is due to commence at 10.00 am on 17 June there is no warrant for fixing the deadline as 10.00 am on 10 June.

Although the Act has been in operation for over 16 years doubt still arises as to the deadline for intimation where a copy of the notice of objection is sent to the applicant by registered post or by recorded delivery (s 16(3)(b): see below).

For example, if a licensing board is due to meet on 17 June the objection must be lodged with the clerk no later than 9 June. Some boards would be prepared to hold that a copy objection *posted* on that day to the applicant has been timeously intimated. Section 7 of the Interpretation Act 1978 suggests, however, that intimation takes place at the time of receipt:

'Where an Act authorises or requires any document to be served by post (whether the expression "serve" or the expression "give" or "send" or any other expression is used) then, unless the contrary intention appears, the service is deemed to be effected by properly addressing, pre-paying and posting a letter containing the document and, unless

1 See *Main v City of Glasgow District Licensing Board* 1987 SLT 305; *McMillan v HM Advocate* 1982 SCCR 309, 1983 SLT 24; and D C Coull '"Not Later Than" Defined' 1987 SLT (News) 353.
2 1992 SCLR 113 (OH), 1992 SCLR 535, 1992 SLT 473 (IH). See also *Tarditi v Drummond* 1989 SCLR 201, 1989 SLT 554.
3 By contrast, s 36(2) of the Licensing (Scotland) Act 1959, from which s 16(2) is derived, employed the phrase 'before the first day of the general half-yearly meeting'.

the contrary is proved[1], to have been effected at the time at which the letter would be delivered in the ordinary course of post'.

In *Adam v Secretary of State for Scotland*[2], a planning case, notice of an appeal against an enforcement notice could be 'served or given' by registered letter or recorded delivery service. Notice was given (a) by ordinary post in a letter sent on the day prior to the expiry of the time limit and (b) by a recorded delivery letter sent on the actual date of expiry. It was established by affidavit evidence that both letters arrived after that date. Rejecting the petitioner's argument that posting per se was sufficient, the Lord Ordinary held that '[T]here cannot be an appeal to someone until that person has knowledge of what is being brought before him'. *Semble* there cannot be intimation to an applicant until the notice of objection is received by him.

Where the last day for lodgement and intimation falls on a Sunday or other *dies non* it would appear that the time limit is extended to the first working day thereafter[3].

In the case of an application by a non-natural person nominating an individual, the 'applicant' is the former alone (see s 11(2)). An application for the regular extension of permitted hours is, however, made by the holder of the licence (s 64(1)); the applicant is thus both the non-natural person and his nominee (see s 11(3)).

Intimation to the applicant must be effected by one of the following methods[4]:
(a) by delivery to him of a copy of the notice of objection lodged with the licensing board (s 16(3)(a));
(b) by sending a copy of the said notice by registered post or recorded delivery in a letter addressed to him at his 'proper address' (s 16(3)(b));
(c) by leaving a copy of the said notice for him at his 'proper address' (s 16(3)(c)).

In *Prime v Hardie*[5] it was held that s 16(3)(a) does not require personal service on the applicant and that an applicant's employer who accepted delivery of the copy objection did so as his agent.

The applicant's 'proper address' depends on a number of variables (s 16(3)(c), as amended by para 5(b) of Sch 8 to the 1990 Act).

Where the applicant is a non-natural person intimation is to the address specified in the application. Except as respects individuals[6] no express provision is made in s 16(3) for a case in which the address of an agent has been published in terms of s 139(5)[7], probably on the assumption that companies, partnerships, etc have no confidentiality requirement. Nevertheless, non-natural persons frequently employ s 139(5) and intimation to the agent is authorised by s 139(6)[7].

1 See *Adam v Secretary of State for Scotland* 1987 SCLR 697, 1988 SLT 300.
2 See above.
3 See *McNiven v Glasgow Corporation* 1920 SC 584 at 588 and *Craig-Na-Brro Sales v Munro Furniture Ltd* 1974 SLT (Sh Ct) 107. The position would appear to be different in England: see *Paterson's Licensing Acts*, 1993 edn, p 61.
4 But see *Morgan v Midlothian District Licensing Board* 1993 SCLR 1, 1993 SLT (Sh Ct) 19, discussed below.
5 1978 SLT (Sh Ct) 71.
6 See below.
7 Added by para 18 of Sch 8 to the 1990 Act.

If the application has been made by an individual natural person the 'proper address' is:

(i)   in all cases where the address of an agent has been published (s 139(5)), the agent's place of business; or

(ii) the applicant's 'place of abode as specified in his application', where the application is for the grant (including the provisional grant) or permanent transfer of a licence; or

(iii) the address of 'the premises in respect of which the application is made', if the application is for renewal of a licence.

In *Morgan v Midlothian District Licensing Board*[1] objections to an application for the grant of a new licence were sent to the applicant's shop, rather than his place of abode. On appeal it was held that while the objectors had failed to obtemper the provisions of s 16(3)(b) or (c), actual and timeous delivery to the applicant satisfied s 16(3)(a).

This decision destroyed the assumption that the prescribed methods of intimation set out in s 16(3) constitute watertight compartments and that once an objector commits himself to postal intimation he must proceed within the four corners of s 16(3)(b). For example, many licensing boards had been prepared to reject as incompetent an objection sent to the 'proper address' by ordinary post, rather than by recorded delivery or registered post, even where receipt of the objection by the applicant was admitted. On the basis of *Morgan*, if actual and timeous receipt is proved or admitted, service in this fashion will be regarded as sufficient under s 16(3)(a).

In practice, certain types of deficiency are common:

(1) The objector may simply intimate to the applicant the bare fact that he has lodged an objection with the clerk, without providing a copy; or fail to provide the applicant with any intimation whatsoever. Some clerks take it upon themselves to intimate the objection to the applicant or his agent. If intimation by the clerk takes place timeously there will probably be no prejudice to the applicant. In *Morgan*[1] it was argued on behalf of objectors that the provisions of s 16(3) are directory rather than mandatory. The sheriff did not require to resolve this issue but it may well be considered that the availability of a dispensing power (s 13(2))[2], negates the existence of common law discretion to waive non-compliance with a preliminary requirement of the Act.

(2) The applicant's 'copy' of the objection may not be a true copy, but simply a resumé. The greatest care should be taken by the applicant when, at the hearing of his application, he is asked whether the objection is admitted. It should not be assumed that he and the clerk have before them identical material.

(3) The objection, which must be directed towards one or more of the grounds of refusal (s 16(5)), addresses irrelevant issues. For example, although a new

1 1993 SCLR 1, 1993 SLT (Sh Ct) 19.

2 Which allows a board to postpone consideration of inter alia an objection in a case of 'inadvertence or misadventure': see 'Power to waive procedural failures', below.

s 17(1)(d)[1] was substituted by para 6 of Sch 8 to the 1990 Act objectors sometimes found on the former provision.

(4) There is a lack of proper specification. It is well-settled that the applicant must have fair notice of the case which he is required to meet. A simple repetition of the ground of refusal is inadequate[2].

The attachment of schedules listing the previous convictions of an applicant company's directors to a letter stating that the company was not 'a fit and proper person' reached the required standard by the narrowest of margins in *Fereneze Leisure Ltd v Renfrew District Licensing Board*[3].

Where an objection takes the form of a petition it cannot be assumed that the signatories are all objecting for the same reason unless the ground is clearly specified:

'[The objection] is not to be treated more leniently . . . On the contrary, it is important that the requirement that the grounds of objection must be specified should be applied as strictly in these cases as it must be in the case of an objection by an individual. If this is not done, the licensing authority may be tempted to attach weight to the objection because of the number of persons associated with it regardless of its content, which is something they are not entitled to do'[4].

Power to waive procedural failures

In terms of s 13(2) where an objector to 'the grant of a licence' has 'through inadvertence or misadventure, failed to comply with any of the preliminary requirements of the Act the board 'may, if it thinks fit, and upon such terms as the board thinks proper, postpone the consideration of the . . . objection to an adjourned meeting'.

This dispensing power is available in relation to applications for the grant (including the provisional grant) and renewal[5] of a licence but does not extend to permanent transfer applications[6].

At the adjourned meeting, which must take place 'during the period of one month next following the first day' of the quarterly meeting (s 4(2)), the board proceeds to consider the objection 'as if the preliminary requirements of this Act had been complied with' (s 13(3)(b)).

In practice, lay objectors are frequently lost in the Byzantine maze of s 16 and ignorant of the provisions of s 13(2), so that the appropriate motion is rarely made. In *Morgan v Midlothian District Licensing Board*[7] an argument to the effect that the board should consider the exercise of its discretion *ex proprio motu* was made but did not require to be decided.

The right of appeal conferred upon a 'competent objector' is 'against the

---

1 'Overprovision' as a ground of refusal of a new licence application.
2 *Chief Constable of Grampian v Aberdeen District Licensing Board* 1979 SLT (Sh Ct) 2.
3 1991 SCLR 751, 1992 SLT 604.
4 *Noble Organisation Ltd v Kilmarnock and Loudoun District Council* 1992 SCLR (Notes) 1006 at 1008.
5 'Grant' includes grant by way of renewal: s 139(1).
6 Similar provision is made in s 13 for an adjournment where an objector, having 'duly lodged' his objection, dies before the board meeting.
7 1993 SCLR 1, 1993 SLT (Sh Ct) 19.

decision of the licensing board to grant, renew or transfer a licence' (s 17(5)). See also s 17(6)). A refusal to entertain an objection in terms of s 13(2) is a separate matter susceptible only to judicial review[1].

Separate provision is made for a late objection by the chief constable. In terms of s 16(4):

'it shall be competent for a licensing board to entertain objections from the chief constable, lodged at any time before the hearing of an application, if the board is satisfied that there is sufficient reason why due notice and intimation of the objection could not be given, and in such a case the chief constable shall cause his objections to be intimated to the applicant before the hearing'.

Where the applicant receives short notice of the objection it may be appropriate to request an adjournment of the application.

Procedure at the hearing

Service of an objection upon the applicant is not tantamount to a citation. In practice, therefore, in the case of renewal and permanent transfer applications, which cannot be refused without a hearing (see s 15), the clerk will usually cite the applicant upon receipt of an objection, if he has not already done so[2]. Otherwise, unless the applicant voluntarily attends the meeting, an adjournment may be required.

When the application is called the clerk of the board informs the meeting that he has received an objection and determines whether the objector is present or represented. The applicant or his agent is asked whether the objection is accepted as competent.

The applicant is well advised to give very careful consideration to the competency issue, since an objector's appeal effectively suspends the grant or provisional grant of a new licence (s 30(1))[3].

A dispute as to competency should be disposed of *in limine* and may (rarely) be considered at a separate, preliminary hearing[4]. Although issues of pure law are frequently involved the matter is one for the board to decide[5].

Prior to the amendment of s 16(5) by para 5 of Sch 8 of the 1990 Act some

---

1 See, for example, *Purdon v City of Glasgow District Licensing Board* 1988 SCLR 466, 1989 SLT 201 for an example of judicial review where the board refused an applicant's s 13(2) motion. Cf *Morgan v Midlothian District Licensing Board*, above, in which an appeal was made to the sheriff against a board's decision that objectors had failed to comply with s 16(3) and no s 13(2) motion had been made.
2 The board may 'decline to consider' inter alia applications for the grant (including the provisional grant) of a new licence where the applicant or his representative do not attend the meeting: s 15.
3 An appeal has no effect on the grant of a renewal application (s 30(2)) nor, it is submitted, on the grant of a permanent transfer.
4 See *Cooper v City of Edinburgh District Licensing Board* 1991 SLT 47.
5 In *Cooper v City of Edinburgh District Licensing Board*, above, it was accepted by the board that the clerk's rejection of an objection was *ultra vires*. Conceivably, the competency of an objection to a renewal application may be purely a matter for the clerk. Section 5(2)(b), read with s 5(6), has the effect of requiring the application to be considered at a quarterly meeting where a *competent* objection has been received: otherwise it may be granted (but not refused) under a 'delegated powers' arrangement (s 5(1)).

licensing boards refused to consider an objection where the objector failed to attend the meeting. Now, by virtue of that amendment, the board 'shall, whether or not the objector appears, consider any competent objection'[1]. Many clerks will only release objections to board members for consideration after any dispute as to competency is resolved. The practice in some areas of distributing objections prior to the meeting is probably unsound, but there are inevitably occasions on which the content of an objection is germane to the competency issue; where, for example, it is argued that the objection is made on irrelevant grounds (s 16(5))[2]. Where a chief constable's objection relates to an applicant's spent convictions, details are not automatically made available: the board must take a decision as to whether the convictions are to be admitted in evidence[3].

A compearing objector should be given an opportunity of addressing the board and, of course, the applicant is allowed rebuttal argument. The objector must not introduce additional grounds of objection nor material for which a foundation has not been laid in his written objection.

Where the refusal of an application is appealed to the sheriff the applicant is required to serve a copy of the initial writ not only on the clerk of the board but also 'all other parties who appeared (whether personally or by means of a representative) at the hearing'[4].

The applicant's agent must therefore ensure that he has a complete record of the objectors who 'appeared'. In *Transition Interiors Ltd v Eastwood District Licensing Board*[5] the sheriff held that 'appearance' required more than mere physical presence at the meeting:

'Parties were agreed that there was no authority to which I might be referred to define "appeared"... As a result I feel obliged to take the straightforward commonly understood meaning of the term when used in relation to proceedings before a Court, Tribunal or Board. It is also significant that paragraph 3 of the Act of Sederunt while making reference to "all other parties who appeared", thereafter in parenthesis specifies "whether personally or by means of a representative". The use of the term "representative" reinforced the view which I formed that the Act did not envisage physical presence as being sufficient to comply with the requirement of attendance [sic] since one would find it difficult to think of a reason to have a representative attend on one's behalf at such a meeting if not to speak on one's behalf and address the forum in support of an objection . . . .'.

It should of course be borne in mind that one objector may speak for a multitude of others who thus 'appear' through a representative.

Obversely, since s 17(5) limits a right of appeal to a 'competent objector who appeared at the hearing' an objector wishing to preserve his position in the event that the application is granted should ensure his 'appearance'.

If the licensing board considers that any objection to the renewal of a licence is

---

1 But only a competent objector who appears has a right of appeal: s 17(5). See also Chapter 14.
2 See *Cooper v City of Edinburgh District Licensing Board*, above.
3 Rehabilitation of Offenders Act 1974, s 7(3). See *Morton v City of Dundee District Council* 1992 SLT (Sh Ct) 2; and Chapter 4, sub voce 'Suitability of the applicant'.
4 Act of Sederunt (Appeals under the Licensing (Scotland) Act 1976) 1977, SI 1977/1622, para 3, as substituted by SI 1979/1520. The appeals procedure and the difficulties caused by the Act of Sederunt are explained in Chapter 14.
5 Paisley Sheriff Court, 2 May 1990, unreported.

'frivolous or vexatious' it may find the objector liable in expenses 'to such extent as the board thinks fit' (s 16(5))[1].

To the regular extension of permitted hours[2]

The provision made in s 64(7) for objections to applications for the regular extension of permitted hours is comparatively eclectic:

'Any person mentioned in section 16(1) of this Act may object to an application for the regular extension of permitted hours, and any such objection shall be in writing and lodged with the clerk of the licensing board and a copy thereof sent to the applicant[3] not less than seven days before the quarterly meeting at which the application is to be considered'.

Although the objection must be in the hands of the clerk not later than seven clear days before the board meeting it seems that the posting of the copy objection on the last day is sufficient[4].

The applicant for a regular extension of permitted hours is made by the 'person holding' the licence (s 64(1)), an expression which includes a nominee of a non-natural person (s 11(3)). The copy objection should therefore be sent to both parties, although it may perhaps be argued that service upon the non-natural person alone is deemed to include service upon his employee or agent[5].

The objection must be on relevant grounds. The physical condition of premises should not be taken into account[6]. In *Perfect Swivel Ltd v City of Dundee District Licensing Board (No 2)*[7] the chief constable objected to an application on the ground that the company applicant could not be trusted to conduct its business during any extension of the permitted hours without causing undue public nuisance or a threat to public order or safety having regard to the previous convictions of its directors. No doubt quite properly this ground of refusal was not supported during a subsequent judicial review.

A licensing board is not empowered to entertain late objections from any source, although it has a discretion to entertain observations from the chief constable 'lodged at any time before the hearing of the application' (s 16(A)(4)).

Although the board is enjoined to consider a competent objection to an application for the grant, renewal or permanent transfer of a licence 'whether or not the objector appears' (s 16(5)) no parallel provision is made as respects regular extension applications.

To the grant of a children's certificate[8]

The only competent objector to an application for a children's certificate is the chief constable. Where he desires to object he must:

1 This antique power is never invoked in practice.
2 See also Chapter 10. Note that applications for occasional extensions of the permitted hours are not liable to objection.
3 Intimation may be made to the applicant's agent: s 139(6).
4 Cf the provisions of s 16(2) and (3), discussed above.
5 See *Prime v Hardie* 1978 SLT (Sh Ct) 71.
6 *Bantop v City of Glasgow District Licensing Board* 1989 SCLR 731, 1990 SLT 366.
7 Outer House, 26 March 1992, unreported on this point.
8 See also Chapter 14 for a consideration of this form of permission.

'not later than seven days[1] before the meeting of the licensing board at which the application is to be considered –
(a) lodge with the clerk of the board a written notice of his objection specifying the grounds of his objection to the grant of the certificate; and
(b) intimate such objection and grounds to the applicant . . .'[2].

No methods of intimation are prescribed, nor are potential grounds of objection specified[3].

The board has no discretion to accept a late objection but may entertain police observations submitted out-of-time (s 16A(4)).

The chief constable is specifically empowered 'to appear at the meeting of the licensing board which considers the application and make objection to the grant of the certificate' (1990 Act, Sch 5, para 4), but must, of course, confine himself to the content of his written objection.

To the grant of an occasional licence[4]

Section 33, which authorises the grant of an occasional licence, makes a single reference to the potential for objections: 'A licensing board shall make such arrangements as it thinks fit as respects the consideration of applications under this section or any objection thereto . . .' (s 33(9)).

In *Hollywood Bowl (Scotland) Ltd v Horsburgh*[5] the Lord Ordinary held that an application for an occasional licence made under s 33 was open to objection at the instance of the persons and bodies listed in s 16(1); and that the petitioners could have informed themselves of the existence of an application by reference to the public register kept in terms of s 20.

POLICE OBSERVATIONS

Section 16A of the Act[6] directs licensing boards to have regard to any observations submitted by the chief constable in relation to the following types of application:
(a) for the grant (including the provisional grant), renewal or permanent transfer of a licence;
(b) the regular extension of permitted hours;
(c) the grant of a children's certificate (s 16A(1))[7].

The procedure for lodgement of the observations with the clerk and intimation to the applicant (s 16A(2) and (3)) is *mutatis mutandis* the same as that prescribed

---

1 Ie seven clear days.
2 1990 Act, Sch 5, para 4. Intimation to the applicant's agent is sufficient: 1976 Act, s 139(6).
3 Presumably an objection must be referable to the requirements of s 49(2) of the 1990 Act; see Chapter 14.
4 See also Chapter 7.
5 1993 SLT 241.
6 Inserted by the 1990 Act, s 53(1).
7 In addition, the chief constable may make observations relative to the proposed suspension of a licence where he has not originated the complaint to the board (1976 Act, s 31(5A), added by the 1990 Act, s 53(2)).

by s 16(2) and (3) in relation to objections[1]. Observations are not to be entertained unless it is 'proved or admitted' that they have been properly intimated (s 16A(2)), but the board has power to consider observations lodged at any time before the hearing on cause shown (s 16A(4), in virtually identical terms to s 16(4)).

While objections to applications of type (a) above must be directed towards one of the grounds of refusal provided by s 17 (s 16(5)), s 16A(5) provides that the licensing board:

'shall have regard to any observations submitted by the chief constable in accordance with this section whether or not they are relevant to one or more grounds on which, by virtue of section 17[2] of this Act, an application may be refused'.

Of course, a licensing board decision based on extraneous considerations is extremely vulnerable to successful attack and the rationale of this provision is unclear. It may, for example, allow the chief constable to report to the board that the notice required by s 10(2)(b) or (3)(b) in connection with an application for the grant or provisional grant of a new licence has not been correctly displayed, such a failure entitling the board to decline to consider (rather than refuse) the application[3].

The origins of s 16A are generally believed to be grounded in *Centralbite Ltd v Kincardine and Deeside District Licensing Board*[4]: the Lord Ordinary reduced the refusal of an application for the regular extension of permitted hours because the board had taken into account a letter from the chief constable which fell to be regarded as an unintimated objection.

This decision did not per se require legislative intervention. It simply served to indicate that the construction to be placed upon police observations was essentially a matter of substance rather than form. Indeed, licensing boards cannot be expected to work 'in the dark'[5]. The police were often called upon to report public disorder incidents in the vicinity of licensed premises and, provided that this information was supplied to the board in an anodyne form, the practice was regarded as unexceptionable. Any difficulty occasioned by a lack of notice could be cured, albeit with some inconvenience, by a motion for an adjournment.

While *Centralbite Ltd* could well have played a part in the introduction of s 16A, its principal *raison d'être* may have been the difficulty experienced in those parts of the country where licensing boards refused to hear the chief constable's representative unless an objection had been lodged.

In any event, if the chief constable is now properly enfranchised clear limitations appear to have been placed on his participation in the licensing process. There is no provision for police (or indeed any other) objections to or observations on a number of applications.

For example, while the chief constable is specifically empowered to oppose or comment upon an application for the regular extension of the permitted hours the

1 As described above.
2 It will be observed that the power to make observations extends beyond the applications embraced by s 17.
3 Subject to the provisions of s 10(4) and s 13(2).
4 1989 SCLR 652, 1990 SLT 231.
5 See *J & J Inns Ltd v Angus District Licensing Board* 1992 SCLR 683, 1992 SLT 930.

Act is silent as respects occasional extensions. There is a virtually irresistible argument that the maxim *expressio unius, exclusio alterius* applies. Yet, such a construction is destructive of the proper operation of the legislation: an applicant for an occasional extension must furnish the chief constable with a copy of his application (s 64(1)) and the board are almost entirely dependent upon a police report if they are to reach a view as to the merits.

Similarly, while a licensing board must consider 'whether it is satisfied' that a new employee or agent substituted in terms of s 25(3) is 'a fit and proper person to be the holder of a licence' (s 25(4)), no provision is made in s 16 or s 16A for police objections or observations at either stage of the procedure.

This difficulty was clearly focused on in *J & J Inns Ltd v Angus District Licensing Board*[1]. An application for the substitution of a new employee in terms of s 25(3) was the subject of a report letter addressed to the board's clerk by the local chief superintendent. This letter expressly acknowledged that the police 'have no power to object or make observations' but placed information before the board which clearly played a material part in the refusal of the application by highlighting the proposed new manageress's association with certain individuals.

Rejecting the petitioners' argument that the board should not have had regard to the police letter since 'there was no statutory provision covering the information which should be before a board when an application under section 25(3) was made', the Lord Ordinary held that:

'The letter from the police was expressed in careful terms, pointing out that there was no power to object or make observations on the petitioners' application. Nevertheless, in my opinion there was nothing to prevent the police from supplying information if they chose to do so and if the operation of the statute in relation to this type of application is to work properly, nothing to prevent the board from taking into account this information or such other information as might properly be laid before it. It would be absurd if a board was required to exercise its discretion by having to work in the dark because it could not entertain any information which might be available'.

To some extent these views echo the dictum of the Sheriff Principal in *Fitzpatrick v Glasgow District Licensing Board*[2]:

'[I]n so far as [a licensing board] is not bound by statute it may conduct its proceedings as it pleases. [They] may, subject to the statutory limitations on them, obtain information to enable them to discharge their functions in whatever way and by whatever means they choose'.

Nevertheless, the soundness of the decision in *J & J Inns Ltd* is open to question on a number of grounds[3]. While the scope of s 16A is patently too narrow the extension of its provisions may properly be a matter for the legislature.

1 See above.
2 1978 SLT (Sh Ct) 63 at 64.
3 See commentary at 1992 SCLR 691.

CHAPTER 7

Occasional licences and permissions

OCCASIONAL LICENCES

The holder of a licence other than a refreshment licence, or an entertainment licence (s 33(10)) may make application to a licensing board in terms of s 33 for an occasional licence:

'. . . authorising him to sell alcoholic liquor during such period of not more than 14 days as the board may determine, in the course of catering for an event taking place outwith the licensed premises in respect of which he is the holder of a licence'[1].

The same facility is available to a registered club for 'an event held outwith the premises of the club if the event arises from or relates to the functions of the club' (s 33(2), as amended by the 1990 Act, Sch 8, para 9(9)).

Where the holder of a public house, hotel or off-sale licence is asked to supply alcoholic liquor (and perhaps also the services of staff) for hospitality purposes at any outside event, in the absence of any sales to guests or otherwise at that event, no occasional licence is required and the liquor so supplied is simply an 'off-sale'. Similarly, there is nothing to prevent an unlicensed caterer from providing customers with alcoholic liquor which he has purchased *as the customer's agent*[2].

Applications for an occasional licence must be made in writing to the clerk, no later than a prescribed number of days before the event, and are required to specify the name and address of the applicant, the premises or place and occasion for which the licence is desired and the hours and period during which alcoholic liquor is to be sold (s 33(7)). At the same time as the application is made, the applicant must send a copy thereof to the chief constable, to whom a copy of the licence is also to be sent by the clerk not later than 24 hours before the commencement of the event (s 33(8)).

As well as being empowered to make procedural regulations (s 37), the board 'shall make such arrangements as it thinks fit as respects the consideration of applications' but 'shall not cause to be published the address of the applicant if the applicant provides the name and address of an agent through whom it may have intimated to him any objections' (s 33(9))[3].

Applications may be (and almost invariably are) considered by the clerk alone or by a committee of the clerk and one or more board members under a 'delegated

---

1 Section 33(1), as amended by the 1990 Act, Sch 8, para 9(9).
2 See *Langmuir v Persichini* 1935 JC 73, 1935 SLT 399; cf *Pasquier v Neale* [1902] 2 KB 287, (1902) 67 JP 49.
3 The advertisement of applications for occasional licences is virtually unknown, but the new provision for publication of an agent's name and address (inserted by the 1990 Act, Sch 8, para 9(b)), is consonant with s 139(5) and (6), added by the 1990 Act, Sch 8, para 18.

powers' arrangement (s 5(1)) without the applicant's appearance but, in accordance with the principles of natural justice an application should not be refused unless the applicant has been afforded the opportunity of a hearing.

The board is under no obligation to state reasons for the grant or refusal of an application[1], nor is there any right of appeal to the sheriff. There is no prohibition on the submission of further applications following a refusal. The grant of an occasional licence may be subject to 'such conditions as [the board] thinks fit including a condition as to the type of alcoholic liquor which may be sold under the licence' (s 33(3)). The occasional licence is not subject to any conditions attaching to the 'parent' licence (see below), such as a condition made under s 29(1) which precludes the sale of spirits.

An occasional licence granted to the holder of a restricted hotel or a restaurant licence *must* be subject to a condition (s 33(3)) that the sale of alcoholic liquor shall be ancillary[2] to the provision of 'substantial refreshment'[3]. There is no obligation to provide a 'main meal' or a 'table meal'. It is sufficient that 'substantial refreshment' be made available and the taking of food is not a prerequisite to the consumption of alcoholic liquor.

Contravention of a condition by a licenceholder or a registered club is an offence (s 33(4) and (5))[4]. As respects clubs, every person named in the current management committee list (s 103(3)(b), (5)) is liable to conviction, subject to the defence that the contravention took place 'without his knowledge or consent' (s 33(5)).

An occasional licence is technically distinct from the 'parent' licence. References in the Act to a 'licence' include an occasional licence[5] and the holder of an occasional licence is a 'licence holder' and 'the holder of a licence'[6]. The premises or place for which the occasional licence is granted are 'licensed premises' as respects the sale of alcoholic liquor[7]. In terms of s 33(6), 'the provisions of the Act and of any byelaws or regulations made thereunder, other than provisions relating to the permitted hours[8], shall apply to the sale of alcoholic liquor under an occasional licence 'as if the sale took place on licensed premises' or, as the case may be, 'as if the sale took place in the registered club'. In the result:

(a) Except in the case of a registered club[9], the police entry powers set out in s 85 apply. Since an occasional licence may be granted in respect of a 'place' rather than simply 'premises', it will be desirable in that event to have the area which is to be the subject of the licence clearly defined by reference to a plan where doubt

1 See *Purdon v Glasgow District Licensing Board* 1988 SCLR 466, 1989 SLT 201.
2 'Ancillary': see consideration of restaurant licences in Chapter 3 and cases cited.
3 'Substantial refreshment': see *Timmis v Millman* [1965] Brewing Tr Rev 23, (1965) SJ 31; *Solomon v Green* [1955] Brewing Tr Rev 313, (1955) 119 JP 289; *Robertson v Mackenzie* 1975 JC 72, 1975 SLT 222.
4 Maximum penalty: level 3. Licenceholder (who has vicarious responsibility) and premises liable to disqualification (s 67, Sch 5).
5 'Licence' is defined in s 139(1) as 'a licence granted under this Act other than under Part III of this Act'. The exclusion relates to seamen's canteens.
6 See definitions of these terms in s 139(1).
7 'Licensed premises': see s 139(1).
8 'Permitted hours': see ss 53, 54 and 139(1).
9 See s 114 for policy entry powers.

may otherwise arise as to the extent of the licensed area. Particularly in the case of temporary structures the board may wish to consult with the local building control department as to the suitability of the proposed venue.

(b) The regulatory mechanism of the Act relative to public order offences and the protection and employment of young persons is substantially brought into operation. It may, however, appear curious that s 33(6) does not specifically apply the provisions of the Act as respects the *consumption* of alcoholic liquor[1].

(c) The sale of alcoholic liquor is deemed to take place in *the* registered club, so that, for example, the rules of that club must be observed. In other cases, sales constructively take place 'in licensed premises', not *the* licensed premises. It would accordingly appear that the operation of the occasional licence is not fettered by restrictions on the 'parent' licence. Thus, the holder of a restaurant licence commits an offence if he sells or supplies alcoholic liquor for consumption in his premises except to persons taking table meals for consumption by such a person as an ancillary to his meal (s 99)[2]. The requirement that he provide 'substantial refreshment' when operating under an occasional licence clearly assumes that, but for such a condition, there would be no obligation as to the supply of food. The board may, of course, impose conditions which would assimilate the occasional licence to the 'parent' licence.

Nevertheless, problems are known to have occurred in relation to occasional licences granted to holders of off-sale licences[3], having regard to the provisions of s 97(4): 'A holder of an off-sale licence or his employee or agent shall be guilty of an offence if he sells wine (including made-wine) in an open vessel'. This view that a difficulty is thereby created, while understandable, is of doubtful validity. For the purpose of the event the holder of an off-sale licence is the holder of a separate occasional licence: he does not hold an off-sale licence in respect of the premises or place which are the subject of the latter. To some extent this argument is fortified by the decision in *Hollywood Bowl (Scotland) Ltd v Horsburgh*[4] in which the Lord Ordinary considered that an occasional licence application was susceptible to objection, in view of the provisions of ss 16, 20 and 139, possibly implying that the occasional licence has a 'stand-alone' status.

Further, it is clear from the heading to s 97 and the terminology of the other subsections that the whole section is applicable to the 'parent' licence. Indeed, it is commonly accepted that occasional licences operated by an off-sale licenceholder allow the *sale and consumption* of alcoholic liquor at the event, which would be prohibited in off-sale licensed premises by virtue of s 97(1) and (2).

(d) The application of byelaws to an occasional licence may in certain districts place additional obligations upon the licenceholder, for example, a responsibility to make foodstuffs available, although s 33(3) only requires the holders of restricted hotel and restaurant licences to provide 'substantial refreshment'. The applicable byelaws are those in force in the district in which the event takes place, rather than, if different, the district in which the 'parent' licence is held.

---

1 Eg under s 68. Cf s 34(4).
2 See *Stainton and Seiler v McNaughtan* 1991 SCCR 339.
3 Under the corresponding provision of the Licensing (Scotland) Act 1959 (s 60) a special permission could only be obtained by holders of hotel and public house certificates.
4 1993 SLT 241.

(e) *Semble* the sale of alcoholic liquor outside the authorised hours would amount to trafficking (s 90(a)). Since the provisions of the Act relative to 'permitted hours' are inapplicable (s 33(6)), the (lesser) offence constituted by s 54(1), (4)[1] appears to have no relevance[2].

Practical applications

Occasional licences are commonly used to allow licenceholders to cater for gala days, agricultural shows, wedding receptions and so on in premises (and places, such as marquees) which are *unlicensed*[3]. The event may take place in another licensing board's area[4].

Since application may only be made where the event takes place 'outwith the licensed premises' in respect of which the applicant is the licenceholder, he may not apply for an occasional licence in respect of his own premises for the purpose of sterilising any restrictive conditions (for example, under s 29).

Otherwise, whether premises may be the subject of an occasional and 'permanent' licence at the same time is more problematical. The sheriff's note in *Donald v Donald*[5] discloses that premises subject to a restricted hotel licence were used for functions by means of occasional licences obtained by the holder of a (full) hotel licence. The case was not concerned with the legitimacy of this device but it is interesting to note that enquiries by the police and the procurator fiscal precipitated an application for a hotel licence in place of the restricted hotel licence to displace 'uncertainty'.

Broadly speaking, the holder of a restricted hotel licence (or his employee or agent) who sells or supplies alcoholic liquor to a member of the public except where a meal is taken commits an offence in terms of s 98. On the other hand, the occasional licence only authorises the sale or supply by *its* holder (s 9(1))[6] (although one suspects that, in practice, sale or supply under an occasional licence often takes place at the hand of another person who is being, as it were, accommodated by the 'parent' licenceholder).

Interestingly, however, that the position is different in England appears to be clear. The 'double licensing' of premises was legitimised in *Brown v Drew*[7]. In circumstances remarkably similar to those in *Donald v Stirling District Licensing Board*[8], justices granted an occasional licence to the holder of a hotel licence, permitting him to operate a bar at a function taking place at premises which were

---

1 Which prohibits inter alia the sale or supply of alcoholic liquor outwith permitted hours, subject to certain exceptions.
2 Cf *Southall v Haime* (1979) 143 JP 245, in which it was decided that Parliament could not have intended the holder of an occasional licence to be convicted of selling without a licence where sales took place outwith authorised hours.
3 In *Hutcheon v Cadenhead* (1892) 19 R (J) 32 the Lord Justice-Clerk expressed the view (at 37) that a 'special permission' could be granted for 'a house, a tent or a portion of a field'.
4 *McDonald v Gordon* (1868) 7 M 45.
5 1992 SLT (Sh Ct) 75 at 78.
6 The Lord Ordinary's decision in *Hollywood Bowl v Horsburgh* 1993 SLT 241 discussed below clearly implies that references in the Act to a 'licence' include an occasional licence.
7 [1953] 2 QB 257, [1953] 2 All ER 689, [1953] 3 WLR 472.
8 1992 SCLR (Notes) 369, 1992 SLT (Sh Ct) 75.

the subject of a limited licence. In the police appeal against the justices' decision it was submitted that premises deemed to be licensed by virtue of an occasional licence[1] could not be actual licensed premises. The Chief Justice (Lord Goddard) said:

'I am unable to give effect to that argument . . . it is obvious that the statutory fiction as to licensed premises is intended to and must apply where the premises are not licensed premises. If they are not licensed at all, then they are deemed to be licensed immediately an occasional licence is given in respect of them. The common case is the refreshment marquee at an agricultural or flower show. When those premises are subject to an occasional licence they are deemed to be licensed premises, but I do not think that that means that premises which are already licensed cannot have an occasional licence'.

Occasional licences may be obtained for the following, additional purposes:

(1) There is English authority for the view that an occasional licence may be granted to allow trading to resume in premises which have become unlicensed because of inadvertent failure to apply for a renewal[2]. The practice is not uncommon in Scotland. Such an expedient will usually be of limited value unless applications are granted for consecutive periods. In *R v Bath Licensing Justices ex parte Chittenden*[3] it was held that under the corresponding provisions of the Licensing Act 1964 occasional licences need not relate to separate and independent occasions, nor need there be a gap between the periods of the licences.

(2) Occasional licences are sometimes obtained to licence on a temporary basis outside drinking areas adjacent to but not included within the premises which are the subject of the 'parent' licence, for example, 'beer gardens' or a marquee in the grounds of a public house or hotel.

(3) Off-sale licences are held by catering companies simply to provide a 'springboard' for occasional licences, although no retail sales take place at the premises in respect of which the off-sale licence is held.

(4) In *Hollywood Bowl (Scotland) Ltd v Horsburgh*[4] an occasional licence had been obtained to overcome the effect of s 30(1)(b) which prevents a new licence coming into force until a competent objector's appeal is abandoned or determined in favour of the applicant. In certain respects the case is now something of a curiosity. It turned in part on the interpretation of the expression 'on such day' occurring in s 33(1), although at the time of the decision (June 1991) it was assumed that the words 'for such period of not more than 14 days' had been substituted[5], an assumption which was subsequently shaken[6]. The petitioners complained that the holders of the occasional licence had effectively circumvented the provisions of s 30(1)(b). The Lord Ordinary (Osborne) held that the petitioners, who had not objected in terms of s 16, had not established a title to sue, drawing a distinction between the conditions attaching to the grant of an occasional licence (which related to a high score bowling competition) and those

1 Cf s 33(6).
2 *R v Bow Street Licensing Justices ex parte Metropolitan Police Commissioner* [1983] 2 All ER 915; see also *R v Woolwich Licensing Justices ex parte Arnold* [1987] Crim LR 572.
3 [1952] 2 All ER 700.
4 1993 SLT 241.
5 1990 Act, Sch 8, para 9(a).
6 See *Mount Charlotte Investments plc v City of Glasgow Licensing Board* 1992 SCLR 311.

which would apply to an operative entertainment licence (the grant of which was the subject of appeal).

The assumption that the petitioners could have availed themselves of the objection mechanism provided by s 16 is questionable. Certainly, an occasional licence appears to be a 'licence granted under this Act' (s 139(1), to which the Lord Ordinary referred). Section 16(1) confers on certain persons or bodies a right to object 'in relation to any application to a licensing board for the grant (including the provisional grant) renewal or permanent transfer of a licence'. The objection must be relevant to one or more of the grounds of refusal contained in s 17; but that section is, quite clearly, concerned exclusively with applications for the grant, including the provisional grant, of a *new* (that is, permanent) licence (see s 17(2)). It is possibly the case that s 33 is, so to speak, self-contained so far as objections are concerned. Section 33(9) provides that the board 'shall make such arrangements as it thinks fit as respects the consideration of any objection', a power which may exclude the operation of s 16.

OCCASIONAL PERMISSIONS

Section 34 empowers a licensing board to:

'. . . grant an occasional permission to a person representing a voluntary organisation or a branch of a voluntary organisation authorising him to sell alcoholic liquor during such hours and for such period of not more than 14 days as the board may determine, in the course of catering for an event, arising from or related to the activities of the organisation, taking place outwith licensed premises'[1].

Prior to the amendment of s 34 the permission authorised the sale of alcoholic liquor 'on such day' as the board determined. The phrase raised interpretational difficulties[2] although the *Report of the Departmental Committee on Scottish Licensing Law*[3] had in view a 'period not exceeding 24 hours'.

'Voluntary organisation' is not defined. *Clayson* refers to 'an established society or organisation' and cited as an example 'a sports club which is not a registered club'[4]. Under the corresponding English provision the organisation must not be carried on 'for purposes of private gain'[5].

Section 34(7) brings into operation s 33(7)–(9)[6].

No more than four occasional permissions may be granted in any one year to the same voluntary organisation or the same branch of a voluntary organisation (s 34(2)).

The board may 'impose such conditions as it thinks fit including a condition as to the type of alcoholic liquor which may be sold under the permission'. Con-

1 Section 34(1) as amended by the 1990 Act, Sch 8, para 10.
2 See *Hollywood Bowl v Horsburgh* 1993 SLT 241, discussed above.
3 (Cmnd 5354) (*Clayson*) para 15.05.
4 Para 15.04.
5 Licensing (Occasional Permissions) Act 1983, s 1(6).
6 See 'Occasional licences', above.

travention of such a condition 'by the person to whom the permission is granted' is an offence (s 34(3))[1].

The premises or place which are the subject of the occasional permission are not 'licensed premises', but the provisions of s 68 apply as if they were, with the substitution of references to 'the holder of the permission' for the references to 'the holder of a licence' (s 34(4))[2] and the police are afforded entry powers under s 85 as if a licence (other than an off-sale licence) were in force (s 34(5)).

The person to whom the occasional permission is granted is deemed to be the holder of a public house licence and 'must ensure that the provisions of this Act or any byelaws or regulations made thereunder relating to the conduct of licensed premises are observed in the premises or place in respect of which the permission was granted' (s 34(6)). Failure to do so is an offence (s 34(6))[3]. (Since regulations are, of course, adjectival rather than substantive in nature it seems peculiar that their breach should attract a penal sanction). The person charged has the defence that 'he used due diligence to prevent the occurrence of the offence' (s 34(6), proviso).

1 Maximum penalty: level 3. No 'due diligence' defence is available.
2 As to the provisions of s 68, see Chapter 14.
3 Maximum penalty: level 3.

CHAPTER 8

Licensing board byelaws and regulations

BYELAWS[1]

Content

Section 38 empowers a licensing board to make byelaws for a number of specific purposes:

'(a) for closing licensed premises wholly or partially on New Year's Day, and on such other days not being more than four in any one year as the board may think expedient for special reasons'[2].

It will not be appropriate to provide for the complete closure of hotel premises so that the normal provision of facilities for residents is usually excepted and an exemption is commonly made for the sale or supply of alcoholic liquor to persons taking table meals. Sometimes, subject to those savings, premises are required to close on 2 January in any year when New Year's Day falls on a Sunday.

'(b) for prohibiting holders of licences from residing in their licensed premises, or for requiring the dwellinghouses of holders of licences to be separate from their licensed premises'[3].

Such a byelaw should clearly not apply to premises which are the subject of a hotel or restricted hotel licence. Even in the absence of a byelaw it is doubtful whether a licensing board would nowadays be prepared to grant a licence for premises which communicate with a private dwellinghouse[4]. The police have powers to enter licensed premises without a warrant (s 85) and comparatively restricted powers of entry to unlicensed premises (s 86). Serious supervisory difficulties would occur if there was the potential for the holder of a licence and his customers to retreat from licensed premises into private accommodation.

'(c) for requiring all wines, made-wines[5] and spirits sold by the holder of an off-sale licence to be sold in corked, stoppered or sealed vessels, cans, jars or casks'[6],

---

1 See also 14 *Stair Memorial Encyclopaedia* paras 270ff; 28 *Halsbury's Laws* (4th edn) paras 1323 ff.
2 Section 38(1)(a); see also *Herkes v Dickie* 1958 SC 51, 1959 SLT 74; *Henderson v Ross* 1928 JC 51, 1928 SLT 449.
3 Section 38(1)(b).
4 See Chapter 4.
5 'Wine' and 'made-wine' are defined in s 139(1) as having the meanings assigned by s 1 of the Alcoholic Liquor Duties Act 1979.
6 Section 38(1)(c).

subject to an exemption for 'licensed premises where no groceries are kept or sold and where a bona fide wholesale business in alcoholic liquor is carried on' (s 38(1), proviso). The words 'corked,' 'stoppered' and 'sealed' are not defined but for the purposes of s 145 of the Licensing (Scotland) Act 1959 (dealing with the delivery of alcohol to children) 'corked' meant 'closed with a plug or stopper' and 'sealed' meant 'secured with any substance without the destruction of which the plug or stopper cannot be withdrawn'. It has been held that gummed paper which can be removed without being ruined is not an adequate seal[1]. Byelaws of this nature are quite common but partially overlap with s 97(4) which provides that 'a holder of an off-sale licence or his employee or agent shall be guilty of an offence if he sells wine (including made-wine) in an open vessel'.

'(d) for requiring every holder of a hotel or public house licence to keep in his licensed premises and to renew from day to day a sufficient supply of drinking water, and such eatables as may be specified in the byelaw, and to display, offer and supply the same as may be prescribed by the byelaw'[2].

A byelaw made under this provision would typically contain a requirement that the licenceholder shall provide specified foodstuffs on demand at reasonable prices. It does not confer a power to make stipulations with regard to the provision or adequacy of kitchen facilities.

'(e) for printing a list of all applications coming before any meeting of the licensing board, with such other information as may be considered necessary by the board'[3].

A number of licensing boards, with and without byelaw authority, prepare (and sometimes sell) agendas which are available to the public. Where a request has been made by an applicant or his agent in terms of s 139(5) to the effect that only the address of an agent is to be published[4] it will not be appropriate to print the applicant's address in an agenda. A number of applications do not require to be published under the Act (for example, for permanent transfer or consent to alterations) and accordingly are not 'protected' by s 139(5). It is debatable whether an agenda prepared by virtue of a byelaw made under s 38(1)(e) is a 'requirement under this Act to cause to be published' an applicant's address but, without doubt, gratuitous and unnecessary publication is destructive of the purpose of s 139(5) and ought to be avoided.

'(f) for setting out conditions which may be attached to licences for the improvement of standards of, and conduct in, licensed premises'[5].

Conditions of this nature may only be attached when a licence is granted or renewed (s 38(3))[6].
    Predictably, the provision which affords licensing boards the greatest measure of discretion has also caused the most difficulty. The conditions which are in fact imposed generally fall into four broad categories:

1 *Mitchell v Crawshaw* [1903] 1 KB 701.
2 Section 38(1)d).
3 Section 38(1)(e).
4 For applications which require to be advertised, see s 12.
5 Section 38(1)(f).
6 'Granting' in that subsection includes granting by way of renewal (s 139(1)).

(1) Negative conditions which absolutely proscribe certain forms of activity in *all* licensed premises, such as entertainment in the form of exotic dancers or the gratuitous supply of alcoholic liquor[1].

(2) Negative conditions which are attached to a *particular* licence prohibiting, for example, the use of premises for live entertainment or the playing of games. This type of condition is rare.

(3) Positive conditions applying to all or some types of premises and requiring, for example, the display of notices setting out the effect of certain sections of the Act, such as s 68, or the separation of the liquor sales area from the remainder of off-sale licensed premises outwith off-sale trading hours or the maintenance of adequate lighting at all times.

(4) Positive conditions stipulating that all forms of musical entertainment (including 'karaoke' and singing by customers) and a host of other facilities such as coin-operated record players, games (including electronic games such as 'space invaders' or quiz machines), video players, tape machines, gramophone players and even wireless and television sets, may not be provided unless with the consent of the licensing board.

Category (4) is extremely troublesome. A number of licensing boards have managed to obtain confirmation from the Secretary of State[2] of byelaws which require a licenceholder to make application to the board for permission to provide the types of facilities mentioned above. The board will usually call for reports from the local environmental health department and possibly also from building control and the police.

Applications are commonly considered at a quarterly or adjourned quarterly meeting or sometimes under delegated powers (in which event a hearing should be arranged if the application is the subject of adverse official comment). They are not advertised nor is there usually any mechanism for objections so that those potentially affected, such as adjoining tenemental proprietors who may be disturbed by musical entertainment, will not be aware of the application. In practice, their interests are taken into account by the environmental health department. Although the possibility of noise nuisance is patently a legitimate concern it requires to be borne in mind that environmental health officers have effective noise control powers under the Control of Pollution Act 1974[3]. The relative informality of their participation in the byelaw process and the latitude which they are often afforded may allow them to achieve results which would be harder to accomplish under the 1974 Act, which provides for a right of appeal to the sheriff against a noise abatement notice; and where a board permits live entertainment subject to a condition, such as noise baffling measures, this may interfere with a statutory defence[4].

---

1 Section 149 of the Licensing (Scotland) Act 1959, which prohibited the sale or supply of a quantity of liquor in excess of the amount requested by the purchaser, was repealed on the recommendation of *Clayson* (para 15.18) but its spirit lives on.

2 As to the confirmation procedure, see below.

3 Control of Pollution Act 1974, s 58.

4 See Control of Pollution Act 1974, s 58; Control of Noise (Appeals)(Scotland) Regulations 1983, SI 1983/1455; articles at [1990] 9 LR 15 (at 16) and [1991] 5 LR 13 (subject to the caveat that ss 58 and 59 of the 1974 Act have not, in Scotland, been replaced by the new provisions of the Environmental Protection Act 1990); and, for an example of a prosecution in which the statutory defences were considered, *Tudhope v Lee* 1982 SCCR 409.

The legitimacy or otherwise of a category (4) byelaw is of considerable commercial importance to the licensed trade. Many hotel and public house businesses are substantially dependent on the provision of entertainment. A hotel would quite simply be unable to cater for function business if no such provision could be made and many public houses effectively compete with entertainment licensed premises by holding discothèques or 'karaoke' evenings.

A decision by a licensing board to refuse byelaw consent upon application being made could only be challenged by way of judicial review (or perhaps by an action of declarator on the ground that the byelaw is *ultra vires*)[1]. However, s 17(6) provides that (author's emphasis):

'any person entitled to appeal to the sheriff against the grant or refusal of a licence may appeal to the sheriff against a decision of a licensing board to attach or not to attach a condition *to a licence*, being a condition mentioned in section 38(3) . . .'.

This provision is a potent indicator that Parliament did not intend category (4) byelaws to be made. Otherwise, if the category (4) type are *intra vires* a licence-holder would have the rather bizarre right to appeal to the sheriff against the imposition of a condition requiring the board's consent, for, say, entertainment in his premises but no appeal against the withholding of permission where application had been made. No provision for application fees has been made in the current Order[2]. It may therefore be surmised that category (4) byelaws sit uncomfortably with the scheme of the Act.

The Scottish Home and Health department now appears to recognise this difficulty and regards category (4) byelaws as tantamount to 'unauthorised sub-delegation'. In the result, the Secretary of State's current practice is to confirm only those of the category (2) type. This is a relatively recent development and a large number of byelaws have managed to escape the net. Nevertheless, in these cases the possibility of a successful challenge remains open, for the reasons suggested above[3].

Where category (2) byelaws are in operation, permitting boards to attach prohibitive conditions to a particular licence, a procedure similar to the application procedure described above will be followed, except that, of course, the matter is raised by the board *ex proprio motu*. Since the condition is attached when a licence is granted or renewed it follows that the imposition of a condition may only take place at a quarterly meeting or any adjournment thereof. The right of appeal noted above and made available by s 17(6) extends to a competent objector but in practice this class of appeal is virtually unknown. The attachment of a condition is not suspended by an appeal.

'(g) for the granting of a licence other than the type applied for'[4].

1 *Allied Breweries (UK) Ltd v City of Glasgow District Licensing Board* 1985 SLT 302.
2 The Liquor Licensing (Fees) (Scotland) Order 1990, SI 1990/2458.
3 Note, however, that a petition for judicial review of a board's refusal to give byelaw consent for performances by a male dance group was dismissed as incompetent because *the specific performance dates had passed* and there was no longer any 'live issue' between the parties: *Marco's Leisure Ltd v West Lothian District Licensing Board* [1993] 13 LR 28.
4 Section 38(1)(g).

This provision may be invoked by the board or, at the board's discretion, by the applicant. It will only be appropriate to grant a substitute licence in a narrower form: for example, a restricted hotel licence in place of a hotel licence. Otherwise there is a risk that potential objectors will be prejudiced. The applicant for the grant or provisional grant of a new licence[1] (other than an off-sale licence) will require to have lodged with the clerk of the board a certificate of suitability in relation to planning (s 23)[2]. It must therefore be kept in view that the substitute licence should not be at variance with the planning permission[3]. Accordingly, where a Class 3 planning use has been authorised[4] permitting 'use for the sale of food or drink for consumption on the premises or of hot food for consumption off the premises' this will probably permit use under a refreshment licence[5] but not under a public house licence.

Where a different type of licence is granted against the wishes of the applicant this is tantamount to a refusal and may be appealed.

Confirmation of byelaws

Byelaws do not have effect until confirmed by the Secretary of State. Section 38(2) brings into operation 'with any necessary modifications' s 202(4)–(12) and (15) and s 204 of the Local Government (Scotland) Act 1973.

At least one month before the board makes application for confirmation, notice of its intention to do so, of the place where a copy of the byelaws may be inspected and of the authority to whom objections may be notified (ie, the Secretary of State) must be given in a newspaper circulating in the board's area or in such other manner as the Secretary of State may determine to be sufficient' (1973 Act, s 202(4)).

During this period a copy of the byelaws must be deposited at the district council's offices and made available for public inspection without payment at all reasonable hours (1973 Act, s 202(5)). Any person may require a copy for which a charge not exceeding ten pence for every hundred words may be made (1973 Act, s 202(6)).

Any person aggrieved by the proposed byelaws may within one month of the publication of the notice referred to above notify his objection in writing and the ground on which it is made to the Secretary of State (1973 Act, s 202(7)) who is bound to take into consideration objections received by him (1973 Act, s 207(8)). If he considers it necessary or desirable a local enquiry may be instituted (1973 Act, s 207(8)).

The Secretary of State may confirm with or without modification or refuse to confirm the byelaws and may fix a date on which they shall come into operation; if

1 Presumably 'granting of a licence' includes the grant and provisional grant of a new licence: see *Kelvinside Community Council v City of Glasgow Licensing Board* 1990 SCLR 110, 1990 SLT 725.
2 See Chapter 4.
3 See *Donald v Stirling District Licensing Board* 1992 SCLR (Notes) 369, 1992 SLT (Sh Ct) 75 in which the planning permission (covering restricted hotel use) was inadequate for the grant of a hotel licence.
4 Town and Country Planning (Use Classes) (Scotland) Order 1989, SI 1989/147.
5 At least one planning authority equiparates refreshment licence to public house use.

no date is fixed they automatically become effective one month after confirmation (1973 Act, s 207(10)). No doubt a decision to confirm byelaws despite objection is susceptible to judicial review.

Newspaper notification must thereafter be given of the confirmation, of the date on which the byelaws come into operation and of the place at which the byelaws may be inspected (1973 Act, s 207(11)). In addition, a print of the confirmed byelaws must be deposited at the district council offices and kept available for public inspection without payment. Copies must be furnished on request at a cost not exceeding twenty pence each (1973 Act, s 207(12)).

The licensing board has an implied power to revoke or amend byelaws[1] subject to compliance with the statutory procedure.

Vires of byelaws[2]

Byelaws must be *intra vires* and not exceed the powers conferred by the Act[3]. For example, where byelaws were authorised for the suppression of nuisance, a byelaw purporting to prohibit bill-posting was held to be *ultra vires*: such activity could, but would not always, amount to a nuisance[4].

They must be certain and may not be unreasonable, oppressive or manifestly unjust[5].

They cannot subvert the general law[6]. For example, it is doubtful whether a byelaw could require licenceholders to remain open for business during the whole permitted hours (see s 54(5)). The Secretary of State has refused to confirm a proposed byelaw which would have enabled a board to place a limitation on the numbers of persons to be admitted to licensed premises, possibly because such a substantive proposal had already been rejected by Parliament during the progress of the 1990 Act.

While the court will generally be reluctant to set aside as unreasonable any byelaw which has been properly confirmed by the Secretary of State, confirmation of itself will not prevent challenge on the ground that it is *ultra vires*[7].

Byelaws will not be valid if the prescribed procedure has been deserted[8].

Byelaws made prior to the commencement of the 1976 Act continue to have effect (s 140(6)).

Breach of a byelaw

The holder of a licence or his employee or agent is guilty of an offence if he commits a breach of any byelaw or any condition attached by a byelaw (s 38(4)).

1 Interpretation Act 1978, ss 14, 21(1), Sch 2, para 3.
2 See 1 *Stair Memorial Encyclopaedia* para 299; 14 *Stair Memorial Encyclopaedia* paras 291 ff.
3 *Kerr v Auld* (1890) 18 R (J) 12.
4 *Eastburn v Wood* (1892) 19 R (J) 100.
5 *Dunsmore v Lindsay* (1903) 6 F (J) 14.
6 *Kerr v Hood* 1907 SC 895.
7 *Scott v Glasgow Corporation* 1944 SC 97.
8 *Dundee Combination Parish Council v Secretary of State for Scotland* (1901) 3 F 848, (1901) 9 SLT 54; and (where no byelaw existed) *Allied Breweries (UK) Ltd v City of Glasgow District Licensing Board* 1985 SLT 302.

Failure to provide potato crisps in licensed premises could thus become a criminal matter[1]. In a prosecution the Crown must prove the byelaw which has allegedly been breached[2]. Section 204 of the 1973 Act provides that the production of a copy of a byelaw endorsed with a certificate by 'the proper officer'[3] stating that the byelaw was made, that the copy is a true copy, that the byelaw was confirmed on a specified date by the Secretary of State and specifying the commencement date, if any, fixed by him, shall be 'sufficient evidence of the facts stated in the certificate'. The accused may, however, seek to impugn the validity of a byelaw, although 'the determination of such a question in a summary process may be inconvenient'[4].

Where the offence relates to the breach of a condition attached to a licence by s 38(3) it will be necessary to produce the licence itself.

The maximum penalty is a level 3 fine. Both the premises and the licenceholder (who has vicarious responsibility; see s 67(2)) are liable to disqualification (see Sch 5) in the event of a conviction, which must be notified by the clerk of court to the clerk of the board (s 129).

A board is entitled to take the breach of a byelaw into account when considering the fitness of an applicant for the permanent transfer of a licence (s 17(3)) or for confirmation of an interim transfer (s 25(4A)) and when considering the possible suspension of the licence (s 31(3)(a)).

REGULATIONS

Permitted content

Section 37, which enables licensing boards to make regulations, falls essentially into four parts.
(1) Regulations may be made:

'. . . with respect to the making of applications for licences (including occasional licences and occasional permissions), extension [sic] of permitted hours and restriction of the terminal permitted hours and the procedure following thereon. . .'.

Section 63 of the Licensing (Scotland) Act 1959, from which s 37 is derived, allowed a licensing court at any general half-yearly meeting to make regulations 'with respect to the making of applications for the grant of certificates and the procedure following thereon'. The draftsman of the 1976 Act has widened the types of applications which are susceptible to regulation but in a curious, eclectic

---

1 In terms of a byelaw made under s 38(1)(d). For an example of the 'extravagant' creation of a criminal offence by means of a byelaw, see *Eastburn v Wood* (1892) 19 R (J) 100.
2 See *Herkes v Dickie* 1958 JC 51, 1959 SLT 74; and *Renton and Brown's Criminal Procedure*, 5th edn, paras. 13-48, 13-49.
3 Presumably the clerk: see 1973 Act, s 235(3).
4 See *Renton and Brown's Criminal Procedure*, 5th edn, para 13-50, and cases cited. It has been suggested in an English case, *Bugg v Director of Public Prosecutions*, Independent, 8 September 1992, unreported, that substantive invalidity (for example, lack of clarity or patent unreasonableness) may be challenged in the context of criminal proceedings, while matters of procedural validity are for the civil courts to determine.

fashion, without much regard for the vocabulary of the Act and, with at least one significant omission.

For example, while regulations may be prescriptive of the procedure to be followed in an application 'for restriction of the terminal hours' (presumably a reference to an evening restriction order but not an afternoon or Sunday restriction order) (s 65), no such power exists in relation to, say, the suspension of a licence (s 31), the making of a closure order (s 32) or a temporary restriction order (s 66). Similarly, there is no regulating ability in relation to applications for consent to the reconstruction, extension or alteration of licensed premises in terms of s 35 (although plans may be required by the board by virtue of s 35(2)), despite a *Clayson* recommendation[1]. However, many boards have not been deterred by this *lacuna* and may require, for example, an inspection of the altered premises by the board's officials.

The words 'applications for licences' are no doubt apt to include applications for the grant or provisional grant of a new licence, a provisional licence in terms of s 27 and, arguably, the renewal of a licence (s 139(1))[2]. They probably do not embrace applications for the affirmation or finalisation of the provisional grant of a new licence, although s 26(5) allows a board to prescribe a notice period for an intention to finalise (while affirmation applications may be disposed of at any meeting held not earlier than 14 days after application is made, in terms of s 26 (3)).

While regulations will generally not be appropriate in relation to regular extensions of the permitted hours, occasional extension applications[3] are usually made subject to time limits for their submission (ranging from 7 to 21 days), subject to a dispensation for applications made in respect of funeral parties. Provision should be made for a hearing before an occasional extension application is refused or granted in part only.

(2) Such regulations may include:

'. . . provisions designed to assist the board in determining the fitness of applicants to hold licences and the expediency of granting licences for the premises in respect of which application is made'.

In practice, boards will usually seek to determine the fitness of applicants by requiring character references. Their utility is open to doubt and a police report is clearly more informative. Since a board is entitled to refuse an application for inter alia the grant or provisional grant of a new licence on the basis that 'the person on whose behalf or for whose benefit the applicant will manage the premises' is not 'a fit and proper person to be the holder of a licence' (s 17(1)(a)) it would appear reasonable that regulations relative to this ground should be permitted, although, on a very strict construction, s 37 only authorises regulatory provisions relative to applicants themselves. At least one board requires a transfer applicant to certify that he is not to manage the premises for another party or to provide details of the true owner of the business.

It is difficult to ascribe much meaning to the words 'the expediency of granting licences for the premises in respect of which application is made', carried over

---

1 Para 14.32.
2 'Grant' in relation to a licence includes grant by way of renewal.
3 For extensions of the permitted hours, see Chapter 10.

from s 63 of the Licensing (Scotland) Act 1959, which contained no requirement as to certificates of suitability (s 23). A board may have a regulation requiring consultation with local authority departments as to the condition of premises before renewing a licence[1], but has a discretion to do so in any event[2].

(3) A licensing board may also make regulations '. . . with respect to the procedure to be followed in transferring licences under this Act'.

A licence may be transferred temporarily and then permanently or simply permanently to 'a new tenant or to a new or existing occupant of any licensed premises'. The consent of the current licenceholder, although not a requirement of the Act, is frequently prescribed by regulation. There will, of course, be circumstances in which such consent is not available, commonly where the holder of a standard security has foreclosed or a lease has been irritated. It is probably more appropriate that the applicant for transfer be required to produce proof of his status as 'a new tenant or a new or existing occupant' by way of his title, lease, missives or other suitable documentation. Some clerks regard consent letters as having virtually no evidential value[3].

Provision is also made in s 25(2) for different types of interim transfers, for example, to the executors of a licenceholder who has died before the expiry of the licence. The applicant must be in possession of the premises and the board may require proof of that fact.

(4) Finally, regulations may be made 'with respect to any matters which, by virtue of this Act, may be prescribed'[4]. For example, provision is made for various types of applications to be 'in such form as may be prescribed'[5]. Regulations are also customarily employed to prescribe time limits for the submission of applications in cases where the Act is silent. While notice of an intention to request finalisation of the provisional grant of a new licence may be prescribed (s 26(5)) and the specific types of applications mentioned in s 37 can no doubt be subjected to deadlines (provided there is no conflict with s 10(1)), in relation to a number of applications (under s 35, for example) no prescriptive power is given but time limits are fixed as a matter of practical necessity.

Vires of regulations

Regulations must not conflict with the substantive provisions of the Act[6]. For example, they cannot alter the time limits for the submission of applications, although one board requires applications for new licences to be lodged seven weeks before the board meeting at which they are to be considered[7]. It is highly doubtful whether they may provide for the charging of fees beyond those prescribed by statutory instrument. The practice of requiring applications in terms of s 25(3) for the substitution of a new employee or agent to be lodged within a

---

1 As in *Coppola v Midlothian District Licensing Board* 1983 SLT (Sh Ct) 95.
2 See *Fitzpatrick v Glasgow District Licensing Board* 1978 SLT (Sh Ct) 63.
3 Transfers are considered in Chapter 5.
4 'Prescribed' is defined in s 139(1) as 'prescribed by regulations made under section 37 of this Act'.
5 Eg those listed in s 10(6).
6 See *McCallum v Buchanan Smith* 1951 SC 73.
7 Cf s 10(1).

specified time from the previous nominee's departure is probably *ultra vires* and its breach may not in any event be visited with any direct sanction[1], but the application may be lodged so late as to preclude disposal within the eight-week period specified in s 11 (4).

A regulation that certificates of suitability in terms of s 23 accompany an application for the grant or provisional grant of a new licence (other than an off-sale licence) may be open to challenge on the ground that it interferes with the discretionary mechanism provided by s 13(2)[2].

As mentioned above, regulations may only be made *quoad* the matters specified.

1 There is no penal aspect to regulations except that in terms of s 34(6) the holder of an occasional permission commits an offence if he fails to observe inter alia regulations relating to the conduct of licensed premises.
2 See Chapter 4.

CHAPTER 9

Duration, renewal and suspension of licences

LICENCES PROVISIONALLY GRANTED

Duration

A licence provisionally granted under s 26(1) or (2) has effect until the quarterly meeting of the licensing board one year after the meeting at which it was granted or last renewed (s 26(8))[1].

A licence provisionally granted under s 26(2), proceeding initially upon a site plan and general description, will however become 'ineffective' unless affirmed in terms of s 26(3) within twelve months of the provisional grant.

Renewal procedure

The Act contains no specific procedural provisions for the renewal of provisional licences. By implication, applications must be lodged not less than five weeks before the first day of the quarterly meeting (s 10(1))[2], subject to the board's discretion to entertain a late application (s 13(2))[3].

The application need not be advertised in terms of s 12, nor is it necessary to display or serve a notice in terms of s 10(3) and (5).

Where no request for Sunday permitted hours was made in terms of s 10(3A) in connection with the provisional grant of a public house or refreshment licence it is doubtful whether the deficiency may be rectified at this stage.

Similarly, it appears that an application for a children's certificate would require to have been made with the provisional grant application[4] but equally that such certificate, where originally granted, does not require to be the subject of separate renewal[5].

Ground of refusal

The Act simply provides that 'A licensing board may refuse to renew a licence provisionally granted . . . if the board considers that there has been unreasonable delay on the part of the applicant in completing the premises' (s 26(9)).

---

1 Substituting in s 30(3) a reference to one year instead of a reference to three years.
2 See below in relation to the renewal of 'full' licences.
3 See below.
4 See the 1990 Act, s 49(1).
5 Note, however, that re-application for a children's certificate is required when the 'full' licence to which it relates is renewed: see Chapter 14 below.

Although there is a right of appeal to the sheriff against a board's decision to refuse affirmation in terms of s 26(2) or finalisation under s 26(4) (s 26(10)), no specific provision is made as respects the refusal of a renewal application; but s 30(5)(b), which provides for the extended currency of a licence on the dependency of an appeal, is expressly applied to provisional grants by s 26(8).

Where the holder of a provisional grant suspects that its renewal may be in jeopardy he may make simultaneous application for a fresh provisional grant, which may only be refused on limited grounds (see s 17(1)).

'FULL' LICENCES

Duration

Where the provisional grant of a new licence has been declared final it appears that the currency of the full licence which then comes into force is initially linked to the expiry date of the provisional grant. In terms of s 26(8), the normal three-year validity (see below) does not apply until the date of the first renewal after finalisation.

For example, if a licence was provisionally granted at the quarterly board meeting in October 1993 and finalised in, say, June 1994, the full licence would require to be renewed at the October 1994 meeting.

Where a finalisation application is approved between submission of an application to renew the provisional grant and the date of the board meeting, bringing the full licence into force, the renewal application could conceivably be regarded as incompetent. Purist clerks may well require the late submission of an application to renew the full licence in terms of s 13(2)[1].

Although the interpretation of s 26(8) suggested above enjoys majority support, the unsatisfactory wording of the provisions has however, generated other constructions. In some districts the view is taken that a licence should be granted for three years after finalisation; in others the licence runs for one year after finalisation, an interpretation which encounters the difficulty that finalisation is often granted outwith quarterly meetings under delegated powers (s 5(1)), in which event the anniversary thereof will almost certainly not coincide with a quarterly meeting.

All licences, including, after the first renewal, those which have come into force following finalisation of a provisional grant, have effect until the quarterly meeting of the licensing board three years after the meeting at which the licence was granted or renewed (s 30(3)).

Surrender

The Act makes no provision for the surrender of licences during their currency. The practice is, however, well-established in Scotland and was homologated in

---

1 As to the consideration of late applications, see below.

D & A Haddow Ltd v City of Glasgow District Licensing Board[1] where the sheriff granted a licence subject to the surrender of another in the area. Indeed, the surrender of an existing licence may be necessary where a new licence application is made for the purpose of removing a condition (for example, under s 29) or where it is desired to change from one type of licence to another.

Some licensing boards are prepared to grant a licence to a manager in his name alone, a practice implicitly approved in *Tominey v City of Glasgow District Licensing Board*[2] (but not appropriate where the premises are to be managed for behoof of a non-natural person)[3].

Although a dismissed manager is bound to deliver his licence to his employer[4], the owner of the business is subject to the obvious risk of surrender. Such a difficulty was addressed in *Drury v Scunthorpe Licensing Justices*[5]. Following his suspension for alleged irregularities, a sole licensee gave written notice to the licensing committee of his wish to 'terminate' his licence with immediate effect (although contractually bound not to do so). The committee purported to accept the letter as surrender of the licence. On appeal by the owners of the premises, the High Court held that the practice of surrender was 'well-established' in circumstances connected with the grant of a substitute licence. However, where an attempt was made to surrender a licence by means of a letter which contained no information as to the reasons, the justices should make enquiry into the circumstances before deciding whether or not to accept surrender; it was desirable, 'if not indeed necessary', such acceptance should take place in open court.

There is also authority for the proposition that where a licenceholder abandons premises the licence is effectively surrendered. Where magistrates refused to renew a transfer, the original certificate holder was convicted of trafficking after resuming possession of the premises. The Lord President (Robertson) said: 'Nothing . . . will ever revive the right of a man who . . . has removed or yielded up possession of the premises to which the certificate relates'[6].

In *West Wemyss United Services Club, Applicants*[7] the sheriff (J A Lillie, KC) held that registration of a club could competently be granted where the club premises were prima facie the subject of a public house certificate whose holder had decamped:

'A pre-requisite of a certificate empowering a particular person to sell liquor in particular premises is . . . possession of the premises by that person. If, holding a certificate in respect of certain premises, he ceases from whatever cause to possess them, the sale of exciseable liquor in these premises becomes illegal unless and until authorised of new . . . the certificate . . . fell to all effects with the surrender of possession'.

More recently, in *Edward Barrett Ltd v City of Dundee District Licensing Board*[8] it was held that a betting office licence could competently be granted to a new

---

1 1983 SLT (Sh Ct) 5. See also *Connelly v Glasgow Licensing Authority* 1964 SLT (Sh Ct) 77; *W S Murphy Ltd v Alloa Burgh Licensing Authority* 1973 SLT (Sh Ct) 2.
2 1984 SLT (Sh Ct) 2.
3 See *Paterson v City of Glasgow District Licensing Board* 1982 SLT (Sh Ct) 37.
4 *Clift v Portobello Pier Co* (1877) 4 R 462, (1877) 14 SLR 344.
5 [1993] 12 LR 13.
6 *Campbell v Neilson* (1897) 24 R (J) 28.
7 1948 SLT (Sh Ct) 33.
8 1992 SLT 963.

occupant of premises where such a licence was already *ex facie* in existence but the holder had ceased to be the tenant. Although it must, of course, be kept in view that the case was decided under different legislation, the following passage is of interest in the present context:

'It may be said, as counsel for [the board] submitted, that upon ceasing to be the tenant and hence have any right to occupy the premises, the licence was implicitly surrendered by the petitioners. Rather, I incline to the view that the licence thereafter ceased to be of effect: it could not be transferred'[1].

Despite the doubts which these authorities may raise, in modern practice, where the licenceholder quits the premises authority for the sale of alcoholic liquor is reinstated by a transfer of the licence, rather than by application for a new licence. This view appears to have been endorsed in *Tong v City of Glasgow District Licensing Board*[2], where the sheriff held that the board had erred by considering that a licence was terminated as soon as the licenceholder ceased trading, although it appears that the possibility of 'constructive surrender' was not fully explored:

'In my view the [board] were wrong in holding that the licence granted to the appellant on 1 December 1988 for a period of three years was no longer in force in October 1991. It still existed ex facie of its terms and no argument or authority was addressed to me by the board to the contrary'.

Renewal procedure

A renewal application requires to be lodged with the clerk not later than five weeks before the first day of the board meeting at which the application is to be considered (s 10(1))[3]. If no application is made the licence expires on the first day of the quarterly meeting (s 30(4))[4]. The application does not require to be advertised and may be granted (but not refused) under a delegated powers arrangement (s 5(1), (2)(c)), except where a competent objection has been lodged (see s 5(2)(b)). In practice, applications are almost always considered at quarterly meetings.

Objection to the application may be taken by the persons or bodies listed in s 16(1) and must be relevant to a ground of refusal (s 16(5)). The chief constable is additionally empowered to submit observations.

It must not be refused unless the applicant fails to attend the board meeting, having been cited to do so (s 15)[5]. He has, of course, a right to be heard in support

---

1 1992 SLT 963 at 966F. It requires to be borne in mind, however, that there is no mechanism for the transfer of betting office licences under the Betting, Gaming and Lotteries Act 1963.
2 1992 GWD 19-1125, Sh Ct.
3 'Not later than': see discussion of time limits in Chapter 1.
4 Subject to the board's power to entertain a late application in terms s 13(2). See *Indpine Ltd v City of Dundee District Licensing Board* 1992 SCLR 113 (OH), 1992 SCLR 353, 1992 SLT 473 (IH), discussed below.
5 Receipt of an objection (s 16) or police observations (s 16A) does not operate as a citation.

of the application[1]. Where he fails to attend, despite receiving a citation, that fact alone will not support a refusal[2].

The board must consult the fire authority for the area and may call for a plan of the premises to be lodged with the clerk (s 24). In practice, boards usually consult the local environmental health and building control departments, as well as the police.

Late renewal applications

A renewal application must be lodged 'with the clerk of the licensing board within whose area the premises are situated not later than five weeks before the first day of the meeting of the board at which the application is to be considered' (s 10(1))[3].

Where the first day of the meeting is rescheduled within the eight-week period stipulated in s 4(1)(a), an application lodged after the original deadline is not thereby rendered timeous[4].

The rejection of an application by the clerk as out of time should be challenged by judicial review[5]. An appeal to the sheriff may only be made against a decision of the board and the correctness of the decision in *M Milne Ltd v City of Glasgow District Licensing Board*[6], in which the sheriff took the view that the clerk's refusal to accept a late renewal application was constructively a decision of the board is open to considerable doubt.

In terms of s 13(2) where an applicant for inter alia renewal[7] has, through inadvertence or misadventure, failed to comply with any of the preliminary requirements of the Act, the board may, if if thinks fit, and upon such terms as the board thinks proper, postpone consideration of the application to an adjourned meeting (s 13(2)(a)). A similar discretion exists where the applicant, having duly lodged his application, has died before the meeting of the board at which the application was to be heard; at the adjourned meeting the licence may be renewed in name of the deceased's executors, representatives or disponees, provided that they are 'possessed of the premises' (s 13(2)(b)). A licence renewed in the name of a deceased person is a nullity[8].

This discretion is very wide. Negligence on the part of an adviser is generally not regarded as a good excuse. Late applicants often advance the explanation that they have in the preceding three years obtained the licence by way of transfer and assumed that it ran for three years from the date of the transfer. Clerks are apt to

---

1 *Baillie v Wilson* 1917 SC 55, 1916 2 SLT 252. See also *C R S Leisure Ltd v Dumbarton District Licensing Board* 1989 SCLR 566, 1990 SLT 200.
2 *Bury v Kilmarnock and Loudoun District Licensing Board* 1988 SCLR 436, 1989 SLT 110.
3 This means, in effect, 'not later than five clear weeks': see *Main v City of Glasgow District Licensing Board* 1987 SLT 305, discussed at 1987 SLT (News) 157 and 353.
4 See *Boag v Teacher* (1900) 2 F 804, (1900) 7 SLT 460. Cf *Ballantyne v City of Glasgow District Licensing Board* 1987 SLT 745.
5 *Tait v Horsborough* 1987 SCLR 310, (sub nom. *Tait v City of Glasgow District Licensing Board*) 1987 SLT 340.
6 1987 SLT (Sh Ct) 145.
7 The subsection refers to 'an applicant for the grant of a licence': 'grant' is defined in s 139(1) as including 'grant by way of renewal'.
8 *Cowles v Gale* (1871) 7 Ch App 12.

point out, however, that upon completion of a transfer licences are reissued or notes of transfer are provided containing the proper expiry date.

If a motion under s 13(2) is successful the consideration of the application is continued to an adjourned meeting, which must be held during the period of one month next following the first day of the meeting (s 4(2)). Although there is nothing to prevent a board holding an adjourned meeting immediately upon conclusion of the other business care requires to be taken that such a procedure does not prejudice potential objectors and that other preliminary requirements are not overlooked[1].

Where the board refuses to exercise its discretion in favour of the applicant the licence expires (see s 30(3), (4), (5))[2]. Such a refusal is not *a refusal of the application*, rather a critically different refusal *to consider* the application, and accordingly is not a 'decision' which is susceptible to appeal in terms of s 39[3].

The board's decision is, however, susceptible to challenge by judicial review, but since there is no obligation to provide a statement of reasons in terms of s 18 the petitioner faces an arduous task. In *Purdon v Glasgow District Licensing Board*[4] the Lord Ordinary (Davidson) observed:

'[I]f an authority is not obliged to give reasons for its decision, it may, as here, become more difficult to present a successful challenge. . . In an application for judicial review the onus rests on [the petitioner] to demonstrate that the decision challenged is irrational. In my opinion the absence of reasons can help an applicant only if on a consideration of the whole averments the court inclines to the conclusion that there is no material upon which a rational refusal could be based'.

A broadly similar view was expressed by Lord Keith in *R v Secretary of State for Trade and Industry ex parte Lonhro*[5]:

'The absence of reasons for a decision where there is no duty to give them cannot of itself provide any support for the suggested irrationality of the decision. The only significance of the absence of reasons is that if all other known facts and circumstances appear to point overwhelmingly in favour of a different decision, the decision-maker, who has given no reasons, cannot complain if the court draws the inference that he had no rational reason for his decision'[6].

Judicial review proceedings do not extend the currency of the licence ad interim[7]. On that account appeals to the sheriff are sometimes taken essentially in an attempt to preserve the *ex facie* validity of the licence until an application for a new licence is granted at the first opportunity, after which the appeal is abandoned. This practice is clearly open to challenge.

---

1 See s 10(7) (application to be made available for public inspection) and s 24(1) (consultation with fire authority).
2 See also *Indpine Ltd v City of Dundee District Licensing Board* 1992 SCLR 113 (OH), 1992 SCLR 353, 1992 SLT 473 (IH), discussed below.
3 Cf *M Milne Ltd v City of Glasgow District Licensing Board* 1987 SLT (Sh Ct) 145. In *Purdon v Glasgow District Licensing Board* 1988 SCLR 466, 1989 SLT 201 the petitioner conceded the absence of a right of appeal.
4 See above.
5 [1989] 1 WLR 525.
6 See also *R v Liverpool Crown Court ex parte Lennon and Hongkins* [1991] 4 LR 22.
7 Cf s 30(5). In *Purdon v Glasgow District Licensing Board* 1988 SCLR 466, 1989 SLT 201, an appropriate declarator was sought.

The law relating to late renewal applications has been significantly developed by *Indpine Ltd v City of Dundee District Licensing Board*[1]. In *Purdon*[2] the renewal application was lodged after the first day of the board's quarterly meeting but three days before an adjourned meeting. No issue was taken as to the competency of this procedure. However, in *Indpine Ltd* the board's clerk rejected as incompetent a renewal application lodged in similar circumstances on the basis that the licence had expired on the first day of the meeting and no licence thereafter existed in respect of which the petitioners could be described as 'an applicant' for the purpose of s 13(2).

The Lord Ordinary (Cameron of Lochbroom) held that the words 'meeting' and 'quarterly meeting' must be intended to cover all of the days on which a licensing board meets for the discharge of its functions in terms of s 4[3]; if the application was made while the board was still meeting nothing in the scheme of the Act prevented consideration in terms of s 13(2). The reference in s 10(1) to the first day of the meeting was 'no more than a convenient way of determining the *terminus ad quem* for the purpose of constituting the period within which an application is to be timeously lodged'. A reclaiming motion was refused.

The view expressed in *Purdon*[4] that the petitioner's licence *had* expired notwithstanding the late submission of a renewal application at the time of the board meeting is effectively overruled by the decision in *Indpine Ltd* that proper weight requires to be given to the words 'Subject to section 13(2)' in s 30(4).

If the licence is lost by reason of a failure to lodge any application or following the board's refusal to adjourn in terms of s 13(2), s 33 which empowers a board to grant an occasional licence for unlicensed premises is potentially available. In *R v Woolwich Licensing Justices ex parte Arnold*[5] a club made application for an occasional licence having failed to renew its registration. The court quashed the magistrates' refusal of the licence and held inter alia that the inadvertent failure to renew the registration was 'an occasion' justifying an occasional licence.

Grounds of refusal

An application for the renewal of a licence may only be refused on the grounds set out in s 17(1)(a)–(c). A refusal on any other ground is incompetent[6].

The relevant grounds are discussed in detail in Chapter 4. The material differences in their applicability to the renewal of a licence are now considered.

(1) Fitness of the applicant. In terms of s 17(1)(a) the renewal application is to be refused if the board finds that:

---

1 1992 SCLR 113 (OH), 1992 SCLR 353, 1992 SLT 473 (IH).
2 See above.
3 See also *Tarditi v Drummond* 1989 SCLR 201, 1989 SLT 554.
4 See above.
5 [1987] Crim LR 572. See also *R v Bow Street Licensing Justices ex parte Metropolitan Police Commissioner* [1983] 2 All ER 915, [1984] 1 WLR 93.
6 *Mount Charlotte Investments plc v City of Glasgow Licensing Board* 1992 SCLR 311.

'the applicant, or the person on whose behalf or for whose benefit the applicant will manage the premises or, in the case of an application to which section 11 of this Act applies, the applicant or the employee or agent named in the application is not a fit and proper person to be the holder of a licence'[1].

If the applicant has committed any offence under the Act since the licence was granted or last renewed an extract of the conviction should have been transmitted to the clerk of the board (s 129). In any event, the police will usually make a fresh criminal records check.

The fitness of limited companies and, to a lesser extent, partnerships, is something of a moving target and altogether more problematic. It would appear that where a company which was once controlled by unsuitable individuals has carried out a restructuring exercise any taint which had existed in the past may be cured when the licence is due for renewal. In *R v Knightsbridge Crown Court*[2] the appellant company was completely restructured pending appeal from the Crown Court and, since it was held that the company's suitability fell to be determined at the time of the appeal hearing, the new owners were able to claim successfully that they were fit to hold a licence.

Similarly, in *Fereneze Leisure Ltd v Renfrew District Licensing Board*[3] the board's appeal to the Inner House as to the fitness of a limited company applicant had become largely academic because of a restructuring and change of directors ad interim; and in *Canavan v Carmichael*[4] the High Court abated the sentence imposed on a licenceholder where the offence had actually been committed by a co-accused who had since been expelled from the partnership which operated the business.

It is a curious feature of the Act that where a licence has been suspended for a period of up to one year or its unexpired portion, on the basis that the holder 'is no longer a fit and proper person' (s 31), it may well be renewed shortly after the expiry of the suspension period.

(2) Suitability of premises. Section 17(1)(b) provides the following ground of refusal:

'that the premises to which the application relates are not suitable or convenient for the sale of alcoholic liquor, having regard to their location, their character and condition, the nature and extent of the proposed use of the premises, and the persons likely to resort to the premises'.

Licensing boards are frequently disinclined to renew licences held in respect of premises which have not been open to the public for some considerable time, where there is no immediate prospect of re-opening.

It has been held that a licensing board erred in law by taking cognisance of

---

1 Where a licence is held in terms of s 11, the director of a company is not a person 'for whose benefit' the premises are operated: *Fereneze Leisure Ltd v Renfrew District Licensing Board* 1991 SCLR 751, 1992 SLT 604.
2 [1982] QB 304, [1981] 3 WLR 640, sub nom *R v Crown Court at Knightsbridge ex parte International Sporting Club (London) Ltd* [1981] 3 All ER 417.
3 1991 SCLR 751, 1992 SLT 604; see also *Singh and Kaur v Kirkcaldy District Licensing Board* 1988 SLT 286 and commentary to *Fereneze Leisure Ltd* 1991 SCLR 751 at 758.
4 1989 SCCR 480.

s 17(1)(d) (the 'overprovision' ground of refusal in relation to new licence applications) where the view was formed that a renewal in such circumstances could adversely affect future applications for new licences in the same locality[1].

However, it may be open to a board to find that prolonged closure is a relevant consideration for the purposes of s 17(1)(b).

In *Mount Charlotte Investments plc*[1] public house premises had not been in operation for two-and-a-half years. No evidence was before the board as to their actual physical condition. The sheriff (F J Keane) said:

'To my mind, "condition" can connote more than a physical state in relation to premises. It can relate to their appearance, physical state and whether they are used or unused, refurbished or otherwise. The words "condition" and "character" where they occur in section 17(1)(b) . . . appear to be of equivalent meaning . . . [The board] were entitled to look at the lack of use of the premises and their proposed refurbishment as their "condition"'.

In the circumstances of the case, however, the board had exercised their discretion in an unreasonable manner:

'in that they formed a view on the condition of the premises apparently based purely on the passage of time and lack of use without providing the applicant with the opportunity to be heard on matters which might have qualified the condition: eg, the premises might be in a pristine state ready for inspection or the decision regarding their future use might be accelerated'.

Although the state of closure is held to be a relevant matter it is less than clear whether this factor would per se justify refusal of a renewal application if the premises were in good condition. Support for the view that no such justification exists may be found in s 54(5) which provides that 'Nothing in this Act shall be taken to require any premises to be open for the sale or supply of alcoholic liquor during the permitted hours'. Indeed, in *West Wemyss United Services Club, Applicants*[2] the sheriff (J A Lillie, KC) observed: 'In England it has been laid down that a public-house which is not an inn involves the holder of a licence in no obligation to the public to keep open the premises or sell liquor to anyone'[3].

The availability of seasonal licences (s 62) seems to suggest that a licenceholder who contemplates periods of closure requires the sanction of the licensing board to exempt himself from criticism. Specific provision is made for the closure of residential parts of hotels (s 62(1)(b)), which may, in any event, be regarded as forming a special category. In terms of s 139(1), by definition a hotel has 'apartments set apart exclusively for the sleeping accommodation of travellers'. For the purposes of the Hotel Proprietors Act 1956, 'hotel' means 'an establishment held out by the proprietor as offering food and drink and, if so required, sleeping accommodation, without special contract, to any traveller presenting himself who appears able and willing to pay a reasonable sum for the services and facilities provided and who is in a fit state to be received'[4], although in *West*

1 *Mount Charlotte Investments plc v City of Glasgow Licensing Board* 1992 SCLR 311.
2 1948 SLT (Sh Ct) 33.
3 Referring to *R v Sussex Confirming Authority ex parte Tamplin & Sons Brewery (Brighton) Ltd* [1937] 4 All ER 106.
4 Hotel Proprietors Act 1956, s 1(3).

Wemyss United Services Club, Applicants[1] the sheriff observed that: 'So far as appears, the public interest to have travellers accommodated in an inn licensed for the sale of liquor does not extend to the supplying of them with liquor'.

In England, where licensing justices enjoy a much wider discretion than their Scottish counterparts, renewal of a licence may be refused where premises have been closed for a significant period so as to suggest that need in the area is not being met or the closure demonstrates the absence of such need.

Before renewing a licence, the licensing board must consult with the fire authority (s 24(1))[2]. In practice, reports will usually also be obtained from the district council's building control and environmental health departments. These reports are frequently a source of difficulty, not least because local authority departments have, since the inception of the Act, adopted in many cases an increasingly expansionist approach to the supervision of licensed premises, possibly because the powers afforded to a licensing board provide a more effective compulsitor than is available under other legislation. It is, for example, not uncommon to find that premises are subject to extensive criticism as to their condition, while no action is contemplated under s 12 of the Food Safety Act 1990.

In an English case[3], a local authority raised objections relating to the suitability and condition of premises on an application for transfer of a justices' licence, based on alleged contraventions of the Food Hygiene (General) Regulations 1970 and the Health and Safety at Work Etc Act 1974. It was prepared to withdraw its objections if an undertaking was given by the applicants that the alleged defects would be remedied. The Divisional court held that the sole issue was the applicant's fitness to hold a licence (also the position in relation to Scottish transfers) but, more materially, that the Licensing Act 1964 could not be used as a means to enforce statutory requirements outside the licensing field. It was, however, prepared to find that the condition of premises was relevant in an assessment of the applicants' fitness to hold a licence.

It has, however, been held in Scotland that the availability of another remedy does not disenfranchise qualified objectors. In *Johnston v City of Edinburgh District Licensing Board*[4] the First Division observed:

'It should be noted that counsel for the appellant argued that the objectors were using the powers of the licensing board to refuse an application for a licence in order to obtain a result in their favour which could and should be the subject of proceedings in court by way of interdict or by referral to an official body such as the Environmental Health Department. The point was not developed but it seems to be suggested that this was a view which had been expressed in England. It is not necessary to give a ruling on that approach, but it would seem somewhat strange to suggest that where "any person owning or occupying property situated in the neighbourhood of the premises to which the application relates" is given the statutory right to object in terms of s 16 of the Act, the right of qualified objectors should be denied them because some other remedy might have been available to them'.

---

1 1948 SLT (Sh Ct) 33.
2 The fire authority is now a competent objector: s 16(1)(e).
3 *London Borough of Haringey v Sandhu*, The Times, 6 May 1987, unreported.
4 1981 SLT 257.

In *Coppolla v Midlothian District Licensing Board*[1] the district council's director of environmental health and cleansing submitted a report to the board which allegedly demonstrated a disregard of cleanliness and food hygiene, suggesting mismanagement of the premises. The application was refused on the ground that the applicant was not a 'fit and proper person', rather than under s 17(1)(b).

Interestingly, in that case the licensing board operated under a regulation made under s 37 which provided that it should consult inter alia the environmental health department before renewing a licence. It is doubtful whether such a regulation is required before consultation may take place. In *Fitzpatrick v Glasgow District Licensing Board*[2] the Sheriff Principal expressed the view that boards may 'obtain information to enable them to discharge their functions in whatever way and by whatever means they chose', subject to the statutory limitations. Similarly, in *Farquhar v City of Glasgow District Licensing Board*[3] the sheriff (I D Macphail, QC) held that:

'I accept that in many cases the officials' reports may well be of assistance to the Board in the discharge of their statutory functions, and I have some difficulty in appreciating on what grounds the Board could properly be said to be acting ultra vires. I understand the law to be that a body such as the Board is entitled to obtain information in any way they think best, provided that they always give a fair opportunity to those who are parties in the controversy to correct or contradict any relevant statement prejudicial to their view . . .'.

However, as suggested below, in view of the local authority's new status as a competent objector, such consultation may be problematic.

It is often difficult to see a connection between the condition of premises and unsuitability for the sale of alcoholic liquor. Gone are the days when 'whitewashing and papering' were considered to be 'in the nature of ornament'[4]. In *Ahmed v City of Glasgow District Licensing Board*[5] renewal of a licence had been refused where a building control inspection revealed a broken toilet ceiling, a broken door closer, a missing lamp cover and an incorrectly fitted fire blanket. Apart from the matter of the fire blanket (which simply required to be placed on a hook) it was accepted that the other defects were trivial. The sheriff said: 'I cannot see that any reasonable body could think that the defects in question could make the premises unsuitable for the sale of alcoholic liquor'.

He also held that the board was required to consider the suitability of the premises 'as at the date when they are considering the application'. Such an approach was followed in *Bantop v Glasgow District Licensing Board*[6]: the Lord Ordinary was 'clearly of the opinion that the relevant date for consideration is the date of the hearing of the application'[7].

This requirement causes practical difficulties, with premises sometimes having to be reinspected in the evening prior to the board meeting.

---

1 1983 SLT (Sh Ct) 95.
2 1978 SLT (Sh Ct) 63.
3 Glasgow Sheriff Court, 31 October 1980, unreported.
4 *Wise v Metcalfe* (1829) 10 B & C 229.
5 1987 GWD 5-156, Sh Ct.
6 1989 SCLR 731, 1990 SLT 366.
7 See also *Dick v Stirling Lawn Tennis and Squash Club* 1981 SLT (Sh Ct) 103, a club registration case, in which the sheriff held that 'It is the suitability of the premises at the date of the application which is in issue'.

The 1990 Act amended s 16 by adding a local authority to the list of competent objectors (s 16(1)(d)). Environmental health and building control departments have been noticeably reticent in their approach to this new freedom, perhaps reluctant to exchange the flexibility of their time-honoured ability to make comments upon applications for the fetters of the statutory mechanism, which requires, of course, advance intimation of the objection. For example, in *Coppolla v Midlothian District Licensing Board*[1] the appellant complained unsuccessfully that the board had acted contrary to natural justice by entertaining an environmental health report which he had received only the day before the hearing of the application. In such a circumstance it will usually be appropriate to move for an adjournment. Following the approach in *Coppolla*, the sheriff observed in *Farquhar*[2]:

'[I]t is not incumbent on the Board to give advance notice to the applicant of any possible difficulties. In many cases it might render unnecessary any motions at the hearing for an adjournment or for time to consider criticisms made in the reports, if the reports were to be intimated to the applicants in sufficient time before the hearing to enable them to have a fair opportunity to come before the Board prepared to correct or contradict anything in the reports. But while that might in many cases be a wise course to follow, it is not obligatory. If it is not followed, it remains the duty of the Board to observe the applicant's right to a fair hearing. . . But an objection to the admissibility of a report from one of these Departments simply on the ground that it had not been previously intimated to the applicant cannot, in my view, be sustained'.

Many reports which masquerade as 'comments' are tantamount to objections. Although boards are known to insist that they cannot take a view as to the suitability of premises without reports it may equally be said that they cannot possibly decide on the fitness of an applicant to hold a licence in the absence of information from the chief constable, who may only place information before a board by way of objection or observation.

Indeed, there is scope for an argument to the effect that in the absence of a specific power to do so a local authority may not make observations. In *Centralbite Ltd v Kincardine and Deeside District Licensing Board*[3] the board's decision to refuse an application for the regular extension of permitted hours was vitiated because it proceeded upon written representations from the police which were tantamount to an objection but which were not lodged with the clerk and intimated to the applicant in the prescribed manner. By parity of reasoning, 'comments' from a qualified objector such as a local authority which are in essence an objection are equally vulnerable to attack.

Ironically, in *Rai v Glasgow District Licensing Board*[4] the sheriff (Lothian) said:

'I was also addressed by the agent for the appellant on the matter of the Board requiring statements from representatives of the two [departments] referred to above. Any statement made by such a representative in response to a request from the Board is the first intimation that an applicant or his agent will have had of a particular criticism. Accordingly, these officials are put in a more privileged position than that occupied by statutory objectors in

1 1983 SLT (Sh Ct) 95.
2 Glasgow Sheriff Court, 31 October 1980, unreported.
3 1989 SCLR 652, 1990 SLT 231.
4 Glasgow Sheriff Court, 17 July 1980, unreported.

terms of section 16(1) of the Act who are required to take certain formal steps before they can be heard'.

It is in this 'privileged position' which many local authorities prefer to remain.

(3) Public nuisance. Section 17(1)(c) provides that a renewal application shall be refused if the board finds that 'the use of the premises for the sale of alcoholic liquor is likely to cause undue public nuisance, or a threat to public order or safety'.

A consideration of this ground usually requires a degree of speculation where application is made for a new licence but where a licence falls to be renewed there is plainly a past record to be considered:

'If the board can find that in the past there was undue public nuisance, and that that nuisance was probably associated with the use of the premises for the sale of alcoholic liquor, then in the absence of any evidence indicating change it would be open to the board to hold that that the use of the premises was likely to cause undue public nuisance'[1].

Where application was made for an entertainment licence the licensing board was entitled to have regard to a history of late-night noise nuisance caused by the applicant's adjacent public house premises[2].

In *Sangha v Bute and Cowal Divisional Licensing Board*[3] the First Division observed that the board had been plainly correct to take into account incidents which had occurred at any time since the grant of the licence, irrespective of whether or not they had previously been brought to its attention. In that case, the appellant, whose application to renew an entertainment licence for a discothèque was refused following an objection from the chief constable based substantially on incidents considered by the board on previous occasions, derived no assistance from the fact that some five months earlier the board had decided not to impose a restriction order (s 65).

The court rejected arguments that (a) it was necessary to distinguish between offences which were prejudicial to public order and safety, such as vandalism and breaches of the peace, and those which were not, such as theft and drug misuse; (b) the board should not have taken into account incidents not demonstrated to be connected with the sale of alcoholic liquor; (c) incidents taking place outwith the premises ought to have been disregarded[4]; and (d) the board should have observed that all but one of the incidents occurred during the extended, rather than the normal permitted hours. It was held that the term 'public' includes customers.

'The emphasis [in s 17(1)(c)] is on public nuisance on one hand and public order and safety on the other. The public for this purpose comprise not only the public at large who live, work, or happen to be close enough to the premises so as to be likely to be affected by what goes on there, but also that section of the public which is attracted to the premises themselves by the entertainment which is on offer. Members of that section of the public are as much entitled to the board's consideration as members of the public at large, and any

1 *Saleem v Hamilton District Licensing Board*, Hamilton Sheriff Court, 13 January 1992, unreported.
2 *Harpspot Ltd v City of Glasgow Licensing Board* 1992 GWD 6-311, IH.
3 1990 SCLR 409.
4 See also *Lidster v Owen* [1983] 1 All ER 1012, [1983] 1 WLR 516 and *Surrey Heath Council v McDonalds Restaurants Ltd* [1990] 3 LR 21.

evidence which might imply that they were at risk of being exposed to criminal activity because of the use of the premises for the sale of alcoholic liquor would be relevant to an objection under this ground'[1].

The attempt to sever the use of the premises for the provision of entertainment on the one hand and the sale of alcoholic liquor on the other, which the court rejected, sits uncomfortably with the provisions of s 41 of the Civic Government (Scotland) Act 1982, in terms of which a public entertainment licence is required for premises where 'on payment of money or money's worth members of the public are admitted or may use facilities for the purpose of entertainment'. Exemptions apply to inter alia 'licensed premises within the meaning of the Licensing (Scotland) Act 1976 in which public entertainment is being provided during the permitted hours within the meaning of that Act'[2]. This single system of control for liquor-licensed places of public entertainment suggests very clearly that both uses may be subject to licensing board supervision.

The fact that no criticism may be levelled at the management of premises is unlikely to be of assistance. In *Surrey Heath Council v McDonalds Restaurants Ltd*[3] Mr Justice Nolan observed:

'The danger of unreasonable disturbance to residents may arise even in the case of a thoroughly well-run restaurant. It may be that such a restaurant, through no fault of its proprietors, has become a focus for unruly behaviour . . . [T]here may be a situation in which the proprietors of the restaurant would be bound to accept a restriction upon their ability to conduct their business in the interest of the community as a whole . . . .'.

McKay v Banff and Buchan Western Division Licensing Board[4] shares with *Sangha* the feature that a regular extension application had previously been granted without opposition. In the former the chief constable submitted a complaint to the board in terms of s 31 (which provides for the suspension of a licence) but did not object to a regular extension application granted some six days later. The licenceholder argued without success that the incidents complained of took place outwith the normal permitted hours and action should properly have been taken under s 65[5]. The court held that:

'. . . taking the nature and cumulative effect of the thirty-three incidents over a two-year period, it was open to the board to conclude that [the] grounds of complaint were proved. It is not appropriate in a case such as this to examine each incident in detail. It is the cumulative effect that counts, and the overall effect of the number and type of incidents. . . .'.

(Reversing the sheriff, who had found some significance in the chief constable's failure to object to the regular extension application).

This approach may be characterised as 'trial by numbers': in other words, the more incidents listed in a complaint the more difficult it will be to escape the sometimes superficial effect which they create. There is, however, shrieval authority for the proposition that, where the factual content of allegations is

1 See also *Freeland v City of Glasgow District Licensing Board* 1980 SLT (Sh Ct) 125.
2 Civic Government (Scotland) Act 1982, s 41(2)(f).
3 [1990] 3 LR 21.
4 1991 SCLR 15, 1991 SLT 20, [1990] 3 LR 23.
5 Section 65 provides for the restriction of the permitted hours.

challenged, evidence must be led. In *Devana Investments Ltd v City of Aberdeen Licensing Board*[1] the sheriff held that:

'To accept a disputed version of the material and vital facts in the teeth of a motion to be allowed to lead evidence is courting disaster and disregarding the natural laws of justice . . . I accept that whether evidence is to be allowed or not is a discretionary matter in the hands of the particular board . . . In my view, the Pursuers have satisfied me that the Defenders' discretion has not been shown to be properly exercised here. The area of dispute has been shown to be sufficiently wide to demonstrate that there was a proper case for allowing evidence'.

While *Devana Investments Ltd* appears to break new ground it is in fact on all fours with two unreported sheriff court cases decided early in the life of the Act.

In *Lennon v Monklands District Licensing Board*[2] the sheriff (A L Stewart), reversing a refusal of Sunday opening, said:

'The main matter which causes me concern . . . is that the Board reached its decision . . . without hearing any evidence. Parliament has clearly provided that, before refusing an application such as this, the Board must be satisfied of certain matters . . . I totally fail to understand how a board can be satisfied of matters which are in contention on the basis of purely *ex parte* statements. How can the members possibly assess which statement is correct? Where there is a dispute on questions of fact. . . the only way in which it can be resolved is by leading evidence from witnesses who can be cross-examined. The Board will then be properly in a position to weigh the evidence and reach a conclusion'.

A broadly similar opinion was expressed by Sheriff I D Macphail in *Lorimer's Breweries Ltd v City of Glasgow District Licensing Board*[3] in which the board's 'erroneous view of their duties deflected them from ascertaining the extent of the undisputed facts and then, if necessary, properly enquiring into the matters in dispute', although:

'. . . they were not required to conduct their enquiry into disputed issues of fact as if it were a trial. Nor were they restricted to hearing evidence which would be admissible in accordance with the rules of evidence which are applicable in a court of law'.

Devana Investments Ltd[4] may have a significant impact on licensing board procedures. Some boards have a large volume of contentious applications to consider and the hearing of evidence could cause substantial administrative inconvenience; but 'convenience and justice are often not on speaking terms'[5].

Proponents of the contrary view will pray in aid the First Division's decision in a gaming licence appeal, *Cigaro (Glasgow) Ltd v City of Glasgow District Licensing Board*[6]. It requires to be kept in view, however, that in this case no motion to allow the leading of evidence was in fact made nor did the appellants make any averments as to prejudice. The rubric to the report, which properly states that 'the licensing board's established practice of hearing only submissions but not

---

1 1992 SCLR 616.
2 Airdrie Sheriff Court, 24 May 1978, unreported.
3 Glasgow Sheriff Court, 20 October 1980.
4 See above.
5 *General Medical Council v Spackman* [1943] AC 627, per Lord Atkin.
6 1983 SLT 549.

evidence from parties was not in breach of the rules of natural justice', requires to be read subject to the following parts of the opinion of the court:

'No motion to allow evidence to be led was made to the board and counsel for Cigaro was quite unable to say that his clients had been in any way prejudiced in the presentation of their application because no evidence had been led. He could not, in particular, identify any particular matter which in the absence of evidence could not be, as was not, fully developed before the board. . . a refusal to hear evidence, whatever else it may amount to is not in itself an act contrary to natural justice. Whether a policy decision in all cases to refuse to hear evidence is open to attack in an appropriate process is another matter but it has nothing to do with the rules of natural justice. . .'[1].

Where complaints of noise, as distinct from disorder, are in issue, originated by local residents often with the support of the local environmental health department, the advocate may be tempted to found on any failure by the local authority to take steps under s 58(1) of the Control of Pollution Act 1974, but in *Johnston v City of Edinburgh District Licensing Board*[2] the court was not prepared to accept the proposition that 'the right of qualified objectors should be denied because some other remedy might have been available to them'. Nevertheless, a failure to take action under s 58(1) may well weaken the credibility of a complainer's case, particularly since, by virtue of that subsection, the local authority 'shall serve a notice' where it is 'satisfied that noise amounting to a nuisance exists, or is likely to occur or recur' and, standing the use of the word 'shall', appears to have no discretion in the matter.

Consequences of refusal

Where a renewal application is refused the licence nevertheless continues to have effect 'until the time within which an appeal may be made has elapsed or, if an appeal has been lodged, until the appeal has been abandoned or determined' (s 30(5)(b))[3].

In the absence of a successful appeal there is nothing to prevent application being made for the grant or provisional grant of a new licence in respect of the same premises: s 14, which prohibits a further application for a new licence during the two years following the refusal of a *new* licence, subject to a contrary direction by the board, is of no relevance.

One licensing board (uniquely, it is believed) allows a further application for *renewal* of the licence during the appeal period where the refusal of the initial application was based on the unsatisfactory condition of the premises (s 17(1)(b)) and remedial action has been taken by the licenceholder.

Where a licence continues to have effect by virtue of s 30(5)(b):

(1) There is nothing to prevent the transfer of the licence to a new tenant or a new or existing occupant (s 25(1)). While such a course may prima facie appear

---

1 See also Chapter 15, sub voce 'Natural justice'.
2 1981 SLT 257.
3 In addition, s 138(2)(a) provides that nothing in the Act shall 'affect the right of any person to carry on his business during the pendency of an appeal against the refusal of a licensing board to renew his licence'.

unlikely it has been known for a licensing board to abandon its resistance to an appeal where the refusal of the renewal was based on the unsuitability of the applicant (s 17(1)(a)) and a transfer to a 'fit and proper person' has taken place ad interim.

(2) The licensing board is bound to consider ancillary applications (for example, for the regular extension of permitted hours) in the usual way[1].

Related applications

Sunday permitted hours

An applicant for the renewal of a public house or refreshment licence requires to state in his application whether it is intended to open the premises for the sale or supply of alcoholic liquor during the permitted hours on Sundays (ie from 12.30 pm to 2.30 pm and from 6.30 pm to 11 pm) (s 10(3A), inserted by the 1990 Act, s 46(2)(a)).

The display of a notice at the premises and service of a notice upon adjoining occupiers are unnecessary, even where Sunday permitted hours have not previously been in operation[2]. (Previously, where the 'old style' Sunday opening permission granted under Sch 4 was to be renewed, para 14 of the Schedule applied para 5 to such renewals and para 5 in turn brought s 10(2)(b) and s 10(5) into play. Paragraph 14 was repealed by s 46(8)(d) of the 1990 Act). No provision is made for press advertisement.

Permitted hours on Sundays may be refused if the board finds that the opening and use of the premises on a Sunday would cause 'undue disturbance or public nuisance[3] in the locality' but 'the refusal of an application on the [sic] ground alone shall not prevent the licensing board from granting the application in respect of days other than Sundays' (s 17(2A))[4]. The board is not obliged to state reasons for its decision.

After its introduction by the 1976 Act Sunday opening was a contentious issue for a relatively short time. It is now seldom the source of opposition. Indeed, by May 1991, shortly after Sunday regular extensions first became available for public houses, approximately two-thirds of public houses in the country had obtained Sunday afternoon extensions[5].

No express provision is made for objections from any source. No doubt it may be said that Sunday permitted hours are now to be treated as an integral and

---

1 See *C R S Leisure Ltd v Dumbarton District Licensing Board* 1989 SCLR 566; 1990 SLT 200.
2 Cf s 10(8) in relation to applications for the grant or provisional grant of a new licence containing a request for Sunday permitted hours.
3 See *Martin v Ellis* 1978 SLT (Sh Ct) 38; *Freeland v City of Glasgow District Licensing Board* 1979 SC 226, 1980 SLT 101; *Freeland v City of Glasgow District Licensing Board* 1980 SLT (Sh Ct) 125.
4 Cf s 65 which allows a board to issue a Sunday restriction order where the use of the premises 'is the cause of undue disturbance or public nuisance having regard to the way of life in the locality on a Sunday'.
5 Source: Scottish Office Statistical Bulletin CRJ /1992/5, August 1992.

material part of the licence[1] and thus the persons and bodies mentioned in s 16(1) may competently object.

Such an argument faces a difficulty caused by the contrasting provisions of s 17(4) and (5). While s 17(4) expressly provides that an applicant for renewal of a licence may appeal to the sheriff against a refusal of a licensing board 'to grant the licence in respect of the permitted hours on a Sunday', s 17(5) simply empowers a competent objector to appeal against a decision to 'grant, renew or transfer' a licence.

Where the whole renewal application, including the Sunday permitted hours component, is refused, a pre-existing Sunday permission appears to continue in force with the licence on the dependency of an appeal (s 30(5)). The position is, however, less than clear where the refusal relates only to the Sunday hours[2]. Certainly, s 138(2)(b) states that nothing in the Act shall 'affect the right of any person to carry on his business during the pendency of an appeal against the refusal of a licensing board to refuse his licence' and it may be the case that s 30(5) temporarily saves not simply the whole licence but the Sunday hours in isolation.

Where a renewal applicant omits to re-apply for opening on Sundays or appeals unsuccessfully against refusal there is no mechanism for re-application until the licence is next due for renewal unless he takes the extraordinary step of applying for the grant of a new licence in respect of the premises. Since some licensing boards employ a 'Yes/No' type question as respects Sunday permitted hours in their application forms it follows that the smallest clerical mistake could have dire consequences. It is doubtful whether the board may consider a request for Sunday hours made only after the last lodgement date[3].

Of course, any pre-existing regular extensions of the permitted hours on Sunday will fall if the basic permitted hours are lost.

Children's certificates[4]

A children's certificate held in respect of the whole or part of public house or hotel licensed premises requires to be renewed with the licence to which it relates (1990 Act, s 49(9)). There is, however, no provision for a simple renewal of the certificate as such: a fresh, separate application is necessary, although the application to renew the actual licence must contain a statement as to whether application is being made for a certificate (1990 Act, Sch 5, para 6).

Schedule 5 of the 1990 Act, which regulates procedure, is reminiscent of Schedule 4 to the 1976 Act and, in the result, is cumbersome in practice. Some boards require a separate application and fee; others do not. Unless there is to be any change in the certificated part of the premises fresh plans are usually not insisted upon.

---

1 Following the reasoning of *Wolfson v Glasgow District Licensing Board* 1981 SLT 17, in which the grant of a licence in a restricted form was equiparated with a refusal of the application. See also *Baillie v Wilson* 1917 SC 55, 1916 2 SLT 252 and *Wallace v Kyle and Carrick District Licensing Board* 1979 SLT (Sh Ct) 12.
2 Although the imposition of a Sunday restriction order is susceptible to appeal: s 64(8)
3 See s 13(2) and discussion of late applications below.
4 As to children's certificates generally, see Chapter 14.

Intimation of the application requires to be made to the chief constable (1990 Act, Sch 5, para 4) who is empowered to object or make observations.

The board requires to be satisfied that:

'(a) that the premises or, as the case may be, the part or parts of the premises constitute an environment in which it is suitable for children to be present; and
(b) that there will be available for sale or supply for consumption in the part of the premises in respect of which the certificate is to apply meals and beverages other than alcoholic liquor . . .'[1]

and, in considering the matter *de novo*, is probably empowered to refuse the application upon a change of criteria, despite any alteration in circumstances.

Unless a direction to the contrary is given, refusal of the certificate prevents a further application being made in the following two years (1990 Act, Sch 5, para 5). The direction need not be given at the time of refusal. There is no right of appeal to the sheriff, but a statement of reasons may be requested.

The currency of certificates appears to be the subject of a drafting mistake. Section 49(9) of the 1990 Act provides that where a certificate is granted at the same time as the grant, provisional grant or renewal of a licence it shall be valid for the period of the licence; otherwise it shall have effect 'until the end of the period for which the licence to which it relates has effect in pursuance of section 30 of the [1976] Act'. Of course, a licence may continue for a considerable time on the dependency of an appeal against refusal (s 30(5)). Inconsistently, however, para 9 of Sch 5 to the 1990 Act provides that where an existing certificate is to be 'renewed' with the licence such a certificate will continue to have effect until granted or refused, potentially a much shorter period than that afforded by s 49(9).

Miscellaneous considerations

Conditions attaching to public house or hotel licences by virtue of s 119, which relates to off-sale departments, should be re-attached at the time of renewal if the applicant so desires, although application forms are usually silent in this respect.

Some licensing boards require consents under byelaws[2] (permitting, for example, the provision of live entertainment) to be renewed every three years with the actual licence, but the majority treat such consents as valid until recalled.

Section 38(1)(f) allows boards to promulgate byelaws for the purpose of setting out conditions 'for the improvement of standards of, and conduct in, licensed premises', which conditions may be attached when a licence is granted or renewed[3]. Existing conditions must be perpetuated at the time of renewal; fresh conditions may be imposed.

Entertainment licences may be renewed subject to a condition in terms of s 101(2).

The licence may be restricted to prohibit the sale of alcoholic liquor other than

1 1990 Act, s 49(2).
2 See Chapter 8.
3 In the absence of a valid byelaw the attachment of a condition will be ultra vires: see *Allied Breweries (UK) Ltd v City of Glasgow District Licensing Board* 1985 SLT 302.

wine, made-wine, porter, ale, beer, cider and perry in terms of s 29(1) but otherwise no prohibition may be placed on the descriptions of liquor which may be sold[1].

At the request of the applicant, the board may if 'satisfied that the requirements of the area . . . make it desirable' insert a condition allowing for closure of the premises for a part or parts of the year to a maximum of 180 days; hotels may be permitted to continue the operation of a bar or restaurant when letting facilities are not available (s 62).

The sale or supply of alcoholic liquor in premises which are the subject of a restricted hotel licence may be confined to residents and their guests, so that the general public, who would normally be permitted to purchase alcoholic liquor with meals, are excluded (Sch 1).

Section 17(6) specifically provides for a right of appeal by an applicant or a competent objector against a board's decision to attach or not to attach a condition in terms of s 38(3) or s 101(2) although, in practice, appeals of this nature by objectors are almost unknown.

The potential for appeals against conditions has, however, been enlarged by case law. In *Wallace v Kyle and Carrick District Licensing Board*[2] the sheriff held that the board's refusal to insert a condition in terms of s 62 could competently be appealed, while a s 29 restriction was considered to be a refusal capable of appeal in *Wolfson v Glasgow District Licensing Board*[3].

In the absence of a successful appeal against unwanted conditions, the licenceholder may only attempt to free his licence from such conditions by application for a new licence[4].

Licensing boards not infrequently call for undertakings when licences are renewed and may purport to grant an application subject to a condition that, say, a kitchen area will not be used until brought up to a satisfactory standard. Conditions of this nature are not enforceable as such[5] but breach of an undertaking may result in a hearing under s 32[6]. In England it has been held that while licensing justices may ask for an assurance as to the manner in which a licensed business will be conducted, they are not empowered to require an undertaking which amounts to a condition[7].

For a licensing board's power to order structural alterations of licensed premises (except off-sale premises) in terms of s 36, see Chapter 11.

---

1 *R v Leicester Licensing Justices ex parte Bisson* [1968] 2 All ER 351, [1968] 1 WLR 729.
2 1979 SLT (Sh Ct) 12.
3 1980 SC 136, 1981 SLT 17, following *Baillie v Wilson* 1917 SC 55, 1916 2 SLT 252, in which the Lord President (Strathclyde) said: 'Refusal of part of the existing licence is refusal of the existing licence. A licence cannot be said to be renewed if it is granted with a material part left out'.
4 See *R v Godalming Licensing Committee ex parte Knight* [1955] 2 All ER 328.
5 *Johnston v City of Edinburgh District Licensing Board* 1981 SLT 257. See also *Chief Constable of Strathclyde v Glasgow District Licensing Board* 1988 SCLR 18, 1988 SLT 128 in which the Inner House considered that the board was in a position to accept an applicant's assurances as to police access.
6 Section 32 provides for the making of a closure order.
7 *R v Edmonton Licensing Justices ex parte Baker* [1983] 2 All ER 545, [1983] 1 WLR 1000. See also *R v Windsor Licensing Justices ex parte Hodes* [1983] 2 All ER 551, [1983] 1 WLR 685.

SUSPENSION OF LICENCES

The *Report of the Departmental Committee on Scottish Licensing Law*[1] considered that the extended validity of licences, from one to three years, should be tempered with 'some form of sanction . . . against misconduct of licensed premises and against any deterioration in matters relating to the suitability of the premises'. The Act provides two suspension mechanisms: the first may be initiated by a competent objector (s 16(1)), the other by the board *ex proprio motu*.

Suspension following a complaint

Where a complaint is made to a licensing board by one of the persons or bodies listed in s 16(1) it may suspend a licence for a period not exceeding one year or for its unexpired portion (s 31(7)) if 'satisfied that it is in the public interest to do so' (s 31(1))[2] on one of the following grounds:

'(a) that the licence-holder[3] is no longer a fit and proper person to be the holder of a licence;
(b) that the use of the premises in respect of which the licence is held has caused undue public nuisance or a threat to public order or safety'[4].

The board may have regard to:

'(a) any misconduct on the part of the holder of the licence, whether or not constituting a breach of this Act or any byelaw made thereunder, which in the opinion of the board has a bearing on his fitness to hold a licence;
(b) any misconduct on the part of persons frequenting licensed premises occurring in those premises or any misconduct in the immediate vicinity of licensed premises which is attributable to persons frequenting those premises'[5].

There is a degree of overlap between these grounds: a failure to provide adequate staffing and stewarding, resulting in incidents of public disorder, may support a finding under both heads[6]. It is nevertheless irrelevant that premises giving rise to nuisance are well-managed[7].

Fitness of the licenceholder

When considering whether the licenceholder is 'no longer a fit and proper person' the board may be entitled to take into account criminal charges which have yet to

---

1 (Cmnd 5354) (*Clayson*) paras. 8.38ff
2 The categories of objector are: persons owning or occupying property in the neighbourhood; the local community council; an organised church; the chief constable; the fire authority; the local authority.
3 A term which includes, where applicable, an employee or agent: see s 11(3).
4 Section 32. The use of the premises need not be related to the sale of alcoholic liquor; cf s 17(1)(c). See also *Sangha v Bute and Cowal Divisional Licensing Board* 1990 SCLR 409.
5 Section 31(3).
6 *McKay v Banff and Buchan Western Division Licensing Board* 1991 SCLR 15, 1991 SLT 20.
7 See *Lidster v Owen* [1983] 1 All ER 1012, [1983] 1 WLR 516; and *Surrey Heath Council v McDonalds Restaurants Ltd* [1990] 3 LR 21.

come to trial. Indeed, according to one shrieval decision, in such a case the chief constable is bound to submit a complaint within a reasonable time of the incident giving rise to the prosecution. In *McKenzie v Renfrew District Licensing Board*[1] the licenceholders were convicted of a contravention of s 68 which had taken place about 18 months earlier, whereupon the chief constable submitted a complaint in terms of s 31. Upholding the licenceholder's appeal against suspension of the licence, the sheriff said:

'I do not believe it was conceived that some twenty months after the sale to a youth of less than eighteen years, a board would then decide that as a result of this lapse some twenty months ago a suspension of twenty-eight days should be meted out. There can be no summary justice in that . . . If Parliament meant such a suspension to be a warning and a form of punishment, the time for its introduction is not nearly two years after the incident to which it gave rise [sic] and a reasonable board would take this into consideration'.

In the absence of any authority to the contrary *McKenzie* has been followed in some districts, with the result that licensing boards are on occasions obliged to conduct proceedings resembling a criminal trial. In the result, a licence may be suspended on the basis of allegations which subsequently fail to produce a conviction[2]. This imperfect state of affairs is rendered even more unsatisfactory by the fact that hearings are usually conducted on the basis of *ex parte* statements, although it would no doubt be open to the licenceholder to move that evidence be led[3].

It also appears that a board may make a finding under s 31(2)(a) on the basis of accusations of criminal behaviour which are not and *do not become* the subject of a prosecution[4].

While the court is empowered to disqualify a licenceholder 'from holding a licence in respect of the premises concerned for a period not exceeding five years' (s 67(3))[5], the fact that it elects not to do so has no effect upon the board's discretion in terms of s 31[6].

Use of the premises

A complaint may competently be made in respect of nuisance and disorder occurring exclusively outwith the normal permitted hours, even where an application for the regular extension of permitted hours has recently been granted without opposition from the complainer[7]. The board may not, however, restrict

---

1 1991 SCLR (Notes) 859.
2 Cf *Clayson*, para 10.38: '[I]t would seem appropriate to enable a licensing authority to suspend a certificate *following conviction* of the certificate holder for a breach of certificate for which the criminal court could have ordered forfeiture . . . but in the exercise of its discretion did not do so'. (Author's emphasis.)
3 See *Devana Investments Ltd v City of Aberdeen Licensing Board* 1992 SCLR 616.
4 See *McKay v Banff and Buchan Western Division Licensing Board* 1991 SCLR 15, 1991 SLT 20.
5 The premises may also be disqualified
   following a conviction for certain offences; see Sch 5.
6 *McKenzie v Renfrew District Licensing Board* 1991 SCLR (Notes) 859.
7 *McKay v Banff and Buchan Western Division Licensing Board*, above.

the permitted hours under s 65 where a complaint has been made solely under s 31[1].

Persons will be regarded as 'frequenting' the premises for the purposes of s 31(3)b) even where they have been denied entry:

'[Counsel submitted] that "frequenting" in terms of s 31(3)(b) only applies to persons who are in or have been in the premises and not to persons who have been refused admission. I do not have to attempt exhaustively to define "frequenting", because the incident which gave rise to this argument related to a youth who had been banned from the premises. It follows that he had "frequented" them in the past and was, notwithstanding the ban, attempting to gain admission again'[1].

Complaints by chief constables are sometimes based on a large number of incidents over an extended period which may not survive individual scrutiny. The court has, however, endorsed the quantitative method:

'[I]n my opinion, taking the nature and cumulative effect of the 33 incidents over a two year period, it was open to the board to conclude that both grounds of complaint were proved. It is not appropriate in a case such as this to examine each incident in detail. It is the cumulative effect that counts, and the overall effect of the number and type of incidents, which were not disputed, entitled the board to find both grounds of complaint proved'[1].

Where there *is* a factual dispute the 'trial by numbers' approach may be less successful[2].

Preliminary procedure

When a complaint is received the board considers whether or not to hold a hearing on the issue and must inform the complainer of its decision (s 31(4)). *Clayson*[3] was of the opinion that the right to complain should be restricted to the chief constable and the local authority since the extension of the right to a member of the public 'would expose the certificate-holder to the possibility of harassment by frivolous or vexatious complaints'. In the result, although this recommendation was not accepted, complaints in practice almost always originate from the chief constable, although the preliminary process is clearly designed to meet *Clayson's* concerns[4]. The licenceholder has no right to be informed that a complaint is under considera-tion. *Semble* the decision to hold a hearing could be taken by the clerk alone under 'delegated powers' (s 5(1)).

If a hearing is to be held the following steps are prescribed:

1 *McKay v Banff and Buchan District Licensing Board* 1991 SCLR 15, 1991 SLT 20.
2 See commentary to *Devana Investments Ltd v City of Aberdeen Licensing Board* 1992 SCLR 616 at 624.
3 Para 8.39.
4 The chief constable's agent may initiate the complaint: see *Stephen v City of Aberdeen District Licensing Board* 1989 SLT 94.

(a) The clerk of the board must 'serve on the holder of the licence not less than 21 days before the hearing[1] a notice that the board proposes to hold a hearing, specifying the complaint and the grounds upon which suspension of the licence is sought' (s 31(5)(a)).

The clerk is not obligated to provide a copy of the actual complaint although the licenceholder should, of course, be afforded fair notice of the case which he requires to meet. A mere reiteration of the grounds of suspension is insufficient[2].

The duty imposed by s 31(5)(a) and the meaning of 'complaint' were both given a narrow interpretation in *Tennent Caledonian Breweries Ltd v City of Aberdeen District Licensing Board*[3]. On 9 April the clerk gave timeous notice to the licenceholder that it was intended to hold a hearing, by means of a letter which re-echoed the terms of s 31(2) (a) and (b), with the addition of the following: 'The chief constable has said that a pattern of incidents of violence and offences connected with drugs has occurred, and that you have failed to adequately supervise the management of the licensed premises'. The chief constable's complaint letter and a schedule of alleged incidents were attached[4].

On 10 June, within the 21 day period (15 days before the hearing), the chief constable sent to the licenceholder and to the clerk a schedule containing details of further incidents upon which he sought to rely.

Rejecting the licenceholder's argument that this additional material could form no part of the complaint, the sheriff (A L Stewart) held that:

'In my opinion the sentence [set out above] clearly specifies the complaint by the [chief constable]. What is contained in the schedules appended to the [chief constable's] letters of 9 April and 10 June is, in my opinion, not a "complaint" but details of allegations made in support of the complaint. Under [s 31(5)] there is no obligation on either [the board or the chief constable] to give any notice of such allegations to the pursuers. There is therefore no question of 21 days' notice being required'.

In *Lawrence v City of Aberdeen District Licensing Board*[5], the clerk of the board advised the licenceholder that a meeting was to be held (in terms of s 31(4)) with a view to determining whether or not a hearing should take place following a complaint by the chief constable. The licenceholder was furnished with a copy of the complaint letter and an accompanying schedule of incidents. Thereafter, under reference to that correspondence, he was given formal notice, purportedly in terms of s 31(5)(a), that the board had resolved to have a hearing on a certain date. An appeal against suspension of the licence was upheld on the ground that the notice of the hearing did not specify the complaint:

'For the purposes of s 31(5)(a) is it effective to serve a notice which contains no specification of a complaint other than by way of reference to past correspondence? In my opinion, the strict provisions contained in s 31(5)(a), requiring the service of a notice

---

1 This means, in effect, not less than 21 clear days: *Main v City of Glasgow District Licensing Board* 1987 SLT 305. 'Serve': see Interpretation Act 1978, s 7.
2 *Chief Constable of Grampian v Aberdeen District Licensing Board* 1979 SLT (Sh Ct) 2.
3 1987 SLT (Sh Ct) 2.
4 For circumstances in which the attachment of a list of previous convictions to a letter of objection was considered to provide barely sufficient specification, see *Fereneze Leisure Ltd v Renfrew District Licensing Board* 1991 SCLR 751, 1992 SLT 604.
5 Aberdeen Sheriff Court, 21 April 1986, unreported.

specifying the complaint and the grounds upon which suspension is sought, will not be met unless the notice, or any schedule annexed to it, contain a specific statement of the complaint and the grounds. Accordingly, a mere reference to past correspondence is insufficient'.

(b) The complainer is to be given notice of the hearing by the clerk (s 31(5)(b)). No time limit is specified.

(c) In terms of s 31(5)(c):

'any person or body mentioned in section 16(1) of [the] Act may, not less than seven days before the hearing, lodge notice with the clerk of the board that he or it wishes to be heard in support of suspension of the licence specifying the grounds on which he seeks such suspension, and any such notice shall be intimated by such person to the holder of the licence'[1].

The purpose of this provision is less than clear. It is sometimes suggested that the *original* complainer must give notice (and intimation) in order to secure a right of audience at the hearing. He would be well-advised to do so, for the avoidance of doubt, but if this interpretation is correct the purpose of the requirement is difficult to determine: no doubt the board could only have decided to hold a hearing in the first instance on the basis of a properly specified complaint. Indeed, in *Tennent Caledonian Breweries Ltd v City of Aberdeen District Licensing Board*[2] it appears to have been assumed that s 31(5)(c) applies only to *other* potential complainers.

(d) Where the chief constable is not the original complainer, he may:

'not less than seven days before the hearing lodge with the clerk of the board observations in respect of the proposed suspension of the licence, and any such observations shall be intimated by the chief constable to the holder of the licence'[3].

The hearing

The hearing may take place at any meeting of the board, not necessarily a quarterly meeting (s 5(2)(j), read with s 5(6)). A suspension order may not be made unless the licenceholder has been heard 'unless after receiving due notice of the hearing' he fails to appear (s 31(5)(d)).

The expression 'due notice' was considered in *Lanvend Ltd v Cunninghame District Licensing Board*[4]. Notice of a hearing was sent to the former registered office of the licenceholding company by the clerk, who had not been advised of a change of address. Thereafter the company's solicitor advised the clerk that no intimation had been received and that the purpose of the proposed hearing was unknown. The board nevertheless proceeded to make a closure order (s 32) in the absence of the licenceholders. On appeal, the sheriff held that the board had erred in law:

1 There is no time limit for intimation.
2 1987 SLT (Sh Ct) 2 at 6H.
3 Section 31(5A), added by the 1990 Act, s 53(2). There is no time limit for intimation to the licenceholder.
4 Kilmarnock Sheriff Court, 10 August 1987, unreported.

'[A]s [the board's agent] persuasively pointed out, where the clerk . . . had correctly sent intimation by post, the provisions of section 7 of the Interpretation Act 1978 deem that the addressee has received the letter; and place upon him the onus of disproving this. [The licenceholder's agent] emphasised that section 32(2)(b) prohibited the making of the order unless the holder fails to appear, "after receiving due notice of the hearing". He pointed out the difference in wording between this provision and, for example, the provision in section 15(2) as to the failure of an applicant to appear, "having been cited by the board to attend the meeting at which his application is to be considered" . . . the information before [the board] . . . was that [the licenceholders] had not received due intimation of the hearing. I have come to the view that [this] submission is correct. The situation would have been different if the defenders had had no information before them, for then the deeming provision of section 7 of the 1978 Act would have applied'[1].

Per contra, in *Dolan v City of Glasgow District Council*[2] the licensing authority had satisfied its obligation to 'notify' an applicant[3] by sending recorded delivery letters to his last-known addresses. Despite non-delivery, notification was deemed to have taken place, the licensing authority having no reason to believe otherwise.

Where the complainer seeks to introduce new material of which the licenceholder has no notice a motion should be made for an adjournment[4] although it may well be considered that the hearing should be confined to matters of which prior warning has been given. Evidence should be led where material facts are in dispute[5].

The board's decision must be taken in public[6], including the decision as to the period of the suspension order[7]. In *Stephen v City of Aberdeen District Licensing Board*[8] it was held that submissions directed at the possible penalty should be made before the board's retiral[9].

The period and effect of suspension

The licence may be suspended for 'a fixed period not exceeding one year or the unexpired portion of the duration of the licence, whichever is the less' (s 31(7)). It seems that once the suspension period has been completed, in the case of a suspension founded on s 31(2)(a) the licenceholder will usually revert to being a 'fit and proper person'. As the sheriff remarked in *McKenzie v Renfrew District Licensing Board*[10]:

---

1 See also *Jolly v Hamilton District Council* 1992 SCLR 88, 1992 SLT 28.
2 1990 SCLR 553.
3 For the purpose of para 4(2) of Sch 1 to the Civic Government (Scotland) Act 1982.
4 *Tennent Caledonian Breweries Ltd v City of Aberdeen District Licensing Board* 1987 SLT (Sh Ct) 2, in which, as explained above, a distinction was drawn between a 'complaint' and allegations in support of a complaint.
5 *Devana Investments Ltd v City of Aberdeen Licensing Board* 1992 SCLR 616.
6 *McKay v Banff and Buchan Western Division Licensing Board* 1991 SCLR 15, 1991 SLT 20.
7 See below; and *Devana Investments Ltd v City of Aberdeen Licensing Board* 1992 SCLR 616.
8 1989 SLT (Sh Ct) 94.
9 Cf *McIndoe v Glasgow District Licensing Board* 1989 SCLR 325.
10 1991 SCLR (Notes) 859.

'How can a person be not a fit and proper person to hold a licence on [sic], say, May 1989 but become a fit person on 26th August 1989 . . . Parliament, it seems, meant this to be some sort of punishment no matter how illogical it may be to say that a person then becomes a fit and proper person once more after they have had their licence suspended for a period of anything up to a year'.

Of course, suspension for the unexpired balance of a licence may be followed by the refusal of a renewal application.

During the suspension period:
(a) the licence 'shall cease to have effect' (s 31(7));
(b) the offence of trafficking (s 90) will be committed if alcoholic liquor is sold by retail[1];
(c) the licence may be transferred to a new tenant or to a new or existing occupant (s 25) provided that the applicant is a fit and proper person, but the transfer has no effect upon the suspension.

The licenceholder may appeal to the sheriff against the making of the order, including the period of suspension (s 31(8))[2]. An unsuccessful complainer has no right of appeal. In *Perfect Swivel Ltd v City of Dundee District Licensing Board (No 1)*[3] it was argued, unsuccessfully, that para 3 of the Act of Sederunt governing the appeal procedure[4] only required service of a copy of the initial writ upon the clerk to the board since the appellant was neither 'the applicant' nor 'an objector'.

In terms of s 31(6), the suspension is placed in abeyance until the time limit for an appeal has expired or 'if the holder appeals to the sheriff or thereafter to the Court of Session, until the appeal has been determined in favour of the suspension or has been abandoned'.

However, as Lord Dunpark observed in *McKay v Banff and Buchan Western Division Licensing Board* (author's emphasis)[5]:

'There is no provision in [s 31(6)] for suspension of the suspension of a licence until the determination of an appeal *by the board* to the Court of Session against the reversal by a sheriff of its decision against the licenceholder'.

The continuing validity of the licence in such a circumstance will thus depend upon a cross-appeal by the licenceholder.

In view of the potential for an appeal it is not appropriate for the board to state a specific date for the termination of the suspension[5].

Closure orders

Where a licensing board considers that licensed premises are 'no longer suitable or convenient for the sale of alcoholic liquor, having regard to their character and condition, and the nature and extent of the use of the premises' (s 32(1))[6] it may

1 See also s 89 in terms of which an offence is committed if premises are kept open for the sale of alcoholic liquor during any time when they are required to be closed by order of a board.
2 For appeals generally, see Chapter 15.
3 1993 SLT 109.
4 Act of Sederunt (Appeals under the Licensing (Scotland) Act 1976) 1977, SI 1977/1622.
5 1991 SCLR 15, 1991 SLT 20.
6 Cf 17(1)(b).

decide to hold a hearing with a view to making a closure order. No provision is made for the initiation of the procedure by means of a complaint, although in practice hearings are usually held following adverse reports to the board by environmental health and building control officials or the firemaster.

Procedure

Not less than 21 days before the hearing the clerk must serve notice on the licenceholder that the board proposes to hold a hearing, specifying the board's grounds (s 32(2)(a))[1]. A closure order may not be made unless the licenceholder has been heard, except where he fails to appear after receiving due notice of the hearing (s 32(2)(b))[2].

Effect of the order

Where the board is 'satisfied as to any one or more of the matters mentioned [above]' it may require closure of the premises by means of an order specifying the matters upon which it is based (s 32(3)). The order is open-ended, remaining in force until the board is 'satisfied that the matters which led to the closure order have been satisfactorily remedied' (s 32(4)), during which time the licence 'shall cease to have effect' (s 32(1))[3].

In certains respects the word 'closure' is misleading:

(a) An order may conceivably be competent in respect of premises which are in fact closed, having regard to the 'nature and extent' of their use, as well as their 'condition and 'character'. In *Mount Charlotte Investments plc v City of Glasgow Licensing Board*[4], an appeal concerning the board's refusal to renew a licence for premises which had been closed for some time, the sheriff observed that:

'To my mind, "condition" can connote more than a physical state in relation to premises. It can relate to their appearance, physical state and whether they are used or unused, refurbished or otherwise. The words "condition" and "character" . . . appear to be of equivalent meaning . . . [T]he respondents were entitled to look at the lack of use of the premises and their proposed refurbishment as their "condition"'.

(b) Section 32 orders have on occasions been made in respect of premises which are palpably unable to open for business because of, for example, serious fire damage or structural defects[5].

(c) While the licence ceases to have effect, there may be circumstances in which premises will remain open but 'dry': for example, premises which are the

---

1 Cf s 31(5)(a).
2 Cf s 31(5)(d).
3 As to offences, see above.
4 1992 SCLR 311.
5 In *Craig v Peebles* (1875) 2 R (J) 90 a certificate-holder was acquitted of trafficking where he continued to conduct his business from premises which had been substantially destroyed by fire. See also *Stevenson v Hunter* (1903) 5 F 761, (1903) 10 SLT 754; and proviso for definition of 'new licence' in s 139(1).

subject of an entertainment licence may continue to provide entertainment under a public entertainment licence[1].

The licenceholder may apply for cancellation of a closure order on the ground that the matters which gave rise to the order have been 'satisfactorily remedied' (although, in some circumstances, the works required to restore the premises to a satisfactory condition may be so radical as to require a new licence). *Pro tem*, the licence may be transferred, subject to the order. *Semble* the licence may be renewed during the closure period, but there would, of course, be a clear risk of refusal where there was no reasonable prospect of remedial action.

An appeal lies to the sheriff (and thereafter the Court of Session) (s 32(7)), placing the closure order in suspense (s 32(6))[2].

---

1 Civic Government (Scotland) Act 1982, s 41.
2 These provisions mirror s 31(6) and (8), discussed above.

CHAPTER 10

Permitted hours

THE SIGNIFICANCE OF THE PERMITTED HOURS

Licensed premises and registered clubs

Subject to a number of special cases[1], 'except during the permitted hours'[2] no person shall:

'(a) sell or supply to any person in any licensed premises, or licensed canteen or in the premises of a registered club any alcoholic liquor to be consumed either on or off the premises[3]; or
(b) consume in, or take from[4], any such premises any alcoholic liquor'[5].

Sale or supply

The words 'sell' and 'supply' are not mutually exclusive and are 'properly regarded as descriptions of different methods of committing the offence'[6]. It is irrelevant that the alcoholic liquor was supplied gratuitously[7]. A prosecution for 'selling' may be sustained although there has been no 'supply'[8].

The extent of the prohibition was considered in *Sinclair v Beattie*[8]:

'Liquor may be sold without being paid for[9]. It may be sold without being delivered at the time of sale. It may be sold and delivered on the premises. It may be supplied on the premises without being sold. In my opinion [the corresponding provision of the Licensing Act 1921] imports a universal prohibition of the sale or supply of liquor on licensed

---

1 Discussed at p 169ff below.
2 In terms of s 139(1) '"permitted hours" means the hours during which by virtue of this Act alcoholic liquor may be sold, supplied or consumed in licensed premises'. Although registered clubs have 'permitted hours' (s 53(1)) they are not 'licensed premises': see s 102(4).
3 Section 54(1)(a), (4). Maximum penalty: level 3. Licenceholder and premises subject to disqualification (s 67, Sch 5). As respects registered clubs, see also s 108(s) as a ground for the refusal of an application to renew a certificate of registration and for the cancellation of a certificate. Under the corresponding provision of the Licensing Act 1921 (s 4), it was considered that a similar prohibition did not extend to temporary club premises occupied on the occasion of a fête: *Watson v Cully* [1926] 2 KB 270.
4 It seems that the offence of 'taking' is not actually committed until the liquor leaves the premises: see *Pender v Smith* [1959] 2 QB 84, [1959] 2 All ER 360.
5 Section 54(1)(b), (4). Maximum penalty: level 3 (Sch 5).
6 *Courage v Smith* 1960 SLT 55; cf *R v South Shields Licensing Justices* [1911] 2 KB 1.
7 See *Jack v Thom* 1952 JC 41, 1952 SLT 161.
8 *Sinclair v Beattie* 1934 JC 24.
9 But see s 87 which restricts credit sales except in certain cases.

premises during the prohibited hours, and it is of no importance in what form the sale or supply is effected'[1].

The licenceholder's vicarious responsibility for sale or supply (s 67, Sch 5) extends only to the acts of his employee or agent.

In *Auld v Devlin*[2] the licensee was properly acquitted where the sale was conducted by an occasional messenger, Lord Mackenzie observing that:

'the mere fact that the money went into the till does not conclude the case from the penal point of view as against the licensee. . . In my opinion what was done here did not make the licensee guilty of an offence any more than would have been the case had a charwoman cleaning the premises handed a bottle of whisky to a purchaser'[3].

More recently, the High Court has held that the prosecution is not obliged to establish the source of the liquor or to exclude the possibility that an employee was acting for his own personal ends[4]. A licenceholder has available, however, the defence provided by the qualification to s 67 in terms of which he may prove 'that the offence occurred without his knowledge or connivance and that he exercised all due diligence to prevent its occurrence'[5].

Where a sale outwith permitted hours takes place in the premises of a registered club a complaint may be laid against the committee of management[6].

Alcoholic liquor may only be bartered, sold, or exposed or offered for sale in wholesale quantities[7] from licensed premises, a licensed canteen or a registered club 'during the hours in respect of which it is lawful to sell alcohol by retail from or in these premises, that canteen or that club' (s 90A(1)(b))[8].

While passenger vessels do not require a licence (s 138(1)(c)) an offence is committed by an person who sells or supplies alcoholic liquor on such a vessel during a voyage beginning and ending on a Sunday, except between 12.30 pm and 2.30 pm and 6.30 pm and 11 pm, being a voyage between two places in Scotland or in a vessel going from and returning to the same place in Scotland on the same day (s 93)[9]. Journeys abroad are thus exempted.

Premises are not required to be 'open for the sale or supply of alcoholic liquor during the permitted hours' (s 54(5)) but a prolonged period of closure may

---

1 At 30 per Lord Morison.
2 1918 JC 41, decided under wartime emergency legislation which made it an offence for any person either 'by himself or by a servant or agent' to sell liquor during prohibited hours, the Lord Justice-General *dubitante*.
3 See *Adams v Camfoni* [1929] 1 KB 95 for a similar English decision; cf *Gair v Brewster* 1916 SC (J) 36.
4 *Courage v Smith* 1960 SLT 55, perhaps echoing the doubts express by the Lord Justice-General in *Auld*: 'I should have been inclined. . . to have held that, if some person in licensed premises had effected a valid contract of sale that person must be held . . . *pro hac vice* an agent of the publican'. See also *Herriot v Auld* 1918 JC 16 for a case involving a 'delinquent servant'; for a recent English case involving agency, see *Moloo v DPP* [1990] Crim LR 54. As to onus, see *Ferguson v Campbell* 1946 JC 28, 1946 SLT 58.
5 The defence is further discussed in Chapter 13.
6 See *Mackenna v Burnette* 1917 JC 20, and the Criminal Procedure Act 1975, s 333; and *Anderton v Rodgers* (1981) 145 JP 181.
7 See Chapter 2.
8 A licenceholder has vicarious responsibility. Maximum penalty: level 5 (s 67, Sch 5).
9 Maximum penalty: level 3 (Sch 5). For a rare example of a prosecution, see *Lord Advocate v D & J Nicol* 1915 SC (J) 735, (1915) 1 SLT 274.

justify the refusal of a renewal application[1]. A condition attached to a regular extension of permitted hours (see s 64(6)) purporting to forbid closure during the period of the extension is probably *ultra vires*.

Consumption

For the purposes of s 54(1)(b), alcoholic liquor need not have been sold or supplied on the premises. In *Caldwell v Jones*[2] the court held that there was no reason to construe the word 'consume' otherwise than in its ordinary sense:

'I can see nothing repugnant . . . in a provision which would prevent, for example, persons purchasing intoxicating liquor in one licensed house, shortly before the termination of the permitted hours, and proceeding to adjoining licensed premises and claiming to be entitled to consume the liquor there on the ground that it had not been sold or supplied in these premises. The word "consume" means what it says; and the fact that the intoxicating liquor being consumed on the licensed premises was not sold or supplied there is an irrelevant circumstance'[3].

Prima facie the offence of consumption outwith the permitted hours is committed only by the consumer, but a licenceholder who connives at the offence may be guilty art and part[4]. In *Thomas v Lindop*[5] the licensee had been unaware that customers were still consuming liquor after time had been called. The Divisional Court held (under analagous provisions) that it was not an offence for the licensee to permit consumption and, in the absence of any knowledge on her part, she could not be considered to have 'aided and abetted' the offence.

The 'occupier or manager' of licensed premises and his employee or agent are entitled to insist that customers quit the premises at the conclusion of the permitted hours (s 79). It has been held in England that the encouragement required for 'aiding and abetting' may be supplied passively by a failure to exercise this right[6].

Use of premises outwith permitted hours

There are no 'opening' or 'closing' times for licensed premises[7], but outwith the permitted hours:
(a) where entertainment or recreational facilities are supplied to the public 'on

---

1 See *Mount Charlotte Investments plc v Glasgow District Licensing Board* 1992 SCLR 311; and consideration of renewal applications in Chapter 9.
2 [1923] 2 KB 309; cf *Blakey v Harrison* [1915] 3 KB 258.
3 At 312 per Lord Hewart, CJ.
4 *Ferguson v Weaving* [1951] 1 KB 814, [1951] 1 All ER 412.
5 [1950] 1 All ER 966.
6 *Tuck v Robson* [1970] 1 All ER 1171, [1970] 1 WLR 741.
7 Persons in licensed premises may be requested to leave at the conclusion of the permitted hours by the management or a constable (s 79) ('Constable': see s 139(1)); refusal to do so is an offence (maximum penalty: level 1 (Sch 5)). Such a request by a constable would not normally be appropriate where one of the licences mentioned below is held.

payment of money or money's worth', a public entertainment licence may be required[1];

(b) 'the sale to or consumption by the public of meals or refreshment' may necessitate a late hours catering licence[2].

In addition, the presence of persons on the premises at such a time may raise the presumption that an offence has been committed, particularly if partly consumed alcoholic liquor is found[3]. It has been held in England that where there is abundant circumstantial evidence it was 'not material that the men were not seen to consume anything. To hold otherwise would be opening a door to a gross abuse'[4].

Unlicensed premises

The permitted hours are also of significance in relation to unlicensed premises. In terms of s 83(1), subject to the provisions of the Act:

'alcoholic liquor shall not be consumed in any premises used for the sale to, or consumption by the public of provisions, refreshments[5], confectionery or tobacco, during any time when the consumption of such liquor in public houses in the licensing area[6] within which such premises are situated is prohibited by or under this Act'[7].

The expression 'any premises' is as broad as it appears: their primary use (for example, as a dance-hall)[8] is irrelevant:

'With regard to the . . . question . . . whether [the premises] were used for the sale or consumption of refreshments? the Sheriff-substitute appears to have decided that question against [the prosecutor] on the ground that the primary use of the premises was to provide facilities for dancing for those interested in that art. I do not think it is essential, to bring the premises with the purview of [the section], that it should be shown that the primary use is for the sale or consumption of refreshments. All that is necessary to satisfy the requirements of the section is that the use made of the premises for the sale or consumption of refreshments should be of a substantial character'[9].

Customers of premises will not cease to be 'the public' where an illusory membership scheme is operated. A club was held to be a place of 'public resort' where there was 'conclusive evidence that there was no discrimination in the

---

1 Civic Government (Scotland) Act 1982, s 41.
2 Ibid, s 42(1). No such licence is required in respect of 'the use as such of licensed premises' (ibid, s 42(4)(a)), nor where the premises are being used in accordance with a public entertainment licence (ibid, s 42(4)(b)).
3 But see exemptions discussed below.
4 *Thompson v Greig* (1869) 34 JP 214, per the Lord Chief Justice (Cockburn).
5 An ordinary fruit shop was held to be occupied for the sale or consumption of 'provisions or refreshments of any kind' in *McIntyre v Wilson* 1915 SC (J) 1.
6 In terms of s 139(1), '"licensing area" means any area for which there is a separate licensing board'.
7 The section does not apply to the consumption of alcoholic liquor at a private function 'related to a particular occasion': s 83(3). It seems that the offences described below are designed to address 'the evils arising from the custom of taking exciseable liquors into ice-cream shops, refreshment rooms etc, and consuming them there during the hours where licensed premises are closed': *Encyclopaedia of the Laws of Scotland* (W Green), para 429.
8 *Adair v Delworth* 1934 JC 83.
9 *Adair v Delworth*, above, at 91 per Lord Fleming.

admission of persons to the premises, and that any person could get in even under an assumed name'[1].

Since the permitted hours of public houses are now capable of extension in a variety of ways[2] it may be very difficult to determine whether consumption has taken place at a prohibited time. An offence is committed by:

(a) any person who in contravention of s 83(1) consumes alcoholic liquor (s 83(1))[3]; and

(b) any person 'keeping or occupying' the premises who permits alcoholic liquor to be consumed but such a person 'shall not be guilty of an offence . . . if he proves that the liquor in question was consumed without his knowledge or consent' (s 83(2))[4].

A person is probably the 'keeper' of premises where they are under his apparent management or control. The keeper or occupier is of course answerable for the defalcations of his employees (subject to the above defence) but they themselves are not open to prosecution.

Although a person charged with permitting consumption does not require to demonstrate that he used 'all due diligence' to prevent the offence[5], proof that it occurred without his 'knowledge or consent' may require evidence of a system to ensure compliance with the provision. A defence in the same terms was considered in *Nicol v Smith*[6]: a licenceholder not directly engaged in the management of a business who, as a matter of fact, had no 'knowledge' of an offence had not 'impliedly consented' to its commission because she trusted her manager and accepted his assurances[7].

The police are given no power of entry to the premises under the section but in terms of s 86(1) a constable[8] may at any time:

'enter and inspect [inter alia] any temperance hotel, restaurant, shop, vessel or other place where food or drink is sold for consumption on the premises or in which he has reasonable grounds for believing that alcoholic liquor is being trafficked in unlawfully'.

THE BASIC PERMITTED HOURS

All licensed premises (except off-sale premises) (s 54(2))[9] and registered clubs enjoy 'core' permitted hours as follows: every day except Sunday, between 11 am and 11 pm; on Sundays from 12.30 pm to 2.30 pm and from 6.30 pm to 11 pm

---

1 *Adair v Delworth*, above.
2 See below.
3 Maximum penalty: level 3 (Sch 5).
4 Maximum penalty: level 3 (Sch 5).
5 Cf proviso to s 67(2).
6 1955 JC 7, 1955 SLT 38.
7 See also *Noble v Heatly* 1967 JC 5, 1967 SLT 26; Sheriff G H Gordon's *The Criminal Law of Scotland*, (2nd edn, 1978), para 8.22 (discussing *Noble*) and paras 8.68ff (considering 'permitting'); and *Mallon v Allon* [1964] 1 QB 385, [1963] 3 All ER 843.
8 'Constable': see s 139(1). See also the proviso to s 86(1).
9 The off-sale departments in certain public houses and hotels are also subject to separate provisions: see below.

(s 53(1)). This is subject to the prohibition of off-sales from premises in respect of which a refreshment licence, an entertainment licence, a restricted hotel licence, a restaurant licence or a licence under Part III of the Act (Seamen's Canteen) is in force (s 53(2)).

Sunday hours are only enjoyed by public house[1] or refreshment-licensed premises where:

'(a) the grant, provisional grant or renewal [of the licence] was in response to an application which stated that it was the intention of the applicant that the premises should be open for the sale or supply of alcoholic liquor during the permitted hours on a Sunday'[2]; or
'(b) before such a licence was renewed, the licensing board has granted an application for Sunday opening in respect of the premises in accordance with the provisions of Schedule 4 to the [1976] Act'[3].

The procedure for making an application under Schedule 4 is now of no significance. The Schedule has effect until all public house and refreshment licences in force at the commencement of the 1990 Act have been renewed (or have ceased to have effect)[4]. The requirement that Schedule 4 be invoked before renewal effectively limited its availability until quarterly licensing board meetings in October 1993.

'Trading' rather than 'permitted' hours apply to (a) premises in respect of which an off-sale licence is held and (b) separate off-sale departments of public houses and hotels which are the subject of conditions inserted under s 119(2). These premises and parts of premises:

'shall not be open for the serving of customers with alcoholic liquor earlier than eight o'clock in the morning and shall be closed for the serving of customers with such liquor not later than ten o'clock in the evening; and. . . shall not be opened for the serving of customers on Sundays'[5].

Contravention of this provision by the holder of the licence (who has vicarious liability) (s 67, Sch 5) or his employee or agent is an offence (s 119(4))[6], the 'rough' description of which is given in Schedule 5 as 'Selling liquor in off-sale premises outwith permitted hours'[7]. *Semble*, however, that the mere act of being open for the serving of customers may be an offence.

There is, of course, nothing to prevent the service of customers with other commodities on Sundays, for example, in a supermarket; but some licensing boards require by byelaw (s 38(1)(f)) that the wines and spirits sales area be screened-off on that day.

A proposal to permit the limited opening of off-sale premises on Sundays was rejected in the House of Commons during the progress of the 1990 Act but

---

1 Note, however, that in terms of s 59 suitable public house premises may enjoy Sunday permitted hours for the sale or supply of alcoholic liquor to persons taking table meals in a restaurant section. The provisions of s 59 are more fully explained below.
2 1990 Act, s 46 (1)(a). The procedure is discussed further in the context of new licence applications (Chapter 4) and applications for renewal (Chapter 9).
3 1990 Act, s 46(1)(b).
4 Subject to immediate partial repeal and modification: see the 1990 Act, s 46(1) and (8).
5 Section 119(3).
6 Maximum penalty: level 3 with the licenceholder and premises subject to disqualification (Sch 5).
7 Although the concept of 'permitted hours' does not apply to off-sale premises: s 119(1).

Parliament appears consistently to have overlooked the ready availability of off-sales from public houses and hotels, often throughout the day (except where s 119(2) conditions are inserted).

Before the insertion of s 90A[1] off-sale licensed 'cash-and-carry' warehouses commonly sold alcoholic liquor in wholesale quantities[2] on Sundays. This practice has been brought to an end (s 90A(1)(b)). In the result, on Sundays the holder of a public house licence (with Sunday permitted hours) or a hotel licence[3] may sell wholesale quantities of alcoholic liquor for consumption off the premises, while the holder of an off-sale licence may not sell a single bottle.

The gratuitous supply of alcoholic liquor in off-sale licensed premises was legalised by the amendment of s 90 by para 15 of Sch 8 to the 1990 Act[4]. A question arises as to whether free-tastings may take place in off-sale licensed premises on Sundays. They must not be opened for the 'serving' of customers on that day in terms of s 119(3). On one view, when the section was enacted the draftsman could not possibly have had in view the subsequent legalisation of gratuitous supply and the 'rough' description of the relevant offence is (as noted above) stated to be 'selling liquor' outwith the prescribed hours (Sch 5). On the other hand, it may be argued that the word 'serving' requires to be given its plain meaning. There is no entirely safe answer.

EXCEPTIONS TO THE PERMITTED HOURS

Relaxations

The prohibitions constituted by s 54(1) are subject to a number of exceptions[5]:

(1) Fifteen minutes are allowed for 'drinking-up' after the conclusion of the permitted hours provided that the liquor was supplied during the permitted hours (s 54(3)(a)). This period may be added to any occasional or regular extension of the permitted hours (s 64), despite not infrequent suggestions to the contrary[6].

(2) Thirty minutes are added to the permitted hours to allow 'the consumption of alcoholic liquor at a meal' provided that 'the liquor was supplied during the permitted hours and served at the same time as the meal and for consumption at the meal' (s 54(3)(h)).

Strictly speaking, consumption of alcohol as an *ancillary* to a meal is not

---

1 By the 1990 Act, s 52.
2 See Chapter 2.
3 Provided that no conditions have been inserted in terms of s 119(2).
4 It may be remarked that no corresponding amendment was made to s 119(2) so that free-tastings in public house or hotel off-sale departments to which the section applies remain illegal (s 119(4)).
5 Note, however, that various offences relating to drunkeness and gaming on licensed premises are not linked to the permitted hours and may be committed even when an exemption applies: see ss 74, 75, 76, 77, 78 and 81.
6 See definition of 'permitted hours' in s 139(1).

enough: a post-prandial drink supplied prior to the conclusion of the permitted hours does not qualify for the exemption[1].

There is no definition of 'meal' in the Act. Whether food constitutes a 'meal' will depend upon the circumstances of the case[2]. The meal need not be a 'table meal'[3], nor is it necessary for the premises to have conventional restaurant facilities[4]. The area in which the meal is served need not be set apart for that purpose.

The thirty-minute period may be added to any extensions in force by virtue of ss 57, 58[5] or 64.

(3) Alcoholic liquor may be taken from any premises within fifteen minutes from the conclusion of the permitted hours, 'if such liquor was supplied in those premises during the permitted hours and was not supplied or taken away in an open vessel' (s 54(3)(b)). This is the last vestige of the former prohibition on any open-vessel off-sales.

(4) There is no restriction on the sale or supply to, or consumption by, any person of alcoholic liquor 'in any premises where he is residing' (s 54(3)(c))[6].

A person may be deemed to 'reside' in premises even where he occupies sleeping accommodation in an annex or overflow building (see s 139(3)). The onus of establishing residence is upon the defence[7].

'Private friends' of a resident whom he bona fide entertains at his own expense may be supplied with and consume alcoholic liquor on the premises outwith the permitted hours (s 54(3)(e))[8].

(5) The 'private friends' of 'the holder of the licence' who are 'bona fide entertained by him at his own expense' may be supplied with and consume alcoholic liquor on licensed premises at any time (s 54(3)(g)). (In terms of s 11(3), the expression 'holder of a licence' includes the employee or agent of a non-natural person).

By implication, the holder of a licence may consume alcoholic liquor as he pleases[9]. There is, however, no express exemption[10]. Under the corresponding provisions of the Licensing Act 1964 (s 63) an exemption is created by equiparating the person carrying on or in charge of the business to a 'resident'.

---

1 Cf ss 57, 58, 59 and 60, discussed at p 194ff below, where the consumption of alcohol simply requires to be 'ancillary' to a meal. The concept of 'ancillary' drinking was introduced by the Licensing (Scotland) Act 1962 but remnants of references to 'consumption at a meal' remain in the 1976 Act.
2 See *Miller v MacKnight* 1954 SLT 251; *Timmis v Millman* [1965] Brewing Tr Rev 23, (1965) 109 SJ 31; and *Solomon v Green* [1955] Brewing Tr Rev 313, (1955) 119 JP 289.
3 See definition of 'table meal' in s 139(1).
4 See *Jackson v Sinclair* [1973] 3 All ER 42, [1973] 1 WLR 840.
5 The operation of these two sections is restricted to the provision of 'table meals'.
6 Residents may also take alcoholic liquor from the premises at any time: s 54(3)(d).
7 See *Jack v Thom* 1952 JC 41, 1952 SLT 161; *Duncan v Smith* 1951 JC 1, 1951 SLT 43; and *Atkins v Agar* [1914] 1 KB 26.
8 For a consideration of 'private friends', see *Jack v Thom*, above and discussed below.
9 See *Smith v Stirling* (1878) 5 R (J) 24, now however effectively overruled on the issue of gratuitous supply to the licenceholder's friends by *Jack v Thom*, above; and *Blakey v Harrison* [1915] 3 KB 258 in which a restricted meaning was given to 'consumption' to avoid the absurdity of the landlord being prohibited from drinking his own beer during prohibited hours.
10 See *Mackenna v Brady* 1918 JC 37 for an unusual wartime case in which the owner of licensed premises was convicted of 'supplying' himself with his own stock during prohibited hours.

The accused must show that he is entitled to the exemption[1], which does not, of course, apply where the friendship is artificial or a sale of alcoholic liquor is disguised as a gratuitous supply[2].

In *Jack v Thom*[3] a group of police constables and a sergeant held a party at a hotel outwith the permitted hours with the permission but not at the invitation of the certificate holder, who supplied them with liquor without accepting payment. The officers did not regard themselves as guests, although the certificate holder was acquainted with most of the group and on first-name terms with some. In an appeal against the hotelier's conviction the court rejected an argument that the magistrates (a) had misdirected themselves by concentrating on the intentions of the persons being entertained and (b) ought to have examined the intentions of the entertainer:

'Entertainment seems to me to be a mutual affair and the thing to be looked at is the whole circumstances and particularly the character of the entertainment. The Court must look at the substance of the matter and ask themselves in terms of the statute whether the recipients of the hospitality were private friends of the appellant and bona fide entertained by him'[4].

(6) Section 54(3)(f) exempts 'the ordering of alcoholic liquor to be consumed off the premises[5] or the despatch by the vendor of liquor so ordered'. Liquor purchased during the permitted hours may be delivered to the customer at any time; and an order placed outwith the permitted hours may be transformed into a concluded sale during the permitted hours.

The provision does not authorise completed sales outwith the permitted hours. In *Valentine v Bell*[6], decided under the corresponding provisions of the Licensing Act 1921, a customer personally ordered and paid for a quantity of wine in a licensed grocer's shop outwith the permitted hours for delivery to her house. The grocer's messenger immediately set off to effect delivery and in fact passed the wine to the customer a short distance from the shop. Rejecting the defence argument that the exemption authorised both the ordering *and* despatch of liquor outwith permitted hours the court held that it applied only to inchoate transactions:

'[I]t would be absurd in one section to prohibit a sale, and in the next section to permit it. [The provision corresponding to s 54(3)(f)] permits not a sale, but ordering; and ordering, I take it, is something quite different from a sale. The section permits what, in England, has been termed "an agreement to sell"[7]; but still, in my judgment, sale remains prohibited . . . [T]he word "ordering" appears to have been very carefully chosen by the Legislature. It is in marked contrast to the word "sale" . . . A grocer may take an order

---

1 *Jack v Thom*, 1952 JC 41, 1952 SLT 161.
2 See *Corbet v Haigh* (1879) 5 CPD 50; and *Atkins v Agar* [1914] 1 KB 26.
3 See above.
4 1952 JC 41 at 46 per the Lord Justice-Clerk.
5 Off-sales which would be unlawful under an entertainment (s 101(1)) or off-sale (s 99(b)) or refreshment (s 100(b)) licence remain prohibited.
6 1930 JC 51, followed in *Sinclair v Beattie* 1934 JC 24 (see below) and *Mizen v Old Florida Ltd, Egan v Mizen* (1934) 50 TLR 340.
7 See *Titmus v Littlewood* [1916] 1 KB 732.

within the prohibited hours but may not, as I read the section, take the order and complete the sale outwith the hours'[1].

The facts of *Sinclair v Beattie*[2] were broadly similar (the liquor was ordered and paid for during prohibited hours) except that the grocer's assistant was intercepted by the police before delivery to the purchaser (also during prohibited hours) could be effected. By a majority[3] the court followed *Valentine* and held that the absence of delivery was 'quite immaterial': 'If the statute had intended that the word "sell" should mean "sell and supply" or "sell and deliver", it would have said so'[4].

The importance of the exemption has, of course, been considerably diminished by the substantial increase in the permitted hours in recent years.

(7) Outwith the permitted hours alcoholic liquor may be sold (but not simply supplied) 'to a trader for the purposes of his trade, or to a registered club for the purposes of the club' (s 54(3)(i)). This provision is probably designed to allow traders[5] and clubs to purchase emergency supplies. The exemption is not available to the holders of licences for off-sale premises, which have 'trading' rather than 'permitted' hours (s 119(1)) and accordingly may not be employed to cater for trade customers on Sundays.

(8) No restrictions are placed on:

'the sale or supply of alcoholic liquor to any canteen in which the sale or supply of alcoholic liquor is carried on under the authority of the Secretary of State or to any authorised mess of members of Her Majesty's naval, military or air forces'[6].

(9) The Secretary of State is empowered to make an order exempting from the permitted hours and off-sale 'trading' hours licensed premises which are within the examination station[7] at an airport 'which appears to him to be an airport at which there is a substantial amount of international passenger traffic' (s 63(1), (2), as amended by the Customs and Excise Management Act 1979, s 177(1), Sch 4, para 12, Table, Pt I).

He must first satisfy himself that arrangements have been made for affording reasonable facilities for obtaining hot and cold beverages other than alcoholic liquor at all times when alcoholic liquor is available for consumption in the licensed premises. An order may be revoked as respects an airport where such arrangements are not being maintained, although a fresh order may subsequently be made (s 63(3)).

---

1 1930 JC 51 at 54 per the Lord Justice-Clerk.
2 1934 JC 24.
3 The Lord Justice-General (Clyde) dissenting.
4 At 31 per Lord Morison. See also *Pletts v Beattie* [1896] 1 QB 519, (1896) 12 TLR 227.
5 The term 'trader' presumably embraces not only a licenceholder but also a wholesaler.
6 Section 54(3)(j). Service canteens themselves are outwith the scope of the Act. The reference to the Secretary of State includes a reference to the service authorities of a visiting force and the reference to members of Her Majesty's forces includes a reference to members of visiting forces: Visiting Forces and International Headquarters (Application of Law) Order 1965, SI 1965/1536; and Visiting Forces (Designation) (Colonies) (Amendment) Order 1958, SI 1958/1262.
7 The 'examination station' is the part of, or place at, a customs and excise airport approved by the Commissioners of Customs and Excise for the loading and unloading of goods and the embarkation and disembarkation of passengers under s 22 of the Customs and Excise Management Act 1979.

At present these provisions apply to the airports at Aberdeen, Edinburgh, Glasgow, Prestwick[1] and Sumburgh[2].

(10) The holder of a licence in respect of any premises[3] may supply alcoholic liquor outwith the permitted hours on an order stating the reason for the supply signed:

(a) by a constable[4] of or above the rank of inspector or by a constable in charge of a police station; or

(b) by the procurator fiscal;

(c) by a medical official[5]; or

(d) in the case of sickness, accident or emergency, by a duly qualified medical practitioner (s 125(1)).

Such an order shall be:

'sufficient defence in any prosecution in respect of the supply of the alcoholic liquor to which it relates if within forty-eight hours after the supply . . . the order is sent by post to the procurator fiscal together with a note of the description and quantity of the liquor supplied and the name and address of the person to whom it was supplied'[6].

The procurator fiscal is required to make a quarterly return to the licensing board of orders received from licenceholders in the board's area (see s 125(3)).

(11) No licence is required for a theatre erected before 1 January 1904 (s 138(1)(b)), which is treated 'as if an entertainment licence were in force' for the purpose of the sale or supply of alcoholic liquor (s 121); and, since such a theatre is not 'licensed premises', the permitted hours do not apply. The conclusion may thus be drawn that, having regard to the definition of 'entertainment licence' in Schedule 1, liquor may be sold or supplied as an ancillary to entertainment at any time; but, suprisingly, the Act provides no mechanism which would ensure that such a connection is maintained[7].

Modifications

Byelaw provisions

A licensing board's byelaws[8] may provide for 'closing licensed premises wholly or partially on New Year's Day, and on such other days not being more than four in any one year as the board may think expedient for special reasons' (s 38(1)(a)).

---

1 The Airports Licensing (Liquor) (Scotland) Order 1977, SI 1977/763.
2 The Sumburgh Airport Licensing (Liquor) Order 1987, SI 1987/838.
3 Including premises from which off-sales are not normally permitted.
4 'Constable': see s 139(1).
5 No definition of this term is offered.
6 Section 125(2).
7 Under s 161 of the Licensing (Scotland) Act 1959 the permitted hours were indirectly applied to theatres erected before 31 December 1903: exciseable liquor could not be sold or supplied during prohibited hours for public houses in the area.
8 See Chapter 8.

Entertainment licences

An entertainment licence may be granted or renewed subject to conditions placing restrictions on the permitted hours 'in order to secure that the sale or supply of alcoholic liquor is ancillary to the entertainment' (s 101(2))[1].

Seasonal licences

A licence may be granted, renewed or transferred subject to a condition that during part or parts of the year (not exceeding 180 days in total) there shall be no permitted hours or, in the case of off-sale premises, trading hours. As respects hotel premises the condition may be refined to allow only the operation of a public bar or restaurant (s 62)[2]. Since the permitted hours do not apply to hotel residents (in terms of s 54(3)(c)), they may still be supplied with alcoholic liquor out-of-season.

Athletic clubs

A registered club may make application to the sheriff for an order providing that there shall be alternative permitted hours on Sundays from 12.30 pm to 2 pm and from 4 pm to 9 pm during 'the winter period' from 1 October to 31 March (s 56(1), as amended by the 1990 Act, s 45(2), (5)).

The sheriff clerk is required to give immediate notice of an application to the chief constable who may, within 20 days of receipt of such notice, lodge objections on the ground that one or more of the conditions mentioned below has not or have not been satisfied. A copy of the objections must be sent to the secretary of the club. The sheriff must conduct a hearing if objections are not withdrawn and 'may order such enquiry as he thinks fit'. Expenses may be awarded against the unsuccessful party (s 56(3)).

The sheriff shall make the order if in his opinion a number of conditions are satisfied (s 56(1)):

'(a) that the premises of the club are structurally adapted and bona fide used, or intended to be used, wholly or mainly for the purpose of providing facilities in connection with the carrying on by members of the club and their guests of athletic sports or athletic games;
(b) that one or more of such sports or games is or are usually carried on out of doors and, when so carried on, can (unless artificial lighting is used) only be carried on during the hours of daylight;
(c) that the said premises are regularly used, or are intended to be used, during the winter period, for providing facilities in connection with the carrying on by members of the club and their guests, during the hours of daylight, of such a sport or game as is mentioned in paragraph (b) above;
(d) that having regard to the time at which the said sport or game is usually carried on by members of the club and their guests, the permitted hours set out in section 53 of [the] Act

---

1 See also discussion of entertainment licences in Chapter 3.
2 See *Wallace v Kyle and Carrick District Licensing Board* 1979 SLT (Sh Ct) 12.

are not suitable for the supply of alcoholic liquor in the said premises to persons who participate in that sport or game'[1].

An order made under these provisions expires with the club's certificate of registration (s 56(4)).

EXTENSIONS OF THE PERMITTED HOURS

Regular extensions

The holder of a licence (other than an off-sale licence) (s 64(1)) and the secretary of a registered club (s 64(5)) may apply to the licensing board within whose area the premises are situated for the regular extension of permitted hours.

An application may only be considered at a quarterly meeting of the board (s 5(2)) and must be lodged not later than five weeks before the first day of the meeting (s 10(1))[2] and requires to be advertised (s 12)[3].

The clerk has no discretion to accept an application which has not been lodged timeously. In *Main v City of Glasgow District Licensing Board*[4] the petitioner argued (unsuccessfully) that the board's clerk had incorrectly computed the last date for submission of his application and sought an order whereby the application would be placed on the agenda for the quarterly meeting but would then be continued to an adjourned sitting to allow for publication and possible objection. The Lord Ordinary (Morison) expressed the opinion, obiter, that:

'[E]ven if I had been satisfied that the respondents' clerk acted contrary to the statutory provisions, I would not have pronounced any order since the petitioner has not thereby suffered any disadvantage. Further difficulty would in any event have arisen in connection with the order sought, in respect that it would have involved a radical departure from the programme envisaged by the Act so as to allow for future publication of the application and possible objection. Such difficulty might have been avoided by an earlier application for an interim order for publication'.

Since the availability of extended hours is crucial for the viability of many licensed businesses, particularly discothèques and other entertainment-licensed premises, it may well be thought that the scope of s 13(2)[5] should be broadened to encompass regular extension applications.

Where a licenceholder has failed to make timeous application for a regular extension of hours he may, in certain licensing board areas, be permitted to obtain a series of occasional extensions[6] to fill the *lacuna* until the next quarterly meeting;

---

1 Section 56(2).
2 As to the computation of the last date for lodgement, see *Main v City of Glasgow District Licensing Board* 1987 SLT 305; and discussion of time limits in Chapter 1.
3 The application may contain a request that the agent's, rather than the applicant's, address be published, in which case any intimation requirement (normally in relation to an objection) may be satisfied by intimation to the agent: s 139(5), (6), added by the 1990 Act, Sch 8, para 18.
4 See above.
5 Which affords licensing boards a discretion to consider certain other types of late applications.
6 See below.

but a number of licensing boards will not countenance such a device unless the applicant is intending to cater for bona fide functions.

The loss of a regular extension of hours may create double jeopardy. Section 41 of the Civic Government (Scotland) Act 1982 provides that a public entertainment licence is required for 'any place where, on payment of money or money's worth, members of the public are admitted or may use any facilities for the purpose of entertainment or recreation'[1], excluding inter alia 'licensed premises within the meaning of the Licensing (Scotland) Act 1976 in which public entertainment is being provided during the permitted hours within the meaning of that Act'[2].

While the operator of, say, an entertainment-licensed discothèque will be disinclined to open for business during a 'dry' period, owners of other types of premises which provide entertainment within the meaning of s 41 may well wish to continue trading during hours which were the subject of the extension to the permitted hours and should accordingly obtain a public entertainment licence as a safeguarding measure.

In suitable cases the licenceholder should make use of the table meal extensions available for dining areas[3] which may provide a measure of comfort upon the loss of a regular extension.

An applicant for the regular extension of permitted hours must at the same time as he makes the application send a copy thereof to the chief constable (s 64(1)). No doubt for reasons of administrative convenience some clerks request that a copy of the application be served not upon the chief constable but upon the senior local police officer. Since the same officer is usually empowered to intimate objections (s 16(1)) to an application on behalf of the chief constable in terms of a force's standing orders (and is presumably entitled to object in any event as the chief constable's agent)[4] this practice would appear to be unexceptionable.

However, at least one licensing board requires the completion of the application form in duplicate, with one copy being sent to the local police by the clerk. No challenge to this procedure has yet been taken but since s 64(1) places the intimation onus upon the applicant the procedure may only be regarded as legitimate if it may be said that, in transmitting a copy to the police, the clerk is acting as the applicant's agent, which is a dubious interpretation of the relationship.

A board may not grant extended hours to the holder of a public house licence on Sundays except (1) where s 59[5] has been applied to the premises and only for the purposes of that section and (2) in the case of other premises as respects any period or periods after 2.30 pm (s 64(4)); but a regular (or occasional) extension may commence on a Saturday evening and continue into the following morning

---

1 Civic Government (Scotland) Act 1982, s 41(2), which, in terms of s 9 of that Act, has effect in a licensing authority's area only if and in so far as the authority have so resolved.
2 Ibid, s 41(2)(f).
3 See below.
4 *Lorimer's Breweries Ltd v City of Glasgow District Licensing Board*, Glasgow Sheriff Court, 20 October 1980, unreported; and *Stephen v City of Aberdeen District Licensing Board* 1989 SLT (Sh Ct) 94.
5 See below.

(s 64(4A)). Sunday extensions are not to be granted if they 'would cause undue disturbance or public nuisance in the locality' (s 64(4A)[1].

Attendance at board meetings

The board 'may decline' to consider[2] an application if the applicant or his representative does not attend the meeting at which the application is to be considered (s 15(1)). The words 'may decline' afford a discretion which must be exercised rationally: the board must ask itself whether non-appearance or non-representation have any significance as to its decision on the merits[3]. A compearing applicant has a right to be heard[4]. Where the board continues an application to an adjourned meeting following non-appearance, an existing grant of a regular extension lapses unless the board decides upon its reinstatement ad interim.

Relevant considerations

A licensing board may grant a licenceholder's application for the regular extension of permitted hours:

'if, having regard to the social circumstances of the locality in which the premises in respect of which the application is made are situated or to activities taking place in that locality, the board considers it desirable to do so'[5].

Similar provision is made for registered clubs (s 64(5)): the licensing board requires to be 'satisfied' as to the matters mentioned above.

In terms of s 64(8), a regular extension is not to be granted if the board considers that the extension 'is likely to cause undue public nuisance or to be a threat to public order or safety'. This provision overlaps with a distinct ground of refusal in relation to public house extensions on Sundays which are not to be granted if the board 'finds that the extension of permitted hours would cause undue disturbance or public nuisance in the locality' (s 64(4)).

It seems clear that the intended relationship between extensions and 'social circumstances' and 'activities' was designed to create real criteria which the applicant required to satisfy and, early in the life of the 1976 Act, regular extensions, even for afternoon periods, were hard won, particularly in urban areas. Eventually, in the absence of any perceived social problems, a more liberal approach became the norm and the amendment to s 53 by s 45(1) of the 1990 Act, which created standard permitted hours on weekdays from 11 am to 11 pm, was essentially in recognition of the fact that this 12-hour drinking period on weekdays was virtually standard throughout Scotland. A similar pattern has emerged in relation to Sunday afternoon extensions in public houses, which only became possible from 1 January 1991; by May 1991, a total of 3,179 such extensions had been granted, an uptake of about 66 per cent[6].

1 Cf s 64(8): see below.
2 A declinature to consider an application is not a refusal so that s 64(9) does not apply: see 'Prohibition on further applications', below.
3 See *Bury v Kilmarnock and Loudoun District Licensing Board* 1988 SCLR 436, 1989 SLT 110.
4 *C R S Leisure Ltd v Dumbarton District Licensing Board* 1989 SCLR 566, 1990 SLT 200.
5 Section 64(3).
6 Source: Scottish Office Statistic Bulletin CRJ/1992/5, August 1992.

On the other hand, late evening extensions have always been and remain much more controversial. In November 1988 the Scottish Home and Health department issued a circular[1] to licensing boards and chief constables suggesting that:

'the proliferation of regular late-night extensions is causing difficulty and distress to local residents and to police in the maintenance of order in the early hours of the morning out of all proportion to any benefit the community may derive from the grant of such extensions'.

There was also a suggestion in the circular that boards had adopted an unjustifiably relaxed approach to the 'social circumstances' and 'activities' tests (which applicants had often been able to meet by reference simply to amorphous factors such as 'local demand' and 'passing trade').

In certain areas the response was immediate, usually in the form of new policies or guidelines for late evening (and indeed other) extensions (see below).

The circular effectively foreshadowed s 47(1) of the 1990 Act which prescribes additional criteria to be met before extensions may be granted, in an effort to fetter the wide discretion afforded to boards by the principal Act. The applicant must demonstrate:

'(a) that there is a need in the locality in which the premises in respect of which the application is made are situated for a regular extension of the permitted hours; and
(b) that such an extension is likely to be of such benefit to the community as a whole as to outweigh any detriment to that locality'[2].

While the lack of detriment may reasonably be inferred from the absence of objections, 'need' is not easily demonstrated. No doubt it is a close relation of 'demand' but is not to be equiparated with 'deprivation'[3]. At least one board requires a regular extension applicant to demonstrate 'need' by having previously obtained a series of occasional extensions.

In *Brechin Golf and Squash Club v Angus District Licensing Board*[4] the petitioners' regular extension application was partially refused for the reason (inter alia) that the board 'was not satisfied . . . that there was a need for persons participating in club activities, ie playing golf or squash, to be able to have a drink on Sundays between 11 am and 12 noon'. The Lord Ordinary (Caplan) considered that this reason fell 'considerably short of being free from ambiguity', but said: 'Local need for a facility cannot be equated with the personal needs of club members', a somewhat cryptic observation which may require to be viewed with a degree of caution. In view of the limited basis upon which alcoholic liquor may be supplied to non-members (see s 107(1)(k)) applications are, of course, generally based on the needs of club members (which can be none other than 'personal').

The introduction of the concept of 'community benefit' may stem from the decision in *Semple v Glasgow District Licensing Board*[5] where doubt arose as to

2 SHHD 20/88, reproduced in the rubric to *Centralbite Ltd v Kincardine and Deeside District Licensing Board* 1989 SCLR 65.
3 These more stringent tests appear to have produced some effect. About 10,700 regular extensions of the permitted hours were granted by licensing boards from June 1991 to May 1992, representing a decrease of 21 per cent from the previous 12-month period. Source: Scottish Office Statistical Bulletin, CRJ/1993/4, July 1993.
4 *R v Sheffield Crown Court ex parte Mead* [1992] 8 LR 19. See also *R v Chester Quarter Sessions ex parte Murray* [1966] Brewing Tr Rev 287.
5 1993 SCLR 191, 1993 SLT 547.
6 1990 SCLR 73, decided before s 47 of the 1990 Act came into force.

whether the satisfaction of 'a wider community need' could be related to the 'social circumstances' and 'activities' criteria in s 64(3). In support of an application for an early-morning regular extension the applicant founded on the demand created by elderly residents who were fearful of leaving their homes in the evening and by a local voluntary organisation which provided support for drug users. The board's statement of reasons for the refusal of the application contained the following passage:

'The board rejected the submissions that public demand and serving a wider community need, on the argument put forward, could be related to either the social circumstances of the locality or the activities taking place in that locality'.

The Lord Ordinary was not prepared to hold that the board had excluded 'wider community need' as a relevant factor but 'saw force' in its submission that the considerations advanced as constituting social need (for example, the service of breakfasts) were not related to the supply of alcoholic liquor.

Conceivably, s 47(1)(b) is designed, at least in part, to remove any doubt as to the legitimacy of the applicant's arguments without, of course, disturbing the board's fundamental discretion.

It requires to be kept in view that there is an onus on the applicant to address the requirements of s 47(1)[1]; but where the appropriate submissions have been made the board is then obligated in accordance with the dictum of Lord Emslie in *Wordie Property Co Ltd v Secretary of State for Scotland*[2] to give informative reasons for refusal[3].

With the passage of time it is becoming clear that in a great many areas applications will continue to stand or fall on the basis of policy considerations (discussed below) and the existence or otherwise of police or public objections.

While boards are generally careful to define 'locality' for the purposes of new licence applications[4], much less attention is paid to that word in the consideration of regular extensions. So far as the possibility of public nuisance is concerned boards will have regard to the potential impact of extended hours on members of the public wherever they may be. In *Bantop v Glasgow District Licensing Board*[5] the Lord Ordinary (Dervaird) remarked that 'clearly undue public nuisance might arise elsewhere than in the locality to which attention is focused by section 64(3)'. The term 'public' includes:

'not only the public at large who live, work, or happen to be close enough to the premises so as to be likely to be affected by what goes on there, but also that section of the public which is attracted to the premises themselves . . . Members of that section of the public are as much entitled to the board's consideration as members of the public at large . . . .'[6]

It is irrelevant that the premises are well-managed[7] or that there is potential for

---

1 *Perfect Swivel Ltd v City of Dundee Licensing Board (No 2)* 1993 SLT 112, 1992 GWD 17-990.
2 1984 SLT 345.
3 *Brechin Golf and Squash Club v Angus District Licensing Board* 1993 SCLR 191, 1993 SLT 547. See also *Ali v Banff and Buchan District Council* 1990 GWD 18-1017, 2nd Div.
4 See *Botterills of Blantyre v Hamilton District Licensing Board* 1986 SLT 14.
5 1989 SCLR 731, 1990 SLT 366.
6 *Sangha v Bute and Cowal Divisional Licensing Board* 1990 SCLR 409. See also *Freeland v City of Glasgow District Licensing Board* 1980 SLT (Sh Ct) 125.
7 *Surrey Heath Council v McDonalds Restaurants Ltd* [1990] 3 LR 21.

bad management[1]. Where the actual record of the premises during the extended hours puts the quality of management and thus the fitness of the licenceholder in issue the actual licence may be suspended in terms of s 31[2].

It is equally irrelevant that incidents of disorder take place outside or even some distance from the premises. Indeed, late-night dispersal problems are the primary source of objections and attempts are frequently made to shift responsibility towards other premises which enjoy similar facilities[3]. In *Lidster v Owen*[4] the applicants argued without success that an excessive number of persons were attracted to the area of their premises because of 'the decisions of the justices to grant further licences in close proximity to the subject premises after the original grant to the applicants and/or the failure of the chief constable to oppose the grants of such further licences'. Lord Justice Slade held:

'[I]t does seem to me that the applicants have been rather unlucky, bearing in mind that theirs was the first of three relevant discothèques on the scene, and their running of the premises has not been criticised in any way. I have, for my part, some sympathy with them. Nevertheless, the evidence before the justices showed that, throughout 1980, what the justices described in the case stated as a "quite unacceptable degree of public disorder" existed in [certain] areas of Bournemouth, and that the principal factor creating this disorder was the number of persons leaving the applicants' premises and the other discothèque premises in Glen Fern Road at one o'clock in the morning'[5].

For reasons which are not immediately apparent, chief constables have on occasions elected to proceed by way of complaints in terms of s 31[6] or s 65[7] rather then object to regular extension applications. In *McKay v Banff and Buchan Western Division Licensing Board*[8] almost all of the incidents relied upon by the chief constable in support of a complaint made under s 31 appear to have occurred after 11 pm. Remarkably, the chief constable submitted his complaint to the licensing board just six days before the consideration of a regular extension application which he did not oppose. The sheriff found some significance in this approach:

'It is not at all clear why the [chief constable] failed to object at the hearing of the renewal of the extensions to the licence and one cannot say whether that was due to maladministration or deliberate tactics or calculated caprice . . . the board may well have taken an alternative course of action . . . by the refusal of the renewal of the regular extension'[9].

The logic of this observation seems virtually unassailable, but the Second Division appears to have been unimpressed and rejected the licenceholder's argument that an evening restriction order would have been more appropriate, on

---

1 *Perfect Swivel Ltd v City of Dundee Licensing Board* 1993 SLT 112, 1992 GWD 17-990.
2 See *McKay v Banff and Buchan Western Division Licensing Board* 1991 SCLR 15, 1991 SLT 20.
3 See *Gordon Highlanders' (Glasgow) Association Club v Mason* 1954 SLT (Sh Ct) 45: the 'clear evidence' of persons living near a registered club gave a reliable indication as to the source of those responsible for drunken behaviour.
4 [1983] 1 All ER 1012, [1983] 1 WLR 516.
5 See also *McKay v Banff and Buchan Western Division Licensing Board*, above.
6 Which provides for suspension of the licence: see Chapter 9.
7 Which allows the board to impose inter alia an evening restriction order: see below.
8 1991 SCLR 15, 1991 SLT 20.
9 An extract from the sheriff's note is printed at 1991 SCLR 23.

the narrow but no doubt correct ground that such an order was incompetent in the context of s 31 proceedings.

In *Devana Investments Ltd v City of Aberdeen District Licensing Board*[1], which concerned a complaint by the chief constable in terms of s 65 initiated in August 1990, it appears that he made no objection to a regular extension application which was granted by the board at the March 1990 meeting. The sheriff, referring to certain incidents relied upon by the complainer, observed that:

'those incidents, if thought important, could have been invoked the year before when the extension of hours was applied for and at that stage the chief constable could have founded on them as a ground for refusing the application for extended hours'.

Devana Investments Ltd is to be contrasted with *McKay* in another material respect. In the latter, the Second Division took a 'broad brush' approach:

'[I]n my opinion, taking the nature and cumulative effect of the thirty-three incidents over a period, it was open to the board to conclude that both grounds of complaint were proved. It is not appropriate in a case such as this to examine each incident in detail'.[2]

However, in *Devana Investments Ltd* a reliance upon 'the volume and nature of the incidents' faltered when some of the alleged incidents were challenged by the licenceholder and the board's refusal to hear evidence was fatal to the restriction order. This decision (which was not appealed to the Inner House) may well encourage chief constables to take a qualitative rather than quantitative approach[3].

It would appear that the fitness of the licenceholder should not be taken into account. In *C R S Leisure Ltd v Dumbarton District Licensing Board*[4] the Lord Ordinary (Prosser) observed: '[I]t does not seem to me to be appropriate for a board, in considering the issue under section 64, to consider the fitness of the licenceholder'[5]. Similarly, in *Perfect Swivel Ltd v City of Dundee Licensing Board (No 2)*[6], in which the chief constable had objected to a regular extension application on the ground that two of the company applicant's directors were the subject of previous convictions and accordingly the company could not be trusted to conduct its business during any extension of permitted hours without causing undue public nuisance or a threat to public order or safety, the board sustained the objection but did not seek to support it in the ensuing judicial review proceedings.

The condition of the premises is an irrelevant consideration. In *Bantop Ltd v Glasgow District Licensing Board*[7] the board, following a practice shared with certain others, had taken the view that an adverse report from the local environmental health department made it undesirable that the licenceholders be permitted to sell alcohol outside the normal hours. The Lord Ordinary (Dervaird) held

---

1 1992 SCLR 616.
2 Per Lord Dunpark.
3 See Chapter 15, sub voce 'Natural justice' for a further discussion of *Devana Investments Ltd* and similar cases.
4 1989 SCLR 566, 1990 SLT 200.
5 But see also *McKay v Banff and Buchan Western Division Licensing Board* 1991 SCLR 15, 1991 SLT 20, as to the possibility of a complaint under s 31.
6 1993 SLT 112, 1992 GWD 17-990.
7 1989 SCLR 731, 1990 SLT 366.

that the board had no power to take this approach and observed that the matters of concern could properly be addressed under s 32[1].

The previous grant of a regular extension in similar terms appears to be of no significance. There is no 'renewal' as such and each fresh application falls to be considered *de novo*[2].

Each application must be considered on its own merits. Section 47(2) of the 1990 Act provides that:

'In determining whether to grant an application for a regular extension of permitted hours in respect of any premises it shall not be a relevant consideration for the licensing board to have regard to whether any application relating to any other premises in its area has, at any time, been granted or refused or the grounds on which any such application has been granted or refused'.

This requirement was initially interpreted as delivering a broadside to licensing board policies (see below) but conventional wisdom now suggests that previous board decisions and policies are distinguishable. The subsection certainly relieves licensing boards from any obligation to be consistent. Its origin is possibly to be found in the following dicta of Lord Dervaird in *Centralbite Ltd v Kincardine and Deeside District Licensing Board*[3]:

'It does not, as it appears to me, necessarily follow that because it is desirable in the views of the board that one extension be granted, it is desirable that all other extensions be granted. That is a matter to be considered in relation to the particular circumstances. The important point here is that the reason which is stated can be read and in my view properly falls to be read as a concern by the board as to the number of applications for extensions with which they might have to deal. If that is a correct interpretation of that, in my opinion that is an irrelevant consideration'.

Licensing board policies

Policies or guidelines have become increasingly popular with licensing boards over the past few years in their treatment of regular extension applications, to the extent that, in many areas, applications within the bounds of the policy will be granted automatically in the absence of objections and only objected applications or those which seek to go beyond policy limits will require a hearing.

A board may provide, for example, that no extensions will normally be granted after a certain evening hour in respect of premises in tenemental property; or fix the limits of extensions by reference to the type of licence, usually (but not always) allowing operators of heavily-invested entertainment-licensed premises an advantage over others; or determine the length of extensions according to geographical location.

This approach has received the support of the court. In *Elder v Ross and*

---

1 Cf the *Report of the Departmental Committee on Scottish Licensing Law* (Cmnd 5354) (*Clayson*), para 9.72: 'As regards public health, if standards of hygiene and cleanliness were not being maintained, perhaps on account of the absence of the compulsory afternoon break, the remedy should lie in proceedings under the relevant statutory powers, and not in any action under the licensing laws'.
2 *Semple v Glasgow District Licensing Board* 1990 SCLR 73; *Elder v Ross and Cromarty Licensing Board* 1990 SCLR 1, 1990 SLT 307, both discussed in the next section.
3 1989 SCLR 652, 1990 SLT 231.

Cromarty Licensing Board[1] the petitioner argued that the board was not entitled to formulate a policy and that in any event the policy was objectionable because it applied to the whole district, ignoring local factors within the area. There had been no objections to his application and his premises had been generally free from complaints. The Lord Ordinary (Weir) adopted the following approach:

'Where a statutory body having discretionary power is required to consider numerous applications, there is no objection to it announcing that it proposes to follow a certain general policy in examining such applications. Indeed, in certain circumstances it may be desirable to achieve a degree of consistency in dealing with applications of a similar character . . . However, such a declared policy may be objectionable if certain conditions are not fulfilled. A policy must be based on grounds which relate to and are not inconsistent with or destructive of the purposes of the statutory provisions under which the discretion is operated[2]. Moreover, the policy must not be so rigidly formulated so that if applied the statutory body is thereby disabled from exercising the discretion entrusted to it. Finally, the individual circumstances of each application must be considered in each case whatever the policy may be. It is not permissible for a body exercising a statutory discretion to refuse to apply its mind to that application on account of an apparent conflict with policy. . .'.

While these views follow a line of English authority[3] the Lord Ordinary's opinion that 'There was no status quo. On the expiry of the previous grant there had to be an application and consideration of that application *de novo*' should perhaps be subject to the qualification suggested by other English cases. In *Re Sheptonhurst Ltd*[4], which concerned the refusal of local authorities to renew sex shop licences, Lord Justice O'Connor observed that (in terms of the relevant legislation) no distinction was to be drawn between grant and renewal of the licence and a 'fresh look' could be taken at the matter but 'when considering an application for renewal the local authority had to give due weight to the fact that a licence was granted for the previous year and indeed for however many years before that'.

It has also been suggested, in Scotland, that an intended change of policy (a) *may*[5] and (b) *should* be intimated to interested parties:

'[I]t may well have been courteous and fair for those members of the board who were considering opposing the application to have given the petitioners' representative some warning of a possible change in the respondents' attitude so that he could have addressed the respondents more fully and also responded to any matter particularly troubling them'[6].

In *Elder* the board's change of attitude towards previously uncontentious applications was precipitated at least in part by the Scottish Home and Health Department circular referred to above and by representations made to it by a local crime prevention panel. There may be other considerations:

---

1 1990 SCLR 1, 1990 SLT 307. See also 1 *Stair Memorial Encyclopaedia* para 241.
2 See also *Mecca Ltd v Edinburgh Corpn* 1967 SLT (Sh Ct) 43.
3 See, for example, *R v Torquay Licensing Justices ex parte Brockman* [1951] 2 KB 784 and *Sagnata Investments Ltd v Norwich Corpn* [1971] 2 QB 614.
4 The Times, 29 June 1989, unreported. See also *R v Windsor Licensing Justices ex parte Hodes* [1983] 2 All ER 551, [1983] 1 WLR 685.
5 *Elder v Ross and Cromarty District Licensing Board* 1990 SCLR 1, 1990 SLT 307.
6 *Brechin Golf and Squash Club v Angus District Licensing Board*, 1993 SCLR 191, 1993 SLT 547, OH.

'[T]he policy of a local authority may quite reasonably change from time to time, for various reasons, such as a change in its composition resulting from an election, or pressure of public opinion, or its own experience of operating the provisions of the Acts. . .'[1].

Per contra, *Semple v Glasgow District Licensing Board*[2] suggests that there need be no substantive reason for a policy shift. In this case early morning extensions, primarily designed to service the needs of local bakery nightshift workers, which had been operated over a four-year period without complaint, were refused because the board, having reviewed its approach to early morning extensions, decided that the presence of shiftworkers in an area was no longer a factor which would per se justify the grant of the application.

The rationale of the policy change was not explained and it may be inferred from the Lord Ordinary's decision that the omission is of no significance. Such an interpretation, if correct, leads to a regrettable result. The advocate whose task is to persuade a board to depart from its general policy will wish to demonstrate that the grant of an application will not undermine the reasons for the policy. In *R v Chester Crown Court ex parte Pascoe and Jones*[3] Lord Justice Glidewell said:

'[W]here there is a general policy and an applicant is seeking to persuade a court to make a proper departure from that general policy, then amongst the most important of matters which the court or justices must consider is the reasons for the policy and whether, if it were to grant what is sought by way of exception, those reasons would still be met.'[4]

Perhaps some comfort may be drawn from *Atherlay v Lanark County Council*[5] (decided under gaming legislation) in which the sheriff held:

'I have already indicated that a local authority is entitled to change its mind and its policy in relation to applications [for amusement with prizes machine permits], and, for aught I know, that is what has happened in the case of the present application. But equally, a local authority is bound to give clear and relevant reasons. . . Had they stated in the grounds of refusal. . . that they had changed their policy and had now come to be of the opinion that the provision of amusements with prizes in public houses was undesirable, for certain specific reasons, this appeal might have had a different outcome . . .'[6].

In *Semple* the petitioner sought, without success, to show that the circumstances of her application could not be distinguished from those surrounding similar applications which had been granted in respect of premises elsewhere in the city. With the introduction of s 47(2) of the 1990 Act (see above) the issue of comparative fairness no longer arises.

Since a board must leave 'its mind ajar'[7] and the 'shadow of the rubber-stamp' is to be avoided[8], it will usually be at pains to declare that each case is examined on its own merits but there is frequently a suspicion that a policy has in fact been rigidly applied or that a small minority of applications are granted 'out of policy' for cosmetic reasons to negate such an allegation. *Elder* and *Semple* demonstrate

1 *Atherlay v Lanark County Council* 1968 SLT (Sh Ct) 71.
2 1990 SCLR 73.
3 [1987] 151 JPR 752.
4 See also *R v Sheffield Crown Court ex parte Mead* [1992] 8 LR 20.
5 See above.
6 See also *In Re Sheptonhurst Ltd* The Times, 29 June 1989, unreported.
7 See *Aitken v City of Glasgow District Council* 1988 SCLR 287 at 291.
8 *R v Cardiff City Stipendiary Magistrate* [1977] BSMD 37.

that a charge of *mala fides* would require to be specifically pled and supported by a plea-in-law.

Objections[1]

In terms of s 64(7):

'Any person mentioned in section 16(1) of the Act may object to an application for the regular extension of permitted hours, and any such objection shall be made in writing and lodged with the clerk of the licensing board and a copy thereof sent to the applicant not less than seven days before the quarterly meeting at which the application is to be considered'.

Accordingly, objections are competent at the instance of persons owning or occupying property in the neighbourhood or any organisation which in the board's opinion represents such persons (s 16(1)(a)); a community council (s 16(1)(b)); an organised church which in the board's view represents a significant body of opinion (s 16(1)(c)); the chief constable (s 16(1)(d)); the fire authority (s 16(1)(e)); and the local authority (s 16(1)(f)).

The requirement to lodge the objection with the clerk and send a copy to the applicant 'not less than seven days' before the meeting means 'not less than seven *clear* days'[2].

Objections must, of course, be on relevant grounds[3], so that while a local authority may object on the ground of noise nuisance it may not do so having regard to the condition of the premises[4].

The chief constable is additionally empowered to make observations (s 16A(1), added by the 1990 Act, s 53) in order, it has been suggested, to nullify the effect of *Centralbite Ltd v Kincardine and Deeside District Licensing Board*[5] in which written police observations, which in substance but not in form amounted to an objection, vitiated the refusal of a regular extension application. However, the strictly factual reporting of, say, public disorder incidents to a licensing board was probably unexceptionable and s 16A is more likely to be related to the fact that, in certain parts of Scotland, the chief constable was not afforded any right to be heard unless he had intimated an objection.

Observations must be lodged with the clerk not later than seven (clear) days before the meeting (s 16A(2)). They must also be intimated to the applicant as prescribed by s 16A(3), which mirrors the provisions of s 16(3)[6].

Since the applicant for a regular extension of permitted hours is *the holder of the licence*, a provision which has caused so much difficulty[7], the objections and observations mechanism may contain a trap for the unwary where application is made by a non-natural person and an employee or agent. Section 64(1) provides that 'any person holding' a licence 'may apply to the licensing board' for a

1 See also Chapter 6.
2 See *Main v City of Glasgow District Licensing Board* 1987 SLT 305 and articles at 1987 SLT (News) 157 and 353.
3 See 'Relevant considerations' above.
4 *Bantop Ltd v Glasgow District Licensing Board* 1989 SCLR 731, 1990 SLT 366.
5 1989 SCLR 652, 1990 SLT 231.
6 As discussed at chapter 6 above.
7 See 'Regular extensions and transfers', below.

regular extension (in contrast to the distinctly different provisions of s 11 in terms of which the applicant for a new licence or for renewal or permanent transfer of a licence is the non-natural person alone). Since s 11(3) provides that 'any reference in this Act to the holder of a licence includes a reference to both of those persons', the objection requires to be intimated to both parties.

On the other hand, in *Prime v Hardie*[1] it was held that the (sole) applicant's employer, a brewery company, had accepted (as his agent) service of an objection to an application for Sunday opening. Obversely, it may perhaps be argued that service of an objection upon the non-natural person alone is deemed to include service upon that person's employee or agent[2].

Conditions

A licensing board may 'attach such conditions as it thinks fit' (s 64(6)) to the grant of a regular extension. Although this power is expressed in very wide terms, conditions cannot be repugnant to the provisions of the Act as a whole nor may they be imposed for some irrelevant purpose[3]. For example, some boards impose a condition to the effect that the premises must be open for business during the whole of the extended hours, but s 54(5) provides that 'Nothing in this Act shall be taken to require any premises to be open for the sale or supply of alcoholic liquor during the permitted hours'. On the other hand, if the licenceholder failed to make use of his extended hours he may have difficulty in establishing 'need' (1990 Act, s 47(1)(a)) when he makes fresh application.

A condition prohibiting the sale of alcoholic liquor (in public house and hotel premises) for consumption off the premises after 11 pm or restricting the admission of customers after a certain hour may be justifiable on the grounds of public order and good management.

Breach of a condition is an offence (s 64(6))[4]. Proceedings may be taken against 'the holder of a licence or his employee or agent', a curious disjunction since 'the holder of a licence' includes the employee or agent (s 11(3)) and, in the case of a registered club, against every official and member of the governing body (s 64(6)). It is a defence to show that the contravention took place without the knowledge or consent of the person charged (s 64(6), proviso).

In terms of s 29 the alcoholic liquor which may be sold under an extension of the permitted hours may be restricted to wine, made-wine, porter, ale, beer, cider and perry. Breach of such a restriction is an offence (s 29(2))[5].

---

1 1978 SLT (Sh Ct) 71.
2 See also *Morgan v Midlothian District Licensing Board* 1993 SCLR 1, 1993 SLT (Sh Ct) 19 for recent evidence of a pragmatic approach by the court to the intimation provisions of s 16(3).
3 See *Fawcett Properties v Buckingham County Council* [1961] AC 636.
4 Maximum penalty: level 3. The licenceholder and the premises are liable to disqualification: s 67 and Sch 5.
5 Maximum penalty: level 5, with the possibility of disqualification of the licenceholder and the premises.

Duration

Regular extensions of the permitted hours may be granted 'during such period in the year succeeding the date of the grant' (s 64(3)) as the board may specify. A strict construction of this provision causes difficulty. If the word 'year' is to be construed as meaning a calendar year it is quite possible that the grant will expire before the date of the corresponding quarterly meeting in the following year[1]. In practice, boards ignore any shortfall. Some support for the view that 'year' should not be literally interpreted may perhaps be found in *Hollywood Bowl (Scotland) Ltd v Horsburgh*[2] in which the Lord Ordinary (Osborne) did not favour a literal construction of 'on such day'. On the other hand, while the Interpretation Act 1978 provides no assistance with the word 'year', it defines 'month'[3] as meaning 'calendar month'[4].

Conjunction of regular extensions and other applications

(1) Renewals and regular extensions. In *C R S Leisure Ltd v Dumbarton District Licensing Board*[5] the board appears to have fallen into the trap of assuming that, because it had refused to renew a licence, the applicants' interest in pursuing a regular extension application had been brought to an end. Where a renewal application is refused the licence nevertheless continues in force *pro tem* by virtue of s 30(5)(b) on the dependency of an appeal and the subsequent consideration of a regular extension (or, indeed, any other) application is perfectly competent. The Lord Ordinary (Prosser) held:

'I am not persuaded that refusal of extended hours was an inevitable consequence of the refusal to renew the licence, either logically or in practical terms. The refusal of renewal could be appealed and pending appeal there would be a period during which the licence would remain current'.

(2) New licences and regular extensions. While an applicant for the grant or provisional grant of a new licence may at the same time make application to permit the opening of the premises on Sundays (s 10(3A)), no parallel provision is made in relation to regular extensions. On the basis that application under s 64 may only be made by 'any person holding' a licence some clerks take the strict view that an application is not competent until a provisional grant, which is not a licence 'in force'[6], has been declared final. Thus, if a provisional grant is finalised shortly after the last lodgement date for a board's (say) June meeting a regular extension application would be delayed for about five months until the October meeting. Operators of entertainment-licensed premises in particular find it

---

1 See article at [1992] 4 LR 4.
2 1992 SLT 241.
3 The maximum period of an occasional extension: see below.
4 Interpretation Act 1978, Sch 1.
5 1989 SCLR 566, 1990 SLT 200.
6 *Ginera v City of Glasgow Licensing Board* 1982 SLT 136; *Baljaffray Residents' Association v Milngavie and Bearsden District Council Licensing Board* 1981 SLT (Sh Ct) 106.

commercially impossible to trade only until 11 pm and many licensed businesses cannot profitably subsist on the basic permitted hours.

Some licensing boards will, however, look sympathetically at applications for occasional extensions[1] during the 'gap' period; others will decline to provide this temporary accommodation except for genuine functions. A few boards are prepared to accept a regular extension application in anticipation of a provisional grant being declared final after the last lodgement date but before the quarterly meeting. On the other hand, in a number of areas, a pragmatic approach is adopted: regular extensions will be granted at the same time as the provisional grant of a new licence, effectively to be held in suspense until the provisional grant is declared final.

There is also a tendency to allow regular extension applications to be conjoined with applications for the full grant of a new licence (which are relatively rare), although at the time of application the applicant has yet to become the holder of a licence.

(3) Regular extensions and transfers[2]. Section 64(3A), as inserted by s 51(5) of the 1990 Act, provides:

'Where a licence has been transferred by virtue of section 25 of this Act and an application under subsection (1) above has been granted under subsection (2) or (3) above to the previous holder of the licence, the reference in subsections (2) and (3) above to the person whose application has been granted shall include a reference to the person to whom the licence has been transferred'.

The amendment was no doubt intended to cure a long-standing problem in certain parts of Scotland where regular extensions were regarded as lapsing when a licence was transferred. The clerks concerned took the view that the benefit of the regular extension attached solely to the holder of a licence to whom it has been granted, with the result that persons acquiring licensed businesses required to operate until the next meeting of the board with only the standard permitted hours, causing considerable hardship.

In order to overcome this problem limited companies were sometimes formed for licenceholding purposes so that they could ultimately be sold with the benefit of a regular extension without the necessity to transfer the licence.

In *Archyield Ltd v City of Glasgow Licensing Board*[3] the *lacuna* in the Act was thrown into sharp focus, the Lord Ordinary (Davidson) holding that the grant of an application to substitute a new employee in terms of s 25(3) terminated the validity of a pre-existing regular extension granted to the company licenceholder and the previous manager:

'I am sufficiently impressed by the considerations persuasively presented by counsel for the petitioners to accept that there may be a gap in the 1976 Act. But I am not convinced that these considerations entitle the court to deny the words "the person to whom it was granted" their plain meaning'.

---

1 See below.
2 See also J C Cummins 'Licensing Reform' 1991 SLT (News) 271.
3 1987 SCLR 191, 1987 SLT 547, doubted in *C R S Leisure Ltd v Dumbarton District Licensing Board* 1989 SCLR 566, 1990 SLT 200.

This decision was studiously ignored by all licensing boards, except one. Some boards continued their practice of treating regular extensions as continuing to be valid, provided that fresh application was made at the first opportunity by the non-natural person and the new manager; and a small minority continues to disregard completely the effect of a s 25(3) substitution.

Such an unsatisfactory state of affairs did no credit to Scottish licensing legislation. A few boards which were prepared to ignore the effect of *Archyield Ltd* did not extend this dispensation to permanent transfers, although paradoxically content to accept regular extension applications by a non-natural person and the new nominee in anticipation of an application to substitute the latter being granted prior to the quarterly meeting.

In one instance, a licensing board refused to consider a regular extension application on the basis that the nominated manager had quit the premises after the last lodgement date, despite the fact that, at the date of the meeting, there had been no change in the identity of the licenceholders, an application in terms of s 25(3) having yet to be granted.

Unhappily, this background to the introduction of s 64(3A) is far from irrelevant because the problem has not been eradicated. Difficulties may still occur where a regular extension is due to be 'renewed' and the licence is to be transferred under s 25. If an application for temporary transfer of the licence (s 25(1A)) is pending at the final lodgement date for a quarterly meeting at which the regular extension expires, application to 'renew' the regular extension is only competent at the instance of the then current licenceholder (who will in any event be well advised to do so as a safeguard against problems or delays developing in connection with the proposed transfer).

In practice the following procedural permutations are possible, depending upon the attitude of the clerk concerned:

(a) The grant of the temporary transfer ad interim results in the board declining to consider the regular extension application by the then former licenceholder.

(b) The clerk will simply change the name of the applicant as shown in the regular extension application when the temporary transfer has been approved (which may well cause problems with objections).

(c) The clerk will accept an application for the regular extension of hours by the prospective licenceholder in anticipation of the temporary transfer being granted.

It follows that the one-step permanent transfer procedure (s 25(1)) may attract similar complications. In a very small minority of districts the grant of a permanent transfer still has the effect of invalidating a regular extension application by the former licenceholder and an extension application by the intending transferee is regarded as incompetent.

The following example illustrates the attitude of some clerks. Suppose that 'A' is selling his licensed premises to 'B'. 'A' lodges a 'safeguarding' application for the regular extension of permitted hours as a precaution against the failure or withdrawal of 'B's' application for permanent transfer. The clerk will not accept a regular extension application by 'B': he is not, at the time of application, the holder of a licence. The grant of 'B's' permanent transfer application results in the board declining to consider 'A's' application for extended hours: he is no longer the holder of a licence.

However, while regular extension applications are usually scheduled for consideration after applications for permanent transfer, the Act does not prevent the continuation of a permanent transfer application until the completion of other business. In the example given, if 'B's' permanent transfer application is granted after 'A's' regular extension application has been approved, 'B' acquires the benefit of the regular extension by virtue of s 64(3A). All that is required is the grant by the board of a motion for a very short continuation. The same result would be achieved if the licence were to be temporarily transferred to 'B' immediately after the board meeting[1].

Otherwise, the transfer of the licence may require to be postponed, or accelerated by the use of the temporary transfer system[1] with a view to ensuring that the licence is vested in the new licenceholder's name prior to the last lodgement date. The seller of the business may also apply 'early' for his regular extension to forestall difficulties.

Where a one-step permanent transfer application has been refused it would appear that the board may not competently consider a subsequent extension application by the same applicant. The transfer is not valid on the dependency of an appeal and the approach taken in *Fereneze Leisure Ltd v Renfrew District Licensing Board*[2], where the sheriff upheld an appeal against refusal of a permanent transfer and directed the board to consider a conjoined regular extension application within a specified time, is of doubtful validity.

However, where a temporary transfer has already been granted, the subsequent refusal of a permanent transfer does not preclude consideration of a regular extension application, since the licence is vested in the applicant pending an appeal.

Remedies

There is no appeal against the board's decision[3] but, since 1985, challenge has been possible by way of judicial review[4] which, if successful, will generally result in the matter being remitted to the board for reconsideration.

OCCASIONAL EXTENSIONS OF PERMITTED HOURS

The holder of a licence (other than an off-sale licence) may apply to the licensing board for an occasional extension of permitted hours:

'in connection with any occasion which the board considers appropriate, and such a grant shall authorise the person to whom it was granted to sell or supply alcoholic liquor[5] in the

---

1 Lenders are, however, usually unwilling to advance funds purely on the basis of a temporary transfer of the licence.
2 1990 SCLR 436 (OH), 1991 SCLR 751, 1992 SLT 604 (IH).
3 *Sloan v North East Fife District Licensing Board* 1978 SLT (Sh Ct) 62.
4 See Chapter 15.
5 The sale of spirits may be excluded under s 29.

premises to which the application relates during such period not exceeding one month[1] and between such hours and on such day as may be specified in the grant'[2].

A board may grant an application made by the secretary of a registered club if it considers:

'that the occasion or circumstances in respect of which the application is made arise out of or are related to the functions of the club or a private function organised by an individual member or groups of members of the club'[3].

Applications are usually processed under a delegated powers arrangement (s 5(1)) under procedures laid down by the board's regulations (s 37). Commonly, 7, 14 or 21 days' notice will be required, with an exception made, for obvious reasons, in the case of funeral parties. The clerk may be empowered to waive the time limit in exceptional circumstances. The applicant is required to send a copy of the application to the chief constable 'at the same time as he makes the application' (s 64(1)).

Although no provision is made for objections or observations from the police or, indeed, any other source, a police report is usually obtained.

Occasional extensions are to be refused if there is a likelihood of 'undue public nuisance' or 'a threat to public order or safety', and may be made subject to conditions, breach of which is an offence. There is no right of appeal.

The tests prescribed by s 47 of the 1990 Act (see above) do *not* apply to applications for occasional extensions. Although the reference in s 47(1) is in general terms to 'an application under s 64 of the principal Act for an extension of permitted hours', which clearly embraces both regular and occasional extensions, para (a) of s 64(1) refers only to 'a regular extension of permitted hours' and para (b) to 'such an extension', ie a regular extension.

Sometimes applicants already holding a regular extension will apply to the board for an occasional extension to commence at the end of the period permitted by the former. This is not a sensible practice. There have been instances of regular extensions being refused after the grant of an occasional extension predicated upon its continuation. Where permitted hours end at 11 pm an occasional extension for a period after, say, 12 midnight, is incompetent.

Where a licenceholder has omitted to apply for a regular extension of permitted hours some licensing boards will permit the period until the next quarterly meeting to be covered by a series of occasional extensions; others will only allow this device to be employed in respect of bona fide events organised by a third party.

The position as respects extensions on Sundays in public houses is as explained above in relation to regular extensions.

Occasional extensions transfer with the licence to which they relate (s 64(3A)). Since some boards do not allow an application to be made in anticipation of a transfer taking place (on the basis that application may only be made by the holder of a licence), in cases where there would be insufficient time for the submission of an application after the transfer the intending transferee may wish to have an

1 'Month' means 'calendar month': Interpretation Act 1978, Sch 1.
2 Section 64(2).
3 Section 64(5).

application lodged in the name of the transferor. Missives for the purchase of licensed premises should obligate the vendor to provide this type of co-operation.

PROHIBITION ON FURTHER APPLICATIONS

Section 64(9), as inserted by para 12 of Schedule 8 to the 1990 Act, provides:

'Where a licensing board has refused an application . . . for the grant of an occasional or regular extension of permitted hours in respect of any premises, the board shall not, within one year of its refusal, entertain a subsequent application for such an extension in respect of the same premises unless the board, at the time of refusing the first-mentioned application, makes a direction to the contrary'[1].

The board's declinature to consider an application because of the applicant's failure to attend or be represented at the meeting (see s 15) is not a 'refusal'.

It should be observed that the potential prohibition embraces both occasional *and* regular extension applications and that the board's permission to allow a further application of *either* nature must be obtained *at the time of refusal*. This requirement raises a practical difficulty in relation to applications for occasional extensions, the vast majority of which are processed administratively by the clerk alone or by the clerk and (usually) one board member upon receipt of a police report. It is therefore not unusual for the applicant to be physically absent at the time of refusal and therefore not in a position to request a direction *instanter*. (Although it should be possible for an applicant to request a hearing, if there has been or is likely to be a refusal, this in practice rarely happens.)

Early indications are that the effect of s 64(9) is often conveniently ignored in relation to applications for occasional extensions but it should not be overlooked. It may be prudent to incorporate a request for a direction in the event that the application is refused *in gremio* of the application form. Presumably a board may decide that directions will automatically be allowed, at least in relation to occasional extensions (as appears to have happened in at least one district).

It will be appreciated that, in the absence of a direction, subject to what is suggested below, a refusal could sterilise the possibility of both occasional and regular extensions in the ensuing year. Indeed, if an occasional extension were to be refused in, say, May of any year and the one-year period happened to expire after the last lodgement date for the June quarterly meeting in the following year, then, arguably, a regular extension application could not competently be presented until the October meeting in the next year, creating a fallow period of 17 months.

As explained above, a question arises as to whether 'year' is to be construed literally. Since it appears to be accepted in practice that extensions for one year are to be regarded as valid until the corresponding meeting approximately one year afterwards, *ex hypothesi* the one-year prohibition should be operated with similar latitude.

---

1 Commonly known as a 'section 64(9) direction'.

The phrase 'such an extension' has also caused perplexity in the absence of any reported decisions. It may be interpreted in several ways, as referring to:
(a) the actual hours sought, on a particular day or days;
(b) any extensions, regular or occasional, whatsoever;
(c) the nature of the extension, that is to say, whether it is for the occasional or regular extension of hours, so that the refusal of a regular extension without a direction would only render incompetent further applications for occasional extensions (and vice versa);
(d) the purpose of the extension, eg an occasional extension to cater for a wedding reception.

If (a) is the correct interpretation, then the applicant would no doubt be in a position to cure the absence of a direction by making re-application with a slight variation in the hours sought, a device which has been acceptable to some clerks but which is clearly outwith the intent of the subsection, presumably designed to spare objectors the necessity of renewing their opposition to applications at successive board meetings and which ignores the use of the word 'such' rather than 'same'.

An unsuccessful applicant for a Sunday afternoon extension would, on the basis of interpretation (b), find himself prevented from applying for evening extensions for one year and, indeed, from making any occasional extension applications in the like period. This possibility suggests that it may be imprudent to make during the currency of the licenceholder's 'core' regular extensions a 'top-up' application for further extended hours which has little chance of success because of, for example, a board's policy. If the board decides to refuse the supplementary application and makes no direction under s 64(9), the licenceholder would thus be deprived of the possibility of 'renewing' the previously enjoyed extensions at the appropriate time.

Interpretation (c) appears to be gathering support in some parts of the country and probably reflects most closely the purpose of the provision.

The construction suggested at (d) has won few supporters but it has the merit of recognising that the actual purpose of the extension may be central to the refusal and, logically, there is no reason why an application for a wedding anniversary party should be prevented from proceeding because a board was not prepared to extend the permitted hours for discothèques.

Opinion is divided as to whether a partial refusal should lead to a motion for a 'section 64(9) direction'; for example, where application for an extension until 1.00 am is only granted *quoad* the period between 11.00 pm and 12 midnight. The safe course is to ask for a direction and to have minuted any suggestion that the direction is unnecessary.

The phrase 'the same premises' is also of significance[1]. It may be that a repeat application will be accepted as competent if there has been a physical alteration to the premises since the refusal. Certainly, where a new licence is necessitated by extensive alterations to premises, the effect of s 64(9) is not carried forward to a new application made under the fresh licence.

The position of the clerk is complicated by the fact that he is enjoined to cause

1 Discussed in *Kelvinside Community Council v Glasgow District Licensing Board* 1990 SCLR 110, 1990 SLT 725.

to be published 'a list of all competent applications' for inter alia the regular extension of permitted hours (s 12). *Main v City of Glasgow District Licensing Board*[1] appears to suggest that where the competency or otherwise of an application turns on a question of law rather than fact[2] the decision is correctly taken by the clerk alone, subject to review by the court with an early application for an interim order for publication.

It may be remarked, however, that if the issue of competency requires to be determined by the board the intention of s 64(9) (to spare objectors from a campaign of attrition) would be substantially frustrated: they would, of course, be obliged to prosecute their objections in the normal way lest the board decided to consider the application.

EXTENSIONS FOR TABLE MEALS

Common features

Sections 57, 58, 59 and 60[3] provide for a variety of extensions of the permitted hours for the purposes of:

'(a) the sale or supply to persons taking table meals in the premises of alcoholic liquor supplied in a part of the premises usually set apart for the service of such persons, and supplied for consumption by such a person in that part of the premises as an ancillary to his meal; and
(b) the consumption of alcoholic liquor so supplied.'[4]

Although 'meal' is not defined in the Act[5], 'table meal' is defined in s 139(1) as:

'a meal eaten by a person sitting at a table, or at a counter or other structure which serves the purpose of a table and is not used for the service of refreshments to persons not seated at a table or structure serving the purpose of a table'.

Thus, a meal taken by a customer seated at a structure which is not a conventional table will not be a 'table meal' if any other customers are taking refreshments, including food and non-alcoholic beverages, while standing.

In order to be 'ancillary', alcohol need not be supplied and consumed at the same time as the meal, so that pre-prandial drinks and digestifs are permissible[6], but must be taken in the area 'usually set apart' when the extended hours provided by the sections are in operation. There will, of course, 'come a point of time when drinks served considerably after the end of a meal cease to be ancillary thereto'[6].

Although 30 minutes drinking-up time may be added to the conclusion of the extra permitted hours (where the liquor was supplied during those hours) drink

---

1 1987 SLT 305.
2 Cf *Kelvinside Community Council v Glasgow District Licensing Board* above.
3 See s 140(2) for the continuing effect of the provisions of earlier enactments.
4 Sections 57(3), 58(3), 59(3) and (by reference to s 58(3)) s 60(1).
5 For a discussion of 'meal', see consideration of restaurant licences in Chapter 4.
6 *Heatly v McIntyre* 1965 JC 1, 1965 SLT 81.

must be served at the same time as and for consumption *at* the meal (s 54(3)(h)). This provision has the rather peculiar result that while an 'ancillary' after-dinner drink could be consumed before the conclusion of the extra permitted hours in an ante-room (provided that it was 'usually set apart'), during the drinking-up period it could not. This paradox no doubt stems from the substitution of the concept of 'ancillary drinking,' introduced by the Licensing (Scotland) Act 1962, for the reference in earlier legislation to consumption at meals.

Where drink is supplied to persons who are not taking meals an offence is committed under s 54(1) and (4). The extension is not thereby invalidated and it is irrelevant that ss 57, 58, 59 and 60 do not contain their own penal provision[1].

The word 'usually' in the phrase 'usually set apart' effectively means 'reserved for at all times'. In *McAlpine v Heatly*[2] the holder of a hotel certificate employed the lounge of his premises between 10 pm and 11 pm for the service of table meals and alcoholic drinks; at other times it was also used for other purposes. It was unsuccessfully argued on his behalf that if the lounge was regularly set apart each evening, albeit for a limited period, it was a part of the premises 'usually set apart'. The Lord Justice-General (Grant) said:

'If a room is set apart for a particular purpose during one hour of the day and is used for other purposes during the rest, it cannot be said to be "usually" set apart for that one purpose, however regular the setting apart is. The statutory provisions have, I think, in view the case where the normal, regular use of a particular room or part of the premises during the day is the supply of meals'[3].

In *Norris v Manning*[4] a meal was distributed to all customers in the dining area (whether or not food had been requested) at the conclusion of the normal permitted hours. The dining area was the only part of the premises being utilised. The licenceholder's conviction for selling liquor after hours was upheld.

Whether part of the premises is 'set apart' will depend on the circumstances of each case. The clerk may request sight of a plan of the premises with the appropriate area delineated. In *Chief Constable of Manchester v Flaherty*[5] the licensing committee accepted the licenceholder's proposal that a dining area would be separated from the remainder of the premises during meal hours by a screen or tubs containing flowers and plants and by the use of a notice indicating that the area was reserved for diners. The separation devices were to be removed outside meal hours. Dismissing the chief constable's appeal, the court held that the words 'usually set apart' were to be given their ordinary meaning and the question of separation was for the justices to determine on the facts.

Difficulties of this nature are unlikely to arise in restaurant licensed premises which are essentially set apart in their entirety for the accommodation of persons taking meals.

---

1 *Stewart v Dunphy* 1980 SLT (Notes) 93; cf s 99(a) and see *Stainton and Seiler v McNaughtan* 1991 SCCR 339, 1993 SLT 119.
2 1967 JC 537, 1967 SLT (Notes) 3; a similar approach was taken in *Timmis v Millman* [1965] Brewing Tr Rev 23, (1965) 109 SJ 31.
3 See also *Clayson*, para 9.70.
4 [1971] Crim LR 419.
5 (1989) 153 JP 242.

Sections 57 and 58

When applied to premises for which a licence (other than an off-sale licence) is held or to the premises of a registered club, these sections make available an extra one and a half hours at the conclusion of the Sunday afternoon permitted hours (ie from 2.30 pm to 4 pm) (s 57(2))[1] and an additional two hours at the conclusion of the evening permitted hours each day of the week (ie from 11 pm to 1 am) (s 58(2))[1], for the purposes set out above.

The holders of restaurant, restricted hotel, entertainment and refreshment licences need only serve notice upon the chief constable that it is intended to bring the additional hours into operation (see below).

Otherwise, the licensing board must first be satisfied that 'the premises are structurally adapted and bona fide used, or intended to be used' (s 57(1) and 58(1)) for the purpose of habitually providing 'the customary main meal at midday for the accommodation of persons frequenting the premises' (s 57(1)); or 'for the accommodation of persons frequenting the premises, substantial refreshment to which the sale and supply of alcoholic liquor is ancillary' (s 58(2)). Just as the Act does not define 'meal', nor is there a definition of 'substantial refreshment', but there is probably no real distinction to be drawn between the two.

It may be observed that the criteria to be achieved before a declaration of satisfaction is granted differ from the requirements to be satisfied when the additional hours are actually operated. Accordingly, while for the purposes of ss 57(1) and 58(1) the board must be satisfied as to the habitual provision of, respectively, 'the customary main meal at midday' and 'substantial refreshment', it seems that for the purposes of ss 57(3) and 58(3) the licenceholder may sell or supply *any* food which qualified as a 'table meal'. While such a meal would no doubt always require to constitute at least 'substantial refreshment' it need not during the Sunday afternoon period amount to a customary midday meal.

In deciding whether premises are 'structurally adapted' the board will no doubt have regard to the adequacy of the kitchen and catering facilities and the ability of the premises to satisfy building control and food hygiene regulations. No account should be taken of extraneous matters, such as whether the premises would be commercially viable or whether the grant of a declaration of satisfaction would encourage applications in respect of other licensed premises[2].

Applications are frequently processed under delegated powers (s 5(1)). There is no right of appeal against a refusal[3].

It may appear curious that the holders of entertainment and refreshment licences should be deemed automatically to satisfy the adaptation and use requirements. Those types of licences were introduced by the 1976 Act and the exemption from the need to obtain the boards *imprimatur* may simply be a drafting oversight.

---

1 Assuming the existence of 'basic' Sunday permitted hours *quoad* public house and refreshment licensed premises.
2 *R v Spelthorne Licensing Justices ex parte Turpin* [1926] 2 KB 519.
3 See *Millen v Walker* 1961 SLT (Notes) 21.

Where the declaration of satisfaction has been given in respect of public house, hotel or registered club premises or at any time in the case of other premises the licenceholder or secretary of the club must, before bringing the additional permitted hours into operation (or, in the terminology of the Act, applying the sections to the premises) serve written notice to that effect upon the chief constable not later than 14 days before the commencement date (ss 57(6) and 58(6)). Notice may be given by post (s 134) and should in practice be effected by recorded delivery. It is both sensible and courteous (but not necessary) to send a copy of the notice to the clerk of the board for his records, especially where the board have not been required to grant a declaration of satisfaction. It is probably incompetent to anticipate the grant of the board's declaration by giving the chief constable notice that the sections will apply on a possibly unspecified date thereafter. Provision is also made for notice to be given when the sections are to be disapplied by the licenceholder (ss 57(5) and 58(5)) although there is no penalty for failure to do so. The sections will cease to apply if the board are no longer satisfied as to their adaptation and use, but no procedure is specified.

While the sections apply to premises, the permitted hours for other than the specified purposes or in part of the premises other than the part 'usually set apart' are the same as if they did not apply, thus creating the potential for an offence under s 54(1) and (4) (ss 57(4) and 58(4))[1]. Where premises are the subject of an occasional or regular extension of the permitted hours, it is doubtful whether an offence is committed if drink is supplied in the area 'usually set apart' to persons not taking table meals during such an extension since ss 57 and 58 do not contain their own penal provisions[1]; the sale or supply of alcoholic liquor would be authorised by s 64 and it is difficult to imagine that in such circumstances an offence would be committed under s 54.

The secretary of a registered club to which the sections apply must notify the licensing board of any reconstruction or extension of, or alteration in, the premises which affects the facilities available in the premises for the provision of the customary main meal at midday (s 57(7)) or of substantial refreshment (s 58(7)). Failure to do so is an offence[2] although no time limit for notification is specified. No parallel provision is made in relation to licensed premises, presumably because alterations to the premises would come to the board's attention by way of an application for consent in terms of s 35.

The holder of a licence (but not the secretary of a registered club) commits an offence if he fails to keep posted in some conspicuous place in the premises a notice stating that the sections apply thereto and setting out their effect[3].

At the conclusion of the additional permitted hours 30 minutes drinking-up time is available in respect of alcoholic liquor served at the same time as and for consumption *at* a meal prior to that conclusion (s 54(3)(h)).

There seems to be nothing to prevent the extended table meal hours being 'added' to an occasional or regular extension, so that, for example, if a regular extension were to be in force until 2 am the supply of drink with meals could take

1 See *Stewart v Dunphy* 1980 SLT (Notes) 93.
2 Maximum penalty: level 3.
3 Ss 57(8) and 58(8). Maximum penalty: level 1.

place thereafter until 4 am in terms of s 58. Mindful of that possibility one licensing board will usually request an undertaking that such a device will not be employed.

Section 59

This section allows the holder of a public house licence in respect of premises with no Sunday permitted hours (s 59(1)) to sell or supply alcoholic liquor for the purposes specified at p 194 above during the periods on Sundays between 12.30 pm and 2.30 pm and 6.30 pm and 11 pm (s 59(2)).

The licensing board must be satisfied that:

(a) the premises are structurally adapted and bona fide used or intended to be used for the purpose of habitually providing the customary main meal at midday or in the evening or both, for the accommodation of persons frequenting the premises; and

(b) the part of the premises 'usually set apart' for the sale or supply of alcoholic liquor to persons taking table meals does not contain a bar counter (s 59(1)(i))[1].

The latter requirement means in effect that drinks may only be dispensed from a counter which is exclusively used for the collection of orders by waiting staff serving customers at table and/or for the service of customers seated at the counter taking meals. This restriction is, of course, imposed by definition upon restaurant and restricted hotel licensed premises (see Sch 1). In relation to public house restaurant areas it is peculiar to s 59. Where, for example, s 57 is in operation, subject to all the requirements of that section, there would be nothing to prevent a customer who was having a table meal at a conventional table from purchasing an ancillary drink by direct approach to the bar counter; if the counter was also being used as an oyster bar by persons seated there consuming meals such meals would not thereby cease to be 'table meals' (s 139(1)) as the drink supplied to this hypothetical customer would be consumed at his table.

The gap period between 2.30 pm and 6.30 pm may be filled by an occasional or regular extension of the permitted hours; or partially filled by the application of s 57 and/or s 60 (see below). After 11 pm the permitted hours may be extended by an occasional or regular extension for the purposes of s 59 (s 64(4)(a)) or by the application of s 58. Where a declaration of satisfaction has been obtained under s 59 as to the provision of 'the customary main meal at midday' it seems that no separate declaration would require to be made prior to the invocation of s 57, but not vice versa. Similarly, s 60 (see below) may simply be brought into operation by notice to the chief constable where the declaration of satisfaction has been given under s 59. As respects s 58 it would appear that a separate declaration of satisfaction is required.

Where the section applies to premises there are no Sunday permitted hours for other purposes or in parts of the premises other than the part 'usually set apart', except as otherwise provided by the Act (s 59(4)). It is difficult to ascribe any meaning to the exception.

1 'Bar counter': see s 139(2).

The section is applied and disapplied to the premises by the notice procedure explained above in relation to ss 57 and 58 (s 59(6)). Similarly, a notice setting out the effect of the section must be kept conspicuously displayed (s 59(7)) and the section ceases to apply to the premises if the board ceases to be satisified as to adaptation and use (s 59(5)).

In all cases, the benefit of the additional hours transfers automatically with the licence. They do not require to be renewed and only come to an end if disapplied by the licenceholder or if the licensing board ceases to be satisfied as to adaptation and use in cases where a declaration of satisfaction is a preliminary requirement. However, where a new licence has been obtained for the premises because of material alterations the sections will automatically cease to apply and require to be brought into operation *de novo*.

RESTRICTION OF THE PERMITTED HOURS

Restriction orders

Section 65 empowers a licensing board to make certain restriction orders, outlined below, in respect of 'any licensed premises' or registered club (s 65(1), as substituted by the 1990 Act, s 48(2))[1]. The order may relate not only to individual premises but also to 'a group of premises in respect of which the same type of licence is held', always provided that a complaint has been made as described below (s 65(3), as amended by the 1990 Act, s 48(3)).

The orders available are as follows.

Afternoon and evening restriction orders

If the board is satisfied that:

'the sale or supply of alcoholic liquor in the afternoon or in the evening in licensed premises or in a registered club is the cause of undue public nuisance or constitutes a threat to public order or safety'[2]

either of the above orders *may* be made.

The effect of an afternoon restriction order is that 'the permitted hours between half-past two and five in the afternoon shall be reduced by such a time and for such a period as may be specified in the order' (s 65(1A), as inserted by the 1990 Act, s 48(2))[3].

An evening restriction order reduces the permitted hours in the evening 'by such a time and for such a period as may be specified in the order but no such

---

1 Despite the reference to 'any licensed premises', orders provide for the curtailment of permitted hours and thus have no applicability to off-sale licensed premises or off-sale parts of other premises which have 'trading hours': see s 119(1).
2 Section 65(1)(a), as substituted by the 1990 Act, s 48(2); cf s 17(1)(c).
3 Afternoon restriction orders are virtually unknown. *Clayson*, whose 'all-day opening' recommendation was not implemented until the passing of the 1990 Act, considered that this power was unnecessary (para 9.72).

order shall restrict the permitted hours before ten in the evening' (s 65(1B), as inserted by the 1990 Act, s 48(2)). This provision is based on the *Clayson* recommendation[1] that 'the terminal hour could be restricted *by not more than an hour* (making it 10 pm as at present)' (author's emphasis). The clear intention was to provide a 'safety net' following the introduction of the later standard terminal hour of 11 pm. *Clayson* no doubt considered that restriction orders and 'extension orders' (the term used for regular extensions of the permitted hours) would pivot independently on the axis of the 11 pm watershed.

In practice, however, restriction orders are employed to curtail regular extensions of the permitted hours. Indeed, chief constables have on occasions chosen to present complaints in terms of s 65, sometimes relying upon alleged incidents said to have taken place over an extended period, despite a failure to oppose applications for the regular extension of permitted hours[2].

There appears to be no impediment to the imposition of a restriction order when permitted hours after 11 pm are operated simply by virtue of s 58[3].

An evening restriction order may not competently be made where the originating complaint has been made under s 31[4]. It will not be appropriate to hold hearings under s 65 and s 31 at the same time[5].

A board's declinature to make a restriction order will not assist the licenceholder where renewal of the licence is subsequently refused on the basis of essentially similar material[6].

Sunday restriction order

A board *may* make this type of order where it is satisfied that 'the use of licensed premises[7] is the cause of undue disturbance or public nuisance having regard to the way of life in the locality on a Sunday' (s 65(1)(b), as inserted by the 1990 Act, s 48(2))[8]. The expression 'the use of licensed premises' is clearly broader as a causal factor than 'the sale or supply of alcoholic liquor'[9]. Where incidents of 'assault, breaches of the peace and general disorder' were found to have taken place, a narrow argument that these could not be related to 'the use' of the premises was rejected:

1 Para 9.71.
2 See *Devana Investments Ltd v City of Aberdeen Licensing Board* 1992 SCLR 616. See also *McKay v Banff and Buchan Western Division Licensing Board* 1991 SCLR 15, 1991 SLT 20 in which the chief constable had presented a complaint in terms of s 31 seeking suspension of the licence on the basis of late-evening disorder.
3 See above.
4 *McKay v Banff and Buchan Western Division Licensing Board*, above.
5 See *Devana Investments v City of Aberdeen Licensing Board*, above.
6 *Sangha v Bute and Cowal Divisional Licensing Board* 1990 SCLR 409.
7 Note that this provision does not apply to registered clubs.
8 Cf s 17(2A). For cases concerning the issue of 'nuisance' on Sundays, see *Freeland v City of Glasgow District Licensing Board* 1980 SLT 101; and *Freeland v City of Glasgow District Licensing Board* 1980 SLT (Sh Ct) 125.
9 See *Sangha v Bute and Cowal Divisional Licensing Board* 1990 SCLR 409 for a consideration of 'the use of the premises for the sale of alcoholic liquor' as the cause of 'undue public nuisance or a threat to public order or safety'.

'The [submission was made] that there was no evidence that "the use" of the premises had caused undue public nuisance . . . This submission is not supported by the evidence for all the incidents occurred during the hours of the late extensions granted to the licenceholder for Friday and Saturday nights during which the premises were "used" as a discothèque'[1].

The reference to 'the way of life in the locality' recognises that the Sunday opening of licensed premises is, historically, a sensitive issue. A Sunday restriction order has the effect that:

'there shall be no permitted hours on a Sunday for such period as may be specified in the order or that the permitted hours on Sunday shall be reduced by such time and for such a period as may be so specified'[2].

Procedure

The procedure is initiated by a complaint to the board by one of the persons or bodies listed in s 16(1) (s 65(1))[3]. The board then decides whether or not to hold a hearing (s 31(4), as applied by s 65(2)). At this stage the board is under no obligation to inform the licenceholder[4] that a complaint is under consideration[5] but it must inform the complainer of its decision (s 31(4), as applied by s 65(2)).

Further procedure prior to any hearing is regulated by s 31(5) and (5A) (as applied by s 65(2))[6]. A licensing board is entitled is make regulations with respect to 'restriction of the terminal hour' (s 37) but these may not, of course, conflict with the substantive provisions of the Act.

The hearing

The hearing must take place at a quarterly meeting of the board (s 5(2)(f), (i), read with s 5(6))[7] and may be held at an adjournment of such a meeting[8]. The licenceholder is entitled to be heard but an order may be made in his absence where he fails to appear after receiving due notice (s 31(5)(d), as applied by s 65(2)[9].

The chief constable may, not less than seven days before the hearing, lodge

1 *McKay v Banff and Buchan Western Division Licensing Board* 1991 SCLR 15, 1991 SLT 20.
2 Section 65(1C), as inserted by the 1990 Act, s 48(2).
3 The categories of objector are: persons owning or occupying property in the neighbourhood; the local community council; an organised church; the chief constable; the fire authority; the local authority. See Chapter 6.
4 All references in this section to a licenceholder include a reference to a registered club.
5 *Lawrence v City of Aberdeen District Licensing Board*, Aberdeen Sheriff Court, 21 April 1986, unreported.
6 This procedure is discussed in Chapter 9 sub voce 'Suspension of licences'.
7 Note, however, that s 5(2)(f) refers simply to restriction of the *terminal* hour and has not been amended to take account of the introduction of *afternoon* restriction orders by s 48(2) of the 1990 Act. Cf suspension and closure order hearings under ss 31 and 32 respectively, which may be held at any board meeting: see s 5(2)(j), (k).
8 *Indpine Ltd v City of Dundee District Licensing Board* 1992 SCLR 113 (OH), 1992 SCLR 353, 1992 SLT 473 (IH); *Tarditi v Drummond* 1989 SCLR 201, 1989 SLT 554.
9 As to notification, see *Dolan v Glasgow District Council* 1990 SCLR 553.

observations with the clerk in cases where he has not originated the complaint and must intimate same to the licenceholder (s 31(5A), as applied by s 65(2)).

Where material facts are in dispute the board should accede to a motion that evidence be heard[1]. The board's decision must be taken in public, *including* the decision as to the period of any restriction order (s 5(7))[2].

It is unclear whether the licenceholder is entitled to make a plea in mitigation directed at the scope of the order once the board's decision has been announced. In *Stephen v City of Aberdeen District Licensing Board*[3] the sheriff held that it was incumbent upon the licenceholder to present his entire case before the board's retiral, while in *McIndoe v Glasgow District Licensing Board*[4] diametrically opposite views were expressed.

Revocation of restriction order

After the expiry of two-thirds of the period for which the restriction order is in force application may be made for its revocation (s 65(4)). The application must be (a) in writing, (b) lodged with the clerk not less than 21 days before a quarterly meeting[5] and (c) copied 'at the same time' to 'the persons whose complaint led to the making of the restriction order' (s 65(5)).

Any person competent to make a complaint (not simply the original complainer) may object to the revocation. The written objection must be lodged with the clerk to the board and a copy sent to the licenceholder not less than seven days before the quarterly meeting (s 65(6)).

The board may 'take such decision in the matter as it thinks fit' after considering the application and any objections. The decision 'may relate to all or any of the premises which are the subject of the restriction order' (s 65(7)).

Appeals[6]

The licenceholder (or registered club) may appeal to the sheriff against:
(a) the making of a restriction order;
(b) the period of a restriction order; or
(c) the refusal of an application for revocation (s 65(8)).

A complainer has no right of appeal against the board's refusal to make an order but revocation is subject to appeal at the instance of 'any complainer who appeared' at the revocation hearing (s 65(8)). *Semble* a complainer will not be regarded as having 'appeared' unless he or his representative addressed the board[7].

---

1 *Devana Investments Ltd v City of Aberdeen Licensing Board* 1992 SCLR 616. The extent of a board's obligation to hear evidence is discussed further sub voce 'Natural justice' in Chapter 15.
2 See *Devana Investments Ltd v City of Aberdeen Licensing Board*, above.
3 1989 SLT (Sh Ct) 94.
4 1989 SCLR 325.
5 Applications cannot be considered other than at a quarterly meeting: see s 5(2)(g).
6 For appeals in general, see Chapter 15.
7 *Transition Interiors Ltd v Eastwood District Licensing Board*, Paisley Sheriff Court, 2 May 1990, unreported.

The effect of the restriction order is suspended pending the determination of the licenceholder's appeal (s 31(6), as applied by s 65(2)); but where the board appeals to the Court of Session (s 39(8)) against the sheriff's reversal of its decision the continued suspension of the order will depend on a cross-appeal by the licenceholder[1].

In view of the potential for an appeal it is not appropriate for the order to state specific commencement and termination dates[1].

Temporary restriction orders

Clayson[2] considered that licensing boards should have power to close individual premises or a group of premises in a locality for a number of hours where there was 'a possibility of disorder arising from a particular event on a given day' (for example, a football match).

Such an emergency power is provided by s 66, in terms of which a constable of the rank of chief inspector or above may apply (at any time) 'for an order making a temporary restriction of permitted hours' (s 66(1)) in relation to any licensed premises or registered club (s 66(4)). Neither the licenceholder nor the registered club concerned has a right to be advised of the application. They may not object (s 66(3)), no provision is made for a hearing, and there is no right of appeal (although the board's decision may be the subject of judicial review). In terms of s 5(2)(f), read with s 5(6), a licensing board may only make 'a decision on the restriction of the terminal permitted hour' at a quarterly meeting. This is clearly a drafting infelicity as respects s 66, whose purpose would be destroyed by such a constraint.

If the board considers it desirable 'in the interests of public order or safety', it may 'order that the premises to which the application relates be closed to the public for such time of up to three hours and on such day or days as may be specified in the order' (s 66(1)).

An order may relate to individual premises or to 'a group of premises in respect of which the same type of licence is held' (s 66(2)).

The limited nature of the board's 'draconian' power and the distinction to be drawn between s 65 and s 66 was emphasised in *Grainger v City of Edinburgh District Licensing Board*[3]. The chief constable successfully applied for an order under s 66(1) in terms of which the late evening operation of premises was curtailed for three hours for a period of 40 days. A court of five judges held that s 66 had been improperly employed:

'The purpose of [s 66] is very limited. It is clearly to allow the board on an application by a senior police officer and no one else, immediately to close the premises . . . on specific days in respect of particular events likely to cause trouble during the limited hours for which closure of the premises is laid down . . . Under s 66(1) there is no provision for a hearing or an appeal, and that clearly indicates that the intention of the legislature was that the power

1 See *McKay v Banff and Buchan Western Division Licensing Board* 1991 SCLR 15, 1991 SLT 20.
2 Para 9.72.
3 1989 SLT 633, overruling *Elantosh Ltd v City of Edinburgh District Licensing Board* 1983 SC 255, 1984 SLT 92.

given to the board was only to be exercised in very limited circumstances . . . What has been done here is to try and use s 66(1) of the Act to bring about the immediate restriction of permitted hours in circumstances which are precisely those envisaged in s 65(1) and in our view that is an improper use of the section'.

Closure by the sheriff

In terms of s 89(1), a sheriff may:

'if riot or tumult happens or is expected to happen, order the holder of a licence in respect of premises situated in or near the place where a riot or tumult happens or is expected to happen to close those premises during such time as may be specified in the order'[1].

This archaic power has not been invoked for many years, although the Home Office has apparently issued guidance to English police authorities regarding strike riots.

A 'riot' is:

'any disorderly assembly which is proceeding "to outrageous deeds of violence against property and persons", and which has reached such proportions and created such a breach of public order, that it cannot be dealt with by ordinary police action'[2].

An offence is committed if premises are kept open for the sale of alcoholic liquor when an order is in force[3] but clearly licenceholders would require to have been made aware of the order before proceedings could be taken.

Offences

A licenceholder or his employee or agent is guilty of an offence if premises are kept open for the sale of alcoholic liquor during any time at which they are required to be closed by virtue of an order made by:
(a) the sheriff under s 89(1)[4]; or
(b) a licensing board under 'any provision of [the] Act' (s 89(2))[5].

The expression 'any provision' prima facie refers to ss 65 and 66 but may also relate to ss 31 and 32[6]. No doubt the breach of a restriction order made under s 65 could result in proceedings under s 54(1), (4)[7].

There is no specific penal provision as respects registered clubs but a finding that 'illegal sales of alcoholic liquor have taken place in the club premises' or that the permitted hours have been breached may result in the refusal of an application to renew the certificate of registration or cancellation of the certificate (see s 108(k), (s) and s 109).

---

1 A suggested form of order may be found in *Purves's Scottish Licensing Laws* (8th edn, 1961, ed by Walker) p 277.
2 *Gordon* para 23.34, quoting Hume I, 197.
3 See below.
4 See above.
5 Maximum penalty: level 3. Premises and licenceholder liable to disqualification; licenceholder has vicarious responsibility. (S. 67, Sch 5).
6 Which respectively provide for suspension and closure orders: see Chapter 9.
7 Sale, supply and consumption outwith permitted hours.

CHAPTER 11

Alterations to licensed premises

APPLICATIONS FOR THE BOARD'S CONSENT

Licensed premises may not be reconstructed, extended or altered without the board's consent first being obtained (s 35)[1], subject to the following exceptions.

(a) Off-sale licences

Although off-sale premises are specifically exempted from the ambit of s 35 (s 35(1)), at least one licensing board purports to require that its permission be obtained for alterations. The licenceholder could, of course, simply refuse to obey such a diktat as being *ultra vires* but there is some sense in off-sale operators making at least a courtesy approach to the board before commencing works. The contemplated alterations could well render the premises unsuitable for the sale of alcoholic liquor in the opinion of the board when the licence comes to be renewed. For example, the owner of an off-sale licensed supermarket may decide to dispense with a counter-service area for the sale of alcoholic liquor, perhaps removing the familiar 'shop-within-a-shop' layout and creating a self-selection area for the display of drink. It is not beyond the bounds of possibility that, for arguably sustainable reasons, perhaps having regard to the type of clientele and the risk of theft[2], the later renewal of the licence would be placed in jeopardy[3].

Section 24(2) empowers the board to call for a plan of the premises on application being made for the renewal of *any* licence, although there is no requirement in s 10 that application for the *grant* of an off-sale licence be accompanied by plans. Paradoxically, s 36, which permits a board to call for the production of plans at the time of renewal and order structural alterations does *not* apply to off-sale licensed premises.

On the face of s 35(1), there would appear to be no requirement for the board's consent to be given even when the premises are extended, but in such a circumstance applications are sensibly made for the grant or provisional grant of a new licence.

---

1 Note also that, in terms of s 27, a board may grant a provisional licence to the holder of any licence to enable him to carry on business in temporary premises during the reconstruction of his premises.
2 Considered to be relevant considerations in *Philip Pearn v Nottingham City Licensing Justices* Nottingham Crown Court, 22 April 1974, unreported. See also *Tesco v Licensing Justices for the Petty Divisional Session of Mold* [1989] CLY 2267.
3 But see *R v Windsor Licensing Justices ex parte Hodes* [1983] LS Gaz R 1138.

(b) Non public or common parts

The reconstruction, extension or alteration must affect a 'public or common part' or *any communication with such a part* (s 35(1)). For the purpose of the section:

'(a) "public part" means a part open to customers who are not residents or guests of residents; and
(b) "common part" means a part open generally to all residents or to a particular class of them'[1].

Accordingly, the board's permission is not required where, for example, it is desired to reconstruct or alter a kitchen, cellarage facilities, guest bedrooms or staff quarters but would be necessary if the reconstruction or alteration is to affect public or common areas within the definition: for example, where a kitchen extension is to take in part of a dining area. It appears that, very strictly speaking, an extension to the building not affecting a public or common part does not require consent. Certainly, as discussed below, in terms of s 35(2) the board may not give approval under the section to a proposal which would materially alter the external appearance, size or shape of the premises, but the subsection appears only to be referable to a change which is 'caught' by s 35(1). Nevertheless, for the reasons expressed above in relation to off-sale licensed premises, it would be imprudent to proceed without agreement from the board.

(c) Alterations required by a lawful authority

No consent is necessary where the reconstruction, extension or alteration 'is required by order of some lawful authority' (s 35(1)), usually the local authority acting under, for example, the Public Health (Scotland) Act 1897 or the Building (Scotland) Act 1959. The suggestion in *Purves's Scottish Licensing Laws* (8th edn, 1961, ed by Walker) that such an order should when received be intimated to the clerk is still sound.

Changes to fixed seating and bar counters, the creation and removal of fixed partitions and so on are clearly within the scope of s 35 but a refurbishment on a like-for-like replacement basis is not. The alterations need not relate solely to the interior of the premises: as explained below, s 35(2) prevents a board from giving its consent under the section to any material external changes. Licenceholders are apt to forget this consideration and practitioners should, as a matter of course, enquire as to the licenceholder's whole intentions when primarily consulted as to the implications of internal proposals.

While s 35 clearly has in view *physical* alterations to premises licensing boards will expect a change in the use to which an area is put to be a matter for their consent, even where no structural alterations are necessary to accomplish that change. However, ss 61 and 62 of the Licensing (Scotland) Act 1959, the precursors of ss 35 and 36[2] of the 1976 Act, were prefaced with the heading: 'Control of licensing courts over *structure* of licensed premises' (author's emphasis). In England a distinction is drawn between s 19 of the Licensing Act 1964 (the

---

1 Section 35(1).
2 Section 36 enables a licensing board to order structural alterations: see below.

counterpart of s 36) and s 20 (the counterpart of s 35) to the effect that s 20 may relate to non-structural matters. In the result, the practice in Scotland appears to follow this distinction although, on this side of the border, it may be out of step with the history of the legislation.

The board is not to give its consent under s 35 to 'any reconstruction, extension or alteration which would materially alter the character of the premises in question or materially alter the external appearance, shape or size of the premises. . .' (s 35(2)). Where proposals are considered to be 'material' application will require to be made for a new licence. It may be considered, however, that such an application is neither necessary *nor competent* where the alterations proposed are purely internal or external alterations are extremely marginal. In terms of s 139(1), 'new licence' means 'a licence granted in respect of premises for which at the time of application for such a grant, either no licence was in force or a licence in a form different from the form of licence so granted was in force' (s 139(1)). Thus, where the holder of, say, a public house licence intends to convert a function room to a restaurant such an alteration could be considered 'material'. Yet, in the absence of any extension to the building, the identity of the 'premises' will be unchanged; no change to the 'form of licence' is required; and it is impossible to place the proposal within the four corners of the definition[1].

A proviso to the 'new licence' definition excludes a replacement licence (of the same type) where premises are rebuilt after destruction by 'fire, tempest or other unforeseen cause'[2]. It would appear that in such a case the new building need not replicate the original. In *Stevenson v Hunter*[3] it was held that a new certificate was not required for premises which were rebuilt with revised internal arrangements and a slight alteration to the outside measurements: the identity of the premises was regarded as unchanged and the existing certificate had not ceased to be valid.

It may also be observed that s 26(1) permits application for the provisional grant of a new licence to be made 'by any person interested in premises about to be constructed or in course of construction for use as licensed premises', terminology which suggests that the procedure is intended to relate only to a 'new build'[4].

There are as many definitions of 'materiality' as there are clerks to licensing boards. Some will permit alterations of a substantial nature to proceed under s 35. Others have been known to exclude from the section mere external signboard changes, new exterior lighting or canopies, which can hardly be said to constitute a 'public or common part'. Indeed, it may be considered that no meaning may be ascribed to the 'materiality' provision so far as it relates to 'appearance'[5]. A separate requirement to obtain planning permission (except perhaps in the case of

---

1 Until recently, recognising this difficulty, one licensing board (uniquely) employed a form of procedure known as 'an application for the grant of *a licence*'.
2 Proviso to 'new licence' definition in s 139(1).
3 (1903) 5 F 761, (1903) 10 SLT 754.
4 The corresponding section of the Licensing Act 1964, s 6(1)(a), while containing a virtually identical provision, also makes express provision for premises which are 'about to be altered or extended' or are 'in the course of alteration or extension' for licensed use, *whether or not they are already used for that purpose* (Licensing Act 1964, s 6(1)(b)).
5 A consideration of the *Report of the Departmental Committee on Scottish Licensing Law* (Cmnd 5354) (*Clayson*) para 8.41 suggests that only extensions to premises were intended to be 'caught' by the provision.

very simple signboard changes) may be an indicator that a new licence is required. Whether the clerk alone has power to decide the competency of an application under s 35 has yet to be firmly decided: perhaps by analogy with *Kelvinside Community Council v Glasgow District Licensing Board*[1] the matter is a mixed question of fact and law for the board to decide with the assistance of the clerk. However, where the clerk refuses to accept an application under s 35 without placing the issue of competency before the board, or the board, having considered the issue, declines to consider the application, the licenceholder's only remedy is to challenge such a decision by way of judicial review. It is more likely that he will proceed to submit an application for the provisional grant of a new licence. The matter is of particular importance in those areas where a regular extension of the permitted hours cannot be applied for at the same time as a provisional grant.

A number of licensing boards provide guidelines setting out their general approach to the 'materiality' issue, providing, for example, that an extension to premises may be allowed under s 35 where the area of the premises will not be increased by more than a certain percentage; or where the cost of the proposed works will not exceed a certain limit. There is certainly no warrant for the sometimes expressed view that *any* extension to a building cannot be considered under s 35: the purpose of the 'materiality' safety-net is to protect the interests of neighbourhood proprietors who would have locus to object to a new licence application (which is, of course, advertised) but not to a consent under s 35[2].

The issue frequently arises where it is proposed to create an outside drinking area or 'beer garden'[3]. Some boards will require the licenceholder to obtain a new licence; others are inclined to permit the use of the s 35 procedure.

In fact, in some instances an application may not only be unnecessary but also undesirable. Public house and hotel licences allow their holders to sell or supply alcoholic liquor for consumption both on and off the premises. In these cases if a customer purchases drink *inside* the licensed area for consumption *outside* no offence is committed. (It should be observed in the passing that some police forces stubbornly cling to the notion that drink may not be sold for consumption off the premises except in sealed vessels. That proposition is quite wrong, subject only to the qualification that, in terms of s 54(3)(b) alcoholic liquor taken from premises within fifteen minutes after the conclusion of the permitted hours must not have been supplied in an open vessel.)

On the other hand, if drink is to be purchased in the outside area the 'beer garden' must be licensed for that purpose. Planning permission may also be required. However, it seems largely to have been forgotten that the outside area may thus become a bar, which, in terms of s 139(1), includes 'any place exclusively or mainly used for the sale and consumption of alcoholic liquor'[4], subject to the restaurant use exception contained in s 68[5]. No such problem arises where alcoholic liquor is only *consumed* in the outside area. If the beer garden does

1 1990 SCLR 110, 1990 SLT 725.
2 See *Clayson*, para 8.41.
3 See Note at [1991] 6 LR 27.
4 See *Donaghue v McIntyre* 1911 SC (J) 61; *Carter v Bradbeer* [1975] 3 All ER 158, [1975] 1 WLR 1204.
5 Section 68 is considered in Chapter 14.

become licensed it may be appropriate for the licenceholder to obtain a children's certificate[1]. Care will require to be taken that no offence is committed under s 59 of the Roads (Scotland) Act 1984[2].

As to the 'character' of premises, it has been held in England that matters of historical character, heritage and aesthetics were irrelevant considerations[3]. It requires to be borne in mind, however, that s 20 of the Licensing Act 1964 is in several material respects different from its Scottish counterpart and cases decided thereunder must be treated with circumspection.

Where the holder of an entertainment licence desires to change the form of entertainment provided (for example, a snooker hall to discothèque conversion) he is usually required to apply for a new licence, irrespective of the extent of the physical alterations in contemplation.

Procedure

Applications for consent under s 35 may be made to 'a quarterly meeting of the board or at such other time as may be appointed by the board' (s 35(1)). In practice, they are frequently considered under delegated powers (s 5(1)) and even when placed before quarterly meetings may sometimes be subject to a lodgement deadline shorter than the normal five weeks.

Despite a *Clayson* recommendation[4], they are not susceptible to regulation in terms of s 37 but boards may require the submission of plans (s 35(2)) and invariably do so. The applicant is not required to satisfy the board that he already obtained any other necessary local authority approvals. While the board clearly has a discretion to refuse the application it must not take extraneous factors into account[5] and is probably bound only to consider whether the proposals will adversely affect the suitability of the premises for the sale of alcoholic liquor and the potential for public nuisance, having regard to the criteria applied when application is made for the grant or provisional grant of a new licence (see s 17(1)(b) and (c)).

Since the provisional grant of a licence is not a licence 'in force'[6] plans approved under s 26 are not subject to alterations by means of an application under s 35. Where changes are desired the holder of the provisional grant must either place his confidence in s 26(4), which allows a board to finalise a provisional grant where deviations from the approved plans 'are of minor importance and have not materially altered the character of the premises or the facilities for the supply of alcoholic liquor thereat' or, for safety's sake, apply for a fresh provisional grant.

Before giving its consent the board must consult with the fire authority for the area (s 35(3))[7]. Some licensed premises, usually hotels, may be the subject of a fire

1 The effect of this certificate and the application procedure are examined in Chapter 14.
2 Ie obstruction of the road or pavement.
3 *R v Chelmsford Crown Court ex parte Larkin* [1990] 2 LR 20.
4 Para 14.32.
5 *R v Liverpool Crown Court ex parte Lennon and Hongkins* [1991] 4 LR 22.
6 *Baljaffray Residents' Association v Milngavie and Bearsden District Council Licensing Board* 1981 SLT (Sh Ct) 106.
7 'Fire authority' has the same meaning as in s 38 of the Fire Services Act 1947 (s 139(1)).

certificate. The Fire Precautions (Hotels and Boarding Houses) (Scotland) Order 1972, SI 1972/382, made under the Fire Precautions Act 1971, applies to premises offering sleeping accommodation for more than six persons (either staff or guests) or where sleeping accommodation is provided beneath the ground floor or above the first floor. If a fire certificate is in force the fire authority will usually require to be advised of the proposed alterations[1] and the board's consultation with the authority under s 35(3) will not be treated as relieving the licenceholder of that obligation[2].

Where consent has been obtained under s 35 the licenceholder is not obligated to carry out the proposed works, although it is courteous to advise the clerk of an intention not to proceed, nor need he do so within any particular time. The benefit of the consent will pass to a new licenceholder; indeed, s 35 does not provide that application may only be made by the holder of a licence. The Act does not require that the finished work be inspected, but at least one board purports to prescribe such an inspection by regulation.

Unauthorised alterations

Where an alteration requiring consent has been carried out without the board's permission first having been obtained:

'. . . the sheriff may on a complaint at the instance of the licensing board, by order declare the licence which is in force for the premises in respect of which the contravention took place to be forfeited or may direct that, within a time fixed by the order, the premises shall be restored to their original condition'[3].

Under s 61 of the Licensing (Scotland) Act 1959 the complaint was instituted by the procurator fiscal in substitution for the clerk to the licensing court, a change 'made in order to bring the procedure into conformity with modern practice with regard to complaints in criminal and quasi-criminal matters'[4]. The draftsman of the 1976 Act chose to place responsibility with the licensing board with the result that, according to *City of Glasgow Licensing Board v Macdonald*[5], the matter should proceed by way of a summary application, rather than at the instance of the procurator fiscal.

It is not entirely clear whether the sheriff has a third option, that is, to make no order or direction, but it is probable that he is bound to select one of the two possible courses of action.

There is no express right of appeal unless such a right may be assumed to exist under the Sheriff Court Ordinary Cause Rules, failing which challenge by way of judicial review is presumably possible.

In England, a complaint must be made within six months of the date on which the contravention arose (and not within six months of the date on which it became known that there was ground for complaint). It would appear that, in Scotland,

1 Fire Precautions Act 1971, s 8.
2 For a prosecution involving failure to obtain a fire certificate, see *Berry v Smith* 1983 SCCR 327.
3 Section 35(4).
4 *Purves*, 8th edn, p 78.
5 1974 SLT (Sh Ct) 74.

the licenceholder is in constant peril of discovery. Persons acquiring licensed premises should make it a condition of the bargain that there has been no contravention of s 35.

No express provision is made for a situation in which a licenceholder fails to comply with an order to reinstate the premises. It may be open to the board to hold a hearing in terms of s 32 (bearing in mind, however, that a complaint to the sheriff may be made even where alterations would in the normal course have been approved) and the renewal of the licence would clearly be placed in jeopardy, at least on the ground of the licenceholder's fitness.

There is no provision for retrospective consent to alterations carried out without approval[1]. Sometimes licensing boards will, after considering mitigating factors, give such permission, but where the alterations are considered undesirable they will be inclined to invoke the sanction available to them. In *R v Croydon Crown Court ex parte Bromley Licensing Justices*[1] Glidewell, LJ observed that:

'. . . if the work had already been carried out, the justices on the application for renewal have the power to require alterations and thus have the power to say what they do require on the premises. In other words they could, effectively, either validate that which had already been done by requiring it, or alternatively, require some of it to be taken away or to be altered in some way or something of that sort'.

If such an approach were to be adopted in Scotland it would be open to deal with the matter by an order under s 36, bearing in mind, however, that the licence may not be due for renewal for some considerable time.

The licenceholder may find himself obliged to remedy the situation by making application for the grant of a new licence. He is not automatically prevented from trading ad interim, although, as suggested above, the board could decide to hold a hearing in terms of s 32 if it considers that the premises are 'no longer suitable or convenient for the sale of alcoholic liquor, having regard to their character and condition'.

In *R v Wyre Licensing Justices ex parte Wilkinson*[2] the licenceholder, without the permission of the justices, commenced the construction of a small extension to his premises. When application was made to incorporate the extension into the licensed area the extension had been substantially completed, but no work had been carried out to knock through from the existing area. The justices refused to consider the application on the basis of the *Bromley* case. Mr Justice Otton observed:

'This was an alteration to be considered as a whole. There was no justification in severing the application to make a hole from the application for the alterations to the premises which would have increased and were intended to increase drinking facilities after the hole had been made . . .',

upholding the justices conclusion that 'this was in reality an application for retrospective consent for the whole of the alterations for which consent had not been applied for at the proper time'.

1 *R v Croydon Crown Court ex parte Bromley Licensing Justices* (1988) 152 JP 245.
2 [1991] 5 LR 21.

ORDERS FOR STRUCTURAL ALTERATIONS

When application is made for the renewal of a licence (other than an off-sale licence)[1] the licensing board may require production of a plan of the premises in terms of s 36(1). The licence may be renewed subject to an order that, within a fixed time, 'such structural alterations as the board thinks reasonably necessary to secure the proper conduct of the business shall be made in that part of the premises in which alcoholic liquor is sold or consumed' (s 36(1)).

An order may not competently be made in respect of non-structural matters such as the locking of a door[2], nor in relation to areas such as kitchens, cellars, toilets and private accommodation, but a board may be empowered to require layout improvements so that, for example, persons under 14 may not have direct access to a bar[3]. In *Bushell v Hammond*[4] the Court of Appeal upheld a justices' order made under parallel English legislation[5] which related to the closure of an entrance by means of a locked gate.

Failure to comply with an order is an offence subject to a level 3 (maximum) penalty with a further fine of £5 for each day that the default continues (s 36(3), Sch 5). The court is also empowered to order disqualification of both the licence-holder and the premises (s 67, Sch 5) while the board may order suspension of the licence (s 36(4)) until satisfied that the matters which led to the order have been satisfactorily remedied (s 36(5)). *Semble* the suspension of the licence may be considered at any meeting of the board, but not under a 'delegated powers' arrangement (see s 5(2)(j)).

The licenceholder has limited avenues of redress. He may apply to the board for cancellation of the suspension order on the ground that the matters which led to the order have been satisfactorily remedied (s 36(6)). The refusal of such an application may be appealed to the sheriff (s 36(8)). The suspension order is also subject to appeal (s 36(8)) in which case the suspension 'shall not take effect until the expiry of the time within which the holder of the licence may appeal to the sheriff or, if the holder appeals to the sheriff or thereafter to the Court of Session, until the appeal has been determined in favour of the suspension or has been abandoned' (s 36(7)). There is a hiatus here, as identified in *McKay v Banff and Buchan Western Division Licensing Board*[6] as respects the similar wording of s 31(6): no provision is made for the suspension order being in abeyance when *the board* appeals from the sheriff to the Inner House.

The use of the word 'order' in s 36 is less than satisfactory. It is used to mean the *original* order under s 36(1) or the *suspension* order made by virtue of s 36(4). Section 36(6) and (8) appear to relate only to a suspension order. Subsection (8) refers to the board's refusal to cancel 'such an order,' clearly a reference to an order under subsection (4), so that, presumably, the power to apply for cancell-

---

1 A plan of off-sale premises may be required in terms of s 24 but there is no power to order structural alterations.
2 *Smith v Portsmouth Licensing Justices* [1906] 2 KB 229.
3 Cf s 69(3)(c).
4 [1904] 2 KB 563.
5 Currently the Licensing Act, 1964, s 19.
6 1991 SCLR 15, 1991 SLT 20.

ation in subsection (6) relates to the suspension order rather than the original order.

It has been suggested that the corresponding English provision may be employed to homologate alterations carried out by the licenceholder without permission[1].

1 *R v Croydon Crown Court ex parte Bromley Licensing Justices* (1988) 152 JP 245.

CHAPTER 12

Gaming and games in licensed premises

AMUSEMENT-WITH-PRIZES MACHINES

Amusement-with-prizes (AWP) machines, colloquially known as 'fruit' machines, are commonly installed in licensed premises, in terms of s 34 of and Sch 9 to the Gaming Act 1968 ('the 1968 Act').

The conditions under which AWP machines may be operated are set out in s 34(2)–(4), (8) and (9) of the 1968 Act. Stakes may be inserted in coins or in tokens and prizes may be monetary, non-monetary or both, subject to limits prescribed by statutory instrument.

In the case of public houses and hotels application for a permit for the provision of machines is made to the licensing board (1968 Act, Sch 9, para 1(c), as amended by the 1976 Act, s 133) 'by the holder of the licence' (1968 Act, Sch 9, para 5(1)(a)); in other cases, application is made 'by the person who is, or by any person who proposes, if the permit is granted, to become the occupier of the premises' (1968 Act, Sch 9, para 5(1)(b)) to the district council (1968 Act, Sch 9, para 1(b)) so that applications made in respect of entertainment, refreshment and (very rarely) restaurant, off-sale and restricted hotel licensed premises will go before a committee of the district council.

Permits are not transferable and cease to have effect if the holder of the permit ceases to be the holder of the public house or hotel licence or, in other cases, ceases to be the occupier of the premises (1968 Act, Sch 9, para 20(1))[1]. These provisions lead on occasions to several anomalies and practical difficulties:

(1) Where a public house or hotel licence is held by a company or partnership or other non-natural person and a nominated employee or agent both are deemed to be the holder of the licence for the purposes of the 1976 Act (see 1976 Act, s11), with the result that some licensing boards require a fresh application for a permit where a change of nominee has been effected under s 25(3). In theory, this should mean that as soon as such a substitution has taken place the permit immediately ceases to be valid[2] but in practice the permit is treated as being in force until re-application is made at the first competent opportunity.

In all cases other than hotels and public houses it is submitted that the 'occupier' of the premises is simply the non-natural person alone so that a change of nominee should not be regarded as invalidating the permit.

(2) While the prospective holder of a licence other than a public house or hotel

---

1 Special provision is made for the death of the permit holder: see 1968 Act, Sch 9, para 20(2).
2 Cf *Archyield v City of Glasgow Licensing Board* 1987 SCLR 191, 1987 SLT 547, the 'mischief' of which has been more or less cured by the 'new' s 64(3A) of the 1976 Act.

licence may make application for a permit in anticipation of the licence being transferred, on the basis that he proposed to become the occupier, a small number of licensing boards will not treat a permit application as competent in respect of public houses or hotels unless the transfer of the licence has actually taken place. In these areas anticipatory applications are not accepted so that no permit will be in force for some time after the grant of the transfer. The vast majority of boards are prepared to accept permanent transfer and permit applications for consideration at the same meeting. So far Parliament has not been prepared to accept a Gaming Board recommendation that a public house licence should automatically confer the right to install two AWP machines.

(3) There is nothing to prevent permit applications in respect of hotel and public houses from being processed under delegated powers but many boards restrict their consideration to quarterly meetings (although not always with the usual five-week lodgement deadline). Where an application for the temporary transfer of such a licence has been approved between quarterly meetings there may thus be no permit in force until an application is granted at the next meeting[1].

Paragraph 3 of Sch 9 to the 1968 Act gives councils (but *not* licensing boards) considerable policy-making powers. Subject to an exemption in respect of 'any premises used or to be used wholly or mainly for the provision of amusements by means of machines to which Part III of this Act applies' (1968 Act, Sch 9, para 4) (in other words, amusement arcades or similar premises)[2], the district council may pass a resolution that it will not grant or will neither grant nor renew permits in respect of certain classes of premises; it may also resolve to limit the number of machines in respect of which a permit may be granted. It will be deduced that no such resolutions may be made in respect of public houses or hotels (in respect of which jurisdiction lies with the licensing board: see above) but, somewhat illogically, they may apply to premises whose primary function is entertainment. Until recently it appeared that so-called 'blanket' resolutions purporting to affect all premises except those protected by para 4 of Sch 9 were probably invalid[3] but this approach has now been approved in *R v London Borough of Barnet ex parte Ellina and Hawrylczak*[4]. Whether this decision would be followed in Scotland is open to doubt.

Where a resolution is in force limiting the number of machines which may be available in the premises the permit may only be granted up to the specified number (1968 Act, Sch 9, para 9). In any event, the licensing board or the licensing committee of the district council, as the case may be (both generally referred to in this section as 'the licensing authority'), has a discretion to limit the number of machines (1968 Act, Sch 9, para 10). Predictably, policy approaches, quite distinct from any resolutions which may competently be made, are frequently in evidence, so that, for example, in some districts a permit for more than one machine will only be granted where the machines are to be sited in different

1 See Chapter 5.
2 It is conceivable that the exemption may not apply to an amusement arcade where there is a preponderance of non-gaming (eg 'quiz' or 'skill-with-prizes') machines.
3 *Walker v Leeds City Council* [1978] AC 403, [1976] 3 All ER 709; cf *Westminster City Council v Lunepalm Ltd*, The Times, 10 December 1985, unreported.
4 [1992] 10 LR 15.

rooms. While this may be a perfectly lawful approach, siting conditions as such cannot validly be imposed[1], although a plan of the premises showing the position of the machine is sometimes required and it is clearly undesirable that machines be so positioned as to compromise customer safety.

The view is sometimes expressed that under no circumstances may a permit be granted in respect of more than two machines, predicated upon a misunderstanding of s 31 of the 1968 Act, which relates to so-called ' jackpot' machines (discussed below) and which provides inter alia as follows:

'(1) Subject to any direction given under section 32 of this Act[2], the following provisions of this section shall have effect where any machine to which [Part III] of this Act applies is used for gaming on any premises in respect of which –
    (a) a licence under [Part II of] this Act is for the time being in force, or
    (b) a club or miners' welfare institute is for the time being registered under Part II or under [Part III] of this Act.
(2) Not more than two machines to which [Part III] of this Act applies shall be made available for gaming on those premises'.

The phrase 'those premises' is only referable to premises licensed under the 1968 Act, not the 1976 Act, or to clubs or institutes registered under Part III of the 1968 Act. Nevertheless, this simple misconception is commonplace.

Where a permit could only be granted or renewed in contravention of a resolution made under para 3 of Sch 9, it must be refused (1968 Act, Sch 9, para 3). If para 4 of Sch 9 applies to premises the grant of the permit is simply 'at the discretion of the appropriate authority' and its renewal may only be refused on limited grounds (1968 Act, Sch 9, para 8(1)). Otherwise, in terms of para 8(2) of Sch 9:

'[T]he grant or renewal of a permit . . . shall be at the discretion of the appropriate authority; and in particular, and without prejudice to the generality of that discretion, the appropriate authority may refuse to grant or renew any such permit on the grounds that, by reason of the purposes for which, or the persons by whom, or any circumstances in which, the premises are to be used, it is undesirable that machines to which Part III of this Act applies should be used for providing amusements on those premises'.

Although entitled to limit the number of machines (1968 Act, Sch 9, para 10) licensing authorities have no power to attach conditions. Otherwise, it has been suggested that they have a discretion which is 'unfettered'[3] and 'about as wide as it can be'.[4] It must, of course, be reasonably exercised. Historically, in Scotland there has been a reluctance on the part of sheriffs to interfere with the decision of the licensing authority[5]. Before the introduction of a right of appeal to the Inner House[6] there was ample scope for inconsistency.

---

1 *R v Luton Licensing Justices* QBD, 13 November 1986, unreported; see also [1990] 3 LR 28; [1991] 4 LR 26; and *Plaza Bingo and Social Club Ltd v Port Glasgow Burgh Council* 1968 SLT (Sh Ct) 3.
2 Which, subject to the discretion of the licensing authority, allows a specified number of s 34 machines to be installed instead of two 'jackpot' machines.
3 *Patullo v Dundee Corpn* 1969 SLT (Sh Ct) 31.
4 *Meade v Brighton Corpn* (1963) 67 LGR 289 per Lord Parker.
5 See, for example, *Clydesdale County Hotels Ltd v Burgh of Falkirk* 1970 SLT (Sh Ct) 71; *Dawson v Lanark Burgh Court* 1972 SLT (Sh Ct) 68.
6 1976 Act, s 133(4), applying s 39(4), (6)–(8) to 1968 Act, Sch 9, para 15. See also Act of Sederunt (Betting and Gaming Appeals) 1978, SI 1978/229.

While this reluctance continues to be in evidence a number of Inner House decisions demonstrate a more muscular approach to the review of the discretion exercised by licensing authorities. For example, in *Noble Organisation Ltd v City of Glasgow District Council (No 1)*[1] an approach which may be characterised as traditional was taken by the sheriff who, having made a number of findings in fact favourable to the appellants' application, nevertheless refused to interfere with the licensing authority's decision, remarking that:

'. . . there are considerable restraints on the question of reversing the decisions of a body which has been given clear statutory provisions to make decisions on which they have been cited to adjudicate'.

An Extra Division of the Inner House appears to have had no hesitation in holding that the sheriff's findings in fact effectively destroyed the basis of the refusal.

A general policy approach may be adopted provided that each case is examined on its own merits. In *Prise v Aberdeen Licensing Court*[2] the Sheriff Principal held that 'A reason which would apply to all premises of a particular class may nevertheless be valid if it can be justified on a consideration of each of the premises in question'[3].

The policy may be subject to legitimate alteration. In *Atherlay v Lanark County Council*[4] the sheriff-substitute (Gillies, QC) observed:

'[T]he policy of a local authority may quite reasonably change from time to time, for various reasons, such a change (sic) in its composition resulting from an election, or pressure of public opinion, or its own experience of operating the provisions of the Acts. There is, accordingly, nothing to prevent a local authority from refusing to renew an existing permit, provided that it has good grounds, of the nature I have indicated, for so doing'[5].

Irrelevant considerations must not be taken into account. In *Mecca Ltd v Edinburgh Corpn*[6] a permit application was refused on the basis that the police had no power to enter the (theatre) premises without a warrant so that, it was suggested, there would be virtually no means of ensuring that the statutory conditions relating to the AWP machines would be observed. Reversing that decision, the sheriff-substitute held that the licensing authority sought:

'to add a requirement for a successful application which the Act does not provide and to deprive from the benefit of the Act a whole class of persons, namely those who occupy property to which the police have no power of entry without a warrant'[7].

There is often an antipathy towards permit applications on the part of licensing authorities because it is feared that they are a corrupting influence on the young. (They may lawfully be 'played' by persons under the age of 18.) For example, in

---

1 1990 SCLR 393. See also *G A Estate Agency Ltd v Glasgow District Council* 1991 SCLR 8, 1991 SLT 16.
2 1974 SLT (Sh Ct) 48.
3 See also *Atherlay v Lanark County Council* 1968 SLT (Sh Ct) 71.
4 See above.
5 See also *In Re Sheptonhurst Ltd*, The Times, 29 June 1989, unreported.
6 1967 SLT (Sh Ct) 43.
7 Police have, of course, a power to enter licensed premises without a warrant: see the 1976 Act, s 85.

G A Estate Agency Ltd v Glasgow District Council[1] the committee's grounds of refusal were based inter alia upon the fact that 'the kind of persons likely to be on the premises' (1968 Act, Sch 9, para 8(2)) included persons under the age of 18, although the appellants had given an undertaking that no person below that age would be admitted to their premises unless accompanied by an adult.

Nevertheless, a Home Office Research Study[2] concluded that: 'Very few young people are at risk of becoming dependent upon amusement machines and no evidence is found of any association between the playing of machines and delinquency'[3]. Indeed, video machines, such as 'space invaders' and so on, with no gaming element, appeared to be equally popular[4] and the research findings suggested that 'there does not appear to be a strong case for imposing further restrictions on the use of amusement machines'[5].

In *J E Sheeran (Amusement Arcades) Ltd v City of Glasgow District Council*[6] applicants for an AWP machine permit relied in part upon the contents of this study, held by the sheriff to be a 'material and relevant consideration' which the council was required to address in its statement of reasons for refusal.

An application for the grant or renewal of a permit may not be refused unless the applicant or his representative has been afforded an opportunity to be heard (1968 Act, Sch 9, para 6)[7].

Generally, the usual rules of natural justice apply. In *Jack v Edinburgh Corpn*[8] it was held, not surprisingly, that the applicant should have been afforded an opportunity to address arguments put forward by the police in her absence.

The licensing authority must not take into account matters which have not been canvassed at the hearing of the application. In *G A Estate Agency Ltd v Glasgow District Council*[9] one of the grounds of refusal had not been discussed and the appellants given no opportunity to dispute it. The Inner House held that there had been 'a blatant, deliberate contravention of the principles of natural justice' and while the court understood the licensing authority's desire to control the number of gaming machines in the centre of Glasgow 'they cannot be allowed to do it by this underhand method'.

Similarly the authority must not proceed upon the undisclosed local knowledge of its members[10].

No specific provision is made for objections (which are, in any event, extremely rare). In *Matchett v Dunfermline District Council*[11] the petitioner had appeared before the respondents' committee in support of his written objection to the grant of an AWP machine permit. It was conceded on his behalf that he possessed no

1 1991 SCLR 8, 1991 SLT 16.
2 'Amusement Machines: Dependency and Delinquency', HORS No 101, 1988.
3 'Amusement Machines: Dependency and Delinquency', foreword.
4 'Amusement Machines: Dependency and Delinquency' p 19.
5 'Amusement Machines: Dependency and Delinquency' p 35.
6 Glasgow Sheriff Court, 3 April 1991, unreported.
7 See *Baskerville v Burgh of Coatbridge* 1967 SLT (Sh Ct) 5.
8 1973 SLT (Sh Ct) 64.
9 1991 SCLR 8, 1991 SLT 16.
10 *Robertson v Inverclyde Licensing Board* 1979 SLT (Sh Ct) 16. See also *Freeland v Glasgow District Licensing Board* 1979 SC 226, 1980 SLT 101 and *Moughal v Motherwell District Licensing Board* 1983 SLT (Sh Ct) 84.
11 1993 SLT 537.

statutory right to object. Lord Kirkwood held that the respondents' indulgence did not confer upon him *locus standi* to challenge grant of the application upon its reconsideration following an initial refusal[1].

A permit may be refused on grounds which are essentially of a planning nature, although planning permission has been granted. In *J E Sheeran (Amusement Arcades) Ltd v Hamilton District Council*[2] the court held that:

'The planning decision was made by [the Secretary of State's representative] as a result of the view which he took of the evidence before him. Another body, discharging a different statutory function for a different purpose, under discretionary powers, was entitled to reach a different conclusion'.

However, in *Leisure Inns (UK) Ltd v Perth and Kinross District Licensing Board*[3], decided under the 1976 Act, some weight was attached to the prior grant of planning permission, the Lord Justice-Clerk observing that:

'I am satisfied that the [licensing board] were entitled to consider the matter of amenity, although, since planning permission had been received . . . the appellants should, in my opinion, have been slow to hold that any detrimental effect on amenity was to be apprehended'.

Where a licensing authority refuses to grant or renew a permit or grant or renew a permit subject to a condition it 'shall forthwith give the applicant notice of their decision and of the grounds on which it is made' (1968 Act, Sch 9, para 15). No request by the applicant is prescribed. There is probably no real distinction to be made between 'grounds' and 'reasons'[4].

In practice, application is made for permission to install a number of machines specified by the applicant and the licensing authority may grant the application in full or authorise a smaller number. In theory, application is simply made for a permit and the specification of a particular number of machines by the licensing authority is a condition.

The reasons must provide 'a rational and substantial ground for refusing a permit' and be 'clear and specific'[5]. There is a right of appeal to the sheriff and, on a point of law, to the Court of Session[6]. Evidence may now be led in appeals: s 39(5) of the 1976 Act is applied by s 133(4) as amended by the Law Reform (Miscellaneous Provisions) (Scotland) Act 1990, Sch 9[7]. The court may remit the case to the licensing authority or reverse or modify its decision. In *G A Estate Agency Ltd v Glasgow District Council*[8] the sheriff considered that the proper course was to remit the matter to the licensing authority 'where the reasons have

---

1 See also *D & J Nicol v Dundee Harbour Trs* 1914 2 SLT 418 at 420, 421 per Lord Dunedin.
2 1986 SLT 289.
3 1991 SCLR 721, 1993 SLT 796.
4 *G A Estate Agency Ltd v Glasgow District Council* 1991 SCLR 8, 1991 SLT 16.
5 *Prise v Aberdeen Licensing Court* 1974 SLT (Sh Ct) 48. See also Chapter 15 for a consideration of the reasons which may be required by s 18 of the 1976 Act.
6 1976 Act, s 133(4), applying s 39(4), (6)–(8) to the 1968 Act, Sch 9, para 15. See also the Act of Sederunt (Betting and Gaming Appeals) 1978, SI 1978/229.
7 As to the difficulty caused by the former position, see *Cigaro (Glasgow) Ltd v Glasgow District Licensing Board* 1982 SC 104, 1983 SLT 549.
8 1991 SCLR 8, 1991 SLT 16.

been so ineptly set out', but on the facts of the case the Inner House held that the committee 'should not be given a second chance to justify their refusal'[1].

The operation of an amusement arcade may necessitate the grant of a public entertainment licence in addition to an AWP machine permit. Section 41 of the Civic Government (Scotland) Act 1982 provides that a such a licence is required for 'any place where, on payment of money or money's worth, members of the public are admitted or may use any facilities for the purpose of entertainment or recreation'[2]. It appears that the licensing authority is entitled to defer consideration of the permit application pending disposal of an appeal against refusal of a public entertainment licence application[3]. The provisions in the Civic Government (Scotland) Act 1982 for advertisement and objections are seen by many as a necessary compensation for the absence of any objection mechanism under s 34 of the 1968 Act when related to amusement arcades.

As to the duration of permits, see paras 18 and 19 of Sch 9 to the 1968 Act. Sections 38 and 39 of the 1968 Act deal, respectively, with offences and the cancellation of a permit.

'JACKPOT' MACHINES[4]

'Jackpot' machines are so called because, unlike AWP machines, they are not currently limited as to their payout, although prizes must be delivered in coins (1968 Act, s 31(4)), and the maximum stake is prescribed by statutory instrument. The potential for a large cash prize (commonly a 'jackpot' of £100 or more) acts as a considerable allurement to customers and, because of their revenue-generating capacity, to certain sections of the licensed trade.

However, the use of these machines is prohibited (1968 Act, s 35) except on premises licensed under the 1968 Act or the premises of clubs or miner's welfare institutes registered under Part II or Part III (1968 Act, s 31(1)).

There is no statutory definition of 'club'. In *J J J Leisure Centre, Applicants*[5] the sheriff (Paterson) observed:

'[O]n the admitted facts the Applicants are clearly, in my opinion, not a club of any sort whatsoever. The essential feature of an association called a club lies not in who owns the property, or who benefits from the running of the association, but rather lies in the constitution of the body claiming to be a club. There must be a constitution, there must be a membership in terms of that constitution, and there must be a committee controlling in some measure the life and well being of the body calling itself a club. If there is no such constitution there can be, in my opinion, no club . . .'.

In *Lunn v Colston-Hayter*[6] clubs were described as 'skeletal' where:

1 See also *Botterills of Blantyre v Hamilton District Licensing Board* 1986 SLT 14.
2 Civic Government (Scotland) Act 1982, s 41(2), which, in terms of s 9 of that Act, has effect in a licensing authority's area only if and in so far as the authority have so resolved.
3 *Noble Developments Ltd v City of Glasgow District Council* 1989 SCLR 622.
4 See also articles at [1990] 1 LR 17 and [1992] 10 LR 9.
5 Selkirk Sheriff Court, 13 April 1982, unreported.
6 [1991] Crim LR 467, [1991] 5 LR 23.

'They served . . . no discernible purpose whatever save to enable the respondent to circulate details of the entertainments which he was organising . . . They had no constitution, no rules, no criteria by which to judge applications for membership and no limitation whatever on the size of membership'[1].

The procedure for registration of a club in Scotland is governed by Sch 8 to the 1968 Act, which applies substantial parts of Sch 7 to Scotland and responsibility for registration and its renewal and cancellation rests with the sheriff whose decision is final (1968 Act, Sch 8, paras 1 and 4), subject only to the possibility of judicial review.

Registration or its renewal *must* be refused where it appears to the sheriff that the relevant premises are 'premises which (for whatever purpose) are frequented wholly or mainly by persons under 18' (1968 Act, Sch 7, para 7) although it is not unusual for proprietary clubs to have a class of junior membership with a numbers limitation.

There is a discretion to refuse:

(1) registration or renewal where it appears that the club:

'(a) is not a bona fide members' club, or
 (b) has less than twenty-five members, or
 (c) is merely of a temporary character'[2].

(2) renewal where there has been a contravention of any of the provisions of Parts I–III of the 1968 Act or any regulations made thereunder (1968 Act, Sch 7, para 9) and

(3) registration where the club or institute's previous registration has been cancelled or its renewal refused (1968 Act, Sch 7, para 10).

While bona fide members' clubs registered under the 1976 Act (for the supply of alcoholic liquor) will usually have no difficulty in obtaining registration, the position of proprietary clubs operated in entertainment-licensed premises is altogether more problematic. There is, however, no automatic impediment to the registration. The Court of Appeal so decided in *Tehrani v Rostron*[3], but, paradoxically and by a majority, also found that the recorder had been entitled to exercise his discretion *solely* on the ground that the club was a proprietary club, a view endorsed in *J J J Leisure Centre*[4] in which the sheriff held: 'One thing the Applicants are not, as is clear from the minute of admissions, is a "members club". That ground alone is sufficient in my opinion for refusing the application'.

Tehrani now has little following and, subject to the satisfaction of certain criteria, clubs of a recreational or sporting nature are likely to qualify.

The approach which now generally finds favour is set out in *Elgin Indoor Bowling Club, Applicants*[5] in which the late Sheriff Wilson gave a careful and commendably clear exposition of the law and a helpful review of a number of authorities, inclining towards the minority view of Lord Justice Phillimore in

---

1 See also 6 *Halsbury's Laws of England* (4th edn), paras 201ff; *Adair v Delworth* 1934 JC 83; *Panama (Piccadilly) Ltd v Newberry* [1962] 1 All ER 769, [1962] 1 WLR 610.
2 1968 Act, Sch 7, para 8.
3 [1972] 1 QB 182, [1971] 3 All ER 790. See also *Walters v Chief Constable of Nottinghamshire*, Nottingham Crown Court, 14 October 1975, unreported.
4 Selkirk Sheriff Court, 13 April 1982, unreported.
5 1989 SCLR 181.

Tehrani. It seems that the sheriff should exercise his discretion in favour of registration if:

(1) the club is under capable and reliable management;
(2) the constitution and rules of the club are so framed as to provide a close resemblance to a bona fide members' club;
(3) the application enjoys the support of club members; and
(4) the proposed division of gaming machine profits between club and members and the proprietor is reasonable.

In *Elgin Indoor Bowling Club* a minute of agreement between the company proprietor and the club provided for an equal division of the net revenue from the machines. The sheriff observed that, in his opinion it would be 'unreasonable to expect that all the profits from the gaming machines should go to the club' as long as a 'substantial proportion' were so destined.

A softer attitude towards the registration of proprietary clubs is also demonstrated in *Chief Constable of Tayside v Dundee Snooker Centre*[1], a case concerning a police application for cancellation[2] of a certificate of registration. While acknowledging the differences between the 1968 Act's registration and cancellation provisions, in his review of the authorities the sheriff (E F Bowen) did not find the decision in *Tehrani v Rostron*[3] to be attractive and considered the majority view that an application could be refused no matter how favourable the circumstances to be 'extreme'. He also distanced himself from the views expressed in *Chief Constable of Strathclyde v Pollokshaws Road Snooker Centre*[4] in which Sheriff Mowat aligned himself with the opinion of the recorder in *Tehrani* who said: 'I should require a lot of persuasion to register a proprietary club under Part III of the said Act'[5]. It may be that 'the heady whiff of commonsense in this arcane field'[6] has arrived.

Nevertheless, in the absence of a right of appeal against the sheriff's decision and of reported judicial review decisions to date, there remains room for a broad diversity of views. For example, the judgment of the sheriff (D B Smith) in *Chief Constable of Strathclyde v Kilmaurs Snooker Club*[7] demonstrates an unequivocally liberal approach. He did not consider it necessary or 'even desirable' that the application should come from the members themselves; nor that there should be a real resemblance to a members' club[8]; nor that the members should enjoy some control over the profits. He added: ' . . . it appears to me that adult human beings can control the profits, if they desire, by restricting their own use of machines'.

---

1 1987 SLT (Sh Ct) 65.
2 As to the provisions for cancellation, see the 1968 Act, Sch 7, paras 13–15 and 18, as applied to Scotland by Sch 8, para 3.
3 [1972] 1 QB 182, [1971] 3 All ER 790.
4 1977 SLT (Sh Ct) 72.
5 In *Elgin Indoor Bowling Club* 1989 SCLR 181 the late sheriff described the approach taken in the *Tehrani* and *Chief Constable of Strathclyde* cases as 'blinkered,' although broadly adopting the tests set out in the latter.
6 2 *Stair Memorial Encyclopaedia* para 1634.
7 Kilmarnock Sheriff Court, 11 October 1982, unreported.
8 Cf *Chief Constable of Tayside v Dundee Snooker Centre* 1987 SLT (Sh Ct) 65, in which the sheriff observed: 'The fact that [proprietary] clubs are permitted to have gaming machines seems to me to make it unrealistic to expect them to give the appearance of something other than what they actually are simply for the purpose of obtaining registration under the Act'.

Application for registration may be made at any time (1968 Act, Sch 7, para 3(1)). The standard, printed form issued by many sheriff clerks (V 71)[1] is not helpful. It requires the applicant to state that the club is a bona fide members' club. This part of the form should be adapted as necessary in the case of an application made on behalf of a proprietary club and the circumstances of the application explained in an accompanying statement, at least loosely following the style of an initial writ. It will probably be prudent to lodge the club's constitution and rules at the outset.

No later than seven days after the date on which the application is made a copy must be sent to the chief constable[2]. Many applications forms contain an execution of service section for completion so that, in practice, lodgement and intimation are carried out *unico contextu*. The application may be granted without a hearing in the absence of police objection[3]. It is not uncommon for the sheriff to require a hearing in chambers in uncontested cases. No time limit is specified for a police objection, nor are any grounds. Applications are usually opposed on the basis that the tests prescribed in *Elgin Indoor Bowling Club*[4] have not been satisfied or, rarely, on the mandatory ground of refusal that 'the relevant premises are premises which (for whatever purpose) are frequented wholly or mainly by persons under eighteen' (1968 Act, Sch 7, para 7).

Certificates last for five years (1968 Act, Sch 7, para 22)[5].

Both the players' stakes and winnings must be in coins (1968 Act, s 31(3)). The maximum stake is prescribed by statutory instrument. As mentioned above there is currently no limit on the amount of prizes. Only two machines may be installed on the premises. In respect of premises licensed in terms of Part II of the 1968 Act the two 'jackpot' (s 31) machines automatically permitted by the licence may, subject to the approval of the licensing board, be 'traded' for a larger number of AWP (s 34) machines (1968 Act, s 31(2))[6].

Section 36(1) of the 1968 Act provides that the machine income may only be removed by 'an authorised person', which means, in the case of a club, 'any officer or member of the club and any person employed by or on behalf of the members of the club in connection with the premises' (1968 Act, s 36(2)(b)). Since members of proprietary clubs will not normally be responsible for the employment of staff, it is suggested that the proprietor's manager be appointed as secretary of the club to ensure compliance with s 36.

There is no requirement that accounts be kept of machine income and expenditure, but this may be a sensible, prophylactic measure to prevent any accusations of *mala fides* on the part of the proprietor when application is made for renewal of the certificate of registration. It is open to the Secretary of State to introduce such a requirement by virtue of s 37(2), but no regulations have yet been made.

While there is an absolute prohibition against the grant of an AWP machine

---

1 As prescribed by the Gaming Act (Registration under Part III) (Scotland) Regulations 1969, SI 1969/1116, reg 2, Sch 1.
2 Ibid, Sch 7, para 3(3).
3 Ibid, Sch 7, para 5(1).
4 1989 SCLR 181.
5 For renewal provisions see para 4.
6 See *Mecca Leisure Ltd v City of Glasgow District Licensing Board* 1987 SLT (Sh Ct) 483.

permit (s 34) to a club or miners' welfare institute registered under *Part II* of the 1968 Act (1968 Act, s 34(7)) in theory at least a club registered under Part III may also hold a permit granted under s 34. A major difficulty is however caused by the conflicting conditions set out in ss 31 and 34, so that AWP machines and 'jackpot' machines may not be operated on the same premises. Nevertheless, it has been suggested that AWP machines may possibly be installed for the use of the general public in a separate part of the club premises[1].

It must also be borne in mind that 'jackpot' machines must not be 'used for gaming on the premises at any time when the public has access to the premises, whether on payment or otherwise' (1968 Act, s 31(8)).

This provision leads to a further consideration. A public entertainment licence is required in terms of s 41(1) of the Civic Government (Scotland) Act 1982 for the use of premises as 'a place where, on payment of money or money's worth, members of the public are admitted or may use facilities for the purposes of entertainment or recreation' (subject to certain exceptions). There is no statutory definition of 'public' but a number of cases provide some assistance.

In *Panama (Piccadilly) Ltd v Newberry*[2] a person proposing to become a member of a club paid a membership entrance fee and filled in a form. In the absence of any selective process, there was no sufficient segregation to make a candidate for membership acquire the status of member and cease to be an ordinary member of the public. Similarly, in *Adair v Delworth*[3] a club was held to be a place of 'public resort' where there was ' conclusive evidence that there was no discrimination in the admission of persons to the premises, and that any person could get in even under an assumed name'.

The test prescribed in *Gardner v Morris*[4], namely, 'could any reputable member of the public on paying the necessary admission fee come into and take part in the entertainment?' is probably of itself insufficient. In *Lunn v Colston-Hayter*[5], in which the organiser of an 'acid house party' sought to avoid the necessity of obtaining a public entertainment licence by restricting entry to members of one or two clubs, described as 'skeletal' and 'transparent devices designed to achieve the effect of circumventing the licensing requirements', it was held that those who had obtained membership and entry tickets 'manifestly remained members of the public'[6].

It is perhaps the case that a person does not cease to be a member of the public unless there is a genuine election procedure.

An exception to s 41(1) is made for inter alia: 'licensed premises within the meaning of the Licensing (Scotland) Act 1976 in which public entertainment is being provided during the permitted hours within the meaning of that Act'[7], but a

---

1 See Smith & Monkcom *The Law of Betting, Gaming and Lotteries* p 324; see also *Fox v Adamson* [1970] AC 522, [1968] 2 All ER 411. As to the meaning of 'premises', see the 1968 Act, s 52; *Commissioners of Customs and Excise v Griffiths* [1924] 1 KB 735 and article at [1991] 6 LR 9.
2 [1962] 1 All ER 769, [1962] 1 WLR 610.
3 1934 JC 83.
4 (1961) 59 LGR 187.
5 [1991] Crim LR 467, [1991] 5 LR 23.
6 See also *Casino de Paris Ltd v Newberry* [1962] 1 All ER 771; *Bytheway v Oakes* [1965] Crim LR 37; *Severn View Social Club and Institute Ltd v Chepstow Licensing Justices* [1968] 3 All ER 289, [1968] 1 WLR 1512 and article at [1991] 6 LR 14.
7 Civic Government (Scotland) Act 1982, s 41(2)(f).

licence under the 1982 Act is frequently obtained as a safeguard against loss of the liquor licence or of a regular extension of the permitted hours or in respect of the operation of premises outwith the permitted hours. Registration of a proprietary club under Part III of the 1968 Act would appear to be judicial confirmation that club members and their guests are not 'the public' thus rendering unnecessary a licence under the 1982 Act; but such a licence is clearly required where entertainment facilities are enjoyed by persons outwith these categories and when such persons have access to the premises s 31(8) applies[1].

NON-GAMING MACHINES

In recent years, amusement-only machines, which charge for participation in a game but offer no prizes, have become increasingly popular. Since no 'game of chance' is involved they are outwith the scope of Part III of the 1968 Act (1968 Act, ss 26 and 52).

Similarly, 'skill' machines, which offer prizes, such as the quiz or 'trivia' variety where a number of possible answers to a question are displayed on a video screen, are unregulated.

However, byelaws promulgated by licensing boards[2] frequently prohibit the playing of games on licensed premises whether by means of electronic machine or otherwise[3], except with the consent of the licensing board[4].

For a brief period it appeared that machines, such as 'space invaders', required a licence under the Cinematograph Act 1909, as amended[5], on the basis that they provided an exhibition of 'moving pictures'. Commonsense only prevailed when the case, *British Amusement Catering Trades Association v Greater London Council*[6] reached the House of Lords.

OTHER GAMES

Section 81 of the 1976 Act provides:

'A licenceholder or his employee or agent shall be guilty of an offence if he permits the playing of any game in the premises in respect of which the licence is held in such circumstances that an offence under the Betting Gaming and Lotteries Acts 1963 to 1971 is committed'.

1 See above.
2 See Chapter 8.
3 Games such as dominoes and cribbage are usually exempted: see below.
4 The *vires* of such a byelaw is open to considerable doubt; and in the absence of any byelaw such a prohibition is certainly invalid. See *Allied Breweries (UK) Ltd v City of Glasgow District Licensing Board* 1985 SLT 302.
5 The current legislation is the Cinemas Act 1985, as amended by the Broadcasting Act 1990.
6 [1985] 2 All ER 535, aff'd (by a majority) [1987] 2 All ER 897, rev'd [1988] 2 WLR 485 (HL).

Of most material concern is s 5(1) of the 1968 Act which prohibits any person from taking part in gaming (see the 1968 Act, s 52(1)) to which Part I of the Act applies in any street or in any other place to which, whether on payment or otherwise the public has access.

The prohibition does not embrace members' clubs, whose premises are not a public place and it is at least arguable that some proprietary clubs with membership schemes[1] may be outwith the scope of the section. Certainly, where 'jackpot' machines are installed they must not be used for gaming on the premises at any time when the public has access (1968 Act, s 31(8))[2].

Members' and proprietary clubs may impose small charges (fixed by statutory instrument) on members and guests for participation in games of chance, the most popular being bingo; banker games are excluded, so that all stakes are returned as winnings (1968 Act, s 40, as amended by the Gaming (Amendment) Act 1973, s 1(2)).

An exception to s 5 is contained in s 6[3] which frees from the restriction:
(a) the playing of dominoes and cribbage (1968 Act, s 6(1)(a));
(b) any other game specifically authorised in respect of particular premises (1968 Act, s 6(1)(b)).

Such specific authorisation may be obtained by the holder of a public house or hotel licence[4] by application to the licensing board (1968 Act, s 6(3)). No form of application is prescribed. A letter addressed to the clerk of the board explaining the circumstances of the proposal will generally suffice. The chief constable will usually be consulted by the board and opposition to the making of the order is generally to be expected; he must be furnished with a copy of any order made (1968 Act, s 6(6)).

Section 6(4) of the 1968 Act allows boards to make:
(a) a global order imposing such requirements or restrictions with respect to gaming by the playing of dominoes or cribbage; and
(b) an order relative to any particular authorisation of a game under s 6(3)
as may be considered necessary to secure that gaming does not take place in a part of premises to which the public have access for 'high stakes' or 'in such circumstances as to constitute an inducement to persons to resort to the premises primarily for the purpose of taking part in such gaming' (1968 Act, s 6(4)(a) and (b)).

This somewhat inept provision is the subject of much misunderstanding and confusion. A licensing board byelaw[5] may typically provide that:

'Unless with the consent of the licensing board, the licenceholder shall not permit the playing of games in licensed premises with the exception of chess, pool, playing cards, cribbage, drafts and dominoes which shall not be played for such high stakes that they

---

1 See above.
2 See above.
3 As amended by the 1976 Act, Schs 7 and 8.
4 Amendments to the 1968 Act contained in the 1976 Act have generally ignored the creation of entertainment and refreshment licences in the latter. Although some clubs operated in entertainment-licensed premises may be outwith the s 5 prohibition others in which the playing of games may be regarded as unexceptionable cannot avail themselves of the type of order explained below.
5 Which may well be *ultra vires*: see Chapter 8.

constitute an inducement to persons to resort to the premises primarily for the purpose of taking part in such games'.

There are, of course, local variations of this wording, which is flawed for a number of reasons:

(1) Section 6(4) certainly enables a board to make a 'blanket' order in relation to dominoes and cribbage, imposing requirements or restrictions of the nature specified above, but it is not appropriate simply to repeat the wording of s 6(4)(a) and (b) without specifying the manner in which the purpose of the subsection is to be achieved.

(2) It would appear that a board may not competently authorise the playing of other games which constitute 'gaming' by what may be described as an edictal approach. If a licenceholder wishes to permit his customers to play small-stake non-banker games[1] he would require to obtain *specific permission*, standing the application requirement of s 6(3).

Byelaws of this type also serve to 'trap' games outwith the scope of the 1968 Act, such as those provided by 'space invader' and 'trivia' machines, briefly discussed above.

Orders made under s 6 are always subject to the provisions of ss 2–4 of the 1968 Act so that, broadly speaking, banker games are prohibited, the game must provide all players with an equal chance (1968 Act, s 2)[2], no charge for participation may be made and there must be no levy on winnings (1968 Act, s 4). A person under the age of 18 may not take part in gaming authorised by s 6 (1968 Act, s 7(1))[3]; the holder of a licence or any person employed by him commits an offence by knowingly allowing such a person to do so (1968 Act, s 7(2), as amended by 1976 Act, s 136(1), Sch 7, para 10)[4].

Contravention of the provisions of *s 6 itself* is not an offence. It therefore seems that no offence is committed for which the licenceholder is liable to prosecution under s 81 of the 1976 Act[5] if, for example, a requirement or restriction made under s 6(3) is breached[6].

EXEMPT ENTERTAINMENTS

It may well be considered that s 15 of the Lotteries and Amusements Act 1976 ('LA Act') substantially dilutes the effect of ss 5 and 6 of the 1968 Act in certain circumstances.

---

1 Banker games are prohibited (s 6(7)): see below.
2 See *Herron v Scholarious* 1970 SLT (Sh Ct) 3.
3 Maximum penalty: level 1 (s 8(6)).
4 The offence is treated as a contravention of s 68(1) of the 1976 Act and thus attracts a maximum penalty set at level 3, with the licenceholder (who has vicarious responsibility) and the premises liable to disqualification (1976 Act, s 67(2), Sch 5), all in terms of the 1968 Act, s 8(7), as amended by the 1976 Act, s 136(1), Sch 7, para 11.
5 Cf the Licensing Act 1964, s 177 in terms of which an offence may be committed if the holder of a justices' licence suffers any game to be played which, inter alia, contravenes a requirement or restriction for the time being in force under s 6 of the 1968 Act.
6 Subject to the caveat that a byelaw may thus be contravened: see above.

Section 15 applies to the provision at 'any exempt entertainment'[1] of any amusement with prizes[2] which constitutes a lottery[3] or gaming or both, but does not constitute:

(1) gaming in a club licensed or registered under Part II of the 1968 Act; or
(2) gaming by means of 'jackpot' or AWP machines regulated by Part III of the 1968 Act[4].

The purpose of the section is to allow group games other than machine games in a non-commercial setting and the following conditions must be satisfied:

'(a) that the whole proceeds of the entertainment, after deducting the expenses of the entertainment, shall be devoted to purposes other than private gain;
(b) that the facilities for winning prizes at amusements to which [the] section applies, or those facilities together with any other facilities for participating in lotteries or gaming, shall not be the only, or the only substantial, inducement to persons to attend the entertainment'[5].

Section 1(2)(c) of the 1968 Act, as amended by s 25 and para 1 of Sch 4 to the LA Act, has the effect of disapplying Part I of the 1968 Act from exempt entertainments under s 15 with the possibly surprising results that:

(i)   No offence is committed under s 5 of the 1968 Act and (except as aftermentioned) the entertainment is outwith the control of the licensing board.
(ii) Persons under the age of 18 may participate.
(iii) There is no restriction on the type of game that may be played.

No doubt unwittingly, some licensing boards have created the potential to close this loophole by providing in byelaws that the playing of games requires their permission. A licenceholder who proposed to hold, say, bingo sessions and comply with the 'exempt entertainment' provisions may thus find the proposal blocked, although it is debatable whether the prohibition of an otherwise lawful activity in this way is *intra vires*.

ENTERTAINMENTS NOT HELD FOR PRIVATE GAIN

A further exemption is found in s 41 of the 1968 Act which allows both members' and proprietary clubs[6] to provide gaming at entertainments promoted 'otherwise than for purposes of private gain' (1968 Act, s 41(1)(a)). Like s 15 of the LA Act, the section excludes clubs registered under Part II of the 1968 Act and gaming by means of 'jackpot' and AWP machines (1968 Act, s 41(1)(b)); it also excludes the

---

1 Defined in the LA Act, s 3(1) as 'a bazaar, sale of work, dinner, dance, sporting or athletic or other entertainment of a similar character, whether limited to one day or extending over two or more days'.
2 'Amusement with prizes' is not defined but the words are to be given their ordinary, natural meaning: *Fox v Adamson* [1970] AC 552, [1968] 2 All ER 411.
3 Where the amusement constitutes a lottery, ss 1 and 2 of the LA Act, dealing with the general illegality of lotteries, do not apply: LA Act, s 15(2).
4 LA Act, s 15(1).
5 LA Act, s 15(4). Contravention of the conditions is an offence: s 15(3).
6 In practice, it may be difficult for proprietary clubs to qualify: see definition of 'private gain' and meaning of 'society' in the 1968 Act, s 51A, inserted by the LA Act, s 25, Sch 4, para 5.

provision of amusements with prizes under ss 15 and 16 of the LA Act (1968 Act, s 41(1)(c), as amended by the LA Act, s 25, Sch 4, para 3[1]).

Part I of the 1968 Act does not apply (1968 Act, s 1(2)(b)) so that, again, no offence is committed under s 5 and, subject to the caveat that the playing of games may require byelaw permission, the exempt games are outwith the jurisdiction of licensing boards. Section 2 of the 1968 Act is, however, applied to s 41 (1968 Act, s 41(2)) so that only equal chance games (eg bingo) are permitted and banker games are prohibited.

No more than one payment (the limit of which is fixed by statutory instrument) may be made by each player, whether by way of entrance fee, stake or otherwise (1968 Act, s 41(3)). The value of prizes and awards is also capped by statutory instrument. The whole proceeds of payments made by players, after deducting expenses not exceeding the reasonable cost of providing facilities for the games, are to be applied for purposes other than private gain (1968 Act, s 41(5) and (6)).

1 For an explanation of s 16, see 2 *Stair Memorial Encyclopaedia* para 1653ff.

CHAPTER 13

Offences and the conduct of licensed premises

The *Report of the Departmental Committee on Scottish Licensing Law*[1] considered that, as a matter of public policy, licenceholders should be required by law to carry a high degree of responsibility for the supervision of licensed premises and for the actings of staff. The committee also recognised the incoherent and unsatisfactory nature of the then current legislation[2], which sought to ensure the proper conduct of premises by means of (a) standard conditions attached to certificates and (b) separate criminal offences. The Act reflects the committee's recommendation that all requirements regarding the conduct of licensed premises should be set out separately in the statute. Provision is made for the licenceholder's vicarious responsibility.

PROSECUTION OF OFFENCES

All offences under the Act are to be tried in a summary manner (s 128(1)(a)). Prosecutions may take place in either the sheriff or district court (s 128(1)(b)), except that the following offences may only be tried by the sheriff (s 128(1)(c)):
(a) acting as a licensing board member while disqualified from so doing (s 2);
(b) proscribed involvement in licensing board proceedings by the clerk and others (s 7(3));
(c) canvassing of a board member (s 19(1));
(d) default in compliance with structural alterations order (s 36(3)).

Section 128(2) provides that any contravention 'which, if it had been triable on indictment, could competently have been libelled as an additional or alternative charge in the indictment, may be so libelled and may be tried accordingly'.

In terms of s 312(x) of the Criminal Procedure (Scotland) Act 1975:

'Where an offence is alleged to have been committed in any special capacity, as by the holder of a licence . . . the fact that the accused possesses the qualification necessary to the commission of the offence shall, unless challenged by preliminary objection before his plea is recorded, be held as admitted'.

Thus, where the holder of a certificate was charged as such and no objection raised, the prosecutor's failure to produce and prove the certificate was of no consequence[3].

---

1 (Cmnd 5354) (*Clayson*) paras 10.01ff.
2 Licensing (Scotland) Acts 1959 and 1962.
3 *Smith v Grant* 1932 JC 36.

Where a licence is held by a partnership, proceedings may be taken against the firm in its own name without the addition of the partners' names[1]. It has been held that office-bearers and management committee members of a registered club could competently be charged as if they were the persons offending where liquor was sold outwith authorised hours 'by the hand of AB, barmaid in the said club'; an objection that the barmaid was not averred to be the servant or agent of the accused was repelled[2].

Where an offence committed by a 'body corporate' is proved to have been committed 'with the consent or connivance of, or to be attributable to any neglect on the part of, any director, manager, secretary or other similar officer of the body corporate, or any person purporting to act in such capacity', such a person shall also be deemed to be guilty and 'liable to be proceeded against and punished accordingly'. The expression 'director' means 'a member' of the body corporate in the case of a nationalised industry (s 67(5))[3].

As respects the specification of the complaint, it was held in *Colthard & Maguire v Reeves*[4] that the names of customers to whom liquor was allegedly sold outwith permitted hours required to be given as a matter of fair notice. The decision here contrasts with the approach taken in a much earlier case, *Muir v Campbell*[5]. Here, the name of a person to whom liquor was 'given out' was not essential to the relevancy of the complaint, although the court observed that (a) where the prosecutor knows the identity of the customer he ought to state it; and (b) otherwise, the words 'to the prosecutor unknown' should be inserted. Although *Muir* was apparently not considered in *Wilson v Allied Breweries Ltd*[6], the dictum of Lord Hunter in the latter case substantially echoes the earlier approach. Referring to *Colthard & Maguire*, his Lordship said:

'[The] charges did not contain in the libel the names of the persons to whom exciseable liquor was alleged to have been sold, and, from the somewhat abbreviated report, it does not appear that there was any statement in either of these charges that the identity or identities of the person or persons alleged to have been supplied were unknown to the prosecutor . . . I wish to guard myself against being thought to say that a charge [of selling to under-age persons] could not be relevantly libelled and proved in circumstances where the prosecutor was unable to identify by name the under-age persons. In such a case proof of the contravention might present difficulties, but it does not follow that a charge, otherwise properly libelled, would necessarily be irrelevant in the absence of such identification'.

In *Wilson* the Crown gave notice of the persons to whom drink was allegedly sold but the identity of the employee or agent effecting the sale was 'meantime to the complainer unknown'. The High Court held that specification of the seller's identity was unnecessary: whether or not he came within the required category was a matter of proof and not of competency. A similar result was reached in *Hall v Begg*[7]; it was unnecessary to state the name of the person who had supplied drink

1 Criminal Procedure (Scotland) Act 1975, s 333.
2 *Burnette v Mackenna* 1917 JC 20, 1916 2 SLT 293.
3 Cf Criminal Procedure (Scotland) Act 1975, s 333.
4 1973 SLT (Notes) 34.
5 (1888) 16 R (J) 20.
6 1986 SCCR 11, 1986 SLT 549.
7 1928 JC 29, (1928) SLT 336.

to an intoxicated customer unless special circumstances required such a statement in fairness to the accused.

Penalties

Offences attract a fine, except that 60 days' imprisonment is an alternative or additional penalty for behaving in a riotous or disorderly manner while drunk in licensed premises (s 78(1)(a), Sch 5). Schedule 5 provides a rough description of all offences, indicates whether the licenceholder has vicarious responsibility, shows whether the licenceholder and his premises may be disqualified and gives the maximum penalty (s 67(1))[1].

Additional penalties of disqualification may be imposed following conviction where (a) column 4 of Sch 5 so indicates; (b) the offence was one of canvassing contrary to s 19 (s 67(3)); and (c) the offence was committed under the Prevention of Corruption Acts 1889 to 1916 (s 67(4))[2]. The court may make one or both of the following orders:

(1) that the licenceholder shall be disqualified from holding a licence in respect of the premises concerned (or to which an application relates or related) for a period not exceeding five years (s 67(3)(a), (4)(a));
(2) that the premises in respect of which the licence is held (or to which an application relates or related) shall be disqualified from being used as licensed premises for a period not exceeding five years (s 67(3)(b), (4)(b)).

Disqualification from licenceholding may only relate to the premises *in quo*: it is not open to the court to disqualify a person from being a licenceholder as such[3]. Even where an offence was of a serious nature, disqualificaton was not appropriate having regard to the licenceholder's previously unblemished record over a long period[4]. One month's disqualification from holding a licence was set aside where serious financial consequences were predicted; the offence had been committed by an employee while the licenceholder was unwell[5]. In *Canavan v Carmichael*[6] the offence of selling liquor outwith permitted hours was committed by the appellant's father-in-law, with whom she had been in partnership. The High Court considered that disqualification from licenceholding was excessive for a first offender, taking into account her father-in-law's subsequent expulsion from the partnership.

---

1 The maximum penalty shown in column 5 of Sch 5 refers to a level on the 'standard scale' set out in s 289G of the Criminal Procedure (Scotland) Act 1975 (added by Criminal Justice Act 1982, s 54), which is subject to amendment by order by the Secretary of State.
2 The Acts are: the Public Bodies Corrupt Practices Act 1889, the Prevention of Corruption Act 1906 and the Prevention of Corruption Act 1916. For a full analysis, see Sheriff G H Gordon's *The Criminal Law of Scotland* (2nd edn, 1978) paras 21.22ff, 44.03ff, and Second Supplement to the principal work.
3 *Canavan v Carmichael* 1989 SCCR 480; *Devaux v MacPhail* 1991 GWD 7-396; *Matchett v Douglas* 1991 SCCR 617.
4 *Matchett v Douglas*, above. The licenceholder, who had held a licence for seven years without committing an offence, was convicted of supplying alcoholic liquor to seven persons under eighteen.
5 *Mackie v Carmichael* 1989 GWD 38-1767. A fine of £50 was, however, increased to £200. See also *Ewing v Carmichael* 1990 GWD 6-325.
6 1989 SCCR 480.

On the other hand, a three-year disqualification from holding a licence was not excessive where the offence related to under-age drinking in a bar and the licenceholder had, in any event, severed his connection with the premises[1].

A certified extract of a licenceholder's conviction requires to be transmitted to the clerk of the board by the clerk of the court (s 129). While the board would be entitled to have regard to the conviction when considering an application to renew the licence, the suspension procedure provided by s 31[2] may only be initiated where a complaint has been received[3]. *Clayson*[4] considered that it was appropriate to provide for suspension of a licence following conviction for a 'breach of certificate' where forfeiture was not ordered by the criminal court. It may be observed that, in some districts, complaints presented by the chief constable in terms of s 31 are entertained where the conduct complained of has yet to come to trial[5].

VICARIOUS RESPONSIBILITY OF LICENCEHOLDERS

In 1916, the Lord Justice-General observed that the doctrine of vicarious responsibility was a necessary adjunct of licensing laws 'for reasons which are singularly obvious', so that 'a publican may be guilty of an offence even although he is not cognisant of the offence having been committed and has given no authority for its commission to his servants or agents'[6].

Half-a-century later, a decision by a court of five judges threatened to render nugatory the accountability of certificate-holders who had delegated the supervision of premises. In *Noble v Heatly*[7] a certificate-holder had devolved responsibility upon a supervisor, who in turn appointed a manager. The High Court held that the certificate-holder could not be convicted of 'knowingly permitting' drunkenness in the premises without any personal knowledge on his part[8]. Although the court did not overrule the decision in *Greig v Macleod*[9], which was founded upon the the Crown, disapproval of Lord McLaren's dicta in that case[10]

---

1 *Stamper v Lowe* 1990 GWD 14-774.
2 The licence may be suspended on the ground that 'the licence holder is no longer a fit and proper person'.
3 In practice, from the chief constable.
4 Para 10.38.
5 Such a course was desiderated by the sheriff in *McKenzie v Renfrew District Licensing Board* 1991 SCLR (Notes) 859, a decision which is unlikely to be the last word on the subject. It also appears that a licenceholder may no longer be a 'fit and proper person' on the basis of accusations of criminal behaviour which do not found a prosecution: see *McKay v Banff and Buchan Western Division Licensing Board* 1991 SCLR 15, 1991 SLT 20.
6 *Gair v Brewster* 1916 SC (J) 36 at 38.
7 1967 JC 5, 1967 SLT 26.
8 'Knowingly permitting' inter alia drunkenness was a 'breach of certificate' offence for which only the certificate-holder could be prosecuted: Licensing (Scotland) Act 1959, s 131 and Sch 2. Cf *Metropolitan Police Commissioners v Cartman* [1896] 1 QB 655.
9 (1907) 5 Adam 445, 1908 SC (J) 14.
10 '[I]f a person . . . delegates the conduct of a business to another, he is responsible for the acts of the persons to whom he has given the institorial power, as if he had made the sale himself'. See the discussion of *Noble* and *Greig* in *Gordon* para 8.22.

effectively excluded from Scots law the English doctrine of delegation, in terms of which knowledge may be imputed from the devolution of management[1].

Noble precipitated demands for legislation to establish a licenceholder's absolute vicarious responsibility for the conduct of his staff[2]. While the majority of the *Clayson* Committee favoured a such a system, Parliament effectively enacted the minority view by providing a 'due diligence' defence. Column 3 of Schedule 5 indicates whether a particular offence attracts vicarious responsibility (s 67(1)); and, where such an offence is committed by his 'employee or agent', proceedings may be instituted against the licenceholder[3] (whether or not the actual perpetrator is prosecuted). The licenceholder may, however 'prove[4] that the offence occurred without his knowledge or connivance and that he exercised all due diligence to prevent its occurrence' (s 67(2)). The issues raised by this form of accountability are now examined.

Responsibility for fellow employees

Typically, an offence is capable of being committed by 'the holder of a licence or his employee or agent'. It requires to be kept in view that, where a licence is held by a non-natural person and his nominee (usually a manager), any reference in the Act to 'the holder of a licence includes a reference to both of these persons' (s 11(3)). Thus, the manager of a company licenceholder may be answerable for the conduct of a fellow employee[5], even where the identity of that employee is unknown to the prosecutor[6].

Acts within the scope of employment

The conduct complained of must be attributable to an 'employee or agent'. The person committing the offence may, in exceptional cases, be excluded from either category. A licensee was acquitted where illegal sales were made by an occasional messenger, employed by a shopman who had no authority to engage bar staff, although the money went into the till:

---

1 Paradoxically, the court in *Noble* found 'considerable support' for its conclusion in *Vane v Yiannopoullous* [1965] AC 486, [1964] 3 WLR 1218, a House of Lords decision which has not prevented the survival of the 'delegated authority' principle in England. See *Ross v Moss* [1965] 2 QB 396, [1965] 3 WLR 416; *R v Winston* [1969] 1 QB 371, [1968] 2 WLR 113; *Howker v Robinson* [1978] QB 178, [1972] 3 WLR 234. Sheriff Gordon's expression of support for the principle (see above, para 8.61) does not appear to take account of the 1976 Act.
2 See *Clayson*, para 10.12.
3 Note that s 67 is extended to offences by wholesalers: s 90A(4).
4 On the balance of probabilities: *King v Lees* 1993 SCCR 28. See also *HM Advocate v Mitchell* 1951 JC 53, 1951 SLT 200; *Neish v Stevenson* 1969 SLT 229.
5 This is an exceptional departure from the general rule that vicarious responsibility does not attach to one servant, even a 'superior servant', for the acts or omissions of another: *Shields v Little* 1954 JC 25, 1954 SLT 146. Where an offence may be committed in terms of s 90A by 'a wholesaler or his employee or agent', the wholesaler alone has vicarious responsibility: see s 90A(4).
6 *Wilson v Allied Breweries Ltd* 1986 SCCR 11, 1986 SLT 549; cf *Colthard & Maguire v Reeves* 1973 SLT (Notes) 34.

'[W]hat was done here did not make the licensee guilty of an offence any more than would have been the case had a charwoman cleaning the premises handed a bottle of whisky to a purchaser'[1].

In the same case, Lord Skerrington observed that the words 'servant' and 'agent' had a definite technical meaning in law and:

'if it had been desired to introduce a new kind of vicarious responsibility nothing would have been easier than to . . . make the licensee responsible if a sale was effected by any person, whether that person was or was not his servant or agent'[2].

In prosecutions taken under earlier legislation it was commonly argued, often without success, that an 'act done contrary to express and particular instructions' or purely in pursuance of the servant's own ends was not conduct within the scope of employment for which 'an absent and innocent licenceholder' should be held responsible[3]. Now, the issue as to whether the employee's act of defiance, disobedience or carelessness took place in the course of his duties is unlikely to arise; a disregard of instructions may, of course, allow the licenceholder to establish the 'due diligence' defence.

On the other hand, it remains the case that there is no vicarious responsibility for a 'private ploy'[4]; or, put another way, an employee who commits an illegal act may not be *pro hac vice* the servant of the licenceholder. The onus of establishing that an employee was acting for his own personal ends rests, however, on the defence and there is effectively a rebuttable presumption to the contrary[5]. In *Courage v Smith*[6] the High Court rejected an argument that the Crown required to exclude the possibility of a private deal for the sale or supply of whisky between a restaurant waiter and a customer.

Lack of knowledge

Under earlier legislation, where the Crown was required to demonstrate the accused's knowledge of an offence, 'wilful blindness' could supply the requisite *mens rea*[7]. This constructive knowledge was difficult to distinguish from a failure to exercise 'all due diligence'[8]. Indeed, in *Knox v Boyd*[9] the High Court appears to have considered that 'knowledge' was excluded by the steps taken to prevent under-age drinking[10]. Absence of knowledge (and connivance) for the purpose of s 67(2) is, however, a straightforward issue of fact and is usually established

---

1 *Auld v Devlin* 1918 JC 41 at 46 per Lord Mackenzie.
2 1918 JC 41 at 46. See also *Herriot v Auld* 1918 JC 16; and, for a similar decision in England, see *Adams v Camfoni* [1929] 1 KB 95.
3 *Ferguson v Campbell* 1946 JC 28, 1946 SLT 58; *Duff v Tennant* 1952 JC 15, 1952 SLT 108; *Simpson v Gifford* 1954 SLT 39. See also *Metropolitan Police Commissioners v Cartman* [1896] 1 QB 655.
4 See *Gordon* para 8.58.
5 *Ferguson v Campbell* 1946 JC 28, 1946 SLT 58.
6 1960 JC 13, 1960 SLT 55.
7 *Knox v Boyd* 1941 JC 82, 1942 SLT 14. See also *Smith of Maddiston Ltd v Macnab* 1975 JC 48, 1975 SLT 86; *Carmichael v Hannaway* 1987 SCCR 236.
8 See *Gordon* para 8.22, where the author's interpretation of *Noble v Heatly* 1967 JC 5, 1967 SLT 26 proceeds upon similar reasoning.
9 1941 JC 82, 1942 SLT 14.
10 See also *Nicol v Smith* 1955 JC 7, 1955 SLT 38.

without difficulty, particularly where the licenceholder is not directly engaged in the management of the business.

It may be observed that a number of long-standing offences which have scarcely been touched by the draftsman's revisionary hand survive with the retention of 'knowledge' as an essential ingredient. For example, s 84[1] provides that a licenceholder commits an offence if he 'knowingly suffers' a constable to remain on the premises in certain circumstances. The imposition of vicarious responsibility by Sch 5 and the concomitant 'lack of knowledge' defence are irreconcilable with the decision in *Noble v Heatly*[2]. A similar oversight is evident in s 126, which virtually re-enacts verbatim s 187 of the Licensing (Scotland) Act 1959 and refers to the offence of 'knowingly permitting' drunkenness: the retention of the word 'knowingly' is repugnant to the provisions of s 78(2), in terms of which the licenceholder need only 'permit' drunkenness (s 78(2))[3].

Exercise of 'all due diligence'

The purpose of a 'due diligence' defence is 'to mitigate the injustice, which may be involved in an offence of strict liability, of subjecting to punishment a careful and conscientious person who is no way morally to blame'[4]. The only requirement is that *the accused* exercised the appropriate level of care necessary for exculpation, which is a question of fact and degree for the court to determine[5]. Thus, in *Tesco Ltd v Nattrass*[6] it was held that the employer need only show that he personally acted without negligence. Lord Diplock said:

'It may be a reasonable step for an employer to instruct a superior servant to supervise the activities of inferior servants whose physical acts may in the absence of supervision result in that being done which it is sought to prevent. This is not to delegate the employer's duty to exercise all due diligence; it is to perform it. To treat the duty as unperformed unless due diligence was also exercised by all his servants to whom he had reasonably given all proper instructions and upon whom he could reasonably rely to carry them out, would be to render the defence of due diligence nugatory . . .'.

There are two reported cases decided under s 67(2):
(1) In *Byrne v Tudhope*[7] a sale outwith the permitted hours took place by the hand of an employee. Although a 'portfolio' of instructions outlining the requirements of the Act was available for staff reference, the employee was not instructed to read it, nor did he do so. The High Court upheld the stipendiary magistrate's finding that the licenceholder's failure to supply 'specific instructions' was fatal to the 'due diligence' defence. It was apparently of no

---

1 Derived from the Licensing (Scotland) Act 1959, s 159.
2 1967 JC 5, 1967 SLT 26.
3 Which effectively recognises the difficulty caused by *Noble v Heatly*, above. See *Hart v City of Edinburgh District Licensing Board* 1987 SLT (Sh Ct) 54 for a consideration of 'repugnancy' caused by the 'erroneous re-enactment' of part of the earlier legislation.
4 *Tesco Ltd v Nattrass* [1972] AC 153, [1971] 2 All ER 127.
5 *Amag Ltd v Jessop* 1989 SCCR 186.
6 [1972] AC 153, [1971] 2 All ER 127, which concerned the 'due diligence' defence contained in s 24(1) of the Trade Descriptions Act 1968.
7 1983 SCCR 337.

consequence that the actual offender was found to have been aware of the necessity to observe the permitted hours.

(2) In *Gorman v Cochrane*[1] the High Court held that the exercise of 'due diligence' was not excluded where the licenceholder absented herself from the premises around the end of the permitted hours and left a barmaid in charge of the service area.

Decisions under food safety and other consumer protection legislation providing a 'due diligence' offer further assistance. It has been suggested that the employer is not to be penalised where he has 'done everything that he can reasonably be expected to do by supervision or inspection'[2]; and that the standard is not one of perfection but it 'cannot be achieved if there are reasonable steps which can [be] and have not been taken'[3].

It would therefore appear that the defence is most likely to be made out where the licenceholder has evidently considered the nature of his obligations and has issued full and specific instructions to staff (including, of course, temporary or part-time employees). The instructions should be acknowledged in writing, periodically re-examined and updated if necessary. A high degree of personal supervision is sensible. Corporate employers holding a number of licences (brewers, for example) will normally discharge their supervisory responsibilites by employing suitably trained area managers.

THE CONDUCT OF LICENSED PREMISES

Police powers of entry to licensed premises

A constable[4] may at any time enter and inspect off-sale licensed premises provided that 'he has reasonable grounds for believing that an offence has been or is being committed' (s 85(1)). As respects all other licensed premises, the entry and inspection power is unqualified; no reason need be given (s 85(1)). There is, however, no provision for entry to premises where liquor is sold in wholesale quantities without a licence[5]. For circumstances in which the potential prevention of police access has given rise to difficulty in new licence applications, see p 73ff above.

An offence is committed where 'any person' (not necessarily the licenceholder or a member of his staff) fails to allow or obstructs entry demanded by a constable (s 85(2))[6]. A conviction was quashed where a constable knocked loudly on the

---

1 1977 SCCR (Supp) 185.
2 *Tesco Ltd v Nattrass* [1972] AC 153, [1971] 2 All ER 127.
3 *Alex Munro (Butchers) Ltd v Carmichael* 1990 SCCR 275. See also *Smith v Miln* 1970 SLT (Notes) 7.
4 'Constable' means 'a constable of a police force maintained under the Police (Scotland) Act 1967': s 139(1).
5 But see s 86 which regulates police access to unlicensed premises where trafficking is suspected.
6 Maximum penalty: level 3. Licenceholder (who has vicarious responsibility) and premises liable to disqualification (s 67(2), Sch 5).

door of an inn after closing time[1] but gave no indication that he was a police officer[2].

In *Hinchcliffe v Sheldon*[3] a licenceholder's son shouted warnings to his father that police officers were outside hotel premises after closing time; the attention of the police had been attracted by two cars in the parking area. After a delay of about eight minutes, the police were admitted and found no evidence of any offence having been committed. It was held that the officers had been wilfully obstructed in the execution of their duty.

A constable is not entitled to require production of a licence for examination[4].

Detection of offences

The court will accept the evidence of police officers whose detection of an offence has resulted in their own technical violation of the Act. In *Marsh v Johnston*[5] two plain clothes police officers saw a hotel customer being supplied with what appeared to be exciseable liquor after closing time. They then ordered and obtained liquor themselves. Rejecting an argument that evidence had been unfairly obtained, the Lord-Justice General (Clyde) said:

'It may be that in ordering a drink outside permitted hours and in tasting it the police were guilty of a technical offence, but this was a sheer technicality and was not done to procure the commission of an offence but to detect and confirm that offences were being committed'.

Similarly, evidence of illegal sales of liquor to a police constable was admissible in *Cook v Skinner*[6]. As in the case of *Marsh*, the court emphasised, however, that there must be no element of entrapment:

'It is clear . . . that where the court has held that the evidence has been obtained unfairly there has been established on the part of the police officers concerned conduct which clearly amounted to a trick upon the accused on the part of the police officers, and in particular a trick which involved positive deception and pressure, encouragement or inducement to commit an offence which, but for that pressure, encouragement or inducement, would never have been committed at all'[7].

Offences in relation to constables

The licenceholder or his employee or agent commits an offence where he:

1 The entry power is not restricted to the permitted hours.
2 *Alexander v Rankin* (1899) 1 F (J) 58.
3 [1955] 3 All ER 406.
4 Cf the Licensing Act 1964, s 185.
5 1959 SLT (Notes) 28, following *Southern Bowling Club Ltd v Ross* (1902) 4 F 405, (1902) 9 SLT 155. See also *Chief Constable of Glasgow v Parkhead and District Railwaymen's Welfare Club* (1962) 78 Sh Ct Rep 121; *Chief Constable of Glasgow v Parkhead and District Railwaymen's Welfare Club* 1968 SLT (Sh Ct) 36.
6 1977 JC 9, 1977 SLT (Notes) 11.
7 See also *Weir v Jessop (No 2)* 1991 SCCR 636, a prosecution under the Misuse of Drugs Act 1971, where the distinction between the procurement and detection of offences was again drawn.

'(a) knowingly suffers to remain in his premises any constable during any part of the time appointed for the constable's being on duty, except for the purpose of the execution of the constable's duty; or

(b) knowingly supplies any liquor or refreshment whether by way of gift or sale to any constable on duty, except by authority of a superior officer of the constable'[1].

The word 'knowingly' refers to the police officer being on duty[2]. Where the licenceholder is held vicariously liable, the 'knowledge' requirement is incompatible with the 'lack of knowledge' defence provided by s 67(2); and *semble* a conviction could not be sustained in the absence of the licenceholder's actual, personal knowledge[3]. The offence under s 84(b) is committed as soon as a 'supply' has taken place: it is immaterial that there has been no consumption of liquor or refreshment[4].

Exclusion orders

It has long been recognised that licenceholders who attempt to operate a 'blacklist' face intimidation from violent 'customers'. An imperfect solution has been attempted in the Licensed Premises (Exclusion of Certain Persons) Act 1980, a well-intentioned but under-utilised measure[5].

An 'exclusion order' lasting not less than three months and not more than two years[6] may be imposed where a person has been convicted of 'an offence committed on licensed premises'[7], where the court is satisfied that 'he resorted to violence or offered or threatened to resort to violence' (1980 Act, s 1(1))[8]. The order may be made in addition to (a) any sentence imposed for the offence or (b) a probation order or absolute discharge, 'but not otherwise' (1980 Act, s 1(2))[9].

The effect of an order is to prohibit the offender from entering the premises *in quo* 'or any other specified premises' without the express consent of the licenceholder or a member of his staff (1980 Act, s 1(1))[10]; the clerk of court is required to send a copy of the order to the licenceholders concerned (1980 Act, s 4(3)).

In the only reported English case, *R v Grady*[11], the Court of Appeal considered that an exclusion order made in respect of all licensed premises in the County of Norfolk was too wide[12]. It appears to be considered in England that the specification of premises is desirable as a matter of good practice, having regard to the duty of intimation imposed upon the clerk of the court. The Scottish High Court

---

1 Section 84. Maximum penalty: level 3. Licenceholder (who has vicarious responsibility) and premises liable to disqualification (s 67(2), Sch 5).
2 See *Sherras v De Rutzen* [1895] 1 QB 918.
3 *Noble v Heatly* 1967 JC 5, 1967 SLT 26.
4 See *Ferguson v Campbell* 1946 JC 28, 1946 SLT 58.
5 See P Coulson 'Problems Over Exclusion Orders' [1990] 1 LR 12.
6 Licensed Premises (Exclusion of Certain Persons) Act 1980 (the '1980 Act'), s 1(3).
7 The Act does not apply to off-sale licensed premises: 1980 Act, s 4(1).
8 Note that an order appears to be incompetent where the offence is committed *outside* the premises.
9 For the equiparation of an absolute discharge or a probation order with a conviction, see s 4(2).
10 'Specified premises' means 'any licensed premises which the court may specify by name and address in the order': 1980 Act, s 4(1).
11 [1990] Crim LR 608.
12 The order was quashed for other reasons: see below.

regards the issue as one of competency. In *Nicolson v Mackenzie*[1] an order purporting to exclude an offender from all licensed premises in Stornoway (for a two-year period) was simply held to be incompetent: the order could only relate to premises specified by name and address.

The *Grady* case is of interest for the view that exclusion orders are designed to curb those who might shortly be described as making a nuisance of themselves in public houses, requiring to be debarred to prevent the annoyance of other customers and possible danger to the licenceholder. Here, a landlady was pushed or punched by the appellant; she fell to the floor, suffering some bruises and tenderness to her back. Although the appellant was sentenced to six months' imprisonment (suspended for two years), the Court of Appeal considered that the exclusion order should be quashed, having regard to her mature years and previous good character.

A person entering licensed premises in breach of an exclusion order commits an offence (1980 Act, s 2(1))[2]. In the event of a conviction, the court may 'if it thinks fit, by order terminate the extension order or vary it by deleting the name of any specified premises' (1980 Act, s 2(2))[3]. The order may not, however, be extended and is otherwise incapable of review.

A licenceholder and his staff are empowered to expel from the premises any person reasonably suspected of having entered in breach of an exclusion order. A police constable is bound to provide assistance for that purpose 'on demand', provided that he also 'reasonably suspects' such a breach; no doubt he is entitled to proceed upon information supplied by the licenceholder (1980 Act, s 3)[4].

Unhappily, the possibility of an order is often overlooked by the prosecutor and the court[5].

Offences involving drunkenness

The meaning of 'drunk'

The Act contains a number of offences prohibiting drunkenness on the part of the licenceholder, his staff and customers. It has been suggested that a person is 'drunk' where he 'has drunk intoxicating liquor to an extent which affects steady self-control; that he is 'intoxicated, inebriated; overcome by alcoholic liquor'[6].

'Intoxication' and 'drunkenness' are not, however, synonymous. In *Keith v Bell*[7] the holder of a public house certificate was charged with being 'in a state of intoxication' on his licensed premises, although he had managed to close the premises for the evening by peforming certain operations 'which were more than of a purely automatic nature'. The High Court upheld his conviction (with

---

1 1993 GWD 7-476.
2 Maximum penalty: level 3 fine and/or one month's imprisonment.
3 Where an order is terminated or varied the clerk of court is required to notify the licenceholder(s): 1980 Act, s 4(3).
4 Cf the 1976 Act, s 79.
5 See further P Coulson'Problems Over Exclusion Orders' [1990] 1 LR 12.
6 *Encyclopaedia of the Laws of Scotland* (W. Green), vol 8, para 931, citing the *New English Dictionary* definition of 'drunk'.
7 1943 JC 65, 1944 SLT 31.

evident regret), the Lord Justice-Clerk (Cooper) expressing the opinion that: '[T]he words "state of intoxication" prima facie suggest a condition graver and more extreme than that which is suggested by such words as "drunk" or "under the influence of drink" . . . '.[1]

The difficulty of giving a precise definition to 'drunk' was considered in *Dunning v Cardle*[2]. Here, the magistrate had correctly concluded that he was faced with 'a question of degree'. The licenceholder was found to have been unsteady on his feet, smelling strongly of alcoholic liquor, his eyes were bloodshot, and his speech was incoherent and slurred. In the opinion of the High Court this evidence was quite sufficient to justify the application of the adjective 'drunk'.

Offences

It is an offence for the licenceholder or his employee or agent to be 'in the premises while drunk' (s 77)[3]. It is of no consequence that the premises are closed to the public[4] or that the consumption of liquor leading to inebriation took place elsewhere.

In terms of s 76, the licenceholder or his employee or agent commit an offence by selling or supplying any alcoholic liquor to a drunken person in licensed premises[5]. The corresponding 'breach of certificate' offence under the Licensing (Scotland) Act 1959 was considered to be absolute. It was immaterial that the certificate-holder did not consider the person supplied to be 'intoxicated'[6]. Alcoholic liquor may be sold, or at least 'supplied', to a drunken person where it is ordered and paid for by a sober companion[7].

Section 75 provides that an offence is committed if a person in any licensed premises (a) procures or attempts to procure alcoholic liquor for consumption by a drunken person (s 75(1)); or (b) aids a drunken person in obtaining or consuming any alcoholic liquor in the premises (s 75(2))[8]. Either offence could, in theory, be committed by a licenceholder or a member of his staff[9], but these provisions are primarily directed at the behaviour of third parties. In both cases the drunken person must be in such a condition prior to the commission of the offence. It seems that the offence of 'procurement' need not relate to liquor which is to be

1 See also *Chief Constable of Glasgow v Parkhead and District Railwaymen's Welfare Club* (1962) 78 Sh Ct Rep 121 in which it was considered that being 'the worse of drink' was 'something less than being in a state of intoxication'; for a description of incidents involving 'manifest intoxication', see *Gordon Highlanders' (Glasgow) Association Club v Mason* 1954 SLT (Sh Ct) 45.
2 1981 SCCR 136, 1981 SLT (Notes) 107.
3 Maximum penalty: level 3. Licenceholder, who has vicarious responsibility, and premises liable to disqualification (s 67(2), Sch 5).
4 *Kessack v Smith* (1905) 7 F (J) 75, (1905) 13 SLT 198. A publican found in a state of drunken collapse in his premises at 3 am was guilty of a breach of certificate. See also *Keith v Bell* 1943 JC 65, 1944 SLT 31.
5 Maximum penalty: level 3. Licenceholder, who has vicarious responsibility, and premises liable to disqualification (s 67(2), Sch 5).
6 See *Purves's Scottish Licensing Laws* (8th edn, 1961, ed Walker) p 34 and cases cited; and *Cundy v Le Cocq* (1884) 13 QBD 207.
7 *Scatchard v Johnson* (1888) 52 JP 389. See also *Brown v McKechnie* 1916 SC (J) 20.
8 In both cases the maximum penalty is a level 3 fine (Sch 5).
9 Although the licenceholder is not rendered vicariously responsible by s 67(2) and Sch 5.

consumed on the premises (unlike the offence of 'aiding'), so that an off-sale purchase for a drunk is forbidden.

Section 74 excludes persons who are drunk from licensed premises and renders them liable to arrest without warrant (s 74(3)). Attempted entry at any time is an offence, except in the case of a resident (s 74(1))[1]. A person who is 'drunk and incapable of taking care of himself' commits an offence by being in (a) licensed premises (s 74(2))[2] or (b) a public place[3] unless under 'the care and protection of a suitable person'. The expression 'drunk and incapable' connotes a condition considerably more serious than mere 'drunkenness'[4].

Drunkenness and other disorderly behaviour

The Act's severest penalty (potentially 60 days' imprisonment) is reserved for a breach of s 78(1), which provides that:

'If any person in licensed premises –
(a) behaves while drunk in a riotous or disorderly manner, or
(b) while drunk uses obscene or indecent language to the annoyance of any person[5], he shall be guilty of an offence'[6].

The phrase 'riotous or disorderly' is clearly intended to embrace a broad spectrum of unacceptable behaviour: at the lower end of the scale, 'disorderly' conduct may be indistinguishable from a breach of the peace[7].

A licenceholder or his employee or agent commits an offence 'if he permits any breach of the peace[8], drunkenness or riotous or disorderly conduct in the premises in respect of which the licence is held' (s 78(2))[9]. This provision is apt to cover the situation where there has been no sale or supply to a drunken person contrary to s 76[10]. It has, however, been held in England that drunkenness is permitted by the supply of liquor to a person who is already drunk[11]; but it is doubtful whether contraventions of ss 76 and 78(2) could be charged cumulatively on the same *species facti*[12].

1 Maximum penalty: level 1 (Sch 5). A person is 'resident' in premises although he occupies sleeping accommodation in a separate building, subject to certain conditions: see s 139(3). No other exceptions are made for residents as respects drunkenness-related offences. In *Thompson v McKenzie* [1908] 1 KB 905 drunkenness was found to have been permitted where a hotel guest was found drunk in a public room.
2 Maximum penalty: level 1 (Sch 5).
3 Civic Government (Scotland) Act 1982, s 50(1). Maximum penalty: level 2.
4 See *Dunning v Cardle* 1981 SCCR 136.
5 A complaint was held to be irrelevant where it did not set forth that various disorderly acts were done to the annoyance of any person: *Rowland v Deas* (1906) 8 F (J) 86, (1906) 14 SLT 293.
6 Maximum penalty: level 3 fine and/or 60 days' imprisonment.
7 Cf *Campbell v Adair* 1945 JC 29; and see *Gordon* para 41.02.
8 See *Gordon* paras 41.01ff and Second Supplement to the principal work.
9 Maximum penalty: level 3. Licenceholder, who has vicarious responsibility, and premises liable to disqualification (s 67(2), Sch 5).
10 *Hope v Warburton* [1892] 2 QB 134.
11 *Edmunds v James* [1892] 1 QB 18.
12 See *Renton and Brown's Criminal Procedure* (5th edn) paras 13.67ff. Cf *Gemmell v Weir* (1897) 14 R (J) 23 in which the accused's conviction on the charge that he 'did permit and suffer drinking and did sell and give out drink' was considered sound: the acts complained of amounting to the single offence of breach of certificate. See also *Courage v Smith* 1960 JC 13, 1960 SLT 55 in which 'sale or supply' were held to be different modes of committing the same offence.

Under previous legislation[1] 'knowingly permitting' inter alia drunkenness constituted a 'breach of certificate' offence. Only the certificate-holder was liable to conviction. In *Noble v Heatly*[2] it was held that his personal knowledge was of the essence. The effect of this decision 'was to cast doubt on the certificate-holder's vicarious responsibility in criminal law for the acts or omissions of his staff' whose 'knowledge' did not render him criminally liable[3]. Thus, the word 'knowingly' does not appear in s 78(2); and the licenceholder is rendered vicariously liable for commission of the offence by an employee or agent. (No doubt the successful prosecution of the person who actually committed the offence would nevertheless depend on proof of his actual or constructive knowledge[4] or a failure to exercise a power to prevent the offence[5].) Nevertheless, the 'burden of proof' provision contained in s 187 of the Licensing (Scotland) Act 1959 has been re-enacted, virtually verbatim, as follows:

'If the holder of a licence in respect of any premises is charged with knowingly permitting drunkenness in those premises, and it proved that any person was drunk in the premises, it shall lie on the holder of the licence to prove[6] that he and the persons employed by him took all reasonable steps to prevent drunkenness in the premises'[7].

The retention of the word 'knowingly' is patently inept. The requirement that 'all reasonable steps were taken' is repugnant to the defence provided by s 67(2), in terms of which the licenceholder need only demonstrate that *he* exercised 'all due diligence'; in other words, he need not prove that all due diligence was exercised which is, in effect, the obligation imposed by s 126[8].

This onus of proof does not apply where the person found drunk on the premises is not a customer but an employee[9]; but did require to be discharged where the drunk was a friend of the certificate-holder[10]. In *Soutar v Auchinachie*[11] the High Court held that all reasonable steps had been taken for the prevention of drunkenness where a person in a state of intoxication had been refused alcoholic liquor; he was supplied with a bottle of soda water and allowed to remain in the premises for about 15 minutes with two sober friends who had undertaken to escort him home. Similarly, a licensee was properly acquitted of 'permitting drunkenness' where he took steps to revive a man who had, without his knowledge, consumed a companion's whisky which had not been sold on the premises[12]. A conviction was sustained in England where two drinks were ordered

1 Licensing (Scotland) Act 1959, s 131.
2 1967 JC 5, 1967 SLT 26.
3 *Clayson*, para 10.11.
4 *Mallon v Allon* [1964] 1 QB 385, [1963] 3 All ER 843.
5 *Townsend v Arnold* (1911) 75 JP 423.
6 On the balance of probabilities: *King v Lees* 1993 SCCR 28. See also *HM Advocate v Mitchell* 1951 JC 53, 1951 SLT 200; *Neish v Stevenson* 1969 SLT 229.
7 Section 126.
8 See *Tesco Ltd v Nattrass* [1972] AC 153, [1971] 2 All ER 127.
9 *Campbell v Cameron* 1916 SC (J) 1.
10 *Kessack v Smith* (1905) 7 F (J) 75, (1905) 13 SLT 198. A conviction was sustained where the certificate-holder and his friend were both found in the licensed premises at 3 am, asleep and intoxicated. Note, however, that a licenceholder does not 'permit drunkenness' by being drunk himself (although an offence will be committed under s 77): *Warden v Tye* (1877) 2 CPD 74.
11 1909 SC (J) 16, (1909) 16 SLT 663.
12 *Townsend v Arnold* (1911) 75 JP 423.

by a sober customer and no enquiry was made as to the identity of the person for whom the second was intended[1].

Expulsion of disorderly customers

Subject to certain statutory exceptions[2], a licenceholder can refuse to serve members of the public as he pleases[3], although an hotelkeeper is obligated to provide food and lodgings for travellers who are able to pay and decently behaved[4].

Nevertheless, the Act recognises that the prevention of an offence may require fortification of the licenceholder's prerogative. Section 79(1) provides that:

'If a person in any licensed premises –
(a) being riotous, quarrelsome or disorderly[5], refuses or neglects to leave such premises on being requested so to do by the occupier or manager thereof, or his employee or agent, or by any constable, or
(b) refuses to leave such premises at the conclusion of the permitted hours in the afternoon or evening, as the case may be, on being requested so to do as aforesaid, he shall be guilty of an offence'[6].

Although licenceholders are often loathe to summon police assistance where a customer has become obstreperous, lest their management ability be called into question, a constable 'may assist' in the expulsion of a person who fails to leave voluntarily (s 79(2))[7]. Such a person may be arrested without warrant (s 79(3)).

Prostitutes, criminals and stolen goods

Section 80 provides that 'any person who occupies or keeps any premises in respect of which a licence is held' commits an offence where he:

'(a) knowingly suffers thieves or reputed thieves or prostitutes or reputed prostitutes or persons convicted of an offence under section 4 or 5(3) of the Misuse of Drugs Act 1971 to remain in those premises, or knowingly permits thieves or reputed thieves, or prostitutes or reputed prostitutes or persons convicted of an offence under section 4 or 5(3) of the Misuse of Drugs Act 1971 to meet or assemble in the premises; or

---

1 *Radford v Williams* (1914) 30 TLR 108. It was observed that drunkenness may be permitted where a drunken man is allowed to consume a sandwich in a bar.
2 Race Relations Act 1976, s 20; Sex Discrimination Act 1975, s 29.
3 The principle was perhaps most concisely expressed in *R v Rymer* (1877) 2 QBD 136: 'no one has a right to insist on being served, any more than in any other shop' (at 140 per Kelly, CB). See also *Sealey v Tandy* [1902] 1 KB 296.
4 There may be no obligation to supply alcoholic liquor: *West Wemyss United Services Club, Applicants* 1948 SLT (Sh Ct) 33. See also *R v Sussex Confirming Authority ex parte Tamplin & Sons* [1937] 4 All ER 106.
5 Cf s 78(1).
6 Maximum penalty: level 1 (Sch 5).
7 Cf the Licensed Premises (Exclusion of Certain Persons) Act 1980, s 3 which *obliges* a constable to assist in certain expulsions.

(b) knowingly permits to be deposited in the premises goods which he has reasonable grounds for believing to be stolen goods'[1].

For a reason which is less than apparent, liability rests with the keeper or occupier of licensed premises (rather than the licenceholder or his employee or agent); but an employee may conceivably be guilty art and part[2].

A conviction may be difficult to sustain. The word 'knowingly' in s 80(a) refers to the type of person described and is necessarily included to prevent the conviction of a person wholly ignorant as to his or her character[3]. Yet, as observed throughout this chapter, the inclusion of the word 'knowingly' in an offence-creating section appears to require proof of the accused's actual knowledge[4]. The prosecution may thus be faced with a virtually insurmountable evidential task, particularly in the case of an absent licenceholder.

It has been suggested that repute as a thief:

'is a question of fact, and although it is usually based on previous convictions for theft, including simple theft, it does not depend exclusively upon proof of convictions . . . The repute must, however, be that of an established thief, and cannot be based solely on one previous conviction for theft'[5].

A 'prostitute' is a person 'who offers her body commonly for lewdness in return for payment'[6].

Section 4 of the Misuse of Drugs Act 1971 contains restrictions relative to the production and supply of controlled drugs; and in terms of s 5(3) it is an offence for a person to have a controlled drug in his possession with intent to supply it to another contrary to s 4(1).

In *Kirton v Cadenhead*[7] it was suggested that a charge of allowing 'men or women of notoriously bad fame to assemble or meet' in a public house required proof that the assembling or meeting was referable to their bad character; but a contrary opinion was expressed to the effect that a conviction could be justified where the character or the premises was such that 'women of bad character resorted there as a rule'[8].

It may be observed that a police constable is not specifically authorised to assist in the expulsion of a person falling within a proscribed category[9].

---

1 Maximum penalty in all cases: level 3. Licenceholder (who has vicarious responsibility) and premises liable to disqualification (s 67(2), Sch 5).
2 See *Gordon* paras. 5.09ff for a discussion of art and part guilt where a statute appears to restrict liability to members of a particular class. Under analagous legislation, it has been held in England that a servant may 'aid and abet' this type of offence where the person primarily liable was the 'keeper' of premises: *Wilson v Stewart* (1863) 3 B & S 913.
3 The offence of 'permitting women of notoriously bad fame to assemble and meet' was, however, made out in *Maxwell v Malcolm* (1879) 7 R (J) 5, although it was not proved that the accused knew of their presence or that his servant was aware of their characters. Cf *Somerset v Wade* [1894] 1 QB 574.
4 *Noble v Heatly* 1967 JC 5, 1967 SLT 26.
5 *Gordon* para 15.67.
6 *Gordon* para 36.40. Presumably the standard of 'repute' as respects a prostitute is *mutatis mutandis* the same as for thieves.
7 (1880 8 R (J) 4.
8 See also *Maxwell v Malcolm* (1879) 7 R (J) 5.
9 Cf s 79.

Miscellaneous offences

Betting and gaming

In terms of s 81, a licenceholder or his employee or agent shall be guilty of an offence 'if he permits the playing of any game in the premises in respect of which the licence is held in such circumstances that an offence under the Betting, Gaming and Lotteries Acts 1963 to 1971 is committed'[1].

Section 5 of the Gaming Act 1968 ('the 1968 Act') prohibits any person from taking part in gaming (see the 1968 Act, s 52(1)) to which Part I of that Act applies in any street or in any other place to which, whether on payment or otherwise, the public have access. The playing of dominoes and cribbage is exempted from the restriction (1968 Act, s 6(1)(a)) together with any other game specifically authorised in respect of particular premises (1968 Act, s 6(1)(b))[2].

For a fuller consideration of this subject, see Chapter 12.

Adulteration of food and drink

Section 88 provides that a licenceholder or his employee or agent commits an offence by fraudulently[3] adulterating the food or alcoholic liquor sold by him or by selling the same 'knowing them to have been fraudulently adulterated'[4]. Prosecutions will normally take place under the Food Safety Act 1990[5].

Deliveries from vehicles[6]

In order to discourage door-to-door sales of alcoholic liquor[7] from taking place under the guise of order fulfilment, section 91 contains detailed provisions regulating vehicle deliveries 'in pursuance of a sale'[8].

---

1 Maximum penalty: level 3. Licenceholder (who has vicarious responsibility) and premises liable to disqualification (s 67(2), Sch 5).
2 Authorisation may only be obtained by the holder of a public house or hotel licence. The licenceholder or his employee commits an offence by allowing a person under 18 to take part in an authorised game: 1968 Act, s 8(7), as amended by the 1976 Act, s 136(1), Sch 7, para 11.
3 'Fraudulently': see *Gordon* para 8.21.
4 Maximum penalty: level 3. Licenceholder (who has vicarious responsibility) and premises liable to disqualification (s 67(2), Sch 5).
5 See the Food Safety Act 1990, s 14(1), which makes it an offence to sell, to the purchaser's prejudice, food (which includes drink) 'which is not of the nature or substance or quality demanded by the purchaser'; s 15 prohibits labelling which is false or misleading.
6 For the effect of the permitted hours upon deliveries, see s 54(1), (3)(f), (i), (j) and Chapter 10.
7 Which would amount to 'hawking', contrary to s 90.
8 The inclusion of these words makes it clear that the section applies only to the transport of alcohol in a commercial context; the Licensing Act 1921, s 7 appeared to encompass all types of delivery. Deliveries to a trader for the purposes of his trade or to a registered club for the purposes of the club are specifically exempted: s 91(4).

'A person'[1] shall not deliver alcoholic liquor 'from a vehicle or receptacle'[2] unless two sets of records are kept. Before despatch takes place, the quantity, description and price of the liquor, together with the name and address of the purchaser, must be entered in a day book kept at the premises (s 91(1)(a)); and the same details must be entered in a delivery book or invoice, which is to be carried by the person effecting the delivery (s 91(1)(b)).

In addition, 'a person shall not, himself or by his employee or agent':
(1) carry liquor for delivery which has not been entered in both the day book and delivery book (or invoice) (s 91(2)(a));
(2) deliver liquor at an address which is not shown in these records (s 91(2)(b))[3];
(3) refuse to allow a constable to examine (a) the 'vehicle or receptacle' while it is in use for deliveries; (b) the day book; or (c) the delivery book (or invoice) (s 91(3)).

Contravention of any of these provisions is an offence (s 91(5))[4]. In *Nicol v Smith*[5] a certificate-holder was charged with offences committed under the corresponding provisions of the Licensing Act 1921 (s 7) by her manager and roundsman. She had supplied the manager with the appropriate record books; and in the course of her weekly visits to the premises obtained assurances that the appropriate entries were being made. The statutory defence then available, that the offence was committed without her 'knowledge or consent', was held to have been made out; but the current 'due diligence' defence would almost certainly not be established in these circumstances (s 67(2)).

Nothing contained in s 91 prevents a licenceholder or his representative from soliciting orders for future delivery from licensed premises[6].

Restrictions on alcohol carriage in hired buses

Section 92[7] makes it an offence for the holder of a PSV operator's licence[8] in respect of any vehicle or his employee or agent to permit the carriage of alcoholic liquor in:

'any container or other device (including a container or device fixed to, or forming part of, a vehicle) constructed or adapted for the purpose of holding two or more bottles or cans or of holding liquid in excess of six pints'[9].

---

1 The reference throughout this section to 'a person' rather than 'the holder of a licence' and the absence of any reference to licensed premises suggests that these provisions apply to wholesalers; cf s 138(2)(b), in terms of which nothing in the Act shall 'prohibit the sale of alcoholic liquor by a wholesaler', save as expressly provided.
2 The corresponding section of the Licensing (Scotland) Act 1959 (s 139) referred to 'any van, barrow, basket or other vehicle or receptacle'.
3 The liquor need not be labelled with the names of the purchasers; cf *Pletts v Campbell* [1895] 2 QB 299.
4 Maximum penalty: level 3. Licenceholder (who has vicarious responsibility) and premises liable to disqualification (s 67(2), Sch 5).
5 1955 SLT 38.
6 See *Cameron v Buchan* (1896) 23 R (J) 46, (1896) 3 SLT 269; *Robertson v Provident Clothing and Supply Co Ltd* 1961 JC 16, 1961 SLT 170.
7 As amended by the Transport Act 1985, s 139(2), Sch 7, para 18.
8 Section 92(5) defines 'PSV operator's licence' by reference to Part II of the Public Passenger Vehicles Act 1981.
9 Section 91(1), (4).

The prohibition only applies where the vehicle 'is being used for the carriage of passengers otherwise than at separate fares' (s 91(1)), that is to say, during a hire[1].

It is also an offence for any person to procure or attempt to procure a contravention of this provision (s 92(2))[2].

Where the holder of a PSV operator's licence is charged with a contravention committed by his employee or agent, he may prove by way of defence that the offence 'took place without his consent or connivance and that he exercised all due diligence to prevent it' (s 93(3)).

Clayson's recommendation that this prohibition be retained was apparently made with some reluctance. The committee recognised the inconvenience caused to persons on long-distance coach tours, for example, but heard evidence that abuses could arise from the carriage of liquor on inter alia vehicles hired by football supporters' clubs[3]. In fact, the possession of alcohol on public service vehicles, railway passenger vehicles or certain other vehicles on journeys to or from designated sporting events is now prohibited by the Criminal Justice (Scotland) Act 1980[4].

1 Penalties in terms of Sch 5: level 3 in the case of a PSV licenceholder; level 1 in other cases.
2 Maximum penalty: level 1 (Sch 5).
3 See *Clayson*, para 15. 35.
4 See the Criminal Justice (Scotland) Act 1980, ss 69 (as amended by the Sporting Events (Control of Alcohol etc) Act 1985, s 10), ss 70, 70A (inserted by the Public Order Act 1986, s 40(1), Sch 1) and s 71. Sporting events have been designated by the Sports Grounds and Sporting Events (Designation) (Scotland) Order 1985, SI 1985/1224.

CHAPTER 14

Children in licensed premises

INTRODUCTION

Historically, the protection of young persons from the dangers of alcohol has occupied a position of special importance in licensing law. While the 1976 and 1990 Acts introduced liberalising measures, with the creation of refreshment licences and children's certificates, and heralded a departure from the view that 'it was better for children to be left outside public houses than for there to be special provision . . . inside'[1], the law remains complex and is often poorly understood.

ENTRY TO LICENSED PREMISES

Children *of any age* have unlimited access to premises in respect of which an off-sale, restaurant, restricted hotel or entertainment licence is held[2]. As respects hotels and public houses, children under 14 are, broadly speaking, excluded from bar areas[3]; and separate provision is made for refreshment licensed premises.

The exclusion of children from bars

The general prohibition

Except in the circumstances explained below 'the holder of a licence in respect of any premises or his employee or agent shall not allow a person under 14[4] to be in the bar of those premises during the permitted hours' (s 69(1), (5))[5]. The act of 'allowing', also relevant for the purposes of ss 68 and 70 (see below), normally requires proof of actual knowledge on the part of the accused or at least 'wilful

---

1 See J Martin 'Children in Pubs – an Historical Perspective' [1990] 3 LR 12 at 13.
2 Subject to the doubt expressed at p 252 below as to the presence of children under 14 in the bar of entertainment-licensed premises.
3 Sensibly, very few licenceholders are prepared to accept the under-age drinking risks associated with permitting persons over 14 but under 18 to be in a bar, a practice which could conceivably jeopardise the 'due diligence' defence made available by ss 67(2) and 71.
4 It is sometimes believed that babies are exempted: they are not.
5 Penalty: level 3 (Sch 5). Licenceholder (who has vicarious responsibility) and premises liable to disqualification: s 67, Sch 5.

blindness' which results in the imputation of knowledge[1]. The suggestion that such an evidential burden rests with the Crown sits uneasily with the statutory defence made available by s 71. Any person charged with an offence under (inter alia) s 69(1) may prove that he used 'due diligence' to prevent its occurrence; or that he had no reason to suspect that the person was under-age[2]. In other words, a defence based on the negation of negligence indicates that the offence of 'allowing' does not require the *mens rea* normally associated with that term. The terms of the corresponding provision in the Licensing (Scotland) Act 1959 (s 143), although employing the word 'allow' were more coherent: where it was simply shown by the prosecutor that a person under 14 was in a bar, the certificate-holder was guilty of an offence unless he established a defence in terms similar to s 71[3]. It may be considered that s 69 imposes a similar type of strict liability and that the use of the word 'allow' is inept.

In addition 'no person shall cause or procure, or attempt to cause or procure, any person under 14 to go to, or to be in, the bar of any licensed premises . . . during the permitted hours' (s 69(2))[4].

Although the meaning of the word 'bar' is of seminal importance, the Act provides no definition as such. In terms of s 139(1) '"bar" includes any place exclusively or mainly used for the sale and consumption of alcoholic liquor'[5].

It is important to appreciate that whether an area constitutes a 'bar' does not depend upon the existence or otherwise of a 'bar counter':

'[O]ne may have a "bar" even though there be no bar counter if, nevertheless, there is within the licensed premises "any place exclusively or mainly used for the sale and consumption of intoxicating liquor"'[6].

A bar offering waiter-service only does not contain a 'bar counter' because the counter, as a dispense bar, is excluded from the definition by virtue of s 138(2)(b); but such a place is nevertheless a 'bar' unless the room is exclusively set apart for table meals (s 68(4), discussed below). An area such as a so-called 'family room' or a 'beer garden' used for *consumption only*, with customers making their purchases elsewhere in the premises, is not a 'bar' because the 'sale' element is missing[7]. The degree of separation required between parts of premises used for 'sale' and 'consumption' is frequently a vexed issue. At one end of the spectrum lies the partition arrangement described in *Donaghue v McIntyre*[8]. Here, a 'box' or room with its own entrance door was separated from the remainder of a public

1 *Knox v Boyd* 1941 JC 82, 1942 SLT 14. See also *Mallon v Allon* [1964] 1 QB 385, [1963] 3 All ER 843, for a consideration of 'admitted to or allowed to remain' for the purpose of rule 2 of Sch 4 to the Betting, Gaming and Lotteries Act 1963.
2 This defence is further discussed below.
3 Licensing (Scotland) Act 1959, s 143(3).
4 Penalty: level 3 (Sch 5).
5 The use of the word 'includes' rather than 'means' precludes this provision from being regarded as a definition: see *Carter v Bradbeer* [1975] 3 All ER 158, [1975] 1 WLR 1204, HL. The onus of proving that an area is a 'bar' rests, of course, on the prosecution: *Donaghue v McIntyre* 1911 JC 61, (1911) 1 SLT 131.
6 *Carter v Bradbeer* [1975] 3 All ER 158, [1975] 1 WLR 1204 (HL) per Lord Edmund-Davies.
7 Note, however, that a point of sale at the threshold between the inside of the premises and a beer garden (a service hatch, for example) would convert the beer garden into a 'bar'.
8 1911 JC 61, (1911) 1 SLT 131.

house by a wooden partition seven feet in height, which did not reach the ceiling, was not an 'open drinking bar' for the purpose of earlier leglisation[1]. Lord Ardwall said:

'[I]n no ordinary sense of the term "bar" can this be held to be part of the bar of the public house. The bar of the public house is, as we know, strictly speaking, the counter over which liquor is served, and it has come to be extended to the space in front of it where the people stand'[2].

On the other hand, there is a modern tendency to divide the bar from other areas by less substantial devices, such as planters, trellis-type partitions and mezzanine areas with railings[3]. It is impossible to give a general indication of the requisite degree of separation with any confidence. From a purely practical point of view, much depends upon police attitude: in many areas the 'visual' aspect is important so that the bar must simply be out-of-sight.

No doubt confusingly, in a House of Lords decision[4], it was suggested that a 'bar'[5] need not be a definable area, the contrary view involving the substitution of 'means' for 'includes' in the 'definition' and thus confining the term 'bar' to a 'place'.

Exceptions to the prohibition

The prohibitions imposed by s 69(1) and (2) only apply *during the permitted hours*, so that children under 14 (even unaccompanied) are allowed to be present in a bar at other times, as, for example, when morning coffee is served. In addition:

(1) Children under 14, accompanied by a person of not less than 18, may be in a bar 'for the purpose of the consumption of a meal' when a children's certificate is in operation (1990 Act, s 49(3))[6].
(2) No offence is committed where the child under 14 is:
   (a) a child of the holder of the licence (s 69(3)(a))[7];
   (b) resident in the premises but not employed there (s 69(3)(b))[8];
   (c) in the bar 'solely for the purpose of passing to or from some other part of

---

1 Children Act 1908, s 120(1), (5). The High Court's finding that the room was not 'exclusively or mainly used for the sale and consumption of intoxicating liquor' turned on the prosecutor's failure to establish that customers in the 'box' had been supplied with 'intoxicating liquor' without food; note that the exception now made for restaurant areas in s 68(4) (see below) depends on the service of 'table meals' and the 'snack of biscuit and cheese' in *Donaghue* would not qualify.
2 Cf *Dominy v Miller* (1923) 87 JPN 793. See also *Carter v Bradbeer* [1975] 3 All ER 158, [1975] 1 WLR 1204 (HL): 'The usual meaning [of 'bar'] is, in my opinion a bar counter over which drinks are sold and also, on occasions, a room' (per Viscount Dilhorne).
3 See, however, *Dick v Stirling Lawn Tennis Club* 1981 SLT (Sh Ct) 103 in which the sheriff appears to have entertained considerable doubt as to the efficacy of a proposed partition arrangement in club premises.
4 *Carter v Bradbeer* [1975] 3 All ER 158, [1975] 1 WLR 1204.
5 For the purpose of s 201 of the Licensing Act 1964, which contains a virtually identical 'definition'.
6 Children's certificates are examined at p 260ff below.
7 The expression 'holder of the licence' includes the nominee of a non-natural person: see ss 11(3), 26(7).
8 This provision is apt to include a hotel resident. See s 139(3) for an expanded definition of residence.

the premises, not a bar[1], being a part to or from which there is no other convenient means of access or egress' (s 69(3)(c))[2];

(3) No offence is committed in respect of a bar:

'which is in any railway refreshment room or other premises constructed, fitted and intended to be used bona fide for any purpose to which the holding of a licence is merely ancillary'[3].

The words 'or other premises' appear to be construed in practice as *eiusdem generis* of 'railway refreshment room', limiting the application of the exception to a place associated with transport, although it may be considered that the ancillary nature of alcohol supply in entertainment-licensed premises (Sch 1) could be sufficient to bring them within its purview[4].

(4) References to a 'bar' in s 69[5] do not apply to:

'a bar at any time when it is, as is usual in the premises in question, set apart for the service of table meals[6] and not used for the sale or supply of alcoholic liquor otherwise than to persons having table meals there and for consumption by such a person as an ancillary to his meal' (s 68(4)).

This exception recognises that the wide meaning of 'bar' could give rise to difficulty in 'mixed use' premises[7]. By pre-supposing that an area predominantly but not exclusively used as a 'dedicated' restaurant could consitute a 'bar', it also accentuates the breadth of 'bar': indeed, the word 'mainly' in the 'exclusively or mainly' test appears to have no application here, nor is there any 'balancing exercise' which may be required to determine whether a 'place' is a 'bar'[8]. References to a 'bar' will apparently include (unless another exemption may be claimed) a dining area in which one person out of fifty is having a drink without a meal.

For the purposes of ss 57, 58, 59 and 60[9], which require part of the premises to be 'usually set apart' for the service of persons taking table meals, an area must be reserved for restaurant use *at all times*; thus, a lounge bar regularly set apart for meals from 10 pm to 11 pm each evening was not 'usually set apart'[10]. *Per contra*, s 68(4) has in view bars which at a customary time are given over to restaurant use.

Because of the reference to 'ancillary' consumption[11] alcohol need not be consumed with the meal or at a table.

---

1 Eg toilets.
2 Note, however, that where application is made for a new licence, boards are generally reluctant to approve a layout which would necessitate reliance on this exception.
3 Section 69(4).
4 Cf *Fife Regional Council v Kirkcaldy District Licensing Board (No 2)* 1991 GWD 18-1110, 2nd Div.
5 And in ss 68 and 72: see below.
6 See definition of 'table meal' in s 139(1).
7 It has, of course, no relevance to the presence of children under 14 in restaurant-licensed premises, which is lawful because of their principal use for the service of meals with the 'ancillary' consumption of alcoholic liquor (Sch 1).
8 See *Carter v Bradbeer* [1975] 3 All ER 158, [1975] 1 WLR 1204 (HL) per Lord Edmund-Davies.
9 See Chapter 10.
10 *McAlpine v Heatly* 1967 JC 537, 1967 SLT (Notes) 3.
11 'Ancillary': see the discussion of restaurant in Chapter 3.

Refreshment-licensed premises

The holder of a refreshment licence or his employee or agent commits an offence if he allows a person under 14:

(a) to be in the premises during the permitted hours, unless such a person is accompanied by a person aged 18 or over;

(b) to remain on the premises after eight in the evening (s 70(1), as amended by the 1990 Act, Sch 8, para 14)[1].

No offence is committed where the person under 14 is (i) a child of the licence-holder or (ii) resident in, but not employed at, the premises (s 70(2)).

RESTRICTIONS ON SALE, CONSUMPTION AND DELIVERY

Sales and purchases[2]

As more fully explained below, a person who has attained the age of 16 may purchase most types of alcohol for consumption at a meal in a restaurant (s 68(4)). Otherwise, an offence is committed where:

(a) a licenceholder or his employee or agent sells alcoholic liquor to a person under 18 in any part of licensed premises (s 68(1), (7))[3];

(b) the holder of a licence allows any person to sell alcoholic liquor to a person under 18 (s 68(1), (7))[3]. The scope of this offence is particularly large: it is not restricted to sales in licensed premises and, since the licenceholder already has vicarious liability for sales by an employee or agent, the reference to 'any person' significantly broadens his responsibility[4];

(c) a person under 18 buys or attempts[5] to buy alcoholic liquor in licensed premises (s 68(2))[6]. It has been held in England that an agency purchase on behalf of persons under 18, who remained outside the premises, did not amount to a purchase *by them* 'in licensed premises'[7]. *Quaere* whether, in such

---

1 Note that the child is required to *quit* the premises by 8 pm; it is sometimes mistakenly believed that it is sufficient to restrict *admission* after that time. The maximum penalty for each offence is set at level 3 (Sch 5); licenceholder (who has vicarious responsibility) and premises liable to disqualification (s 67, Sch 5).

2 Note that s 68, with which this section is concerned, is specifically applied (with necessary modification) to any premises or place in respect of which an occasional permission is granted: see s 34(1), (4). See also s 33(6) for the importation of the Act's sale provisions where an occasional licence is held.

3 Penalty: level 3. Licenceholder (who has vicarious responsibility) and premises liable to disqualification (s 67, Sch 5).

4 For a consideration of criminal responsibility where powers and duties have not been delegated, see Sheriff G H Gordon's *The Criminal Law of Scotland* (2nd edn, 1978) para 8.62.

5 'Attempt': see index to *Gordon*.

6 Penalty: level 3 (Sch 5).

7 *Woby v B and O (Juveniles)* [1986] Crim LR 183. Note that the agency offence contained in s 68(3) (see (d) below) does not appear in the parallel provisions of the Licensing Act 1964 (s 169).

a circumstance, the licenceholder (or his employee or agent) would be guilty of an offence if he knew that the real purchasers were under-age[1];

(d) a person 'knowingly'[2] acts as agent for a person under 18 in the purchase of alcoholic liquor (s 68(3))[3]. The purchase need not take place in licensed premises;

(e) a person 'knowingly' buys or attempts to buy alcoholic liquor for consumption *in a bar* in licensed premises by a person under 18 (whether as an agent or otherwise) (s 68(3))[3];

(f) a wholesaler or his employee or agent sells alcoholic liquor to a person under 18 (s 90A(2))[4]; here, no offence is committed by the under-age purchaser since the premises are not 'licensed premises'[5].

Supervision of off-sales

The holder of an off-sale licence, or of a public house or hotel licence with off-sale part conditions (s 119), or any employee or agent of his, commits an offence if he 'causes or permits' a person under 18 to sell alcoholic liquor on the premises without the sale 'having been specifically approved' by a person over that age 'acting on his behalf' (s 97A, inserted by the 1990 Act, s 54)[6]. A similar offence may also be committed by a wholesaler (s 90A(3), inserted by the 1990 Act, s 52)[7].

Consumption

Section 16 of the Children and Young Persons (Scotland) Act 1937[8] provides that:

'If any person gives, or causes to be given, to any child under the age of five years any alcoholic liquor, except upon the order of a duly qualified medical practitioner, or in the case of sickness, apprehended sickness, or other urgent cause, he shall, on summary conviction, be liable to a fine not exceeding level 1 on the standard scale'.

Otherwise, the consumption of alcoholic liquor by a person over the age of five is subject to remarkably few restrictions. An offence is committed where:

1 See also 'Practical Points' [1990] 3 LR 28.
2 'Knowingly': see *Gordon* paras 8.22ff.
3 Penalty: level 3 (Sch 5).
4 Penalty: level 3 (Sch 5). The wholesaler is vicariously responsible where the offence is committed by his employee or agent: s 67 (and Sch 5), applied by s 90A(4). Section 90A was inserted by 1990 Act, s 52.
5 Cf s 68(2).
6 Penalty: level 3 (Sch 5). Licenceholder (who has vicarious responsibility) and premises liable to disqualification (s 67, Sch 5). For a consideration of 'causing or permitting', see *Gordon* paras. 8.68ff.
7 The maximum penalty in this case is set at level 1 (Sch 5).
8 As amended by the Criminal Justice Act 1967, Sch 3 and the Criminal Procedure (Scotland) Act 1975, s 289F.

(a) a licenceholder or his employee or agent allows a person under 18 to consume alcoholic liquor *in a bar* (s 68(1))[1].

(b) a person under 18 consumes alcoholic liquor *in a bar* (s 68(2))[2].

Consumption in any part of licensed premises which is not 'a bar' is perfectly lawful, causing the *Report of the Departmental Committee on Scottish Licensing Law*[3] to observe that 'Some of the potential effects of the present law are perhaps not widely realised'. The Act reflects the committee's recommendation that one particular 'loophole' should be closed[4], but it remains the case that while the child's own purchases are prohibited by s 68(2) and *agency* purchases by an adult on behalf of a child are 'struck at' by s 68(3): 'It is . . . possible for an adult to buy a drink in a bar of a public house and give it to someone under 18 to drink elsewhere on the premises which is not a bar'[5].

Deficient drafting may, in fact, have opened up a new loophole. It may be considered that premises which are the subject of a refreshment licence are not and do not contain a bar[6] so that consumption here (although plainly very ill-advised) may not be unlawful.

Sales and consumption in restaurants

Section 68(4) specially authorises the sale to or purchase by a person aged 16 or over of 'beer, wine, made-wine, porter, cider or perry' for consumption *at a meal* in a part of the premises 'usually set apart for the service of table meals' which is not a bar, or in a bar during its regular use as a restaurant (when, as explained above, the bar ceases to be a 'bar'). This rather inelegantly worded provision may be 'de-coded' as follows:

(1) A child over the age of 16 may purchase these types of alcohol in:
   (a) restaurant-licensed premises;
   (b) a restaurant within premises which are the subject of a restricted hotel licence;
   (c) a restaurant area within public house or hotel-licensed premises which is either (i) 'usually set apart' for the service of persons taking table meals in terms of licensing board approval (ss 57, 58, 59 and 60);[7] or (ii) set apart at a usual time for table meal purposes.

(2) The consumption of alcohol must take place at the meal so that merely 'ancillary' consumption of, for example, an aperitif, is not permitted.

   The subsection also allows a person over 18 to purchase the specified drinks as the child's agent; but the child's own purchasing-power does not allow him to buy alcohol for consumption by a person under 16.

Since the restaurant areas described at (1) above are not 'bars', any type of

---

1 Penalty: level 3. Licenceholder (who has vicarious responsibility) and premises liable to disqualification (s 67, Sch 5).
2 Penalty: level 3 (Sch 5).
3 (Cmnd 5354) (*Clayson*) para 11.23.
4 See the proviso to s 68(4). Previously, a person of 16 or over could buy most types of alcohol for a younger person to drink with a restaurant meal.
5 *Clayson*, para 11.23.
6 See consideration of refreshment licences in Chapter 3.
7 See Chapter 10.

drink may be consumed there (not necessarily at a meal) by children over the age of five, provided it is bought for them by an adult not acting as an agent.

Deliveries

The sale and purchase prohibitions in s 68 are fortified by restrictions on off-sale deliveries. An offence is committed where:

(a) a licenceholder or his employee or agent delivers to a person under 18 alcoholic liquor sold in licensed premises for consumption off the premises.

(b) a licenceholder 'allows' any other person to effect such a delivery. In both cases, an exception is made for deliveries which take place at the purchaser's home or place of work: the person taking-in the liquor need not be over 18.

(c) any person 'knowingly' sends a person under 18 for the purpose of obtaining alcoholic liquor from premises[1] where the liquor is delivered in pursuance of an off-sale.

None of these offences is committed where 'the person under 18 is a member of the licenceholder's family or his servant or apprentice and is employed as a messenger to deliver alcoholic liquor' (s 68(5))[2].

RESTRICTIONS ON EMPLOYMENT

Since young persons under the legal age for alcohol consumption in a bar should not be subjected to 'undesirable influences'[3], the Act makes it an offence for 'the holder of the licence or his employee or agent'[4] to employ a person below 18 'in any bar of licensed premises' when the bar is open 'for the sale or consumption of alcoholic liquor' (s 72(1))[5].

A person will be regarded as 'employed by the person for whom he works' although he receives no wages (s 72(3)). No exemption is made for training purposes, for members of the licenceholder's family, or for areas which are the subject of a children's certificate, but:

'a person shall not be deemed to be employed in a bar of licensed premises by reason only that in the course of his employment in some other part of the premises[6] he enters the bar for the purpose of giving or receiving any message or of passing to or from some other part of the premises, not a bar, being a part to or from which there is no other convenient means of access or egress'[7].

---

1 Which need not be 'licensed premises' so that wholesale premises are included.
2 Penalty: level 3 (Sch 5) for all offences. Where an offence is committed by a licenceholder (who has vicarious responsibility) both he and the premises are liable to disqualification (s 67, Sch 5).
3 *Clayson*, para 11.53.
4 The word 'or' is conjunctive: see *Stainton and Seiler v McNaughtan* 1991 SCCR 339, 1993 SLT 119.
5 Note that the bar need not be in use for sale *and* consumption. A bar set apart for restaurant use only is not a 'bar' for the purpose of this provision: see s 68(4). Penalty: level 3 (Sch 5). Licenceholder (who has vicarious responsibility) and premises liable to disqualification (s 67, Sch 5).
6 For example, as a waiter in a restaurant.
7 Section 72(2)(a).

While the service of drinks in a restaurant is not prohibited, the 'giving or receiving of a message' dispensation would not allow the person under 18 to execute a drinks order in the bar and take the liquor to restaurant customers.

Section 73 makes it an offence to employ a person under 18 in refreshment licenced premises 'if the purpose, or one of the purposes, of his employment is to serve alcoholic liquor to persons in those premises' (s 73(1), (3))[1].

PROSECUTION OF OFFENCES

Corroboration of age

At common law in Scotland, the prosecutor must prove, with unimpeachable evidence, that the child was under 14, or 18, as the case may be[2]. In *Paton v Wilson*[3] a barmaid had been convicted of selling alcoholic liquor to a 16-year-old[4] on the evidence of (a) the youth himself, who gave parole evidence of his date of birth but did not produce his birth certificate, and (b) two police officers who witnessed the transaction and considered that the purchaser was 'obviously' under-age. The sheriff considered that he was entitled to take into account the appearance of the youth at the date of the trial (ten months after the alleged offence) and, in so doing, concurred in the view formed by the police officers. Upholding the barmaid's appeal against conviction, the High Court held that the sheriff's impression of age could not be used to corroborate the evidence of the youth himself. Referring to the decision in *Lockwood v Walker*[5] the Lord Justice-Clerk said:

'One can readily understand that if the boy had been a very young child, well under the age of 18 years, then evidence of a police officer to the effect that he was obviously under the age of 18 years might be relevant and might be capable of amounting to corroboration. But in the present case the boy was 16 and it is notorious that around that age an individual may present an appearance of either a younger or older age than he or she in fact is. That being so, in the circumstances of this case, we are satisfied that the evidence which the two police officers gave to the effect that the boy appeared to them obviously to be under the age of 18 years is not sufficient to corroborate the evidence of the boy himself'.

As Sheriff G H Gordon appears to suggest in his commentary to the case[6], this decision admits the possibility that police evidence could, in extreme circumstances, provide corroboration, while a sheriff's observations will never be capable of performing such a function.

---

1 Penalty: level 3 (Sch 5). Licenceholder (who has vicarious responsibility) and premises liable to disqualification (s 67, Sch 5). A person is deemed to be employed despite the absence of remuneration (s 73(2)).
2 *Lockwood v Walker* 1910 JC 3, (1909) 2 SLT 400. Cf *Wallworth v Balmer* [1965] 3 All ER 721, [1966] 1 WLR 16.
3 1988 SCCR 286, 1988 SLT 634.
4 In contravention of s 68(1).
5 1910 JC 3, (1909) 2 SLT 400.
6 1988 SCCR at 288.

Exceptions to the common law rule

The common law rule is abrogated as respects offences arising under:
(a) Section 69, which excludes persons under 14 from bars.
(b) Section 72, prohibiting the employment of persons under 18 in bars.
(c) Section 73, prohibiting the employment of persons under 18 for the service of alcoholic liquor in refreshment-licensed premises.

In these cases, where it is alleged by the prosecutor that a person was 'at any time' under the relevant age, and 'he appears to the court then to have been under that age', the onus of demonstrating the contrary rests on the accused (ss 69(6), 72(4), 73(4)). Rebuttal evidence need not be corroborated and the presumption may be displaced on the balance of probabilities[1].

Defences

A licenceholder charged on the basis of his vicarious responsibility following the alleged commission of an offence by his employee or agent may seek to establish the 'due diligence' defence contained in s 67(2)[2]. In addition, *any person* charged with certain offences is entitled to the defence ('the s 71 defence'):

'(a) that he used due diligence[3] to prevent the occurrence of the offence, or
 (b) that he had no reason to suspect that the person in relation to whom the charge was brought was under 18 or under 14, as the case may be'[4].

The offences referred to are:
(a) the sale of liquor to persons under 18 (s 68(1));
(b) permitting consumption of alcoholic liquor by persons under 18 in a bar (s 68(1));
(c) the delivery of alcoholic liquor (sold for consumption off the premises) to a person under 18 (s 68(5));
(d) 'knowingly' sending a person under 18 to collect alcoholic liquor which has been sold for consumption off the premises (s 68(5))[5];
(e) allowing persons under 14 to be in a bar during permitted hours (s 69(1));
(f) permitting unaccompanied persons under 14 to be in refreshment-licensed premises during the permitted hours (s 70(1));
(g) permitting persons under 14 to remain in refreshment-licensed premises after 8 pm (s 70(1));
(h) the sale of alcoholic liquor to a person under 18 by a wholesaler or his employee or agent (s 90A(2))[6];
(i) causing or permitting unsupervised sales by persons under 18 in wholesale

---

1 *King v Lees* 1993 SCCR 28. See also *HM Advocate v Mitchell* 1951 JC 53, 1951 SLT 200; *Neish v Stevenson* 1969 SLT 229.
2 See Chapter 13.
3 Cf 'all due diligence' in s 67(2).
4 Section 71, as amended by the 1990 Act, s 54(2).
5 Since the prosecutor must prove that the accused knew the age of the child or acted with 'wilful blindness', the essence of the offence (normally committed by a customer) and the defence provided by s 71 are mutually exclusive.
6 The s 71 defence is applied to this offence by s 90A(5).

premises (s 90A(3))[1], off-sale licensed premises or the off-sale part of a public house or hotel premises (s 97A);

(j) the breach of the provisions of the 1990 Act as respects children's certificates or of any condition attached to such a certificate (1990 Act, s 49(6))[2].

The s 71 defence is 'without prejudice' to the 'due diligence' defence afforded to a licenceholder charged vicariously as a result of the defalcations of his staff (s 67(2)) and is available where the sale (or other conduct complained of) took place as a result of his own actings. It has been held that s 71 may also be invoked by a licenceholder where the offence was committed by an agent. In *Akhtar v Procurator Fiscal (Airdrie)*[3] a licenceholder had been convicted of contraventions of s 68(1) 'by the hands of her agent'. Observing that the relevant sections of the Act are 'somewhat unhappily drafted', the Lord Justice-General said:

'[W]e are of the opinion that there was a defence open to a licensee under s 67(2) of the Act . . . There are also defences under s 71 of the statute. There are, indeed, two defences. The first is in subsection (a) of s 71 and we need not refer to that again since it is not now contended that the defence was established . . . [His Lordship narrated the terms of s 71(b) as set out above and continued:] Although it may be difficult on a literal reading of s 71(b) to see to whom the pronoun 'he' refers, the plain common sense of the matter searching for the intention of Parliament, is that if the licensee is charged, whereas his agent is not, the licensee is entitled to prove if he can that the agent in question had no reason to suspect that the persons to whom the drink was sold was [sic] under 18 years of age'.

Establishing the s 71 defence

As the Lord Justice-Clerk observed in *Paton v Wilson*[4] it is 'notorious' that young persons around the age of 16 may present an older appearance. The operation of a policy restricting purchases to persons over 21 and excluding persons under that age from bars is a valuable step towards 'due diligence'. Licenceholders exercising their liberty to allow persons over 14 but under 18 to be present in a bar court disaster. 'Proof of age' schemes involving the production of identity cards with photographs are desirable.

A rebuttable presumption as to a child's age applies in only one case where the s 71 defence is available. Thus, for the purposes of s 69(1) a child may appear to the court to be under 14 (s 69(6)). If the accused fails to displace the presumption it seems unlikely that the court would be sympathetic to a 'due diligence' or 'no reason to suspect' argument. In other cases it requires to be kept in view that the court's impression of a child's age does not fill an evidential *lacuna*[5]; but it has been held in England[6] that the appearance of under-age purchasers in court may entitle magistrates to conclude that a licensee who accepted assurance as to age must nevertheless have been aware that they were under 18.

Clear risks attach to the use of drink vending machines, sometimes installed in

1 The s 71 defence is applied to this offence by s 90A(5).
2 The s 71 defence is applied by the 1990 Act, s 49(7)(b).
3 High Court, on appeal, 27 June 1989, unreported.
4 1988 SCCR 286, 1988 SLT 634.
5 *Lockwood v Walker* 1910 JC 3, (1909) 2 SLT 400; *Paton v Wilson* 1988 SCCR 286, 1988 SLT 634.
6 *Wallworth v Balmer* [1965] 3 All ER 721, [1966] 1 WLR 16.

hotels to facilitate residents' purchases when bars are closed; in the absence of any supervision, it is difficult to imagine a circumstance in which the s 71 defence could succeed[1].

The s 71 defence need only be established on the balance of probabilities[2].

CHILDREN'S CERTIFICATES

Purpose and procedure

The holder of a public house licence or a hotel licence or an applicant for the grant, provisional grant or renewal of such a licence may make application to the licensing board for a children's certificate, in respect of the whole or part of his premises (1990 Act, s 49(1); see also Sch 5, para 2).

The effect of a certificate is to create for meal-taking purposes (as more fully explained below) a limited exception to s 69(1) which forbids the presence of any child under the age of 14 in a bar of licensed premises during the permitted hours and to s 69(2) which prohibits any person from causing or procuring or attempting to cause or procure any person under that age 'to go to, or to be in' a bar during those hours[3].

Application cannot competently be made by the holder of an entertainment licence. The rationale of this exclusion may be quite simple but perhaps not immediately apparent. No offence is committed under s 69(1) or (2) '. . . in respect of a bar which is in any railway refreshment room or other premises constructed, fitted and intended to be used bona fide for any purpose to which the holding of a licence is merely ancillary' (s 69(4)).

Since an entertainment licence authorises the sale by retail or supply of alcoholic liquor 'as an ancillary to the entertainment provided' (1976 Act, Sch 1) it would appear that entertainment-licensed premises may claim this immunity virtually by definition.

Nevertheless there has in Scotland been a tendency to construe the words 'or other premises' as *eiusdem generis* of 'railway refreshment room', limiting the application of the subsection to airport departure lounges and other places associated with transport.

There is no reported case in point which provides assistance. However, in *Fife Regional Council v Kirkcaldy District Licensing Board (No 2)*[4] where an application for the provisional grant of an entertainment licence in respect of a swimming pool and sports centre was refused on the ground that young people could be 'unduly exposed to drink' the court was not prepared to interfere with the board's conclusion that the premises were thereby to be regarded as not suitable or convenient for the sale of alcoholic liquor.

---

1 See *Clayson*, para 15.20; and 'Alcohol Sales From Vending Machines' [1992] 11 LR 22.
2 *King v Lees* 1993 SCCR 28. See also *HM Advocate v Mitchell* 1951 JC 53, 1951 SLT 200; *Neish v Stevenson* 1969 SLT 229.
3 Section 69 contains its own exceptions; see above.
4 1991 GWD 18-1110, 2nd Div.

The application may only be considered at a quarterly meeting (1976 Act, s 5(2)(1), read with s 5(6)) and must be lodged with the clerk of the board not less than five weeks before the first day thereof (1990 Act, Sch 5, para 2). There is no provision for the discretionary consideration of late applications. Advertisement is not required nor need mention be made of the application in the notices prescribed by s 10 of the 1976 Act in connection with applications for the grant or provisional grant of a new licence.

Where the certificate is to apply to only part of the premises the board may require a plan of the premises to be produced to it and lodged with the clerk, such as will enable the board to ascertain to which part of the premises the certificate is to relate (1990 Act, Sch 5, para 3)[1]. There is no provision in the 1990 Act requiring the plan to be lodged *with* the application.

A copy of the application (but, curiously, not of any plan) requires to be sent to the chief constable by the applicant (1990 Act, Sch 5, para 4). No time limit is prescribed.

The board may grant a certificate in respect of the premises or a part or parts if it is satisfied:

'(a) that the premises or, as the case may be, the part or parts of the premises constitute an environment in which it is suitable for children to be present; and
(b) that there will be available for sale or supply for consumption in the part of the premises in respect of which the certificate is to apply meals[2] and beverages other than alcoholic liquor within the meaning of [the 1976] Act'[3].

Where a certificate is in force it is lawful:

'for a person under 14 years of age accompanied by a person of not less than 18 years to be present in [the approved] part at any time when the premises are open to the public between eleven in the morning and eight in the evening for the purpose of the consumption of a meal sold or supplied in the premises'[4].

Although hotel premises may conceivably have permitted hours on a Sunday commencing at 11 am (or even earlier) by virtue of a regular extension of the permitted hours (s 64) public house Sunday permitted hours (where granted) do not commence until 12.30 pm.

There is no requirement that a meal actually be taken although that is clearly the intention of the section. Where a child under the age of 14 enters the certificated part of the premises for the *purpose* of consuming a meal but ultimately elects not to do so the legitimacy of his presence in that area is open to doubt. It may be remarked in the passing that, in refreshment-licensed premises, where a broadly similar regime applies, it is sufficient that food and non-alcoholic beverages be available (see the 1976 Act, s 100(b) and Sch 1).

The board is empowered to attach to the certificate:

---

1 The board is not empowered to make regulations in this regard: see 1976 Act, s 37.
2 As to the meaning of 'meal', see discussion of restaurant licences in Chapter 3.
3 1990 Act, s 49(2).
4 Ibid, s 49(3); cf the 1976 Act, s 70(1). In refreshment-licensed premises food need only be made available for purchase: see the 1976 Act, Sch 1.

'such conditions . . . including conditions restricting the hours during which and days on which children may be present in any premises or part of premises to which the certificate relates, as appear to the board to be appropriate'[1].

This widely expressed power has largely been responsible for the conspicuous unpopularity of children's certificates in many parts of Scotland. By December 1992, about 1,400 certificates had been granted, representing an increase of about 12 per cent from the 1991 total. In some districts, however, the uptake has been extremely low, in one case just one per cent[2]. The conditions which some boards attach are frequently onerous or nebulously expressed and impose standards far beyond those normally and reasonably expected of places of family resort. While it is proper that the safety of children be protected by a requirement that electrical sockets and open fires be guarded, the excessive zeal of some environmental health departments who, in many areas have almost made the certification process their own, has resulted in conditions such as the following: 'Nothing shall be done to prevent or dissuade breastfeeding from taking place'; and 'If the part of the premises under application is a public bar as opposed to a lounge bar, the applicant, as far as possible, shall ensure that small children are not subjected to offensive language'. Conditions of this nature are particularly dangerous since the contravention of a condition attached to a children's certificate (or of any provision in s 49 of the 1990 Act) is a criminal offence, attracting a level 3 fine upon summary conviction (1990 Act, s 49(6)). The licenceholder has vicarious responsibility for an offence and both he and the premises are liable to disqualification (1990 Act, Sch 5, s 49(7)(a), applying the 1976 Act, s 67(2) and (3)). The defence of 'due diligence' is available (1990 Act, s 49(7)(b), applying the 1976 Act, s 71). It may well be thought remarkable that such draconian consequences may flow from the imposition of inept conditions, although board byelaws, which also have a penal aspect (1976 Act, s 38(4)), require to be confirmed by the Secretary of State.

A common requirement that the certificated area must have direct access to toilets ignores the dispensation afforded by s 69(3)(c), in terms of which a child under the age of 14 may be in a bar 'for the purpose of passing to or from some other part of the premises, not a bar, being a part to or from which there is no other convenient means of access or egress'[3].

Where a condition is in force limiting the hours of operation of the certificate there is nothing to prevent children removing to another, uncertificated part of the premises which is not a 'bar' after the terminal hour, or so removing at 8 pm in the absence of such a condition.

The introduction of children's certificates was recommended by *Clayson*[4] but not, of course, implemented in the 1976 Act. *Clayson* expressed the hope that

---

1 1990 Act, s 49(4).
2 Sources: Scottish Office Statistical Bulletins, CRJ/1992/5, August 1992, CRJ/1993/4, July 1993.
3 Note, however, that the latitude allowed by s 69(3)(c) may not be sufficiently wide to allow passage from the entrance to the premises through a bar to a certificated area.
4 Paras. 11.10ff. It is interesting to note that at least limited approval for the presence of accompanied children in a meal-taking environment was given as long ago as 1911 by the Lord Justice-Clerk in *Donaghue v McIntyre* (1911) 1 SLT 131 at 135: '[A]s long as children are prevented from frequenting or from being brought into the bar, there is much to be said in favour of their being along with their parents when the latter are getting food and drink in a reasonable way'.

'licensing authorities will not frustrate our general intention by adopting too restrictive a policy' towards applications and suggested a right of appeal to the sheriff against refusal or the imposition of conditions. No provision is, in fact, made for an appeal.

As to the suitability of premises, *Clayson* had in mind:

'. . . such factors as the type of clientele, the provision of seats and tables, any record of misconduct or disorder, the availability of food and drink other than alcoholic liquor, toilet facilities, and the number of people likely to use the premises at any one time'.

It may be thought unfortunate that the legislation both in substance and in operation has not more closely followed these recommendations.

The only competent objector to an application for a children's certificate is the chief constable (1990 Act, Sch 5, para 4)[1].

In practice, the greatest influence of any agency is that exerted by environmental health departments, at least in some parts of Scotland, primarily because they have, in the main, been responsible for the formulation of standard conditions for attachment to certificates. However, since a local authority now has an express right to object to certain types of applications (see the 1976 Act, s 16(1)) but not to applications for children's certificates, it may well be argued that they are not empowered to comment here and that observations upon a children's certificate application which are tantamount to an objection will vitiate a refusal[2].

The board may decline to consider the application if the applicant or his representative does not attend the meeting at which the application is to be considered (1976 Act, s 15(1)). The applicant has a right to be heard[3]. Where he does not attend that fact alone will not justify refusal[4].

Where an application has been refused the board shall not within two years of its refusal 'entertain another such application in respect of those premises[5] unless it has made a direction to the contrary in respect of that refusal' (1990 Act, Sch 5, para 5). The direction need not be made at the time of refusal[6]. One may only speculate that the appropriate request may otherwise be submitted for consideration at the next meeting, in which event it is possible that the request will be heard by a differently constituted board.

There is no right of appeal to the sheriff against a refusal or the attachment of conditions, although challenge may be made by way of judicial review. The board is however required to state reasons for its decision when requested to do so in terms of s 18 of the 1976 Act.

As one has come to expect, there are a number of drafting and procedural problems:

(1) While s 49(1) of the 1990 Act allows application to be made by an applicant for inter alia the grant or *provisional grant* of a public house or hotel licence, para 2 of Sch 5 refers to an 'applicant for a new public house or hotel licence'. Presu-

---

1 The objection procedure is explained in Chapter 6.
2 Cf *Centralbite Ltd v Kincardine and Deeside District Licensing Board* 1989 SCLR 652, 1990 SLT 231.
3 See *C R S Leisure Ltd v Dumbarton District Licensing Board* 1989 SCLR 566, 1990 SLT 200.
4 *Bury v Kilmarnock and Loudoun District Licensing Board* 1988 SCLR 436, 1989 SLT 110.
5 See *Kelvinside Community Council v Glasgow District Licensing Board* 1990 SCLR 110, 1990 SLT 725, in which the expression 'the same premises' was considered.
6 Cf the 1976 Act, s 14.

mably the former provision is the correct one[1]. That being so, there would be nothing to prevent application being made by an applicant for the provisional grant of a new licence in terms of s 26(2). Such an application proceeds simply upon a plan identifying the site of the premises and a general description of their proposed size and character with particular reference to the sale of alcoholic liquor. It seems improbable that a licensing board could reach a view as to the suitability of premises or any part on the basis of such information. Where application is made in respect of only part of the premises a plan could be required in terms of Sch 5, para 3 which will 'enable the board to ascertain to which part of the premises it is proposed the certificate should relate'. Layout plans are not submitted as part of the s 26(2) process until application is made for affirmation of the provisional grant. No provision is made for a children's certificate application to be made at the affirmation stage (and, in any event affirmation applications are sometimes disposed of other than at quarterly meetings). In such circumstances it would appear that the certificate application may require to be delayed until the first quarterly meeting after finalisation of the provisional grant, at which stage the applicant will be the holder of a licence. Some boards will be prepared to accept the application in anticipation of finalisation between the last lodgement date and the date of the quarterly meeting; others will not.

(2) Section 49(10) of the 1990 Act provides that where a licence is transferred in terms of s 25 of the 1976 Act:

'. . . any children's certificate in respect of the premises or any part of the premises to which the licence relates shall be transferred to the new licence holder subject to the same conditions as were applied to the original grant of the certificate'.

Unfortunately, the draftsman's persistence in adhering to the concept of 'the holder of a licence' which has caused so much difficulty in relation to regular extensions of the permitted hours[2] presents difficulties in some areas where a licence is or is about to be transferred without a certificate. If the person acquiring the premises desires the benefit of a certificate a number of clerks will not accept his application in that regard in anticipation of the grant of his temporary or permanent transfer application.

(3) In terms of s 49(5) of the 1990 Act:

'There shall be displayed at all times in any premises or part of such premises to which a children's certificate applies a notice of the fact that a children's certificate has been granted in respect of such premises or part'.

A notice simply stating that 'A children's certificate applies to this part of the premises' appears to be sufficient, but it seems peculiar that the draftsman has not chosen to follow the wording of, for example, s 57 of the 1976 Act by requiring that the effect of the certificate be explained and equally odd that the notice need not set out any conditions attaching to the certificate, such as the operational hours, for ease of police supervision. However, at least one board requires the display of a suitably informative notice by the attachment of a condition to that effect.

---

1 For the purposes of s 14 of the 1976 Act 'new licence' has been held to include an application for the provisional grant of a new licence: see *Kelvinside Community Council*, above.
2 See Chapter 10.

(4) Section 49(9) and Sch 5, para 9 of the 1990 Act contain inconsistent provisions as to the currency of certificates[1].

(5) Although a licenceholder can choose to disapply ss 57, 58, 59 or 60 of the 1976 Act, no provision is made for the surrender of a children's certificate, a course which may be desirable where it has been granted subject to conditions which prove to be unacceptable or, indeed, impossible to fulfil; but, equally, actual licences are in practice surrendered despite the absence of any enabling provision[2]. *Clayson* recommended that the licenceholder 'should have the right to extinguish the certificate on his own initiative by giving two weeks' notice to the clerk of the licensing board'[3].

(6) Regrettably, the unpopularity of children's certificates in certain areas has thoroughly confused many members of the licensed trade who wish to encourage family business but who are unable or unwilling to comply with some of the more outré conditions imposed by boards. The view that ss 57, 58, 59 or 60 of the 1976 Act[4] provide the only alternative is prevalent but far from logical. Instead, in such circumstances, resort should be made to s 68(4) of the 1976 Act which, broadly speaking, permits children under the age of 14 to be in bars when they are set apart exclusively for restaurant use. Where the s 68(4) exemption is available, the application of, say, s 57, is not an indispensable addition.

Suspension of certificates

Section 50 of the 1990 Act appears to allow a licensing board to suspend a children's certificate *ex proprio motu*:

'Where a licensing board considers that the premises or part of the premises to which a children's certificate relates no longer constitute an environment in which it is suitable for children to be present they shall decide whether or not to hold a hearing for the purpose of determining whether to suspend the certificate'[5].

The power to suspend is implied rather than express and it may also be thought that this provision is curiously and somewhat illogically framed. Where the board has *already* reached a conclusion as to unsuitability (without a complaint from an external source) there remains a discretion as to whether a hearing is to be held, at which the issue will have been partially prejudged. Doubtless the procedure may only be invoked where the licenceholder has altered his *modus operandi* rather than where the board has changed its general policy towards children's certificates.

The clerk of the board is required to serve not less than 21 days' notice of the hearing upon the licenceholder, specifying the grounds upon which suspension of the certificate may be made (presumably these grounds must be more than a simple repetition of s 50(1)). Notice of the hearing must also be given to the chief constable (no time limit is specified for this purpose) and, although he is given no

---

1 Discussed in the context of the certificate renewal procedure in Chapter 9.
2 See *D & A Haddow Ltd v City of Glasgow District Licensing Board* 1983 SLT (Sh Ct) 5.
3 Para 11.14.
4 See Chapter 10.
5 1990 Act, s 50(1).

power to initiate the procedure by way of a complaint, he may, not less than seven days before the hearing, notify the clerk that he wishes to be heard in support of the suspension and specify the grounds on which suspension is sought. He must intimate such notice to the licenceholder; again, no time limit is prescribed (1990 Act, s 50(2)).

A suspension order may not be made unless the licenceholder is afforded a hearing, unless he fails to appear, having received due notice (1990 Act, s 50(2)).

The period of the suspension may be a fixed period not exceeding one year or the unexpired portion of the duration of the certificate, whichever is the less, and during the suspension period 'the certificate shall cease to have effect' (1990 Act, s 50(3)).

The licenceholder may not make application to the board to have the suspension order lifted on the basis that he has cured the difficulties which gave rise to the hearing, nor is there right of appeal to the sheriff. On the contrary, where it appears to the board that the grounds giving rise to the suspension continue to obtain it may, not more than one month before the expiry of the suspension period determine 'that the suspension shall continue for a further period of not more than one year' (1990 Act, s 50(4)). Provision is also made for a series of further suspensions *ad infinitum* (1990 Act, s 50(4)) although there would, of course, come a point at which the board may be required to determine an application to renew the certificate, or, more correctly, to grant *de novo*, although a second or subsequent suspension is not expressly subject to the limitation that it may not exceed the unexpired portion of the certificate. By virtue of s 50(4), s 50 as a whole 'shall have effect as regards any such further suspension as it has for the purposes of an initial suspension', suggesting that before any second or subsequent suspension may be imposed another hearing would require to be held, to which the notice requirements of s 50(2) would apply, and at which the licenceholder would be entitled to oppose the order.

Where a licence with a suspended children's certificate is transferred by virtue of s 25 the new licenceholder cannot operate the certificate until the suspension period has expired.

CHAPTER 15

Appeals and judicial review

APPEALS

The scope of the appeal provisions

As noted at the appropriate section of the text, the majority of licensing board decisions are subject to appeal to the sheriff at the instance of an applicant, licenceholder, objector or complainer (s 39(1)). The sheriff's decision may be appealed to the Court of Session on a point of law (s 39(8)).

The most significant omission is in relation to applications for the regular extension of permitted hours[1].

The right of appeal may not be immediately obvious. For example, where a licensing board entertains or refuses to entertain an application for a new licence where no direction has been given under s 14 following the refusal of a previous application, *ex facie* that decision is not susceptible to appeal. It has, however, been held that while Parliament has purposefully denied such a remedy to the applicant[2] objectors nevertheless have an unrestricted right of appeal[3].

On the other hand, an imagined right of appeal may be non-existent. It appears to have been assumed that an objector to the grant, permanent transfer or renewal of a licence may appeal to the sheriff against a board's ruling that his objection is incompetent as, for example, in *Morgan v Midlothian District Licensing Board*[4] and *Prime v Hardie*[5]; or, more, precisely, a board's refusal to 'entertain' the objection (see s 16(2))[6].

The right of appeal conferred by s 17(5) upon a *competent* objector is, however, purely against the board's decision to grant the application. It may be that an aggrieved objector's only remedy is to petition for judicial review of the board's decision not to entertain the objection. Certainly, on a narrow reading of s 16(1) and (2) an objector's status as 'competent' may simply depend on his inclusion in

---

1 See *Fereneze Leisure Ltd v Renfrew District Licensing Board* 1990 SCLR 436 (reported on appeal at 1991 SCLR 751, 1992 SLT 604 on other issues) for a case in which the sheriff upheld an appeal against refusal of a permanent transfer and directed the board to consider an associated regular extension application.
2 *Fife & Kinross Motor Auctions Ltd v Perth and Kinross District Licensing Board* 1981 SLT 106.
3 *Kelvinside Community Council v City of Glasgow District Licensing Board* 1990 SCLR 110, 1990 SLT 725. An applicant denied a 'section 14 direction', as it is commonly known, could no doubt seek judicial review of that decision.
4 1993 SCLR 1, 1993 SLT (Sh Ct) 19.
5 1978 SLT (Sh Ct) 71.
6 See also *Kelvinside Community Council v Glasgow District Licensing Board* 1990 SCLR 110 at 116D, where the Lord Justice-Clerk refers to a right of appeal in these circumstances.

the list of competent objectors set out in s 16(1). Thus, it would be argued, a procedural failure on the part of a qualified objector does not rob him of that status but simply results in the board's declinature to 'entertain' his objection.

Nevertheless, even by that reasoning, some support for the 'judicial review' argument may be found in a comparison of the respective positions of the applicant for and objector to a new licence application who are met with a decision that there has been a failure to comply with a preliminary requirement of the Act. Both have available a motion in terms of s 13(2) based upon 'inadvertence or misadventure' which, if granted by the board, allows postponement of the consideration of the application to an adjourned meeting. If the board refuses (or declines to consider) the motion, that decision is not a decision to grant or refuse the application which is susceptible to appeal, even if predicated upon an error in law which is later corrected by the court[1].

The position is further clouded by the provisions of s 5(2). A board may arrange for the grant of a renewal application[2] under a 'delegated powers' arrangement by virtue of s 5(1) but *not* where a *competent* objection has been lodged (s 5(2)(b)). In practice, objected applications are always placed before the board and, where doubt arises as to the competency of an objection, submissions will be heard. Nevertheless, s 5(2)(b) may arguably suggest that a decision on competency is a preliminary matter for the clerk, in which event the existence of a right of appeal would appear to be even less likely.

Where an applicant appeals against the refusal of an objected application he may take issue with the acceptance of the objection as competent.

It may be considered that the clerk's rejection of an application on competency grounds is properly the subject of judicial review, rather than an appeal to the sheriff, and that *M Milne Ltd v City of Glasgow District Licensing Board*[3] was wrongly decided.

There is normally no appeal from the sheriff to the Sheriff Principal[4] but it has been held that such an appeal is competent on a point of procedure, where, for example an appeal has been dismissed or decree granted by the sheriff following a party's failure to appear at a diet[5].

On the other hand, where the sheriff refused to allow an appellant's adjustment which would 'have significantly widened the scope of the enquiry' at a very late stage, and leave to appeal to the Sheriff Principal was refused[6], the Sheriff Principal held:

'[T]he sheriff's discretion not to allow further adjustment was not purely a matter of procedure, it was the exercise of [his] particular discretion. The sheriff principal's respon-

---

1 See commentary to *Indpine Ltd v City of Dundee District Licensing Board* 1992 SCLR 353 at 356.
2 Note, however, that the refusal of such an application may only take place at a quarterly meeting: see s 5(2)(c), read with s 5(6).
3 1987 SLT (Sh Ct) 145.
4 *Troc Sales Ltd v Kirkcaldy District Licensing Board* 1982 SLT (Sh Ct) 77.
5 *Charles Watson (Scotland) Ltd v Glasgow District Licensing Board* 1980 SLT (Sh Ct) 37, followed in *Khawar v Eastwood District Licensing Board*, Paisley Sheriff Court, 30 July 1991, unreported; see also *Ladbrokes the Bookmakers v Hamilton District Council* 1977 SLT (Sh Ct) 86; cf *Saleem v Hamilton District Licensing Board* 1993 SCLR 266, in which the court entertained under s 39(8) an appeal against dismissal.
6 Thus excluding the possibility of an appeal in terms of s 27 of the Sheriff Courts (Scotland) Act 1907.

sibility for the proper regulation of the conduct of judicial business does not extend to regulating a sheriff's exercise of a discretion'[1].

As respects members' clubs, the decision of the sheriff in dealing with an application for the grant, renewal or cancellation of a certificate of registration is final (s 117); but where an interlocutor is 'procedural in character and the issues raised concern the regularity of the procedure before the sheriff and the competency of his actings' an appeal lies from the sheriff to the Sheriff Principal[2]. Where an objection to an application for the grant of a certificate was repelled by the sheriff as neither relevant nor competent and no evidence was heard, the Sheriff Principal refused the objector's appeal as incompetent:

'[The sheriff] was quite entitled to dispose of the application on preliminary pleas and to hold, as he did, that there is not relevantly stated in the objections a ground of objection which can competently be made in terms of section 108. There is nothing procedural about such a decision; it was a decision on the merits'[3].

The *nobile officium* of the Court of Session may not be petitioned where no provision is made for an appeal[4]. This remedy is available 'to meet a *casus improvisus* in the statutory code or to cure some procedural technicality where *per incuriam* some formal step in procedure has been omitted'[5], but it may not:

'. . . be invoked to extend the provisions of an Act of Parliament so as, for instance, to give a remedy to someone other than the parties to whom Parliament has chosen to give a remedy . . . [nor] to enable the Court to supplement the statutory procedure by what would in effect be an amendment of a statute'[6].

Where a party to an appeal dies before its determination the appeal may presumably be continued by his representatives[7].

The effect of an appeal

An appeal will place in abeyance a board's decision to:
(a) refuse the renewal of a licence (s 30(5)(b), s 138(2)(a))[8];
(b) refuse to renew a licence *quoad* Sunday permitted hours (s 30(5)(b), s 138(2)(a));

---

1 *Cambridge Street Properties Ltd v City of Glasgow District Licensing Board*, Glasgow Sheriff Court, 6 April 1993, unreported per Sheriff Principal N D MacLeod, QC.
2 *Chief Constable of Strathclyde v Hamilton and District Bookmakers Club* 1977 SLT (Sh Ct) 78. See also *Edinburgh North Constituency Association SNP Club v Thomas H Peck Ltd* 1978 SLT (Sh Ct) 76; *Ladbrokes the Bookmakers v Hamilton District Council* 1977 SLT (Sh Ct) 86.
3 *Stephen v Woodend Bowling Club* 1993 SCLR (Notes) 574.
4 But as to the availability of judicial review, see p 305ff below.
5 *McLaughlin, Petitioner* 1965 SC 243.
6 *Maitland, Petitioner* 1961 SC 291, 1961 SLT 384, approved in *Fife & Kinross Motor Auctions Ltd v Perth and Kinross District Licensing Board* 1981 SLT 106. In the latter case it was held that Parliament had not intended an appeal based on a decision under s 14; cf *Kelvinside Community Council v City of Glasgow District Licensing Board* 1990 SCLR 110, 1990 SLT 725, in which it was held that such a decision was appealable at the instance of objectors.
7 *Cooke v Cooper* [1912] 2 KB 248. See also ss 13 and 25(2).
8 An objector's appeal has no effect on the *grant* of a renewal application. In terms of s 30(2), 'A renewed licence shall come into effect on being renewed by a licensing board'.

(c) suspend a licence (s 31(6), s 36(6));
(d) impose a closure order (s 32(6));
(e) impose a restriction order (s 31(6), as applied by s 65(2));
(f) grant or provisionally grant a licence (s 30(1)).

A lacuna in s 31(6) (and consequently in s 32(6) and s 36(6)) was identified in *McKay v Banff and Buchan Western Division Licensing Board*[1]: there is no provision for the 'freezing' of a suspension, closure or restriction order pending the determination of a *board's* appeal to the Court of Session from the decision of the sheriff and in such a circumstance a cross-appeal by the licenceholder is necessary to preserve the validity of the licence.

A licence 'shall have effect' on the dependency of an appeal against a board's refusal to grant a permanent transfer following a temporary transfer (s 25(1C)) or to confirm under s 25(4) a transfer under s 25(2) or a substitution under s 25(3) (s 25(4C)).

Where the grant or refusal of an application is under appeal there is nothing to prevent the submission of a further application (except where a prohibition is in place in terms of s 14).

The *same* application may not, however, be reconsidered. In *Matchett v Dunfermline District Council*[2] an appeal against the refusal of an amusement-with-prizes machine permit[3] was sisted by agreement between the applicant and the district council. The council's licensing committee thereafter reheard the application and granted the permit. Dismissing an objector's petition for judicial review in the absence of *locus standi*, Lord Kirkwood expressed the opinion that once intimation of the original decision had been intimated and an appeal initiated, the district council were *functus* in relation to that particular application and, but for his decision on the preliminary issue, would have taken the view that the district council acted *ultra vires* in proceeding to reverse its earlier refusal[4].

Statement of reasons

The starting point in any appeal should be the statement of reasons for the board's decision which may competently be requested in respect of any of the decisions mentioned in s 5(2) of the Act (s 18(1))[5] (although an appeal may proceed where the appellant has omitted to obtain such a statement)[6]. In other cases the board is under no obligation to provide reasons[7].

It may be remarked in passing that the legislature has chosen to align an

---

1 1991 SCLR 15, 1991 SLT 20.
2 1993 SLT 537.
3 Gaming Act 1968, s 34 and Sch 9.
4 See also *Thomson v City of Glasgow District Council* 1992 SLT 805.
5 The *Report of the Departmental Committee on Scottish Licensing Law* (Cmnd 5354) (*Clayson*) para 8.32 considered that a statement of reasons should be available 'in the interests of openness, fairness and impartiality'.
6 In the unlikely event of the clerk failing to provide reasons the appellant is not thereby entitled to decree in absence: see *Mecca Ltd v Kirkcaldy Burgh Licensing Court* 1975 SLT (Sh Ct) 50.
7 *Purdon v City of Glasgow District Licensing Board* 1989 SLT 201; see also *R v Secretary of State for Trade and Industry ex parte Lonhro* [1989] 1 WLR 525 and *R v Liverpool Crown Court ex parte Lennon and Hongkins* [1991] 4 LR 22.

entitlement to reasons with applications which may not be disposed of under a delegated powers arrangement, rather than with the types of application covered by the appeal provisions of the Act. In the result, reasons may be required for the board's decision in relation to a regular extension or children's certificate application, although such a decision may only be challenged by judicial review; and, obversely, while a board's refusal to affirm or finalise a provisional grant may be appealed (s 26(10)) there is no right to written reasons.

The request for a statement of reasons must be made: 'not more than 48 hours after the decision is made, by the applicant or, as the case may be, by the holder of the licence, or by any objector, or by any complainer who appeared at the hearing' (s 18(2)). The request may be made orally at the hearing when the board's decision is announced, in which case it is probably good practice to confirm the request immediately thereafter in writing; or application may simply be made in writing. The 48-hour time limit is mandatory, and the request must be in the clerk's hands within that period. The authority usually cited for that proposition is *H D Wines (Inverness) Ltd v Inverness District Licensing Board*[1], in which the Lord Justice-Clerk (Wheatley) rejected the argument that 'once the applicant had committed himself to a request by handing his letter of request over to the postal system he had satisfied the requirements of [s 18(2)]' (Lord Kissen concurring). However, Lord Stott did not find it necessary to express a concluded opinion and observed:

'All that is required is that a request shall be made within 48 hours of the decision. An aggrieved applicant is not in my opinion to be deprived of a right of appeal conferred on him by an Act of Parliament unless that result is a necessary implication from the terms of the Act and since there is no evidence that this request was not timeously made in the sense of having been despatched outwith the prescribed period of 48 hours I should be inclined with some hesitation to hold that the request was not shown to have been out of time notwithstanding that it did not come into the hands of the depute clerk until a later date'.

The board must give the reasons 'within 21 days of being required to do so' (s 5(1)). The 21-day period and the 48-hour time limit 'shall not include a day which is a Sunday, Christmas Day, New Year's Day, Good Friday, a bank holiday, or a public holiday, or a day appointed for public mourning' (s 18(4)).

It is not clear whether the reasons must be *received* by the applicant within 21 days of the request. If that is indeed the case (by analogy with *H D Wines (Inverness) Ltd*[1]) the provisions of s 39(2)[2] should be borne in mind.

Before composing the statement of reasons the clerk should consult with board members.[3] In *Ladbroke Racing (Strathclyde) Ltd v Cunninghame District Licensing Court*[4] the clerk appears to have formed the view that it would have been improper so to do, but the sheriff (D B Smith) observed:

'I can see that there are practical difficulties in consulting the often large number of members of the court – in this case there were 10 – but although I am certain that the clerk

---

1 1982 SLT 73.
2 See below.
3 *Clayson* (para 8.32) endorsed the views of the Guest Committee (Second Report, Cmnd 2021, 1963), which considered that the reasons given would be those which actuated the court as a whole in reaching its decision, although the views of individual members might differ in a particular case.
4 1978 SLT (Sh Ct) 77.

acted from motives of complete propriety . . . I am of the opinion that this practice . . . is wrong'.

If reasons have been requested by one party to a hearing, the board 'shall give copies of those reasons to all other parties to the hearing' (s 18(3))[1].

The sufficiency or otherwise of the statement of reasons will come under close scrutiny in the course of an appeal. Indeed, the inadequate statement is a rock upon which licensing board decisions regularly perish. It was made clear as long ago as 1978 that boards are not 'fulfilling [their] statutory obligation if they merely repeat, without further explanation or clarification, the words used in the statute'[2].

The standard of sufficiency which must be achieved is perhaps most clearly explained in a planning, rather than a licensing, case:

'[In] order to comply with the statutory duty imposed upon him the Secretary of State must give proper and adequate reasons for his decision which deal with the substantial questions in issue in an intelligible way. The decision must, in short, leave the informed reader and the court in no real and substantial doubt as to what the reasons for it were and what were the material considerations which were taken into account in reaching it'[3].

In another non-licensing case the Lord President (Emslie) said:

'The statutory obligation to give reasons is designed not merely to inform the parties of the result of the committee's deliberations but to make it clear to them and to this court the basis on which their decision was reached, and that they have reached their result in conformity with the requirements of the statutory provisions and the principles of natural justice. In order to make clear the basis of their decision a committee must state: (i) what facts they found to be admitted or proved; (ii) whether and to what extent the submissions of parties were accepted as convincing or not; and (iii) by what method or methods of valuation applied to the facts found their determination was arrived at'[4].

Since appellants are 'entitled to know what it is they are appealing against', the board's decision must stand or fall by the reasons given: the court may not look for reasons to support the decision other than those supplied nor may it infer reasons which have not been made explicit[5].

There may, however, have been at least a limited departure from this principle in *J & J Inns Ltd v Angus District Licensing Board*[6]. The petitioners brought a petition for judicial review of the board's decision to refuse an application in terms of s 25(3)[7]. The intelligibility of the board's reasons[8], criticised 'with some

1 As to the meaning of 'parties', see 'Procedure', below.
2 *Martin v Ellis* 1978 SLT (Sh Ct) 38. See also *Ladbroke Racing (Strathclyde) Ltd v Cunninghame District Licensing Board* 1978 SLT (Sh Ct) 77; *Troc Sales Ltd v Kirkcaldy District Licensing Board* 1982 SLT (Sh Ct) 77; *Moughal v Motherwell District Licensing Board* 1983 SLT (Sh Ct) 84; and *Speedlift Auto Salvage v Kyle and Carrick District Council* 1991 SCLR 801, 1992 SLT (Sh Ct) 57.
3 *Wordie Property Co Ltd v Secretary of State for Scotland* 1984 SLT 345 at 348 per Lord President Emslie. See also 1 *Stair Memorial Encyclopaedia* para 292.
4 *Albyn Properties Ltd v Knox* 1977 SC 108 at 112, 1977 SLT 41 at 43, a 'fair rent' appeal. See also *Noble Organisation Ltd v City of Glasgow District Council (No 1)* 1990 SCLR 393, 1990 SLT 554.
5 *Loosefoot Entertainment Ltd v Glasgow District Licensing Board* 1990 SCLR 584.
6 1992 SCLR 683, 1992 SLT 930.
7 For the substitution of a new manager.
8 Reasons need not be given for a decision upon this type of application (see s 18, read with s 5(2)) but in this case were volunteered.

vigour' by counsel for the petitioners, appears to have depended upon the board's decision in another matter, namely a refusal to renew the petitioners' licence about one year earlier. The Lord Ordinary (Weir) was, however, prepared to hold that by reference to extraneous material '. . . the position becomes quite clear and must have been perfectly clear to the persons who matter, namely the petitioners'.

The introduction of a reason which was not canvassed at the hearing of the application will point to a breach of the rules of natural justice:

'The sheriff found that there had been no discussion at the hearing in relation to the sufficiency of permitted machines in the city centre and that to produce this as a ground of refusal of the application for the first time in the decision letter contravened the principles of natural justice in respect that the appellants have been given no opportunity to dispute it. We agree . . .'[1].

Obversely, a reason omitted from the statement supplied pursuant to s 18 cannot subsequently be put before the court, even where the reason may have formed a valid ground for a decision[2].

The board is not required to make findings-in-fact and a failure to do so will not amount to an error in law:

'The Statute prescribes no particular form for a Statement of Reasons. In particular, it does not require the making of findings-in-fact. A Licensing Board is a lay body and I am not sympathetic to arguments which depend upon an examination of the form rather than the substance . . .'[3].

The statement should not be scrutinised line by line and word by word as if it was 'a closed record or a trust disposition and settlement'[4]. Indeed, reasons need not be 'immaculately precise and exhaustive' provided that they are free from confusion and ambiguity[5]. Brief reasons which are not lacking in clarity are acceptable and the fact that certain matters are not referred to in detail will not necessarily yield the inference that they have not been considered[6], provided that there is no global dismissal of relevant material:

'[We] do not consider that each and every objection requires to be dealt with in the statement of reasons, but the general purport and effect of the objections should receive recognition and attention. The way that the reasons are expressed gives rise to the suspicion that the rejection of the claims of crimes, vandalism, etc., by reason of the police evidence simply resulted in a package rejection of the other objections without any explanation for that rejection'[7].

1 *G A Estate Agency Ltd v City of Glasgow District Council* 1991 SCLR 8, 1991 SLT 16.
2 See *Midlothian District Council v Kinnear* 1993 GWD 3-193, Ex Div; cf the sheriff's power to obtain an amplification of reasons, discussed below.
3 *Granite City Bowling Centre Ltd v City of Aberdeen District Licensing Board*, Aberdeen Sheriff Court, 31 October 1991, unreported per Sheriff D J Risk.
4 *Loosefoot Entertainment Ltd v Glasgow District Licensing Board* 1990 SCLR (Sh Ct) 584.
5 *Brechin Golf and Squash Club v Angus District Licensing Board* 1993 SCLR 191, 1993 SLT 547.
6 *Fife Regional Council v Kirkcaldy District Licensing Board (No 1)* 1991 GWD 10-611, Ex Div.
7 *R W Cairns Ltd v Busby East Church Kirk Session* 1985 SLT 493.

At the other end of the spectrum, prolixity brings its own dangers. It will usually be assumed that everything contained in the statement has a bearing on the reasons for a decision and it is difficult to argue that material is 'innocuous' or 'irrelevant'[1].

Where responsibility lies with an applicant to satisfy the board as to certain matters the licensing board is not obligated in giving its reasons to prove the negative: '[I]n deciding to refuse to grant the application, there is no onus on the board, in giving its reasons, to demonstrate positively that the applicant is not a fit and proper person'[2].

Until recently it was assumed that reasons lacking in specification were always capable of being amplified by the invocation of para 5 of the Act of Sederunt (Appeals under the Licensing (Scotland) Act 1976) 1977, SI 1977/1622 which provides as follows:

'Where an appeal is made to the sheriff against a decision of a licensing board and that board has given as reasons for its decision one or more of the statutory grounds of refusal, the sheriff, may, at any time prior to pronouncing a final interlocutor request the licensing board to give their reasons for finding such ground or grounds of refusal to be established'[3].

In *Augustus Barnett Ltd v Bute and Cowal Licensing Board*[4] reasons given by the board for the refusal of the grant of an off-sale licence went beyond a mere reiteration of a statutory ground of refusal. In his dissenting opinion Lord Murray suggested that the board be required to amplify its reasons in terms of para 5.

Considerable doubt has now been cast upon the competency of such procedure. In *Leisure Inns (UK) Ltd v Perth and Kinross District Licensing Board*[5] the Second Division declined to express a concluded view but the Lord Justice-Clerk (Ross) observed:

'[I] am inclined to the view that such a remit [ie under para 5] can only be used where the licensing board have given no reasons and where they are required by the sheriff to give their reasons for finding a ground of refusal to be established. Paragraph 5 empowers the sheriff to request the licensing board 'to give reasons', not 'to give or amplify their reasons'[6].

This interpretation, though no doubt correct, leads to peculiar results. If a statement of reasons issued following the refusal of a permanent transfer application simply discloses that the applicant was found not to be a fit and proper person, enlargement is possible by the use of para 5; but if the statement narrates that 'the applicant is not a fit and proper person to be the holder of a licence because of his previous convictions', no resort to para 5 may be made.

But, paradoxically, if the statement of reasons is no more than a bald repetition of the statutory ground, it is more likely that the board will lose the appeal

---

1 See *Givaudan & Co Ltd v Minister of Housing and Local Government* [1967] 1 WLR 250 at 259.
2 *J & J Inns Ltd v Angus District Licensing Board* 1992 SCLR 683 at 690; 1992 SLT 930 at 935.
3 The Inner House may competently remit to the sheriff with a direction that he exercise his powers under para 5: *Leisure Inns (UK) Ltd v Perth and Kinross District Licensing Board* 1991 SCLR 721, 1993 SLT 796.
4 1989 SCLR 413, 1990 SLT 572.
5 See above.
6 1991 SCLR 721 at 726.

substantially for that reason than that the sheriff will make a request for amplification[1].

The difficulty seems to stem at least in part from the unsatisfactory use of the word 'reasons' in para 5. Following the Lord Justice-Clerk's analysis in the *Leisure Inns* case[2] it is used in two senses:

(1) reasons simply amounting to a statutory ground of refusal without any elaboration; and

(2) reasons for arriving at that decision.

(Of course, in tending to the view that a remit under the paragraph 'can only be used where the licensing board have given *no reasons*', [author's emphasis] his Lordship is no doubt referring to a situation in which *unsupported* reasons have been supplied[3].)

This may be a very narrow interpretation. In the first place, for the reasons explained above the simple repetition of the statutory ground is nothing less than a kamikaze approach; and secondly boards really have no option but to embody a statutory ground in a statement of reasons. It is axiomatic that the only ground of refusal is a statutory one. Lord Murray's view[4] may therefore be the preferred, purposive interpretation.

In *H D Wines Ltd v Inverness District Licensing Board*[5] the sheriff employed para 5 as a means of ordaining the board to specify *which* ground of refusal had been found to apply where this information could not be clearly deduced from the statement of reasons. This approach is almost certainly incompetent. Equally, reasons may not be required by the sheriff where the appellant has failed to make a request under s 18.

Time limit for appeal

In terms of s 39(2) an appeal requires to be lodged with the sheriff clerk:

'within 14 days from the date of the decision appealed against or in a case where reasons for a decision have been given under section 18(2) of this Act, within 14 days from the receipt of those reasons, which shall be presumed to have been received on the day after the date on which they were posted, except that in the case of reasons posted on a Friday or Saturday, they shall be presumed to have been received on the Monday next following'.

The sheriff may hear an appeal 'on good cause shown' although it was not lodged within the time limit (s 39(3))[6].

Circumstances may arise where this discretionary power will give rise to difficulty. Section 30(1) provides that where an application for a new licence was the subject of objections the licence comes into effect when 'the time within which an appeal may be made has elapsed' (s 30(1)(a)); or, if an appeal is lodged by an

---

1 See, for example, *Martin v Ellis* 1978 SLT (Sh Ct) 38.

2 1991 SCLR 721 at 726.

3 On occasions sheriffs have invoked para 5 where the appellant has failed to make a request for reasons and *none* have been given: this is plainly incompetent.

4 As expressed in *Augustus Barnett Ltd v Bute and Cowal Licensing Board* 1989 SCLR 413; 1990 SLT 572: see above.

5 Inverness Sheriff Court, 14 February 1980, unreported.

6 See *H D Wines (Inverness) Ltd v Inverness District Licensing Board* 1982 SLT 73.

objector, when the appeal has been abandoned or determined in favour of the applicant (s 30(1)(b)). If an objector lodges his appeal out of time the licence will have come into force by virtue of s 30(1)(a). *Semble* the licence would require to be reduced at the instance of the objector if the appeal were to proceed under s 39(3). Such course appears improbable.

A statement of reasons issued pursuant to a request made out of time is not 'given under section 18(2)' and an appeal is only made timeously if lodged within 14 days from the date of the decision, although in such a circumstance the sheriff's discretionary power to hear a late appeal may be invoked[1].

Where an application for the provisional grant of a licence has been made under s 26(1) and a competent objector has appeared at the hearing of the application, thus creating the potential for an appeal, practitioners should take steps to determine whether a statement of reasons has been requested by that objector within the prescribed period. Otherwise it is possible that the applicant will proceed to incur expense in the progressing of work at the application site oblivious to the risk of an appeal subsequently being initiated.

Procedure

The appeal proceeds by way of a summary application[2] and is commenced by an initial writ[3]. The parties should be designed as 'Pursuer(s)' and 'Defenders'[4]. The board may competently be a party to the appeal (s 39(2A), inserted by para 11 of Sch 8 to the 1990 Act).

It has been suggested that provision for adjustment of the pleadings may usefully be made in the interlocutor appointing answers to be lodged[5]. In *Cambridge Street Properties Ltd v City of Glasgow District Licensing Board*[6], the Sheriff Principal (N D MacLeod, QC) expressed the opinion, obiter, that the sheriff had exercised his discretion properly by refusing to allow late adjustments which would have significantly broadened the scope of an appeal. An informal closed record will be of assistance to the court[7].

Where two or more decisions share common features separate appeals need not be taken[8].

Where the appellant has received a statement of reasons from the board he must lodge a copy with the sheriff clerk (Act of Sederunt, para 4).

1 *H D Wines (Inverness) Ltd* 1982 SLT 73.
2 Sheriff Courts (Scotland) Acts 1907 and 1913. See Macphail *Sheriff Court Practice* (1988) paras 26-01ff.
3 Paragraph 2 of the Act of Sederunt (Appeals under the Licensing (Scotland) Act 1976) 1977, SI 1977/1622, as amended by SI 1979/1520, which regulates procedure and is referred to in this section as 'the Act of Sederunt'.
4 *Clydesdale & County Hotels Ltd v Burgh of Falkirk* 1970 SLT (Sh Ct) 71; *Mecca Ltd v Kirkcaldy Burgh Licensing Court* 1975 SLT (Sh Ct) 50.
5 *Macphail* para 26-22, doubting the suggestion in *Hutcheon v Hamilton District Licensing Board* 1978 SLT (Sh Ct) 44 at 46 that adjustment may take place at any time. See also *Jackson v City of Glasgow District Council* 1992 GWD 22-1236.
6 Glasgow Sheriff Court, 6 April 1993, unreported.
7 See the sheriff's comments in *Devana Investments Ltd v City of Aberdeen Licensing Board* 1992 SCLR 616.
8 *Wright v Renfrew District Council* 1993 SCLR (Notes) 585.

In appeals arising from the grant or refusal of an application in name of a non-natural person and an employee or agent (s 11) for a new licence or for the renewal or permanent transfer of a licence, the employee or agent is not 'the applicant' and should not be a party to the appeal[1]. In terms of s 11(2), the application requires to name 'both the applicant *and* the employee or agent of the applicant' (author's emphasis). However, as respects applications for the occasional and regular extension of permitted hours, application is made by the person holding the licence (s 64(1)) and, by virtue of s 11(3) any reference to the holder of a licence includes a reference to both these persons. Judicial review proceedings[2] should thus be commenced in name of the non-natural person and the employee or agent.

As to the content of the initial writ, see *Hutcheon v Hamilton District Licensing Board*[3].

Where the defender fails to appear or be represented at the calling of the case the sheriff is entitled to grant decree against him. Such a course will not normally be appropriate as respects an absent pursuer. In *Saleem v Hamilton District Licensing Board*[4] the pursuer's solicitor was absent when the case was called, having been detained in another court. The sheriff granted the board's motion for dismissal. When the solicitor eventually appeared, some ten to fifteen minutes late, the sheriff took the view that he could not recall the case, the board's solicitor having left the court. The First Division held that:

'[I]f the pursuer is not present or represented we are of the opinion that the sheriff should normally drop the case from the roll and that only in exceptional circumstances should he dismiss the application at that stage. We consider that the sheriff has a discretion as to how to dispose of the application if such a situation arises, but in our view he should drop the case from the roll unless he has strong reasons for not doing so'.

Approving *Macphail*[5] the court suggested that after the case is dropped from the roll the pursuer may thereafter lodge a motion to enrol the cause for further procedure and of new to grant warrant to cite the defender. When that motion is heard the defender may move for dismissal, while the pursuer may move the sheriff to grant his motion for further procedure.

Preliminary pleas must be disposed of *in limine*[6]. The appellant must not merely recite the statutory grounds of appeal (see below) but should give proper notice of the matters sought to be argued[7].

The Act of Sederunt is an unhappy piece of drafting which contains a number of dangerous traps for the unwary and has given rise to several interpretational difficulties.

In terms of para 3:

1 *Lorimer's Breweries Ltd v City of Glasgow District Licensing Board*, Glasgow Sheriff Court, 20 October 1980, unreported.
2 See p 305ff below.
3 1978 SLT (Sh Ct) 44.
4 1993 SCLR 266.
5 Para 26-19.
6 *Sutherland v City of Edinburgh District Licensing Board* 1984 SLT 241. See also *Harpspot Ltd v City of Glasgow District Licensing Board* 1992 GWD 6-311.
7 *Sutherland v City of Edinburgh District Licensing Board*, above; see also *Fife Regional Council v Kirkcaldy District Licensing Board (No 1)* 1991 GWD 10-611.

'At the same time as the initial writ is lodged with the sheriff clerk or as soon as may be thereafter, the appellant shall serve a copy of the initial writ –
(a) on the clerk of the licensing board; and
(b) if he was the applicant at the hearing before the licensing board, on all other parties who appeared (whether personally or by means of a representative) at the hearing; and
(c) if he was an objector at that hearing, on the applicant'.

This provision has been construed as imposing a mandatory requirement with no statutory power given to the sheriff to waive compliance. In *Binnie v City of Glasgow District Licensing Board*[1], service was not effected upon 'all other parties' until more than five weeks after lodgement of the writ with the sheriff clerk. The sheriff reached the view that such service had not occurred 'as soon as may be', and, in rejecting an appeal from that decision, the First Division observed:

'As the [appellant's] submission was developed it became clear that [her] only hope of success was in substituting for the words "as soon as may be thereafter" in s 3 of the act of sederunt the words "as soon as it suits the personal convenience of the solicitor concerned"'.

Binnie obliquely suggests that an appellant may not be faulted where he promptly and diligently obtains details of the compearing objectors from the clerk, although a delay may thereby ensue[2].

In *Kaur v Motherwell District Licensing Board*[3] the initial writ was lodged with the sheriff clerk on 21 February; a warrant was granted the following day; and service was effected on 27 February. The delay, which appears to have been attributable to the appellant's difficulty in obtaining an objector's address, was not held to be excessive.

The mandatory effect of para 3 was underscored in *Perfect Swivel Ltd v City of Dundee District Licensing Board (No 1)*[4] in which the initial writ was lodged with the sheriff clerk on 1 May but service upon the chief constable was not effected until 20 June. The First Division rejected the appellants' argument that rule 5 of the Act of Sederunt (Ordinary Cause Rules, Sheriff Court) 1983, SI 1983/747) which came into operation on 1 September 1983, had the effect of extending the dispensing power of the sheriff in terms of rule 1 of the Sheriff Court Ordinary Cause Rules to inter alia para 3, agreeing with the sheriff that rule 1 only applies to breaches of the Sheriff Court Rules and not to statutory rules controlling particular appeals.

Although para 3 is clearly 'mandatory' in the sense that service of the initial writ upon 'all other parties' cannot be waived, the court does, of course, have a discretion to treat *ex facie* late service as having been effected 'as soon as may be' if there are compelling reasons for the delay. The reported cases referred to above provide little assistance as to the manner in which such a discretion should be exercised, mainly concerning as they do appeals in which agents have been dilatory or oblivious to their responsibilities. *Per contra*, in *Padda v Strathkelvin*

---

1 1979 SLT 286.
2 See also the sheriff's comments regarding *Binnie* in *Crolla v City of Edinburgh District Licensing Board* 1983 SLT (Sh Ct) 11.
3 Hamilton Sheriff Court, 4 December 1990, unreported.
4 1993 SLT 109, 1992 GWD 16-932, IH.

District Licensing Board[1], where a delay of only eight days from lodgement with the sheriff clerk to service upon the board and an objector was held to be fatal, the sheriff (A C McKay) observed that: '[I]n this case . . . unlike *Binnie*, the situation does not reveal that the solicitor concerned acted without regard for the time-limits set by the Act of Sederunt' but held that: '[T]hose provisions are mandatory and I have no dispensing power. The delay in service in the present case is short but not *de minimis*'.

Practitioners should thereafter approach the requirements of the Act of Sederunt with a diligence approaching neurosis. In those sheriff clerks' offices where immediate warrants to serve are not usually granted and there is a risk that the warranted initial writ will be delayed in its transmission to the agent, an immediate warrant should nevertheless be requested. It will often be the case that the continued operation of licensed premises is entirely dependent upon the currency of a competent appeal[2] and it is an unhappy solicitor who must explain to his client that he must cease trading and reconcile himself to the licensing board's decision.

In the exceptional circumstances of *Crolla v City of Edinburgh District Licensing Board*[3] it was held that a second appeal, commenced within the time limit, could competently proceed where the original appeal was defective by reason of a failure to crave warrant for service upon an objector. However, where an appeal was dismissed in the pursuer's absence, a second appeal commenced out-of-time was held to be incompetent on the basis that the dismissal should properly have been appealed to the Sheriff Principal[4].

Where there has been a failure to effect timeous service on 'all other parties' the correct plea is to the competency of the appeal, rather than a plea of 'all parties not called'[5]. The expression 'all other parties' has itself created serious difficulty.

In *Padda v Strathkelvin District Licensing Board*[6] the chief constable's representative appeared at the hearing of the appellant's application, not as an objector but simply to provide factual information to the board. The sheriff held that the appellant's failure to serve a copy of the initial writ upon the chief constable was a fatal omission:

'I regard matters of competency such as this as *pars judicis* and I myself raised the question of service of the appeal upon the Chief Constable . . . I was informed that service was not effected upon him . . . The Act of Sederunt requires service on those "who appeared (whether personally or by means of a representative) at the hearing" as I read it; in other words, I do not read the immediately preceding word "parties" as meaning "all others who appeared as parties" . . .'.

This opinion is diametrically opposed to that expressed by the Sheriff Principal (C H Johnston, QC) in *Hutcheon v Hamilton District Licensing Board*[7]:

---

1 1988 SCLR 349.
2 For example, following the refusal of a renewal application: see s 30(5)(b).
3 1983 SLT (Sh Ct) 11.
4 *Khawar v Eastwood District Licensing Board*, Paisley Sheriff Court, 9 May 1991, unreported.
5 See Maxwell *Court of Session Practice* p 193 and *Sangha v Bute and Cowal Divisional Licensing Board* 1990 SCLR 409 at 415–417.
6 1988 SCLR 349. See also 'Licensing Reform' 1991 SLT (News) 271 at 273.
7 1978 SLT (Sh Ct) 44.

'The test of whether, in any particular case, the chief constable is a party "who appeared at the hearing before the licensing board", must be whether or not he has lodged objections at any time before the hearing . . ."[1].

More recently, in *Kaur v Motherwell District Licensing Board*[2] the sheriff considered but declined to follow *Padda* for reasons which were not articulated.

While *Padda* is probably a freakish decision it may not safely be ignored. Indeed, it now has wider implications. Local authorities are now competent objectors (s 16(1)(e)). They have no express entitlement to submit observations but frequently provide the licensing board with factual information[3]. Although the sheriff remarked that: 'The Chief Constable has a statutory interest and certain statutory duties. I do not require to spell out the practical difficulties which would arise were he unaware of an appeal in good time'. If the ratio of *Padda* is correct there is an inevitable logic in the proposition that para 3 would require service of the initial writ upon the local authority where informal comment is made upon an application. As a more marginal consequence, all 'parties', as construed in *Padda*, would require to be furnished with a copy of the statement of reasons (s 18(3)).

The appellant's position is likely to be complicated where the appeal is against the refusal of an application which has attracted a large number of objectors, some or all of whom have appeared at the hearing[4]. The completion of a sederunt sheet by the clerk may help to eliminate later confusion in the appeal process.

In *Transition Interiors Ltd v Eastwood District Licensing Board*[5] the sheriff held that objectors who attended the hearing of an application but did not address the board had not 'appeared' for the purpose of para 3:

'It is . . . significant that para 3 . . . while making reference to "all other parties who appeared", thereafter in parenthesis specifies "Whether personally or by means of a representative". The use of the term "representative" reinforced the view . . . that the Act [of Sederunt] did not envisage physical presence as being sufficient . . .'.

Nevertheless, while this decision may well be correct, it cannot be followed with any degree of safety.

It also requires to be kept in view that where objections to an application take the form of a petition it is commonplace for a limited number of signatories to address the board, essentially as representatives for other signatories who are in attendance but choose not to speak.

Where an appeal arises from the determination of a complaint (eg under s 31 or s 65) there is no 'applicant' as such, leading to the suggesting in *Macphail*[6] that there is a *lacuna* in para 3 of the Act of Sederunt. An argument to that effect was

---

1 The chief may now submit observations in relation to certain types of applications (see s 16A) and no doubt thus becomes a party.
2 Hamilton Sheriff Court, 4 December 1990, unreported.
3 Although the supply of information is sometimes open to construction as an objection in substance if not in form; cf *Centralbite Ltd v Kincardine and Deeside District Licensing Board* 1989 SCLR 652, 1990 SLT 231.
4 There is, of course, no requirement for an objector/appellant to serve a copy of the initial writ upon other objectors, although this was the effect of the Act of Sederunt until it was amended by SI 1979/1520. See *Russell v Ross* 1980 SLT 10.
5 Paisley Sheriff Court, 2 May 1990, unreported.
6 Para 26-13 and footnote.

advanced but rejected in *Perfect Swivel Ltd v City of Dundee District Licensing Board (No 1)*[1], an appeal from the board's decision to suspend the appellant's licence for one year under s 31. The First Division held that the chief constable was to be regarded as 'the applicant' because he had applied for suspension of the licence, while the licenceholder was 'the objector' at the hearing of the complaint because he objected to the suspension being granted.

Grounds of appeal

Section 39(4) provides that:

'The sheriff may[2] uphold an appeal under this section only if he considers that the licensing board in arriving at its decision:
(a) erred in law;
(b) based its decision on any incorrect material fact;
(c) acted contrary to natural justice; or
(d) exercised its discretion in an unreasonable manner'.

The boundaries between these categories (which are discussed further below) are apt to be blurred and there is therefore an understandable tendency for pleaders to seek safety by founding appeals on all four grounds.

A failure to define 'locality' for the purpose of s 17(1)(d) is not, as one might imagine, an error in law. In *Scott Catering & Offshore Services Ltd v City of Aberdeen District Licensing Board*[3] the sheriff held inter alia that:

'In the circumstances I must sustain the pursuers' argument on lack of definition of the locality for the purpose of assessing over-provision. To that extent the respondents must be deemed to have erred in law. . .',

but in *Botterills of Blantyre v Hamilton District Licensing Board*[4] the board's failure to decide upon the locality amounted to the grounding of its decision upon an incorrect material fact. This distinction was emphasised in *Art Wells Ltd (t/a Corals) v Glasgow District Licensing Board*[5] in which the sheriff (A C Horsfall) said:

'[Counsel for the appellants] relied on the opinion of the court in *Botterills of Blantyre v Hamilton District Licensing Board*. In my opinion, however, that provides no authority for the proposition that such a failure constitutes an error in law. As was pointed out in *Botterills*, where a licensing board is considering the provision applicable to liquor licensing which relates to the over-provision of facilities in any locality, it must first decide what is the locality which is to be looked at. But it is clear that it must do so, not as a matter of law, but as an essential first step in the reasoning process . . .'.

1 1993 SLT 109, 1992 GWD 16-932, IH.
2 For a consideration of the effect of the word 'may' see *McIndoe v Glasgow District Licensing Board* 1989 SCLR 325 at 330.
3 1987 GWD 22-823, Sh Ct.
4 1986 SLT 14.
5 1988 SCLR 48, aff'd 1988 SCLR 531.

Where a board granted an application for the grant of a new licence which proceeded upon an inaccurate certificate of suitability in relation to planning, it was held that it had erred in law; but if it had been aware of the inaccuracy it could be inferred that it had based its decision on an incorrect material fact[1].

Irregularities in voting procedure (see below) amount to an error in law, rather than a breach of natural justice. In *Najafian v Glasgow District Licensing Board*[2] the sheriff held:

'I am satisfied that the respondents failed to observe the provisions of section 5(7) by failing to express their individual votes in public and thus erred in law. I am not satisfied, however, that such a failure also constitutes a breach of the principles of natural justice',

although it has also been observed that a board's failure to vote in public may preclude parties:

'from appealing upon the ground that the principles of natural justice were not applied because a member of the board ought to have declined to vote upon the ground that he had a personal interest to vote as he did'[3].

The rigid application of a policy which fetters the exercise of discretion may amount both to an error in law and a breach of the rules of natural justice[4].

A licensing board's failure to put to an applicant for comment matters considered to be germane has been held to be contrary to natural justice[5] and an unreasonable exercise of discretion[6].

The sheriff may hear evidence by or on behalf of any party, irrespective of the ground of appeal (s 39(5), as amended by the 1990 Act, Sch 8, para 11(3)) to overcome the difficulty identified in *Tennent Caledonian Breweries Ltd v City of Aberdeen District Licensing Board*[7].

Error in law

Error in law 'includes ignorance or disregard or misinterpretation of any rule of statute'[8]. It occurs where the law has been misapplied or misunderstood as, for example, by the refusal of an application on incompetent grounds[9]; or where the licensing board has asked itself the wrong question[10]. A failure to follow the correct voting procedure also amounts to an error in law.

Section 5(7) provides that proceedings in relation to the matters mentioned in

---

1 *Donald v Stirling District Licensing Board* 1992 SCLR (Notes) 369.
2 1987 SCLR 679.
3 *Simpson v Banff and Buchan District Licensing Boards* 1991 SCLR 24, 1991 SLT 18 per Lord Dunpark.
4 *Aitken v City of Glasgow District Council* 1988 SCLR 287.
5 *William Hill (Scotland) Ltd v Kyle and Carrick District Licensing Board* 1991 SCLR 375, 1991 SLT 559.
6 *Mount Charlotte Investments plc v City of Glasgow District Licensing Board* 1991 SCLR 311.
7 1987 SLT (Sh Ct) 2.
8 Walker *Civil Remedies* p 166. See also 1 *Stair Memorial Encyclopaedia* paras 285ff.
9 *Mount Charlotte Investments plc v City of Glasgow Licensing Board* 1992 SCLR 311; see also *D & A Haddow Ltd v City of Glasgow District Licensing Board* 1983 SLT (Sh Ct) 5.
10 *Singh and Kaur v Kirkcaldy District Licensing Board* 1988 SLT 286. See also *Fereneze Leisure Ltd v Renfrew District Licensing Board* 1991 SCLR 751, 1992 SLT 604.

s 5(2) (which may only be considered at a meeting of the board and not under a delegated powers arrangement):

'shall be held in public, but a licensing board may retire to consider its decision in any such matter and the clerk of the board shall accompany the board when it so retires unless the board otherwise directs'.

In *Najafian v Glasgow District Licensing Board*[1] the board simply announced its decision in public after considering the application in private. No voting took place. The sheriff held that:

'[T]he mere declaration by the chairman of the result of deliberations held in private, whether that declaration is said to be unanimous or not, cannot be said to constitute voting in the context of this section. When the section is read as a whole it is perfectly clear that it was the intention of Parliament that the whole decision making process of a licensing board, including voting, should be carried out in public'.

The Inner House has emphasised the high standard which is required for compliance with s 5(7). In *Simpson v Banff and Buchan District Licensing Boards*[2] the board had retired to consider its decision. Upon its return a motion for suspension of the licence was made and seconded. Without further procedure the chairman pronounced suspension of the licence. The Second Division held that there had been a failure to observe the provisions of s 5(7): '[T]he board's decision must be taken in public in such a way that it is plain to the public how each member of the board would have voted, if a formal vote had been necessary'. It would apparently have been sufficient if the board's chairman had ascertained that (a) there was no counter-motion and (b) the decision to suspend the licence was unanimous without any abstention.

Although it is frequently obvious that licensing boards have reached concluded decisions during private retirals and the subsequent public voting is simply an open declaration of the result, in *Simpson* Lord Dunpark gave the clearest indication that such a practice is unsound:

'I do not consider that it can be said positively that this decision to suspend the respondent's licence was *made* in public . . . "the decision" must undoubtedly be made in public and not in the back room'.

It thus appears that where a board returns to the public meeting after a retiral and, as sometimes happens, the chairman immediately announces the existence of a division among members such a statement alone constitutes a fatal flaw, even if motions for grant and refusal are properly made, seconded and voted upon.

On the other hand, in *Stephen v City of Aberdeen District Licensing Board*[3] the sheriff (A M G Russell, CBE, QC) recognised without any disapproval the realities of decision-making and voting:

1 1987 SCLR 679, following *Solway Leisure Ltd v Perth and Kinross District Licensing Board*, reported as an addendum to *Najafian* at 681.
2 1991 SCLR 24, 1991 SLT 18, followed in *McKay v Banff and Buchan Western Division Licensing Board* 1991 SCLR 15, 1991 SLT 20.
3 1989 SLT (Sh Ct) 94.

'On returning to the hearing the call over how each member voted was, in accordance with practice, to show publicly the decision that each member *had already reached* [author's emphasis] during their retirement'.

Where the board's chairman announced refusal of an application it was not sufficient for other board members to signal their agreement by simply nodding their heads in assent[1].

Per contra, silence was construed as indicating assent in *David Kelbie Properties Ltd v City of Dundee Licensing Board*[2]. Following submissions on behalf of the appellants and the chief constable (who was an objector) and without any retiral, the board's chairman invited members to propose motions. Silence ensued. The chairman then moved refusal of the application. The motion was not seconded and no one actively expressed agreement. The chairman then announced that the application had been refused. The sheriff (A L Stewart) found 'with some hesitation' that the board had narrowly complied with the terms of s 5(7), distinguishing *Najafian* and *Simpson* on the basis that: 'There could thus be no question of a decision taken in private during retiral simply being rubber-stamped in public without a vote', while emphasising that he did not intend to approve of the procedure which had been adopted[3].

The public voting requirement embraces all aspects of the board's decision. Where a board had determined to impose a restriction order in terms of s 65 its decision was vitiated by a failure to vote in public upon the duration of the order[4].

It is an error in law for a licensing board to find a ground of refusal established where there is 'insufficient material before it to entitle it to establish that ground'[5].

Incorrect material fact

The appellant must set forth the incorrect material facts founded upon and aver that the board's decision was affected by these errors.[6] Where an appellant has failed to request a statement of reasons it may be impossible to do so.[7]

This ground of appeal is apposite not only where statements of fact made to the board are found to be incorrect but also where there has been an erroneous inference from *correct* facts:

'[A] conclusion in fact drawn by inference is in no different a position from a finding in fact based upon direct evidence. If there are no reasonable grounds to support the inference from established facts the conclusion is factually incorrect and, if material, this would justify the intervention of the sheriff . . .'[8].

1 *Transition Interiors Ltd v Eastwood District Licensing Board*, Paisley Sheriff Court, 2 April 1992, unreported.
2 Dundee Sheriff Court, 7 August 1991, unreported.
3 See also *Ladbroke Racing (Strathclyde) Ltd v Cunninghame District Licensing Court* 1978 SLT (Sh Ct) 77.
4 *Devana Investments Ltd v City of Aberdeen Licensing Board* 1992 SCLR 616.
5 *Moughal v Motherwell District Licensing Board* 1983 SLT (Sh Ct) 84.
6 *Aitken v City of Glasgow District Council* 1988 SCLR 287.
7 *Coppola v Midlothian District Licensing Board* 1983 SLT (Sh Ct) 95.
8 *Art Wells Ltd (t/a Corals) v Glasgow District Licensing Board* 1988 SCLR 531; see also the sheriff's comments in *Loosefoot Entertainment Ltd v Glasgow District Licensing Board* 1990 SCLR 584 at 588 (Sh Ct), aff'd 1991 SLT 843, IH.

A finding in fact with no evidential basis may possibly also amount to an error in law[1] and an unreasonable exercise of discretion[2].

A board's failure to disclose to the applicant a material fact influencing its decision constitutes a breach of natural justice[3]. The approach which should be taken where material facts are in dispute is discussed below.

Since the sheriff may hear evidence in the course of the appeal (irrespective of the ground) (s 39(5)) it is perfectly conceivable that he may be 'in a better position than the board to evaluate the factual evidence'[4]. It is virtually (but not absolutely) unknown for licensing boards to put witnesses on oath[5] and render them liable to cross-examination so that where the court hears evidence in the usual way the board's factual findings will not 'have the sanctity of the verdict of a jury'[6].

Where an appeal succeeds on the ground that the board has acted contrary to natural justice[7] such a finding has a 'concussive effect' on its decision[8] and a failure to advance an argument based on 'incorrect material fact' is of no significance[9].

Natural justice[10]

The Act provides little assistance as to the manner in which licensing boards should approach applications, objections or complaints[11], although they have a limited opportunity to supplement the statutory provisions by the making of regulations (s 37). They are bound to 'consider' applications (s 15(1)) and objections (s 16(5)) and to 'have regard' to observations by the chief constable (s 16A(5)).

There are sundry references throughout the Act to hearings (eg in s 13(1) and s 15(2)) but even where no express right to be heard is conferred it will usually be implied[12].

Although a board has the freedom to perform its functions as it pleases 'in so far as it is not bound by statute'[13] proceedings must be conducted in a quasi-judicial manner[14] and with proper regard for the rules of natural justice[15].

This requirement has produced a large number of reported decisions which fall

1 See *Moughal v Motherwell District Licensing Board* 1983 SLT (Sh Ct) 84.
2 *Noble Organisation Ltd v City of Glasgow District Council (No 1)* 1990 SCLR 393, 1990 SLT 554.
3 See below; and *Freeland v City of Glasgow Licensing Board* 1980 SLT 101 at 104.
4 *Martin v Ellis* 1978 SLT (Sh Ct) 38, where it was also suggested that 'it may be misleading' to examine a board's decision on an issue of fact as an exercise of discretion (s 39(4)(d).
5 Whether they have the power to do so may be open to doubt: see *Board of Education v Rice* [1911] AC 179 and *Local Government Board v Arlidge* [1915] AC 120.
6 *Martin v Ellis*, above. See also 'The hearing of evidence', below.
7 See below.
8 *McIndoe v City of Glasgow District Licensing Board* 1989 SCLR 325 at 329 and 330.
9 *McIndoe*, above; *Lorimer's Breweries Ltd v City of Glasgow District Licensing Board*, Glasgow Sheriff Court, 20 October 1980, unreported.
10 See also 1 *Stair Memorial Encyclopaedia* 249ff.
11 See *Martin v Ellis* 1978 SLT (Sh Ct) 38 at 40.
12 *C R S Leisure Ltd v Dumbarton District Licensing Board* 1989 SCLR 566, 1990 SLT 200. See also *Inland Revenue v Barrs* 1961 SC (HL) 22 at 30 per Lord Reid.
13 *Fitzpatrick v Glasgow District Licensing Board* 1978 SLT (Sh Ct) 63.
14 *Kieran v Adams* 1979 SLT (Sh Ct) 13.
15 See generally Walker *Civil Remedies* pp 165 and 166.

into the broad categories discussed below. If an appeal is set to succeed on this ground the court will not entertain an argument that the board in any event arrived at the right decision: 'I think we should be slow to encourage the idea that these principles [of natural justice] could be safely disregarded so long as it could be proved that no positive injustice had resulted[1].'

The hearing of evidence

In *Cigaro (Glasgow) Ltd v City of Glasgow District Licensing Board*[2], an appeal against the refusal of a gaming licence, the First Division held that '[A] refusal to hear evidence, whatever else it may amount to is not *in itself* an act contrary to natural justice' (author's emphasis). However, this statement requires to be viewed with some caution. In *Cigaro* the board was not invited to hear evidence (because, it was averred, such a motion would inevitably have been refused); the appellants did not contend that they were prevented from putting material before the board; and there was no evidence of the nature and scope of the evidence which the board would have been invited to hear[3].

Indeed, in *McIndoe v Glasgow District Licensing Board*[4] the sheriff (G Evans) observed that:

'The coolness of these comments [in *Cigaro*] was, I would venture to suggest due to the fact that. . . there was no overt breach of natural justice by the [licensing] board . . . in the sense of actively refusing to allow evidence to be heard . . . the appellants not being able to point to any feature that might have amounted to prejudice'.

Here, the appellant was unable to demonstrate that he had received less than a sufficiently full hearing, despite the refusal of a motion to allow the leading of evidence and the showing of a video recording.

Where an uncontested application for a new licence was refused on the ground inter alia that the premises would be frequented by children and young persons, the sheriff rejected the appellants' argument that no factual conclusion could be reached without enquiry:

'It should be made clear that no evidence, in the court sense of that word, was heard at all in this application. The case was presented, as is very frequently the practice, by the pursuers' solicitor in an *ex parte* statement[5]. A licensing board itself is not in a position to lead evidence – it is an administrative decision not based on adversarial grounds like cases in court. Therefore, when the defenders heard that young persons came in family groups

---

1 *Barrs v British Wool Marketing Board* 1957 SLT 153 at 160 per Lord Sorn, referred to in *McIndoe v Glasgow District Licensing Board* 1989 SCLR 325 at 330; see also *R v Thames Magistrates Court ex parte Polemis* [1974] 1 WLR 1371 at 1375 and 1376; and *Maxwell v Department of Trade* [1974] QB 523 at 540.
2 1983 SLT 549.
3 Cf *W S Murphy Ltd v Renfrew Burgh Licensing Court* 1973 SLT (Sh Ct) 18, in which the sheriff said: 'In my opinion, where a party intimates to a licensing court that he desires to lead competent evidence which is relevant to the matter in issue before them, and the court refuse to hear that evidence and then go on to make an order that is adverse to that party, they act quite unreasonably and unjustly, and cannot be said to have conducted their proceedings judicially'.
4 1989 SCLR 325.
5 See also *Fitzpatrick v Glasgow District Licensing Board* 1978 SLT (Sh Ct) 63 at 64 for the express approval of *ex parte* statements.

that was not an adminicle of evidence that they were bound to accept wholly as put by the pursuers'[1].

Nevertheless, despite some disharmony among the authorities, there are a number of shrieval decisions which suggest that a board should not proceed on the basis of *ex parte* statements where material facts are in dispute, creating a real *lis* between, say, an applicant and an objector (provided, of course, that the appropriate motion is made).

In *Lennon v Monklands District Licensing Board*[2], a contested Sunday opening application, the sheriff (A L Stewart) held that a board could only resolve matters in contention by 'leading evidence from witnesses who can be cross-examined'. Similarly, in *Richmond v Renfrew District Licensing Board*[3] the sheriff held that it was the board's duty to investigate the authenticity of signatures to an objection petition where they had been called into question by the applicant's agent:

'No evidence was led from any of the petitioners to support the truth of the allegations contained in the petition. This practice might be acceptable where the contents of the petition are not in dispute, but where there is any question as to the authenticity of any signatures . . . and where the facts stated therein are disputed it is the duty of the board to investigate the matter'.

The ethos of these decisions is in more or less direct opposition to the view expressed by the late Sheriff Principal (F W F O'Brien, QC) in *Martin v Ellis*[4]; and in *Russo v Hamilton Licensing Court*[5] the sheriff-substitute thought that it would be 'monstrous' if a chief constable were to be subject to cross-examination when making a report to the court.

The approach in *Lennon* was approved in *Lorimer's Breweries Ltd v City of Glasgow District Licensing Board*[6], in which the board had refused a motion to allow evidence to be heard regarding alleged incidents of disorder reported to them by the chief constable.

Many licensing boards have, of course, a large volume of applications to consider, many of which may be contentious. An obligation to put factual disputes to enquiry raises the spectre of extremely lengthy meetings. Sheriff Macphail expressly rejected such a consideration:

'Much has been said in this appeal, and, in others, about the volume of business which this board is required to transact . . .; but administrative convenience, in itself, cannot be accepted as a valid excuse for failure to comply with the requirements of natural justice. "Convenience and justice are often not on speaking terms" '[7].

1 *Scott Catering and Offshore Services Ltd v City of Aberdeen District Licensing Board* 1987 GWD 22-823, Sh Ct.
2 Airdrie Sheriff Court, 24 May 1978, unreported.
3 Paisley Sheriff Court, 9 June 1983, unreported.
4 1978 SLT (Sh Ct) 38 at 40.
5 1971 SLT (Sh Ct) 63.
6 Glasgow Sheriff Court, 20 October 1980, unreported.
7 This aphorism is taken from *General Medical Council v Spackman* [1943] AC 627 at 638 per Lord Atkin.

It may be remarked in passing that the potential protraction of board meetings was not a factor which impressed the sheriff (I G Pirie) in *Najafian v Glasgow District Licensing Board*[1] when it was argued on behalf of the board that a vote upon each application would result in the proceedings being 'unnecessarily prolonged'.

Curiously, more than a decade elapsed before the appearance of a reported decision which essentially homologates the judgment in *Lorimer's Breweries Ltd*. In *Devana Investments Ltd v City of Aberdeen Licensing Board*[2] the licenceholders, who were the subject of a complaint by the chief constable in terms of s 65, were denied an opportunity to lead evidence in relation to ten out of twenty incidents of alleged disorder found to be 'established' by the board. The sheriff (A M G Russell, CBE, QC) held that:

'To accept a disputed version of the material and vital facts in the teeth of a motion to be allowed to lead evidence is courting disaster and disregarding the natural laws of justice'.

If these shrieval decisions are correct, there remains to be considered the manner in which evidence should be obtained by boards. The paucity of helpful material makes it impossible to arrive at any clear conclusion. It may be that boards are not empowered to put witnesses on oath[3].

In *Lorimer's Breweries Ltd*[4] the sheriff tended to the view that cross-examination should be permitted, but was, however, at pains to emphasise that:
(a) the board was not restricted to hearing evidence which would be admissible in accordance with the rules of evidence which are applicable in a court of law; and
(b) hearsay evidence would be admissible provided that the party against whom it is adduced has a proper opportunity of controverting the case against him.

He also referred to the following dicta of Diplock, LJ (as he then was) in *R v Deputy Industrial Injuries Commissioner ex parte Moore*[5]:

'The requirement that a person exercising quasi-judicial functions must base his decision on evidence means no more than it must be based upon material which tends logically to show the existence or non-existence of the facts relevant to the issue to be determined, or to show the likelihood or unlikelihood of the occurrence of some future event the occurrence of which would be relevant. It means that he must not spin a coin or consult an astrologer, but he may take into account any material which, as a matter of reason has some probative value . . .'.

In England, it has been held that:

'Licensing courts and authorities dealing with licensing matters are not bound by the strict rules of evidence and they can therefore, and properly do, accept hearsay evidence or unproved documents. Again, what weight they attach to such evidence is a matter for them to consider'[6].

The nature and extent of a board's obligations in this troubled area are patently ripe for clarification.

---

1 1987 SCLR 679.
2 1992 SCLR 616.
3 See *Board of Education v Rice* [1911] AC 179; *Local Government Board v Arlidge* [1915] AC 120.
4 See above.
5 [1965] 1 QB 456 at 488.
6 *R v Manchester Crown Court ex parte Dransfield Novelty Co Ltd* 1972 unreported, per Glidewell, J.

The right to make representations

Parties to an application have a right to be heard, even where the Act is silent as to procedure:

'[T]he silence of s 64 as to hearings would not in itself suggest to me that there is any right in a board to proceed to a refusal without giving the applicant some opportunity . . . to deal with any adverse points raised by objections or regarded by the board as possible grounds for refusal'[1].

If a board is minded to reach a decision for particular reasons it is 'elementary justice . . . that the applicant or objector should be told about it so that he may have an opportunity of meeting it or commenting upon it[2].'

Similarly, it must not proceed upon confidential information which a party to an application has no opportunity of correcting or contradicting[3].

While licensing board members may bring their personal knowledge to bear the nature and extent of that knowledge must be disclosed[4]. There is otherwise a risk that a party will be precluded from appealing on the ground that the board based its decision on incorrect material fact (s 39(4)(b)). Accordingly, in *Freeland v City of Glasgow District Licensing Board*[5] the Second Division held that:

'[T]he rules of natural justice preclude a board from taking a decision against a party . . . which is based, either wholly or in part upon a fact or facts within the knowledge of the board without disclosure of that fact or those facts to that party for his comments'[6].

It is an unreasonable exercise of discretion for a board to suppose that a defect of this nature may simply be rectified upon appeal[7].

In *Khullar v City of Glasgow District Licensing Board*[8] a failure by the board to challenge the applicant's description of locality for the purpose of a new licence application was held *not* to amount to a breach of natural justice. The sheriff (B A Lockhart) considered that it was 'quite impractical' to expect the board to retire, make a provisional decision on the question of locality and then put that

1 *C R S Leisure Ltd v Dumbarton District Licensing Board* 1989 SCLR 566, 1990 SLT 200; cf *J & J Inns Ltd v Angus District Licensing Board* 1992 SCLR 683 in which Lord Weir reserved his opinion as to whether an applicant under s 25(3) is entitled to a hearing.
2 *Freeland v City of Glasgow District Licensing Board* 1980 SLT 101 at 104 per Lord Kissen, followed in *William Hill (Scotland) Ltd v Kyle and Carrick District Licensing Board* 1991 SCLR 375, 1991 SLT 559. See also *Tomkins v City of Glasgow District Licensing Board* 1991 GWD 39-2410, Ex Div; *Hunt v City of Glasgow District Council* 1987 SCLR 244; *G A Estate Agency Ltd v City of Glasgow District Council* 1991 SCLR 8, 1991 SLT 16; *Tong v City of Glasgow District Licensing Board* 1992 GWD 19-1125, Sh Ct.
3 *R v Secretary of State for Home Affairs ex parte Hosenball* [1977] 1 WLR 766. See also *University of Ceylon v Fernando* [1960] 1 WLR 223; and *Kanda v Government of the Federation of Malaya* [1962] AC 322.
4 *Robertson v Inverclyde Licensing Board* 1979 SLT (Sh Ct) 16. See also *Goodall v Bilsland* (1909) 1 SLT 376 at 380 and 381.
5 1980 SLT 101.
6 See also *Charles Watson (Scotland) Ltd v Glasgow District Licensing Board* 1980 SLT (Sh Ct) 37, in which it was held that non-disclosure also amounted to an error in law; *Mecca Ltd v Kirkcaldy Burgh Licensing Court* 1975 SLT (Sh Ct) 50; *Ahmed v Stirling District Licensing Board* 1980 SLT (Sh Ct) 51; and *Moughal v Motherwell District Licensing Board* 1983 SLT (Sh Ct) 84.
7 *Ahmed v Stirling District Licensing Board*, above.
8 Glasgow Sheriff Court, 21 August 1991, unreported.

decision to the applicant for comment: it was simply sufficient that the applicant's agent had been given an opportunity to address the board on the matter.

On the other hand, a refusal of a new licence based on a finding of overprovision was unfair where that ground had not been put in issue by the board at the hearing of the application[1].

Each party must be given an equal opportunity to state his case. In terms of the familiar dictum of Lord Hewart, CJ in *R v Sussex Justices ex parte McCarthy*[2] it is '. . . of fundamental importance that justice should not only be done, but should manifestly and undoubtedly be seen to be done'.

Accordingly, the mere silent presence of an interested party during a board's private discussions will vitiate its decision[3].

In *Coppola v Midlothian District Licensing Board*[4] the Director of Environmental Health's retiral with the board to their deliberations on a renewal application was held to be a breach of natural justice:

'No matter what the director might have said or not said at the private discussion, the appellant was bound to feel that the respondents had had an opportunity to hear more of one side of the case than the other'[5].

Similarly, the failure of a licensing committee to allow an applicant for an amusement-with-prizes machine permit[6] to deal with representations made by the assistant chief constable after she had left the committee meeting was held to be contrary to the rules of natural justice[7].

Although 'the clerk of the board shall accompany the board when it . . . retires unless the board otherwise directs' (s 5(7)), in the somewhat unusual circumstances of *Low v Kincardineshire Licensing Court*[8] it was held that the refusal of a betting office licence was vitiated by the presence of the depute clerk of the licensing court during the court's private deliberations where he had signed a letter of objection to the application on behalf of the town council.

It is unclear whether a licenceholder is entitled to make a plea *ad misericordiam* in an attempt to limit the nature of the penalty where a licensing board has decided to impose a sanction[9].

In *Stephen v City of Aberdeen District Licensing Board*[10] the sheriff (A M G Russell, CBE, QC) found that it was incumbent upon the licenceholder's agent 'to present all his arguments in favour of his client before the board retire', dismissing any similarity with criminal trial procedure. *Per contra*, a diametri-

1 *Tomkins v City of Glasgow District Licensing Board* 1991 GWD 39-2410, Ex Div.
2 [1924] 1 KB 256, [1923] All ER Rep 233.
3 *Barrs v British Wool Marketing Board* 1957 SC 72, 1957 SLT 153, followed recently in *Intascot plc v Inverclyde District Council* 1992 GWD 21-1238, Sh Ct.
4 1983 SLT (Sh Ct) 95.
5 See also *Kanda v Government of the Federation of Malaya* [1962] AC 322 at 337 per Lord Denning.
6 Gaming Act 1968, s 34.
7 *Jack v Edinburgh Corporation* 1974 SLT (Sh Ct) 64. See also *R v Merthyr Tydfil Justices* (1885) 14 QBD 584.
8 1974 SLT (Sh Ct) 54.
9 Under, for example, s 31.
10 1989 SLT (Sh Ct) 94.

cally opposite view was expressed in *McIndoe v Glasgow District Licensing Board*[1]. In virtually identical circumstances the sheriff (G Evans) held that:

'[T]he fact that [suspension of a licence] may have penal consequences to the licence holder has the result that a licensing authority must be very careful to ensure that they adhere strictly to the principles of natural justice. . . If I may adapt the words in *Falconer*[2] to fit the instant context: "It should be said very clearly that no licensing authority is entitled to depart from the ordinary rules of fair conduct and one of the rights which a licenceholder has is to speak in mitigation before suspension is passed".'

It would appear that where information is laid before a board by one party of which another has no prior notice the rules of natural justice will not be broken unless the party averring prejudice moved for and was refused an adjournment:

'There is no suggestion that [the board] told counsel [for the pursuers] that no postponement . . . would be allowed. It must therefore be assumed that, if any such motion had been made, it would have been considered by [the board] . . .. If [the board] had refused such a motion there would almost certainly have been a breach of the rules of natural justice. However, neither of these things happened as no such motion was in fact made. I therefore reject counsel for the pursuers' submission on this point'[3].

Prejudice and bias

Apart from the categories of statutory disqualification (s 2)[4] a licensing board member may in certain circumstances also be disabled from adjudicating upon applications at common law if his impartiality is open to challenge. The protection of the grant of a new licence from objection on the ground of disqualification under s 2 (see s 2(6)) does not apply[5].

While the maxim *nemo iudex in causa sua*[6] applies, objection may be 'not in the nature of interest, but of a challenge to the favour'[7].

The effect of a finding of prejudice or bias is not entirely clear. It has been said that where a board has acted contrary to natural justice the effect on its decision is 'concussive'[8]. A board member's temporary absence from the bench during the hearing of an application[9] may vitiate the whole proceedings[10]; but in *Blaik v Anderson*[11] Lord Strachan remarked that a (putative) statutory disqualification 'would probably go no further than to discount the vote'[12].

Much more recently, in an appeal under the Civic Government (Scotland) Act

---

1 1989 SCLR 325.
2 *Falconer v Jessop* 1975 SLT (Notes) 78.
3 *Tennent Caledonian Breweries Ltd v City of Aberdeen District Licensing Board* 1987 SLT (Sh Ct) 2.
4 See Chapter 1.
5 *Ower v Crichton* (1902) 10 SLT 271; *R v Gee* (1901) 17 TLR 374.
6 'I do not know any rule more fundamental than that a man shall not be judge in his own cause': *Blaik v Anderson* (1899) 7 SLT 299 per Lord Strachan. See also *Lockhart v Irving* 1936 SLT 567.
7 *R v Rand* (1866) 1 QB 230 per Blackburn, J.
8 *McIndoe v City of Glasgow District Licensing Board* 1989 SCLR 325 at 329 and 330.
9 See p 295 below.
10 *Goodall v Bilsland* 1909 SC 1152, (1909) 1 SLT 376. See also *Barrs v British Wool Marketing Board* 1957 SC 72 at 78, 1957 SLT 153 at 160; and 1 *Stair Memorial Encyclopaedia* para 284.
11 (1899) 7 SLT 299.
12 At 301.

1982[1], the Second Division expressed the opinion obiter that 'even if the views of one particular member were prejudiced this would not necessarily invalidate the decision of the committee taken as a whole'[2].

The mere possibility of bias is not sufficient for disqualification but actual bias need not have been established. Various tests have been suggested: 'real likelihood'[3], 'reasonable suspicion'[4], 'real risk'[5], and 'probability'[6] of prejudice.

It now seems settled that the court will apply the 'reasonable man' standard propounded as follows in *Law v Chartered Institute of Patent Agents*[7]:

'[I]f there are circumstances so affecting a person acting in a judicial capacity as to be calculated to create in the mind of a reasonable man a suspicion of that person's impartiality, those circumstances are themselves sufficient to disqualify although in fact no bias exists'[8].

Emphasising that 'justice must be rooted in confidence', in *Metropolitan Properties Co (FGC) Ltd v Lannon*[9] Lord Denning observed that:

'There must be circumstances from which a reasonable man would think it likely or probable that the justice, or chairman, as the case may be, would, or did, favour one side unfairly . . . The court will not inquire whether he did, in fact, favour one side unfairly. Suffice it that reasonable people might think he did'[10].

A pecuniary interest will raise a presumption of bias no matter how small if it is personal and direct[11]. The grant of a public house licence was reduced where three of the justices who participated and voted were shareholders in the company owning the application premises, although the whole profits of the public house were to be devoted to public purposes[12].

The organising secretary of 'The Vigilance Society' (dedicated to the promotion of temperance and the suppression of drunkenness) was 'rightly interdicted' from taking part in licensing court decisions[13].

1 *Piper v Kyle and Carrick District Council* 1988 SLT 267.
2 At 269. The issue in this case was whether discretion had been reasonably exercised.
3 *McDonald v Finlay* 1957 SLT 81; *R v Sunderland Justices* [1901] 2 KB 357; *R v Peterborough Compensation Authority* [1934] BTRLR 102. Cf *Kanda v Government of the Federation of Malaya* [1962] AC 322 at 337 per Lord Denning: 'The court will not go into the likelihood of prejudice. The risk of it is enough'.
4 *R v Sheffield Confirming Authority ex parte Truswell's Brewery Co Ltd* [1937] 4 All ER 114. The conflict between 'real likelihood' and 'reasonable suspicion' is discussed by Davies, LJ in *Metropolitan Properties Co. (FGC) Ltd v Lannon* [1969] 1 QB 577 at 604–606. See also de Smith's *Judicial Review of Administrative Action* (4th edn) p 262ff.
5 *Tennent Caledonian Breweries Ltd v City of Aberdeen District Licensing Board* 1987 SLT (Sh Ct) 2.
6 *R v Tempest* (1902) 18 TLR 433.
7 1919] 2 Ch 276 at 289.
8 Approved by the High Court in *Bradford v McLeod* 1985 SCCR 379; 1986 SLT 244. See also *Tennant v Houston* 1987 SLT 317, criticised in P W Ferguson 'Nemo Iudex in Sua Causa?' 1987 SLT (News) 149; and *Hannamm v Bradford Corpn* [1970] 1 WLR 937 at 949 per Cross, LJ.
9 [1969] 1 QB 577 at 599.
10 Cf *R v Barnsley Licensing Justices ex parte Barnsley and District Licensed Victuallers' Association* [1960] 2 QB 167 at 187 per Devlin, LJ; and *R v Cambourne Justices ex parte Pearce* [1955] 1 QB 41, [1954] 2 All ER 850.
11 *Wildridge v Anderson* (1897) 25 R (J) 27. See also *McDonald v Finlay* 1957 SLT 81.
12 *Blaik v Anderson* (1899) 7 SLT 299.
13 *Goodall v Bilsland* 1909 SC 1152, (1909) 1 SLT 376.

It has also been held, in England, that the refusal of an application could not be allowed to stand where a licensing justice, who was a crusading teetotaller, subsequently wrote that he would have been 'nothing less than a traitor' if he had voted in favour[1]; and that a licensing justice was not entitled to adjudicate upon a transfer application where, as a member of a voluntary association hostile to all licences, he had attended a meeting which resolved to oppose the transfer, although he had left the meeting prior to that decision[2].

In such circumstances it will make no difference that the interested party, while sitting on the bench, does not vote[3].

However, a member of a temperance society merely in sympathy with the society's objects who took no active rôle in its 'practical campaign' was unlikely to be disqualified, even where he subscribed to its funds: 'There is nothing illegal in persons thinking that the more you reduce licences the more you promote the cause of temperance'[4].

The canvassing of licensing board members by another member may result in a decision being set aside[5]. Where a justice wrote to his colleagues in opposition to the confirmation of a new licence and took part in its refusal the justices' decision was quashed[6]; but bias was not established where justices whose decision was the subject of appeal encouraged other justices to attend the appeal hearing[7].

It is now possible to lead evidence that a board member has demonstrated prejudice by improper behaviour[8], a development which will no doubt lead to further, understandable discomfiture on the shrieval bench[9]. In *Tennent Caledonian Breweries Ltd v City of Aberdeen District Licensing Board*[10] it was averred that one board member 'brandished his papers and stated in a loud voice that the complaint [by the chief constable] and its schedules manifested a "disgraceful catalogue" of events' before any submissions as to the merits of the complaint had been made on behalf of the licenceholder. While the sheriff could not look behind the board's denials on record[11], he expressed the opinion that a full admission of the pursuers' averments would have compelled him to hold that the continued

1 *R v Halifax Justices ex parte Robinson* (1912) 76 JP 233.
2 *R v Fraser* (1893) 9 TLR 613. See also *R v Maldon Justices* [1930] BTRLR 85.
3 *R v Justices of Hertfordshire* (1845) 6 QB 753, cited with approval in *Blaik v Anderson* (1899) 7 SLT 299; *R v Malvern Justices ex parte Cosgrove* [1948] Brewing Tr Rev 413; cf *R v Howard, Licensing Justices of Farnham* [1902] 2 KB 363, (1902) 18 TLR 690 where, in analogous circumstances, proceedings were not invalidated on the basis that the justice left the bench as soon as objection was taken to his presence and he was 'not shewn to have committed himself to any opinion on the subject of inquiry'.
4 *Goodall v Bilsland* 1909 SC 1152, (1909) 1 SLT 376. See also *McGeehen v Knox* 1913 SC 688, (1913) 1 SLT 283.
5 *Macdougall v Miller* (1900) 8 SLT 284; cf *Ahmed v Stirling District Licensing Board* 1980 SLT (Sh Ct) 51. As to the prohibition of canvassing by an applicant, see s 19.
6 *R v Ferguson* (1890) 54 JP 101.
7 *R v London Justices ex parte Kerfoot* (1896) 60 JP 726, (1896) 13 TLR 2.
8 Prior to the amendment of s 39(5) (by the 1990 Act, Sch 8, para 11) evidence could only be led where the appeal was based on s 39(4)(b) (incorrect material fact) leading to the difficulty exemplified in *Tennent Caledonian Breweries Ltd v City of Aberdeen Licensing Board* 1987 SLT (Sh Ct) 2.
9 See Sheriff A L Stewart's remarks in *Tennent Caledonian Breweries Ltd v City of Aberdeen District Licensing Board*, above, at 4.
10 See above.
11 See above.

presence on the bench of the member *in quo* 'must have put in doubt the impartiality of the *whole* board and demonstrated a real risk of bias . . .' (author's emphasis). It was, however, favourable to the board's position that the alleged innuendo was made at an early stage in the proceedings and not repeated; and that no similar allegations were made against the other nine board members.

Board members are well-advised not to make public comment on matters which have yet to come before them; but it has been suggested that an expression of scepticism is not indicative of bias unless it conveys an invincible unwillingness to be persuaded to a particular point of view[1].

Since a local authority[2] may now competently object to certain types of application (s 16(1)(f), added by the 1990 Act, Sch 8, para 5) there may be a danger that board members are prejudiced by their involvement in a decision to object. It has, however, been held in England that disqualification by bias was not made out where a licensing confirming authority included members of the city council which had already withheld approval for the application site under planning legislation[3].

While licensing boards are, broadly speaking, entitled to take a policy approach to applications[4] the rigid application of a policy which admits of no exceptions and amounts to prejudgment is likely to constitute an error in law rather than a breach of the principles of natural justice[5].

Subject to the possibility of prior interdict[6] objection on the ground of bias should be taken at the hearing of the application; otherwise, on appeal, it may be necessary to demonstrate prior ignorance of the disqualification. In *Smillie v Hamilton Burgh Licensing Court*[7] an unsuccessful applicant for a betting office licence appealed on the ground inter alia that two members of the licensing court were members of a church which it was alleged had lodged objections. The sheriff said:

'It is not averred that, after the hearing, a sinister aspect came to the notice of the pursuer who was unaware that bias might be present. He should, if aware that his cause was liable to be adversely effected, have objected to the composition of the court at the court and at the time when the matter could, and should, have been disposed of there and then; but to come along now, and in a vague way, indicate that two members of the court might have been influenced by the action of others with whom it is said they were associated, will not help the pursuer'[8].

1 See *Arab Monetary Fund v Hashim*, Court of Appeal, Independent, 30 April 1993, unreported.
2 Defined in s 235(1) of the Local Government (Scotland) Act 1973 as 'a regional, islands or district council'.
3 *R v Sheffield Confirming Authority ex parte Truswell's Brewery Co Ltd* [1937] 4 All ER 114. See also *Low v Kincardineshire Licensing Court* 1974 SLT (Sh Ct) 54 at 55.
4 *Elder v Ross and Cromarty District Licensing Board* 1990 SCLR 1, 1990 SLT 307. See p 182ff for a fuller discussion.
5 See *Aitken v City of Glasgow District Council* 1988 SCLR 287.
6 *Goodall v Bilsland* 1909 SC 1152, (1909) 1 SLT 376. See also *Lockhart v Irving* 1936 SLT 567 in which interdict was granted to prevent a chief constable investigating complaints made against him.
7 1975 SLT (Sh Ct) 44.
8 See also *R v Byles ex parte Hollidge* [1911–13] All ER Rep 430.

Disqualification from voting through absence

A board member who has been absent for part of the hearing of an application is thereby disqualified from voting[1]. It has been suggested that the maxim *de minimis non curat lex* applies:

'[T]his must be regarded from a common-sense point of view . . . No one supposes that if [a board member] were out of the room for a minute, or two minutes, that the judgment to which he contributed would be vitiated by that fact'[2].

Despite the provenance of that dictum, it should not be relied upon and where, as sometimes happens, a member requires to leave the bench an adjournment may be the only safe course.

It is axiomatic there where an application requires to be adjourned and is therefore 'part heard' it will require to be heard *de novo* if the composition of the board is different at the adjourned meeting; but where the difference in composition simply arises from the absence of a member or members present at the original hearing and no new members have been added, then, provided the board is quorate (s 5(3)), it will not be necessary to recommence the proceedings[3].

Where a board member may not take part in the decision because of his temporary absence he '. . . vitiates the whole decision, and does not merely disqualify his own vote'[4]. Accordingly, the decision will not be allowed to stand where the discounting of a vote would still result in a majority decision.

It has also been held that the rules of natural justice were breached where licensing committee members who had not been present throughout the whole of a hearing were present during (but did not take part in) the committee's private discussion[5].

Unreasonable exercise of discretion

It has been suggested that the purpose of this ground of appeal is '. . . to enable a sheriff to correct decisions which are on the face of them arbitrary, capricious or perverse'[6]. This approach probably goes too far, echoing the 'irrationality' test applied on judicial review[7]. Rather, it may be considered that the basis of review

1 *Goodall v Bilsland* 1909 SC 1152, (1909) 1 SLT 376. See also *McGhee v Moncur* (1899) 1 F 594.
2 *Goodall v Bilsland* above, per the Lord President.
3 Where a decision is taken by an inquorate board it is nevertheless *ex facie* valid and 'remains so until . . . reduced, withdrawn or recalled': see *Mecca Ltd v Kirkcaldy Burgh Licensing Court* 1975 SLT (Sh Ct) 50 at 52.
4 *Goodall v Bilsland* above, per the Lord President.
5 *Black v Perth and Kinross District Council*, Perth Sheriff Court, 5 November 1991, unreported; cf *Barrs v British Wool Marketing Board* 1957 SC 72.
6 *Kieran v Adams*, Glasgow Sheriff Court, 7 February 1978, unreported but reproduced in part in *Loosefoot Entertainment Ltd v City of Glasgow District Licensing Board* 1990 SLT 843. See also *Sharp v Wakefield* [1891] AC 173.
7 See, for example, *Council of Civil Service Unions v Minister for the Civil Service* [1985] AC 374, [1984] 3 All ER 935. In *Latif v Motherwell District Licensing Board* 1993 GWD 20-1256 the First Division expressly rejected such a test as 'inappropriate' for the purpose of s 39(4)(d). See also *Loosefoot Entertainment Ltd v City of Glasgow District Licensing Board*, above, in which the sheriff was reluctant to concede that a licensing board's decision could only be overturned if 'arbitrary, capricious or perverse'. For a further consideration of the difference between 'statutory unreasonableness' and 'irrationality', see p 306ff below.

by the court is satisfactorily stated by Sheriff G H Gordon, QC in *Loosefoot Entertainment Ltd v City of Glasgow District Licensing Board*[1]:

'[I]t is open to me to accept that the board's decision must be upheld in an appeal under section 39[4](d) unless they can be said to have acted in the absence of any factual basis[2] or that their decision was so unreasonable that no reasonable board[3] would have reached it or, of course, on the ground that they took account of matters which they should not have taken into account and failed to take into account matters which they should have taken into account'[4].

Where the board takes irrelevant considerations into account and asks itself the wrong question this may amount to an error in law[5].

An unreasonable exercise of discretion may be inferred where the board's statement of reasons contains omissions which warrant the conclusion that it has failed to give due consideration to representations as, for example, by a 'package rejection' of objections; but the brevity of a board's retiral to consider an application does not of itself justify such a finding[6].

A refusal to hear evidence has been held to be an unreasonable exercise of discretion as well as a breach of the rules of natural justice[7].

The rigid exercise of a policy approach to applications which disables a board from exercising its discretion in an individual case should be appealed against under s 39(4)(a) (error in law); on the other side of a thin line the application of a general policy to a particular set of circumstances may be an unreasonable exercise of discretion[8].

The prior grant of planning permission does not fetter a board's discretion:

'The planning decision was made by [the Secretary of State's representative] as a result of a view which he took of the evidence before him. Another body, discharging a different statutory function for a different purpose, under discretionary powers, was perfectly entitled to reach a different decision'[9].

The position could hardly be otherwise: an application for the grant or provisional grant of a new licence (other than an off-sale licence) may not be entertained unless it is supported by a certificate of suitability in relation to planning (s 23). Nevertheless, in *Leisure Inns (UK) Ltd v Perth and Kinross District Licensing*

1 1990 SCLR 584 at 597 aff'd 1991 SLT 843.
2 See also *Leisure Inns (UK) Ltd v Perth and Kinross District Licensing Board* 1991 SCLR 721, 1993 SLT 796; cf s 39(4)(b).
3 The test is that of 'the reasonable board', rather than 'the reasonable person': see *Latif v Motherwell District Licensing Board* 1993 GWD 20-1256, 1st Div.
4 See also *Wordie Property Co Ltd v Secretary of State for Scotland* 1984 SLT 345, a planning case which is now frequently cited in licensing appeals; and the observations of Lord Morison as to the standard of 'unreasonableness' in *Noble Organisation Ltd v City of Glasgow District Council (No 3)* 1991 SCLR 380 at 387, 1991 SLT 213 at 217 and 218 (decided under the Civic Government (Scotland) Act 1982 whose appeal provisions are largely similar to those contained in the 1976 Act).
5 See, for example, *Fereneze Leisure Ltd v Renfrew District Licensing Board* 1991 SCLR 751, 1992 SLT 604; *Mount Charlotte Investments plc v Glasgow District Licensing Board* 1992 SCLR 311.
6 *R W Cairns Ltd v Busby East Church Kirk Session* 1985 SLT 493.
7 *Devana Investments Ltd v City of Aberdeen Licensing Board* 1992 SCLR 616.
8 *Aitken v City of Glasgow District Council* 1988 SCLR 287. See also *Bury v Kilmarnock and Loudoun District Licensing Board* 1988 SCLR 436.
9 *J E Sheeran (Amusement Arcades) Ltd v Hamilton District Council* 1986 SLT 289 at 291, an appeal against the refusal of an application for a permit under s 34 of the Gaming Act 1968.

Board[1], which concerned an application for the provisional grant of a new public house licence, the Lord Justice-Clerk (Ross) observed that:

'It was plain that the planning authority had had regard to the question of amenity . . . Contrary [counsel for the applicant's] submission I am satisfied that the [board] were entitled to consider the matter of amenity, although since planning permission had been received . . . the [board] should, in my opinion have been slow to hold that any detrimental effect on amenity was to be apprehended'.

The exercise of discretion is a collective process. Where one licensing committee member was alleged to have prejudged an applicant's fitness to hold a private hire car driver's licence[2] the Second Division expressed the opinion that:

'[I]n general the court will not attempt to look into the minds of individual members of a committee which is exercising a discretion. What is in issue is the collective exercise of discretion by the committee . . . even if one does have regard to what one particular member is alleged to have stated, we are not satisfied that anything which he said was sufficient to vitiate the committee's collective discretion in dealing with the appellant's application'[3].

A board may not be bound by its own previous decisions. In *Sangha v Bute and Cowal Divisional Licensing Board*[4] the renewal of an entertainment licence was refused on the basis of incidents of disorderly and criminal conduct, almost all of which had been considered by the board at previous hearings when decisions had been taken not to impose a restriction order in terms of s 65 and to grant a regular extension of the permitted hours despite police objection. Before the sheriff (Palmer), counsel for the board submitted, apparently with success, that:

'. . . it was important to bear in mind that when a Licensing Board sits, the Board consist not necessarily of the same members. In his submission there was no way that a Board could be bound by its previous decisions and I did not understand it to be seriously suggested that it was. As an illustration, he said that it was not uncommon when applications are made for members of the public to object under Section 16(1) of the Act. Where such an objection is sustained, the application falls. Thereafter, a subsequent application is lodged. If, in such a situation, a differently constituted Board grants the application, then it is not open for an unsuccessful objector to come back and argue that the second Board had exercised its discretion in unreasonable manner because it disagreed with the first Board'[5].

On appeal, the Lord President (Hope) observed that the appellants were 'plainly right' to concede that the board had been entitled to take into account all incidents which had occurred since the original grant of the licence 'irrespective of whether or not they had previously been brought to the board's attention'. Similarly, in *Kieran v Adams*[6] the Sheriff Principal said:

1 1991 SCLR 721, 1993 SLT 796.
2 *Piper v Kyle and Carrick District Council* 1988 SLT 267, under the Civic Government (Scotland) Act 1982.
3 At 269.
4 1990 SCLR 409.
5 Dunoon Sheriff Court, 6 October 1988, unreported.
6 Glasgow Sheriff Court, 7 February 1978, unreported. The Sheriff Principal's note is, however, partly reproduced in *Loosefoot Entertainment Ltd v Glasgow District Licensing Board* 1990 SCLR 584, 1991 SLT 843.

'I think it is quite clear that it is no part of the court's duty to exercise a general supervision over the decisions of the board to ensure that they are uniform . . . There may be cases in which a sheriff would have to consider a complaint by an appellant that he had, for no reason, been singled out for prejudicial treatment. In the present case there was information before the board . . . which would have justified refusal of the application'.

On the other hand, in *Cashley v City of Dundee District Council*[1] where an applicant for a taxi licence appeared to have been 'singled out', it was held that, although the court did not require 'an inflexible uniformity of approach', a licensing authority was bound to 'act consistently' in pursuit of its policy of attaching weight to an applicant's criminal convictions. In the only case where the policy had been 'applied severely', the licensing authority had exercised its discretion in an unreasonable manner[2]. It may be observed, however, that the factual background to this case could be regarded as quite exceptional:

(1) The applicant's criminal record consisted of three minor theft convictions, all approximately ten years old; the successful applicants' criminal records 'appeared to be significantly more serious and more relevant', leading the sheriff to remark that the grant of licences was 'a quite astonishing exercise of discretion'.

(2) The licensing authority's inconsistency was to be found in its treatment of numerous applications *at the same committee meeting*. It is, however, a much more difficult matter to plead for consistency from meeting to meeting (for the reasons suggested in *Sangha*, above), as the sheriff appears to have recognised in *McLeod v City of Aberdeen District Council*[3]:

'[The solicitor for the applicant] intimated that he proposed to add . . . an averment that on two occasions subsequent to the refusal of the [applicant's] application for a licence, an application for the grant of a licence and an application for the renewal of a licence had been granted despite the fact that the applicants had worse records . . . [This] bare averment adds nothing to the article. There is no requirement (and it is too much to expect) that every case is dealt with in precisely the same fashion as its predecessors'.

Cases decided under (former) gaming legislation arguably offer a more coherent approach to the problem of consistency, where the exercise of discretion was the subject of challenge. For example, in *Keith v Dunfermline Town Council*[4] the owner of a public house was refused a permit for the provision of amusement-with-prizes machines[5] although the same licensing authority had granted an *ex facie* indistinguishable application two months previously. The sheriff said that:

'[W]here a general ground of refusal has been departed from in even one instance, it can no longer be relied upon in later cases, without some explanation which shows that the later applications were considered in a reasonable way . . . [T]he defenders relied entirely upon the general ground which would exclude all applications relating to public houses, without reference to any distinction between the premises for which a permit was previously granted and those for which it has been refused, and without any other explanation as to

---

1 Inner House (Ex Div), 11 June 1993, unreported.
2 Lord McCluskey observed that they may also have acted contrary to natural justice.
3 Aberdeen Sheriff Court, 13 February 1992, unreported.
4 1968 SLT (Sh Ct) 51.
5 Now regulated by the Gaming Act 1968, s 34 and Sch 9.

why the applications were treated differently. On the face of it, this was an unreasonable exercise of discretion . . .'[1].

The shrieval bench has traditionally exhibited a marked reluctance to interfere with the decisions of elected members of the community. In *Ahmed v Stirling District Licensing Board*[2] it was observed that 'Much of the decision of a licensing board is . . . a matter of discretion and it is not in the ordinary case necessarily an easy matter to show that this discretion has been unreasonably exercised'.

Similarly, in *Martin v Ellis*[3] the Sheriff Principal (F W F O'Brien, QC) referred approvingly to the view expressed in *Bruce v Chief Constable of Edinburgh*[4] that the sheriff should exercise the unusual jurisdiction conferred upon him 'with great care and circumspectness'[5].

On occasions, however, such caution is taken to extremes. For example, in *Noble Organisation Ltd v City of Glasgow District Council (No 1)*[6] the sheriff (A A Bell), having made findings-in-fact favourable to the application, nevertheless refused to interfere with a licensing authority's decision, observing somewhat enigmatically that:

'[T]here are considerable restraints on the question of reversing the decisions of a body which has been given clear statutory provisions to make decisions on which they have been cited to adjudicate'.

An Extra Division of the Inner House held that the sheriff had erred in law by failing to recognise that the licensing committee had exercised its discretion in an unreasonable manner in the absence of any factual basis for its decision.

The sheriff may also fall into the opposite trap of substituting his own view for that of the licensing board: there is 'a band of decisions within which no court should seek to replace the individual's judgment with [its] own'[7]. In *Latif v Motherwell District Licensing Board*[8] the sheriff:

'was not acting objectively as he should have done and was purporting to do. He was in fact acting subjectively and leaving out of account the very important fact that a licensing board has had the advantage of hearing many such applications, knows its own area and may be assumed to have developed some expertise in assessing problems such as the overprovision of licensed premises'[9].

1 For a similar approach, see *Brodie v Kilmarnock Town Council* 1967 SLT (Sh Ct) 85. It requires to be kept in view, however, that *a change of policy* will not generally be open to attack. See *Cooper v Leven Town Council* 1967 SLT (Sh Ct) 82; *Semple v Glasgow District Licensing Board* 1990 SCLR 73; cf *Atherlay v Lanark County Council* 1968 SLT (Sh Ct) 71.
2 1980 SLT 51 at 53.
3 1978 SLT (Sh Ct) 38.
4 1962 SLT (Sh Ct) 9 at 11.
5 Cf the observations of the Second Division as to the value of cases decided under earlier legislation in *Freeland v City of Glasgow District Licensing Board* 1980 SLT 101 at 104: 'The Act of 1976 has introduced a new concept into licensing law and has ended the wide discretion conferred on licensing courts under earlier legislation . . .'.
6 1990 SCLR 393, 1990 SLT 554.
7 *In Re W (an Infant)* [1971] AC 682 at 700 per Lord Hailsham, LC.
8 1993 GWD 20-1256.
9 See also *Ranachan v Renfrew District Council* 1991 SLT 625; *Hughes v Hamilton District Council* 1991 SLT 628; *McGill v Clackmannan District Council* 1991 GWD 18-1111, 1st Div.

Disposal of the appeal

Where an appeal is upheld the sheriff must decide whether to:

'(a) remit the case with the reason for his decision to the licensing board for reconsideration of its decision; or
(b) reverse or modify the decision of the licensing board'[1].

If option (a) is selected the sheriff may:

'(a) specify a date by which a rehearing by the board must take place;
(b) modify any procedural steps which would otherwise be required in relation to the matter by or under any enactment'[2].

In the event of a rehearing 'any decision of a licensing board on any such case shall be valid as if reached at a quarterly meeting as mentioned in section 4(1)(a) of this Act'[3].

The sheriff must proceed upon 'relevant' reasons[4] in exercising the discretion afforded to him by s 39(6) but it is extremely difficult to extract clear guidance from reported cases.

For example, where the board's failure has been purely in respect of the public voting requirement in s 5(7) there has been a marked diversity of approach.

In *McKay v Banff and Buchan Western Division Licensing Board*[5] the Second Division expressed the opinion that the board was entitled to find the grounds of the chief constable's complaint proved 'taking the nature and cumulative effect of the thirty-three incidents over a two year period'; yet for reasons which were not enunciated the board's decision to suspend the licence was reversed *de plano* purely because of a breach of s 5(7)[6].

On the other hand, the opposite course was taken in *Transition Interiors Ltd v Eastwood District Licensing Board*[7] where the sheriff held that:

'. . . the [board] made only a simple error in law. Their decision was not capricious or unwarranted, but they failed to vote properly. This error can be easily rectified and I think they should be given an opportunity to do so. I do not read the cases of *Simpson* and *McKay*[8] as precluding this course of action; the matter is discretionary and accordingly I see no inconsistency with those decisions in remitting this case, where no breach of natural justice nor misuse of discretion has occurred'.

---

1 Section 39(6).
2 Section 39(7).
3 Section 39(7). The purpose of this provision is simply to protect the decision taken at a re-hearing from challenge on the ground of competency: see *Clayson*, para 15.48.
4 See *R W Cairns Ltd v Busby East Church Kirk Session* 1985 SLT 493 where the sheriff's reasons for not remitting an application were 'not convincing'.
5 1991 SCLR 15, 1991 SLT 20.
6 A similar decision by the sheriff (for reasons which do not appear in the reports) was upheld in *Simpson v Banff and Buchan District Licensing Boards* 1991 SCLR 24, 1991 SLT 18.
7 Paisley Sheriff Court, 2 April 1992, unreported. See also *Najafian v Glasgow District Licensing Board* 1987 SCLR 679.
8 See above.

If it is clear that the board will be incapable of reviewing the matter objectively a rehearing will not be appropriate. The sheriff should remit the case to the board and ordain it to issue a licence. He may not grant the licence himself[1]. In *Botterills of Blantyre v Hamilton District Licensing Board*[2] the sheriff concluded:

'This has been a long drawn out affair. I think it inevitable that by this time attitudes must have hardened. I would have thought it very difficult for the [board] with the best will in the world to re-examine this application with complete detachment'.

The Second Division found this to be a 'perfectly legitimate attitude'.

Per contra, in *Scotia Leisure v City of Glasgow District Council*[3], although counsel for the appellants outlined 'the long and, to say the least, most unfortunate history of this application', which appeared to amount to a war of attrition between the appellants and the licensing committee, the Second Division was not prepared to interfere with the sheriff's 'wide discretion in deciding which of the alternatives he should adopt'[4]. In a now familiar approach, the sheriff had concluded that:

'. . . weighing the competing factors as best I can . . . in view of the wide discretion which Parliament has entrusted to the licensing committee to decide whether to grant a permit of this kind . . . I should not assume the role of the licensing committee but rather remit the case to it . . .'.

Scotia Leisure must represent the high water mark of the non-interventionist philosophy. Indeed, one may be forgiven for concluding that the adoption of such an approach effectively disables the sheriff from exercising the discretion afforded to him by s 39(6).

Where there has been a gross breach of the rules of natural justice an order for reconsideration is unlikely:

'As it is abundantly clear that the committee gave no reasons for their refusal, we deal with this case upon the basis that there was a blatant, deliberate contravention of the principles of natural justice. In our opinion the result is that the committee should not be given a second attempt to justify their refusal and that the sheriff exercised his discretion wrongly in remitting this case to the committee'[5].

Where the board behaved with impropriety (by allowing a local authority official to retire with them) it was held that:

'[T]he appellant could not feel confident that the [board] would be able to afford him justice at a rehearing of the same case where formerly they had not been seen to do so . . . I think that acting contrary to natural justice to the extent that happened here can only be met by a reversal of the decision in question'[6].

---

1 *Latif v Motherwell District Licensing Board* 1993 GWD 20-1256, 1st Div.
2 1986 SLT 14 at 16.
3 1991 SCLR 232.
4 At 234 per Lord Dunpark.
5 *G A Estate Agency Ltd v City of Glasgow District Council* 1991 SCLR 8 at 13, 1991 SLT 16 at 18.
6 *Coppola v Midlothian District Licensing Board* 1983 SLT 95 at 98.

However, where the denial of natural justice was neither blatant nor deliberate and the board was not precluded from dealing further with the matter through loss of objectivity the sheriff should have remitted an application for reconsideration[1].

A similar conclusion was reached in *Ahmed v Stirling District Licensing Board*[2] where the board had acted 'in good faith, without malice'; but in *Tong v City of Glasgow District Licensing Board*[3] the sheriff was not prepared to remit an application where the board, although acting in good faith, had not raised with the applicant the basis of its refusal.

Where the only evidence properly before the licensing authority was favourable to the applicants and 'no committee, acting reasonably, could come to any other conclusion than to grant the licence' it was appropriate to do so[4].

Similarly, where the court found that:

'there was no adequate material before the [board] to justify their holding that this ground of refusal had been made out, there would be no point in remitting the case to the sheriff so that he could remit the case to them'[5].

The extent of the sheriff's ability to 'modify' the licensing board's decision (s 39(6)(b)) is not clear. He may possibly be empowered to remove or attach a condition to a licence, even where the condition is not part of the *lis inter partes*[6].

While it requires to be kept in view that a licensing committee has far greater powers to impose conditions[7] than a licensing board, the position under the Civic Government (Scotland) Act 1982[8] may provide some guidance.

In *G A Estate Agency Ltd v City of Glasgow District Council*[9], which concerned the refusal of a public entertainment licence[10], the Second Division formulated conditions to meet 'the only two reasons given by the committee [for refusal of the licence] which the sheriff was unwilling to regard as unreasonable'.

By so doing they removed any doubt as to the competency of such an approach, as expressed by the sheriff (J P Murphy) in *Noble Organisation Ltd v City of Glasgow District Council*[11]:

'To attempt to do now what the licensing authority might have done, but did not do so, particularly in the light of [para 18(9)(b) of the 1982 Act][12] which says only that the sheriff may reverse or modify the decision of the authority, seems to me, at least in the circum-

---

1 *Tomkins v City of Glasgow District Licensing Board* 1991 GWD 39-2410, Ex Div.
2 1980 SLT (Sh Ct) 51.
3 1992 GWD 19-1125, Sh Ct.
4 *Speedlift Auto Salvage v Kyle and Carrick District Council* 1991 SCLR 801, 1992 SLT (Sh Ct) 57, under the Civic Government (Scotland) Act 1982.
5 *Leisure Inns (UK) Ltd v Perth and Kinross District Licensing Board* 1991 SCLR 721, 1993 SLT 796.
6 For appeals against condition see s 17(6), as enlarged by case law: *Wolfson v Glasgow District Licensing Board* 1980 SC 136, 1987 SLT 17; and *Wallace v Kyle and Carrick District Licensing Board* 1979 SLT (Sh Ct) 12.
7 Civic Government (Scotland) Act 1982, Sch 1, para 5.
8 The appeal provisions in Sch 1, para 18 are very similar to those contained in s 39 of the 1976 Act.
9 1991 SCLR 8, 1991 SLT 16.
10 Civic Government (Scotland) Act 1982, s 41, Sch 1.
11 1990 SCLR 64 at 72.
12 Which is in identical terms to s 39(6)(b) of the 1976 Act.

stances of this particular case, to be putting myself in the place of the licensing authority. Consequently I am not prepared to impose any conditions'.

In *McIndoe v Glasgow District Licensing Board*[1] the sheriff assumed that he could competently order reconsideration of an application by a differently constituted committee. This power, if it exists, seems to be rarely used.

Similarly, the extent of the sheriff's ability to modify 'any procedural steps which otherwise would be required in relation to the matter by or under any enactment' (s 39 (7)(b)) has been the subject of doubt.

Where a licensing board refuses an application for the grant (or provisional grant) of a new licence no further application in respect of 'the same premises' may be entertained in the ensuing two years unless the board makes a direction to the contrary at the time of refusal (commonly known as a 'section 14 direction'). If the sheriff upholds an objector's appeal against the grant of a licence and elects to reverse the board's decision a question arises as to the manner in which a 'section 14 direction' may be granted, if at all. This important difficulty was neatly focused, but did not require to be resolved, in *Flannagan v City of Glasgow Licensing Board*[2]. The sheriff (B Kearney) said:

'I would . . . expressly reserve my opinion as to whether the reversal by the sheriff of a decision of the licensing board should be equated, for the purpose of section 14 . . . with the refusal by a licensing board of an application for a new licence. Section 14 makes reference to "at the time of refusing the first mentioned application" and . . . when the board grants the licence there can be no such time of refusing. I think it might therefore be regarded as inappropriate to interpret the sheriff's decision as being equatable with the board's decision when the result is to deny to a citizen a right which he would otherwise possess'.

He then considered whether 'this supposed problem' could be circumvented by the use of s 39(7)(b), and, reserving his view, added:

'I would have some fears that remitting a case back to a licensing board with instructions, say, to refuse the application and then further instruct it to entertain an application under section 14 might go beyond what is conveyed by the phrase "modify any procedural steps which would be required in relation to the matter by or under any enactment"'.

Where the application is remitted to the board for reconsideration the appeal process is, of course, capable of being commenced *de novo* after the board's new decision.

The sheriff's decision 'may include such order as to the expenses of the appeal as he thinks proper' (s 39(1)). As expenses usually follow success[3] under-funded objectors such as private individuals and community councils often encounter serious financial difficulty in maintaining their opposition to licensing board decisions.

---

1 1989 SCLR 325.
2 Glasgow Sheriff Court, 18 November 1992, unreported.
3 See the sheriff's comments in *Troc Sales Ltd v Kirkcaldy District Licensing Board* 1982 SLT (Sh Ct) 77 at 80; see also *Prise v Aberdeen Licensing Court* 1974 SLT (Sh Ct) 48.

Appeal to the Court of Session

Any party to an appeal who is dissatisfied with the sheriff's decision may appeal on a point of law[1] to the Inner House of the Court of Session within 28 days of the date of the decision (s 39(8))[2].

An appeal may only succeed if it can be demonstrated that the sheriff proceeded upon a wrong principle of law or that 'his decision was so unreasonable that no sheriff, properly directing himself on the facts before him, could have reached it'[3].

The court may thus require to ask itself the arcane question as to whether any 'properly directed' sheriff could have reached the conclusion that a licensing board's decision was so unreasonable that no reasonable board would have reached it.

Grounds of appeal which simply reiterate the provisions of s 39(4) without affording proper notice of the matters sought to be argued will not be sufficient to allow argument to be developed[4].

A competency issue may be canvassed in the Inner House although not argued before the sheriff[5].

The court may allow the lodgement of late grounds of appeal. But where a motion was made after the By Order hearing[6] the First Division held that:

'[T]he purpose of the By Order hearing is to eliminate, so far as reasonably practicable, disruption to the court's timetable by late adjournments or inaccurate forecasts of the duration of a hearing on the Summar Roll. That is the stage at which consideration should have been given to the grounds on which the appeal was to be argued . . . Since no good reason was advanced as to why the point . . . could not have been mentioned at that stage, we were not prepared to grant an adjournment'[7].

In *Chung v Wigtown District Licensing Board*[8] the sheriff had upheld the applicant's appeal on the ground that the board had exercised its discretion unreasonably but felt unable to sustain an argument directed at an alleged breach of natural justice. In the board's appeal to the Inner House, the First Division held that the applicant was disabled from pursuing such an argument in the absence of a cross-appeal:

'[T]he sheriff held that the procedure was not so flawed as to amount to a departure from the rules of natural justice and the [applicant] has not lodged any ground of appeal directed

---

1 See Walker *Civil Remedies* p 166; and 1 *Stair Memorial Encyclopaedia* paras 285ff.

2 In *Saleem v Hamilton District Licensing Board* 1993 SCLR 266, the sheriff's dismissal of an appeal following the pursuer's non-appearance amounted to an 'error in law'; cf *Charles Watson (Scotland) Ltd v Glasgow District Licensing Board* 1980 SLT (Sh Ct) 37.

3 *Scotia Leisure Ltd v City of Glasgow District Council* 1991 SCLR 232 at 234, referring to *Wordie Property Co Ltd v Secretary of State for Scotland* 1984 SLT 345. See also *Britton v Central Regional Council* 1986 SLT 307.

4 *Fife Regional Council v Kirkcaldy District Licensing Board (No 1)* 1991 GWD 10-611, Ex Div. See also *Sutherland v City of Edinburgh District Licensing Board* 1984 SLT 241.

5 *Wolfson v Glasgow District Licensing Board* 1980 SC 136, 1981 SLT 17. See also *Padda v Strathkelvin District Licensing Board* 1988 SCLR 349 for circumstances in which a matter of competency was regarded as *pars judicis*; cf the sheriff's observations in the note to *Sangha v Bute and Cowal Divisional Licensing Board* 1990 SCLR 409 at 416, 417.

6 Under Rule of Court 294C(7).

7 *Kilmarnock and Loudoun District Council v Noble Organisation Ltd*, 1st Div, 25 June 1992, unreported.

8 1993 SCLR 256.

to this point. We also note that some of the points which [counsel for the applicant] sought to raise were not the subject of averment in the appeal in the sheriff court. The only question which we can consider . . . is whether the sheriff was right to hold that . . . the [board] exercised their discretion in an unreasonable manner'[1].

Appeals are not infrequently restricted to the single issue of the sheriff's decision as to the course to be adopted under s 39(6)[2].

JUDICIAL REVIEW[3]

Procedure

Decisions of licensing boards and their clerks which are not susceptible to appeal in terms of the Act[4] may be challenged in the Outer House of the Court of Session by judicial review[5].

The procedure, introduced in 1985[6], is endowed with the advantages of speed and flexibility.

In terms of Rule of Court 260B(4) the court may in a judicial review application:

'(a) grant or refuse the application or any part of it, with or without conditions;
(b) make such order in relation to the decision in question as it thinks fit, whether or not such order was sought in the application, being an order that could be made if sought in any action or petition, including an order for reduction, declarator, suspension, interdict, implement[7], restitution, payment (whether of damages or otherwise), and any interim order;
(c) subject to the provisions of this rule, make such order in relation to procedure as it thinks appropriate in the circumstances'.

Petitioner's qualifications

The petitioner must possess *both* title and interest to sue[8]. Parties to and persons entitled to make an application are clearly qualified[9].

1 1993 SCLR 256 at 263 per the Lord President (Hope).
2 See p 300 above; and *Scotia Leisure Ltd v City of Glasgow District Council* 1991 SCLR 232 in which it was suggested that the sheriff has a 'wide discretion' in deciding which alternative to select.
3 See also St Clair & Davidson *Judicial Review in Scotland* and 1 *Stair Memorial Encyclopaedia* paras 345ff.
4 Review is incompetent where the Act confers a right of appeal.
5 The remedy is only available in the Court of Session.
6 Act of Sederunt (Rules of Court Amendment No. 2) (Judicial Review) 1985, SI 1985/500, inserting Rule of Court 260B.
7 For an unusual case in which judicial review was competently employed in an (unsuccessful) attempt to secure specific performance under the Court of Session Act, 1868, s 91 (now Court of Session Act 1988, s 45) see *Noble Developments Ltd v City of Glasgow District Council* 1989 SCLR 622.
8 See, for example, *Hollywood Bowl (Scotland) Ltd v Horsborough* 1992 SLT 241; *Matchett v Dunfermline District Council* 1993 SLT 537 (interest but no title); *Patmor Ltd v City of Edinburgh District Licensing Board* 1987 SLT 492; and *Edward Barrett Ltd v City of Dundee District Licensing Board* 1992 SLT 963.
9 See *Main v City of Glasgow District Licensing Board* 1987 SLT 305; and *Tait v Horsborough* 1987 SCLR 310, (sub nom *Tait v City of Glasgow District Licensing Board*) 1987 SLT 340.

In a case decided under the Gaming Act 1968[1] it was held that competent objectors who had no statutory right of appeal possessed title and interest to seek review of the grant of a licence.

Where a licensing board rejected an objection as incompetent an appeal to the sheriff was allowed although it may be argued that the aggrieved objector's only remedy is to petition for judicial review[2].

In contrast to the position in England[3] there is no time limit for the commencement of a petition but mora, taciturnity and acquiescence may operate as a bar to proceedings[4].

Delay in seeking an interim order for publication where an application requires to be advertised (s 12) may give rise to difficulty[5].

Scope of the remedy

Judicial review invokes the supervisory rather than the appellate jurisdiction of the court[6]. The scope of the remedy, as compendiously stated in *Stewart v Monklands District Council*[7], is virtually co-extensive with the grounds of appeal provided in s 39(4):

'The grounds of review cover matters of illegality, improprieties of procedure and of improprieties in the exercise of power but not a reconsideration of the merits of the case where no such illegality or impropriety is alleged . . . the petitioner makes no attempt to challenge the decision . . . on any ground of abuse of power, perversity, illegality or unreasonableness. It is not for example said that some relevant fact was ignored or some irrelevant fact considered. It is not said that the respondents acted dishonestly or unfairly. What is sought is a simple review of the decision on a matter of fact [that the petitioner was intentionally homeless] which was determined by the respondents in a legitimate and proper exercise of their discretion. Such a review is not within the supervisory jurisdiction of the court . . .'[8].

Nevertheless, it seems that 'unreasonableness', one of the most complex legal concepts imaginable, will be judged according to different standards, depending on whether the issues arise in the context of a statutory appeal (under s 39(4)(d)) or on judicial review, although the test to be employed for both purposes is formulated in very similar terms. Thus, as is well-settled, the court is not to interfere with the discretion entrusted to a licensing board unless its exercise demonstrates that no reasonable licensing board could have reached a particular

---

1 *Patmor Ltd v City of Edinburgh District Licensing Board* 1987 SLT 492.
2 See *Morgan v Midlothian District Licensing Board* 1993 SCLR 1, 1993 SLT (Sh Ct) 19; *Prime v Hardie* 1978 SLT (Sh Ct) 71; and p 267ff above.
3 See *Caswell v Dairy Produce Quota Tribunal for England and Wales* [1990] 2 AC 738.
4 See *Hanlon v Traffic Commissioner* 1988 SLT 802, discussed in N Collar 'Mora and Judicial Review' 1988 SLT (News) 309 and considered in *Perfect Swivel Ltd v City of Dundee District Licensing Board (No 2)* 1993 SLT 112.
5 See *Main v City of Glasgow District Licensing Board* 1987 SLT 305.
6 For a consideration of this distinction, which is less than clear-cut, See 1 *Stair Memorial Encyclopaedia* paras 242ff.
7 1987 SLT 630.
8 At 632, 633. See also *West v Scottish Prison Service* 1992 SLT 636.

decision[1]. Prima facie this test is no more than a restatement of the familiar '*Wednesbury* unreasonableness' principle:

'The court is entitled to investigate the action of the local authority with a view to seeing whether they have taken into account matters which they ought not to take into account, or conversely refused to take into account or neglected to take into account matters which they ought to take into account. Once that question is answered in favour of the local authority it may still be possible to say that although the local authority have kept within the four corners of the matters which they ought to consider they have nevertheless come to a conclusion so *unreasonable that no reasonable authority could have come to it* [author's emphasis]. In such a case again, I think the court can interfere'[2].

According to Lord Greene, to prove a case of this kind requires 'something overwhelming', while in *Council of Civil Service Unions v Minister for the Civil Service* ('the CCSU case')[3] Lord Diplock equiparated *Wednesbury* unreasonableness with 'irrationality':

'It applies to a decision which is so outrageous in its defiance of logic or of accepted moral standards that no sensible person who had applied his mind to the question to be decided could have arrived at it'[4].

While 'irrationality' in this sense was the test applied in the judicial review case of *Purdon v Glasgow District Licensing Board*[5] (under reference to the CCSU case), in *Latif v Motherwell District Licensing Board*[6], a statutory appeal against the refusal of a licence, the court declined to endorse Lord Diplock's test, observing, without elaboration, that it was 'inappropriate' where the question to be examined was whether a licensing board had exercised its discretion in an unreasonable manner for the purposes of s 39(4)(d).

A fuller articulation of the difference between 'statutory unreasonableness' and 'irrational unreasonableness' is to be found in *Noble Organisation Ltd v City of Glasgow District Council (No 3)*[7], an appeal under the Civic Government (Scotland) Act 1982 on a ground identical to that provided by s 39(4)(d) of the 1976 Act[8]. It was submitted on behalf of the district council:

'on the basis of the familiar dicta contained in cases such as *Associated Provincial Picture Houses v Wednesbury Corporation*[9] and *Wordie Property Co Ltd v Secretary of State for Scotland*[10], that the court's entitlement to intervene in a decision based on the exercise of an authority's discretion could only be justified if the decision was "so unreasonable that no reasonable tribunal could have reached it"'[11].

---

1 See, for example, *Loosefoot Entertainment Ltd v City of Glasgow District Licensing Board* 1990 SCLR 584, aff'd 1991 SLT 843.
2 *Associated Provincial Picture Houses Ltd v Wednesbury Corpn* [1948] 1 KB 223 at 233 per Lord Greene, MR. See also *Edinburgh District Council v Secretary of State for Scotland* 1985 SLT 551; *Wordie Property Co Ltd v Secretary of State for Scotland* 1984 SLT 345.
3 [1985] AC 374, [1984] 3 All ER 935.
4 [1985] AC 374 at 410, [1984] 3 All ER 935 at 951.
5 1988 SCLR 466, 1989 SLT 201.
6 1993 GWD 20-1256, 1st Div.
7 1991 SCLR 380.
8 Civic Government (Scotland) Act 1982, Sch 1, para 18(7)(d).
9 [1948] 1 KB 223.
10 1984 SLT 345.
11 1991 SCLR 380 at 387.

The relevance of these dicta was doubted by Lord Morison:

'[A]ccepting that these authorities may indicate that, in order to justify the court's intervention on the ground that a tribunal has exceeded its jurisdiction, something more is required than merely to show that a decision is unreasonable, they do not in my view apply in this respect to the appellate function of the sheriff . . . That function is the subject of express statutory provision in paragraph 18(7) of Schedule 1 to the 1982 Act which provides inter alia that the sheriff may uphold an appeal if he considers that the licensing authority "(d) exercised their discretion in an unreasonable manner". *No further definition of the basis upon which the sheriff is entitled to intervene is required*' [author's emphasis][1].

In the result, the standard of 'unreasonableness' required for judicial review purposes is now well-settled but probably falls to be distinguished from the 'reasonable board' test applied in statutory appeals, in a manner which has yet to be clearly focused. Nevertheless, the *Wednesbury* formula has been employed in appeals under s 39: see, for example, *Donald v Stirling District Licensing Board*[2].

Limitations

While the availability of judicial review is of considerable value in the licensing field, principally because it partly fills the vacuum created by the absence of an appeal against the refusal of a regular extension of permitted hours, there are a number of limitations:

(a) The petitioner may have difficulty in demonstrating that the decision challenged is irrational where the board has not been obliged to state its reasons[3].

(b) The court has no power to grant (or indeed refuse) an application[4] but may reduce the board's decision, grant declarator and order the board to consider or reconsider an application[5].

(c) Although the validity of a licence is generally preserved on the dependency of an appeal, judicial review proceedings have no such effect[6]. Where, for example, the continuing validity of a licence is at stake interim orders may be required to preserve the status quo.

(d) The court will only deal with live issues, not with matters which are, or have become, hypothetical or academic[7].

The final determination of the petition may be reclaimed (appealed) without leave of the judge within 21 days of his interlocutor[8]; as respects other interlo-

---

1 1991 SCLR 380 at 387.
2 1992 SLT (Sh Ct) 75 at 77K.
3 *Purdon v Glasgow District Licensing Board* 1988 SCLR 466, 1989 SLT 201. See also *R v Secretary of State for Trade and Industry ex parte Lonhro* [1989] 1 WLR 525.
4 Cf s 39(6).
5 See *Tait v Horsborough* 1987 SCLR 310, (sub nom *Tait v City of Glasgow District Licensing Board*) 1987 SLT 340; *Bantop Ltd v Glasgow District Licensing Board* 1989 SCLR 731, 1990 SLT 366; and *C R S Leisure Ltd v Dumbarton District Licensing Board* 1989 SCLR 566, 1990 SLT 200.
6 See *C R S Leisure Ltd v Dumbarton District Licensing Board*, above.
7 *Marco's Leisure Ltd v West Lothian District Licensing Board* [1993] 13 LR 28. See also *McNaughton v McNaughton's Trs* 1953 SC 387, 1953 SLT 240. Cf *Air 2000 v Secretary of State for Scotland (No 2)* 1990 SLT 335.
8 Rule of Court 264(a).

cutors no reclaiming motion may be made except with leave of the judge, which must be applied for not later than seven days after the date of the order in question[1].

1 Rule of Court 260B(21), (22).

CHAPTER 16

Registered clubs

MEMBERS' AND PROPRIETARY CLUBS

A distinction falls to be drawn between a members' club[1], in which the supply of alcoholic liquor requires to be authorised by a certificate of registration granted by the sheriff under Part VII of the Act; and a proprietary club, operated as a commercial business for the benefit of its owners, where liquor sales are conducted in terms of a licence[2] granted by a licensing board. Registration is effectively limited to a bona fide members' club, with not less than 25 members, whose whole assets, including the liquor stock, are owned jointly by the members and which is managed by elected officials[3].

Members' clubs may be (but rarely are) incorporated under the Companies Acts, normally as a company limited by guarantee.

THE REQUIREMENT FOR REGISTRATION

Prior to the introduction of a system of club registration[4], there was 'nothing illegal in working men having a club where they will be supplied at times and in a manner convenient to themselves within their own club premises with such refreshment as they desire', provided that the club was bona fide in nature[5] and not 'a mere pretence and pretext of a club'[6]. The clear scope for abuse was eventually considered to be unacceptable. Section 120 of the 1976 Act, essentially replicating s 83 of the 1903 Act, provides that an offence is committed by any person who:

1 For a consideration of members' clubs generally, see 2 *Stair Memorial Encyclopaedia* paras 803ff.
2 Usually an entertainment licence.
3 See s 107, containing a list of peremptory club rules; and the grounds of objection to registration in s 108. These sections are further considered below. For an example of a commercial enterprise attempting 'to obtain for itself the privileges of a members' private club' see *Chief Constable of Glasgow v Piccadilly Club* 1968 SLT (Sh Ct) 33. See also *Chief Constable of Strathclyde v Pollokshaws Road Snooker Centre* 1977 SLT (Sh Ct) 72 for a consideration of the differences between bona fide members' clubs and proprietary clubs.
4 Licensing (Scotland) Act 1903, which, as amended by the Temperance (Scotland) Act 1913 and the Licensing Act 1921, forms the basis of the current legislation.
5 *McWilliams v Main* (1902) 4 F (J) 54, (1902) 9 SLT 503.
6 *McNally v Main* (1902) 4 F (J) 105, (1902) 10 SLT 230. See also *Madin v McLean* (1894) 21 R (J) 40, (1894) 1 SLT 604.

(a) sells or supplies, or authorises the sale or supply of, alcoholic liquor in the premises of an unregistered club[1] to a member or other person;

(b) pays for alcoholic liquor so sold or supplied (s 120(1))[2].

In addition, every officer and member of the club is guilty of an offence if alcoholic liquor is 'kept in any such premises for sale or supply in those premises' (s 120(2))[3], subject to the defence that the liquor was kept 'without his knowledge or consent' (s 120(3))[4]. Where there are reasonable grounds for believing that liquor is being illegally sold or supplied or stocked, a justice of the peace may, after hearing evidence on oath[5], grant a warrant authorising a constable to:

(i) enter the unregistered club's premises at any time (by force, if necessary), carry out a search, seize documents relating to the club's business and take the names and addresses of persons found in the premises (s 120(4))[6];

(ii) seize and remove liquor which the constable reasonably supposes to be in the premises for the purpose of sale or supply, together with the vessels containing the liquor (s 120(5)).

Where a conviction ensues under s 120(2), the liquor and containers are to be forfeited and sold, with the proceeds paid into the general fund of the district or islands area (s 120(6)).

If the unregistered club is a genuine members' club, the only appropriate prosecution is under these provisions since the 'supply' cannot amount to trafficking without a licence (see below); but where the club is, in fact, a proprietary club in disguise the complaint should be brought under s 90[7].

'Supply' outside club premises

The introduction of a registration requirement did not alter the principle that the supply of liquor to a member of a bona fide club does not amount to trafficking:

'It is supplying members of the association with their own goods upon terms arranged by themselves. Such supplying does not constitute a contract of sale or trafficking of any kind'[8].

In *Crossgates British Legion Club v Davidson*[9] a registered club, through certain officials, was convicted of trafficking without a certificate. During a country

1 'Unregistered club' means a club in respect of which a certificate of registration under Part VII of the Act is not in force: see definition of 'registered club' in s 139(1).
2 Maximum penalty: level 3 (Sch 5).
3 Maximum penalty: level 3 (Sch 5).
4 'Knowledge or consent': see *Nicol v Smith* 1955 JC 7, 1955 SLT 38.
5 'Evidence that persons have on several occasions been seen entering an unregistered club sober and leaving intoxicated' would be suitable: MacPherson *Police Powers and Duties* (2nd edn, 1922) p. 92.
6 A person who fails to give his name and address or supplies false details is guilty of an offence: s 120(7). Maximum penalty: level 1 (Sch 5).
7 See *Purves's Scottish Licensing Laws* (6th edn, 1949, ed by Shearer) p 153. It appears that the only method of impugning the bona fides of a registered club is by objection to the renewal of the registration (s 108); or by an application for its cancellation (s 109). See *Gallagher v Davidson* 1915 SC (J) 52, 1915 2 SLT 9.
8 *McWilliams v Main* (1902) 4 F (J) 54, (1902) 9 SLT 503. It is immaterial that the liquor is 'sold' at a profit and paid into club funds: *Graff v Evans* (1882) 8 QBD 373.
9 1954 SLT 124.

outing, a marquee was erected in which club members were supplied with liquor upon payment. Upholding the club's appeal, the High Court adopted the dictum of Mr Justice Darling in *Humphrey v Tudgay*[1]:

'The liquor being the liquor of the whole association, the member who takes some of it puts back into the club, not the liquor but its equivalent in money. That is not a "sale" of the liquor to him. He only takes what is his own and replaces it with something of his own although not of the same kind or quality'[2].

Despite the clarity of the *Crossgates* decision, the *Report of the Departmental Committee on Scottish Licensing Law*[3] received a representation to the effect that a certificate of registration should confer authority for the supply of liquor at a function held outwith the club's own premises[4]. In the result, s 33(2) of the Act enables a licensing board to grant an occasional licence authorising a registered club to 'sell' alcoholic liquor 'at an event held outwith the premises of the club if the event arises from or relates to the functions of the club'[5]. The use of the word 'sell' is no doubt confusing: the 'sale' of alcoholic liquor is effectively circumscribed by s 33(6), in terms of which the Act's provisions (other than those relating to the permitted hours) are deemed to apply 'as if the sale took place in the registered club'.

In *Chief Constable of Lanarkshire v Auchengeich Miners' Welfare Society and Social Club*[6] the sheriff considered that it was 'a glimpse of the obvious' to say that 'when a club is registered under the Act it is entitled to sell or supply exciseable liquor in the club premises stated to be occupied by the club in the application'. The possibility that a certificate could embrace separate but adjacent premises was considered, but not resolved, in *Blantyre Miners' Welfare Society, Petitioners*[7]. Here, a club, already registered, applied for registration in respect of a new building, within the same fenced precinct, about 20 feet distant from the original facilities. Thereafter the club's agent argued that the fresh application should be refused as unnecessary. The sheriff considered that such a course 'would be highly dangerous' and the club 'might well be prosecuted for a contravention of the Licensing Acts'. The application was granted on the narrow basis that the proposed refusal was incompetent.

It may, however, be considered that the operation of secondary club premises without further formality sits uneasily with the scheme of Part VII. An application for the grant or renewal of registration is open to objection on the ground that 'the premises are, or the situation thereof is, not suitable or convenient for the purposes of a club' (s 108(d))[8]; and the register kept by the sheriff clerk contains 'the address of the premises in respect of which the certificate has been granted' (s 102(3)(b)). On the other hand, if the *Blantyre* club had abandoned its new application and proceeded to conduct the affairs of the club at the new premises,

---

1 [1915] 1 KB 119 at 123.
2 See also *Watson v Cully* [1926] 2 KB 270.
3 (Cmnd 5354) (*Clayson*) para 13.58.
4 Apparently, clubs had considered themselves obliged to engage a certificate-holder for such a purpose.
5 The application procedure is considered in Chapter 7.
6 (1962) 78 Sh Ct Rep 114.
7 1964 SLT (Sh Ct) 61.
8 An application for cancellation of a certificate may also be made on this ground: s 109(1).

the nature of the prosecution apprehended by the sheriff is not immediately apparent[1].

THE REGISTER OF CLUBS

The sheriff clerk of each sheriff court district, referred to in Part VII as 'the registrar', is required to maintain a register of clubs to which a certificate of registration has been granted (s 102(1))[2], disclosing, in each case, the following information (s 103):
(a) the name of the club[3];
(b) the address of the premises in respect of which the certificate of registration has been granted[4];
(c) a statement whether the club is the tenant or the proprietor and occupier of the premises[5];
(d) the name and address of the secretary;
(e) the date of the certificate; and
(f) a statement whether the certificate has been granted for the first time or on renewal.
The register is open to public inspection 'at all reasonable times', subject to payment of a twenty-pence fee. The public purse is spared this expense where the chief constable wishes to examine the register or gives written authorisation to a constable for that purpose (s 115(1), (2)).

APPLYING FOR REGISTRATION

An application for registration may be made at any time. The form, supplied by the sheriff clerk[6], and lodged with him as registrar, requires to be signed by the chairman, secretary or solicitor of the club. The signatory must hold one of these offices at the time when the application is made[7]. The following information is to be supplied (s 103(2)):
(a) the name of the club;

---

1 See also *Clarke v Griffiths* [1927] 1 KB 226, considered at p 318 below.
2 A sheriff clerk depute may exercise the registrar's functions: s 102(2).
3 A club is not obliged to re-apply for registration simply because of a change of name.
4 In terms of s 116, any citation of a registered club may be made in its registered name in accordance with the Citation Amendment (Scotland) Act 1882 or by a copy of the citation being left by an officer of the court at the registered address. The purpose of this provision is obscure.
5 An applicant club is not, however, required to 'aver whether it is owner or tenant'. If the club does not fall into one of these categories, the registrar 'will make some other suitable entry': *Hampden Tenpin Bowling Club v Chief Constable of Glasgow* 1965 SLT (Sh Ct) 22.
6 The form of application is not prescribed.
7 *Scottish Homosexual Rights Group, Petitioners* 1981 SLT (Sh Ct) 18, in which it was also held that application could not 'be competently made before the club has been instituted'.

(b) the objects of the club[1];
(c) the address of the premises occupied by the club.

In *Bayview Club, Petitioners*[2] objection was taken on the ground inter alia that the club premises were not 'occupied'. A club which was already registered purchased new premises subject to the fresh grant of a certificate of registration. The sheriff considered that the *tempus inspiciendum* was the time of grant of registration:

'[T]he applicants' right of legal occupation will, in this case, attach to the premises coincidentally with the issue of a certificate of registration, so that its issue will in fact be to a club which occupies, in the sense of having a title to occupy, the premises'[3].

The position is likely to be different in the case of a newly-formed club; and registration has been refused in a number of cases where the premises have not been ready for occupation[4]. In two cases concerning Freemasons' lodges it has been held that occupation of premises need be neither exclusive nor continuous[5].

In addition, s 103(3) requires that the application shall be accompanied by:
(i) two copies of the rules of the club (s 103(3)(a))[6];
(ii) a list containing the name and address of each official and each member of the committee of management or governing body of the club (s 103(3)(b))[7];
(iii) a certificate granted by two members of the local licensing board and the owner of the premises (where the club is not the proprietor) to the effect that the club is bona fide in nature and not mainly conducted for the supply of liquor (s 103(3)(c), (4))[8].

Mandatory club rules

Registration may not be granted unless the rules of the club contain certain provisions, as follows (s 107(1))[9]:

---

1 The club need not realise all of its stated objects (*Glengarnock Social Club v Chief Constable of Glasgow* 1971 SLT (Sh Ct) 35). Objection may, however, be made on the ground that it is not conducted 'in good faith' or is 'used mainly as a drinking club' (s 108(f), (h)).
2 1954 SLT (Sh Ct) 43.
3 Cf *Glasgow Rangers' Supporters' Social Club, Petitioners* 1960 SLT (Sh Ct) 27, (1960) 76 Sh Ct Rep 44.
4 In *Bayview*, the new premises required extensive adaptation, but no objection was taken as to their suitability. See 'Suitability of premises', below.
5 *Lodge Liberton No 1201, Petitioners* 1966 SLT (Sh Ct) 90; *Lodge Regal No 1422, Petitioners* 1972 SLT (Sh Ct) 61.
6 See below.
7 As noted at the appropriate section of the text, these officials and members are vicariously liable for a number of offences. After registration, a new list must be lodged immediately where changes have taken place: s 103(5), as amended by the Law Reform (Miscellaneous Provisions) (Scotland) Act 1980, s 21.
8 The form of certificate is contained in Sch 6. Note that the word 'continued' in the Schedule was intended to be 'conducted': this misprint has yet to be corrected. A licensing board member may, within ten days, withdraw his signature from the certificate: s 103(4), proviso.
9 Note, however, that in terms of the proviso to this subsection, 'any lodge of Freemasons duly constituted under a charter from the Grand Lodge of Scotland' is wholly exempt; in *Lodge Regal No 1422, Petitioners* 1972 SLT (Sh Ct) 61 it was suggested that their preferential treatment is based on 'a limited requirement for the sale [sic] of alcohol'.

(1) Section 107(1)(a):

'that the business and affairs of the club shall be under the management of a committee or governing body who shall be elected for not less than one year by the general body of members and shall be subject in whole or in part or in a specified proportion to annual re-election, or of whom not more than one-third may be non-elected persons from outwith the club and the remainder shall be elected and subject to annual re-election as aforesaid'.

This provision is designed to 'distinguish between a members' club and one run by private interest for gain [and to] ensure that the management of a registered club is answerable to the members and not to some other person or body'[1]. In the mid-1960s, chief constables were apt to object to applications on the ground that the management committee was not elected by 'the general body' since certain classes of members were disenfranchised[2]. The resultant shrieval decisions clearly show that it is acceptable for a club to provide that certain categories of members are not to have voting rights, so long as 'the control of the club is bona fide in the hands of a committee elected by a substantial body of the members'[3].

The term 'general body' is to be construed on all the facts and circumstances of each case[4]. Registration was not considered appropriate in the following cases:
(a) where membership was divided between 1,350 voting (ordinary) members and 1,103 non-voting (lady associate) members[5];
(b) where voting membership was confined to those who were members of another organisation[6];
(c) where the 'vast majority' of the membership had no vote[7].

(2) Section 107(10(b):

'that no member of the committee or governing body and no manager or servant employed in the club shall have any personal interest in the sale of alcoholic liquor therein or in the profits arising from such sale'.

In *Drongan and District Working Men's Social Club, Petitioners*[8] the club's rules provided for the payment of a discretionary honorarium to the club's officers. The chief constable opposed registration, arguing that a personal interest was thereby created since club income was to be derived from liquor sales. Rejecting this objection as being 'without merit', the sheriff said:

'The terms of section 173(b)[9] are specifically incorporated in . . . the club's rules. It is not to be presumed in my view that the only profits to be made by the club will necessarily be derived from the sale of liquor. In any event, section 173(b) is clearly restricted to personal

1 *Baillieston Miners' Welfare Society and Social Club v Chief Constable of Lanarkshire* 1966 SLT (Sh Ct) 31.
2 In terms of s 108(b), objection may be made on the ground that the rules do not conform to the provisions of the Act.
3 *Largs Golf Club, Petitioners* 1966 SLT (Sh Ct) 71.
4 *Ardeer Golf Club, Petitioners* 1966 SLT (Sh Ct) 10; *Largs Golf Club, Petitioners* 1966 SLT (Sh Ct) 71; *Drongan and District Working Men's Social Club, Petitioners* 1966 SLT (Sh Ct) 73.
5 *Prestwick Bowling Club, Petitioners*, Ayr Sheriff Court, 25 May 1965, unreported.
6 *Hibernian Social and Recreation Club* 1972 SLT (Sh Ct) 38.
7 *Chief Constable of Strathclyde v Hamilton and District Bookmakers Club* 1977 SLT (Sh Ct) 78.
8 1966 SLT (Sh Ct) 73.
9 Ie of the Licensing (Scotland) Act 1959, virtually identical to s 107(1)(b) of the 1976 Act.

interest in the sale of liquor or profits arising from such sale, and does not fetter the actings of the committee or members in their financial administration of the club'.

(3) Section 107(1)(c): 'that the committee or governing body shall hold periodical meetings'.

(4) Section 107(1)(d): 'that . . . all members of the club shall be elected by the whole body of members or by the committee or governing body, with or without specially added members'. This rule is not required in the case of a students' union of:

'a university, central institution, college of education or a further education college under the management of an education authority, which is recognised and certified as such to the registrar by the Senate or Academic Council of the university or the governing body of the central institution or college of education, or by the education authority, as the case may be'[1].

An objection to the renewal of a certificate of registration was sustained where prospective members made application for membership in response to large newspaper advertisements of a commercial nature: see *Chief Constable of Glasgow v Piccadilly Club*[2].

(5) Section 107(1)(e):

'that . . . the names and addresses of persons proposed as ordinary members of the club shall be displayed in a conspicuous place in the club premises for at least a week before their election, and that an interval of not less than two weeks shall elapse between the nomination and election of ordinary members'.

The students' union exemption applies. The corresponding ground of objection is found in s 108(p). This provision and the immediately preceding rule are designed to discourage instant membership purely for drinking purposes; they were particularly important at a time when alcoholic refreshment was virtually unobtainable on Sundays except in clubs or where the customer was a bona fide traveller.

(6) Section 107(1)(f): 'that no alcoholic liquor shall be sold or supplied in the club to any person under 18'.

(7) Section 107(1)(g)[3]: 'that no person under 18 shall be admitted a member of the club unless the club is one which is devoted primarily to some athletic purpose . . .'.

(8) Section 107(1)(h):

'that no persons shall be allowed to become honorary or temporary members of the club or be relieved of the payment of the regular entrance fee or subscription, except those possessing certain qualifications defined in the rules and subject to conditions and regulations prescribed therein'.

---

1 Section 107(1)(d), (4). This exemption will be referred to below as 'the students' union exemption'.
2 1968 SLT (Sh Ct) 33.
3 Subject to the students' union exemption.

The nature of these qualifications, conditions and regulations is a matter for the club.

(9) Section 107(1)(i): 'that there shall be a defined subscription payable in advance by members'.

The imposition of an additional entrance fee may suggest that the club is not being conducted in good faith as a club (s 108(f)). In *Chief Constable of Glasgow v Piccadilly Club*[1] the sheriff said:

'I do not doubt that a registered club may impose on its members a charge for the use of some facility, but the imposition of [a] charge before a member can even cross the threshold is at variance with the accepted concepts of registered clubs and points in the direction of commercial enterprise'.

(10) Section 107(10(j)): 'that correct accounts and books shall be kept showing the financial affairs and intromissions of the club'.

A finding that a club's accounts were presented only to a commercial concern which provided the club's facilities pointed to the conclusion that the club was a sham[2].

(11) Section 107(1)(k):

'that a visitor shall not be supplied with alcoholic liquor in the club premises unless on the invitation and in the company of a member and that the member shall, upon the admission of such visitor to the club premises or immediately upon his being supplied with such liquor, enter his own name and the name and address of the visitor in a book which shall be kept for the purpose and which shall show the date of each visit'.

Thus, a visitor may only consume liquor which has been purchased by a member. The reference to 'such visitor' is, of course, to a visitor supplied with liquor and, strictly speaking, his admission to the premises does not per se require to be recorded in a visitors' book; this is, however, the normal and sensible practice. In *Chief Constable of Glasgow v Parkhead and District Railwaymen's Welfare Club*[3] non-members had been admitted purely for the purpose of obtaining drink: their names were entered in the visitors' book and counter-signatures by members were provided either in advance or on a later occasion. The signing member might never have seen the non-member against whose name he signed. The certificate of registration was cancelled. Evidence of this practice could legitimately be obtained by police officers entering the club under false names.

(12) Section 107(1)(l): 'that no alcoholic liquor shall be sold or supplied in the club premises for consumption off the premises, except to a member of the club in person for consumption by him or to a person holding a licence or a wholesaler's excise licence[4] for the sale of such liquor'[5].

It is appropriate to note in this context the off-sale offence contained in s 95:

---

1 1968 SLT (Sh Ct) 33.
2 *Chief Constable of Glasgow v Piccadilly Club*, above.
3 1969 SLT (Sh Ct) 36.
4 Wholesaler's excise licences were, however, abolished by the Finance Act 1981, Sch 19.
5 Spirits could not be sold to the holder of a licence subject to a restriction in terms of s 29.

'If any person sells or supplies alcoholic liquor in the premises of a registered club for consumption off the premises, or authorises such sale or supply of alcoholic liquor or pays for alcoholic liquor so sold or supplied, he shall, unless such liquor was sold or supplied to a member of the club in person for consumption by him or to a person holding a licence for the sale of such liquor, be guilty of an offence'[1].

A person entered in the committee of management list lodged with the sheriff clerk (s 103(3)(b), (5)) is liable to be convicted unless he proves that the offence 'took place without his knowledge or consent' (s 95(2), as amended by the Law Reform (Miscellaneous Provisions) (Scotland) Act 1980, s 21)[2]. Where the prosecutor establishes that any liquor has been received or delivered inside, and removed from, the premises 'such liquor shall, unless the contrary is shown, be deemed to have been so taken for consumption off the premises' (s 95(3)).

The sale or supply requires to take place 'in the premises of a registered club'. The offence of supplying intoxicating liquor 'in a club for consumption off the premises except to a member on the premises'[3] was not made out where the supply took place on additional, unregistered premises[4]:

'[The prosecution argument] involved the construing of the words "in a club" as meaning "in or from the premises of a club". The legislation might be more complete if those words had been inserted . . . "In a club" means, I think, in the premises of a club . . . It is not necessary to consider whether there were not other means of punishing what was done in this case, as, for example, by a charge . . . that the club was not being conducted in good faith as a club[5] when it was supplying liquor to members in the High Street premises'[6].

Reciprocity rules

Club rules may provide for the admission of members of 'another club' to whom alcoholic liquor may be sold or supplied for consumption on the premises (s 107(2)). Guests of these members may also be supplied, subject, of course, to the 'visitors' book' rule required by s 107(1)(k) (s 107(3)). This arrangement may only be operated if:

'(a) the other club is a registered club whose premises are in the locality and are temporarily closed; or
(b) both clubs exist for learned, educational, or political objects of a similar nature; or
(c) each of the clubs is primarily a club for persons who are qualified by service or past service, or by any particular service or past service, in Her Majesty's Forces, and are members of an organisation established by Royal Charter, and consists wholly or mainly of such persons;
(d) each of the clubs is primarily a club for persons who carry on the same trade, profession or occupation, and that trade, profession or occupation is the same in the case of either club; or
(e) each of the clubs is a working men's club, that is to say, a club which is, as regards its

1 Section 95(1). Maximum penalty: level 3 (Sch 5). A conviction may result in cancellation of the certificate: see s 109(2). Illegal sales are also a ground of objection in terms of s 108(k).
2 'Knowledge or consent': see *Nicol v Smith* 1955 JC 7, 1955 SLT 38.
3 Contrary to the Licensing (Consolidation) Act 1910, s 94.
4 *Clarke v Griffiths* [1927] 1 KB 226.
5 Cf s 108(f).
6 See also *Watson v Cully* [1926] 2 KB 270.

purposes, qualified for registration as a working men's club under the Friendly Societies Act 1974, and is a registered society within the meaning of that Act or of the Industrial and Provident Societies Act 1965;

(f) each of the clubs is one to which [the students' union exemption] applies'[1].

Although paragraph (a) specifically refers to 'a registered club', with the remaining paragraphs simply referring to 'clubs', it has been held that '[W]here section 17(1) of the Licensing (Scotland) Act 1962 [now s 107(2)] uses the word "club" it means a registered club within the meaning of the statute'[2]. The arrangement need not be restricted to one other club[2].

Amendment of rules

Where an application for the grant (or renewal) of registration is imperilled because the rules are considered to be unsatisfactory, the application may not be continued to allow amendment. In *British Legion (Scotland) Tiree Branch, Petitioners*[3] the sheriff considered that his discretion extended only to the grant of refusal of the application. Similarly, in *Chief Constable of Strathclyde Police v Hamilton and District Bookmakers Club*[4] the sheriff considered that application would require to be made *de novo*:

'I suspect that the applicants, finding the objections to be well-founded, wished an opportunity to change their ground, to amend the rules lodged with the application and reorganise their membership. They were not entitled to do so . . . If they could not establish their right to a renewal of their certificate, their remedy was to abandon the application for renewal, put their house in order, and thereafter apply for a new certificate'.

On the other hand, an amendment to a club's rules after lodgement of the application but before the hearing was considered permissible in *Scottish Homosexual Rights Group, Petitioners*[5].

False statements

An offence is committed by any person who 'makes any statement which he knows to be false in a material particular, or recklessly[6] makes any statement which is false in a material particular' in:

(a) an application for the grant (or renewal) of a certificate of registration;
(b) the club rules;
(c) the committee of management list;
(d) the 'bona fide' certificate which is to be granted by two licensing board members and the proprietor of the premises (where the club is not the owner)

---

1 Section 107(2)(a)–(f).
2 *Parkhead and District Railwaymen's Welfare Club* 1964 SLT (Sh Ct) 18.
3 1947 SLT (Sh Ct) 65.
4 1977 SLT (Sh Ct) 78.
5 1981 SLT (Sh Ct) 18.
6 'Recklessly': see index to Sheriff G H Gordon's *Criminal Law* (2nd edn) sub voce 'Recklessness'.

(s 103(6), as amended by the Law Reform (Miscellaneous Provisions) (Scotland) Act 1980, s 21)[1].

A person charged vicariously is not to be convicted of such an offence if he proves that the contravention took place 'without his knowledge or consent' (s 103(7), proviso)[2].

While an objection to the bona fides of licensing board members is competent, 'such an objection would require to be clear and precise with due notification to the applicants':

'I do not consider that the sheriff would be entitled to allow a roving enquiry to ascertain if the certifying gentlemen have fulfilled their duties. There is a presumption that they have done so, and such presumption could only be displaced by a precise statement of their failure, and evidence would require to be led on both sides'[3].

Notices

The applicant club requires to give public intimation of the application by –

'(a) publishing a notice thereof twice in the seven days immediately following [lodgement of the application] in a newspaper circulating in the area in which the club is situated[4];
 (b) displaying a notice thereof in a conspicuous place on or near the premises occupied by the club for the period of 21 days immediately following [lodgement of the application]'[5].

The content of the notice is not prescribed by the Act. It need not explain the objections procedure (below) for the benefit of potential objectors, as would normally be the case where application is made for the grant of a new licence.

The sheriff clerk as registrar is required to give notice of the application 'forthwith'[6] to (a) the chief constable, (b) the local district or islands council and (c) the fire authority for the area (s 105(2)).

OBJECTIONS

Competent objectors

Objection to the application may be made by:
(1) Those to whom the sheriff clerk has given notice (above) (s 105(3)(a)).

---

1 Persons named in the committee of management list are vicariously liable: s 103(7). Maximum penalty: level 5 (Sch 5).
2 'Knowledge or consent': see *Nicol v Smith* 1955 JC 7, 1955 SLT 38.
3 *British Legion (Scotland) Tiree Branch, Petitioners* 1947 SLT (Sh Ct) 65. See also *Wellington Athletic Club v Magistrates of Leith* (1904) 12 SLT 570. In the City of Glasgow District, and no doubt elsewhere, licensing board members will only grant a certificate after a police report has been obtained.
4 Section 105(1)(a). Copies of the newspapers should be lodged with the sheriff clerk.
5 Section 105(1)(b).
6 'Forthwith' is a relative term, meaning as soon as possible in the circumstances: see *Chief Constable of Dundee v Dundee & District Railwaymen's Social and Welfare Club* 1958 SLT (Sh Ct) 40.

(2) 'Any person owning or occupying property in the neighbourhood' of the club premises (s 105(3)(b)). Residence per se may not constitute a qualification[1]. While objection to inter alia the grant of a new *licence* may be taken by an organisation representing neighbourhood occupiers (see s 16(1)(a)), there is no parallel provision here. In *Glasgow Fire Service & Salvage Corps Social and Athletic Club, Applicants*[2], where the secretary of a ward committee sought to appear for unnamed residents, the sheriff considered that:

'A ward committee unless it owns or occupies property cannot have standing as objectors. It might be permissible, but I express no firm opinion, for the secretary of a ward committee to appear for named owners or occupiers as objectors in their own right'.

The objections of specified occupiers grouped under the name of a residents' association were allowed in *Astor Dance Club v Chief Constable of Strathclyde*[3].
(3) 'A community council for the area in which the premises are situated which has been established in accordance with the provisions of the Local Government (Scotland) Act 1973' (s 105(3)(c)). It is doubtful whether a community council for an adjoining area could claim to be qualified as representing owners or occupiers under s 105(3)(b)[4].
(4) 'Any church which in the opinion of the sheriff represents a significant body of opinion among persons residing in the neighbourhood' (s 105(3)(d)).
Where objections are lodged and not withdrawn, the sheriff shall, 'as soon as may be' hear parties and 'order such enquiry as he thinks fit' (s 105(6)(b)).

Time limit

Objections require to be lodged with the sheriff clerk and a copy sent to the secretary of the club[5] within 21 days of the first publication of the newspaper notice (s 105(4))[6].
    Objections intimated only to a club's solicitor were considered incompetent in *Chief Constable of Dundee v Dundee & District Railwaymen's Social and Welfare Club*[7]:

'Normally I should have held that notice to the solicitor acting in the matter was notice to the party, but section 79(2) [now s 105(4)] falls to be contrasted with section 78(1) [now s 103(1)] providing that applications may be signed by the chairman, secretary or authorised law agent of the club and if it had been intended that notice might be given to the last mentioned I think these words would have been repeated in [s 105(4)]'.

1 See *McDonald v Chambers* 1956 SC 542, (sub nom *McDonald v Finlay*) 1957 SLT 81; and Chapter 6.
2 1968 SLT (Sh Ct) 47.
3 1977 SLT (Sh Ct) 43.
4 Cf *Kelvinside Community Council v Glasgow District Licensing Board* 1990 SCCR 110, 1990 SLT 725.
5 References in Part VII to 'the secretary' include references to 'any officer of the club or other person performing the duties of secretary': s 118.
6 'Within': 'Where an act must be performed within a specified number of days, it can be timeously performed at any time up to midnight on the final day of the period, the period being calculated exclusive of the *terminus a quo*'. See 22 *Stair Memorial Encyclopaedia* para 826.
7 1958 SLT (Sh Ct) 40.

Per contra, the sheriff was prepared, 'in the very special circumstances', to entertain objections sent on police advice to the president of a club[1].

The 21 day time limit is 'unequivocal and mandatory', with 'no saving provision or means of avoidance'[2].

Grounds of objection

There are no less than 19 grounds of objection, some of which overlap:
(1) 'that the application made by the club is in any respect specified . . . not in conformity with the provisions of this Act' (s 108(a)).
(2) 'that the rules of the club are in any respect specified . . . not in conformity with the provisions of this Act' (s 108(b)).
(3) 'that the club has ceased to exist or has less than 25 members' (s 108(c)).
(4) 'that the premises are, or the situation thereof is, not suitable or convenient for the purposes of a club' (s 108(d))[3].
(5) Section 108(e):

> 'that the club occupies premises in respect of which, within the period of 12 months immediately preceding the formation of the club, an order had been made under section 67(3) of this Act or the renewal of a licence under this Act has been refused, or in respect of which at the time when the premises were first occupied by the club an order was in force under section 110 of this Act that they should not be used for the purposes of a club'.

Section 67(3) provides for the disqualification of licensed premises from being used as such[4]. The grounds upon which the renewal of a licence may be refused are contained in s 17(1). Section 110 provides for an order that premises are not to be used as registered club premises for at least 12 months where a certificate has been cancelled or its renewal refused.
(6) 'that the club is not conducted in good faith as a club, or that it is kept or habitually used for any unlawful purpose or mainly for the supply of alcoholic liquor' (s 108(f))[5].
(7) 'that there has been a failure to intimate to the registrar forthwith any change in the rules of the club or in the list containing the names and addresses of the officials and members of the committee of management or governing body of the club' (s 108(g))[6].
(8) 'that the club is to be used mainly as a drinking club' (s 108(h))[7].
(9) 'that there is frequent drunkenness in the club premises, or that drunken persons are frequently seen to leave the premises' (s 108(i))[8].

1 *United Biscuits (Tollcross) Sports and Social Club, Applicants* 1973 SLT (Sh Ct) 25.
2 *Three Steps Social Club v Chief Constable of Strathclyde* 1977 SLT (Sh Ct) 18. It was held here that the commencement of the 21-day period was not delayed by the club's initial failure to lodge rules.
3 This ground is examined further below.
4 See Chapter 13.
5 A club is 'not conducted in good faith' where it is something less than a bona fide members' club, as, for example, in *Chief Constable of Glasgow v Piccadilly Club* 1968 SLT (Sh Ct) 33.
6 The intimation requirement is contained in s 103(5).
7 This ground is considered further below.
8 'Drunkenness': see Chapter 13. The expression 'seen to leave' is not to be construed literally: see *Gordon Highlanders' (Glasgow) Association Club, Petitioners* 1954 SLT (Sh Ct) 45, (sub nom *Gordon Highlanders (Glasgow) Association Club v Mason*) (1954) 70 Sh Ct Rep 144.

(10) 'that the club is or, in the case of an application for the renewal of a certificate of registration, has been, at any time during the currency of the certificate of registration . . . conducted in a disorderly manner' (s 108(j), as amended by the 1990 Act, Sch 8, para 16)[1].

(11) 'that illegal sales of alcoholic liquor have taken place in the club premises' (s 108(k))[2].

(12) 'that persons who are not members of the club are habitually admitted to the club premises merely for the purpose of obtaining alcoholic liquor' (s 108(l))[3].

(13) 'that the supply of alcoholic liquor to the club is not under the control of the members of the club or of the committee of management or governing body of the club' (s 108(m))[4].

(14) Section 108(n):

'that the officials and committee of management or governing body of the club, or the manager, or a servant employed in or by the club, have or will have a personal interest in the purchase by the club or in the sale in the premises of the club of alcoholic liquor or in the profits arising therefrom, or, where the said premises are not owned by the club, that the owner or the immediate lessor of the premises has or will have such a personal interest'[5].

(15) 'that any of the rules of the club referred to in section 107(1) . . . are habitually broken' (s 108(o)).

(16) 'that persons are habitually admitted or supplied as members of the club without an interval of at least two weeks between their nomination and election as ordinary members, or for a subscription of a nominal amount' (s 108(p)).

(17) 'that the officials and committee of management or governing body of the club, or the members of the club, are persons of bad character or persons who follow no lawful occupation and have no means of subsistence' (s 108(q)).

(18) 'that the club has been, is or will be used as a resort of persons of bad character' (s 108(r)).

(19) 'that alcoholic liquor is sold or supplied for consumption on or off the premises outwith the permitted hours' (s 108(s)).

Two grounds of objection which have produced the bulk of reported decisions are now examined.

---

1 The amendment precludes a club from arguing that it is no longer conducted in a disorderly manner.

2 For example, in contravention of s 95, which restricts off-sales.

3 This ground overlaps, to a degree, with s 108(f), (h). In *Dick v Stirling Lawn Tennis and Squash Club* 1981 SLT (Sh Ct) 103 the sheriff observed that: 'In terms of the rules, there is no limitation as to the number of guests a member may introduce . . . and it seems to me that there would be a likelihood which cannot be discounted of the main purpose of the club becoming the consumption of alcoholic liquor'.

4 This ground was not made out where a club received a brewery loan linked to an obligation to purchase the lender's beer: *Drongan and District Working Men's Social Club, Petitioners* 1966 SLT (Sh Ct) 73.

5 See *Lord Advocate v Trotter* (1903) 5 F 43.

Suitability of premises[1]

State of completion

Although the provisional grant of a new licence may be obtained for premises yet to be constructed (s 26), there is no analogous mechanism whereby registration may be obtained in respect of club premises which have yet to be made ready for occupation. It has been suggested that:

'It may at first sight seem strange that club premises should be discriminated against in this way, but the provisions of the Licensing Acts were probably intended to secure that only genuine clubs in active existence should be able to obtain the benefit of registration . . . and were perhaps prompted by the fact that any less restrictive measures might lead to the establishment of clubs intended mainly for drinking purposes'[2].

While a certificate has been granted for premises requiring 'extensive adaptation'[3], no objection had been taken as to their suitability; and the sheriff's decision may in any event have been influenced by the fact that the applicant club already enjoyed the benefit of registration at other premises.

Per contra, in *Glasgow Rangers' Supporters' Social Club*[4] the sheriff considered that the legislation envisaged 'an existing club in legal occupation of existing premises to the suitability of which for the purpose of a club no objection is taken'. Since registration immediately authorised the supply of liquor, a former cinema which required to be converted was considered unsuitable. Similarly, an application was refused where the club premises had yet to be built, although the sheriff observed that registration might have been reasonable if the club was 'waiting for premises already built, but unable to be occupied until a previous tenant moved out'[5].

Where a club was being renovated and contained neither furniture nor seating, the sheriff considered that a measure of latitude was appropriate:

'It seems to me that where work is in progress where an application for a new certificate is lodged and is sufficiently advanced at the date of the hearing to render the premises suitable the application should not be refused on that ground'[6].

Facilities

The paucity of recreational facilities may render premises unsuitable, as well as suggesting that the consumption of alcohol may be the primary activity (see below). Registration has been refused where:

---

1 Section 108(d).
2 'The Pleader' (1960) 76 SL Rev 62, on a consideration of *Glasgow Rangers' Supporters' Social Club, Petitioners* 1960 SLT (Sh Ct) 27, (1960) 76 Sh Ct Rep 44.
3 *Bayview Club, Petitioners* 1954 SLT (Sh Ct) 43.
4 See above.
5 *British Legion Club Ltd v Burgh of Invergordon* (1936) 52 Sh Ct Rep 295. See also *Chapelhall Community Social Club v Chief Constable of Lanarkshire* 1969 SLT (Sh Ct) 8.
6 *Scottish Homosexual Rights Group, Petitioners* 1981 SLT (Sh Ct) 18. Cf *Dick v Stirling Lawn Tennis and Squash Club* 1981 SLT (Sh Ct) 103: registration was refused where alteration works had not commenced.

(1) the club premises consisted of a single room occupying 483 square feet, with limited games facilities (darts, cards and dominoes)[1];

(2) a club room constituted a very small part of an indoor bowling complex, with no room to develop facilities 'beyond those of conversation and the consumption of food and drink'[2].

Police supervision

A number of cases have concerned police objections arising from apprehended supervisory difficulties[3]. In *Free Gardeners (East of Scotland) Social Club v Chief Constable of Edinburgh*[4] club premises occupied the basement and ground floor of a building; the remaining three floors were let to other bodies. Access to all parts of the building was shared through an inner hallway. The chief constable contended that it would be impossible to distinguish between persons leaving the club premises and meetings or functions on upper floors. Holding his objection to be incompetent, the sheriff said:

'This argument presupposes that the applicant's premises will be run in such a way as to offend against the provisions of the Act, a presupposition which I am not prepared to make. But further it substitutes for the test laid down in s 174(d) [now s 108(d)] (viz a situation which is not suitable or convenient for the purpose of a club) an entirely different test; a situation which is not suitable or convenient for the purposes of police supervision. In my view the language of the Act will plainly not bear such a construction'[5].

On the other hand, in *Astor Dance Club v Chief Constable of Strathclyde*[6] the sheriff was not willing to go so far:

'I was not prepared to hold that the possibility of police supervision could never be a factor in deciding the suitability of premises for use as a registered club. For example, I could see that if two different registered clubs had a common entrance, the impossibility of deciding which club a person was leaving would grossly hamper supervision'.

Mixed use

Although premises may not simultaneously be the subject of two *licences*, it has been held that two masonic lodges may be registered as clubs in respect of the same premises:

'The proviso to s 173 [now s 107(1)][7] clearly places a lodge of Freemasons . . . in categories apart from other applicant clubs. If an application were to be made from a club which fell outwith [this category] for registration in respect of premises in which there already

---

1 *Muirhead Celtic Supporters Social Club v Chief Constable of Lanarkshire* 1966 SLT (Sh Ct) 22.
2 *Hampden Tenpin Bowling Club v Chief Constable of Glasgow* 1965 SLT (Sh Ct) 22.
3 Police powers in relation to registered clubs are considered below.
4 1967 SLT (Sh Ct) 80.
5 The soundness of this decision is open to considerable doubt. Note that police supervision considerations are most certainly relevant as respects the *licensing* of premises.
6 1977 SLT (Sh Ct) 43.
7 Which exempts Freemasons' lodges from the mandatory rules.

operated a registered club, I would not regard myself as bound by this decision in looking at the wider issues involved'[1].

Difficulty may arise in other cases where a club proposes to hire out its facilities. In *Glengarnock Social Club v Chief Constable of Glasgow*[2] the sheriff considered 'at least arguable' the suggestion that a club, with one large hall, may not be conducting itself as a bona fide club 'if it allows its accommodation and facilities to be used with frequency by outside bodies'. In stark contrast, no objection was taken in *Chief Constable of Lanarkshire v Auchengeich Miners' Welfare Society and Social Club*[3] where the sheriff noted, apparently with approval, that part of a club's premises were used for dances and bingo sessions:

'The club is drawing a quite substantial revenue from the letting of the hall for these purposes. It does not seem to me to matter much whether the club is directly responsible for the provision of entertainments or whether it merely makes its premises available to someone else at a rent to provide the entertainment, always providing that the use made of the premises is in furtherance or fulfilment of the club purposes'[4].

Neighbourhood amenity

Where it is suggested that registration of a club will result in a loss of local amenity regard must be had to:

'the nature and purposes of the club, the age and probable degree of responsibility of the members, and, where there is proximity to housing, the likelihood of noise and nuisance to adjoining proprietors'[5].

It was 'preposterous' to assert that premises which had been used for sports activities for over 30 years were unsuitable[6]; but registration was refused where it was proposed to establish a motoring club in 'a valuable west-end locality':

'The introduction of such a club would turn the street from a quiet street into a noisy one, especially at the times of the motor trials. It would introduce an element of danger, especially to children crossing the road. It would materially diminish the value of property in the neighbourhood'[7].

The sheriff also observed that 'motoring and alcoholic refreshment make a notoriously bad combination' and that 'the proposed situation is not convenient for the purpose of a licensed [sic] motoring club'. Yet, in *Woodend Bowling Club v*

---

1 *Lodge Regal No 1422, Petitioners* 1972 SLT (Sh Ct) 61. Registration was also granted where a lodge enjoyed a let of premises for only two nights per week and the premises were used at other times by other organisations: *Lodge Liberton No 1201, Petitioners* 1966 SLT (Sh Ct) 90.
2 1971 SLT (Sh Ct) 35, distinguished (by the same sheriff) in *Lodge Regal No 1422, Petitioners*, above.
3 (1962) Sh Ct Rep 114.
4 Objection was taken (unsuccessfully) on the ground that the club was not conducted in good faith and was kept or habitually used mainly for the supply of liquor; but the certificate was cancelled for other reasons.
5 *Sandyhills Bowling Club v Tollcross Council of Churches* 1967 SLT (Sh Ct) 31.
6 *Motherwell and Wishaw Miners Welfare Society and Social Club, Petitioners* 1962 SLT (Sh Ct) 70.
7 *Edinburgh and District Motor Club Ltd, Applicants* (1934) Sh Ct Rep 165.

Stephen[1] the sheriff declined to construe this decision as creating a *nexus* between suitability and the supply of alcohol:

'The selling [sic] of alcoholic refreshment in a registered club is always ancillary to the purposes of the club and, therefore, the objection has to be that the premises, or the situation thereof are not suitable or convenient for the purposes of a club, whether or not alcoholic refreshment is to be available'.

The following extract from the sheriff's note in *Dick v Stirling Lawn Tennis and Squash Club* perhaps suggests the opposite approach[2]:

'[T]here would in my view be a reasonable expectation of an increased use of the club during the permitted hours for drinking purposes with a consequential adverse effect upon amenity, car park congestion and the use of the present access facilities . . .'.

Use as a 'drinking club'[3]

This is possibly the most formidable ground of objection. Where a club was admittedly in financial difficulties and hoped to obtain additional revenue from the supply of alcoholic liquor, the suggestion that 'members by and large would give up their games facilities and resort to drinking' was rejected without hesitation[4]. An objection is, however, likely to be sustained where the club's financial commitments may only be serviced through the consumption of substantial quantities of alcohol[5]. In *Hampden Tenpin Bowling Club v Chief Constable of Glasgow*[6] it was conceded that without profits drawn from alcohol the club could not pay rent. The sheriff said:

'While it is not abnormal for a club to derive a substantial part of its income from bar profits, and even to derive most of its income from such a source, it is unique in my experience for an applicant club with a nominal subscription to expect to derive so large a proportion of its income from bar profits'.

Where a club was prohibited by a title condition from supplying liquor in its premises and sought registration for new premises too distant to be regarded as an annexe, it was inescapable logic that the latter were to be used mainly for drinking[7].

In the unusual case of *West Wemyss United Services Club, Applicants*[8] police objection was taken on the ground that the club was to be used mainly as a drinking club because the premises were the subject of an *ex facie* current public house certificate. The holders of the certificate had parted with possession of the premises. The sheriff held that registration was competent: in such a situation, the public house certificate 'necessarily becomes of no effect and the way is open

---

1 Aberdeen Sheriff Court, 18 January 1993, unreported.
2 1981 SLT (Sh Ct) 103.
3 Section 108(h).
4 *Motherwell and Wishaw Miners Welfare Society and Social Club, Petitioners* 1962 SLT (Sh Ct) 70.
5 *Tinto Club v Chief Constable of Glasgow* 1964 SLT (Sh Ct) 54.
6 1965 SLT (Sh Ct) 22.
7 *Shotts Miners' Welfare Society and Social Club, Petitioners* 1960 SLT (Sh Ct) 25.
8 1948 SLT (Sh Ct) 33.

to the person thereafter in right of possession to make such use of the premises as he may choose and is able'.

THE SHERIFF'S DECISION

The sheriff may only grant or refuse the application[1]. If the club's rules do not conform to the mandatory requirements the application must be refused (s 107(1)). Otherwise, if no objections are lodged or maintained an application 'duly made' in accordance with the Act must be granted (s 105(6)(a)). It seems that the sheriff may grant a certificate even where a ground of objection has been established[2]. Although this course would be competent but 'exceptional' where the club was considered to be a 'drinking club'[3], such a finding in *Shotts Miners' Welfare Society and Social Club*[4] caused the sheriff to observe: 'On complying with the statutory provisions a club is entitled to registration. If it offends against those provisions the sheriff has no option but to refuse registration'[5].

The sheriff may accept undertakings as to the future conduct of the club. Such undertakings subsist for the duration of the certificate and may only be discharged by a fresh application[6].

Expenses may be awarded against an unsuccessful party (s 105(6)(b)). The form of certificate to be issued by the registrar is set out in Schedule 6 (s 105(7)).

In terms of s 117(2): 'The decision of the sheriff in dealing with an application for the grant of a certificate or registration or for the renewal of such a certificate or in cancelling such a certificate shall be final'. It has been held that an appeal to the Sheriff Principal is competent where there has been no final disposal on the merits and the sheriff has dealt only with matters of procedure[7]. In *Stephen v Woodend Bowling Club*[8], however, the Sheriff Principal (R D Ireland, QC) considered that an appeal by an objector whose objection had been held to be incompetent and irrelevant could not be entertained:

'There is nothing procedural about such a decision; it was a decision on the merits. The sheriff was exercising the discretion conferred upon him by section 105(6)(b), which was, after hearing parties . . ., to decide whether to grant or refuse the certificate. When he made that decision, it was a decision covered by section 117(2) and no appeal to the Sheriff Principal is competent'.

1 *British Legion (Scotland) Tiree Branch, Petitioners* 1947 SLT (Sh Ct) 65. His jurisdiction is not excluded 'by reason only of the fact that he is a member of the club': s 117(1).
2 *Hampden Tenpin Bowling Club v Chief Constable of Glasgow* 1965 SLT (Sh Ct) 22.
3 *Tinto Club v Chief Constable of Glasgow* 1964 SLT (Sh Ct) 54. 'Exceptional' is no doubt an under-statement.
4 1960 SLT (Sh Ct) 25.
5 There was no suggestion here that the club rules did not comply with the Act and the sheriff can only have been referring to the objection.
6 *United Biscuits (Tollcross) Sports and Social Club, Applicants* 1974 SLT (Sh Ct) 91.
7 *Chief Constable of Strathclyde v Hamilton and District Bookmakers Club* 1977 SLT (Sh Ct) 78; *Edinburgh North Constituency Association SNP Club v Thomas H Peck Ltd* 1978 SLT (Sh Ct) 76; *Ladbrokes the Bookmakers v Hamilton District Council* 1977 SLT (Sh Ct) 86.
8 1993 SLT (Notes) 574.

Although judicial review of the sheriff's decision would no doubt be competent, no petitions have so far been brought[1].

THE AUTHORITY OF THE CERTIFICATE

Registered club premises are not 'licensed premises', nor does a certificate authorise any sale of alcoholic liquor 'which would otherwise be illegal' (s 102(1)). Nevertheless, although the distinction between a certificate of registration and a licence 'is by no means nominal'[2], reference is commonly made to a 'club licence'.

The certificate authorises the supply of alcoholic liquor to members and their guests, in accordance with the club's rules and the provisions of Part VII, during the permitted hours: Mondays to Saturdays from 11 am to 11 pm and Sundays from 12.30 pm to 2.30 pm and from 6.30 pm to 11 pm (s 53(1))[3].

The local licensing board's jurisdiction is confined to applications for: occasional and regular extensions of the permitted hours (s 64), table meal related extensions (ss 57, 58), and occasional licences (s 33). In certain circumstances, restriction orders may be imposed (ss 65, 66)[4].

No provision is made for the approval of alterations to club premises except that an offence is committed where approved meal facilities are altered without the licensing board having first been notified (ss 57(7), 58(7)).

CURRENCY AND RENEWAL OF CERTIFICATE

A certificate of registration remains in force for three years from the date of issue (s 106). A renewal application requires to be lodged with the registrar not later than 21 days[5] before its expiry (s 104(1)). The sheriff has a discretion to entertain an application lodged within this period 'but shall not grant the application unless he is satisfied that the failure to lodge it timeously was due to inadvertence' (s 104(2)). This discretion is not available where the renewal application is lodged after the 21 days, when the certificate has expired[6].

Where a renewal application has been duly made, the certificate remains in force pending the sheriff's final decision for a period not exceeding three months from the expiry date; and, 'if the sheriff thinks fit', for a further three months (s 106, proviso). The second extension period is not automatic and must be allowed before the expiry of the initial period[7].

---

1 Judicial review: see Chapter 15.
2 See the sheriff's observations in *Sandyhills Bowling Club v Tollcross Council of Churches* 1967 SLT (Sh Ct) 31.
3 Alternative permitted hours are available during the winter months for some athletic clubs: s 56.
4 The effect of the permitted hours, and the extensions available, are considered in Chapter 10.
5 Ie 21 clear days: *Main v City of Glasgow District Licensing Board* 1987 SLT 305.
6 *Royal British Legion Club, Petitioners* 1984 SLT (Sh Ct) 62.
7 *Chief Constable of Strathclyde v Hamilton and District Bookmakers Club* 1977 SLT (Sh Ct) 78.

The application requires to be accompanied by:

(a) the 'bona fide' certificate granted by two licensing board members and the owner of the premises (where the club is not the proprietor) (s 103(3)(c), (4), as applied by s 104(4)); and

(b) a certificate stating that there have been no changes in the club rules or in the management committee list since grant of the certificate or its last renewal or that any such changes have already been intimated to the registrar (pursuant to s 103(5)) (s 104(3)).

There is no requirement that the application be advertised, either in a newspaper or by means of a notice at the premises. The registrar is, however, obliged to give notice of the application to the chief constable, the district or islands council and the fire authority (s 105(3)). An objection by any of these parties must be lodged with the registrar and intimated to the secretary within 21 days of such notice (s 105(5)). The other persons and bodies who may competently object to the grant of a certificate may also object to a renewal application (s 105(3))[1]. Curiously, no time limit is specified, as the sheriff observed in *Hampden Tenpin Bowling Club v Chief Constable of Glasgow*[2] when he refused to allow new objections to be raised after the conclusion of the applicant's case. The grounds of objection are identical to those provided in the case of a new application (s 108), as is the procedure before the sheriff (see s 105(6), (7)). His decision is final (s 117(2))[3]. A disqualification order may be made where the renewal is refused (s 110).

POLICE POWERS

Police have very limited supervisory powers[4]. Under the authority of a warrant granted by a justice of the peace, a constable may enter club premises at any time, if need be by force, search the premises, seize any club business documents and take the names and addresses of any persons found in the premises (s 114)[5]. The justice of the peace must first be satisfied by evidence on oath that there are reasonable grounds for believing:

'(a) that any registered club is being so managed or carried on as to give rise to a ground of objection to the renewal of its certificate of registration . . .; or

(b) that an offence under the Act has been or is being committed in any registered club'[6].

Section 115(3) permits the chief constable or any constable with his written authorisation to inspect the current club membership list which is to be kept on the premises.

1 See above.
2 1965 SLT (Sh Ct) 22.
3 See above.
4 This has long been a contentious area of licensing law: see *Clayson*, paras 13.20ff. The committee's recommendation that police should have the same right of entry to registered clubs as licensed premises was not enacted. A similar proposal was defeated during the Parliamentary progress of the 1990 Act.
5 Any person refusing to give his name and address or supplying false details is guilty of an offence: s 114(2). Maximum penalty: level 3 (Sch 5).
6 Section 114(1).

Despite these limitations, the court has on a number of occasions condoned 'undercover' operations. In *Southern Bowling Club v Ross*[1], an unsuccessful attempt was made to interdict the police from entering a club in disguise. More recently, where two police officers pretended to be otherwise employed, the sheriff rejected an argument that evidence had been obtained in an unfair and irregular manner:

'It seems to me . . . that the police must often employ such devices and subterfuges where they have reason to suspect that the law is being flouted, and there is need to investigate the matter'[2].

In another case, apparently involving the same club, policemen had obtained entry without being introduced by a member; two officers used fictitious names. The sheriff said:

'On each occasion, the doorman was told that they were not members. I see no impropriety in that course of conduct. Policemen are not entitled forcibly to enter private club premises any more than any other private premises without a warrant, but entry by a policeman to a private club which admits anyone who cares to come in does not constitute an entry under false pretences'[3].

PROTECTION OF YOUNG PERSONS

Club rules must provide that no alcoholic liquor shall be sold or supplied in the club to any person under 18 (s 107(1)(f)). An infraction of this rule is not *ipso facto* an offence[4]; but it may give rise to an objection to registration (s 108) or to cancellation of the certificate (s 109)[5].

Persons under 14 are not to be allowed in a bar during the permitted hours (s 112(1))[6]; otherwise persons entered in the current management committee list are guilty of an offence (s 112(2), as amended by the Law Reform (Miscellaneous Provisions) (Scotland) Act 1980, s 21) unless it is proved that the contravention took place without the accused's 'knowledge or consent' (s 112(2), proviso). It is also an offence for any person to 'cause any person under 14' to be in a club bar at such a time (s 112(3))[7].

For a case in which bar facilities gave rise to difficulty where children were to resort to club premises, see *Dick v Stirling Lawn Tennis and Squash Club*[8].

Persons under 18 are not to be employed in a registered club for the service of alcoholic liquor (s 113(1))[9]. If the person *in quo* appears to the court to have been under 18, 'for the purpose of the proceedings he shall be deemed to have been

1 (1902) 4 F 405, (1902) 9 SLT 155.
2 *Chief Constable of Glasgow v Parkhead and District Railwaymen's Welfare Club* (1962) 78 Sh Ct Rep 121.
3 *Chief Constable of Glasgow v Parkhead and District Railwaymen's Welfare Club* 1969 SLT (Sh Ct) 36.
4 Cf s 68(1).
5 See below.
6 Maximum penalty: level 3 (Sch 5).
7 Maximum penalty: level 3 (Sch 5).
8 1981 SLT (Sh Ct) 103.
9 A person working in a club is deemed to be 'employed' even where he receives no wages: s 113(3).

then under that age unless the contrary is shown' (s 113(4))[1]. Again, persons named in the current committee of management list are guilty of an offence (s 113(2))[2], subject to the 'lack of knowledge or consent' defence (s 113(2), proviso).

CANCELLATION AND DISQUALIFICATION

On application being made by any competent objector (s 105(3))[3], the sheriff may make a finding that:

'the club is being or has been, at any time during the currency of the certificate of registration, so managed or carried on as to give rise to a ground of objection to the renewal of its certificate, being one of the grounds of objection specified in section 108'[4].

In such a case, or where a conviction has taken place under s 95[5], a certified copy of the finding or conviction is to be transmitted to the registrar within six days (s 109(2)). Thereafter entries are made in the register, which is laid before the sheriff (s 109(3)). He may proceed to cancel the certificate of registration 'if he thinks fit, after such further enquiry as he may think necessary, and having regard to the grounds specified in such finding or the magnitude of the offence' (s 109(3)). Expenses may be awarded against an unsuccessful party (s 109(5)). The sheriff's decision is final (s 117(2)). Under earlier legislation, there was nothing to prevent a renewal application being made if the certificate expired during a cancellation period[6]. Now, the club may not apply for renewal earlier than 12 months from the cancellation date (s 109(4))[7]; a fresh application for the grant of a certification of registration is not, however, required.

Cancellation places the club in further jeopardy.

Disqualification

Following cancellation or where renewal of the certificate has been refused, the sheriff may 'if he thinks fit, order that the premises occupied by that club shall not be occupied and used for the purposes of any registered club' (s 110(1)). The length of the disqualification period is at the sheriff's discretion, except that the maximum period is twelve months where there had been no previous order; and

---

1 There is no parallel provision as respects the 'under fourteen' offence in s 112, above. Cf ss 69(6), 72(4), 73(4).
2 Maximum penalty: level 3 (Sch 5).
3 See above.
4 Section 109(1), as amended by the 1990 Act, Sch 8, para 17. An application for cancellation current before the expiry of a certificate should be disposed of prior to the determination of a renewal application: *Inch v Buckhaven Burgh Ex-Service Men's Club* 1953 SLT (Sh Ct) 108.
5 Which restricts off-sales from club premises: see above.
6 Licensing (Scotland) Act 1959, s 175(4).
7 An application would not be competent if the premises were the subject of a disqualification order in terms of s 110: see below.

in other cases five years (s 110(2)). The sheriff may subsequently cancel or vary the order 'on good cause being shown' (s 110(3)).

Section 117(2) does not provide that a decision under s 110 is final.

Offences

Persons named in the committee of management list at the relevant time are guilty of an offence where a finding has been made under s 109(1) that a registered club is being so managed or carried on as to give rise to one or more specified grounds of objection to the renewal of the certificate (s 111(1), as amended by the Law Reform (Miscellaneous Provisions) (Scotland) Act 1980, s 21)[1]. The grounds are those mentioned in s 108(f)[2], (i)[3], (j)[4] and (l)[5].

A person is not to be convicted of the offence if he proves that the club was improperly managed or carried on 'without his knowledge or consent and that he exercised all due diligence to prevent the club from being so managed or carried on' (s 111(2))[6].

---

1 Maximum penalty: level 3 (Sch 5). It appears that the finding requires to have been made in the context of cancellation proceedings; in other words, although there are grounds of objection to a renewal application, no potential for an offence exists under s 111(1) where the renewal is refused.
2 Club not conducted in good faith, habitually used for unlawful purpose or mainly for supply of liquor.
3 Drunkenness in, or drunks seen leaving, the premises.
4 Club conducted in disorderly manner.
5 Non-members admitted merely to obtain alcohol.
6 Cf s 67(2): see Chapter 13.

Index

Outside drinking area, 60, 121, 208, 209, 250
Over provision of licensed premises
criteria, 79–82
generally, 78
locality, meaning, 78, 79

Partnerships
appeals by, 277
applications from, 56, 57
fit and proper person test, 71, 72, 141
prosecution of, 231
Passenger trains
exemption for, 32
Passenger vessels
exemption for, 32
permitted hours, 164
Pavement
obstruction of, 209
Penalties for offences, 232, 233, 239
Permanent transfer of licence. *See* TRANSFER OF LICENCE
Permits
gaming. *See* GAMING
Permitted hours
basic, 167–169
closure allowed during, 164, 165
'drinking up' time, 169, 170
entertainment licence, 46, 47
extensions for table meals. *See* EXTENSION OF PERMITTED HOURS
generally, 163
hotel, 38, 58, 59, 167, 168
meaning, 163
modifications, 173–175
occasional extension of. *See* OCCASIONAL EXTENSION OF PERMITTED HOURS
occasional licence, 120
off-sale licences, 27, 58, 167–169
offences,
    consumption outwith, 163, 165
    sale or supply outwith, 163, 164, 168
passenger vessels, 164
public house licence, 34, 58, 59, 167, 168
refreshment licence, 44, 45, 167, 168
registered club, 329
regular extension. *See* REGULAR EXTENSION OF PERMITTED HOURS
relaxations, 169–173
restaurant licence, 167, 168
restricted hotel, 40, 167, 168
restriction of. *See* RESTRICTION OF PERMITTED HOURS
Sunday. *See* SUNDAY PERMITTED HOURS
table meal extension. *See* EXTENSION OF PERMITTED HOURS
unlicensed premises, 166, 167
use of premises outwith, 165, 166
Person
meaning, 103

Petrol stations
licensing of, 53, 75
Planning certificate. *See* CERTIFICATES OF SUITABILITY
Plans
applications, accompanying, 59, 60, 205, 261
warranty as to, 93
Police
complaint leading to suspension of licence, 156–158
evidence obtained by, 238
objectors, as, 67, 78, 104, 105, 111, 113, 114, 263, 320
observations by, 88, 114–116, 137, 185, 201, 202
offences against, 237–239
powers of entry,
    licensed premises, 73, 74, 118, 237, 238
    occasional permission premises, 123
    registered club, 330, 331
    unlicensed premises, 30, 167
temporary restriction order, applicants as, 203
Premises
licensed. *See* LICENSED PREMISES
suitability of,
    alterations, effect of, 205, 209
    character, condition and proposed use, 75, 76
    closure, effect of, 142, 143
    generally, 73
    location, access, 73, 74
    location, amenity, 74, 75, 296, 297
    persons likely to resort, 76, 77
    registered clubs, 324–327
Price of liquor
controls over, 22
Private friend
meaning, 39, 40
Promotional activities
control of, 48
Proper address
meaning, 108, 109
Proprietary club
Gaming Act registration, 221, 222
generally, 310
See also REGISTERED CLUB
Prosecution of offences, 230–232, 257–260
Prostitutes
licensed premises, on, 244, 245
Provisional grant of new licence. *See* APPLICATIONS
Provisional licence, 50, 205
Public
meaning, 77, 146, 179, 224
Public entertainment licence
amusement arcade, 220
generally, 35, 38, 50, 83, 147, 165, 166, 176, 224, 225
warranties as to, 93, 94
Public house
beer garden, 208, 209